£18 9\
LIB/04/00l

OPERATIONS MANAGEMENT

is book is to be returned on or before
the last date stamped below.

1 2

1

OPERATIONS MANAGEMENT

John Naylor

Liverpool Business School
Liverpool John Moores University

PITMAN PUBLISHING
128 Long Acre, London WC2E 9AN

A Division of Pearson Professional Limited

First published in Great Britain 1996

© Pearson Professional Limited 1996

British Library Cataloguing in Publication Data
A CIP catalogue record for this book can be obtained
from the British Library.

ISBN 0 7121 1054 2

10 9 8 7 6 5 4 3 2 1

Typeset by PanTek Arts, Maidstone, Kent.
Printed and bound in Great Britain by Bell and Bain Ltd, Glasgow

The Publishers' policy is to use paper manufactured from sustainable forests.

CONTENTS

PREFACE

This book gives a comprehensive coverage of operations management for those who come to the subject for the first time. It assumes a general awareness of, and orientation towards, business and management. It does not, however, assume strong backgrounds in areas such as finance or mathematics. The numerical tools and techniques that are introduced are to illustrate application rather than give a complete coverage of every aspect of each model. Application is reinforced by reference to real organisations that have been disguised in only a few cases.

I wrote the draft manuscript using WordPerfect®, with DrawPerfect® or Chartist® for the figures. Teachers who adopt the book can obtain copies of the figures in WPG and CHT formats, with a shareware version of Chartist. Please write directly to me at Liverpool Business School, 98 Mount Pleasant, Liverpool, L3 5UZ, UK; mailname j.b.naylor@livjm.ac.uk.

In preparing *Operations Management*, I have benefited greatly from the advice, information, cooperation and comments from individuals and firms. There is no space to note every contribution. Anyhow, some informants asked, for clear reasons, not to be identified and I have respected their wishes. In the Business School, many colleagues made informal comments and suggestions. In particular, Graham Padgett and Bernard Tabernacle looked carefully at two chapters and suggested improvements. At Pitman, John Cushion was most encouraging throughout the project.

Finally, I must acknowledge the debt I owe to my family. My children Rachel, Emma and William offered friendly rivalry. Maureen, my wife, spent almost a year coping with a rival in the house. Without her, the book could not have happened.

John Naylor

NOTE: a reference in the text such as see **12** refers to numbered section 12 in that particular chapter; a reference such as **7.23** refers to section 23 of chapter 7.

1

THE SCOPE OF OPERATIONS MANAGEMENT

Chapter objectives

When you have finished studying this chapter, you should be able to:

- Define the term operations management and distinguish it from the notion of operational-level management.
- Define management and explain how managers have to balance efficiency, effectiveness and equity.
- Compare the production of goods and services.
- Explain and illustrate the types of resource used in an operating system.
- Sketch diagrams which set out the features of operating system structures.
- Identify and illustrate the key decision areas for operations managers and relate them to time horizons.
- Use the value chain and organisation charts to show how the operations function fits within an organisation.

INTRODUCTION

1. Why study operations management?

A general answer to this question is that operations management is important, all pervasive and can be done well by competent people. This is because:

- Operations is the core function of the organisation and continuously manages the flow of resources through it. In many organisations, operations accounts for 80% of the employees and hence most of their added value.
- The output of the operations system is the bundle of goods and services which is consumed in society. An organisation which does not continuously satisfy the needs of customers fails.
- All organisations have an operations activity. The techniques and skills of operations management can be applied across a range of apparently diverse businesses, institutions, authorities and so on, whatever sector of the economy they are in. This means that many skills learnt in one context can be transferred to another and, further, it is possible to learn directly applicable knowledge from sources such as this book.

- Operations management is management in that it offers the challenge, the complexity and the responsibility which are part of any managerial role. A good operations manager does not define the task as merely tinkering with techniques to run part of the business on a day-to-day basis. The role is larger than this, being also concerned with developing operating processes, products, locations and so on to meet the demands and pressures of the changing environment.
- In a broader sense, a nation depends heavily, for its international competitiveness, on the efficiency and effectiveness of the operations in its organisations. So much talk has been about getting the strategy right that the need to invest in, develop and manage competitive operating systems is lost sight of. It is in all our interests to have properly functioning operating systems whether within manufacturing organisations or in the more public domain of services whether from banking to buses or hairdressing to health care.

2. What is operations management?

Before moving on to discuss the position of operations management in the organisation, we can set out and explain the following definition:

Operations management is concerned with creating, operating and controlling a transformation system which takes inputs of a variety of resources and produces outputs of goods and services which are needed by customers.

The definition contains key ideas which require further explanation. These concern operations management:

- as a management activity
- producing outputs of goods and services needed by customers
- using resources
- creating, operating and controlling a transformation system.

The following sections explain these points in more detail but before moving on to them we should look at two difficulties with terminology. First, some authors use the label *production/operations management* (abbreviated to POM) but in this book we shall use the more general *operations management*. Not only is our label easier to use but it takes us away from the connections which the idea of production management has with an emphasis on the engineering aspects of manufacture. As we shall see, most production systems furnish a mixture of goods and services and use of the single term underlines this point. Secondly the terms *operating or operational* are often used to describe a level in a managerial hierarchy or a phase of a planning cycle.

- Strategic planning is concerned with pursuit of long-term aims which are themselves identified within the planning process. A typical time scale would be one to six years, or even longer.
- Intermediate (or administrative) planning may occur in large organisations and is concerned with the contributions of subunits to the general plan. The time scale may be six months to three years.
- Operational planning is concerned with achieving specific tasks with known resources. This level plans for a maximum of a year down to weeks, days or even hours.

We should not allow the notion of the operational level to be confused with operations management. All the functions of the organisation, from personnel to purchasing, engineering to sales, can be seen to have the above hierarchy of planning and decision making. We shall look at these levels again in Chapter 2. Operations management, on the other hand, is concerned with transformation of inputs into outputs and has, as its concerns, decisions at all levels of the managerial hierarchy.

A MANAGEMENT ACTIVITY

3. A definition of management

Good management is the key to good organisational performance. A poorly managed taxi business uses unreliable vehicles, not-so-polite staff, arrives late for, or misses, pick-ups and handles its finances carelessly. It quickly earns a bad reputation. A well managed business does not fail on any of these counts and prospers. The choice is the choice of the managers - it is possible to succeed or fail within the same general circumstances. What are the key features of the management process?

Management is the process of achieving organisational objectives within a changing environment by:

- *balancing efficiency, effectiveness and equity,*
- *obtaining the most out of limited resources, and*
- *working with and through other people.*

The next sections, **4** to **7**, examine the parts of this definition.

4. Achieving organisational objectives

An objective is a target to be striven for. Individuals and organisations are more successful if they have targets which are clear, challenging and achievable. The targets are means by which the individual can plan and coordinate work with others and how the leaders of an organisation communicate its overall aims in order to mobilise effort. For example, as we shall see in our discussion of quality, leading organisations have identified world-class standards in terms of 'Six Sigma', which means less than three faults per million elements of output. Such standards are used to guide individual management decision making, whether it concerns plant maintenance, staff selection or inspection rates.

We shall see in Chapter 2 how the organisation cannot fix several objectives for all time. Continually changing environments impose new demands and problems, whether they concern shortage of raw materials, rising energy prices, new customer requirements or tougher competitive policies of rivals. A key part of the management function is to maintain an awareness of such changes and prepare responses to them.

5. Balancing efficiency, effectiveness and equity

Separating the three Es of the management balance is worthwhile because it enables us to understand something of the dilemma faced by managers in making

3

decisions. Efficiency is a measure of how well resources are transformed into outputs. We are encouraged to compare things we buy in terms of their efficiency. Washing machine suppliers state the energy consumption per cycle; car manufacturers are required to state fuel consumption under standard test conditions; audio equipment manufacturers stress minimal distortion losses. In all these cases, efficiency is being assessed according to the use of a key resource, be it energy or incoming sound. But what if the washer doesn't wash very well, the car is too small or the hi-fi not powerful enough? The product, in other words, may not be capable of achieving its purpose. We have fallen into the trap of overemphasising efficiency at the expense of effectiveness.

Effectiveness, then, is an assessment of how far a stated objective is achieved. Often, a focus on 'getting the job done' is important, for example when managing a crisis. The ultimate crisis, war, requires managers who believe in 'winning at all costs'. In the main, however, a manager's overemphasis on effectiveness leads to a loss of efficiency in terms of wasted resources. On the other hand, too much stress on efficiency may mean that the task does not get done at all. The right balance is a management decision. To take a case of customer service, narrow considerations of efficiency would suggest that hotels and shops should not employ lift attendants as lifts are easy to operate. Yet the well known Galeries Lafayette department store in Paris has an attendant in every lift. It is an effective way of providing customers with guidance and assistance at the instant when they demand it, although such demands may not be made very frequently.

Equity is the third of the 3 Es in the manager's mixture. This concerns the distribution of outputs among customers and is particularly important in public sector and not-for-profit organisations whose outputs are not traded in the conventional market place. The manager in the private business has no qualms in supplying only those who will pay. The manager of the hospital or social work department has to ensure that all clients are treated fairly according to their needs, irrespective of how well off they are. Who gets to use the kidney machine; which village gets the by-pass; which schools have to close: these are questions which not only

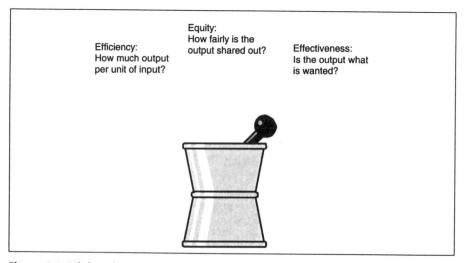

Efficiency:
How much output
per unit of input?

Equity:
How fairly is the
output shared out?

Effectiveness:
Is the output what
is wanted?

Figure 1.1 Mixing the 3 Es

include issues of efficiency and effectiveness but are also concerned with equity. If the balance goes wrong and, for example, equity becomes bound up with political considerations, then resource allocations are badly made.

The best blend of the 3 Es is a changing decision. Not only do different organisations tend to have distinct patterns which help to give them their character but, as has been suggested, the mixtures will vary according to circumstances. The crisis may require action at all costs, while in calmer times the manager may be expected to achieve a defined output while operating as efficiently as possible. The operating manager is not normally faced with questions of equity except in public service organisations where such choice, on a case by case basis, can make the task very difficult.

6. Obtaining the most from limited resources

We can stress the limitation of resources available to managers as it takes us beyond basic questions of efficiency in the current operations. Managers have to recognise that resources have to be found and obtained, that they often have a limited life and, therefore, the processes and products of the organisation have to be adapted accordingly. Low energy consumption is not simply part of the efficiency equation for products and processes but it also concerns the search for new products and processes whose overall performance is even better. We shall return to identifying the resources used in operations management below.

7. Working with and through other people

Management is primarily a social process. We should recognise that, while much of operations management has been presented in terms of techniques for optimising the levels of stock or the flow of goods through a warehouse or machine shop, all such changes are both carried out and constrained by the people who work within those functions. An example which is to be discussed in detail later is the quality improvement programme. Without the cooperation of all the staff involved, such initiatives are doomed to failure. Ambitious managers who do not work well with others find that, whatever good ideas and plans they come up with, they will be unsuccessful in implementing any change.

PRODUCING OUTPUTS OF GOODS AND SERVICES NEEDED BY CUSTOMERS

8. Goods and services as products

Goods are manufactured. They are material, made, distributed, sold and then used by buyers at their will. Services are immaterial, transitory and consumed at the moment that they are produced. At first sight, the production of goods, which is manufacturing, appears to be quite different to the production of services. One can contrast the manufacture of furniture to having a haircut. Yet although the scale, technology and location of these two examples are not the same, the two sectors can have much in common. Comparing furniture making with hairdressing, both producers will experience variations in demand and will have to vary capacity or make allowances for queuing; both will have made location decisions;

both will have to set the production activity in the context of a business so as to manage and control it effectively.

Useful goods and services are the products. Operations managers use the term *product* to describe the outputs which are supplied to customers, whether they are physical objects or intangible services. Viewing all outputs in this general way is an important perspective because it enables us to seek out the similarities in operations as apparently diverse as oil refining, printing, shoe repair and banking.

9. A service economy?

It is often suggested that modern western capitalist societies are moving away from being based on manufacturing towards becoming service economies. Consumption patterns change and reflect rising incomes, education levels and interest in leisure of most of the population. This trend, however, is often seen as full of risk for future national prosperity. Frequent references are made to the fall in the United Kingdom's manufacturing output during the past decades. Many advocate policies which will 'rebuild the manufacturing base' and return the country to being a net exporter of manufactured goods, a state which had been maintained for almost two hundred years. This type of argument creates two difficulties for study of production in its societal context, firstly whether there is indeed a trend towards a service economy and, secondly, the implication that the production of services is somewhat inferior to the production of goods.

To verify the existence of a trend towards a service economy is not easy. There are problems both with definitions and data. One common way of measuring industrial trends is to examine the nature of employment. A glance at the *Situations Vacant* columns suggests many more openings in the service sector than there used to be. Yet do such changes mark real shifts in the nature of what is produced? Compare the jobs of electrician and lawyer where the difference between their roles may not be so great as appears at first.

> An electrician can work on the production of goods for sale, for example an item of capital equipment. Alternatively, the same person may work on theatre lighting or aircraft maintenance. The remoteness of these jobs from the production of material goods must surely place the electrician in the service sector.
>
> The lawyer appears to produce a service and would clearly be doing so when representing a client in a dispute over, say, a family matter. On the other hand, the lawyer could represent the interests of a kitchen equipment manufacturer in protecting patent rights. Indeed, the lawyer could be a permanent employee of this manufacturer, filling the role of company secretary. In such a case it could be argued that the lawyer is as closely concerned with the production of material goods as is the maintenance electrician.

We can see that the same role can be classified as delivering service (providing legal advice) or manufacturing (participating in the manufacture of equipment) depending on one's point of view. Drawing distinctions has been made more difficult in recent years by the trend in many companies towards subcontracting of functions which were previously performed in-house. For example, a factory which contracts its cleaning or security services to specialist companies transfers jobs, which would previously have been counted as being in manufacturing, into the service sector. Yet the same tasks may be carried out by the same people. Whether workers fall into one or the other category is, therefore, rather arbitrary.

Even when the difficulties of categorisation are overcome, data does not support the notion of a long-term, steady shift towards service employment. A simple model of the employment split sees the rising labour productivity of manufacturing leading to a static or declining labour force in that sector. Surplus labour is then taken up by the service sector, which is inherently more labour intensive and for which demand is rising. Yet evidence from the past hundred years or so shows that many manufacturing industries have boomed and died. In 1841, 35.5% of the British population were employed in manufacturing, a figure that did not vary by more than three percentage points during the next 130 years. Table 1.1 gives some data from more recent years showing the relatively rapid fall in employment in manufacturing.

Beyond more subcontracting of functions there were two other main trends during the 1970s and 1980s. First there was a fall in manufacturing output resulting from lost international competitiveness; secondly the output per employee continued to rise steadily, the many firms which did survive were those which used their resources more efficiently and effectively.

The general rise in service employment hides many trends in different directions. The increase in service employment in the nineteenth century was mainly a result of more women going into domestic service. This role has all but disappeared yet at one time it employed one quarter of all women. Later, the domestic servant was partly replaced by the laundry and then the launderette. Yet even these services have largely come and gone and been replaced by a manufactured good, the washing machine. The domestic kitchen now contains more powerful machinery than many factories in the early stages of the industrial revolution. For many functions, self-service is the order of the day.

10. Goods superior to services?

My washing machine performs a function equivalent to the domestic servant or laundry. This is but one example of the interchangeability of many goods and services. Yet there remains an attachment to the notion that it is rather better to

Table 1.1 Employees in employment, United Kingdom

	1973	1979	1985	1991
All employment	22,662	22,920	21,423	22,628
Agriculture, forestry and fishing	434	378	341	291
Construction	1,743	1,638	1,021	963
Production*	8,172	7,521	5,953	5,261
... of which Manufacturing	7,828 (35%)	7,176 (31%)	5,362 (25%)	4,882 (22%)
Service	12,747 (56%)	13,761 (60%)	14,108 (66%)	15,754 (70%)

* Production includes manufacturing and the supply of energy and water
Source: *Annual Abstract of Statistics 1981* and *1993*, London, HMSO

manufacture than to deliver services. These are historical ideas, possibly related to the nineteenth century notion of the inherent nobleness of work. Adam Smith, for one, classed the work of servants as 'barren and unproductive', seeing it as having no value.

'[It] consists in services which perish generally in the very instant of their performance, and does not fix or realise itself in any vendible commodity which can replace the value of their wages and maintenance. The labour, on the contrary, of artificers, manufacturers and merchants, naturally does fix and realise itself in some such commodity.' [1]

Smith saw the work of merchants as essential adjuncts to the manufacturing process and, therefore, valuable. The merchant of Smith's day could just as well be the financial adviser of today, a role that is much further removed from a manufacturing process. Yet one could surely not sustain an argument for the superiority of one role over another.

It is evident, then, that the distinction between goods and services is not as clear as the original definitions suggest. Nor is it clear whether there is a single general trend towards service delivery in the post-industrial age. Furthermore, the notion that the production of goods is in some way superior to the production of services breaks down when distinctions between roles are attempted.

Many businesses both manufacture and supply service. Manufacturers primarily produce goods. For them, processes such as advice giving, delivery and installation are adjuncts to the manufacturing. Service producers such as taxi companies do no manufacturing. There are, however, many hybrids. To take a case in point, a newly completed washing machine stands in the warehouse at the Hotpoint factory. This is a manufactured good. Yet, as soon as the distributor places an order and the delivery process starts, service begins to be important. The value of the washing machine is enhanced by its despatch from Colwyn Bay

approaching 100% goods

↑↑↑↑↑↑↑↑↑↑↑↑↑↑↑↑↑↑↑↑↑↑↑↑

Self-service petrol
Food from discount retailer
Water supply
Hamburger, ready to eat
Dinner in restaurant
Supply and fitting of carpets
House painting
Gardening
Hospital operation
Car wash
Financial advice
↓↓↓↓↓↓↓↓↓↓↓↓↓↓↓↓↓↓↓↓↓↓↓↓

approaching 100% service

Box 1.1 Goods/service mixes in different purchases

to its destination. When displayed in the retail shop, the offer is a mixture or bundle of good and service. The machine has been manufactured, delivered and is about to be sold and delivered again complete with a guarantee of further service. If a fault develops, Hotpoint sends out a technician to perform a repair service which may include the exchange of a manufactured component. Box 1.1 suggests some other purchases in which you may be involved. The items are ranked according to a rough estimate of the proportions of good and service contained in each transaction.

Peters underlines the emerging recognition of the importance and integration of the service element. He goes beyond the data of Table 1.1 in saying, 'Would you believe that 96 per cent of us ply service trades? ... 79 per cent of us work in the service sector ... and of the 19 per cent still employed in so-called manufacturing, 90 per cent do service work (design, engineering, finance, marketing, distribution and so on).'[2] One of the reasons given for the recovery of competitiveness of the United States' economy in the middle 1990s is its edge in service productivity.

11. Comparison of manufacturing and service provision

The distinction between goods and services is not made in order to classify firms into one or other category as we have seen that many contain elements of both. Nor is it done to identify a preference for one over the other as such debate is sterile. In identifying these *ideal types*[3], however, we can discuss the likely characteristics which distinguish them. Then, in studying a case of an actual firm, we can recognise the degree to which it produces goods or services and therefore identify the sort of policies and operations systems it will require to produce them. The balance of manufacturing and service in any firm is decided by its business strategy which is itself a response to the environment in which the firm operates and is determined by the long-term goals.

Manufacturing and services: similarities

In many manufacturing organisations, there is a rigid separation between the production of goods and the associated activities of dealing with the customer. Marketing is often called a boundary-spanning function because, in one sense, it connects the organisation to the outside market yet, at the same time, provides a buffer between the uncertainty of that market place and the production system which can then operate more efficiently if undisturbed.

The same kind of separation can be advantageous in a service operation. Those activities which can be isolated from the interaction of the customer and the organisation are uncoupled and carried out either at another time or in another place. The number of staff who are engaged in direct dealing with customers is then reduced and the 'isolated' operations can be managed using similar methods to those used in manufacture.

Aircraft maintenance is carried out by specialists located at various bases throughout the world. Not only is it important for the airline to have a short down-time for maintenance but a predictable time is also needed. Major components such as engines are not, therefore, maintained *in situ* but are exchanged for replacements which have already been serviced. The engines can then be taken apart and rebuilt under factory conditions after the aircraft has resumed flying.

9

Manufacturing and services: differences

Manufacture and service operations are most similar when much of the service operation can be isolated from the point of delivery. It follows, then, that differences will become most apparent when the service has to be wholly produced at the delivery point. Examples include entertainment, fast food and medical diagnosis. In the case of routine service such as that delivered in a hamburger bar or by a travel company, it is possible to reduce costs by standardisation of products and incorporation of rules to make operations and control straightforward. But such 'mass service' operations are different to 'mass production'. The emphasis is on the use of interactive skills in customer care rather than technical skills in arranging flows of goods. The most successful firms have discovered ways of getting staff to apply interactive skills routinely and repetitively when the customer is so directly involved in the process.

USING A VARIETY OF RESOURCES

12. Categories of resources

Our definition of operations management includes the use of resources not just because these are obviously needed, there being no such thing as a free lunch. The emphasis is placed on the resources because the operations function consumes such a variety and, in most organisations, such a large proportion of the total used by the organisation. They can be categorised as follows:

- **Material resources** The raw materials and components which are consumed, or converted, by the system. Besides the material which is to be processed, the system will require energy and consumables such as processing tools and other variable items used in the process. Furniture factories use sandpaper and polishing materials, hospitals consume bandages and blood.
- **Capital equipment** The plant and property required to carry out the operations function. Buildings include depots, stores and factories while the plant ranges from machine tools to oil refineries, refrigerators to freight vehicles.
- **Labour** The people who run the operations function. These range from servers, drivers and operators to managers and controllers. Each has a vital role to play in the success of the function.
- **Information** Information is not often seen as a management resource in the same way as the others listed here. This is partly because it is not valued and accounted for as a business asset. At the same time, the operations function depends on information from many sources concerning orders, supplies, technology, competition and so on. For some organisations such as computer bureaux, market research companies, broadcasting organisations and universities, information is a critical raw material which the operating system converts into refined information as its key activity.

CREATING, OPERATING AND CONTROLLING THE TRANSFORMATION SYSTEM

13. Operations as a transformation process

The transformation system converts the resources into the appropriate bundle of product for the customer. The simplest system model of this process, Figure 1.2, shows the transformation process receiving inputs from suppliers and making them available as outputs to customers. While this is a very simple model, and you may easily pass over it with a glance, you should recognise that it is a basic building block of operations models which are developed in more detail throughout this book. We shall use it here to show the different configurations of systems which occur when the roles of stock and the customer are taken into account.

14. Operations within the manufacturing and supply chain

First, we can look at the role of inventory which is often used as a buffer between the operating system and its suppliers and customers. As we shall see later, this is because of uncertainty in both supply and demand as well as because the flow rates through the different stages cannot easily be matched. Figure 1.3, drawn from Wild's rather more complex presentation[4], shows four arrangements for manufacturing, supply or isolated service chains which result from whether and where inventories are placed. As Figure 1.3 shows, they may separate the transformation process from both suppliers and customers.

The first arrangement, Type 1, can be called *Process stock to stock*. It is very common. For manufacturing systems, it has the benefit of using inventories to isolate the internal processes from interruptions and variations in the patterns of supplier performance and customer requirements. It is also a model of other stages of the supply chain to the ultimate consumer. It demonstrates how a distributor can transform goods stored in bulk, say at an import depot by moving them to local cash-and-carry warehouses where retailers can draw on them as needed. The diagram brings out the most obvious drawback of such a system in that expensive stock has to be stored between each stage of what can become a long chain.

The remaining examples of Figure 1.3 follow from Type 1 by eliminating one or both of the inventories. In Type 2, *Direct inputs*, the supplier and transformation process are closely matched and not separated by the buffer. Sometimes the firms decide that the input material is so perishable that it is worth tying the two stages together very closely. Canners and freezers of vegetables have for many years had

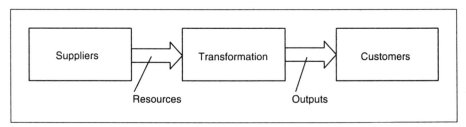

Figure 1.2 Operations as a transformation process

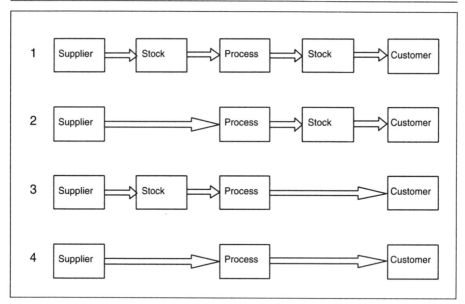

Figure 1.3 Flows through manufacturing and supply chains

plant whose packing capacity copes with the very seasonal flows of product from the fields and for the rest of the year remains idle. This ensures that the food is packed in the best condition. At the other end of the temperature scale, manufacturers have found it valuable to transport molten iron from plant to plant using special rail wagons. This avoids the costs of reheating but requires that the outputs of one plant must be balanced with the inputs of the other.

Ideas of saving inventory have gained ground in recent years through the introduction of just-in-time (JIT) supply systems which reduce the buffer stock sizes almost to zero. We shall look at this in more detail later but can note here that JIT is not a simple solution. Management attention is shifted from stocks to maintaining carefully balanced supply chains.

Type 3, *Direct outputs*, eliminates the stock holding after the transformation process. It can also represent JIT from the point of view of the supplier in the Type 2 case. Generally, however, the case covers customers who have goods made to order and these are supplied when they are ready. Examples range from Pizza Express' delivery service to Pronuptia, which specialises in the making of wedding dresses. Neither firm likes to carry finished stock.

Type 4, *Direct connections*, covers jobbing firms in large-scale engineering which aim not to carry inward stocks unless under specific contracts and supply the finished items when they are ready. Shipbuilders and civil engineers fall into this category. As with 2 and 3, Type 4 can also represent part of a chain of organisations which are fully linked by JIT arrangements.

Electricity supply is a rather special example of Type 4 because of the perishable nature of both inputs and outputs. With no storage capacity, the distribution companies such as MANWEB have to continuously supply customers according to their demands. This burden is in turn placed upon the power generators who have some storage capacity yet have to use flexible power stations to match variations minute by minute.

15. Operations within service-oriented systems

Operations such as transport and personal service differ from the examples covered by Types 1 to 4 for two reasons. First, the customer is more closely involved in the process, providing inputs as well as receiving the outputs. Secondly, the outputs of the transformation cannot be stocked. If a freight train fails to pass through a bottleneck, such as a tunnel or busy junction, at the appointed time, this represents capacity lost by the system for ever. Similarly, it is no use the hearses arriving a day before or after the funeral.

Seeing the customer as part of the transformation process and recognising the impracticability of storing service takes us on to three further models which are illustrated in Figure 1.4. The most general case, Type 5, *Flexible service*, is very typical. It shows service resources being present and offering some spare capacity, known as slack. At the same time, the customer arrives and, in principle, joins a queue before being served. The model shows the process as delivered to the customer who is seen as 'passing through' the transformation and receiving its outputs.

The Type 5 arrangement seems to be illogical as there would not normally be spare service capacity and the need for a queue at the same time. This is indeed true but the model represents the case where uncertainties cause continual imbalances between customer demands and the capability of satisfying them. Visit many a public house around 7 on a Saturday and you will see under-used service resources. By 10 o'clock, you will be lucky if you are served immediately or can

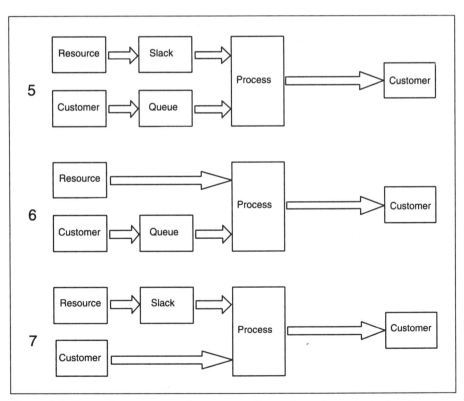

Figure 1.4 Flow of resources and customers through service-oriented systems

get a seat. Hospital accident departments are busy an hour or so later as well as on Sundays after the morning football. The balance between having queues at peak times and offering excess capacity at others is a critical problem for service operations managers which we shall look into later.

The Type 6 configuration, *Instant service*, is Type 5 without queues. It sets out to offer surplus capacity at all times. Examples range from the fast-service restaurant to the expensive private hospital, from the motel which advertises 'Rooms always available' to the fire service where the spare capacity means that fire crews become expert at billiards. Again, management of the high costs of such service operations is a problem. Sometimes, the excess capacity, especially of labour, can be used for other functions when it is not needed.

The Type 7 organisation offers *Low cost service*. Here, efficiency in the use of resources takes precedence over effectiveness and, sometimes, equity. The dentist, who in the United Kingdom is mostly paid per task carried out, cannot maintain enough income for the practice unless its facilities are in full use throughout the working day. A queue of two or three weeks, with exceptions for emergency cases, enables efficiency to be maintained while recognising the equitable treatment of those in greatest need.

16. Issues within the transformation system

What are the decisions which the operations manager must make when setting up and running the transformation process? Four areas have particular significance. They are capacity management, activity scheduling, inventory management and control. Through these elements, which are summarised in Figure 1.5, the operations manager seeks to create value for the customer. The systemic nature of the

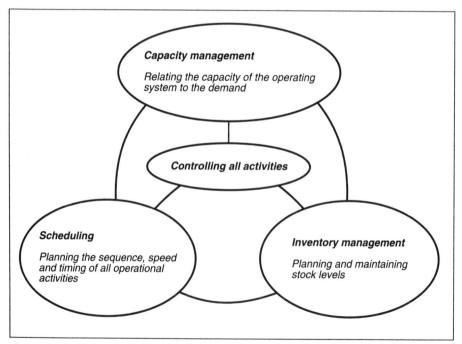

Figure 1.5 Principal decision areas within the operations system

operations function is seen in the way that these functions are interlinked and can be related back to the seven models of the transformation process given above.

In the short term, the capacity of operating systems can only be changed within certain limits. The doctor, faced with an outbreak of infectious disease, can respond by working harder and longer and, perhaps, by delaying visits to non-urgent cases. Manufacturing facilities may rely on overtime working to increase capacity by up to 20 per cent. In each case it is unwise to attempt to sustain the high output for long. In the medium term, the medical centre may take on another partner or the factory may set up a second shift. Each requires careful planning, a task not to be undertaken lightly. Capacity changes outside these ranges require even longer lead times, perhaps up to a decade in the case of construction and commissioning of brand new facilities.

Operations managers are not just concerned, then, with the short term. They have to be involved in choices about system capacity well into the future. It is here that the function interacts with strategic management, which is the long-range planning and policy accomplishment of the organisation.

Generally speaking, activity scheduling has a shorter time horizon. While some industries engage in operations which themselves take several years to complete, civil engineers being a notable example, the state of mind remains very much the same. The plans are made to suit the agreed overall productive capacity and activity scheduling involves itself with the sequence, speed and timing of all the tasks which are required to meet customers' needs. Within Model 1 schemes which operate between stocks, scheduling is very much an internalised process, working out the best ways of transforming the inward inventory into product ready for despatch to customers on demand. Models 2 to 4, on the other hand, dispense with the buffers. They require an integration of scheduling systems of the linked organisations which can increase the complexity of the task. For the service systems of Models 5 to 7, scheduling is more responsive to customers' immediate needs and the operations manager has to focus on questions of how much spare capacity to have in place as well as how to manage queues to best effect.

We have seen that the importance of inventory management will vary according to how much is carried. It is very easy to carry high stocks, yet these are expensive to hold. The skills of inventory management are concerned with maintaining an effective service to users while limiting the costs of capital devoted to stockholding.

Finally, control is placed at the centre of Figure 1.5. All operations activities need to be monitored and controlled so that they achieve their targets in terms of efficiency, effectiveness and, where appropriate, equity. At the same time, control can be expensive and intrusive for those engaged in the tasks. The manager must, therefore, understand how control can be exercised as well as how much is needed.

THE OPERATIONS FUNCTION WITHIN THE WHOLE ORGANISATION

17. The organisation's value chain

The value chain has become well known tool for setting out the key processes of the organisation as a whole. First proposed by Porter[5], its essential features are

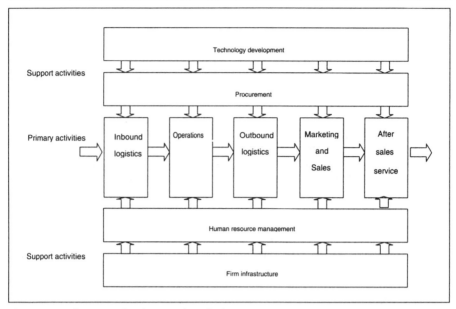

Figure 1.6 The organisation's value chain

activities, both internal and external, and integration. Through the nine generic activities which the model identifies, the firm can add to, or reduce, the total value of its product. Porter divides business activities into those which directly operate upon the product or service eventually delivered, the so-called primary activities, and the other necessary functions, or support activities, which provide a framework to back up the main line. Figure 1.6 shows the *primary* activities set out as links in a chain. These are reinforced by the four *support* activities which can be explained as follows:

- *Procurement* The obtaining of purchased inputs of all kinds.
- *Technology Development* Basic research and the design and development of both products and processes.
- *Human Resource Management* Recruiting, training, developing and organising of personnel.
- *Firm Infrastructure* Managerial processes such as planning and control, quality management, obtaining and allocating funds, the work of the legal department and dealing with governments.

As presented here, the model is made up of the elements which form the quintessential profit-making firm which produces a bundle of goods and services. The labelling of the model should be adapted to suit organisations which carry out other significant primary activities, such as social work departments, or where key support is needed from different functions such as a legal or international department.

The purpose of introducing the model here is to use it to illustrate how operations fits within a typical organisation. The function forms the working core of the organisation yet it should not be seen as embracing every part of it. Good organisation requires both the separation of functions and giving them clearly defined roles together with methods by which the functions are to be linked together. This is the nub of the classic study of Lawrence and Lorsch[6] who also showed that the degree of such differentiation and integration should be related to the setting in which the organisation was established.

18. Operations management and organisational structure

Firms have a choice about how to allocate tasks and fit them together. Figure 1.7 shows the scope of the operations management task in two businesses. First, the ellipse with the solid line shows the scope in a manufacturing firm. Of the primary activities, the operations manager is responsible for production, and some aspects of stockholding. The manager is also heavily involved with support activities from product and process development to quality assurance. Primary activities of delivery, sales and marketing and after-sales service are handled by other departments.

The second firm, outlined with the dotted line, is a supermarket retailer. Here store operations from inbound logistics through to selling are more closely integrated at the operational level. Support activities are frequently head-office functions carried out by specialists. The outline, therefore, identifies stores management as responsible for all aspects of the flow of goods from the unloading of incoming transport through to the consumer.

Organisation structure

To examine how these choices work out in practice, we can compare the organisation structures of the two firms of Figure 1.7. In the manufacturing company, the attention of the operations function (here called production) is on converting stock to stock. Consequently, production is separated from suppliers and customers by the purchasing and sales departments whose role is to deal with the

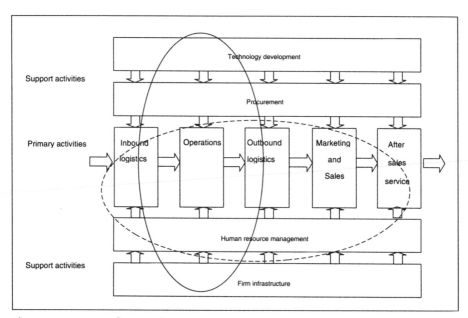

Figure 1.7 Scope of operations in two firms

inputs and outputs. This typical arrangement is illustrated in Figure 1.8. To manage continuous operations, the Production Director is responsible not only for the manufacturing facility but other functions with which it has to be closely integrated on a daily basis. These include:

- production planning, scheduling and control
- jig and tool design and manufacture
- maintenance of plant and equipment
- industrial engineering, which includes work measurement, method study and the management of any related payment scheme
- quality assurance.

In the supermarket firm, illustrated in Figure 1.9, the main operations activities are divided into two parts under the Distribution Director and the Stores Operations Director. One involves the receipt and storage of supplies from manufacturers and their distribution to the stores, the other is store management itself. Other functions at head office include merchandising which looks after relations with suppliers and studies the introduction of new lines. The Stores Managers, reporting to Area Operations Managers, manage the flow of goods in the stores from the moment they are received at the goods-inward bay until they are taken away by the customer. Figure 1.9 shows just some departments which may be established, depending on the size of the store. Others could be bakery, pharmacy, delicatessen, white goods, textiles and so on. At the local level, therefore, the Store Manager, as operations manager, is responsible for all stages of the firm's value chain as follows:

- inbound logistics, including unloading, unpacking and storing
- sales, including display, pricing and promotion
- outbound logistics from checkout operations to enabling customers to take purchases away conveniently
- in-store and after-sales customer service.

Comparing the responsibilities of the operations managers in the two cases, we can see several similarities and differences. The roles are similar in that they lie at

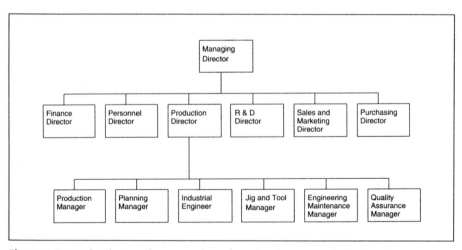

Figure 1.8 Production as the operations function in a manufacturing firm

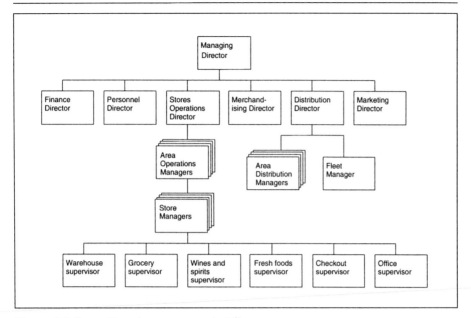

Figure 1.9 Operations in a supermarket firm

the heart of the business and drive it along on a day-to-day basis. The roles differ in that the manufacturing operations are isolated from direct contact with customers and will also be more involved with other functions in long-range questions such as product and process development. In the supermarket case, decisions about new products, new locations and so on are taken by specialists at head office.

It can be seen then that the scope of the operations manager's responsibilities varies from organisation to organisation and depends upon issues such as the operating system structure, the size of the activity and the personal choice of those involved.

Case study: Operations management in a nursing home.

Nursing homes are set up to satisfy the needs of those who require 24 hour nursing care. They are inspected and approved by local authorities but are owned and managed by a range of bodies including individuals, companies and charitable organisations.

The Newton Nursing Home has space for 40 patients in a three-storey building converted from a pair of large Victorian houses. It is part of a business which operates 25 similar establishments throughout north-west England. The local manager is the Matron who is responsible for all operations at the home. Helped by qualified sisters who work shifts, the Matron has to ensure that care to the required standard is available at all times. One third of the patients are confined to bed, only a handful of the others can walk unsupported. The operations managers must, therefore, ensure that each patient is looked after according to his or her needs. The care tasks include: providing and supervising personal care; preparing and serving meals; cleaning and washing; dealing with visiting medical practitioners; arranging visits to the hospital; providing ancillary services such as hairdressing and chiropody. Beyond these direct service responsibilities the managers deal with friends and relatives of the patients and arrange occasional events such as outings and informal concerts.

Staffing is a continual problem. There are standards, enforced by the licensing authority, for the minimum number of staff on the premises at any time. To cover the periods when permanent staff are unavailable, the managers maintain lists of carers looking for occasional employment They also use agencies and sometimes fall back on persuading a member to work an extra shift.

Patients pay for their accommodation and care, prices varying from £290 to £360 per week depending on the room. Most patients receive some support from the social security system, in some cases they are paid for entirely. Payments from public funds can be made directly to the company. For the rest, patients or their representatives are invoiced by head office and Matron is responsible for chasing slow payers. The Matron also looks after the day-to-day repairs of the building and equipment. To do this she employs a repair person who possesses skills from gardening to interior decorating.

Few patients recover. When a room becomes vacant, the Matron arranges to have it redecorated and let as soon as possible. To this end she maintains a waiting list of a few names and sometimes places an advertisement in the local paper.

Questions

1 *Is Newton Nursing Home a 'pure service' business? What operating system structure exists at the home? What resources are converted into what outputs?*

2 *What, in terms of the 3 Es, are the operating system objectives?*

3 *Relate the principal operating decisions to the categories of Figure 1.5.*

References

1. Smith, Adam, *The Wealth of Nations* London, Methuen, 1981
2. Peters, Tom (1984) 'Hit and run strategy for hypercompetition' *The Independent on Sunday, Business News* 9 October, p.22
3. The ideal type is not the same as a simple classification or an empirical model. In constructing such a description one is searching for the basic characteristics of a particular sort of organisation and not attempting to describe any actual situation.
4. Wild, R. (1991) *Production and Operations Management* 4th edition London, Cassell pp.7–11
5. Porter, M.E. (1985) *Competitive Advantage* New York, Free Press
6. Lawrence, P.R. and Lorsch, J.W. (1967) *Organisation and Environment* Homewood Ill., Irwin

2

OPERATIONS MANAGEMENT IN THE ORGANISATIONAL CONTEXT

Chapter objectives

When you have finished studying this chapter, you should be able to:

- Define a system, explain the key elements of systems and justify the use of systems thinking in analysing operations.
- Distinguish between structural and process models of systems and organisations.
- Describe an organisation in terms of input-output models and classify flows between the elements in terms of input, output, planning and control.
- Explain the term market orientation and describe the key activities of the marketing function.
- Describe the marketing mix and the communications mix.
- Identify the main processes involved in design and development and discuss how and why these are being modified in modern organisations.
- Explain and illustrate the concept of manufacturability.
- Demonstrate the construction of budgets for operation and investment and show how these form links between finance and operations.
- Define and explain the significance of the break-even point to operations managers.
- Compare different financial methods of appraising investment proposals, including those involving discounting of future cash flows.

SYSTEMS THINKING

1. Structure and process

Organisations can be seen as consisting of elements which are almost stable and others which change continually. The former are called structural elements and the latter as processes.

- The term *structure* refers to the set of relatively unchanging elements within a system. In an operations system, they include buildings, facilities, vehicles or machinery, the basic organisation, information systems, work rules and trade union agreements.

- The term *process* refers to those features of a system which change continually within the structure. In operations, they include flows of goods and service, energy, new recruits, cash and information.

2. Systems as wholes

When we observe something we call *a system* we tend to speak of it as a whole and ascribe to the whole system attributes which cannot be attached to any particular part of it. It is as though the system behaves in a way which is different from simply a sum of the behaviour of all its parts. While it is true that, if we knew enough about each element in detail, we could predict the behaviour of the system as a whole, in reality this is not usually possible because systems are characterised by complexity. The following are examples of systems:

a shoal of fish, the electricity supply grid, FIAT, the Football Association, the insurance industry

'But,' you may say taking the first example, 'a shoal of fish is a system comprising a vast number of fish which are themselves systems!' That is indeed true. One could also add that the shoal is but one small element of life in the ocean which is often itself referred to as an ecosystem. And the oceanic ecosystem is part of the planet which is part of the solar system and so on. These are reasonable responses. They refer to two further important features of the way we think about systems, recognition of the existence of a hierarchy and the notion of a boundary used to separate one system from another.

3. System definition

These ideas lead us to the definition of a system:

A system is a set of parts which are connected together in significant ways.

Central to the idea of system, captured by this definition, are the significant connections or relationships among the components. It is as though the arrangement of these parts, and the way they work together, are at least as important as the parts themselves. The following important general features of all systems are illustrated in Figure 2.1:

- **Holism** - the notion that the whole of the system behaves in a way which is greater than the sum of its parts. The attributes which are displayed by the system as a whole are called *emergent properties*.
- **Hierarchy** - each system consists of parts which are themselves systems. We may refer to these parts as *subsystems* when we are interested in the elements from which they are made, otherwise we use the term *component*. Does the fact that systems are composed of subsystems mean that we require an immensely complex and deep investigation each time we want to answer a question? The answer is, 'No,' for we only need to investigate what we need to.

The notion of hierarchy makes us sensitive to the possibility of complexity both in relation to subsystems and to systems of which the system under investigation is a part. The depth of investigation, that is the degree of resolution of these systems, will depend on the relevance it has for our investigation[1].

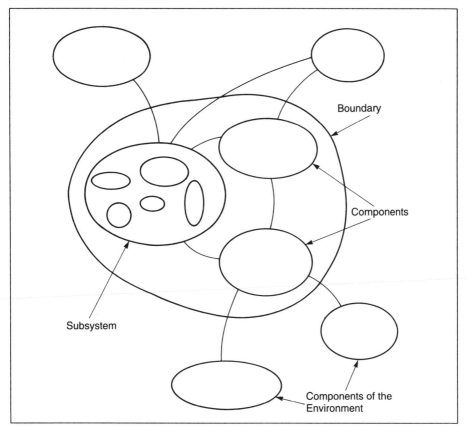

Figure 2.1 A general system and its elements

- **Boundary** - the boundary is the notional line which separates the system from those elements outside it. For a business organisation, what is owned by it and who is employed by it are usually easy to define. But what of charitable organisations which rely on volunteers? What about groups of organisations which, from time to time, cooperate with each other? The boundary in these cases is not easy to draw.
- **Environment** - the collection of elements which are outside the system but interact with it in meaningful ways. Systems which have environments are called *open systems*.
- **Significance** - the use of the term *significant* in the definition is important. Just as a marine biologist can see meaning in fish forming shoals to enhance survival, an operations manager sees particular forms of production system as more likely to achieve the set goals. Others, such as employees or customers, may perceive the system and its goals in quite different ways. These contrasting perceptions of operating systems, especially those brought in by customers of service systems, have to be considered by the effective manager.

4. Justification for systems thinking

One response to being introduced to systems thinking is that it introduces a great deal of unnecessary complexity. Why be concerned with notions of boundary and hierarchy and this mysterious idea of emergent properties? The answer is that systems ideas help us to do several things: we can more easily picture and cope with the complexity of operating systems; we can recognise the different perspectives brought by different people in these complex situations; we can find features in common among such systems and thus transfer learning from one to another. This last point was given at the start of Chapter 1 as one of the reasons for studying operations management.

- *Complexity*
  Decision making about simple issues, such as which loaf of bread to buy, requires limited investigation and costs little if the wrong decision is made. But what about if you are seeking to make a long-term deal over millions of buns for a restaurant chain? There are many issues to be explored, many variables to be taken into account. A thorough investigation, recognising the complexity of interactions, would be needed here. Systems thinking assists in recognising and coping with the complexity.
- *Subjectivity*
  Gathering an appreciation that different people will define systems, and therefore problems within them, in different ways may be regarded as an unfortunate hindrance to progress. In some situations it may be possible to impose a particular point of view or discover a consensus which can be sustained. In others, the perspectives of different groups (managers, workers, customers) will be so different that the manager will have to cope by trading off the needs of one group against those of another. Again, systems thinking can help in the management of this complexity.
- *Generality*
  General Systems Theory examines systems in all spheres of reality, for example biology, ecology, politics, economics, business. In so doing, it seeks universal statements about organisation, complexity, control and so on[2]. Notwithstanding the difficulties of comparing systems, in different fields, it is useful to think of general notions, especially the nature of control, when considering effective management of operations systems. Again, if we learn one of the approaches to problem solving developed in later chapters, we can, by recognising its general properties, apply it in many situations in many organisations.

OPERATIONS WITHIN THE ORGANISATIONAL SYSTEM

5. Process models

The organisation, as a system, is a set of parts which are connected together in a significant way. The significance is that which is provided by the owners or managers in arranging the components in order to achieve the chosen plan. The organisation is set in a complex environment consisting of elements such as competitors, customers, suppliers, the government, the legal system, the labour market, trades unions, banks and so on. In organising the business, the managers seek to take advantage of the opportunities which the environment provides while avoiding or coping with the threats that it imposes. We shall take up this model of organisation and environment when we come to look at planning in Chapter 4.

The organisation is made up of several subsystems which interact with each other and with the environment. There are almost as many ways of presenting the arrangement of these components as there are authors writing on the subject. The value chain model of a business organisation was presented in Chapter 1. This type of model, which presents the business as an input-output (I-O) system within an environment, is very common. One way of doing this in more detail for the functions of a manufacturing business is shown in Figure 2.2.

In Figure 2.2, the output of each stage of the flow of goods is the input to the next stage. Thus the subsystems of the business are themselves perceived as I-O (input-output) systems. By extension, each component of these subsystems can be analysed in the same way. For example the paint shop, part of the production system, takes in unpainted goods and sends out painted ones. This transformation is the contribution of the department to the total production system which takes in raw materials and transforms them into finished goods.

Figure 2.2 shows how the flow of goods passes from purchasing to production to sales and finally to customers. What of the other departments such as personnel? Are they less involved in the purpose of the business? No, these back-up activities are important links in the chain because, for example, the production subsystem requires people who have to be recruited, trained and looked after. Indeed, from the point of view of the personnel manager, the personnel function is also an I-O system. Among other activities it takes in recruits and provides competent staff to the other subsystems.

6. The roles of subsystems

Other subsystems in Figure 2.2 fulfil different roles. The finance function controls the flows of cash into, out of and around the business. Information is exchanged

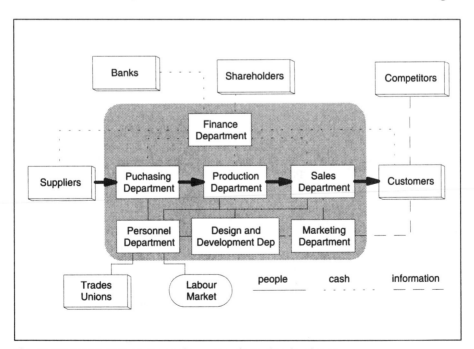

Figure 2.2 Input-output stages in a manufacturing business

among the departments. This information is operational, such as orders and immediate plans, or it supports other decision areas of management including planning and control, discussed in detail in Chapter 4.

A planning system looks ahead and decides what is to be done in the future. Production planning entails day-to-day scheduling; process and pre-production planning involves looking further ahead to make it possible for production to take place, for instance by the provision of special equipment; strategic planning for production has a time scale of several years and includes decisions about new processes, changes in capacity or location.

A control system includes, on a day-to-day basis, activities such as inspection, standard costing, progress monitoring and stock control. Looking further ahead, progress towards long-term plans is monitored. In all these cases, data is collected, compared with original plans and corrective, control action taken where necessary.

Thus we can draw up an inventory, as in Box 2.1, which outlines the relationships among various components of the production system and other systems within the business. Box 2.1 demonstrates that the links between the production

System	Relationship to operations system	Relevant features
Purchasing	Input	Buying, quality assurance, vendor rating
Stock holding	Input Control Output	Raw materials Intermediate stocks Finished stocks
Distribution	Output	Close links if distribution integrated with production
Sales	Planning	Short-term production plans tuned to demand
Marketing	Planning	Longer-term product and process plans
Personnel recruitment	Input Planning	Staff required at once Staff required in the future
Training	Input Planning	Training for immediate needs Training for future needs
Finance	Control Input Planning	Costs of all inputs Working capital Budgets
R&D and Design	Input Planning	Manufacturing instructions Future processes

Box 2.1 Links among subsystems of the business

system and the rest of the business are many and complex. These links include the fundamental ones of inputs and outputs between stages of the process to the managerial links of planning and control. The relationships between planning, operating and control are developed in Chapter 4.

7. Structural models

Process models, which stress the flow of inputs and outputs through the operating system, are not the only way that the system can be conceived. Structural models examine the relationships among the relatively fixed components. We have already seen one type, the organisation expressed in terms of functions such as operating and marketing. Systems thinking, however, encourages us to take a wider view than this, recognising that the organisation consists of several linked subsystems of different types. The *socio-technical systems* view examines the organisation in terms of the intertwining of the technical system with the social system. This is examined in more detail in Chapter 3. Kast and Rosenzweig[3] advanced a more general model, stressing that the organisation had several major subsystems as shown in Figure 2.3.

The diagram shows that it is possible to look at the organisation in several ways. The traditional management approach was to emphasise the structural system and describe the organisation in terms of hierarchical charts such as those

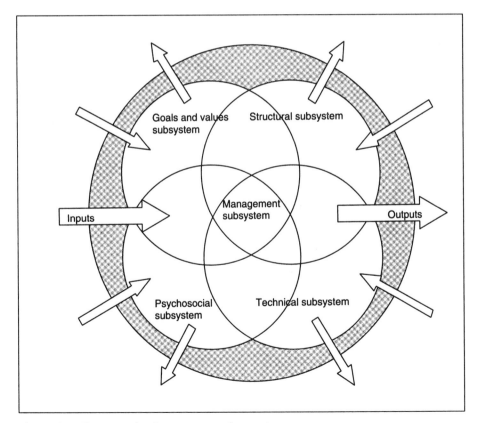

Figure 2.3 The organisation as a complex system

used in Chapter 1. The behavioural scientist focused on the psychosocial subsystem, concentrating on developing ideas about the behaviour of individuals and groups. The political scientist would start by looking at goals and values. The traditional production management specialist saw the organisation in terms of a collection of facilities which were to be optimised. The technical system was the centre and other factors were seen only in terms of constraints upon choice. The modern view of organisations considers all the subsystems and the interactions between them. Not only does each subsystem have some interactions with the environment but the important point is that it is the system *as a whole* which works to convert inputs into outputs. For the operations manager, understanding interactions is important. An example is the relationship between the psychosocial and the technical subsystems which is covered fully in Chapter 3. Building on the general input-output picture presented in Figure 2.2, we can now examine links between operations and three other functions in more detail.

MARKETING AND THE OPERATIONS FUNCTION

8. The marketing approach

Of all the business functions, marketing is the one which most clearly links the organisation to the outside world. Indeed its prime focus is boundary spanning in that it is concerned with relations with the customer.

The marketing approach to business involves a fundamental commitment to satisfying the needs of customers. It is both a set of beliefs (concerning market orientation) about the direction in which businesses should be facing and a set of processes which express the beliefs in practice. The commitment to satisfying customer needs has been interpreted differently throughout history. During the industrial revolution firms produced goods and services in rapidly increasing volumes. Prices fell so dramatically and demand was so great that success in manufacturing stemmed from obtaining raw materials and using machinery to reduce costs and maximise output. James Watt's steam engine was four times more efficient than the ones it replaced. In 1813, there were about 2,000 power looms in the Lancashire cotton weaving industry, by 1820 some 14,000 and the 100,000 mark was reached in 1833. In these circumstances it is not surprising that most companies focused their efforts on production to overcome the shortages which had hindered economic growth.

Rising competition among companies made them realise that something more would have to be done to encourage the customer to buy products, especially when there were so many to choose from. Firms began to consider what the customers wanted. They were, however, still conditioned by the desire to produce in large volumes to keep costs and prices down. The early *production orientation* changed to a *sales orientation* in which the accent was on selling whatever the company had to offer. The tools of selling and promotion came into widespread use. These included advertising, personal persuasion and offering financial incentives and discounts. Yet even sales-oriented firms were not good at keeping up with rapidly changing customers' tastes. As these tastes shifted, the firms faced the struggle to keep costs below the prices that increasingly disenchanted customers were prepared to pay.

9. Market orientation

Market orientation begins with the customer. It recognises that products are bought to satisfy needs. This implies two broad stages of marketing activity - discovering and interpreting needs and then devising ways of satisfying them. Of course, customers' needs are not independent of what firms have to offer and many take active steps to mould or create needs through various forms of persuasion. All in all, having a market orientation means that the firm sees itself as engaged in a continual exchange with its customers. Consider the early years of rivalry between Ford and General Motors in the United States:

Ford had defined customer needs for motoring in terms of basic transportation at the cheapest possible price. Starting from this definition, the astonishingly successful Model T was produced at low cost by the new manufacturing systems which Ford had developed. In 1926, Ford's output was one million vehicles, twice that of GM. In emerging as one of the first major companies with clear marketing orientation, GM reinterpreted the customer need to include the notion that customers also wanted to travel *in comfort.* New technology, that of being able to press sheet steel cheaply to make body panels, allowed GM to introduce a range of cars with enclosed bodies. By 1930, Ford's 2:1 lead was reversed. The Model T became obsolete and GM has never relinquished its place as the world's leading manufacturer.

It was GM's exploitation of the pressing technology that made the difference. The new cars were more expensive than Ford's. They had to be made affordable, convenient and desirable. Instalment payments were introduced, as were trade-ins. A distribution and servicing network was formally established. There was the idea of a *model range* with different sizes and styles, with annual changes to keep the car up to date. GM was bringing together the *marketing mix* (see section **18**) in offering a combination of *product, promotion, price and place* to satisfy the customer. It recognised that a customer wanted more than a manufactured good. Service was just as important[4].

It must be said that not all companies have adopted a market orientation. This may be because of blinkered management or because circumstances do not warrant it. Witness a recent example of production orientation:

When asked about the competition between rail and road transport in his country, the General Manager of Pakistan National Railways replied, 'The question is not whether the roads are a problem for Pakistan railways. I am unable to cope with the load which is laid upon me. In the passenger sector I am responsible for 50 percent of the traffic yet the demand is 20 percent more than that. In the freight sector, the figures are similar. I do not have the equipment to carry the demand. Road transport, therefore, is not a problem for me.'[5]

Throughout the interview the manager frequently used the first person. In so doing he presented himself as the embodiment of the railway company. Note also the way in which he showed his production orientation both by denying the significance of competition and in the choice of words he used to describe his problems.

10. Marketing definition

We can define marketing as follows:

Marketing is the process of identifying, anticipating, influencing and supplying customer requirements efficiently and profitably.

Figure 2.4 emphasises the four main processes implied by this definition which we shall examine in turn.

11. Identifying customer requirements

Market research includes finding out about markets, customers and their requirements. For example, the firm benefits from knowing the location of its customers and potential customers as well as other information such as their tastes, buying habits and consumption of competitors' goods and services. Market research information is used by both Research and Development and Design functions to create successful products as well as by market planners to provide forecasts of demand.

Incorporating the 'voice' of the customer has become more and more important in surviving in competitive environments. One method of involving customers in design which has gathered ground in recent years is QFD, or Quality Function Deployment. QFD aims to relate the features valued by the customer to the factors which must be considered in making a product work. Clearly different customers attach different values to product attributes. In designing a car, for example, attention may be focused on doors. Customers may recognise the value of those that are easy to open and close, those that provide extra side-impact protection, those which carry features such as electric windows. The balance among these could be the subject of a survey.

Meanwhile, designers may explore different approaches to door design which offer the attributes identified among customers. QFD establishes specific measures for combinations of these engineering characteristics. Some will score highly on one dimension but not well on others. Electric windows may be valued for their convenience but the presence of the motor within the door increases its weight and makes it less easy to open and close. They also put up the costs of materials and assembly.

QFD then brings the preferred attributes and engineering characteristics together in a planning matrix which points the way towards optimal design selection[6]. The method is covered in more detail in **16.6**.

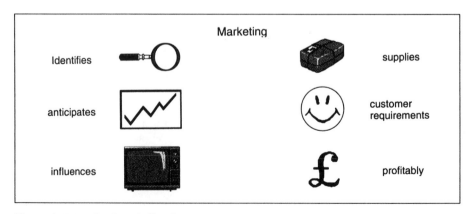

Figure 2.4 Marketing defined

12. Anticipating customer requirements: the product life cycle

Anticipation is the province of market forecasting in which, by methods such as projection of historic trends, an organisation seeks to be ready for change. Attention could be paid to annual growth rates or seasonal fluctuations in demand for current products or, with rather more difficulty, new products.

Marketers often use the *product life cycle* (PLC) for describing the way the fortunes of individual products change as time passes. Used in the right way, the PLC is a tool which gives valuable insight into planning and strategy formulation as we shall see in Chapter 4. It also aids communication among managers when discussing plans.

Many products go through a cycle, after their introduction to the market, of growth, stability and subsequent decline. The PLC is a representation of such a sequence. In our version, four phases can be identified, as in Figure 2.5. The PLC is a time series model representing the volume of sales after the product has been introduced to the market. Let us examine what happens when a new product is brought in. In the initial stages, the business is faced with making potential customers aware of the product, explaining to them the way it is used and when or where it is to be supplied and establishing effective channels of distribution.

After this *introduction* phase, if successful, sales growth is likely to be rapid. In the *growth* phase, the business will begin to recoup its investment in development and the production system will be working at its planned capacity. Success, however, attracts competition and rivals will begin to take a share of the market. The business will need to continue its selling efforts to defend market share. The sales rate then begins to slow as the market enters its *maturity* phase. During this time

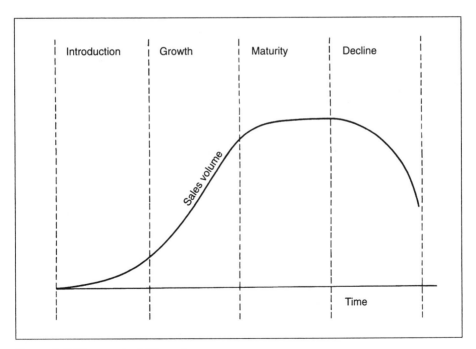

Figure 2.5 The product life cycle

several factors may contribute to stabilisation of sales: it may be that most potential customers have bought the product and confine themselves to replacement purchases; customers may tire of whatever features the product has to offer; it may be that there is a gradual shift towards alternatives which satisfy their needs in a better way. Finally, the product goes into *decline*. Competitors gradually drop out as sales fall and the residue of demand is shared among the remaining firms.

13. Limits of the PLC

We shall see in Chapter 4 how operations policies should be deliberately changed to match stages of the life cycle. It is sufficient to note here that while the model gives a basic general view of market behaviour it has its weaknesses:

- The PLC is a generalised model which does not apply always. The sales of some basic products, such as domestic piped water, hardly change decade by decade and variations depend much more on weather and (to a lesser extent) price than any underlying trend towards water going out of fashion! Other products have a long history - Beecham's Powders have been sold for more than 100 years and are 'Still going strong'.
- The life spans of products within industries may be changing. We have already looked at the example of General Motors' introduction of annual styling changes. Relaunches of this nature began to be seen by the market as wasteful and manufacturers increased the periods between model changes, especially as the costs of new model development rose rapidly. Recently, however, competition has intensified and new computer aided design processes have cut the cost of model changes. The trend in the European automobile industry is towards shorter periods between new launches.
- The PLC is simply a *descriptive* model. As we have seen, it should not be seen as capable of making forecasts. Nor should it be treated as *prescriptive*, that is being a statement of the way markets ought to behave. A marketing manager, then, should only use the PLC for thinking about the policy issues at various stages of a product's life.

14. Linking the PLC to operations and finance

Figure 2.6 links the PLC to the operations and finance functions. Products require cash investment, not only for product and process development but also for the initial marketing activity. The figure extends the time line back into the development period. It shows the cumulative negative, or outward, flow of cash spent on investment throughout this period. Recovery only begins after sales revenue comes in. When the cash line crosses the zero axis, the project has recovered all its initial expenditure. This is the *project break-even point*. For example, in the case of development of a new pharmaceutical, break-even comes eight or more years from start up. (Note that this break-even point is a point in time and should not be confused with the one identified in cost-volume-profit analysis as in section **30**, below.)

The operations manager must also be aware of the general form of the PLC although, as has been said, it should not be used on its own as a predictive tool. It can be seen that the rate of required output gradually builds up during the introduction phase. During the growth phase, the operations function must increase its capacity at a high rate. As the mature phase is entered, extra capacity is no longer required and the operations manager must ensure that the investment programme is slowed down.

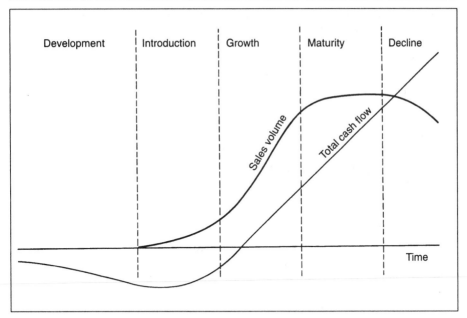

Figure 2.6 Cash flow during the PLC

15. Influencing customer requirements: the communications mix

Influencing customers is the third part of the marketing definition. To achieve this, marketers think in terms of the communications mix which consists of:

- *Advertising*
  This has many purposes depending on whether a product is well known or is being introduced for the first time. In the former case the idea may be to persuade a customer to consume more and then repeat the purchase; in the latter, the advertisement may focus on product information and persuading someone to try it out. Marketing managers have to choose the amount to spend on advertising, its pattern and intensity, the media to be used and the message to be conveyed. Plans in this area must take into account operating implications. Increased demand would be worthless without the ability to supply. Benefits may flow from timing advertising to boost demand during slack periods, especially where they coincide with a known pattern such as the seasons.
- *Public relations*
  This usually refers to communications addressed to a wider audience than just customers and markets, for example the safety assurances continually stressed by the nuclear industry. Yet PR can affect sales by giving general support to the image of a supplier.
- *Promotion*
  This is the range of activities and product features which give that last little 'push' in achieving a sale. In some goods, packaging may be an important feature of the product's image as well as contributing to its value in use. Luxurious wrappings aid image building. For services, the working environment has a significant influence on customers: consider how you compare

33

different greengrocers shops. Promotional campaigns may affect sales in the short term and, hence, the operations function.

- *Selling*
  Personal selling is a significant feature of influencing customers. This is especially true where the sale involves a complex bundle of goods and service. Good children's shoe shops, such as Clark's, measure feet as a matter of course; this involves selling and providing service simultaneously. This close relationship of selling and the service operations is something we shall return to in Chapter 3.

16. Supplying customer requirements

In order to supply products to its customers organisations have to make two types of decision:

- *Channels of distribution*
  The range of available channels is very wide. They vary from the simplest 'direct to the consumer' through to involving several intermediate stages such as distributors or international agencies. The selection of channel will depend on the scale and location of the supplier and the number of final customers. For example, national newspapers seek to have as short a time as possible from printing to being made available at a large number of outlets before breakfast. New technology allows for printing at several locations using page settings which have been distributed electronically. The distribution system from the print works relies on major contractors, such as TNT, to deliver to wholesalers who then break down the loads and take them to shops in their own vans. Distribution is, of course, the operation function of the transport companies. The pattern of the complete network emerges from a complex interaction of decisions among many companies.
- *Management of channels*
  Having selected broad patterns of distribution, logistics managers are concerned with questions such as: detailed process design including warehouse layout and equipment as well as choices of vehicle sizes and routes; the levels of stock to keep within the distribution channel and how to combine it with the appropriate level of service. The service level decision is one which lies at the interface of marketing and operations.

17. Balancing stocks and service in distribution channels

One way to regard the interface between operations and marketing is to see the functions separated by the buffer of finished goods stock. This is the relationship in the upper part of Figure 2.7. The production system is isolated from variations in the market by the finished goods stock and the sales department is engaged in the boundary spanning between the firm and the market. The light arrows suggest the flows of goods and the black arrows are orders which pass from sales to the stock warehouse and from the stock warehouse to the production system.

The problem for operations managers here is that the only information received about customer demand is through the stock information. The problem for sales is that nothing is known directly about operating performance or plans. Stock levels of finished goods can be optimised under this system, as shown later in the book,

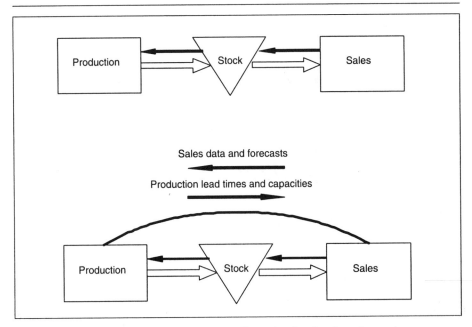

Figure 2.7 Using information to manage flows in distribution channel

but a much greater improvement is available if the two functions share information on current activities as well as forecasts and plans for the future. The possible extra communication link is shown in the lower half of Figure 2.7. Such integration allows the sales and marketing function to understand the consequences of demand changes for the bundle of goods and service and hence work with the operations function to satisfy them.

18. The marketing mix

The marketing mix was referred to briefly in section **9**. It consists of the various factors to be considered by marketing managers in successfully carrying out their function. Each has interactions with and implications for operational decisions.

The marketing mix of any one company is a unique balance of four elements, the first two of which we have only looked at in passing. The mix is often called *The 4 Ps.*

- *Product* - the bundle of goods and service which is offered to the customer.
- *Price* - sometimes the initial purchase price may be stressed but the costs of ownership, from running expenses to finance costs, are also often relevant.
- *Place* - the place at which the bundle is offered. This was discussed in sections **16** and **17**.
- *Promotion* - the publicity, advertising and final selling effort. This has been covered in section **15**.

19. The product and the customer

In the end, the enterprise attempts to exploit its chosen markets through matching its offering to market needs. The way this is done is again at the heart of the connections between operations and marketing. Markets are composed of individual buyers, whether they act on their own behalf or buy for other organisations. Each demands a different product bundle. For example, at the simplest level, both my father and I like a certain brand of mild. But he wants to buy it in his club and I in mine.

The appropriate response depends on many factors from competition to technology. To give each customer a unique service is expensive, to offer no variety leads to failure. Take the example of milk.

> The approach of the Milk Marketing Board for many years was to support dairy farmers by minimising the costs of getting the product to the consumer. This meant that processing, from pasteurisation to bottling, was carried out at large plants before delivery. The need to deliver to the doorstep and collect empty bottles was another pressure for standardisation. The market was supplied with pints of full-cream milk. Advertising reinforced both the goodness of the product and its packaging - 'Drinka pinta milka day.' Variations in customer demand were largely ignored.

This policy is one of *market aggregation*, that is the widest possible range of customers are satisfied with offerings from a very limited product range. There is no attempt to match different offerings to identified groups. At the other extreme lies *customisation* in which each customer is given a unique offering. While possible for single contracts or expensive products such as individually designed houses or clothes, full customisation is not feasible for the average producer. In the middle lies *market segmentation* in which potential customers are separated into groups with common features such as needs, tastes, life style and so on. The supplier then attempts to match product features to the different segments.

Market segmentation may be clearly defined or the boundaries may be unclear. *Product differentiation*, in either case, responds to the existence of segments by offering products with discernible differences, both from others within the same range and from those of competitors. This has a bearing on the operations system as extra costs are incurred in achieving the differentiation. Not only is the range of offerings likely to be increased but the goods-service bundle may be changed for each segment. Bases of differentiation may be quality, speed of service, time of service, design and so on. Branding, supported by image-building advertising, is a means of sustaining perceptions of differences in consumers' minds.

20. Price

Pricing has an indirect effect on the operations function in that changes in price usually have effects on demand and on the mix of products that are sold. The interaction between pricing and operational issues can be important in some service industries where demand fluctuations are difficult to cope with. Peak tariffs exist in many cases, from transport to telephones, holidays to haircuts. In such cases the supplier is trying to optimise revenue by raising prices at the times when demand is excessive. There is some hope that some demand will be transferred to slack times.

Price is important in those markets which are sensitive to it. Generally this occurs where product differentiation is low and customers have, or can obtain, enough information to compare one offering with another. Examples range from petrol, where filling stations are required to have prominent price displays, to standard package holidays. In each of these industries, however, suppliers attempt to raise perceptions of differentiation through branding and adding on extra items of service to the bundle.

In situations of price sensitivity, the operations manager may be encouraged to focus on reducing costs, thus enabling price to be cut further and market share increased. This is a wasteful policy in other situations.

DESIGN, DEVELOPMENT AND THE OPERATIONS FUNCTION

21. Product and process design and development

Product design is another route along which the influence of the market reaches the operations system. We need to distinguish product design, which is the creation of a set of specifications for the product, from process design which concerns how the product is to be created. In the supply of services, the two are clearly related as the process is part of the service offered. What is not so obvious is the intrinsic closeness of product and process design in manufacture. Not so long ago, product designers would pass the specification 'over the wall' to the process engineers who would then have the task of finding a way to make it. Modern ideas of parallel engineering and manufacturability recognise the waste that this can create. Disassembly, from nuclear plant to plastic vehicle parts, has also become a design issue in recent years.

Good design in business is about discovering what people want and taking steps to deliver it. Marketers know that satisfied customers tend to tell a few others, dissatisfied ones tell many more. The design process may not seem very costly in itself but it is a stage where up to 90 percent of the costs of supplying a product are decided. In other words, the design function has a very significant effect upon operations.

Design and development have many features in common and are not separated in many organisations. Differences, if any, lie in the starting points of the process. Design starts from an expression of customer need, such as an architect being requested to design a health centre, a furniture designer working on a range of seats for a new airport lounge or a fashion designer creating some new clothes for the next season. Development, on the other hand, is usually considered to spring out of basic research where initial 'blue-sky' ideas are taken forward to practical application. These differences are ones of emphasis rather than basic process for effective basic research is still focused on customer needs.

22. The design and development processes

Design and development decisions have much in common with other managerial decisions, including those in operations management. They can be set out in terms of a process, or methodology, which takes the decision making from an initial awareness of a question through to a completed specification. Outlined in Figure 2.8, the stages are as follows:

- *Problem awareness*
  Identification of opportunity or problem setting within which a solution is to be found. Either this is quite clear ('I need a house built here.') or a result of an

37

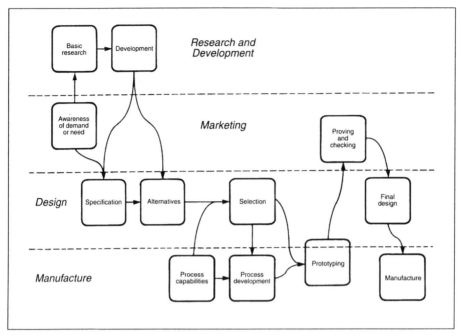

Figure 2.8 Links between marketing, R&D, design and production during design and development

unease about a complex situation ('Our products don't seem to be as good as those of our competitor.') An opportunity would be expressed as: 'This chemical may have applications in crop protection if only we can find a safe way of making and applying it.'

- *Specification*
  The problem identification leads on to the brief which sets out what is required. For design carried out by a third party, there will be an agreement between the designer and client about what is required.

- *Generation of alternatives*
  Given time, a range of alternatives will be created and investigated. These may be candidates for the final product. This phase involves divergent thinking and depends on experience and skill. (Note that these two stages may be supported by research studies as shown in Figure 2.8.)

- *Selection from alternatives*
  Proposals are gradually reduced in number by a process of selection which may involve the client. Whereas the original brief may be detailed and have tried to make it clear what is required, clients often prefer to make choices from a limited range presented to them. This is especially true for products with high aesthetic values.

  Selection should also consider the costs and capability of manufacturing.

- *Prototypes*
  The success of any design may not be apparent until a product has actually been produced. Prototypes have various purposes.

  They can be in the form of scale models to display in three dimensions the relationships between components and to make sure they all fit together. In the design of a nuclear power station, for example, staff work with carefully constructed scale models to ensure that the work of different groups fits together well.

They can be used to test performance before resources are invested in full-scale production. Aircraft are always tested in prototype form before production lines are equipped with expensive jigs and tools.

Prototypes may be used to test client or market reaction to include not only their preferences but questions of safety and reliability.

- *Final selection and implementation*
The design brief may be satisfied once the completed design is handed over to the client. In other cases, the designer is required to supervise the implementation of the design (an architect supervises construction from the design point of view) or continue involvement with adaptations in the light of changing circumstances.

23. The design–production sequence

Figure 2.8 may suggest that the process is a simple chain of events. On the contrary, the design and development methodology is iterative. This means that it may be necessary to return to earlier stages in the light of later experience. For example, unsatisfactory performance of a prototype may lead to the immortal phrase, 'Back to the drawing board!' How are such problems reduced?

Many companies have drawn design staff, especially those involved in engineering design, from among qualified staff in the production departments. This has advantages in ensuring an intuitive acceptance among designers of the limitations of production processes. But it also underpins a culture of design dominance where, in effect, completed designs are passed over to the production department with the instructions 'Here you are. Make that!' without an effective analysis of the production department's capability.

24. Manufacturability

The sequential relationship is one of the causes of the costly design modifications as, for example, production finds that it cannot produce to quality standards without a high rate of rejects. Stressing *manufacturability*[7], the capability of being manufactured, is a key factor in finding a solution. Apart from technical analysis of production issues, however, the dominance of design should be reduced. Rather than design serving customers through the marketing function, it may be better to see design serving production which in turn serves marketing.

The problem is not confined to manufacturing. For example, in civil engineering, it has been argued[8] that attention to 'constructibility' and value engineering typically yields construction cost savings of 10 to 20 times the costs of the extra design input. In other cases, design difficulties lead to construction delays which in turn mean that revenue streams start to flow late. The Channel Tunnel project was delayed by changing specifications during the construction phase. Before operating licences were granted, the fire in King's Cross underground station led to the British and French governments changing the safety standards. Particularly affected was the design of passenger rolling stock.

25. Improvements to design–production relationships

In contrast to the traditional design-production link, the production function can be seen as imposing a constraint upon what technologists and designers would wish to produce and marketers would wish to sell. In the production area, with its usually clear cost structures, the tensions between customer quality perceptions and costs can be felt acutely. Yet one of the functions of good design must be manufacturability. The example of the milk carton (see Box 2.2) shows the problems created by a market demand for an improved design which cannot be supplied using existing materials and processes.

DFMA (design for manufacturability and assembly) is an example of parallel, or concurrent, design which moves away from reliance on the traditional sequential approach. It focuses on improving both component manufacture and assembly through:

- simplifying designs
- reducing the number of components
- using standard components
- sharing components among several products
- speeding processes through new forms of fixing and finishing.

More generally, *parallel design* uses computer graphics to enable a range of experts from different departments to work together on design projects. The software

---

Milk cartons

Cardboard milk cartons have advantages over other packaging methods yet these advantages would be forgotten by the consumer during the daily struggle between weak fingers and carton tops which never seem to tear. Suddenly the milk gushes out down your suit and you wonder how it is that such a design failure ever reached the shelves.

In spite of the problem of opening, the cardboard carton has strong advantages over its rivals. Milk turns sour more quickly when exposed to light. The opacity of the cartons coupled with the absence of questions over their disposability mean that they easily beat glass or plastic bottles for supermarket distribution. In addition, their rectangular form yields economy in transport and display. Cardboard is easier to print than plastic or glass so there are better opportunities for the display of promotional messages and so on.

The problem of opening stems from the need to line the cardboard with thin polythene. The cardboard supports the polythene yet must tear easily enough, and bring the polythene with it, to form the spout. Some boxes work better than others, those with the 'pitched roof' causing less mess than the 'bricks'.

Manufacturers have tried various designs, including a polythene ring-pull similar to the openers found on soft drinks cans. The market leader, Tetrapak, is one firm devoting resources to this question and sees a solution as necessary to push up sales by increasing acceptance of its cartons for use with other liquids. It has proved difficult to combine, within acceptable cost, ease of opening with reliability of seal in transit. In the end, Tetrapak's customers will not pay enough to cover the costs of the design changes which have been tried so far. The production technology to insert a cheap and reliable ring pull opener has not yet been developed.

Box 2.2 Manufacturability of milk cartons

allows proposed design changes to be evaluated very quickly and, by the time the design is complete, a manufacturing specification is already available, complete with schedules and costs. Not only is the total development time reduced but many expensive prototypes can be avoided.

Another modern development, *design for disassembly*, brings recycling issues into the original design. One problem with the use of plastics in cars, for example, is the range of applications within the car and the corresponding detailed variations in choice of materials. This can make recycling difficult. Studies are aiming at reducing this variety so that all of the plastic material can be recycled. Other studies of assembly processes seek to avoid the use of glues and hidden screws to aid disassembly.

26. Assessing outcomes

The assessment of an innovation or design will be made according to company criteria. These usually include:

- *Innovation and engineering*
How valuable are the technical aspects of the new product? What contributions will they make to company success?
- *Manufacturability*
What are the operations implications of the new product? How much change is required? Is the product compatible with existing lines? Will manufacturing costs be made higher than the added value to be gained in the market place?
- *Marketing*
How does the new product gain competitive edge in the market place? Does it offer advantages that customers are willing to pay for?

Different firms will have different mixes of such questions. One product which had high innovative and engineering content and was capable of being manufactured is *Concorde*. Its relative failure came from the unwillingness of customers to pay such premium prices for the added benefit of high speed travel. Box 2.2 shows another example where production is possible but not at a price acceptable in the market place.

FINANCE AND THE OPERATIONS FUNCTION

As outlined in Box 2.1, the links between the finance function and operations consist of the provision of working capital and a contribution to both planning and control through the budgeting process. The eventual survival of all organisations, whatever their sector, depends on their *stewardship*, that is how well they have acquired, allocated and controlled the funds to which they are entitled. Cash is not only a necessary ingredient to many transactions in which the organisation is involved but it also forms a useful common denominator in evaluation of performance. In other words, the measuring stick has a single scale. For example, we shall see throughout this book how comparisons between different operations policies are made principally on the basis of their financial outcomes. We shall also note, in section **34**, that even though organisations have economic goals, an overemphasis on the financial measures can lead to problems.

Central to the interaction between finance and operations is the budget. In the following sections we shall illustrate the different types of budget, operating and capital, and their use within the organisation.

27. The operating budget

A budget is a formal projection of performance set out in financial terms. The operating budget covers a period of up to a year and is valuable to the manager because it not only incorporates the plan but it provides an objective measure against which outcomes can be assessed.

Budgets are prepared for operations activities according to whatever processes are involved. They may start from estimates of demand during the next period. In a simple case, such as the annual budget for Farndon Forge Company, Box 2.3, the costs are broken down into categories representing the costs of various systems such as raw materials supplies, direct labour, and so on. Following a hierarchy of systems, these costs can, in turn, be separated into further categories, for instance factory overhead can be divided into items covering heating and lighting, rates, maintenance and so on.

The other means of division, useful for operational managers, is to express the annual plan as a set of monthly, or even weekly, budgets. These enable control to be reasonably close to the activities being monitored.

Managers exercise control when comparing actual figures with the budget. They focus their attention on differences known as *budget variances*. Box 2.3 shows how the outcomes of FFC's year indicate both overspending and underspending, that is favourable and unfavourable variances. Sales revenue was higher than planned, but so were the costs. Possibly as a result of higher production levels, there were

Farndon Forge Company				
Operating Budget for 1997				**£000**
Item	**Budgeted revenue and cost**	**Actual revenue and cost**	**Variance**	
			Favourable	**Unfavourable**
Sales income	1,300	1,380	80	
Raw materials	315	325		10
Direct labour costs	340	319	21	
Indirect labour	220	227		7
Equipment maintenance and consumables	70	90		20
Training	40	40		
Factory overhead	112	118		6
Total costs	1,097	1,119		22
Operating profit	203	261	58	

Box 2.3 Operating budget and outcomes for FFC

increases in most items. The exceptions were direct labour where there was a favourable variance which may have resulted from increased efficiency or lower than expected hourly payments. Further cost analysis, especially within the context of monthly budgets, would enable the reasons to be pinpointed more closely.

One of the weaknesses of the type of budget set out in Box 2.3 is that many of the variances arise because of changing output levels. They do not arise from the skill, or fault, of the operating managers. Flexible budgets use standard costs to overcome this difficulty. To understand the basis of flexible budgeting, we must first of all distinguish between direct and indirect costs.

28. Direct and indirect costs

Products to be supplied incur *direct* and *indirect* costs. In manufacturing, direct costs are those, such as item-by-item component purchase costs, which can be considered as being directly part of each item being manufactured. The labour used in assembly can also be measured and seen as a direct cost. Indirect costs, on the other hand, cannot be attributed to each individual item of production; examples include heating, administration, training and accounting costs. These are often budgeted as *overheads*, although, for the purposes of working out total costs of each item, accountants in most companies derive methods to share out the overheads among all produced items.

Service organisations also have difficulties in establishing the cost base. A solicitor who charges a client £75 for a half-hour interview is not only recovering the cost of her own time but also having to charge for the firm's overheads, which include administration, premises, insurance and so on. There will also be an element of profit.

Farndon Forge Company				
Operating Budget for 1997				**£000**
Item	Actual revenue and cost	Standard cost of actual output	Variance Favourable	Unfavourable
Sales income	1,380			
Raw materials	325	334	9	
Direct labour costs	319	361	42	
Indirect labour	227			
Equipment maintenance and consumables	90	74		16
Training	40			
Factory overhead	112			
Total costs	1,097			
Operating profit	261			

Box 2.4

As sales increase, indirect costs remain unchanged while direct costs rise in proportion. It can be said that indirect costs are a function of time while direct costs are a function of volume. We can speak of rent, building maintenance, general lighting and training budgets in terms of pounds per year. For direct costs we can think of costs of components per item and we can calculate the cost of direct labour or process energy from basic measurements.

29. The flexible budget

Standard costs separate the volume effect from the other factors which make up the budget variance. For example, in the case shown in Box 2.3, FFC may recognise that the budget allows for 315/1300 or £0.24 to be spent on raw materials for each pound of sales revenue. If the price per item sold is £1,000 then the standard cost of material per item is £240.

The flexible budget adjusts for changes in volume by recalculating the budgeted direct costs. For example, if sales revenue at FFC is higher than the budget, assumed in this simple example to result from increased volume of sales, then the amount spent on raw materials would be expected to rise in proportion. In this case the budgeted cost of raw materials is adjusted, in proportion to output, to £334,000. Box 2.4 outlines how the direct costs could be analysed. The only variances now presented are those which arise from changes in the methods of operations management rather than from the change in the total volume of output.

Note how the variances now show the following:

more was spent on maintaining equipment or supplying consumables such as
    grinding discs or welding rods;
the better than expected use of direct labour;
the cost of materials was under budget.

The first two points in the list confirm, with different figures, the impression gained from the fixed budget comparison. The third, in contrast, tells a different story about raw materials. There were savings per unit of output, indicating that buying was more effective or there was less waste in the manufacturing process.

Indirect costs are not adjusted in this simple example although there are methods of adjusting allocations which are beyond our scope.

30. Break-even analysis

Budgets are not just tools for control after the event. As we shall see in Chapter 4, the budgeting procedure is part of the planning process, designed to ensure that profit is a forethought of active managers rather than an afterthought discovered after the books have been added up. The notion of dividing costs into *variable*, or direct, and *fixed*, or indirect, costs has an important application in break-even analysis. Often called *cost-volume-profit* analysis, the technique is used to look for the *break-even point* of output at which the firm makes neither a profit nor a loss. For sales below the break-even point, there is a loss; above break-even a profit is made.

A graphical representation of costs and revenues at various output levels is shown in Figure 2.9. The firm is selling its products at £500 per unit. The break-even point is shown as the intersection of the revenue and total cost lines, in this case at an output of 10,000 units worth £5 million. At outputs below the break-even point, total costs exceed revenues. Above break even, revenues exceed costs. The shaded areas represent the loss or profit obtained.

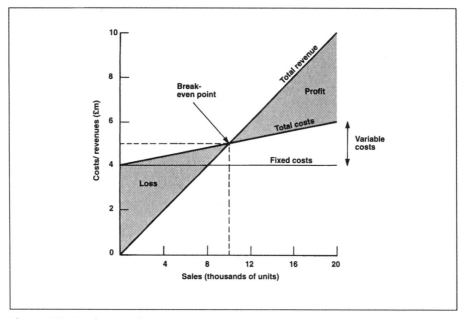

Figure 2.9 Break-even chart

Normally, a firm will budget to operate above the break-even point. We shall not go into a detailed graphical analysis of such changes here but it will be clear that the actual profit earned will be sensitive to shifts in fixed and variable costs as well as revenue. The chart can be redrawn to represent such changes. It the firm is budgeted to operate close to the break even point then small shifts may cause it to slip into loss. The *margin of safety* is a measure of how far the output is above the break-even point:

$$\text{Margin of safety} = \frac{\text{Budgeted output} - \text{Break-even output}}{\text{Budgeted output}} \times 100\%$$

The margin of safety is a measure of the risk to which the operations system is exposed if costs or revenues change.

31. Patterns of fixed and variable costs

As part of their strategic planning process, organisations can choose between different patterns of fixed and variable costs to achieve the same outputs. For example, an investment in robots to replace labour on an assembly line changes that part of the work from a variable, direct labour, to a fixed cost.

Figure 2.10 shows a comparison between two possibilities for the business in Figure 2.9. For a budgeted output of, say, 15,000 units, both firms earn the same profit. The budgeted output is the point BO on the output scale in each case. The low fixed costs of Firm A mean that it operates with a high margin of safety (55%) and its profits are little affected by small changes in output. Firm B, on the other hand, operates closer to its break-even point (its margin of safety is 33%) and its profits are more sensitive to changes in volume of output. If business is good,

45

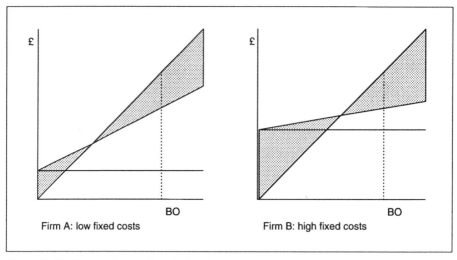

Figure 2.10 Comparison of cost structures

with sales above budgeted levels, then Firm B would do better as its profits expand more quickly. On the other hand, B would do worse if sales were weak. Firm B is said to have higher *operational gearing* than Firm A.

Newspapers have high fixed costs and this accounts for the continual pressure to maintain market share through promotions of all kinds.

32. Advantages and drawbacks of break-even analysis

In common with other techniques discussed throughout this book, break-even analysis is not a universal solution. Its advantages are that it enables operations managers to understand the implications of different cost structures and perform analyses on them. The main drawback lies in the nature of the cost and revenue patterns themselves. Variable costs are not always linearly related to output as in the case of overtime payments for a few extra hours, shift premiums and changes in machine efficiency caused by running them away from their designed capacities. Similarly, fixed costs are often not truly fixed. Increased demand on a distribution system may require managers to rent or purchase extra warehousing space. In spite of these difficulties, the principle of identifying the behaviour of different costs remains a valid one. Operations managers, especially in those organisations with high fixed costs such as airlines, cinemas and car assembly plants, are very aware of the need to keep output well above the break-even point.

33. The capital expenditure budget

The capital expenditure budget is the result of decisions about the allocation of an organisation's capital resources. It is clear that many operational systems are based on huge amounts of invested capital and are dependent upon a continual stream of new investment if products and processes are to be kept up to date in terms of standards of efficiency and effectiveness. Examples of investments from the current business press include:

- A new ceramic coating process to extend the life of kitchen knives; development by Sheffield University and Richardson, makers of *Laser* knives.
- Information technology development to support the growth of People's Phone Company.
- Ford Motor Company's announcement of the development of a new 'world car'.
- Richard Branson's proposal to convert the GLC County Hall into a shopping, leisure and hotel complex.

It can be seen that each of these involves new products and processes and, therefore, has considerable implications for the operations functions within the organisations.

The financial evaluation of a proposed investment should be made according to two broad criteria:

- Is the investment worth proceeding with?
- Is the investment the best of the alternatives which are presented to the company?

The first criterion requires a critical evaluation of the investment in terms of inputs and outputs during its life. The second, on the other hand, compares the evaluation with all of the others on an agenda of possibilities. In circumstances where the amount of capital available to the organisation is limited, which is especially true in the public and voluntary sectors, there is a situation of capital rationing and projects may be selected according to rankings. Models of decision making under capital rationing are complex. We shall, in this chapter, concentrate on the framework for analysing individual investments and making simple comparisons..

34. Analysing investments: strategic and financial perspectives

The strategic perspective considers the relationship between the proposed use of funds and the objectives of the company and how they fit in with other developments in the long term. This is a broad approach which is examined in Chapter 4.

The financial perspective considers the link between capital to be used, especially its cost, and the return to be made in terms of flows of funds and the risks associated with them. This perspective considers not only the question of whether an individual project is worth the investment it requires but it also takes into account whether the same funds can be better used on other schemes.

The two perspectives should be complementary, yet there is sometimes conflict. The strategic view may stress issues in the long-term development of the company and investment benefits which may not be easily measured in financial terms. The financial view, on the other hand, focuses on measurable values and possibly presents an over-rigid framework for comparison.

We can see the contrast between the two perspectives in the following example of a company setting up a joint venture in a foreign country:

The company, Elco, is considering a 50-50 joint venture with a foreign government to manufacture pharmaceutical products. Elco can make a broad estimate of the market size using data supplied by its partner. Its familiarity with the production technology enables it to estimate costs quite accurately. From this information, Elco can provide a broad picture of the likely financial return from the development. If this analysis shows a poor return, should Elco not go ahead? This is where the strategic perspective may conflict with the financial.

There may be considerable benefits in the longer term which lie outside the basis financial analysis. They could include the opening up of further opportunities, the gaining of operating experience in a new territory or the restriction of the scope of rivals.

35. Financial comparisons

Methods of comparing proposed investments, when based on financial criteria, can be complex. Not only are the technical details of some of the techniques beyond the scope of this book, they are beyond the scope of many small and medium sized companies! We shall concern ourselves with an outline of four methods here. They are named after the measures they use, as follows:

- Accounting Rate of Return (ARR)
- Payback
- Net Present Value (NPV)
- Internal Rate of Return (IRR)

The simplest methods are ARR and Payback, which are often used for quick calculations especially where the data can only be roughly estimated. NPV and IRR require more careful analysis and depend on at least some of the data being known with more confidence.

36. The accounting rate of return (ARR)

The most simple and unsophisticated approach to appraisal, the ARR method, is based on the following calculation:

$$APR = \frac{Profit\ from\ investment}{Amount\ of\ investment} \times 100\%$$

As with all of the methods, the ARR is compared with a target figure (say, 18%) which acts as a target level of return required. In addition, proposals can be compared with each other in order to rank them in order of return.

There are several difficulties with this formula which makes the ARR difficult to settle in practice. The most significant of these is the ignoring of the timing of the profits earned by the investment. Consider the two projects, A and B, of Table 2.1. Each requires an investment of (say) £60,000 and each produces the same ARR.

Profit after depreciation

Year	Project A	Project B
1	15,000	0
2	15,000	10,000
3	15,000	10,000
4	15,000	25,000
5	15,000	30,000

Table 2.1 Profits for two projects, A and B

It is assumed that the initial capital expenditure is fully depreciated as a charge against profits over the 5 year period covered by the table. Each project earns the same total profit over the 5 years and it would seem that there would be little to choose between them. Yet there is an important difference between the timing of the profits from the projects. Those from Project B come later and only exceed those from Project A in years 4 and 5. This means that Project A would be chosen on the basis of the above information. Why is this?

The answer lies in the time-value associated with money. If it is possible to receive a given sum of money at two different future dates, then the earlier date will be preferred. Similarly, if one has to spend a given sum at a future date, a later date will be preferred. This brings out the weakness of the ARR measure. By treating all profits as being the same it ignores the time preferences of those involved in the decision.

37. The payback method

Investments in projects mean that money is 'tied up' in the projects until profits are earned to repay the investment. This is called the *opportunity cost* of the investment. Managers will recognise that early repayments of investments will enable them to re-use the money for others. The payback method recognises this argument. For example, consider Table 2.2 in which two projects, C and D, are set out. Each has an initial capital expenditure of £60,000 to purchase assets with a 5 year life.

Project C is the same as Project A in Table 2.1. But, in using the payback method, we table *profit before depreciation* as a measure of income as we are estimating the timing of the cash transactions in the project rather than the less concrete notion of profits.

Comparing the proposals, it can be seen that C (£135,000) earns more total cash returns than D (£120,000). In an ARR calculation, C would have a higher apparent return than D. But would Project C always be chosen?

Suppose the management of the company sees a need for a quick payback on its investment. This may be because it is short of cash, or it has a number of other competing projects in which it would invest were cash available. In such a case, Project D may be chosen. Overall it reaches the target ARR and has the advantage of paying back the original investment more quickly. At the end of the second year, Project D will have paid back £77,000 whereas only £54,000 will have been returned by Project C.

Profit before depreciation

Year	Project C	Project D
1	27,000	40,000
2	27,000	37,000
3	27,000	28,000
4	27,000	15,000
5	27,000	0

Table 2.2 Profit from two projects, C and D

We can formally compare the payback periods, that is the time it takes for the original cash outlay to be returned. That of Project D is about 1½ years against 2¼ years for C. On the criteria of payback, therefore, Project D will be selected.

38. Exclusivity and independence

It is often found that projects such as C and D concern the same area of the business. For example, they could be alternative ways of changing the service delivery system to realise cost savings. Such pairs are said to be *operationally exclusive*. In other cases, they will be *operationally independent*, one being new machinery and the other covering the initial expenditure on opening up a new market.

Although operationally independent, C and D may still be financially exclusive if they seek to use the same investment funds. If the organisation has access to plentiful financial resources, through bank loans for example, then this situation will not arise. Many, however, face *capital rationing* and have to choose between one project and the other. One solution is to select the project with the shortest payback period and then re-use the funds in the next shortest project, and so on.

39. Discounted cash flow (DCF)

The ARR method concentrates on nominal returns on investments throughout the life of a project but ignores the timing of these returns. The payback method, on the other hand, focuses its attention on the time it takes to recover the original expenditure but passes over the total profits during the life of the project.

The concept of discounted cash flow (DCF) goes some way to resolving these difficulties by recognising income over the life of a project while at the same time acknowledging the time value of money. DCF has two important features, cash flows and discounting.

Cash flows

Cash flows are used in the appraisals because they focus on liquidity of the enterprise, not its profitability. The timing of cash flows, for example those involved in buying land and plant at the start of a project, can be very different from the representation of these as depreciation charges in financial accounts.

The cash flows to be taken into account are those future flows which arise as a result of the project. They include outgoings such as capital expenditure on the project and changes in income such as sales revenue. Changes in other costs, such as overheads, resulting from the project should also be considered but not those notional changes which arise solely from the methods of bookkeeping being used.

Discounting

Discounting assigns a higher value to cash flows which occur earlier. See Box 2.5 to explain the principle. From Box 2.5, it can be seen that £1,200 in 8 years time from now is worth less than £900 in 5 (£392 against £447). The concept of DCF is used in the last two methods, Net Present Value and Internal Rate of Return.

40. NPV and IRR methods

The *net present value* (NPV) is obtained by adding the discounted present values of all cash flows and inflows using the company's target discount rate. If the NPV is

An explanation of discounting

Imagine that you are taking part in the following hypothetical game show:

You have been given £1,000 which is in a bank and will be made available to you in 1 year's time. How much is the money worth to you now? Would you take the host's offer of £990 now instead? It would be surprising if you wouldn't. Or £980 now? Yes. And so on... At the other end of the scale, you wouldn't accept a rubber duck so the bank deposit is worth more than that.

Continuing with the game, you may eventually agree that the deposit is worth the equivalent of (say) £900 now. In doing this you have discovered how to discount the value of future money to a present value. In assessing the discounted value of the deposited money, you have made an assessment of the likely interest rates you could obtain in the interim and also the various risks involved with the agreement.

The trouble with such a game is that it shows how individuals have different ways of valuing future cash flows, depending not only on the urgency of their current needs but also on the size of the sums involved. For example, would you apply the same discounting ratio to £100 as to £1,000,000?

Within companies, DCF techniques are formalised so that standard discount rates are used. The Table illustrates the effect of discounting. It shows the present value of a sum of £1,000 were it made available at different times in the future. The discount rate 15% is a widely used one, although some businesses look for 20%, or even 25%.

Year	Present Value
1	870
2	756
3	658
4	572
5	497
6	432
7	376
8	327
9	284
10	247
15	123
20	61

Present Value of £1,000 at a discount rate of 15%

Box 2.5 Discounting

positive, the project is expected to give a return on investment greater than the target rate and the project should be accepted. If it is negative, the project should not be proceeded with.

Instead of the company deciding in advance on a discount rate, the IRR method calculates the discount rate implied by the project. The *internal rate of return* is the discount rate at which the NPV is zero. The example shown in Table 2.3 gives the main features of the process.

In Table 2.3 the cash flows associated with an 8-year project are presented. An investment of £800,000, assessed to occur entirely at the start, yields cash flows which build up to year 4 and then decline to the end of the project's life in year 8. While the project yields a positive cash flow of £880,000 if the cash flows are not discounted, the application of discounting shows a different picture. At a 15% discount rate, the net present value of the project is £94,000, a positive value but perhaps not large enough to justify going ahead. Errors in estimates may swallow up this figure.

The IRR calculation looks for the discount rate which yields a zero NPV. It proceeds as follows:

Starting without a defined target, take an initial guess of (say) 15% as the discount rate and calculate the NPV. Repeat for other values (as in the 20% and 18% columns of Table 2.3) until the NPV is near to zero. This is the best estimate of the IRR, in this case 18%. Note that it would be unwise to calculate the IRR to fractional decimals because the accuracy of the forecasted data could not justify it.

Data for IRR calculations from discount tables are easily set out in spreadsheets on personal computers. Most of the leading packages enable NPVs to be calculated automatically.

41. Comparison of appraisal methods

Of the techniques demonstrated here, those based on the concept of discounting make the most sophisticated attempt to incorporate the time value of money into

Cash flows	£000			
Year	Actual cash flow	Discounted at 15%	20%	18%
0	-800	-800	-800	-800
1	50	43	42	42
2	150	113	104	108
3	250	164	145	152
4	300	172	145	155
5	330	164	133	144
6	300	130	100	111
7	200	75	56	63
8	100	33	23	27
Total	880	94	-53	2

Table 2.3 NPV and IRR estimations

assessments which also recognise the total benefits of a project over its life. Discounting builds in some allowances for uncertainty as well as recognition that individuals inherently prefer income now rather than in the future.

There are penalties with the application of such sophisticated procedures. Their outcomes require careful estimates of cash flows in an uncertain future and also the selection of an appropriate discount rate. In response to uncertainty, sensitivity analysis can be used to check whether possible changes in future cash flows have a great impact on the outcome of the calculation. Small and medium sized firms, however, do not use discounting methods but tend to rely on a combined view of the accounting rate of return and an estimate of the payback period.

42. Sensitivity analysis

It is good management practice to test the outcomes of complex calculations by changing parameters and studying their implications. The changed parameters may represent difficulties with estimating size of cash flows (uncertainty) or actual delays in the implementation of a project (risk). Delayed timing of incurred cash flows caused, for example, by unexpected difficulties during the start-up phase, may seriously reduce the NPV of a project. Consider the case of EuroDisney shown in Box 2.6.

Shares in EuroDisney were offered in France in 1989. The company, most of whose equity was held by The Walt Disney Corporation, was established to develop the park near Paris to be opened in 1992.

The prospectus accompanying the share sale showed a projected IRR of 13.3% for the first 25 years of operation. It was unusual in showing the outcomes of sensitivity analysis of the basic assumptions. Below are some of the assumptions tested together with their effect on IRR of low and high estimates of the parameters.

Parameter	IRR range %
Attendances	12.7 - 13.8
Customer spending	12.3 - 14.1
Property income	13.0 - 13.5
Inflation	11.2 - 15.3
Interest	13.2 - 13.3
Residual value after 25 years	13.1 - 13.4

Investors could, from the share data, reach their own conclusions about the risks involved in buying shares. They could see, for example, that the project's prospects were particularly sensitive to different inflation assumptions yet not at all sensitive to interest rates. An investor would, therefore, have to include a view of inflation in determining whether or not to buy the shares.

Box 2.6 Sensitivity analysis of EuroDisney investment

Case study: Improvements at IBM, Lexington

At the start of the 1980s, the IBM typewriter plant at Lexington, Kentucky faced problems of levelling off of demand in a static market. There were 9 major competitors in 1979, growing to 30 by 1984 and 44 by 1986. Most were located in east Asia and competed on costs and quality.

In response, IBM invested $350 million during the period 1983-86 in order to become the lowest-cost typewriter maker with its new product, the QuietWriter. The new line included keyboards and printers as well as related office machines.

As part of the new strategy, IBM streamlined the product line and improved productivity. For example, the keyboard of the QuietWriter was very similar to the one used on the IBM PC. They shared many components. Furthermore, the QuietWriter's printer became letter quality printer option for the PC.

Streamlining was not the only policy carried out during the 3 year programme. About 300 robots and 200 minicomputers were installed. The number of parts suppliers was cut. Inspection was automated. Of the 700% improvement in productivity, however, about 200% came from automation and 500% from design for manufacturability. Cutting the number of parts and the number of suppliers was a decisive step towards streamlining the direct production activities and in removing much of the bureaucracy which had accumulated over the years[9]. The results of the new policy can be seen below.

Cost element	Before	After
Labour as % of cost	57%	23%
Material as % of cost	43%	77%
Direct labour per unit	7 hr	0.4 hr
Floor space (000 sq.m)	400	200
Staff	7,500	2,000
Plant capacity per year	0.75 M	1.7 M
Different parts per unit	2,900	1,000
Average repairs per year	6	0
Number of suppliers	400	60
Time to produce product	?	2.5 hr

Questions

1 Discuss the changes at IBM in terms of the linkages between operations and other functions of the business.
2 Using the diagrams presented in this chapter, show how graphical methods can be used to represent the themes set out in the case study.

References

1. The systems message is not expressed as follows:
   Little fleas have smaller fleas upon their backs to bite 'em,
   And smaller fleas have smaller fleas and so ad infinitum.
2. von Bertalanffy, Ludwig (1950) 'An outline of general systems theory' The British Journal for the Philosophy of Science 1.2. Bertalanffy pioneered the search for GST. It is fair to say that the search for general principles has not been as successful as its pioneers may have wished.
3. Kast, F.E. and Rosenzweig, J.E. (1974) Organisation and Management 2nd edn Tokyo, McGraw-Hill Kogakusha p.112

4. Cannon, T, (1992) *Basic Marketing* 3rd edition London, Cassell p.12
5. Television interview conducted by Mark Tulley (1994) *Great Railway Journeys of the World* BBC2, 17 February
6. For more details, see Hauser, J.R. and Clausing, D. (1988) 'The house of quality' *Harvard Business Review* **66.3** May-June, pp. 63–73
7. See Heidenreich, P. (1988) 'Designing for manufacturability' *Quality Progress* May, pp. 41–44
8. McGeorge, J.F. (1988) 'Assuring quality in design engineering' *Journal of Management in Engineering* **4.4** pp.350–62
9. The decription of IBM is based on Ernst, R.G. (1987) 'How to streamline operations' *The Journal of Business Strategy* **8.2** pp.32–36

3

TECHNOLOGY AND OPERATIONS MANAGEMENT

Chapter objectives

When you have finished studying this chapter, you should be able to:

- Identify the main external factors which influence process choice.

- Set out the differences between service provision and manufacture and relate them to differences in scale.

- Describe and compare four types of service and two types of self-service facility and show how they are chosen and changed.

- Identify the main features of the five basic systems of manufacture and isolated service provision and show how they relate to each other.

- Explain why hybrid systems are commonly found.

- Outline how profiling can be used to investigate the appropriateness of a production system design.

- Give an overview of how the boundaries between production technologies are becoming blurred.

- Show the significance of Woodward's studies of socio-technical systems.

INTRODUCTION

We shall begin this chapter by examining the technical subsystem of the organisation. In doing so, we are not concerned with the detailed analysis of the engineering aspects of each operation. Such studies of *process technologies* lie in the domain of specialists whether they are mining engineers, systems analysts, tailors or chefs. Our interests, on the other hand, rest in the planning, organising and control of the processes in so far as they form elements of the complete operations system. Exploring the technical subsystem, therefore, gives us an understanding of the different ways in which operational systems are organised efficiently.

An important problem in efficient operations is the link between the technical system and the people who work in and around it. This combination is the socio-technical subsystem. We shall complete the chapter by looking at ways in which the technology affects the human organisation and *vice versa*.

PRODUCTION SYSTEM CHOICES

1. Scale in manufacturing and service supply

The type of production used by a firm is decided by a variety of factors:

- Market demand in terms of quantity to be supplied, the places at which it is to be supplied, the range of different products required and the fluctuations in demand.
- Product design, including size, complexity, and means of supply.
- Process technology for manufacture or service.
- Whatever system is already installed. While one may argue for an ideal match between the operations system and the items in the list above, the possibilities of change are limited and many organisations end with something of a mismatch. This issue can be investigated using *profiling*, as in section **16**.

The single most important variable affecting the organisation of production is scale. Large-scale production enables manufacturers to use plant which is dedicated to either one, or a limited range, of purposes. The production of large quantities enables plant and equipment designs to be tuned to achieve low costs for a given volume, that is to achieve *production economies of scale*. Examples of large-scale production are oil refining, paper making, bicycle assembly, newspaper printing and, among services, directory enquiries, banking and film processing.

Small-scale operations, often called *jobbing shops*, take business which is characterised by variety. While the holding-down of costs remains important, such businesses achieve success by offering flexibility and producing a wide range of products to satisfy the needs of small and specialised sectors of the market. Examples of manufacturing jobbing are customised oil blending, printing of visiting cards, tailoring, bookbinding, and, among services, medical treatment, bespoke training courses and television repairs.

2. Differences between service and manufacture

The key difference between service and manufacture lies in the degree of involvement of the customer directly in the service operation. As shown in **1:11**, direct services are supplied in the presence of the customer, while isolated, or indirect, services are performed separately. The isolated service becomes more like manufacture and can be organised in a similar way.

Box 3.1 classifies operations according both to scale and to the degree of customer involvement. The basic focus is different. Direct services require that attention be paid both to inter-personal skills, that is an understanding of the needs of the customer in relation to the way the service is provided, and to some technical skills. Manufacturing and isolated service, in contrast, are not so concerned with personal interaction and depend more heavily on the technical skill in managing the production system. We shall look at each in turn, starting with services.

SERVICE SYSTEM CHOICE

3. Types of service process

We can think of service provision in terms of processes which have distinct characteristics. Schmenner[1] identifies four categories:

	Services direct to the customer emphasising inter-personal skills	*Manufacturing or isolated service activities emphasising technical skills*
Small scale	Personal service: legal advice, shoe repairs, gardening	Jobbing: building, *haute couture*, wedding cars
Large scale	Mass service: banking, buses, supermarkets	Mass production: car assembly, newspapers, pension management

Box 3.1 Service and manufacturing operations affected by scale

Professional Service
Often regarded as the typical service operation, professional service describes those activities which are supplied in the presence of individual customers by trained personnel. Examples include doctors, counsellors, beauticians and individual music teachers.

Mass Service
Mass services try to replicate the supply of professional services on a large scale. They are carried out in the presence of groups, or even crowds, of customers. Examples include higher education, large-scale retailing, television and concerts.

Service Shop
The service shop is the means through which isolated service is made available to the customer. Each customer's needs are treated individually but the service takes place without the customer being present. Garages, some shoe repairers and estate agents operate in this mode.

Service Factory
This is the service shop operating at large scale. The range of services available is standardised so that they can be offered, but not necessarily provided, by staff with limited specialised knowledge or skill. Much of the skilled supply activity of banks, post offices, large hotels and restaurants takes place away from the customer.

4. Issues in service process design

The issues for managers vary according to the two dimensions of scale and customer involvement:

Scale issues

Small scale (Professional Service and Service Shop)
The labour intensity of these operations means that managers are continually concerned with overcoming the effects of labour cost increases while maintaining quality of service. The service may be offered at many small-scale outlets so there are problems of supervision and control. Because of the non-standard nature of

the tasks to be carried out, staff must be flexible and be able to offer a variety of service on request.

Large scale (Mass Service and Service Factory)

Large-scale service operations seek efficiency increases through capital investment and reducing the reliance on labour. Managers have to face capital investment decisions concerning sites, buildings and equipment. Also, there is the challenge of establishing and maintaining the feeling of good quality service through having appropriate physical surroundings and sufficient staff to offer personal contact when needed. Standardisation of the range of services offered reduces the reliance on individuals to cope with a large range of possibilities. In the main, they need not be as highly trained as in small-scale operations. On the other hand, the organisation relies on the staff being able to provide the limited service politely and quickly. This implies training and motivation aimed at high quality, repetitive delivery. Successful large-scale organisations such as the major retailers, pay great attention to the detailed steps of customer transactions and train their staff accordingly. Box 3.2 is taken from the staff training manual of Superdrug, the major retailer of household and personal care products[2]. The company stresses its commitment to offering high quality goods at competitive prices.

Customer involvement issues

Direct service (Professional Service and Mass Service)

The focus is on the customer. This can be achieved through improving the service quality which comes mainly from recruiting, developing and motivating staff. Questions of supervision and control also arise when the service is delivered in small outlets spread across different locations.

Isolated service (Service Shop and Service Factory)

Isolated service operations are managed, in the 'back room', in similar ways to manufacturing activities. Questions range from capital investment in new equipment to scheduling tasks and quality control. Customers access through designated 'gateways' and the emphasis in the service element is on effective and efficient gatekeeping. The gatekeeper must combine personal service skills with the ability to identify customer needs and arrange for the required service to be provided by others where necessary. With the large-scale Service Factory, the range of services is standardised and the gatekeeper offers whatever is appropriate out of the defined range.

'The price has gone up again'

A customer walks up to you, complaining that the price of a product is higher than it was last week. List the things you would say and do:

- *Listen to the complaint in a polite way.*
- *Offer to check the price.*
- *Explain the increase and suggest a cheaper alternative, if possible.*
- *Report to management if the customer has found an item cheaper elsewhere.*

Box 3.2 Detailed attention to service

5. Self service

Self service represents another means by which the provider seeks to control the costs of delivery. Compared with the direct service operations discussed above, the relative involvement of the customer in the service process is increased. Cost savings arise, in effect, from the employment of the customer. Physical labour, as in carrying goods out of a supermarket, and decision making, such as selecting choices from a menu presented on a screen, are passed over to the customer. Self service represents a step of *detachment* of the service provider from direct contact with the customer.

Detachment can be achieved in two ways:

Replacement of the human server
Replacement of the service provider by capital equipment depends on a recognition that costs can be reduced through automating some tasks carried out by humans. In large-scale service, dispensing machines replace humans for routine processes from the sales of tickets and coffee to the supply and deposit of cash. In small-scale service, the matching to individual needs requires equipment with more sophisticated programming based on expert systems technology. Proposals for medical diagnosis machines fall into this category. Such equipment needs to be interactive so that it responds to information from the user.

Removal of barriers
Many self-service facilities such as stores and restaurants depend on the removal of barriers which have traditionally separated the customer from the service. These barriers are both physical and psychological, that is customers must be enabled to access the facility and be willing to use it. Consequently, the skills required to provide the service have to be simplified and standardised and sufficient information given to enable the customer to cope. The layout of supermarkets is clearly designed to enable customers to reach the goods. At the same time there needs to be appropriate information, equipment and packaging to enable the transaction to take place.

6. Summary of service patterns

Figure 3.1 summarises the service delivery patterns discussed in sections **3** to **5**, together with the relationships between them. The three basic patterns are *self service*, *personal service*, and *isolated service*. Within each pattern, a shift from small to large scale means more than an increase in the volume of output. The search for cost reductions implies the standardisation of the service. In addition there are the specialisation of roles and the deskilling of much of the process delivery. Trends in the opposite direction require customisation to more closely match the separate needs of each individual.

The other change directions suggested in Figure 3.1 are the switches between the patterns. Personal service becomes self service through the process of detachment, again often as a means of maintaining quality while fighting against increases in price. Personal service becomes isolated service through the policy of isolation. The opposite policies of *attachment* and *integration* are also shown.

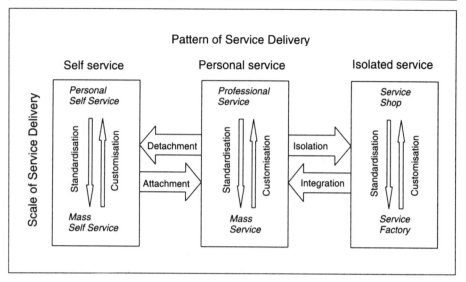

Figure 3.1 Service delivery patterns and scale

7. Examples of service patterns

We can illustrate the service patterns with three examples:

Car Repairs

General car repairs were traditionally carried out in Service Shops which provided an isolated service based on a diagnosis of the requirements of each customer's car. Rising costs and competition led to several changes in this industry. First, the suppliers and vehicle manufacturers identified standardised service packages which should be applied at intervals throughout the life of the car. The standardisation enables the garage to reduce its costs and improve the planning of its work. Secondly, specialists entered the repair business. Focusing their attention on the repair and service activities which are most frequently required, they reduced costs through scale economies. Tyre suppliers, for example, gain through intensive use of fitting and balancing equipment as well as through bulk purchasing, reductions in input prices. They also benefit from using more specialist labour which requires a narrower range of skills and therefore less training. Exhaust suppliers have gained similarly with such companies as Kwik Fit and Superdrive also offering exchange of other items such as brakes. The specialists have transformed the industry from a series of Service Shops into a mixture of Service Shops and Service Factories.

Insurance

Direct selling of motor insurance has grown rapidly in recent years. Direct Line, a subsidiary of The Royal Bank of Scotland, provides insurance cover for one million motorists in 350,000 households. It claims that low premiums result from higher efficiency, close control of approved repairers and the absence of broker commissions. Conventional brokers respond, however, with accusations of 'cherry picking', which is building up a profile of low risk customers. Guardian

Direct only insures customers who have three years without claims and are over 21. Others only accept older customers, Royal Direct has a 30 minimum and Churchill 25[3].

We can see in this example two trends:

Standardisation: the offering of a defined range of standard services to a limited range of customers. This enables the service to be provided by operators trained in the use of computer screens. Decisions are made by algorithms based on customer information.

Detachment: rising awareness among customers of the products on offer, a readiness to take on the responsibility to shop around and the technology to access the information easily, in this case the telephone.

Travel tickets

Apart from the simplest ticket sold from mechanical dispensers, automatic sales of travel tickets have been held back by complexity. This results from multiple fare structures and the great variety of possible journeys which can be made over larger systems. Information system developments have changed all that. At main stations in France, for example, one can use machines to plan a journey to any station on the SNCF system and then buy an appropriate ticket. The compulsory seat reservations on the TGV trains can also be made in this way, minutes before departure. While payments can be in cash, most customers use bank cards.

Developments such as these result from on-line information systems. As well as storing and displaying information including times, routes, prices and seat availability, they can receive information from the customer to discover wishes, offer options and verify travel and credit status. In the introduction of simple dispensing machines, train ticket sales moved from Mass Service to Mass Self Service. The new systems, by incorporating much of the variety of services offered by SNCF and responding to the customer's needs, customise ticket sales and move towards Personal Self Service.

MANUFACTURING SYSTEM CHOICE

As with direct service systems, the choice of overall process design of manufacturing and isolated service operations is based on several variables. Again, the most important is scale but other factors, such as the size and homogeneity of the output, have to be considered. The number of possible arrangements of equipment to produce given outputs is unlimited. In sections **8** to **12**, however, we shall present the five main categories of manufacturing system, illustrated in Box 3.3.

8. Project

Project systems are used to manufacture goods which are difficult to move during assembly or after they have been completed. Reasons for immobility include scale

---

Project ↔ Jobbing ↔ Batch ↔ Line ↔ Continuous

Box 3.3 The spectrum of manufacturing systems

and complexity of the output or of the tasks involved. Industries from civil and marine engineering to film making and research centres work on a project basis. While appearing dissimilar on the surface, these manufacturing tasks face many common challenges.

- Different people and equipment are required to participate at different times. It is usual to bring these to the project location when they are needed. Consequently, there is a problem of scheduling the availability of such resources so that they are ready on time. Yet they must not be wasted at other times.
- Much project work involves the use of specialist staff and equipment which are usually obtained through subcontracting. This again suggests an emphasis on accurate timing and coordination of the multiple roles involved.
- The tasks involved in the project have to be properly sequenced within the total time allowed for completion. Frequently, many items which make up the final product are fabricated in stages and transported in parts to the assembly position. Their fabrication involves many skills and technologies. A power station needs coal handling equipment, furnaces, boilers, turbines and generators, all of which require specialists in their supply. This variety underlines the need for planning, monitoring and control of progress.
- The quality of the product depends on the skills and application of all those involved.
- Since many projects are unique, they are designed and planned under much uncertainty and the managers have to be flexible in overcoming technical and operational problems as they arise. In contrast to other manufacturers, they work to a single goal, the completion of the project, which may be over a long period.

9. Jobbing

The jobbing shop is noted for its flexibility in being established to carry out a wide range of tasks. The products are supplied in small batches, even down to single items, as with the specialist car repairer mentioned above. The jobbing shop differs from the project operation in that its outputs are transportable. In engineering manufacture, many general machine shops, moulding plants and patterns makers work in this flexible way, making or repairing items to customer orders. Yet the jobbing shop is apparent in most manufacturing industries from printing to concrete moulding, electronic equipment to high fashion makers.

Since the patterns of demand for a jobbing shop are unpredictable and the size of any one order relatively small, the layout of the plant cannot be adapted to form product-related flow lines. It is conventional to group similar activities and staff together in departments such as casting, plating machining, painting and assembly. This enables the highly skilled staff to be used flexibly. There are often physical advantages, from ventilation to insulation, in keeping families of processes in one area.

As we shall see, the flow of materials through a jobbing shop is far from regular. The uninitiated will always feel a sense of chaos when entering such a plant. Good management is concerned with making plans which work under this uncertainty and then tracking all the work to ensure that it is completed on time and within budget. Managers must offer customers reliable delivery dates and know their costs in detail to ensure that profits are made.

Jobbing printers produce items from single colour wedding invitations to full colour promotional brochures for small and medium company clients. The smallest orders may be for 100 posters while the largest may be for several thousand mail shots. The printers compete by offering high quality goods within the frequently near-impossible time scales demanded by the clients. The many combinations of printing machine designs and ink processes mean that most jobbing printers cannot offer the full range. On the other hand, they seek to satisfy all the needs of their regular customers. This is achieved by subcontracting specialised work to others in the district.

10. Batch

Batch processing is a step up from jobbing in terms of scale. While the two may overlap, there is no clear divide. Batch operations concentrate their attention on a more limited range of products produced in larger quantities than in the jobbing shop. Many batch companies organise their production stages through separate departments as with the jobbing shop. As we shall see, however, modern methods of production planning and control have led to significant changes in these arrangements. Examples include the creation of machining cells and an identification of critical bottlenecks.

Batch processing involves dividing the production activity into the tasks which must be carried out. Then a schedule is made which is designed to enable the batch to pass through each stage in the required sequence. The reduced product range means that complexity is less than in the jobbing shop, yet the setting out and achievement of the schedule remains a daunting task.

Batches are frequently derived from larger customer orders. For example, a contract to supply 20,000 garments over a period of a year may be divided into batches of a month's supply. In this way the work load is spread out, stock levels are kept low and other garment contracts are fulfilled by the same processes. Other items made in batches include: moulded plastic car components; office furniture; castings and architectural masonry. In these cases, the size of any order does not justify the laying down of a dedicated production line.

11. Line

Line systems are established when demand for a product, or small range of similar products, is so great that it is worthwhile investing in a dedicated production line. The process is often called mass production.

The best known example of line production is car assembly. Because of the demand for model variants, most assembly lines produce a small range of similar products rather than cars which are identical. The cars are similar enough to be handled on the same line and are specified to require mainly the same components. Variations in major items such as engine sizes and doors are managed by delivering these to the work stations in the sequence required. On General Motors' *Astra* lines, one sees what appears to be a random mix of vans and cars, saloons and hatchbacks and so on. On any day, their common feature is colour since the paint process cannot be changed in the short interval between the vehicles arriving at the booths.

The line layout differs from the batch layout in the following respects:

- The line moves the product from each work station to the next. There is no build up of items between the stages of production except those that are on the line. This means that all work stations must operate at the same rate. One problem for managers is to achieve *line balance*, that is to ensure that resources are deployed effectively among the work stations, see Chapter 8.
- Each work station fulfils only a small part of the complete task. From the employees' point of view, the resultant short cycle time and limited skill requirement mean that personal involvement in the work is severely limited. This problem is explored further in Chapter 5.
- The plant layout is dedicated to one product or a small family.
- The scheduling of production through the line is, in principle, much more simple than in batch production. On the other hand, the line is much more sensitive to the absence of a key component so managers have to monitor supplies very carefully.

Line layouts may require expensive specialist equipment as with assembly of cars or electronic products or, in isolated service, mail sorting and despatching. They may also be created to improve the efficiency of labour-intensive work. Examples are packing hampers or large clerical tasks such as counting votes at a general election. In such cases, the lines created are only temporary yet they still incorporate the ideas of moving product and work specialisation.

12. Continuous

The four production systems described in sections **8** to **11** deliver so-called *integral* products, see Box 3.4. Continuous production systems produce high volumes of dimensional products. Continuous process plant is characterised by the way raw materials flow through it continuously with very little build up of stocks at any intermediate stage. While again it is possible to build flexibility into the plant design, variations in the product family are usually very small. Chemical plants producing soap, for example, can cope with different mixes of ingredients but remain dedicated to soap. Similarly, breweries will produce batches of different grades of beer.

It can be seen that continuous plant either runs with the same product all the time, as with electricity generation, or operates in large batch mode. Its distinction from the other production processes comes from the dimensional nature of the product. High investment in specialised processing plant and automatic monitoring and control are usually required although some very specialised plant runs at small scale. Examples lie in pharmaceuticals where the small demand for some products is measured in kilogrammes per year.

Integral products are those which can be counted. Thus a batch shop has an order for 1,000 stop valves; a car assembly line produces 11 cars per hour; the local sandwich bar produces 300 filled rolls between 10 o'clock and lunch time.

Dimensional products are those which are measured by weight, volume or similar measures. A quarry supplies 600 tonnes of ore per day; a brewery produces 25,000 gallons per year; a power station produces 1,200 megawatts.

Box 3.4 Integral and dimensional products

It is often difficult to run a continuous process plant at an output other than the designed standard. Like mass production, the high fixed costs mean high operational gearing so that success is very sensitive to the volume of sales (see section **2.31**).

13. Hybrid systems

The five production processes are presented here as ideal types. Many firms combine two or more at different stages of the production process. The choice depends on the nature of the product and details of the manufacturing process. Some common examples are:

- *Batch → Line*
  In this frequently found arrangement, components are made in batches ready to be assembled on a line. The upstream batch processes may run much faster than the assembly process or they may be geographically distant from the assembly plant. In the latter case, the transport system requires the items to be produced in batches. Many car components from engines to tyres are made in batches, ready for line assembly. Biscuit ingredients are mixed in batches while the biscuits themselves are formed, baked, coated and packed on lines.
- *Continuous → Line or Continuous → Batch*
  Raw materials, made in continuous plant, are finished and packed on dedicated lines or even in batches if the variety is great. Bulk aspirin manufacture is a continuous process while packing is line. For most pharmaceutical production, pelleting and packing lines can be used for a range of products to be sold in the same form. Batch finishing is found in oil refineries. Lubricating oil is normally packed on filling lines but some markets require special sizes or shapes of packaging. These are filled off-line in batches.
- *Jobbing → Project or Batch → Project*
  Project work is frequently rendered difficult by the need to work in unfamiliar and exposed conditions. Modern developments in construction have led to more items being pre-assembled in factories before delivery and erection on site. Reinforced concrete bridge beams are an example. The quality of materials and dimensional accuracy are improved if the beams are made in special plant. There they can be protected from the weather during the curing time. This switch in process technology has an influence on design since structures have to be made of transportable components rather than cast from concrete in larger and freer forms. They look more like *Lego* than *Plasticene*.
  High specification windows are frequently batch assembled in factories before delivery and fitting on site. This replaces that traditional method of building frames into walls as they go up. Simple glazing was fitted later.

The examples suggest two main reasons why hybrids are formed from two production processes. First, there is the nature of the product itself. Project and continuous processes are quite different from the others in this respect. The individual nature of the project and the dimensional form of the continuous product set them apart from jobbing, batch and line which, in principle, can produce the same product. The latter three relate to the scale of production rather than its basic physical characteristics. Secondly, the different processes run at different optimal speeds so they tend to be separated by buffer stocks, which are semi-finished goods in quantities which rise and fall with the production cycles. These buffer stocks tend to physically separate the different sections of a hybrid plant.

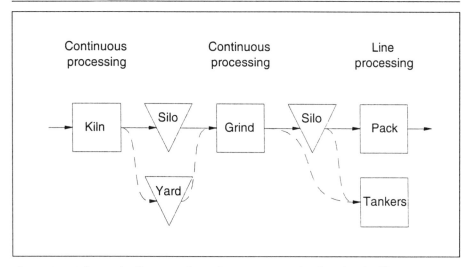

Figure 3.2 Schematic diagram of Castle Cement works showing buffer stocks

The Castle Cement works at Padeswood, Clwyd, North Wales is a continuous →
line hybrid, see Figure 3.2. It manufactures Portland cement and related products
from the limestone found in the Clwydian range. The process involves heating a
mixture of limestone, shale and sand to 1500 degC in a rotating kiln. Output is in
the form of glass-like clinker which is then ground to cement dust in high-speed
ball mills. Additives to modify the cement properties are put in during the grinding. Some cement is despatched in bulk tankers while most is passed to the
packing line to fill the familiar 50 kilogramme sacks. Although the grinding stage
has a higher capacity than the kiln, the two are normally balanced so that the
small intermediate silo carries just a few minutes inventory. Again, the packing
line has a higher capacity than is usually required so its feed silo is also small.
Any section can be stopped for cleaning or maintenance. So as not to lose output
when the grinding or packing are stopped, an open yard enables an overflow
inventory of clinker from the kiln to be stacked for several days. Cement dust
cannot, of course, be stored in this way.

14. System choice

Manufacturing managers have to choose among the range and mix of process
technologies. This is an important decision since selection of an inappropriate
system leads to high operating costs or a waste of capital investment. As
explained in section **13**, the project and continuous processes are clearly determined by the nature of the product. The choice of jobbing, batch and line, on the
other hand, is dependent on scale and managers have to relate process choice to
considerations of demand and product variety.

This problem is illustrated in Figure 3.3. Line processing suits operations of high
volume of standard products. At the other extreme, jobbing shops produce small
quantities of a variety of items. Batch processing occurs somewhere between the
two, the transitions between the stages, illustrated by the dotted line, depending
on circumstances. Through decisions to seek larger orders, for example, jobbing

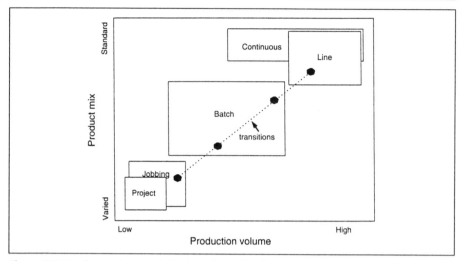

Figure 3.3 Scale, variety and choice of production systems

shops move towards becoming batch processors and batch shops begin to lay down dedicated production lines. Within batch processing itself, managers can look to narrow the product range, reduce flexibility and increase the scale of output. In practice, there is little difference between a jobbing shop and a small batch operation. Similarly, the step from large batch to line processing can be imperceptible. Large steps rarely occur successfully as they require complete overhaul of the physical plant and operating systems.

Table 3.1 summarises the key factors in the choice of process in manufacturing and isolated service systems. As with the process descriptions, the processes are ideal types and the factors generalisations. The table is intended to set out the important differences among the processes. It can be seen that batch production is presented as something of an intermediate between jobbing and process. Its position on the scales in the table, such as high to low, depends on the particular circumstances. There is never a single, correct set of choices of operating systems. The choice is a blend of issues from how a firm embraces competition through to the current process layout which is itself an accumulation of many related decisions in the past.

15. Developments in production systems

We mentioned in **2.9** how Ford's line assembly revolutionised manufacturing and brought cheap vehicles to the mass market. Technical advance is often seen in this light, the creation of systems for production on larger and larger scales. Yet such developments do not mean that the older systems of production organisation become obsolete. Each has its own application. Jobbing will continue for as long as single items are required. Indeed, as we shall see in Chapter 4, the more markets are dominated by mass-produced items, the more likely there will be demand for individual, or customised, items.

Intolerance of the apparent chaos of jobbing and batch shops has a long history. Urwick, a writer of the classical school of management thought, argued, 'To allow the individual idiosyncrasies of a wide range of customers to drive administration away from the principles on which it can manufacture is suicidal.'[4] To such

	Chosen process technology				
	Project	*Jobbing*	*Batch*	*Line*	*Continuous*
Product factors					
Product range	Diverse	Diverse	↔↔↔↔↔↔↔	Standard	Standard
Quantity produced	One	Small	↔↔↔↔↔↔↔	Large	Large or very large
Design	Unique	Customers' needs	↔↔↔↔↔↔↔	Standard	Fixed
Technology focused on..	Product	Product	↔↔↔↔↔↔↔	Product/ process	Process
Value offered to market	Skill, time capability	Skill, time capability	↔↔↔↔↔↔↔	Price	Price, uniqueness
Process factors					
Process changes	Flexible	Flexible	↔↔↔↔↔↔↔	Inflexible	Inflexible
Capital	Low	Low	↔↔↔↔↔↔↔	High	High
Speed	Flexible, worker paced	Flexible, worker paced	↔↔↔↔↔↔↔	Fixed, machine paced	Process paced
Impact of breakdown	Low	Low	↔↔↔↔↔↔↔	High	Very high
Inventory in process	High and rising	High	↔↔↔↔↔↔↔	Low	Very low
Control of production	Supervision and simple records	Supervision and simple records	↔↔↔↔↔↔↔	Machine paced	Automated
Control of quality	External verification	Individual obligation	↔↔↔↔↔↔↔	End of line checking	Built into process

Table 3.1 Product and process factors in the choice of process technology

writers, standardisation and simplification were the keys to success. To Urwick, such truths were self-evident for we base our high standard of living on the ability to carry out many functions more efficiently than did our ancestors. At the same time, however, our rising wealth enables us to demand at least some goods and services which more closely match our idiosyncrasies. The growth of McDonald's has not made lunching at the Savoy any less desirable.

There is room, then, in markets for both individual and mass produced goods. We should, therefore, not be learning that one production system is superior to another but that each must be used appropriately. Having selected a system which matches the needs of the environment, the challenge lies in running it well.

16. Profiling

Hill[5] has developed the method of profiling to investigate the relationships between the different production processes, the rest of the business and its markets. Many companies fail to understand and incorporate these trade-offs. Furthermore, as market environments or business policies change, they fail to see how their internal processes become increasingly unmatched. A firm's new policy to reduce work in progress may cause its production managers to reduce batch sizes. This means an increase in the cost of machine idle time as more effort is put into changing them over from one product to another. A business can, of course, compete for the sort of business which looks for smaller quantities but the one in question may not be successful if it tries to win large orders with a small batch mentality.

Table 3.2 illustrates the profiling process. It is drawn from Table 3.1, removing project and process technologies and cutting the number of rows for simplicity. The firm selects relevant characteristics of products and processes as shown in the left hand column. The product and process characteristics are then positioned on the scale (jobbing to line) whose measures are set out in each row. Three product

	Chosen process technology		
	Jobbing	Batch	Line
Product range	Diverse ∇	◆ ▼	Standard
Quantity required	Small ∇▼	◆	Large
Process changes	Flexible ∇	◆ ▼	Inflexible
Speed	Worker paced ∇	◆ ▼	Fixed, machine paced
Inventory in process	High ∇▼	◆	Low
Control of quality	Individual obligation ∇	◆ ▼	End of line checking

Table 3.2 Effective and ineffective profiles

profiles are shown in the table. Two represent products which display a consistent pattern and one does not:

- Product ∇ represents the manufacture of *haute couture* clothing or the installation of fitted kitchens. Such products are demanded in ones or, at most, very small batches. The company accepts the role of workers in deciding output and quality and motivates and trains them accordingly. Expected levels of inventory in process are high. The firm is consistent in its process choices. In the fitted kitchen example, it will use components made in batches but each order is treated as an individual job. Indeed, in taking place on the customer's premises the service offered has many of the characteristics of a project.
- Product ♦ is similarly well balanced, being a varied family of goods or services, such as printed cards or restaurant meals. In batch processing, the product range, process flexibility and inventory are smaller than in the jobbing shop. Production rates are partially determined by machines and quality will be controlled by end of production inspection combined with a reliance on the skills of individual workers.
- Product ▼, in contrast, has an inconsistent profile. The supplier is using line production methods to produce small quantities of standard products. This yields the worst of both worlds; high inventories are set alongside high running costs as the production lines are stopped to switch from one product to another.

The profiling approach is intended to be illustrative and exploratory rather than definitive. Its value lies in the generation of insights and debate among operating managers as to the sorts of production systems which they require.

17. Transitional process technologies

We have seen how the gap between jobbing and small batch production is not clear cut. Furthermore, there is little to choose between the layouts of some large batch and line producers. The distinctions have become even less clear with the developments of process innovations which have attempted to bridge these gaps and gain corresponding benefits. We shall look at each transition in turn:

The jobbing – batch transition

The costs of setting up machines for different items set lower limits to economical batch sizes. For smaller volumes, it is often more economical to use simpler equipment.

Figure 3.4 shows how costs vary with volume in printing. Conventional presses apply one colour at each stage. Therefore, to produce four colours, a printer may pass the same material through the press four times, using different inks and plates on each occasion. Figure 3.4 shows the total cost of such a job; this comprises the set-up cost S1 and the variable cost which is related to volume. A four-colour press enables the work to be printed in one pass. This machine consists of four stages linked in sequence with sophisticated paper handling and control equipment. The set-up cost S4 is higher than for setting up the single-colour machine four times. The running cost per item, however, is much

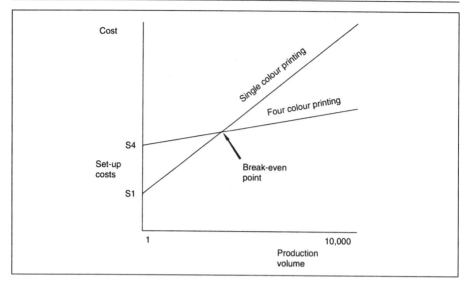

Figure 3.4 Printing costs for the same job on different presses

lower as only one pass is required. The four-colour cost line, therefore, climbs less steeply than the single-colour one. At volumes above the break-even point (see **2.30**), the more sophisticated machine comes into its own. Break-even is typically several thousand copies.

Developments using information technology in the control of machine tools have reduced the break-even points. Computer numerically controlled (CNC) machine tools have reduced set-up times compared to the machines they replace. The programming of such machines takes place off-line instead of by manual adjustment of trains of gears and control cams which has to be carried out while the machine is stationary. Machining centres are another development. They group machines together under the control of a computer. Robots and conveyors allow products and tools to be moved under software control. While these arrangements are hardly simple, their complexity is lower than mechanical transfer lines and the cost of switching from batch to batch is again reduced.

The batch – line transition

At the batch–line transition lie processes which have their roots in either process. *Group technology*, also known as *cell-based manufacturing*, identifies common characteristics among batched products so that they form a basic pattern with variations, see **8.4**. On the basis of commonality, groups of machines are laid out to carry out the basic processes with ancillary machines to handle the variations on the way. The same mode of thinking has led to increasing the flexibility of assembly lines so that they can cope with a wider range of products while operating without interruption.

The transitional processes are shown in Figure 3.5. At their appropriate mixes of volume and flexibility, these new applications modify the scope of the basic processes. For example, group technology enables higher outputs from batch layouts without resort to laid-down assembly lines. Flexible assembly lines allow for the efficient production of high volumes of varied products.

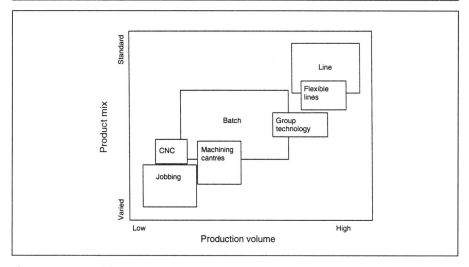

Figure 3.5 Transitional processes

18. Organisational factors

So far we have discussed process technologies with a focus on their technical features. Yet, as explained in **2.7**, operations managers need to understand the close relationship between people and processes within the *socio-technical* subsystem. Among the first to relate process technology to human behaviour was Woodward[6] in her classic study of firms in south Essex. It led her towards a theory of production organisation.

In the study of 92 manufacturing firms in south Essex, England during the 1960s, Woodward collected data on many aspects of production operations and management as well as measures of success. Data included, for example, the percentage of total costs allocated to payment to employees, the number of levels in the hierarchy and the span of control[7] of supervisors.

Woodward concluded that, according to similarities among key organisational variables, the different systems of production fell into three clusters of firms whose characteristics were broadly similar. These she called *unit and small batch*, *large batch and mass*, and *process* systems. They correspond to the jobbing, line and continuous categories we have been using so far.

Table 3.3 summarises some of the many observations made. If they were the only output of the work, then it may not have been regarded as particularly significant. So far, we can see that she described the firms in one area of the country and fitted them into clusters according to similarities among their production systems. She went further than this, however. In collecting data about the success of firms in the sample, Woodward investigated what features distinguished the better performing firms from the rest. In doing so, she was looking to see whether it was possible to make statements about the ways firms *ought* to be organised, that is to develop a *normative theory* of the organisation of production.

The way Woodward presented the data is illustrated in Table 3.4. This example shows that the more successful process firms had spans of control which

73

	Jobbing	Line	Continuous
Mean number of levels in hierarchy	3	4	6
Percentage of costs allocated to wages and salaries	40	35	15
Mean span of control of first line supervisors	22	49	13
Mean ratio of managers and supervisors to all staff	35	17	7

Table 3.3 Selected data on firms with different production systems

	Number of people controlled					
	<10	11–20	21–30	31–40	Median	No.
All firms	6	12	5	2	13	25
More successful	1	5	–	–	–	6
Less successful	1	–	1	2	–	4

Table 3.4 Spans of control in continuous process firms

were close to each other and to the median of the group as a whole. The less successful firms tended to be scattered. Woodward's observations of other organisational factors showed similar patterns with the more successful firms being more similar to each other and closer to the mean values. This pointed the way to the normative theory.

> 'The figures relating to the span of control of the chief executive, the number of levels in the line of command, labour costs, and the various labour ratios showed a similar trend. The fact that organizational characteristics, technology, and success were linked together in this way suggested that not only was the system of production an important variable in the determination of organization structure, but also that one particular form of organization was most appropriate to each system of production. In unit [jobbing] production, for example, not only did short and relatively broadly based pyramids predominate, but they also appeared to ensure success. Process production, on the other hand, would seem to require the taller and more narrowly based pyramid.'[8]

These conclusions leave us a long way from a general theory of production organisations. Woodward, in order to achieve rigour in her research, was taking a narrow perspective. She took the production systems in each company as given and did not investigate, for example, whether each was appropriate to its market situation. Furthermore, there was no allowance made for the historical development of each company - structures often exist because they have always been that way. Despite these comments, however, the study did enlighten the debate about the implications of different type of production technology.

19. Supervisors and employees

One resemblance between jobbing and continuous production is that both employ a greater proportion of skilled workers than line production systems. In jobbing shops, the skilled workers are engaged directly in manufacture, doing it, so to speak, with their own hands. In continuous production systems, no worker is engaged in direct work upon the product. There are few workers and the skill required in such systems is directed at overall process control and plant maintenance. Again, these require highly competent workers. It is in line assembly that we find many more semi-skilled or unqualified employees engaged in specialised repetitive tasks requiring less general skill. Naturally, these tasks themselves can be automated and many firms have taken the investment route towards achieving lower costs.

Recognising the different mixtures of skills among shop-floor workers in the three production systems, it may be surprising to encounter Woodward's conclusion on the spans of control at the first level. This was much larger (1:49) in line production than in jobbing (1:22) or continuous systems (1:13). The explanation lies in understanding the nature of the supervisory role. In jobbing and continuous production factories, the workforce is broken down into small groups. In this situation, the supervisor is expected to display leadership in problem solving related to tasks as well as maintaining links with other departments. These involve obtaining tools and materials, arranging for despatch and so on. The work groups, therefore, tend to include the supervisor and the consequent personal relationships are informal.

Line production is different. Detailed process planning has been carried out before the line is laid out. Repetitive jobs throw up few technical problems as the perceptual and conceptual skill elements typical of jobbing work have been removed. Workers are employed for their dexterity. Problems that do arise tend to be dealt with by specialist engineers. The supervisor is, therefore, less involved in the workers' tasks. Leadership concentrates on ensuring that assemblies are carried out at the predetermined line speed. Having allocated workers to the line, the supervisor maintains discipline, arranges work breaks and so on. The relationship is formal and, with the pace having been set by the machine, each supervisor can manage many more workers.

Case study: Meubles Grange

Meubles Grange makes furniture in its factory in the Rhone valley some 40 km from Lyon, France. The styles, mainly in cherry wood, follow French traditions from about 1750 to 1900. They include *Trianon*, *Louis Philippe* and *Consulat*. With beds, wardrobes, mirrors, book cases, sideboards, bureaux, tables and chairs, the number of designs shown in the catalogue is about 180, not counting size options for items from beds to shelves. This variety is increased by three colour shades and three levels of distressing, making nine possible finishes in all. The furniture is expensive; a medium sized buffet sideboard retails at over £1000. For a premium, Grange prides itself in meeting special customer requests for dimensions, colour finishes or interior fittings.

The range is updated annually with a new catalogue. Items which sell less than about 100 per year are considered for replacement. The company has been broadening its range in two directions. First there are complementary soft furnishings which enable Grange to offer a total look, *le savoir-vivre à la française*, to customers. Secondly, the company offers traditional designs in metal or rattan made by subcontractors in the Far East. These sell well in the spring whereas the timber products peak in the autumn.

The company, founded by cabinet maker Joseph Grange in 1905, has grown to a £25 million turnover with some 400 employees. About 75% of output is exported, the most important markets being Germany, the United States and the United Kingdom although others including Australia and New Zealand are also served. Sales are through distributors to specialist furniture stores who display room settings showing the company's products. Deliveries are by road trailer in Europe, each distributor receiving a delivery every two weeks. US traffic goes in containers.

While the look of the furniture is traditional, Grange does not replicate old methods of manufacture. Rough sawn timber is dried in modern kilns. Furniture components, many of which are common across several lines, are made on high quality wood machines. Assembly is aided by modern fixings and special jigs to ensure accuracy of fit. Finishing, in contrast, is done by hand. One craftsman works on all the items of a customer's order, applying the appropriate varnishes and waxes to give the required finish. The aim is to give a consistent high quality finish across all items ordered by the customer. Grange seeks to reduce the number of complaints from the present 0.3% of orders.

Making to customers' orders means that the only stocks of finished goods, apart from goods in transit, are the metal and rattan lines.

Questions

1 *What bundle of goods and service has Grange chosen to offer?*
2 *Identify the types of production system found at Meubles Grange and how they relate to the market the company serves.*

References

1. Schmenner, R.W. (1993) *Production/Operations Management* New York, Macmillan pp. 18–22
2. Superdrug (1993) *Success: Customer Care and Service Skills Programme* Unpublished company materials
3. Hunter, T. (1994) 'Direct insurers picking low-risk cherries in a battle for the premium customers' *The Guardian*, 5 March, p.31
4. Urwick, L. (1943) *Elements of Administration* London, Pitman
5. Hill, Terry (1991) *Production/Operations Management* Hemel Hempstead, Prentice-Hall p.69
6. Woodward, Joan (1971) *Industrial Organisation: Theory and Practice* London, Oxford University Press
7. The span of control is the number of subordinates who are directly responsible to a manger or supervisor, that is occupying the next lower level in the hierarchy. Firms often try to even out responsibilities among staff at a particular level by taking span of control into account. Other

factors, such as spatial dispersion or technical content are also brought into play. Woodward's comparisons use averages for each firm.

8. Woodward, op. cit. pp. 69–71

4

PLANNING AND CONTROL

Chapter objectives

When you have finished studying this chapter, you should be able to:

- Explain the key roles of planning and control in the management of organisations and their operations.

- Set out the planning and control cycle and how planning and control relate to the strategic and operational levels of management.

- Illustrate the uncertainty under which plans are made and how organisations respond to it.

- Define and explain the purpose of objectives; identify the features of good objectives; discuss their limitations in practice.

- Show how a sequence of actions and decisions can be set out in a flow chart.

- Define strategic management and outline the features of its main stages: analysis, choice, implementation and control.

- Give details of competitive and cooperative strategies and identify the implications that each has for operations management.

- Relate in broad terms two strategic lessons from Japan - Just-in-Time and Total Quality Management.

- Explain why control systems are needed at all levels of organisations; identify three categories useful in understanding control processes.

- Outline some control problems in human activity systems.

INTRODUCTION

Planning and control are fundamental management activities. Without them an organisation stands little chance of achieving its objectives. Planning selects the direction and points the organisation along the route; control ensures that the direction is maintained. These activities form the planning and control cycle shown in Figure 4.1. While in practice they form a continuous loop, we can think of the cycle being initiated by top management formulating strategic plans. These plans are carried out through their interpretation into more detailed intermediate and operating plans. These are the more local planning and control cycles nested in the *Carry out plans* cell of Figure 4.1.

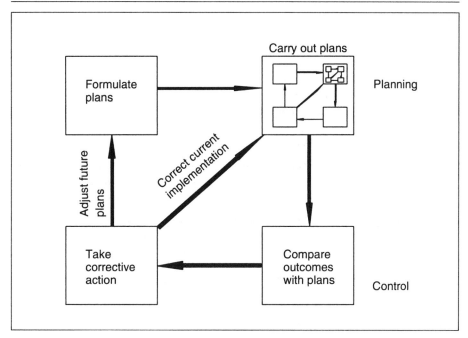

Figure 4.1 The planning and control cycle

The control function comes into play when the plans are set in motion. Through comparison of results with the plans, either in anticipation or measurement after the event, corrective control action is taken. The control action can, if taken early enough, change the current implementation. On the other hand, gaps between results and plans should be considered in the next round of planning formulation. Thus, the cycle is completed through feedback control.

This chapter examines in detail the planning and control cycle. It explains how the operations function is involved with all planning levels, picking out the strategic level as particularly important. It then shows how various types of control can be used to ensure that objectives are achieved.

PLANNING

1. What is planning?

We are all planners, more than we might imagine. We plan meal menus, shopping trips, examination revision, holidays and careers. These plans, formal or informal as they may be, give shape and purpose to our lives and enable us to assemble resources and cooperate with others in their achievement. In the same way, business plans enable managers to gather their resources and impose their intentions upon the organisation. A plan in the business context is usually formal and can be defined as follows:

A plan is an explicit formalised statement of intention which consists of objectives and statements of actions which are to be taken to achieve them.

79

Note that a plan is more than a statement of wishes. To be effective it must clarify what actions are required for its accomplishment. There is, however, a danger of overemphasis on formal plans if users become committed to them in spite of changing circumstances. The infamous 'five year plans' of the soviet system illustrated how sticking closely to rigid plans could contribute to the ruin of economies. In the planning and control cycle, performance must be monitored and, if necessary, plans adjusted when circumstances change.

2. Planning under uncertainty

All plans are made in uncertain conditions. The uncertainty usually arises in the business environment. The plan is a means by which it can be taken into account and an effective response produced. There are four types of uncertainty:

- *State uncertainty* refers to difficulties in predicting the future state of the environment. Operations managers are continually faced with this problem. The return from investments in new facilities depends on future demand which depends on many factors. For example, the sales of a petrol station may depend on changes in road layouts or the success of a new estate agency depends on the unpredictable state of the housing market.
- *Timing uncertainty* refers to circumstances where an environmental state or event is confidently expected, the only question being when. Instances include: the timing of the introduction of a competitor's new service; the failure of a piece of equipment; the sale of a certain quantity of stock; the opening of a new transport link.
- *Effect uncertainty* describes the unpredictable impact of environmental changes. Again, this problem affects operating managers. Organisations may be well aware of the changes yet remain uncertain of their impact. Examples include: the expansion of production facilities by a competitor may reduce one's own demand; a change in safety legislation may affect operating costs of different companies in different ways; growing shortages of key raw materials may increase prices by an unknown amount; introduction of new taxes may reduce demand, again by an unknown amount.
- *Response uncertainty* refers to the indeterminate consequences of a management decision. For operating managers: the results of changing production processes or layouts may not be fully clear; the impact on quality of increasing production line speeds may be difficult to assess; market responses to product innovation are difficult to forecast; employee trade unions may respond unfavourably to plans for increased efficiency.

All four types of uncertainty may be seen in the same situation. In the early 1990s British Airways was seeking to develop its routes in continental Europe. One objective was to obtain landing rights at Orly, the second airport of Paris. BA faced state uncertainty in not knowing whether the route licensing system was to be liberalised. The French government eventually agreed, at first without stating a date when operations could start. This timing uncertainty made marketing the new service difficult. When the routes were opened to competition, BA could not know whether other airlines would try to operate them. This was effect uncertainty. Finally, BA recognised that an existing French operator, Air Inter, would respond vigorously to its own entry to the Orly market. BA, therefore, faced response uncertainty which made estimating demand very difficult. BA opened its service in 1994.

Being able to respond to uncertainty is a mark of good operations management. We saw in **1.14** how internal operating structures with spare capacity or stocks of materials respond to short-term fluctuations in demand. We shall see later in this chapter how strategic management attempts to change relationships between the organisation and its environment to either influence it or reduce its effects. Forecasting can play its part also. Uncertainty would be eliminated if either:

- the organisation could forecast the environment with sufficient accuracy, or
- the organisation had sufficient influence over the environment to ensure that the planned-for future actually came to pass.

Both are impossible in the long term. In the first case, there is no known way of forecasting the future in the detail required. Further, the logic of such 'future models' would mean that all firms would have one. Therefore, all firms would have to consider all other firms' models within their own. This would make the models more complex than the systems they were trying to model in the first place! The second case is an example of attempting to make the future come true. Some large organisations have succeeded for while in using, say, monopoly power to control their environments. But such success does not last long.

3. Forecasting

Forecasting, that is the making of predictions of future states or events, is not an exact science. The forecasts vary in their reliability and may vary from confident statements of conditions for the next few hours to little more than educated guesses covering five years or more. The process is, however, important to operations managers.

Box 4.1 shows how, for each type of uncertainty, a forecast could be useful in enabling managers to make effective plans to cope. In many businesses, the operations manager is not responsible for forecasting key variables such as demand and input prices and this may lead to conflict. Demand forecasting is the province of sales and marketing yet many an operations manager is aware of the optimism of sales people. The consequence is that operations managers are wary of establishing service capacity or producing stocks according to forecasts which they 'know' are unlikely to turn out. This behaviour, in turn, causes sales to overestimate even more wildly and so on. Forecasting is one of the most important interactions between marketing and operations and needs to be managed more seriously than in this example. We shall see in our chapters on both capacity management and operations planning and scheduling how forecasts are incorporated into operations decision making.

The type of forecast to be used depends not only on the time scale covered but also on the resources of time and effort which the organisation can devote to the process. In a small business there are only resources for educated guesses, that is estimates illuminated by the awareness which comes from being close to operations and customers. The large enterprise, on the other hand, employs its own researchers and consulting groups so it gets an early warning of change in the environment. The time scale to be covered by the forecast relates to the planning process itself.

4. Levels of planning

As we saw in Figure 4.1, there are several levels of planning in an organisation. They are nested so that each level relates to the ones above and below. These

Type of uncertainty	Type of forecast	Typical questions to be answered
State uncertainty	Time series forecast	What will be the sales of microwave ovens for the next two years?
Timing uncertainty	Event timing forecast	When will the rival company introduce its patented technology in the domestic market?
Effect uncertainty	Event outcome forecast	What will be the effect on our sales of the new product?
Response uncertainty	Response forecast	What will the competitor do if we lower our prices and increase our output now?

Box 4.1 Uncertainty and forecasts

levels can, for discussion, be divided into three - *strategic, intermediate* and *operational* - although in practice there may be fewer or more and the boundaries may not be as clear cut as suggested here.

5. Links between levels

The three notional planning levels are shown in Box 4.2. Notice that senior managers display a greater scope in the plans they are responsible for. They have to decide allocations of greater resources within broader constraints and are expected to take a longer view of the impact of their decisions. There are links both down and up the hierarchy of levels:

- Downward links are shown by the way that each level establishes broad parameters for the level below. These refer to objectives to be aimed for and the resources with which they should be achieved. Thus a *means-ends chain* is established in which each level provides the means to achieve the ends of the next higher layer. This is illustrated by the case of the mail order film processing company in Box 4.3. The Director of Operations is responsible for the strategic plan to increase profits over three years. The intermediate and operations level managers, of whom only two are shown, each have objectives and plans which are blended into this overall strategy. To the more senior managers, the lower-level objectives are the means by which their own ends are achieved.
- Upward links, in a well planned business, are found in the way that each level needs to consider the capacity and capability of the levels below in formulating plans. Otherwise, plans would be simply unrealistic. Good planning should involve a blend of leadership from the senior managers, *top-down planning*, with consultation over what is feasible with junior managers, *bottom-up planning*. This process can be carried out informally although in large organisations it tends to use formal methods such as Management by Objectives.

Type of planning	Managers involved	Typical time scale
Strategic: Achieving overall objectives by managing the long-term relationships between the organisation and its environment.	Senior managers of all key functions including Directors responsible for operations.	One to ten years or more
Intermediate: Allocating resources among sub-units and functions to give each a direction and to ensure coordination.	Middle managers working together and also within their functions: production, logistics and operations managers.	Six months to two years
Operational: Accomplishing closely defined tasks with available resources.	Managers of operating units including supervisors or first line managers.	A few hours up to one year

Box 4.2 Levels of planning

Type of planning	Manager involved	Typical objective
Strategic	Director of Operations	To increase company profits to £500,000 per year in three years time ↑ end ↓means
Intermediate	Processing Plant Manager	To reduce operating costs per order by 5% this year ↑ end ↓means
Operational	Despatch Department Supervisor	To reschedule staff hours before July 31st to reduce labour costs by 5% while maintaining output.

Box 4.3 The means-ends chain of objectives and plans

Vertical links may be unintended. Changes in strategic plans may have unanticipated operational consequences. Indeed, many operations managers will count them among their greatest headaches. In the upward direction, operating decisions may have unintended strategic consequences, especially if the organisation is already prone to crisis. The lack of care in operations on the ferry *The Herald of Free Enterprise* not only led to a disaster for its passengers but severely damaged the reputation of the operating company.

6. Objectives

We have seen that a plan contains objectives and a statement of the means by which they are to be achieved. There is some difficulty for the management student because the terms aim, objective and goal tend to be used interchangeably both by managers themselves and in the literature. While some try to draw out differences among their own definitions they just add to the confusion. Therefore, we shall use the one term *objective* here.

An objective is a defined, measurable result which is to be achieved within a stated time.

Objectives have a pivotal role in the planning process. Without them, planning, which looks for statements of how objectives are to be achieved, cannot begin. Objectives have more value than this, however. Overall, they serve to:

- Provide managers with *clear targets* which they can work towards. Lacking organisational objectives managers would tend to interpret situations in their own ways and would find it difficult to act in unison.
- Decide *priorities*. Among the objectives at any level of an organisation, the achievement of some will be more critical to success that others. It may be valuable to highlight these 'must do' objectives to separate them from others which may be desirable but could well be postponed if resources are not available.
- Build *commitment*. The process of objective setting involves encouraging all employees to commit themselves to the ends of the organisation. In so doing, clear objectives help in building commitment towards the combined ends.

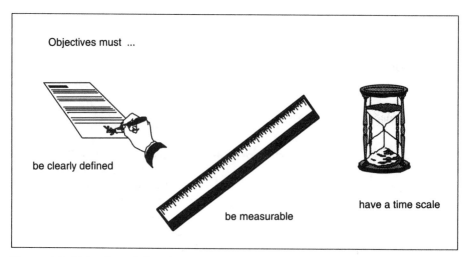

Objectives must ...

be clearly defined

be measurable

have a time scale

Figure 4.2 Objectives defined

- Objectives serve as *measuring rods* against which *choices can be made*. Many techniques of operations management presented later in this book are dependent for their application upon a choice of objective. For example, operating schedules are dependent on the objectives given to those who have to set them out.
- Objectives serve as *measuring rods* against which *performance is appraised*. Whether performance is measured for the allocation of the weekly production bonus or to assess promotion potential, the use of consistent standards helps in maintaining confidence in the appraisal scheme.
- Objectives influence *motivation*. This goes beyond the inclusion of measurable standards within a formal appraisal scheme. Clear and achievable objectives can offer a sense of personal achievement to the individual.

7. Good objectives

From the definition given in 6, we can see that a good objective should be stated in terms which are quantitative, both in terms of measure of achievement and period. Furthermore, since objectives represent an agreement over means and ends among managers, they should be written. The tests of a good objective should be threefold:

- Is the intended result clearly stated?
- Is it possible to measure whether the result has been achieved?
- Is the time scale made clear?

The examples given in Box 4.3 all satisfy these tests. They also bring out a further point which we shall meet again later, namely *constraints*. Take the example of the Despatch Department Supervisor. This manager's objective is 'To reschedule staff hours before 31st July to reduce labour costs by 5% *while maintaining output.*' It would be easy for a line manager to cut total costs if output was also permitted to fall. However, the italicised part of the objective statement mentions a constraint upon cost cutting, emphasising that changes must take place within a framework of continuing activity. The framework defines the scope of decision making within which the objective has to be achieved. Objectives and constraints, then, usually go together. The constraints may be explicitly stated in a similar way to the objectives or implied by the conventions of the operations department.

8. Problems with objectives

There are three problems with the formal, explicit setting of objectives which should be mentioned here.

Change

However minor and trivial they may appear, objectives form part of the carrying out of a general plan for the organisation. Relatively stable environments enable planning to be done with confidence while rapidly changing, or turbulent, environments pose great difficulties for the planner. No sooner is the plan made then it is out of date. Change outside a manager's control may make the pursuit of an objective either impossible or no longer relevant to success. Such situations need constant review and a much more flexible approach to the establishment and modification of plans and their objectives.

Conflict

As opposed to the single objectives given here as examples, managers are usually faced with multiple objectives which will almost certainly be in conflict. This is the managerial problem of 'keeping all balls in the air'. Almost anyone can juggle with one ball, focusing attention and energy on maintaining its movement. Having more than one makes the task more interesting yet less heed and fewer resources are then devoted to any one ball. For the manager, then, multiple objectives may mean that achieving one can be only done at the expense of another. Balancing efficiency and effectiveness, mentioned in **1.5**, is a general example of this difficulty.

Measurement

The achievement of some managerial tasks is very difficult to measure. Managers have to combine operational roles, such as ensuring short-term schedules are achieved, with other dimensions which can be seen in the definition of management given in **1.3**. These include building and creating work teams, developing subordinates and so on. The danger with having a mix of measurable and unmeasurable objectives is that managers will be tempted to focus their efforts on what can be measured in order to look good. There is also the problem of *measurementship* where employees deliberately set out to set low objectives so that they can appear good at the period end review.

Having noted these problems, it is important to recognise that operations managers use objectives extensively in planning and controlling. Planning techniques have been developed by management scientists to add clarity and precision to the process. Their use stems from the desire to achieve clear objectives, through planning how they are to be achieved and monitoring the level of success so that control can be exercised. We shall be using examples of Gantt charts, networks, linear programmes and other methods later in the book. To illustrate the approach, however, we shall use a flow chart.

9. The flow chart

Flow charts have many designs and applications. Generally, they set out sequences of events and decision points which, together, model action and decision sequences. All these are important in planning and we shall meet several versions in later chapters. The illustration in Figure 4.3 shows the sequence in the case of overcoming what the authors, rather charmingly, call 'improper idling' of a petrol engine[1]. The objective of the process is to return the fuel system to good condition. Rather than be too concerned about the nature of the activities within the model, you should note how it is built up from a set of boxes, rectangles for actions, diamonds for binary (yes/no or OK/no good) decisions.

This type of flow chart is used by information specialists as a basis for designing systems. While this design may also be useful for other managers, there are two limitations. First, there is no representation of time or cost within the diagram. It is useful for thinking about the sequence of events but less useful if one were allocating resources to them on an industrial scale. Secondly, operational processes quickly become too complex for representation in this way. We shall examine how these problems can be overcome in later chapters.

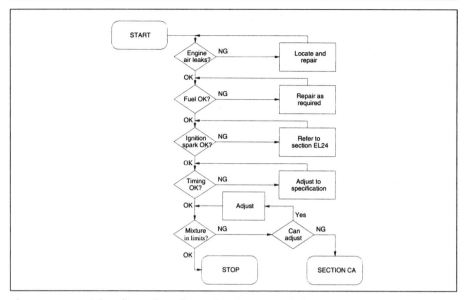

Figure 4.3 Decision flow chart for curing improper idling

STRATEGIC MANAGEMENT

In the long term, an organisation thrives if it can establish effective relationships with the many parts and elements of its environment. For most business organisations this means that they have to find ways to compete successfully through obtaining resources and serving customers. Competition does not necessarily mean titanic struggles with rival companies. On the contrary, most organisations seek to limit the direct rivalry they face. They look for those parts of industries and markets within which they can protect themselves from larger and stronger competitors. Furthermore, many build their own defences through cooperation, an important and growing feature of the policies of many organisations. We shall examine strategic management as a process involving planning, control and reviewing policies in the context of both competition and cooperation.

10. Strategic management defined

The modern view of strategic management is set out by Kreitner[2]. It has developed from *strategic planning* which was concerned with how to plan for the use of the organisation's resources to pursue long-term objectives. This did not, however, concern itself with implementation or control. Accomplishment of plans was, somehow, left to people other than planners and control adjustments were only considered when the plans came round for review. Experience has shown that the best written plans frequently failed because of unanticipated problems and the basic resistance to change within many organisations.

The modern view, then, is that planning, implementation and control should be integrated into the complete process of *strategic management*. Ansoff gives the definition of strategic management as:

87

The positioning and relating of the organisation to its environment in a way which will assure its continued success and make it secure from surprises.[3]

The implications of this definition and our discussion are that strategic management involves the following activities:

- Understanding of the environment, including making forecasts about the way its various features are changing.
- Relating the organisation to key features of the environment which have a significant influence upon it. Depending on the organisation, these include suppliers, financiers, sources of labour, governments and so on.
- Deciding upon how the organisation will serve chosen sections of the environment through the supply of bundles of products.
- Obtaining and using resources so that the needs of the environment may be satisfied by the right balance of effectiveness, efficiency and equity.
- Monitoring, forecasting and controlling performance so that the plans made during the process can be achieved.

11. The strategic management process

As stated in the previous section, strategic management is planning, implementation and control. To look at the planning process in a little more detail we can divide it into stages of analysis and choice. Analysis is the process of deciding the general direction and goals of the organisation and understanding, in terms of the goals, both the environment and the internal strengths and weaknesses. Box 4.4[4] shows the way results can be presented as a SWOT profile, so called because of the four categories of strengths, weaknesses, opportunities and threats under which the internal and external appraisals are categorised. The idea is to focus managers' attention on the most important external and internal factors which will have an impact in the long term. By presenting them together, a comparison can be made among the items so that, for example, users could question whether an organisation with good opportunities for new products is devoting sufficient resources to their development.

Many tools and techniques can be used during the appraisal process to interpret the fit between the organisation and its environment[5]. We have no space to detail them here. The general purpose, however, is to compare the expected future fit with the business objectives. A difference between the two, the so-called *planning gap*, means that corrective action is required. While it may be that the objectives are unrealistic and need modification it will normally be the case that the firm must reconsider its activities and make plans to bridge the gap. This could involve introducing new or updated products, entering new markets, improving customer service, investing in facilities and operational processes, financial restructuring and other possibilities which fundamentally change the nature of the organisation.

The identification of how best to bridge the planning gap forms the selection, or choice, stage of planning. The comparisons made in the appraisal would normally present the organisation with several possible means of closing the gap. The selection stage means looking at these in detail, comparing each for the benefits it brings and the related costs and risks. For example, for the operations manager, there may be a recognition of the opportunities in a new, emerging market for a firm's goods. This is known as *market diversification*. Having decided upon the

---

ENVIRONMENTAL APPRAISAL

Opportunities	*Threats*
Maintain market leadership in instant picture cameras.	Some technological problems.
	Market saturation in some countries.
New uses for current products and process.	Competition from Kodak and 35mm cameras with 1-hour printing services.
Markets for *Spectra* camera.	Internal resistance to change.
Economic recovery in major markets.	
Video printouts.	
Strengths	*Weaknesses*
Market leadership in instant cameras.	Management changes.
Strong R&D and marketing functions.	Over capacity.
Customers prefer Polaroid brand.	History of forecasting mistakes.
High quality.	Price of product.
Strong financial position.	Narrow product range.

INTERNAL APPRAISAL

Box 4.4 SWOT analysis, Polaroid Corporation

main thrust of strategy, the managers will have to select a way of achieving it. The market could be supplied by export, manufacture by a local company under licence or by the firm itself establishing a new production facility within the target country. These choices will have to be analysed for their effects, especially on production and distribution.

Implementation forms the next step in the strategic management process. Good plans take into account four key factors which have strong influence on their success:

- Is the *organisational structure* appropriate to the plans being proposed?
- Is it possible to develop a coherent set of *policies* so that every member of the organisation understands the contribution each must make to the plan?
- Are *people* available with the appropriate training and experience?
- Are *systems* in place both for carrying out the policies and monitoring their outcomes?

The final element of strategic management is control. The relationship between this activity and the other parts of the process are illustrated in Figure 4.4. This has been developed from Figure 4.1 to emphasise the two steps in strategy formation, analysis and choice, and the different ways in which corrective action can be taken. Strategic control involves comparisons not only of current performance with plans but also of forecasts of future performance. Corrective action can take place in the operational subsystem of the organisation, that is to change what and how things are currently done. Alternatively, two other forms of adjustment are shown in Figure 4.4. There can be adjustments to plans and, if it turns out that this does not bridge the planning gap, the company can review its strategic analysis. These actions are examples of feedforward, concurrent and feedback control which are examined further in section **21**.

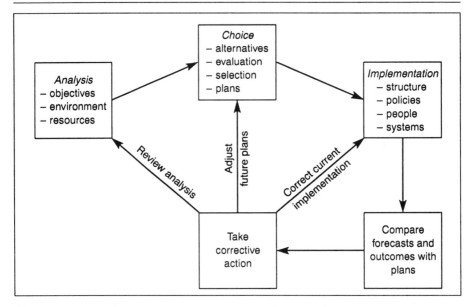

Figure 4.4 Strategic management processes and connections

12. Strategy during the product life cycle

For many organisations, competitors are a critical part of the environment in which they operate. We saw in **2.12** how the idea of the product life cycle enables us to understand how the intensity of competition rises and falls with time. This has implications throughout the operations function as indicated in Box 4.5. The usefulness of the PLC idea varies from industry to industry. Sometimes, experience shows that new products follow fairly regular patterns. Examples range from pesticides, which may have a useful life of about seven years before they are superseded, to some toys which may only last a season if they are sold as tie-in merchandise connected with films or television series.

As mentioned in section 9, competition does not necessarily take the form of head-on clashes with rivals. Indeed, there are many ways in which firms compete depending on the structure of the industries in which they find themselves.

13. Generic competitive strategies

The best-known model of competitive strategies is that developed by Porter[6]. As shown in Figure 4.5, Porter's model combines two strategic variables, *competitive advantage* and *competitive scope*.

Competitive advantage is the sustainable strategic edge which an organisation has in relation to its competitors. Improvements in performance, for example in reducing costs or increasing responsiveness of the operations function, enable the organisation to choose more ways to compete, that is to gain the edge. Well chosen strategies gain ground more effectively. Porter argues that firms must choose between competing on low prices, and therefore low costs, or through differentiation. A firm which differentiates provides superior value, in terms of quality, service,

Stage of product life cycle			
Introduction	Growth	Maturity	Decline
Thrust of competitive strategy			
Plan for competition.	Monitor competitors' behaviour.	Compete through minor innovations and updating.	Compete on price.
Basic operations implications			
Build scale of operations: links with suppliers; production systems; distribution.	Seek economies of scale throughout the whole operations system.	Reduce investment in growth; concentrate on cutting costs throughout operations system; make low cost improvements in product–service bundle on continuous basis.	Reduce scale of operations to match decline in demand.

Box 4.5 Competitive and operations strategies during the product life cycle

extra features and so on, compared with the lower-priced rivals. To be successful, enough customers must recognise the added value and be prepared to pay a premium price for it.

Competitive scope is the range or breadth over which the organisation chooses to compete. The range may be defined in terms such as the number of industries, countries, markets and products. To give two extreme examples: a very narrow scope may be one customer group in one area, such as a nursery school; a very broad scope is the many countries and markets served by a global corporation such as Unilever.

14. Four generic strategies

Porter's model encourages managers to think of their choice of combination of competitive advantage and scope which leads to one of the four *generic strategies* set out in Figure 4.5. The first two are built on broad competitive scope while the last two are narrow.

Cost leadership

Organisations which pursue this strategy aim to keep their total costs lower than those of their competitors. In most industries this means operating at high volumes so that economies of scale are realised. Managers concentrate their attention on maintaining lower costs in relevant phases of their value chains. Large-scale

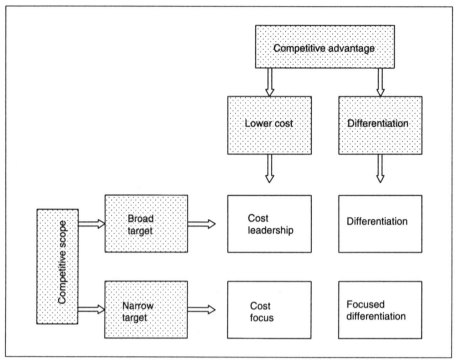

Figure 4.5 Generic competitive strategies

buying means low input prices. High volumes of throughput mean great efficiency in operations, distribution and marketing. The supermarket chain Asda is one which stresses price as a key part of its competitive strategy. It offers keen prices every day and thinks that customers prefer this to a continually changing range of offers, see Box 4.6[7].

Asda turns price screw

Asda ... is demanding price cuts from suppliers to pass on to its customers, in an attempt to strengthen its market position.

It has written to selected suppliers demanding that they turn promotional deals into permanent price reductions. ...

In the letter, the Leeds-based company states its intention to operate permanent prices 'below those prevailing in the market place'. Customers resented 'yo-yo' pricing, the letter added. ...

... the letter is in line with the strategy ... of offering better value to its relatively poor customers who are based in the urban North of England.

The company has a policy of reducing promotional discounts, which it believes lead to distrust of its pricing.

It has about 300 promotional discounts a month now, compared with about 1,000 a few years ago.

Box 4.6 Asda's competitive strategy

Asda also illustrates the problems for this strategy if newcomers enter the industry with even lower costs of operations. Competition from the LADs (limited assortment discounters) intensified in the 1990s. The home-based chains, such as Kwiksave and Lo-Cost, were first augmented by firms from other EU countries such as Aldi (Germany), Netto (Denmark) and Ed (France). Then came warehouse clubs, including Costco, which claimed to shave another 10 per cent off prices with their new form of trading. All the entrants threaten the established firms.

Differentiation

Only a few companies within an industry aim to compete using price as their most important weapon. Most differentiate by establishing in the customers' minds the idea of value for money. While Asda stresses price, Sainsbury offers variety, innovation and a high quality image. Both Asda and Sainsbury have a broad competitive scope within the UK market. They are located in most regions and appeal to the large group of customers who seek the convenience of the large store with parking. Yet Sainsbury, with its differentiation strategy, has been more successful than Asda. It has used advertising to establish its brand, widely recognised as being synonymous with quality, and in its operations it has striven for value for money in the mix of goods and service which it provides. Value for money must be stressed because a differentiator will not succeed if the extra prices it charges are greater than the extra value perceived by the customer.

Cost focus

The firm following the cost focus strategy seeks competitive advantage by supplying a narrowly defined market with an operations system designed to operate at low cost. The market is often defined by region or urban area. For example, free newspapers draw their revenue solely from advertising. They first competed with conventional local newspapers by cutting costs of production, especially of journalists and editorial staff. Yet they quickly learned that they needed some news items among the advertising to encourage readers to turn the pages! Hence we see the use of column fillers and cheap syndicated articles on subjects such as travel, astrology and heraldry.

Focused differentiation

In following a strategy of focused differentiation, the organisation delivers a superior product to a narrowly defined market segment. Again, the market could be defined geographically, although it could be split by social group, gender, age and so on. The company operating the Newton Nursing Home, see Chapter 1, serves aged people in north-west England. It aims to offer a superior service to its customers by providing numerous little extras and comforts not provided by rivals. Through doing so it has established a reputation for good service and can charge a rate some 10 per cent above the market average.

Porter argues that organisations need to select a generic strategy and stick to it. Otherwise there is a danger of being 'stuck in the middle', losing to threats from both cost leaders and differentiators. Others have argued that this is false since it may be possible to arrange operations systems so that both cost leadership and differentiation are achieved simultaneously. *Customisation* is one trend which we shall return to in Chapter 17. Under this policy, the organisation

93

produces individually tailored outputs from systems which are almost entirely based on mass production or mass service principles.

15. Strategic cooperation within the firm

So far we have focused our attention upon the competitive view of strategic management. Yet many organisations have found that they can use their resources better if they cooperate. Indeed, one of the arguments for building up a diversified firm consisting of several related divisions is that advantage based on *synergy* can be gained. In sharing resources and functions such as finance, operations, marketing, distribution and so on, more can be gained than if they operated independently. Synergy is often called the 'two plus two equals five' effect.

To gain synergy, relationships among business units can exploit three types of connection, according to Porter[8]. First, the connections can be *tangible* in that the measurable extra costs of forging the link are exceeded by the benefits in terms of total cost savings or enhanced differentiation of products. Activities to be considered for linking are those which represent both a substantial proportion of costs and are sensitive to increases in scale or utilisation. Examples could be reaching common customers or transferring process technologies to improve quality.

Intangible connections form the second group. Here business unit functions are similar in general terms such as facing the same type of buyer, making the same type of purchase or running the same type of manufacturing process. For instance, two units may be engaged in large batch production and hence may share knowledge of the development of planning systems or materials handling technology. Costs and benefits of linking are, however, more difficult to measure than those in the tangible category.

Figure 4.6 illustrates both tangible and intangible connections. Two divisions are represented by their value chains, see **1.11**. It can be seen that tangible links could arise, in this case, from shared sales forces, distribution or technology. Intangible links lie in sharing ideas on manufacturing or in making common approaches to the government.

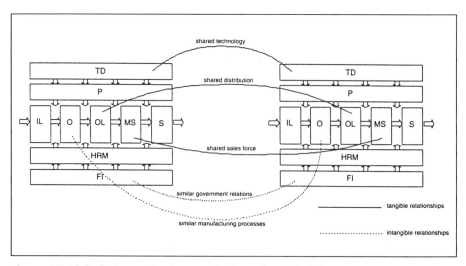

Figure 4.6 Links between business units in a diversified form

The third type of link is based on *competitor interrelationships*. Large corporations compete in many ways, often on a large scale. Taking a passive stance against a multifaceted competitor runs the risk of each business being 'picked off' in turn as the opponent allocates promotional resources around its various units. An active protagonist should be prepared to match, indeed preempt, this sort of behaviour.

Despite the potential advantages of these links between divisions, many diversified firms do not cement such bonds effectively. Impediments may arise from human factors, such as different cultural and value systems, and technical reasons such as the way financial systems set up transfer prices which affect one unit less favourably than another. Head offices may be reluctant to intervene as this would run counter to the spirit of operational decentralisation.

16. Strategic cooperation between firms

In the light of such difficulties, it is not surprising that firms look outside the group for coalition partners. Such ventures have been attempted for many years with varying degrees of success[9] and there has been much recent discussion of alliances in the literature[10]. We shall illustrate three links with tangible benefits, namely resource pools, combination alliances and deescalation alliances[11].

Resource pools

These involve two or more organisations in putting their resources together. They do so to:

- reduce duplication or redundancy
- share or alleviate risk
- combine efforts to compete with rivals
- reach a scale threshold where they can become effective entrants to a market.

The agreement may link primary activities of the value chain. Figure 4.7 uses the value chain concept, introduced in **1.17** to illustrate the 1991 agreement between Sears and le Groupe André to reorganise and reestablish distribution facilities in Benelux and Germany. The agreement called for sharing of operations and both inbound and outbound logistics. Links between the secondary activities were also needed to sustain those between the primary ones.

The example of Sears – Groupe André focused on primary activities. In other pools, the stress is on the secondary activities themselves, especially technology development. In the EU since 1980, such groupings have become common in information technology, biotechnology and new materials[12]. These alliances have been promoted by various EU joint development programmes.

Combination alliances

These occur when partners combine or exchange complementary functions. For example, clusters of companies engaged in the fields of broadcasting, consumer electronics and distribution have combined to promote projects in areas such as satellite broadcasting and high definition television. Such a combination of technological alliance is illustrated in Figure 4.8. Here the partners, A, B and C, set up a joint venture company to which they contribute complementary skills and resources to the various value activities. Here, the joint venture is responsible for its own sales, marketing, distribution and human resource management but draws on the partners for the other value chain activities as shown.

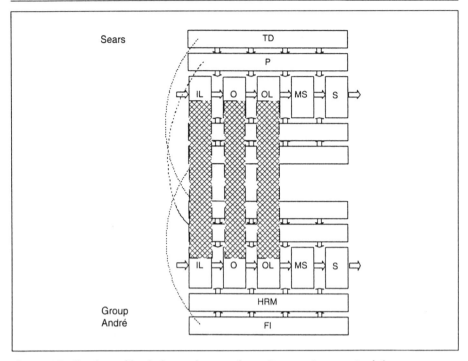

Figure 4.7 Sharing of logistics and operations, Sears – Groupe André

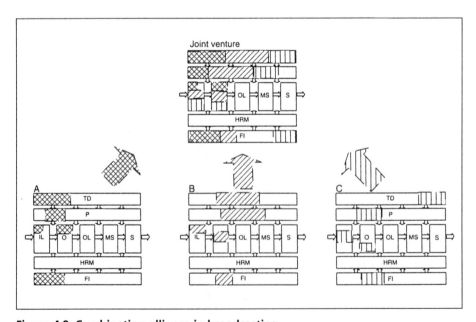

Figure 4.8 Combination alliance in broadcasting

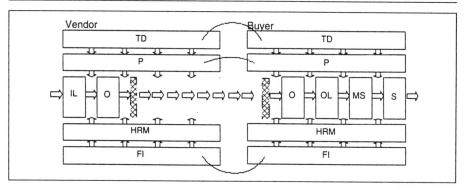

Figure 4.9 Vendor-buyer strategic alliance

The division of labour between partners may be vertical when they combine different stages of the supply chain. Figure 4.9 presents partnership sourcing, an increasing trend in some industries where just-in-time supplies and high quality standards are sought. Firms which combine their outbound logistics with the downstream partner avoid the need for strength in sales and marketing and service. Again, partners link their secondary activities, for example by having joint design activities for product modification or replacement. Effective partnership sourcing goes deeper than integrating stock control and quality monitoring. Just-in-Time (JIT) is one approach to initiating and developing such strategic links. It is discussed further in **4.18**.

Deescalation alliances

Deescalation alliances are those in which members agree to reduce competition or attacks upon each other. Each company can differentiate and focus its value activities, for example by providing complementary services. Timetabling cooperation between cross-channel ferry companies in the light of a new entrant to the business, Eurotunnel, is a case in point.

Besides the links described above, firms take part in alliances with less tangible benefits. These are less readily explained by the above classification. As Badaracco[13] points out, there are other issues which come to the fore in these loose, tenuous arrangements. One is the transfer of embedded technical and managerial knowledge. 'How to make cars at the lowest cost in the world' is not knowledge which is possessed by an individual: nor is it written down. It is embedded within teams. Such transfer gradually occurs within any alliance and is the express purpose of many cooperative agreements in high technology.

17. Strategic lessons from Japan

Some Japanese companies have gradually achieved competitive advantage in leading manufacturing industries, especially automobiles and consumer electronics. There have been many studies seeking to explain this success. Reasons advanced vary from government policy and the social environment to the details of process planning and organisation. Common to these studies is a recognition that leading Japanese companies concentrate on eliminating waste and making continuous improvements. Tied in with these efforts are two general managerial philosophies, *just-in-time* and *total quality management*. These are called philosophies rather than techniques because a commitment to them is part of the way Japanese managers think that organisations ought to be managed.

Some westerners have mistakenly seen both JIT and TQM as means of setting up operations policies, as if they are techniques to be chosen when planning models suggest they are the best way forward. For Japanese firms, on the other hand, both JIT and TQM are general approaches to producing improved results. Strategic thinking in Japan is as much grounded in incremental or continuous improvement (*kaizen*) as it is in formally setting out long-range plans and analysing new opportunities outside the organisation.

18. Just-in-time (JIT)

JIT concentrates on eliminating waste by ensuring that only just enough of the input items for a manufacturing process are made available just in time and at the point at which they are to be used. At the operational level JIT aims to cut the high stocks which hinder the performance of many companies. In this sense it can be seen as a set of production management techniques designed to:

- improve purchasing procedures by linking suppliers more closely into the production schedules
- identify and eliminate bottlenecks
- ensure higher quality and hence eradicate scrap and rework, and
- cut machine and other process failures.

We shall be dealing with these issues at appropriate stages later in the book. At this point, however, we should recognise that JIT, successfully carried out, has deeper implications than are suggested by merely listing a set of techniques for use at the operational level. JIT is both a cause and a result of strategic change.

Improved performance of leading firms over the past few decades greatly affects the strategic environment of all business. The demands of customers have increased substantially, especially in so far as:

- the volume and type of demand have become more variable. More models are on offer, product life cycles have become shorter, it is necessary to improve products more rapidly than ever.
- delays in supply are no longer acceptable. Customers increasingly seek products which closely match their requirements but are not satisfied if this implies that each item is made from scratch with consequent long delays.
- quality must be perfect yet the price must be as low as possible.

The strategic response to this emerging business environment is to create a manufacturing and distribution system which is capable of supplying a rising variety of products while being very flexible and offering very short delivery times. This dilemma facing many modern manufacturers is summarised in Box 4.7. As we saw in Chapter 3, the production of long runs of products with little variety can be achieved through setting out production lines which convert raw materials to finished goods without the build up on intermediate stocks of work in progress.

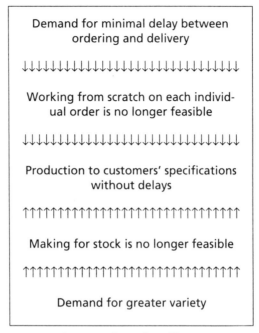

Box 4.7 The manufacturing dilemma

Yet most firms do not experience demand sufficiently large to justify this. They are committed to supply in limited batches. The basis of JIT in these firms is to achieve rapid rates of flow, as on the production line, through machines which are, in effect, independent.

JIT, then, looks to limit stocks and increase the speed of flow through all stages of the production system. Batch sizes are reduced so as to increase the speed of flow of items. For companies which fully take into account the JIT philosophy, the production system is seen as extending beyond their own boundaries to imply integration with both suppliers and customers.

The changes are sometimes cosmetic. In a recent conversation with a logistics manager of a component manufacturer, the author was told:

> Of course some customers pay lip service to the just-in-time philosophy. They use the idea as an excuse. They want us to deliver in smaller batches at no extra cost and because we are in a recession we are forced to do so. But we still deliver into the receiving warehouse where the goods get stuck for days or weeks before being released on to the shop floor.

Integration of manufacturers' and suppliers' systems to increase flow rates requires more effort than this. When set up with full commitment, JIT implies changes at all levels of management.

19. Implantation of JIT

For illustration, we can take just two of the levels suggested in **4**, *strategic* and *operational*. Using these as the categories, Box 4.8 summarises the impact that JIT philosophy has right through the organisation which takes it fully into account.

The increased flow speeds and greater flexibility of JIT are achieved, according to Japanese managers, by *jidoka*, making things visible. Eliminating inventory means that irregularities and delays in production, poor quality and uncertain planning are all exposed. The Japanese use the parable of a river. Figure 4.10 shows, at the top, the river flowing along slowly and, at the surface, smoothly. Yet it does not flow at the same pace everywhere. Rocks, deep pools and other obstructions hinder the smooth flow and cause some water to, so to speak, lag behind. The water in the parable represents the flow of goods through the plant. The pools are the stocks and the rocks the barriers to smooth operations. These are problems of machine failure, poor quality, uncertain supplies and so on. To make the stream run faster, the obstacles must be removed. To accomplish this, the level in the river is gradually reduced so that the rocks become visible and can be taken away. In the plant, a policy of gradually reducing safety stocks and work in progress means that the imperfections become clear and action must be taken to correct them.

Issue	Impact on operations management	Impact on strategic management
Flows	More speed; smaller batch sizes; more switches between orders; emphasis on reducing switching time.	Changes in manufacturing layouts; integration with suppliers' and customers' flows; selection of single sources of supply.
Stocks	Smaller input stocks received close to the point where they are to be used; processed items move on quickly.	Stocks reduced throughout whole system; switch of resources from building warehouses; development of small lot delivery systems.
Flexibility	Increased need for changes in processes; responsive and flexible procedures; flexible, multi-skilled work force.	Focus on developing total systems which match flexibility demanded in the environment; implications for training.
Quality	High quality the goal at every stage; errors to be studied and learnt from.	Developing total quality throughout the whole chain.
Responsibility	The worker is the expert; local detailed operations control; each employee is responsible for quality.	Recognising and instilling the philosophy of just-in-time.

Box 4.8 Levels of planning

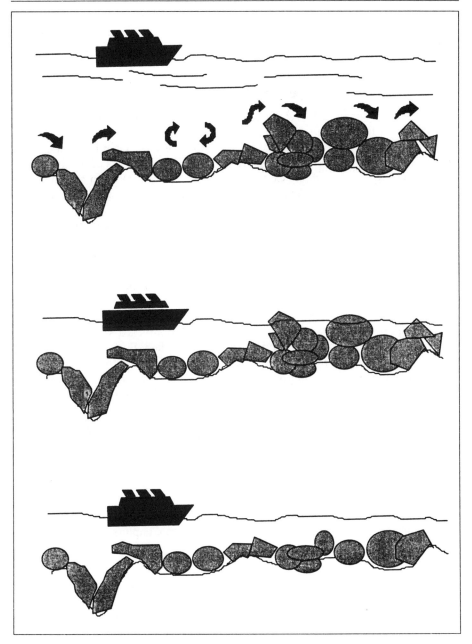

Figure 4.10 Lowering the river brings problems to the surface

As it is not possible to have a river without water, some stocks are necessary for the process to work. This is not denied. Proponents of the JIT philosophy argue that manufacturing can be run with much less stock than is usually imagined. We shall return to the detailed means by which this can be achieved in Chapter 12.

101

JIT development implies the removal of hazards to the smooth flow of materials through the plant. A key hazard is quality and this takes us on to the second application of the Japanese ideas of waste elimination and continuous improvement - total quality.

20. Total quality management (TQM)

The gradual lowering of the water level exposes the hazards which account for why the water level is kept so high in the first place. In the same way, the factory tries to protect itself from diverse hazards, many of which can be seen as poor quality - defective components, breakdowns or maladjustments of machines and late delivery to the next stage. Continuous improvement relies on making these defects more visible so that every weakness in the system becomes noticed and ways are found of eliminating them.

Total quality management applies these ideas to every process in the whole organisation. Each department, section and individual must be seen as contributing to the quality of the organisation's output. Applications in manufacturing are obvious and programmes aiming for zero defects (ZD), no delays, and machine breakdowns are common. TQM goes further than this, recognising how employees in service functions have to make their contributions. For example, the first point of contact for many customers is the front gate of the plant or the reception desk of the hotel. The contribution of staff at these points is a key element in the customers' appreciation of the product they are supplied. Furthermore, there are many staff who see neither the product nor the ultimate customer. Yet, if their work does have value, it is important to others in the organisation - their internal customers. Each link shows as a supplier–customer link with the effectiveness of the latter being strongly influenced by the quality of the work of the former.

TQM is, therefore, a system which needs to be embedded within the culture of an organisation. Teamwork, leadership and communication sustain TQM. Yet it cannot work in a vacuum. As shown in **6** and **7**, continuous improvement is not possible without a framework of analysis and measurement. Therefore, TQM also requires:

- a formally planned system of quality management, and
- measurement systems which collect performance information.

We shall be examining the details of these processes in Chapters 15 and 16.

CONTROL

Robert Burns wrote, 'The best laid schemes o' mice and men gang aft a-gley.'[14] Probably more well known is Murphy's Law, 'If it is possible for something to go wrong, then it will.' Each of these statements may seem to be unduly pessimistic. They emphasise, however, that the outcomes of plans frequently deviate from intentions. This may be because of the hidden defects mentioned in **19** but also results from the point made in **2**, that plans are made within a framework of uncertainty. We should not simply set plans in motion and expect them to succeed. Systems out of control lead to spectacular disasters such as plant explosions or ship collisions. They may also lead to gradual, almost unnoticed, decline in performance so that, in the end, no-one really knows why a business has failed.

The failure to control the system may have been temporary, as with the disaster, or permanent, as happens with gradual decline. In either case we can see that we must not expect plans to succeed unless the planning and control cycle of Figure 4.1 is complete. In the following sections, we shall be looking more closely at types of control as they apply to strategy and operations.

21. The control function

The general function of control is defined as follows:

Control ensures
that the plan is achieved
in spite of obstacles, variations and uncertainties
in both the organisation and its environment.

To be effective, the control process must know the objectives and plans to be achieved, be able to assess performance and then take the necessary actions to correct deviations between the measured performance and the plans. This is the classic control loop whose presence is observed in many systems. Living systems frequently have built-in control mechanisms which maintain the delicate balance necessary for survival. The human body has thousands of them. For instance, the temperature of the brain must be maintained to within 0.1°C to allow effective functioning.

Organisations, on the other hand, do not have natural controls. They must be designed and installed as part of each process. They can, however, operate in one way that natural systems usually cannot. They can forecast outcomes of current behaviour and take control action in anticipation of future deviations from the plan. Recognition of this enables us to distinguish between three types of control which are detailed below.

Feedback control

This is perhaps the most widely recognised form of control. Figure 4.11 shows the elements which go to make up the control process. The system converts *inputs* into *outputs*. This system could represent one day-to-day operational process, such as delivery, or the whole business working over a period of several years. The *controller* gathers information about, or *monitors*, the outputs to assess the performance of the system and compares these with the *goals* set out in the plan. In the light of this comparison, the controller takes *control action* to change the inputs or the system itself so that the progress towards the goals is restored.

In feedback control systems, managers use information about past activities to discover and learn from discrepancies and make changes to avoid them in the future. One of its problems is that corrections occur after the event, that is when errors have occurred and the costs or waste have already been created. For instance, budgetary control is based on reports of past events and, while delays can be reduced by use of shorter intervals between those reports, their usefulness is limited by their historic nature.

Concurrent control

Often called real-time control, concurrent control works as closely as possible with the present performance of the system. It means that the stages of monitoring, comparison and taking action are all rolled into one and the controller is

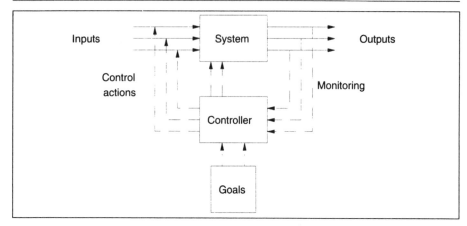

Figure 4.11 Feedback control: monitoring and making changes after tasks are completed

brought very close to the system, see Figure 4.12. Concurrent control is normal in work where the individual or team is responsible for performance. There will be a continual awareness of the need for efficiency, timeliness and quality and the group will continually check that such goals are being achieved.

End-of-line inspection is an example of feedback control where the errors are picked up on completion of the job. Using the notion of concurrent control, total quality management improves upon the final inspection by building in quality monitoring at all stages of production, making every person responsible for the quality of their output as it happens.

It is argued that concurrent control is merely a variant of feedback control where the monitoring is carried out very quickly. To an extent this is true but there is an important difference in perspective. An analogy may be seen in a domestic task such as cutting a hedge. Before starting the job I find a stick whose length matches the height I want. Then I cut short sections, keeping a line by eye

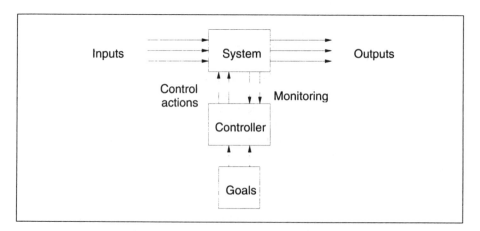

Figure 4.12 Concurrent control: monitoring and making changes while work is in progress

and using the stick to check the height from the path. I could examine these two monitoring processes as feedback mechanisms where control signals pass through my eyes, brain and muscle system. But this is the view of the biologist and not the gardener, who is not interested in such detail. Feedback control of the hedge height occurs when I stand back and judge whether the whole process was successful. If I then judge the hedge to be uneven or too high I can repeat the task, if it is too low I have to wait until the next year.

Feedforward control

As the name implies, feedforward control involves the anticipation of problems and the taking of action before they arise. Conceptually, the data on current performance of the system is used to produce a forecast of its future state, as shown in Figure 4.13. Control action is taken on the basis of this forecast. In a sense this implies the making of a plan within a plan. Yet its focus is not planning which is about where to go and how to get there. Feedforward control is about supporting the plan to give it the greatest chance of success. Preventive maintenance, such as painting the outside of my house, is based on anticipation of the well known consequences of not doing the work in time. This is a key point in feedforward control; the system needs to be sufficiently well understood to enable the forecasting stage to work successfully.

Because of the difficulties that managers have in understanding all the consequences of actions in a complex system, feedforward control is the one which is most difficult to install and use. If, for example, a delivery driver is late because of heavy traffic, he may be able to warn the customer's purchasing department which can then arrange for unloading to be rescheduled. Yet the consequences of the delay may be severe in a JIT system where, depending on the items being delivered, the production of an important order may be held up. In other cases a slight delay would be of little consequence, being overcome by a simple resequencing of assembly. It is often difficult for the purchasing manager to recognise the significance of a delay and therefore pass forward the warning to the production department.

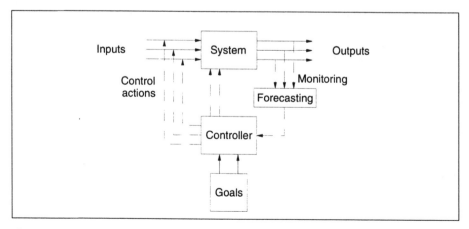

Figure 4.13 Feedforward control: forecasting deviations and taking control action in advance

22. Control in the operations system

We have given several examples of control in the above sections. None is, in principle, superior or more effective than the others. In modern organisations it is clear that all three types must be used. Each has its own focus. Feedforward control helps in the avoidance of hazards and errors, concurrent control enables operators to be given the scope to identify and eliminate the consequences of errors as they occur, and feedback control emphasises adjustment after the event so that the organisation learns not to repeat errors by finding better ways of doing things. To illustrate this combination, Box 4.9 shows how they can be used in the management of both quality and stocks. The methods mentioned in the box are referred to again in later chapters.

What if the control system, as set out in Figures 4.11 to 4.13, simply cannot work? As suggested at the beginning of this section, it may be that the process has got out of hand through momentary inattention. On the other hand, there may have been years of neglect. The system can no longer be driven along the planned route and to continue to do so only makes things worse. This takes us to our last variation of the control model, one that incorporates the possibility of changing the goals themselves. Figure 4.14 builds on Figure 4.11 by adding a feedback loop from the controller to the goals, suggesting that it may be necessary to change them in the light of circumstances. The same approach could be taken to the concurrent and feedforward loops but it is more likely that goals will be changed after some reflection on progress.

This extra feedback loop is another way of looking at the levels of planning set out in 4. This time, however, we have taken the bottom-up rather than the top-down perspective. In parallel with planning, there will, in any organisation, be a hierarchy of control systems which are interlinked. These can be seen as follows:

- *Strategic control* Monitoring the performance of the organisation in relation to its environment and how well it is achieving its strategic plans. Taking strategic action.

	Feedback	Concurrent	Feedforward
TQM	Finished goods inspection. Customer complaints. Demand for repairs and spares.	Monitoring of work in process. Preventive maintenance. Continuous improvement.	Monitoring quality of supplies and suppliers. Investment in new equipment. Skills training.
Stock Control	Monthly stock counts and checks on condition.	Continuous monitoring.	Forecasts drawn from extrapolations of sales figures and production plans.

Box 4.9 Applications of control types to Total Quality Management and Stock Control

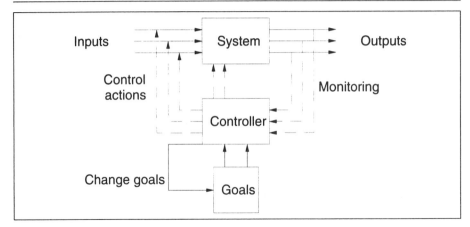

Figure 4.14 Feedback control with goal adjustment

- *Intermediate control* Monitoring the performance of divisions or functions according to annual budgets and non-financial performance indicators such as meeting schedules, quality, safety and so on. Taking action in the short and medium term to correct deviations from plans, budgets and performance standards.
- *Operations control* Monitoring performance of the operations function on a moment-by-moment or day-to-day basis in relation to production schedules. Taking immediate action to correct deviations from the detailed plans, for example by moving staff or changing schedules.

23. Control problems in the real organisation

The danger with presenting control as a series of diagrams with loops around which information flows is the suggestion that somehow the process is straightforward and automatic once it has been designed. The reality is some way from this. Control systems themselves are prone to difficulties and failure, not least because they exist within human activity systems which are, of course, staffed by managers. Kreitner[15] points out three special problems of control systems: *goal displacement*, *measurementship*, and *budget games*.

Goal displacement is the phenomenon of the means becoming the ends. Organisations, in striving to maintain efficiency, effectiveness and equity, may become so bound up with rules that their members forget why they were set up in the first place. Bureaucratic paperwork becomes more important than human needs. We hear of cases (in America) of dying patients not receiving treatment until their insurance status is confirmed while in many countries the military type who sticks to procedures through everything is the butt of much derision.

Measurementship stems from the desire to appear good. It involves manipulating reports and the data that go to make them up. This goes right to the top of some organisations where various means of 'off-balance-sheet financing' enabled firms to present a sound impression to their shareholders while being as much in hock as ever. At lower levels, many directors are keen on seeing low finished goods stocks and take steps to stop the flow into finished goods warehouses in the days before the count is to be taken. This, of course, causes or increases the chaos elsewhere.

107

Budget games are played especially by those managers who perceive their bosses to have a punitive leadership style. For example, in project management, they seek a budget which is larger than necessary so as to protect themselves from later overruns. They then, naturally, have to find ways of spending the money, often in a hurry before the period end. Among the most common tactics are asking for incremental increases on the previous year, asking for some items which will definitely be rejected while hoping to slip others through, only asking for a small funding for a new idea and talking up a crisis to put pressure on the boss.

24. Budgetary control

We will illustrate the practical application of control by reference to budgeting. Notwithstanding the difficulties mentioned in the previous section, all managers who are responsible for consuming resources should be given a budget. They should contain targets for revenue or, in the case of most operations, expenditures which are for those areas for which the manager has responsibility.

The principles of budgeting have already been explained in **2.27** to **2.29**. The process normally works on an annual cycle, sometimes with a one or two year extension which is itself updated every year. The idea of the extension is to combine relatively tight control of money while giving the manager scope to plan beyond the end of the immediate year. In many cases, there is scope to adjust budgets in the light of changing circumstances, indeed this is sometimes automatic as in the *flexible budget*, see **2.29**. Allowances are made in advance for changed levels of activity which may occur during the period. Hence, if demand for a product line were to rise in response to, say, unexpectedly good weather, then production output may have to rise. Naturally the production budget would have to flex in relation to this change. This expansion of costs would not necessarily be in proportion to output as this may be achieved less efficiently than the norm, as in the case of extra shifts or overtime, or more efficiently as expensive equipment is used more intensively than expected.

Applying our ideas of planning and control we can see that sound budgeting practice has the following features:

- Targets should be clear and agreed between managers and their superiors.
- The budgets should be integrated so that they are mutually consistent and contribute to the overall plan.
- Feedback should be clear, as early as possible and enable managers to identify differences between outcomes and the budget, the so-called *variances*.
- Where several managers are responsible for activities in a particular function, the process must recognise and sustain the communication and cooperation which are necessary.
- The budget reports should help in deciding upon control action.

Case study: Jaeger

Jaeger is famous for manufacturing and selling high quality clothing. It is a vertically integrated company in that it manufactures and distributes through its own wholesale and retail outlets. More than 90% of its goods are made in the United Kingdom. There are 80 Jaeger ladies' shops in the UK with a similar number abroad. Jaeger sells its products through other outlets so the wholesale operations both at home and for export are as important as the retail. This is a successful business widely recognised for excellent design.

In common with other leading firms in the retail industry, Jaeger has moved away from having just two sales seasons each year, spring and autumn, towards a more continuous replenishment of the stores with new designs. According to the Chairman[16] , this means five seasons per year, there being two (early and late) for spring.

It takes 11 months from conception of a range to the delivery of the first batch to the shops. This represents the minimum time for everything to be done. Clearly it is in the interests of the company to delay the start of this design process for as long as possible so that decisions can be based upon knowledge of the latest trends. Colour is the starting point. For a spring range, the colours are decided between December and January and discussed with fabric suppliers. Mid-February is the deadline for the merchandise director to decide the direction of the range. From February to May, cloth selection and ordering of sample lengths take place. From 1st April to the middle of June, Jaeger goes through fabric modelling and sampling. Designing and modelling of garments runs from May to late-June while fabric is being obtained for pattern cards and swatches. By 1st June, the merchandise director and product managers review the design work. This gives one month for pilot and sample orders to be placed and filled. While these activities are progressing, the company buys cloth. Cloth has a long lead time so that 70% of purchase orders are committed by 10th May and the final purchase order is placed by 10th September, a date which the manufacturers find quite late.

Sales are estimated and Jaeger's factories are expected to have production plans for the new range ready by 20th July. Delivery dates are agreed by the end of that month. This means that the sales department can begin to accept firm orders during August. Before any orders are received, however, Jaeger has itself to place firm garment requisitions on its own factories. It does this by 1st August. One quarter of estimated sales are ordered on the first of each month until November.

1st August is also the decision date for the range information including prices. The samples, ordered in June, are delivered to the warehouse on the 10th August and selling starts in earnest on the 20th.

Managers, right up to the Chairman, receive weekly reports of progress against plans which remind every one of the decisions which are due and who has to make them.

Questions

1 *Identify the types of uncertainty faced by Jaeger.*
2 *Give examples of the sort of planning described in the case study. From your general knowledge of retailing, what would comprise strategic planning at Jaeger?*
3 *Choose examples of three types of control and set them out using suitable diagrams.*

[Incidentally, if you found the description of the series of dates difficult to take in, you will be in good company! It is an ideal example of the way Gantt charts can clarify time sequences, see **12.1**.]

References

1. Based on Nissan Motor Company (1982) *Nissan Prairie Service Manual* Tokyo, Nissan p. EF–13
2. Kreitner, Robert (1992) *Management* 5th ed. Boston, Houghton-Mifflin p.176
3. Ansoff, H. Igor (1984) *Implanting Strategic Management* Englewood Cliffs. Prentice Hall
4. Based on Rowe, A.J., Mason, R.O., Dickel, K.E., Mann, R.B. and Mockler, R.J. (1994) *Strategic Management* 4th ed. Reading, Mass., Addison-Wesley p.201
5. For example, see Thompson, John L. (1994) *Strategic Management: Awareness and Change* London, Chapman and Hall
6. Porter, Michael E. (1980) *Competitive Strategy* New York, Free Press
7. Bruce, Rupert (1994) 'Asda turns price screw' *The Independent on Sunday: Business* 13 March, p.1
8. Porter, Michael E. (1985) *Competitive Advantage* New York, Free Press p.323
9. See, for example:
   Bertodo, R.G. (1990) 'The strategic alliance: automative paradigm for the 1990's' *International Journal of Technology Management* **5.4** pp.375–88
   Sasaki, Toru (1993) 'What the Japanese have learned from strategic alliances' *Long Range Planning* **26.6** pp.41–53
   Turpin D. (1993) 'Strategic alliances with Japanese firms: myths and realities' *Long Range Planning* **26.4** pp. 11–15
10. See, for example
    Gugler, P. (1992) 'Building transnational alliances to create competitive advantage' *Long Range Planning* **25.1** pp.90–9
    Lei, D. (1993) 'Offensive and defensive use of alliances' *Long Range Planning* **26.4** pp.32–41
    Lyons, M.P. (1991) 'Joint-ventures as strategic choice – a literature review' *Long Range Planning* **24.4** pp.130–44
    Murray, E.A. and Mahon, J.F. (1993) 'Strategic alliances: gateway to the New Europe?' *Long Range Planning* **26.4** pp.102–11
    Shenkar, O. (1990) 'International joint ventures' problems in China: risks and remedies' *Long Range Planning* **23.3** pp.82–90
    Snodgrass, C.R. (1993) 'The use of networks in cross border competition' *Long Range Planning* **26.2** pp.41–50
11. Devlin, G. and Bleakley, M. (1988) 'Strategic alliances: guidelines for success' *Long Range Planning* **21.5** pp.18–23
12. Hagedoorn, J. and Shakenraad, J. (1990) *Leading Companies and the Structure of Strategic Alliances in Core Technologies* Discussion paper, MERIT, Limburg University Maastricht
13. Badaracco, J. (1991) *The knowledge link: How firms compete through strategic alliances* Harvard Business School Press
14. *To a mouse.' . . . often go wrong.'*
15. op. cit. p.531
16. Young, G. (1985) Untitled seminar paper in McAlhone, B. (ed.) *Directors on design: The 1985 SIAD design management seminar* London, The Design Council

5

ORGANISING AND STAFFING FOR OPERATIONS

Chapter objectives

When you have finished studying this chapter, you should be able to:

- Explain the common features of organisations and interpret organisation charts.
- Compare common forms of departmental and matrix structures in terms of differentiation and integration.
- Identify current trends in the development of organisations.
- Define the scope of human resource management as it supports operations.
- Outline how recruitment and appraisal are carried out; show how difficulties with the unstructured interview may be overcome.
- Describe the main features of a good training programme.
- Set out the elements of the interpersonal communication process and how it may be improved; clarify why and how organisations can improve communications.
- Review the key theories of motivation and show how these can be applied to management of the operations function; explain the advantages of good job design and participation in motivation.
- Outline the range of rewards available from employment and relate these to various schemes of payment.
- Explain the importance of good leadership.

INTRODUCTION

Operations are usually carried out by organisations. These groupings of people are an omnipresent feature of modern life. Without the social cooperation which is implied by productive organisations, very little would be achieved. Yet how often does one hear the complaints, 'There's no organisation round here,' or, 'Why don't they get themselves organised?' The trouble in such cases lies not in the absence of organisation, since this is evidenced by the fact that some sort of activity is taking place. It stems from the poor quality of the organisation. Some are clearly more successful than others. Their management requires the application of many skills from staffing to strategy making and communicating to controlling. These need to be coordinated. Study of organisations is, therefore, very important to the operations manager who is often responsible for many staff whose work has to be coordinated.

Organisations have been defined in many ways yet the well-known definition of Barnard[1] remains one of the simplest and clearest:

> *An organisation is a system of consciously coordinated activities or forces of two or more persons.*

We have encountered many features of this definition. For instance, the notion of system was developed in Chapter 2, see Figure 2.3, and the suggestion of conscious choice was brought out in the comparison of two formal structures in **1.18**. We shall develop themes from Barnard's definition in this chapter. In particular, we shall look at the use of structure to achieve coordination, the management of individuals and groups within the organisation and the application of communication and motivation to achieve the vital order without which little of value would happen.

ORGANISATIONS

1. Common features of organisations

Barnard's definition implies the following features present in all organisations:

- *Common goals*
  In our discussion of goals in Chapter 4, an underlying implication was that people within an organisation come together to achieve common ends. For productive organisations to function, this is clearly necessary and the goals, effectively communicated among members, act as a banner around which they can be expected to rally.
- *Specialisation*
  Organisations achieve their success through specialisation of work. The total task is divided so that individuals can bring their skills to each part and, in total, achieve more than they could do separately. There are dangers in excessive specialisation, however. The organisation may lose the flexibility which comes from having individuals who can perform many tasks and the individual may lose motivation if the job is too repetitive and boring.
- *Conscious coordination*
  While they may often appear to have emerged 'like Topsy', organisations are designed by those who are responsible for them. Coordination is the counterpart of specialisation. If the work is to be shared among individuals then the relationships between them have to be managed effectively. As we saw in Chapter 3 in the discussion of socio-technical systems, some patterns of organisation are better suited to different process technologies. This is, however, only one feature which needs to considered and we shall consider others in **3**.
- *Hierarchy*
  The goals, specialisation and coordination of organisations imply a hierarchy of authority. Hierarchy means that some people are given the *authority* to direct and coordinate the work of others. Along with this authority goes the *accountability* for its use. The authority and accountability are defined and clarified

through the *chain of command* which is itself often represented by the levels and links of the organisation chart. Therefore, for the organisation represented in Figure 5.1 (copied from 1.8), the Managing Director has the authority to direct and coordinate the work of the other senior managers. In turn, the Production Director has authority with respect to others in the production department, and so on. At the same time, each manager is responsible to the superior in the hierarchy, known as the *line manager*.

The above features are the least required before an organisation can be said to exist. They do not, however, describe or define organisations in any detail. It all depends on how the features are implemented. Hierarchical relationships can sometimes be oppressive, eliminating initiative and denying creativity. On the other hand, they can both be highly efficient and bring satisfaction to the people who are employed within them.

2. Organisation charts

Organisation charts display the official positions and formal lines of authority and responsibility. In showing the organisation's skeleton, they do present a basic structure but that is all. Just as the human body is only partly described by its skeleton, so the organisation is only partly represented by its chart. They are useful, however, in studying the lines of command and formal communication and the way in which people are deployed.

Each organisation chart presents us with a description along two dimensions:

- *Vertical* The hierarchy – the number of levels and the chain of command
- *Horizontal* Specialisation – the way tasks are divided between managers and departments and who is responsible for coordinating them at each level.

To clarify accountability, it is normal to allocate each individual to a single line manager. In Figure 5.1, the Production Director's role as line manager of six subordinates is to ensure that work, which may have been done by one person in a much smaller firm, is effectively coordinated. Thus, as organisations grow, they can reap the benefits of specialisation of work yet have to pay the penalty of the

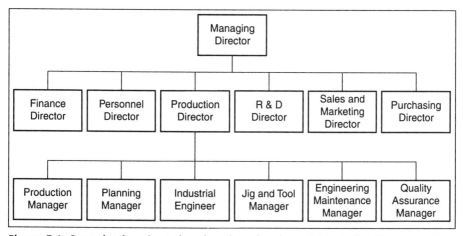

Figure 5.1 Organisation chart showing three levels and the chain of command

extra effort required in coordinating that work. The challenge for organisational designers is to ensure that the right balance between specialisation and coordination is achieved.

3. Departmental organisation structures

The vertical and horizontal dimensions of the organisation chart help us to distinguish between various organisational forms. These can all be seen as attempts by managers to solve the problem of specialisation of work while simultaneously achieving coordination between relevant employees. The organisation structure both *differentiates* and *integrates* at the same time. This is an important issue for the operations manager. From the operations perspective, the identification of the tasks required to take a product through each step of its value chain (see **1.17**) is one thing, whereas to allocate these differentiated tasks to staff and then to integrate their work is quite another. The most common way this is achieved is through departments. A department groups together employees whose jobs are more or less related – the problem is that they can be related in various ways and each situation demands its own solution. We can identify four criteria for the creation of departments.

Function

Functional departments are created around the similarity of tasks performed, or technical skills required, by the people within them. They are based on disciplines such as production, marketing, finance or personnel. Figure 5.1 is an example of a company creating functional departments at two levels. First, the whole business is split into production, personnel and so on. At the next level, the production department itself is separated into sub-departments around the disciplines indicated.

The advantage of functional departments lies in the affinity which staff with similar skills feel with one another, thus making coordination straightforward. They appear frequently in small, growing organisations as each manager takes on assistants to cope with the increasing work load. Their disadvantages lie in the narrow outlook which may develop among departmental members whose concern with the specialism may outweigh broader considerations of the success of the company as a whole. Especially in the case of large functional departments, they emphasise differentiation at the expense of integration.

Hospitals often have functional departments, based around medical and paramedical specialities. This arrangement rightly encourages the professional development of staff within each discipline and the need for departmental heads to have specialised knowledge. On the other hand, hospitals have a history of inter-departmental rivalry with professional interests being advanced at the expense of the system as a whole. Box 5.1 lists the functional departments, known as directorates, within Huddersfield NHS Trust. The horizontal line is placed in the list to separate the medical and paramedical directorates from the business functions. The former can be said to be primary value chain activities, delivering services directly to clients while the latter are the support activities. The switch to increased operational control of medical functions by general managers has created much tension in the health service.

Directorate	Responsibility
Surgery	All surgical activity; accident and emergency; audiology; orthoptics.
Medicine	Medical, including elderly in Royal Infirmary; general out-patients.
Mental Health	Mental illness; learning difficulties; clinical psychology; child and adolescent psychiatry; community psychiatric nurses.
Children and Women's Services	Paediatrics; child health; obstetrics; gynaecology; family planning.
Clinical Support	Anaesthetics; radiology; pathology; pharmacy; intensive care unit; theatres; therapy.
Elderly	Geriatric medicine; geriatric units.
Community	Community nursing clinics; community dental services; health centres; family planning services.
Finance	All financial functions.
Business Development	Planning and development; information; contracting.
Operations Management	Estates; site management; support services; medical photography.
Personnel	Human resources; personnel; training.
Nursing and Training	Professional nursing guidance; nursing training; quality leadership.

Box 5.1 Directorates of Huddersfield NHS Trust in 1994

Product

The unifying theme of the product department, often called *division*, is its output. Each division operates as if it is almost an autonomous business within the whole organisation. This type of organisation is valuable where:

the size of each division is sufficient for it to be able to provide its own specialisms, such as accounting and personnel, and
the work of each division is relatively independent so that their operations do not have to be closely coordinated.

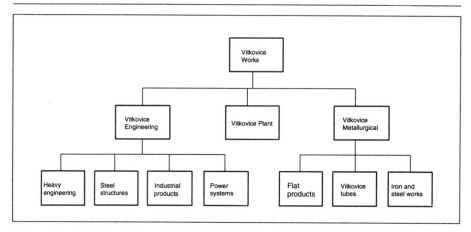

Figure 5.2 Organisation structure for the market economy: Vítkovice Company

Many large organisations are organised on this basis. Its advantage lies in the unification of effort towards the supply of a particular bundle of goods and services. Figure 5.2 shows the organisation structure created at the Vítkovice Works in Ostrava, The Czech Republic shortly after the revolution of 1989[2]. The reorganisation was to prepare for privatisation. Employing more than 20,000 people in total, the product divisions can be seen within each of the main sections of the business, namely basic iron and steel making and heavy engineering. Focus on products as the main factor in divisionalisation was not, however, complete. While the responsibility for operations within each division should in principle be autonomous, the sales and marketing activities remained centralised as a unit. This was because of so much output being exported and the company's unwillingness to change to having duplicated selling functions where, before the revolution, all sales had been handled through a single government agency.

Duplication through a proliferation of support functions is one of the difficulties of product divisions. Furthermore, there is danger that divisions forget they are part of a larger organisation. Then they fail to take opportunities to coordinate activities among themselves in order to face competition more effectively.

Geographic location

Geography is a common basis for structural design, especially in large companies whose operations are widely dispersed. Service companies, from transport to retailing, can offer the same group of products to customers in many locations. They may then be best organised by region. British Airways has geographic divisions, such as BA Manchester; large bus operators such as Badgerline run services in different towns and cities in separate divisions usually keeping the names of previous companies; the electricity company MANWEB organises its maintenance operations by district.

Differences between regions push managers towards organising geographically so that the business can respond more effectively to local conditions. International organisations face variations in cultural settings and economic conditions which can have strong influences on every aspect of marketing, employment, finance and so on. Oxfam's charitable work in central African countries, for example, has to take into account famine and the displacement of peoples from one country to another. In Brazil, on the other hand, work is among disadvantaged groups within a country whose economy is among the world's top ten.

Customer facing

The fourth basic structural form is based on the type of customer. This approach is useful when different customer groups demand different products or require them to be supplied in different ways. A business can compete more effectively against a rival which targets principally one of its customer groups. BT switched from a geographical to a customer oriented organisation when it was privatised in 1991. Box 5.2[3] describes the main departments. Business Communications and Special Business were the areas where competition was becoming more intense.

We have presented each of the four bases for departments in its ideal form. In practice, organisations do not use the ideals, they adapt these principles according to circumstances. This point is shown in the example of the Hospital Trust structure of Box 5.1. It can be seen as a mixture of customer facing and functional designs at the same horizontal level. Organisations, moreover, may use different criteria at each level in the hierarchy. The supermarket firm of Figure 1.9 starts with a functional division at board level, then has two levels divided geographically and finally has product departments within the store.

Each organisation structure is something of a compromise from the operations manager's point of view. If one principle is used to create and integrate departments or divisions, and some staff are brought more closely together in teams, this is at the expense of linkages which may have been created if another principle was used. For example, BT moved from a regional to a customer-type structure. In

---

'As part of a major reshaping of the Group, a new organisation structure was introduced on 1st April 1991 aimed as serving customers in BT's chosen markets more effectively.

BT is now organised into three customer-facing operating divisions: Business Communications, Personal Communications and Special Businesses, and a number of support units ...

Business Communications and Personal Communications provide the primary interface between BT and its customers, whether business or residential, for the provision of UK and international calls, exchange lines and equipment supply, while the Special Businesses division is responsible for providing customers with [private circuits, managed networks and mobile communications].'

The support services are:

Worldwide Networks, for the UK and international trunk networks
Products and Services Management
Development and Procurement, and
Finance, Personnel and other services.

Box 5.2 BT's organisation after 1991

urban areas where all types of customer appear in abundance, it will be relatively easy to maintain service levels to both. In remote rural areas, on the other hand, a community may have a few domestic subscribers and even fewer businesses. There it would be less sensible to provide separate installation teams for the two types of customer. BT clearly judged that the focus on the customer which was provided by the new organisation in the areas of high competition was the more important factor to be considered.

4. Matrix organisation structures

The problem of seeking to integrate organisations in several ways simultaneously has led some companies, especially large ones, to consider having dual lines of authority. Companies engaged in large project work in civil engineering or aero-space found that it was difficult to keep these projects going while operating within a traditional departmental structure. The emerging organisation, referred to under the general title of *matrix organisation*, originally involved staff reporting to both their functional departmental manager and, for the duration, to a manager designated for the particular project.

The organisation shown in Figure 5.3 illustrates how Vítkovice sets up change projects. These may mean the introduction of new products or processes, control systems and so on. The work is carried out by multi-functional teams which are led by project managers. Shown as engineers in the diagram, the team members may work on the project full time or just for part of their time. Their attachment to the team is temporary. Otherwise, they report to their line managers. The chart

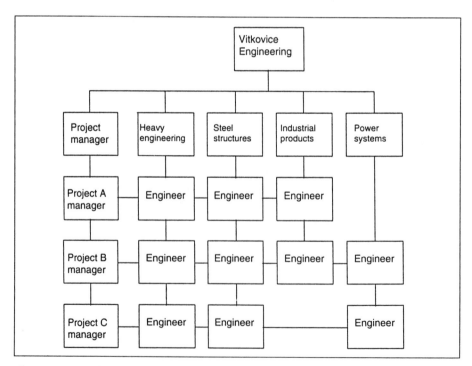

Figure 5.3 Matrix structure for projects at Vítkovice

resembles a chess board. In Figure 5.3, projects A and C span three departments while B requires that the efforts of four are integrated. Normal manufacturing operations are not affected by the project structure.

In some multinational companies, matrix structures are made permanent. Work of operating and marketing managers in different countries has to be coordinated along both product and geographic dimensions: the company wants to integrate the supply and demand for each product line on a world scale while, at the same time, it wishes to coordinate different activities in each country from the point of view of finance and taxation, employment, training and so on.

A complex example of a matrix structure occurs in the 'major appliances' (or 'white goods') product division of Electrolux[4]. This widely dispersed organisation has about 500 business units. Each is a nationally based company with its own balance sheet and profit and loss account. The white goods division has some 43 factories in 15 countries grouped in three 'product areas', namely cold, hot and wet. Within the product areas, the national 'product divisions' have at most two factories each. Generally, the factories do not duplicate production so each is responsible for the supply of its lines for all markets where the item is sold. There are 135 marketing and sales companies in 40 countries, their work coordinated by one of the two international marketing coordinators.

Electrolux does not ignore variations between countries, as in many global firms. It sees the country managers as having an important role in achieving high performance among the companies within each territory. They deal with national issues such as relations with large retail customers and trades unions and overseeing national salary structures. Figure 5.4 gives a simple summary of the structural relationships referred to here.

The arrangement of the white goods division at Electrolux is, therefore, designed to integrate both operational and strategy making activity in three dimensions:

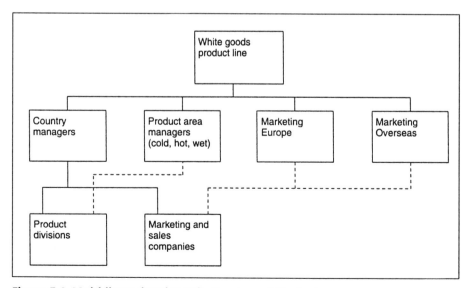

Figure 5.4 Multidimensional matrix structure at Electrolux

- Country managers monitor performance of production and sales companies in their territories.
- Product area managers are responsible for product design and development, deciding where each is to be made and planning output flows in liaison with the marketing groups.
- Marketing managers control sales and marketing including the co-ordination of brands (such as Electrolux and Zanussi) and promotion across frontiers using satellites and other cross-border media.

The claimed advantages of the arrangement lie in good coordination and allocation of responsibility. These, however, are at the expense of internal tensions between the various managers and coordinators. Many questions and problems do not fall readily into the remit of one or the other type of manager. They are expected to resolve these problems quickly by direct contact.

This example of a fully fledged, permanent matrix design emphasises both the advantages and disadvantages of such structures. These have been summarised in Box 5.3. Problems arise because a basic notion of each person in the organisation having a single supervisor is breached. This can lead at least to stressful ambiguity and, at worst, to destructive power struggles among managers. We should not forget, however, that such difficulties also frequently arise in the simpler departmental structures we discussed earlier. Structures do not of themselves create well-managed organisations. More than anything, success depends on the skills and willingness of the managers to interact within them in a positive way.

For some organisations, such as Electrolux, the matrix organisation in seen as the only way to coordinate large groups effectively. Others have found that the excessive complexity leads to such loss of efficiency that detailed co-ordination of operations by central managers is dispensed with. Texas Instruments, for example, gave up its matrix structure in the early 1980s in favour of a simpler structure to coordinate more independent business units. These units are expected to decide what coordination is necessary and make the relevant arrangements themselves.

Advantages	Disadvantages
Integration of important functions such as sales and marketing, production and project management.	Conflict between managers over range of responsibility.
Improved information flow.	Some doubt about whether more information is at the expense of quality.
Flexibility in response to changing market and competitive environments.	Possible loss of efficiency through extra managerial overhead.
Coordination at appropriate levels in the organisation.	Conflict that has to be referred to higher levels for resolution.
Managers report directly to those who are responsible.	Stress caused by having several bosses with potentially conflicting interests.

Box 5.3 Summary of advantages and disadvantages of a matrix organisation structure

5. New organisational trends

In many industries the pace of change has been increasing. The problem of increasing complexity of traditional organisations has become more acute. They are seen as too inflexible, slow, uncreative and expensive. The trend for the 1990s is towards simpler structures with lower costs. The main trends are:

- *Fewer layers*

  Removing layers of middle management, leading to so-called *lean structures,* can have a great impact on the number of managers and therefore costs. In the early 1990s, General Motors Europe reduced its layers from 7 to 6. Toyota, on the other hand, has only 7 for its whole organisation, the third largest producer in the world. The dramatic effect of reducing layers can be illustrated by a simple calculation. With 100,000 employees and an average span of control for each supervisor of 7, the organisation requires

  $$14,286 + 2,041 + 292 + 42 + 6 + 1 = 16,668 \text{ managers in 6 levels}$$

  whereas were the span of control to be 9, there would be

  $$11,111 + 1,235 + 137 + 15 + 1 = 12,499 \text{ managers in 5 levels.}$$

  This argument does not mean that hierarchies are unnecessary but that changes in culture, management style and information systems mean that old assumptions must be questioned and changed.

- *Team work*

  Delegation of responsibility to teams which blend the work of different functions is another trend. Rather than the top-down coordination of the matrix structure, however, self management is becoming more important. The teams for, say, quality improvement, may set their own patterns of work and focus attention on the issues which they consider to be the most important. Their success depends on having access to more information as well as developing individual skills and mutual trust among members.

- *Reduction of scale and complexity*

  The division of large corporations into semi-autonomous units reduces the degree of complexity which the top managers have to cope with and hence enables their numbers to be cut. Coordination is achieved through strategic planning and budgeting but not through detailed operating management.

The reorganisation of the UK National Health Service was justified partly by a need to remove the heavy and complex central management. Coordinated planning was perceived as not delivering health care which was responsive enough to the needs of the people. Individual operating units, from district hospitals to ambulance services, are now established as semi-autonomous units which are, in principle, free to make contractual arrangements with health authorities who purchase their services on behalf of patients.

The philosophy behind this decentralisation is that, for large, complex systems, management cannot improve over the resource allocation which would occur if buyers and sellers were operating in a free market. Such benefits are not free, however. Each unit within the system has to take the responsibility of managing its own affairs as a business and of forging its own links with others in what is becoming a competitive market. The complete effects of changing the balance between centralisation and decentralisation will only be seen after several years of operation.

HUMAN RESOURCE MANAGEMENT

6. Scope of human resource management

We are all encouraged to participate in organisations, whether as member of voluntary groups, teams and clubs, participants in higher education or employees. Most work of economic significance takes place within organisational contexts. The relationship between the individual and the organisation is, therefore, very important; if constructive the collective effort can lead to excellent results, but if disharmonious the relationship can be counterproductive. From the point of view of the organisation, the processes of bringing in an individual and achieving a harmonious relationship is the domain of personnel management. This has two aspects, providing and developing the staffing resource, now usually called *human resource management*, and leading, motivating and controlling staff within their assigned roles. The latter aspect is the responsibility of line managers although uniformity of treatment in terms of appraisal, remuneration and so on is achieved through having consistent personnel policies throughout the organisation.

Human resource management is concerned with ensuring that the appropriate number of skilled people are available at the right time to fill the roles required. A general model of this process is presented in the flow diagram of Figure 5.5. Many techniques of operations management which we shall examine later in this book have equal applicability to the personnel management function. In other words,

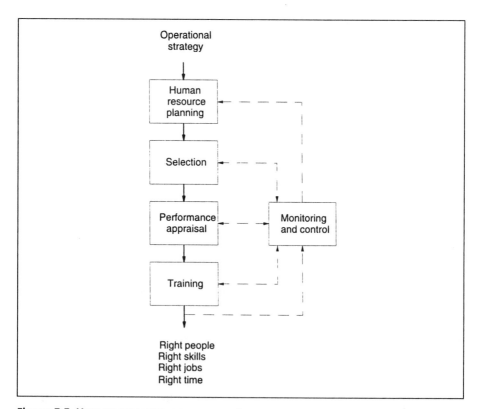

Figure 5.5 Human resource management

personnel management has its operational as well as administrative and strategic aspects. It manages the flows of people. We shall look in turn at each step given in Figure 5.5.

7. Human resource planning

Human resource planning starts from the total strategy of the organisation. Like planning in general, it means the development of an overall approach to satisfying future human resource needs. In most cases, recruitment and development of employees should be treated as investment, expensive decisions which are often difficult to reverse if errors are made. If hiring is carried out on an *ad hoc* basis, continuity and development may be put at risk. Planning should involve not only an analysis of current human resources and needs but also take into account future changes in the business. Changes within the environment can quickly lead to a mismatch between the ideal and actual staffing levels. Consider the following examples:

Nuclear Electric
Nuclear Electric is responsible for the construction and operation of nuclear power stations. It awards contracts for station building to civil engineering companies but, during the construction phase, requires a continually changing mix of design, supervisory and commissioning engineers of its own. When a station is complete, the company needs operating engineers whose skills and experience differ from the others.

To maintain continuity of employment of the teams of engineers of the various disciplines, Nuclear Electric used to rely on a steady construction programme. When, in the late 1980s, it became clear that the Government may not place any new orders, the company had to work out how to maintain sufficient staff to complete its current contracts. Furthermore, it had to develop a policy of what to do with its staff after the building ceased. In so doing, the company examined the skills, age and other details of all its engineering staff. It offered severance terms to those it no longer could employ and retraining to others who could eventually become operating engineers. With the company being the major employer of nuclear experts in the country, it was not feasible to recruit new staff directly from the labour market.

Banking
Throughout the recession of the 1980s, the clearing banks recruited very few junior staff. This policy was partly in response to the need to control costs but also because many banking services were becoming automated. This had curious effects on staffing in branches. The most junior staff are often confined to mundane backroom tasks, but eventually move on to jobs requiring more experience. With a five-year gap in recruitment and, therefore no replacements, managers faced the problem of motivating the maturing juniors while at the same time having the routine tasks carried out.

The outcome of the planning process is a detailed analysis of the staffing requirements for the organisation in the future. Included within the plan will be means by which any gaps will be filled. Large organisations use a blend of recruiting and training to fill posts - recruiting can be internal and external and may, in either case, be followed by an appropriate amount of training.

8. Recruitment

Recruitment involves finding staff with the appropriate attributes to fill available jobs. A simplified version of the procedure is shown in Figure 5.6. Starting from an agreement over the availability of a job, together with its definition, the personnel manager would plan the recruitment process so that sufficient candidates of appropriate calibre come forward for selection. At the same time, decisions are made about how the choice is to be made. For all but temporary or casual appointments, there is usually a series of screens which filter out less suitable prospects until a short list is presented to a group of managers for the final choice. The screens may include checks on qualifications, skills and experience, physical and psychological tests, work tests and so on.

It is important to note that, as in all aspects of employment, it is unlawful to discriminate against members of minority groups. Sometimes discrimination can occur unwittingly. For example, the methods of inviting applications may be biased against some groups. Many employers used to rely on word of mouth to spread the news that there were vacancies. The effect of such a policy is that the applicants would tend to represent the backgrounds of those already in employment and therefore not give equal opportunities to all.

Selection procedures must likewise be shown to be fair as well as effective. The interview is the most widely used technique in personnel management and is especially important in the selection process of most organisations. Operations managers are often involved in interviewing short lists of candidates set up by the personnel department. It is important to guard as far as possible against the defects of the *unstructured interview*. This has no prepared schedule or format, nor does it involve systematic scoring. A strength of the interview lies in its flexibility

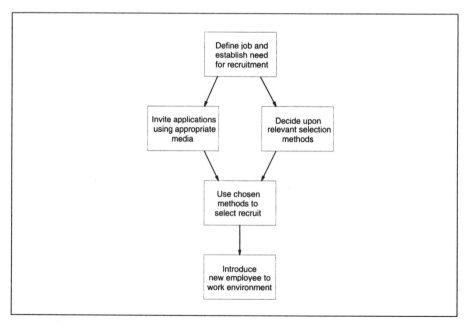

Figure 5.6 Recruitment process

yet this feature can be a weakness too. Without structure it is notoriously ineffective in selecting the best candidate. Many managers believe they are good interviewers and, lacking feedback on results, also place a heavy reliance on the process itself. Unstructured interviews often stray into discussion of irrelevant and personal issues which, when meeting the preferences and prejudices of the interviewer, distort decisions. Legal challenges to these selection and promotion decisions have been mounted in recent years under equal opportunities legislation. Unstructured selection procedures have proved to be difficult to defend.

It is important, then, that all managers use the interview as effectively as possible. The *structured interview* is built around a series of job-related questions which are asked of all candidates. Box 5.4 shows four question categories which are often sought. The information could be elicited at interview but that concerning job knowledge and ability could be gathered from practical tests or observation of behaviour in a simulated situation. Giving candidates full information about the job helps to clear up many potential misunderstandings over personal matters before the interview stage is reached. Yet it is wise to invite candidates to show their willingness to meet the demands of the job, possibly by reference to previous experience.

The four categories of Box 5.4 should not be regarded as a complete list. For example, in the recruitment of young trainees, an organisation may be as concerned with potential as with current ability. Qualifications and school reports would be important and the interviewer may seek to probe learning ability rather than current technical skills.

Using a panel of interviewers can be expensive but helps in removing personal bias. Whether interviewers act alone or in a group, the schedule provides a formal

Question category	Information looked for	Example of a supervisor's job in a jobbing machine shop
Situational	The applicant's capacity to handle the range of circumstances met with on the job.	What would you do if you saw a long-serving employee using a grindstone without wearing goggles?
Job knowledge	The applicant's knowledge of practical, technical, legal etc aspects of the job.	Can you explain the differences between the various grades of aluminium used in ... manufacture?
Job simulation	The applicant's ability to carry out critical aspects of the job.	Demonstrate the instructions you would give if you were asked to arrange for ... to be done.
Personal requirements	The applicant's ability to meet the demands of the job in terms of hours, travel, location and so on.	Are you willing to work nights if required to do so?

Box 5.4 Schedule for a structured interview

basis for personnel records as well as being available later to show that the process was conducted equitably.

The difficulties of effective recruitment are highlighted by the case of trainee pilots in the RAF. The air force needs to maintain its planned ratio of pilots to aircraft. Pilots both fly and are officers; they must have appropriate physical skills and be leaders of others. Initial selection is based on tests and interviews to cover these two aspects. All those who pass the initial selection move on to various courses: Initial Officer Training; Basic Flying and then streaming into one of three categories – Fast Jet, Multi-Engine or Helicopter. The Fast Jet role is seen as the most demanding. These trainees move on to Advanced Training and then Operational Conversion. Each stage builds up the accumulated investment in the trainee, who can fail at any point. The cost of training a Fast Jet Pilot is approximately £1.5 million. The problem for the RAF is to minimise wastage in training while maintaining a supply of pilots of the necessary quality[5].

9. Performance appraisal

Performance appraisal means evaluating the performance of persons within their jobs in order to make reasoned personnel decisions. These decisions cover salary, giving general advice, development and training, promotion opportunities and human resource planning. While formal systems are gradually being extended to cover more managers and supervisors, they are little used for those employees for whom the relationship with the organisation is treated much more in terms of a temporary economic link. These include many shop floor workers, sales staff and so on. In such cases, performance is measured, where possible, in output terms and rewarded under a bonus scheme. With so many employees in this category, the operations manager has to be very familiar with methods of direct payment by results and we shall look at this aspect in Chapter 6 on Work Study.

Within a formal appraisal system, there will be an appraisal interview. This raises many of the difficulties of fairness and consistency which were discussed in the previous section. The interview should, then, be set within a framework of planning and control to counter these problems. An effective and equitable appraisal system should contain:

- An analysis of the range and number of jobs to be appraised and the organisational context in which the system is to be established.
- Clarification of, and agreement over, the purpose of the appraisal.
- Training of appraisers in the necessary skills.
- A statement of the procedures to be followed and the outcomes expected.
- Regular review of the process as the basis for improvement.

Kreitner[6] identifies three general orientations for appraisal – trait, outcome and behaviour. Of these, the last is the least common yet is the most strongly recommended by experts.

- *Trait-oriented* appraisal is widely used yet, since it concentrates on personality traits, is one of the weakest and most susceptible to prejudice. Traits such as 'charm', 'ambition' or 'initiative' have been found irrelevant or inconsistently held in different job situations. They do not account for achievement of job outcomes.

- *Outcome-oriented* appraisal focuses on outcomes. Management by Objectives (see **4.5**) assesses how well employees meet previously agreed goals. Yet, since goals are individualised in this way, a serious drawback of the approach is that there is no consistent basis for comparing one person with another. This makes outcome-oriented approaches unsuitable for appraisal systems which are primarily designed to rank employees for merit pay or promotion.
- *Behaviour-oriented* appraisal highlights behaviour which is relevant to the job. This is because it is behaviour which is, in the end, the root of success or failure in a job.

Whatever system of performance appraisal is used, the manager should be aware of its limitations and the basic contradictions which it sets up. For example, appraisal systems frequently seek to combine evaluation of an employee's performance with advising and agreeing upon routes to improving that performance. Each is a laudable purpose yet, in combination, they create problems. The manager is to be seen as both an evaluator, being prepared to note under-performance, and, simultaneously, an advisor. In the latter role, the manager is being presented as a supporter or trusted friend at court who can arrange to have development opportunities made available.

10. Training

Training is critical to good operations management. Kreitner[7] defines training as:

> *the process of changing employee behaviour, attitudes or opinions through some type of guided experience.*

Implied within this definition is the notion that the changes are to be related to the job. The planning of a training programme should, therefore, start with a comparison of the attributes required to perform the job effectively and the attributes of the employee. This *training needs analysis* identifies gaps in the person's capabilities. In turn, the *training gaps* form the basis of a training plan.

The delivery of instruction is a personal service. In principle, each needs analysis establishes an individualised plan. Managers are then faced with the problem of supplying the service to each employee within budget constraints. It is not surprising that a compromise has to be reached and employees are given standardised training courses in spite of their not needing every element of them. To some extent, training resources are wasted.

Training takes place either within the workplace, *on-the-job training*, or away from it, *off-the-job training*. Each has its advantages and disadvantages as summarised in Box 5.5. Off-the-job training is often criticised because of the difficulty of transferring any learning directly back to the work situation. Unless the training is fitted in with other changes, the employee immediately unlearns whatever learning has been provided. A combination of both modes of training will ensure retention and optimise the new skills which are transferred to the job. For this to happen the training should:

- take place in circumstances which are similar to the job
- enlarge the trainee's experience
- offer a range of experience not normally met by the trainee
- enable learning of underlying ideas rather than simple rote following of instructions
- be planned at a time when the trainee can appreciate and use the benefits of the programme.

	Advantages	Disadvantages
On-the-job training	Skills learned are directly applicable. May not need special trainers. Trainee can contribute to productive effort. Cheap.	May provide too narrow experience. Bad habits passed on. Trainee may be in the way.
Off-the-job training	Suitable for tasks not currently carried out. Necessary where trainee's errors can be expensive or disastrous. Provides wider experience and practice in unusual situations. More readily controlled by professional trainers.	Difficult to relate back to current job situation and to match to individuals' needs. May require expensive development and testing if it is to be successful. Expensive to operate. Attendance at special training centres often used as reward for good performance.

Box 5.5 Comparison of styles of training

For example, to train a clerk in the use of new software, off-the-job training may be advisable so that it can take place without interruption. There may be a series of modules which teach procedures and give understanding of the reasons for them. As the programme advances, the trainee should have access to the software and begin to use it within the job situation. Other instances are the off-the-job training in simulators for airline pilots and the on-the-job methods used for car drivers. In the former case a great deal can be done, and indeed has to be done, to prepare potential pilots before they take the controls of a real aircraft. In the latter, on the other hand, most people come to the driving school with a high awareness of the context of the task. The learner is rehearsing a set of skills which have to be combined and made intuitive before being able to drive successfully.

Training contrasts

There is a danger in job-based needs analysis. It can lead to very narrow training prescriptions if the behavioural approach brought out in this brief analysis is overemphasised. For example, bank trainees expect their employers to teach them all the processes which working in a branch entails. These range from counting cash to checking customers' accounts and so on. Yet the service function must go further than this. Service in banking involves being able to relate to customers at the personal level. Generally, western employers try to achieve this by using training to influence trainees' *attitudes*. For instance, they stress that the customer is always right and that it is better if staff are always pleasant. They may go so far as to suggest to staff what they may do in critical service situations, as with a complaint, see Box 3.2 in 3.4. Within the general frameworks set out, however, staff are encouraged to express their own personality in the way they give service. Banks rely on effective initial recruitment and gradual development to produce staff with appropriate interpersonal skills.

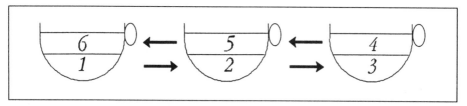

Figure 5.7 Pouring tea for three persons

Compare this with the way service training can be given in Japan. Figure 5.7 is based on one of many sketches in the training manual of a Japanese bank[8]. The book features dozens of instructions of how to behave within the work environment. Greetings, addressing clients, colleagues and superiors and many other aspects of social behaviour are laid out in detail. The formal processes of social interaction are, of course, much more important in Japan than in most western countries. Therefore, employers stress behaviour in their training. This example illustrates how important it is to take cultural differences into account when managing a service facility.

Safety training

Training is an important factor in ensuring that work is conducted in a safe manner. The focus of responsibility has shifted over the years. For employers, there has been a shift from compliance with detailed regulations towards a more general duty to ensure safe premises, products and working practices. Each process must be studied for safety implications. The process should be designed to be as safe as possible and workers should be trained accordingly. It has been found that conformance is best achieved if staff are encouraged to develop positive attitudes towards, and opinions about, safety.

COMMUNICATING, MOTIVATING AND LEADING

While the personnel department provides a valuable support service in the functions described above, the ultimate responsibility in ensuring that the primary activities of the organisation are carried out lies with the line manager. This is, in our case, the operations manager. In the following sections we shall study the role of the line manager in leading and motivating the staff, using communications skills to do this effectively.

11. The importance of good communications

To carry out their function, managers spend their time communicating. They are responsible for planning, controlling, development, decision making, problem solving and so on. Few of these activities can take place without sharing of information with others. Kreitner[9] presents the results of several studies, summarised as follows:

- Organisational and individual performance improves when there is effective communication.

- Managers spend most of their time communicating. (Typically 80% of the working day.)
- Managers communicate primarily face to face. (75%, compared with 10% by telephone.)
- Managers in small organisations (less than 50 employees) rely heavily on horizontal communication, interacting with other specialists.
- Managers in large organisations (more than 500 employees) direct 58% of their communication vertically, to their superiors or subordinates.

Good communication is not only required between pairs of individuals working on the details of a task. It is required to gain cooperation of all members of the organisation in achieving the common goals. Within any organisation there are two systems of communication: the formal system controlled by management and the informal system or *grapevine*. The latter is frequently very fast with news; it operates through a network of relationships which are based on family ties, club memberships, physical proximity or even chance meetings on the bus. The grapevine can be influential and can operate destructively. It must, however, be recognised that it will always exist. It is part of the organisation's culture.

Managers can respond to the tendency to rely on informal communications by:

- Having good, coordinated formal communications. This extends from giving clear information and instructions on issues that matter through to using corporate newsletters to tell staff about wider developments.
- Monitoring the grapevine as one means of eliciting general feelings over organisational issues.
- Taking steps to counter malicious rumours. (They may be tempted to do this by feeding information, or leaks, into the grapevine, but their lack of control may mean that the outcomes are negative.)

Two aspects of communications stand out from this discussion, the need for individual managers to be effective communicators and how organisations can design good communications systems. We shall examine these in turn.

12. Interpersonal communication

Communication can be defined as:

the transfer of information and understanding from one person to another.

There are two important features in this definition:

- The accent is on person-to-person flow. While it may appear that many situations involve large numbers of senders or receivers – the televised speech or the audience cheering the soloist at the end of the concert – each link is from individual to individual. This makes analysis very complex.

At the 1994 Eurovision Song Contest, the entry for Bosnia-Herzogovena received loud and long applause from the Irish audience. Did they all think it was a good song? Was there an element of sympathy for an oppressed nation? Was there a political gesture towards the inactive European powers? One can only say that each person probably had intentions in the simple act of applauding which went beyond approval of the performance.

- Communication is more than the sending of data. It is inevitable that the receiver interprets the information in some way. The purpose of good communication is to ensure that the recipient interprets the information in the *intended way*. Then common understanding will be achieved.

Recipients often interpret messages which the other party had no intention of sending. I bought some roofing timbers from a demolition site in the centre of our town. Having sorted out the pile of material and agreed the price, I asked the seller if he would take a cheque. Hearing that he wanted cash, I walked a hundred metres to the bank, put my tools on the counter, pulled out my cheque book and began to write. The teller, meanwhile, summoned assistance. She thought it was a hold-up. I hadn't realised how much soot was covering my face and clothes.

The elements of the communication process can be picked out of this discussion and set out as in Figure 5.8. This figure displays one-way communication by telephone in which the sender, on the left, wants to ensure understanding by the receiver, on the right. In most conversations, where the flow is two-way, we would have to double up our model to cater for the continual switching of roles by the participants. The features of the process are as follows:

Encoding Encoding involves the translation of internal ideas into a common language which the receiver can understand. In our case this code or language is speech which uses not only a shared vocabulary but also pace, tone of voice and non-verbal sounds. In other circumstances gestures, pictures and so on can be used.

Encoding is a skill. It should recognise the purpose of the message as well as the strengths and limitations of the medium being used. Telephones are good for sending simple messages but poor for complex technical data.

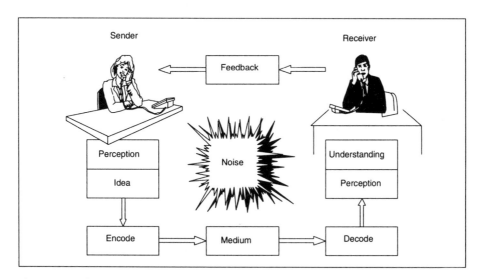

Figure 5.8 The communication process

131

Medium The medium both constrains the message and becomes part of it. Each medium has advantages and disadvantages. When the sender has a choice, the match between message purpose and medium should be considered. The capacity of a medium to carry information and facilitate understanding is called its *richness*. Face-to-face meetings are rich because there are many language cues, from words to gestures, feedback is immediate and the context is personally involving. Our telephone contact is less rich because some cues are eliminated and each participant has less awareness of the environment of the other. Lean media are impersonal and have no immediate feedback, such as most forms of printed text.

Lean media are best used for routine messages such as production instructions or monthly budget reports. Rich media are better for non-routine situations in which, say, the manager seeks to persuade someone of a change of plan. A mismatch can be frustrating. There are too many boring meetings used by a boss to present detailed information (rich medium – routine information). Even worse is the use of memoranda to give people surprising or shocking personal information such as decisions over redundancy (lean medium – non-routine information).

Decoding However well the message is composed, understanding depends on the receiver's decoding and perception. Successful decoding requires that both parties use the same coding system, that is they use the same language. Much military training is devoted to learning and using common codes which can be used successfully in situations of great stress. Organisations and professions develop their own codes, referred to as jargon. Perception of the sender's intention is also conditioned by what the receiver already knows both of the message and the purpose of the sender as well as the receiver's own psychological make-up.

Feedback The communication process will hardly be complete without some feedback from the receiver. Again, referring to the military context, the sender seeks assurance of 'Message received and understood.' Feedback completes the loop, as in the ubiquitous control model. Responsibility for feedback rests on both parties – the sender to establish and monitor feedback links, the receiver to supply the feedback messages, to ask questions and to express any feelings of not having understood.

Noise Noise is any interference with the transfer of understanding from one person to the other. This is not simply sound interference but covers a wide range of influences which can disturb any stage. They include:

Encoding – unfamiliar language; poor literacy, numeracy, drawing or modelling skills; physical disabilities

Message – poor transmission technology; competing messages; interference of all kinds

Decoding – unfamiliar language; poor listening or reading skills; aural or visual disabilities

Perception – negative attitudes towards sender or message; unanticipated outside influences.

To overcome the effects of noise, managers have available two remedies. First, they should search for and remove sources of noise. Secondly, they can improve the quality of messages to make them as clear as possible. Often, messages contain a high degree of *redundancy*, which is information above the minimum required for encoding the sender's meaning. Natural languages are full of redundancy and good communicators deliberately include an appropriate amount of repetition to ensure that their messages get through. A maxim for a good oral presentation is, 'First tell them what you are going to say. Then say it. Then tell them what you have said.'

13. Organisational communication

Organisations work through communication. Given the problems reviewed in the preceding section, one may wonder how information can ever be transmitted through an organisation. Extra barriers to communication arise from organisational divisions, either between levels or between the specialists of different departments. Approaches to resolving these difficulties include:

- removing physical barriers between people through the choice of facility location and layout
- using training to help colleagues understand the language and attitudes of other specialists
- avoiding disputes over semantics which touch on personal beliefs while ensuring that the language in use does not demean others
- building an atmosphere of trust so that staff feel free to communicate.

This latter point is one of the most intractable. Subordinates may feel unconfident in communicating with superiors, especially in settings such as formal meetings. These feelings impose constraints on the vital process of upward communication.

Upward communication

Leaders of large organisations need information from lower levels for two reasons. The first can be termed *intelligence*. People at the grass roots are frequently in close contact with customers, suppliers and, sometimes, competitors. They may observe operating problems, customer reactions or changes in the organisation's environment but not appreciate their significance. At the same time, others would recognise the significance if only they had the information! The problem is to ensure that the two aspects are brought together. The second reason for upward communication is to collect the ideas and understand the feelings of subordinates. With many at the base of the pyramid and few at the top there is a problem. How can upward communication be achieved?

In the Army, the problem of intelligence is addressed by having a separate department specialising in its collection. Among its many tasks, the role of military intelligence is to collect information from soldiers who have been on missions, debriefing them on what they have seen of the enemy's behaviour. By assembling this collective observation as soon as possible, the significance of what may otherwise seem a disparate pattern of events may be appreciated.

In non-military organisations such an approach would normally be unacceptable and too expensive. Managers, though, do have several means of gathering and encouraging the upward flow. These are summarised in Box 5.6.

14. Motivation

For the operations manager, who is usually responsible for the majority of staff in the organisation, motivation is important. For the individual, it is defined as

the internal processes which direct behaviour.

Information on employee attitudes	*Regular formal surveys*. To gain commitment from those expected to complete questionnaires, managers should be committed to publishing their results and making changes.
	Grievance procedures. Usually confined to the problems of an individual, most large organisations have agreed formal processes for listening to and dealing with complaints.
	Informal listening. Management by wandering around (MBWA) was popularised at Hewlett-Packard by its founders. It means what it says, managers must spend time going round listening. Other managers use an *open-door policy*, which encourages any employee to bring forward a problem.
	Exit interviews. Often conducted by specialists in the personnel department, exit interviews are designed to find out why an employee is leaving. Results are compared in order to pick out trends.
Employee ideas and intelligence	*Suggestion schemes*. Based on the notion that it is the people doing the job who often have the best ideas about it, these schemes are used by many employers with varying degrees of success to reward good technical ideas.
	Working parties or task forces. Cutting across levels and functions, work teams will break down barriers if there is sufficient confidence in the value of their outcomes. This approach has been used in *quality circles*, see **17** and Chapter 15.

Box 5.6 Encouraging upward communication

Managers must attempt to understand these processes so that they can persuade employees to accept and follow the objectives of the team, department or organisation.

The manager's desired outcome is job performance. This comes from a combination of factors internal and external to the employee. As set out in Figure 5.9, an individual carries to the job a blend of personal motivation and ability. Personal ability accumulates from experience and training, some of which can be provided by the employer. The design and context of the job must also be recognised: the job may offer demanding and interesting activity; it may give the opportunity for the employee to participate in management; it may offer a range of rewards from cash to recognition and personal satisfaction. Each of the elements of this general model are covered in the next sections.

15. Theories of motivation

Four of the most influential theories of motivation are summarised in Box 5.7. Each takes a different approach to the issues and hence illuminates them in a different light. Such is the complexity of the field that it is unlikely that a universally applicable theory will emerge.

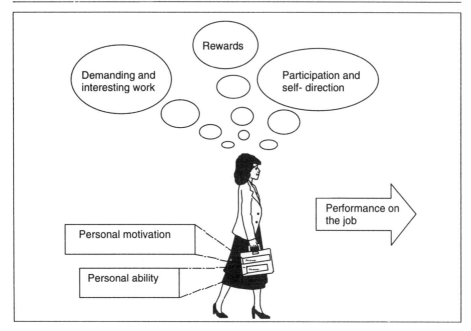

Figure 5.9 Motivation factors in job performance

Maslow's theory is perhaps the most widely known. Developed in a clinical, rather than employment, context, the theory has a weak empirical base. Its popularity stems from simplicity and surface plausibility. While a practising manager would be unwise to base policy upon a slavish following of the hierarchy, the theory does point out that employees are unlikely to respond to appeals to presumed needs for self-actualization if their basic pay and conditions are well below par.

Herzberg's contribution, again based on shaky evidence, was to focus on the psychology of work and pick out the difference between dissatisfiers and satisfiers. The former will demotivate workers. Above a satisfactory level however, no amount of extra investment in their improvement will bring gains in motivation. Satisfiers, on the other hand, are the true motivators. Managers should focus on these, having eliminated the dissatisfiers. The theory points to the inherent value of work itself and how gains can result from job enrichment. One problem is that later evidence suggests that some of the factors are treated differently by different people, especially pay. Some are motivated by incremental increases in income while others are not so influenced provided that pay is at a satisfactory level. For the former, it is a satisfier, whereas for the latter it is a dissatisfier.

The theories of both Maslow and Herzberg generalise about reward factors in a search for universal applicability. Expectancy theory, in contrast, says little about rewards and returns to a study of the individual. Whatever the rewards, each person will make a different evaluation of the combined probabilities of achieving performance from effort and reward from performance. For example, it has long been recognised that output-related rewards for workers on a long assembly line have little motivational effect because, for an individual, there is no link between effort and output. In taking the analysis to the personal level, the theory also recognises how motivation changes through time. Telling a subordinate that there

Theory	Summary	Comment
Maslow's Hierarchy of Needs (1943)	Five levels of needs arranged in hierarchy. People not conscious of needs but all proceed along predictable route from bottom to top: physiological → safety → affection → esteem → self-actualization.	Widely known and influential mainly because simple and plausible. Maslow made original tentative proposal after studying mentally ill patients. Little supporting evidence from employment studies.
Herzberg's Two Factor Theory (1950)	Motivation results from satisfaction. Factors divided into *dissatisfiers* (supervision, conditions, pay, security and so on) and *satisfiers* (achievement, advancement, responsibility, recognition and work itself). Points out that dissatisfaction and satisfaction are not opposites.	As well known and influential as Maslow's theory but less well understood. Based on study of professional engineers and accountants but challenged by many others since. Only weak evidence found elsewhere.
Vroom's Expectancy Theory (1964)	Motivational strength depends on expectations of outcomes and rewards. Increases if a person's perceptions of both *outcomes of efforts* and *rewards from these outcomes* increase. Takes into account different people's assessments of circumstances and rewards and how these may change in time.	Focuses on the individual's appraisal of the situation. Supported by empirical evidence and in line with common sense. Explains how motivation can quickly change with circumstances.
Locke's Goal-Setting Theory (1984)	Stresses participation to achieve personal ownership of goals. These motivate through *pointing* towards a target, *encouraging effort* in moving towards the target, *promoting tenacity* in the effort in spite of problems and *enabling the creation of strategies and plans*.	General theory which clearly applies to those motivated by goals. Research emphasises the value of feedback. Basis of programmes such as MBO (see **4.5**) and employee participation.

Box 5.7 Some significant theories of motivation

is no chance of promotion may change that person's motivation for the worse; telling them, some time later, that there is a possibility may rekindle the wish to perform better. For the manager, the stress is on understanding the meaning of rewards to individuals and ensuring that they have a good chance of achieving them. Therefore, the links in the effort–performance–rewards chain must be clear to all.

Advocates of goal-setting theory attempt to bridge the gap between an individual's wants within the job and organisational objectives. This is achieved by encouraging a shared ownership of the goals as well as making feedback on performance available to all. The approach suggests that there should be both a high degree of participation in the goal-setting process and feedback systems for self-control to be exercised.

A study by Hackman and Oldham[10] questioned the causal link from satisfaction to motivation proposed by Maslow and Herzberg. At the same time they returned to the search for general factors within the job tasks which would lead to high motivation. They suggested that there are certain *core job characteristics* which have an influence on both job satisfaction and job motivation. In other words, the last two elements are outputs of the job system. The mechanism proposed by Hackman and Oldham is set out in Figure 5.10. The outcomes of the job are the results of *critical psychological states* which are in turn caused by *core job characteristics*. Differences between individuals are recognised by suggesting that each link in this chain is influenced by mediating factors – personal knowledge and skill, desire for personal growth and satisfaction with the job context. Figure 5.10 shows the way each of the elements of the chain is made up and these items are returned to in the next section.

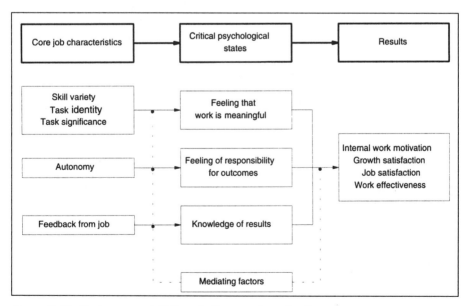

Figure 5.10 Hackman and Oldham's theory of motivation

16. Job design

Job design refers to the identification and arrangement of tasks which together form a job. It is clear that boring jobs carried out under adverse conditions are demotivating. At the same time, challenge, variety and excitement can be excessive and themselves also be demotivating. In designing jobs, managers have to pay attention to the relationship between the demands that they make and capabilities and motivation of their employees. There are two basic approaches to the relationship - matching people to jobs and matching jobs to people.

Matching people to jobs

The design of many jobs is closely determined by technology. Within the socio-technical system (see 2.7), the technological element may be the stronger partly because of economic circumstances but also because of the current state of knowledge. Assembly line jobs are created because competition forces manufacturers to supply high volumes at low cost and they are at present unable to devise ways of replacing all the workers by robots. Many surveillance tasks are also dull yet require that the employee remains vigilant. Again they exist through necessity and because they have yet to be automated. People are expected to fit within these frameworks.

Accepting the unsatisfactory nature of many of these jobs, what can managers do to relieve some of their negative consequences? There are three possibilities:

- *Establishing clear expectations*
  The nature of the job is made clear to potential employees. Far better to advertise 'The most boring job in the world' than to pretend that there are numerous possibilities of variety and job satisfaction.
- *Job rotation*
  Moving people from one task to another at intervals may prevent stagnation and even relieve physical fatigue if the various tasks involve different working positions. A balance needs to be struck between the benefits of change and the disturbance caused by this change being too rapid.

  > In line with common practice, surveillance staff at the Museum of Anatolian Cultures in Ankara change their positions at every break. In discussion, one told me, 'I'd rather stay in one place. In that way I would only have one boring job instead of four.'

- *Earning relief*
  Kreitner[11] reports on the success of some employers with *contingent time off*. In one example, a group were producing 160 units in an eight-hour day with a 10% reject rate. They agreed a new target of 200 per day plus 3 every rejected unit. Within one week of the agreement, output rose to over 200 and defects fell to 1.5%. The average working time was 6.5 hours, after which the staff could go home. Notwithstanding the poor state of affairs which must have existed before this change, it is clear that the workers found the possibility of earning time off to be highly motivating. Yet, in spite of reported successes, formal CTO agreements are rare.

Matching jobs to people

The limited possibilities within the people-to-jobs matching have led many firms to redress the balance between the two aspects of the socio-technical system. Here, the nature and boundaries of the job are considered alongside concern with the needs of employees. The aim is to achieve productivity and satisfaction for the people simultaneously. Two approaches are common:

Job enlargement Some degree of involvement and variety can be created if several tasks which have been divided are combined into a single job. This may be easy to achieve as when four clerical staff handling different stages of order processing each take over dealing with one quarter of the orders. In other cases, process design may have to be altered and more equipment made available. For example, on a line putting together electrical items, each worker would need to have all components available and be furnished with a complete set of tools and assembly jigs. These can, however, often be supplied at low cost.

Critics point out that combining a few boring tasks does not of itself make an interesting job. Yet if the job cycle time is increased substantially by combining a dozen or more tasks, employees' feelings of frustration and boredom may recede.

Job enrichment The accent on job enrichment is to redesign the job with the express intention of increasing its influence on motivation. In section **15**, we saw how Hackman and Oldham saw both motivation and satisfaction as outputs from the job. Hence they could both be affected by job design. Their model is one approach to understanding the ways in which jobs can be enriched and we can use it to look at some possibilities. In many cases, the core job characteristics can be changed:

Skill variety. Requiring that a range of skills is used, for instance manual, planning, leading, communicating, calculating, monitoring and so on.
Task identity. Enabling a person to complete a whole task with a meaningful outcome, for example assembling a complete unit or handling all the requirements of a customer.
Task significance. Designing the job to be important so that others depend upon its successful completion. Encouraging staff to see others as customers of their work is one element in the development of a total quality approach.
Autonomy. Allowing the individual discretion in how the job is paced, sequenced, checked and so on. This does not imply personal isolation for, as we shall see below (**17**), autonomy can be given to a group.
Feedback from job. Providing the person with information on how effectively they are working.

The other theories of motivation will also enable us to understand issues concerning job redesign. For example, Maslow's or Herzberg's models underscore the fact that employees may not be interested in such changes if their basic needs, or dissatisfiers, are not supported. It should also be noted that some employees do not seek enriched jobs. There are two difficult questions here:

Could an employee prefer a job with very low skill which requires merely surface mental attention? There are, possibly apocryphal, stories of doctoral students working on General Motors' assembly lines to earn their keep. The job gave them eight hours a day to think about their theses.

Does enrichment increase managerial power? Some workers regard the process as a further example of management's manipulation. This is reinforced in those cases where managers retain the control of job design. In encouraging conformance to the new arrangements, those in charge may demonstrate that it is only they who can set the boundaries of control and responsibility. A more open approach, with consultation, increases uncertainty over outcomes yet may gain greater long-term commitment.

17. Motivation from participation

Participation means that managers give power to subordinates to take control of their work situation. Instead of managers carrying out the managerial tasks from goal setting, through planning and implementation, to control, some of these are given to lower levels. This is not new. Organisations would never work if every task were to be carried out at the top. The point about participative management is that it has to be a positive programme. It counters the tendency of many managers, through habit, fear or lack of confidence, to draw all decision making and control into themselves.

In general, coercive management styles do achieve some level of output. This is, however, at the expense of creating an alienated and instrumental workforce. Improvements to performance require more coercion which continues the vicious circle of alienation. In many processes, managers can never supervise tasks closely enough to overcome the negative effects of dissatisfied staff. Box 5.8 quotes one of the acts of sabotage reported by Beynon[12].

Participation can be achieved through the creation of teams who share ownership of groups of tasks. This enables the core job characteristics of task significance and autonomy to be brought out. There are two types of team which can be noted:

- *Quality circles*
  Improvements to quality often require changes cutting across traditional functional boundaries. They also benefit from the detailed knowledge held by staff currently engaged in the relevant tasks. Quality circles are usually made up of groups of volunteers who work together on projects which they select as potentially fruitful. The circles can break up and reform as projects change. Success requires management encouragement and recognition. QCs are discussed in greater detail in Chapter 15.

'In the Paint Shop the car, after an early coat of paint, passes through the Wet Deck where a team of men armed with electric sanders - 'whirlies' - sand the body while it is being heavily sprayed with water. ...

'If there was a problem on the Wet Deck – a manning problem, speed-up, if the foreman had stepped out of line – they always had a comeback. They could sand the paint off the style lines – the fine edges of the body that gave it its distinctive shape. And nobody could know. The water streaming down, the whirlies flailing about, the lads on either side of the car, some of them moving off to change their soaking clothes. The foreman could stand over them and he couldn't spot it happening. Three hours later, the body shell would emerge with bare metal along the style lines. They *knew* it was happening.'

Box 5.8 The Wet Deck at Ford, Halewood, in 1970

- *Job teams*

  In contrast to quality circles which meet outside the immediate job context, these autonomous work groups are permanently engaged in the productive task. Many manufacturing plants and service facilities have changed over to such arrangements, the groups taking responsibility for decisions such as task allocation and rotation, quality, rest breaks, flow of materials, minor maintenance and cleanliness of the work area.

The introduction of teamwork presents two immediate problems. The first is the resistance of supervisors whose roles are changed, reduced in scope or eliminated altogether. The second is resistance from the workers themselves who may be suspicious of managerial motives, especially where relations have not been healthy. Teamwork demands higher commitment and ability on behalf of workers and change may be costly in terms of the extra training required.

18. Motivation from rewards

Expectancy theory stresses the importance of rewards and the probability of gaining them as essential ingredients in motivation. For the individual, they are the ultimate pay-offs for carrying out tasks at work. The work may be willingly done, with the rewards flowing accordingly, or carried out grudgingly as with the alienated workers of Ford's Wet Deck in Box 5.8. In this case, the workers took the pay for the job but also gained satisfaction from sabotage.

Rewards can be divided into those supplied by others, *extrinsic rewards*, and those which are experienced within the person and hidden from the public domain. The latter were referred to by Jahoda[13] as the *latent functions of employment*. Employment brings a bundle of both types, see Box 5.9. Some of the latent functions may not seem pleasant and are only noticed when a job is lost. 'It is not uncommon for unemployed people to report that, while they hated the sniping, nagging and gossip which went on when they had a job, when they lost it they missed it terribly.'[14]

Heading the list of extrinsic rewards is money. There are almost as many payment systems as there are employers but we can make some generalisations, firstly about principles and then about practical examples. How should payment systems be designed if they are to effectively motivate performance? Our review of motivation theory suggests the following points:

- Staff should see a link between effort and performance, and performance and reward.

Extrinsic rewards	*Latent functions*
Pay	Achievement
Employee benefits	Personal identity
Advancement at work	Regular activity
Recognition by managers, colleagues and wider society	Self-regard
	Self-fulfilment
Status	Satisfaction from work itself
Status symbols	Time structure to the day

Box 5.9 Rewards from employment

- The distribution of rewards must be fair and be seen to be fair.
- The rewards must appeal to each individual.

These principles are easily stated yet most difficult to achieve in practice. Not all jobs have easily measured outputs, often performance is not related to the person's own effort, sometimes individuals can only gain at the expense of others. In many jobs pay is only loosely related to achievement and, therefore, much reliance is placed on the non-pay extrinsic rewards together with the latent functions. Such are the employment arrangements for many doorkeepers and doctors, shop assistants and surgeons.

Formal pay schemes may include rewards which are tied to performance. Box 5.10 lists some common schemes of which there are many variations. Piecework, production bonuses and commission are the methods which tie effort, performance and pay most closely together. Modern production bonus schemes are often tied to time standards using formulae which are explained in the next chapter. The schemes do have such disadvantages that their use in business operations is declining. Technological developments sever the links between personal effort and outcomes and the schemes may encourage excessive striving after bonus, especially where it represents a large proportion of income. For example, insurance companies have been heavily criticised for relying on high commissions to motivate their sales people. Customers rely on advice from these personnel because insurance, especially pensions and life insurance, is something they rarely buy and little understand. This relationship has been exploited by unscrupulous staff selling unsuitable products.

In other schemes in the list, the proportion of personal income covered by the bonus rarely exceeds ten per cent. It could be stated that the use of money assures formality of appraisal. The rewards given then mean more as statements of recognition than as radical changes to the receiver's standard of living. As a colleague stated, 'It's better than a slap on the back.'

19. Leadership

We have focused on motivation methods as the way to persuade people to accept and then follow the objectives of the organisation. There are, however, other important persuasive influences. Managers have formal power vested in them by their position in the organisation. In using this power they can exercise formal leadership with respect to those in positions beneath them. Their power is limited by the power possessed by others. Workers, for example, can exercise economic power, particularly strong if they act collectively to resist managers' efforts.

Leadership is the process of persuading others to voluntarily accept the organisation's goals. When we say that an organisation has succeeded through 'good leadership' we probably mean that the people at the top, the leaders, are good managers. This means that they have succeeded as much by making good decisions about marketing, investment, technology and organisation structure as they have at influencing everyone to march in the same direction. Indeed, as Perrow[15] points out, the non-personal decisions appear to have more effect on performance than the methods used to lead people. Leadership, however, is important in getting that extra drop of commitment from others in the team.

Many theories of leadership have been advocated, the more modern ones rejecting universal models and emphasising the importance of situational factors.

Pay scheme	Method	Advantages and disadvantages
1 Piece work	Payment per unit produced.	Direct relationship with output, but has reputation for exploitation among out workers; individual absorbs business risk in cyclical market.
2 Production bonus	Payments related to output by formula.	Clear relationship with output, but requires the establishment of time standards and can be complex to administer.
3 Commission	Formula based on sales revenue.	Clear relationship to sales personally achieved, but encourages competition between staff; can be seen as unfair by those not receiving the bonuses.
4 Profit sharing	Formula based on end of period profits	Invites interest in company's performance, but profits not obviously related to personal effort.
5 Share options	Free or discounted shares in company.	Personal stake in long-term performance of company, but capital growth not obviously related to personal effort; resented by non-participants and increases problems if company suffers setbacks.
6 Benefit sharing	Distribution of benefits from gains in productivity.	Encourages individuals and teams to improve performance, but may create problems in other departments; can be difficult to calculate.
7 Merit pay	Bonus for excellent performance.	Applies to staff whose output not directly related to effort, but requires subjective assessment and therefore difficult to operate fairly.
8 Pay based on skills	Bonuses for achieving and maintaining capabilities.	Inspires staff to reach high standards and keep them up, but may be unnecessary and hence waste training resources.
9 Fixed rate	Rate per hour or year.	Simple and clear; hourly rates encourage attendance, but little incentive to produce more at work.

Box 5.10 Incentive payment schemes

From these contingency theories, we shall pick out Fiedler's to illustrate the issues[16]. Fiedler showed that the climate of the group had a substantial impact upon whether a particular leadership style would be effective. The climate could be favourable, with good relations between a well-established leader and the group and with tasks relatively easily planned and controlled. An unfavourable climate refers to an unestablished leader not enjoying good personal relations with staff where tasks to be performed are unclear. Interacting with the climate are the leader's own basic motivations. According to Fiedler, leaders are either task-oriented or relationship-oriented. The former are more concerned with production, whereas the latter are more concerned with people. A simple best match between styles and climate was not found. Indeed, where the situation was either highly favourable or highly unfavourable, task-oriented managers did better. This can be explained as follows. In a favourable climate, the best leader is one who provides task direction, the group itself being able to sort out the interpersonal relations. In an unfavourable climate, close supervision of tasks is called for because any effort by the manager to counter the bad personal relations will be wasted. It is only in intermediate situations where a people-oriented leader will be of value in building group relations and resolving subordinates' concerns over tasks and rewards.

We must, therefore, look beyond the notion of motivation as applying a set of techniques to job design and reward. Encouraging commitment to the aims of the organisation requires managers to exercise a wide range of approaches including: participation in planning and controlling; appealing to reason; giving inspiration; politicking and bargaining; applying pressure; flattery; and appealing to the influence of third parties such as senior managers or outsiders.

Case study: Levi Strauss & Co

Levi Strauss & Company employs some 30,000 people in the United States, making and distributing its famous jeans and related products. Now a private company after a mid-1980s buy-out, profits in 1992 were $360M. In that year it became the first private company to appear in *Fortune's* annual list of 'most admired' companies. The company had been through great changes since its previous successful period in the 1970s. Then it was riding the crest of a wave with sales to the baby-boomer market supported by the strong brand name and product quality.

Success led to complacency and, by 1982, sales were in serious decline. Levi's tried to overcome this by supplying large chains and discounters for the first time. This only served to cut margins in the declining market. A series of plant closures and lay-offs began in 1984.

Bob Haas, five generations removed from the company's founder, was appointed chief executive in that year. He presided over the reduction in the number of product lines by two-thirds, closure of 59 factories and the dismissal of 17,000 staff. Of greater concern to Haas than the profit slump was the internal authoritarian and bureaucratic structure which was rife with conflict and politics. Haas wanted better interpersonal relations and more teamwork, better communications and more trust. At first, other managers did not want to know. Sales had been falling and attempts at diversification had been unsuccessful. Under threat, people are not interested in appeals to a greater purpose.

Yet by 1987, when the financial health of Levi's began to improve, Haas was able to join with other senior managers in producing the Aspiration Statement.

This document supplemented Levi's rather dry and technical strategy and mission statements. The mission statement referred to 'responsible commercial success as a global marketing company of branded casual apparel'. It also made reference to ethical behaviour, a safe and secure work environment, opportunities for the staff to advance and responsibility towards the wider community. To animate these policies, the Aspiration Statement was intended to express the 'soul' of the company. Written on a single sheet, it was distributed to all employees. The following extract captures its tone:

> We all want a company that our people are proud of and committed to, where all employees have an opportunity to contribute, learn, grow and advance based on merit, not politics or background. We want our people to feel respected, treated fairly, listened to, and involved. Above all, we want satisfaction from accomplishments and friendships, balanced personal and professional lives, and to have fun in our endeavours.

The statement called upon all leaders in the organisation to help bring the aspirations nearer.

Change is being introduced at all levels. Supervisors report that, whereas they used to be praised for being tough, they are now encouraged to share their authority. Participation is encouraged and productivity sharing is now widespread. At one plant in the Blue Ridge mountains of Tennessee, gains are split 50-50 provided that the plant meets its normal outputs. This increases the average take-home pay by about $600 per year. Smaller contributions are rewarded with T-shirts, coffee cups and coupons.

The Aspiration Statement was little understood by shop-floor workers used to the previous authoritarian culture. Levi's started an educational programme built around concepts of leadership, ethics, and understanding and valuing individual diversity. The company also began literacy and numeracy training. It wanted staff to perform better in their jobs but also felt an obligation to prepare staff for the possibility of more plant closures. In spite of its expressed intentions, Levi's had, in 1990, to shut down a plant in Texas where Dockers slacks were made. What managers felt were generous redundancy terms did overcome strong feelings of betrayal.

As in many countries, individual piecework has been the norm in the United States apparel industry. Levi's ran experiments with work teams who were empowered to make changes to production processes. They proved successful. In the 1990s, plants have begun to be reorganised into teams of about 36 people. Each team is responsible for one product line right through from cloth cutting to despatch. They determine their own production targets subject to minima set by management. In the changed plants, throughput time for jeans has fallen from six days to one, allowing a faster response to customers' requests and hence improving competitiveness. While many clothing companies have, in effect, *hollowed-out* their production by producing off shore in countries from Nicaragua to The Philippines, Levi's is looking to the benefits of improved quality and flexibility to keep its activities in the United States. The company recruited 2,500 staff in manufacturing during the early 1990s.

One employee of the Blue Ridge plant, with 17 years service, said, 'A year ago I hated my job. I took night classes to improve myself, determined that when my children got through college I was leaving. But now I've changed my mind, and the Lord willing, I'll probably be here until I retire ... a new pride in our job and commitment to our company makes it a better place to work.'

Haas argues, 'You don't work for Levi's, you work for yourselves; you just happen to work at Levi's.'[17]

Questions

1 *How effective do you think the Aspiration Statement would be in bridging the gap between company and individual goals?*
2 *How is Levi's improving production performance? Why?*
3 *Comment upon Haas' statement given in the last paragraph of the case study.*

References

1. Barnard, C.I. (1938) *The Functions of the Executive* Cambridge, Mass., Harvard University Press p. 78
2. Macák, František (1991) 'Re-structuralization and privatization of the Vítkovice Works of Ostrava' *Vítkovice 91* No. 4, December
3. S.G. Warburg and Co. Ltd. (1991) *British Telecommuncations public limited company, Offer for sale* London, 21 November, p. 9
4. Lorenz, Christopher (1994) 'Management: How to bridge functional gaps' *The Financial Times* 25 November, p.14
5. Moffat, J. (1992) 'Three case studies of operational research for the Royal Air Force' *Journal of the Operational Research Society* **43.10** pp. 955–960
6. Kreitner, R. (1992) *Management* 5th ed. Boston, Houghton-Mifflin, pp. 324–5
7. op. cit. p. 329
8. Hiroshima Sogo Bank (1994) *Watashitati no tekisuto [Our textbook]* 32nd edn. Hiroshima Sogo Bank, Personnel Training Section, p. 114
9. op. cit. p. 349
10 Hackman, J.R. and Oldham, G.R. (1980) *Work Redesign* New York, Addison-Wesley
11. op. cit. p. 395
12. Beynon, H. (1973) *Working for Ford* Harmondsworth, Penguin, pp. 140–1
13. Jahoda, M. (1992) *Employment and Unemployment* Cambridge University Press
14. Naylor, J.B. and Senior, B. (1988) *Incompressible Unemployment* Aldershot, Gower p. 26
15. Perrow, C. (1972) *Complex Organisations: A critical essay* Glenview, Illinois, Scott, Foresman and Company, p. 101
16. Fiedler, F.E. (1967) *A Theory of Leadership Effectiveness* New York, McGraw-Hill
17. Waterman, R. (1994) *The Frontiers of Excellence* London, Nicholas Brealey Publishing

6

STUDYING WORK

Chapter objectives

When you have finished studying this chapter, you should be able to:

- Outline and illustrate the contribution of ergonomics to work design.

- Compare the performance of humans and machines and demonstrate problems of their interaction through displays and controls.

- Suggest reasons for vigilance decrement and variations of human performance over time.

- Identify key issues in the design of the working environment for efficiency, health and safety.

- Outline why and how accidents occur at work and how they can be prevented.

- Describe the main reasons for formal work study and suggest areas where it can be used to advantage.

- Explain the role of *method study*, demonstrate the use of flow diagrams, process charts and multiple activity charts and show how motion study is used for close analysis.

- Define *work measurement* and show how industrial engineers can establish normal and standard times for jobs using different methods.

- Explain the usefulness of productivity measures to the operations manager.

- Compare different methods of incentive payment for work performance and compare such systems with *job evaluation*.

INTRODUCTION

In Chapter 5 we examined questions of organising, leading, motivating and controlling people within the operating organisation. This general approach enabled us to identify key issues for the manager in planning and developing the organisation and its people. Within this context, however, there are many complex processes that need to be planned and managed so as to achieve objectives. Most of these processes require human involvement. In some cases people do the physical work themselves, while in others their role may be that of controller of machinery in which skills of setting up, monitoring and maintenance are brought to the fore.

It is easy to slip into thinking of people as components of these operating systems and treat them as equivalent to, or even part of, machines whose performance can be predicted and can be expected to be consistent. Humans sometimes show inferior task performance compared with machines whereas, in other aspects, their performance is superior. The differences are important. Therefore, in this chapter we will look at the relationship between people and machines at work. This physical and psychological approach contrasts with the mainly social aspects considered in Chapter 5. As well as forming a basis for *work study*, it brings out issues in *health and safety*. This is an important area which should be of great concern to all operations managers.

Whether we examine operations that involve people, machines or a combination of both, we need to search for the best ways of carrying out tasks, especially when these are done frequently. This is the role of *method study* which analyses the sequencing and layout of tasks, sometimes in close detail to find the best ways of doing things. Since we must also bear in mind that organisations are engaged in economic activities, it is common to use some form of *work measurement* to both plan the resources required to carry out tasks and to control performance against established standards. This comparison produces various measures of productivity that can be used as the basis of bonus payments which form part of work motivation as discussed in Chapter 5.

1. Humans and machines

In **5.15** we noted that job design refers to the identification and arrangement of tasks that together form a job. Then we went on to consider the socio-psychological effects of jobs and the how far the task or the person can be adapted to improve what otherwise would be difficult and tedious activities. In studying both humans and machines at work, however, we can move closer to the tasks than we did in Chapter 5. This is the realm of *ergonomics*, the study of work. Ergonomic studies focus on designing jobs and work environments that are efficient and safe. Questions for ergonomists include the layout of work stations, human-machine communication and the quality of the working environment itself. We can use studies of typing, word processing and data input tasks to illustrate these questions.

The conventional keyboard is an example of poor ergonomic design, see Box 6.1. In spite of attempts to overcome its deficiencies, the threat of strain injury from continual data input remains[1]. Taking a broader view of the work system, ergonomists have also studied the design of office work stations, for instance the height and shape of desks and chairs, to reduce the strain caused by sitting in one place for long periods, see section **3**. Even wider solutions to physical stress could include job enlargement so that no individual spends excessive periods in one position carrying out a single task.

Problems of human-machine communication are illustrated by the design of displays and controls. Where information is difficult to read, errors will almost certainly follow. Physical and cost constraints often lead to information being presented in less than ideal ways. The need for cheap and simple gearing in a small space meant that gas meters installed until the 1980s had pointers on alternate dials turning in opposite directions. Figure 6.1 illustrates how difficult they were to read. Meter readers could, through practice, avoid errors and, in any case, the consequences of such errors are minor.

The dominant QWERTY typewriter keyboard was deliberately arranged to slow down typists. In the early mechanical typewriters, the levers tended to jam when efficient typists were working. Hence the keys were placed in an inconvenient arrangement. For instance, many key sequences used in common words require consecutive use of the same finger or hand so the movements between key strokes slow down the speed.

In mechanical typewriters, the user not only has to expend effort in moving the levers but also has to perform other motions such as moving the paper carriage at the end of each line. Word processors have reduced the distance moved and effort expended in each key stroke and have curtailed the frequency of other movements. This change has resulted in an increase in carpal tunnel syndrome, a form of wrist injury caused by small repetitive movements using little effort.

Different keyboard layouts can improve typing speeds on modern equipment yet these may result in even more wrist problems. Other innovations include adjustable key spacings and the splitting of the board into two sections, each of which is contoured to fit the shape of the hand and allow each wrist to rest in a more natural position. The conventional keyboard demands a horizontal palm position which, if the upper arms are to hang vertically from the shoulders, means that the forearm is permanently twisted.

Box 6.1 Ergonomics of the keyboard

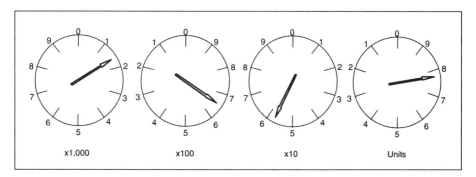

Figure 6.1 Reading the gas meter ...

Contrast this with the dial of an altimeter, Figure 6.2, as fitted to some aircraft in the second world war. Again, space demanded that alternate pointers rotated in opposite directions and that they shared a common dial. We can see that the aircraft is flying at something more than 3,000 feet but to be more precise than that requires some practice! Making consistently accurate readings in the difficult conditions of a cockpit would be a challenge.

These illustrations are of analogue displays, now often superseded by digital presentation. This area of information seems, however, to be particularly prone to technology-driven innovations that add complexity and are not based on careful

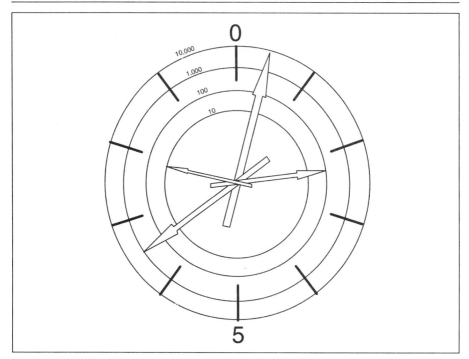

Figure 6.2 Altimeter reading ...

Reading a traditional watch is an acquired skill. This skill enables us to judge angles on the dial and estimate the time to the nearest minute, an accuracy which is quite satisfactory for most purposes. When wanting a rough idea of the time, a glance will suffice. Yet another advantage is the way we use angles on the face to estimate elapsed time, for example if a train is to leave at twenty minutes to the hour, a quick look will tell if we have to hurry. In contrast, reading a digital face requires the same degree of concentration whatever accuracy is required and estimates of elapsed times require computation.

When resetting the time we develop a concept of a geared linkage between the knob and the fingers. Turn one way for forwards, the other for back. The controls on the digital watch bear no relation to these ideas. One cannot, for example, move the numbers *backwards*. What has happened is that what is good for the chip designers is not good for the user. Old watches used to operate in more or less the same way; now one needs a book of instructions, a magnifying glass, fine fingers and about 20 minutes to change to summer time. When the alarm goes off during a funeral one is left pressing knobs at random while trying to pretend the sound is coming from somewhere else.

Box 6.2 Failings of digital watches

analysis of function. Take the everyday example of the digital watch, Box 6.2. The digital watch promised high accuracy and reliability at very low cost. Yet it is flawed. It has been packaged in many ways to incorporate radios, games, alarms and chimes. Yet defects occur at the interface with users.

150

Controls are another area where ergonomists have studied difficulties. The conventional gate on the gearbox of a vehicle allows drivers to change without looking down. (For the same reason, head-up displays in military aircraft present key information to the pilot by reflection off the windscreen.) Drivers are engaged in the general task of process control. In such cases, careful attention to the form and location of control levers can assist in promoting safe and accurate operations. This applies whether the process is driving a vehicle, a machine tool or a piece of domestic equipment. For instance, we are used to gas and water valves opening anti-clockwise whereas electric rheostats (such as volume controls on a radio) turn clockwise. What happens on one of those domestic cookers that has both gas and electric rings? Errors in such cases are irritating rather than serious and can be prevented with both interlocks and warnings.

The control problem becomes more acute as machines, equipment and even whole plants become larger and more complex. This is clearly illustrated in the case of the near disaster at the nuclear power plant at Three Mile Island, Harrisburg, Pennsylvania.

The emergency started on 28 March 1979 around a misunderstanding over the condition of a valve in the cooling system. The reactor ran out of control for some hours. This resulted in the emission of radioactive material into the surrounding area. Although they were, by all accounts, competent, the operators were unable to cope with the sequence of events. The control systems continued to operate in as far as the controllers were presented with information on the state of the plant. Yet the rate of delivery of this information and the design of some dials and gauges meant that the controllers were very quickly overloaded. They did not have time to appreciate one alarm before another went off. At one stage more than fifty alarms were sounding in the control suite at the same time. The controllers were capable of managing the plant under normal conditions yet, once these no longer applied, they were unable to manage a plant that was out of control.

2. Human abilities

We have seen how weaknesses of ergonomic design can at best lead to loss of efficiency and, at worst, threaten safety. Links between humans and machines need to take into account their characteristics. Humans and machines are radically different, not different versions of the same sort of information processor. Table 6.1 illustrates some differences in human and machine capability when it comes to information handling. For instance, the limitations of humans as *data sensors* have many implications for the operations manager. The sensory organs are more responsive to some kinds of information than others: they will detect some dangerous gases but not others; they do not notice dangerous radiation; sensitivity to sound waves is limited to frequencies up to about 20 kHz, declines with age and can easily be impaired. On the other hand, with training and experience, humans can discriminate among complex information such as assessing the quality of a beer. In spite of control automation, the brewer tastes the product at each stage before it is passed to the next.

Data processing by people is remarkably good in those areas for which the body has been 'designed', such as the processing of visual or aural signals to recognise a pattern, say a friend's face or voice. On the other hand, it is clear that machines

151

Table 6.1 Data processing of humans and machines

Data activity	Human capability	Machine capability
Data sensing		
– infrequent events	Can appreciate unlikely or low frequency events	Complexity limited by design
– sensitivity	Good under right conditions but limited range	Not so good, depends on design
– noise	Can sort out signals from noise	Poor
– incidental information	Able to collect incidental information	Depends on design
Data processing		
– pattern recognition	Good	Limited, but improving
– reliability	Good but limited by conditions	Very high
– computation	Poor	Unlimited
– channel capacity	All channels have slow rates of data transmission	Unlimited
– memory	Poor	Unlimited
Scope and vigilance		
– monitoring physical phenomena	Limited range, low accuracy	Very high range and accuracy
– time	Performance deteriorates	No deterioration

are better for computation and rapid storage and retrieval of large quantities of data. Machines are also being developed to pick out patterns from complex data. Statistical smoothing algorithms are a common example. Furthermore, machines generally score well on *scope and vigilance* criteria, whether it be the smoke detector or thickness gauge in a paper mill.

Vigilance refers to the capability of a person to perform a task over a long period. It is known that over long periods, people experience the feeling that their efficiency deteriorates and that they have to increase their efforts to maintain their performance. This problem is important to operations managers and their staff. Tasks such as driving, machine control, data entry, surveillance and so on are all subject to this *vigilance decrement*. Explanations vary from psychological to physiological.

Various proposals give a psychological basis for the decline in performance:

- *Arousal*
  A person's level of arousal has an impact upon their performance. In any task, there is an optimal level. If they are too active or too drowsy, they will not do so well. Since arousal itself varies with time then there will be a deterioration in achievement.

- *Inhibition*

  There is the possibility of a build up of resistance or inhibition within the nervous system. This may result from an event having occurred very frequently or not at all during the vigilance period. In either case, the person may find it difficult to react to the next occurrence.

- *Filtering*

  When carrying out difficult tasks or working in distractive environments, humans may develop the ability to filter out all but the information that they learn to be relevant to their role. The consequence may then be that they fail to detect rare signals or appreciate their significance.

Whatever the explanation, and none is complete, it is clear that tiredness, arousal and attention contribute to decline in performance. Jobs that are affected need to be carefully designed and attention should be paid not only to rest but also to the work environment. There should be sufficient stimulus to maintain arousal but not so much that excessive filtering has to take place.

Studies of the physiological factors in changing human performance over long periods have identified the so-called *bio-rhythms*, especially the *circadian rhythm*. A continuous daily cycle has been observed in measures such as body temperature and chemical concentrations such as cortisone levels. For instance, young people with normal sleep patterns show oral temperatures varying from 36.1 degrees in the early morning, through 36.6 degrees by 9 am up to a peak of 36.9 degrees by the mid-evening. It has also been shown that efficiency on continuous tasks is highest at peak body temperature. There are implications in this data for all work patterns, especially shift work. Where an employee works the same shift permanently, it is found that the circadian rhythm shifts after about a week to become entrained in the person's work cycle. Under rotating shifts, however, measures show that the rhythm retains the normal pattern.

Longer cycles in human performance have been detected and it has been suggested, for example, that pilots do not fly on certain days of the month. It is important, however, to keep the study of rhythms in perspective. While the physical measures may be well established, the resulting differences in performance may not be so clear and other social and psychological factors are likely to be much more important.

3. The work environment

The efficiency and safety of staff are affected by environmental factors, many of which are within the managers' control.

Lighting

Obviously, the level of illumination necessary for tasks involving detail, such as sewing or surgery, will be higher than for a warehouse where large objects are stored. In general, brighter lighting is required where the following apply:

- fine work – working with small objects and tools, reading fine scales accurately
- low colour or brightness contrast – including inspection or surveillance where special colour lighting can increase contrast
- high speed – care must be taken to avoid stroboscopic effects where moving objects can appear stationary

- high standards of accuracy, surface finish and cleanliness
- tasks are carried out over long periods.

Noise

Working areas always have some sound noise. High levels damage hearing, extended exposure to levels above 90 dB being regarded as dangerous although, depending on the nature of the sound, lower levels can be distracting. Table 6.2 illustrates some examples. Decibels are a logarithmic scale with zero as the quietest sound that can be heard; the second column gives the ratio of sound power compared with this notional minimum.

Physical demands

Mention has already been made of the design of work stations to minimise fatigue. Much work is carried out in the sitting position and efforts have been made to improve chairs for office and industrial use. When sitting on an ordinary office chair for example, most of the right angle between thighs and trunk is achieved by bending the hip joint. After 60° however, unless we are very supple, further flexing is resisted by tension in the hamstrings. The final 30°, therefore is taken up by rotation of the pelvis. This in turn makes us lose the concave curve in the spine, the lordosis, which is normal in the standing position, see Figure 6.3. To sit up straight, then, requires effort to overcome the hamstrings whose tension comes from their being stretched beyond their relaxed length. The conventional design solution to this problem includes a back support that slopes backwards and is adjustable and shaped to the desired profile of the spine[2]. More radically, other designs have the seat sloping forward[3]. To prevent sliding, however, the feet have to exert a backward force. This is not helpful if the chair is on castors! Some designs incorporate a kneeler to resolve this problem.

This example of chair design is but one of many issues facing the designer of tools and equipment. Humans developed tools as extensions to their own bodies, the direct contact and personal source of power ensuring human-machine integration. The modern machine tool, with its own separate power sources and indirect contact through programmes, is a much more complex problem. The information transfer between the two is the most significant design issue.

Table 6.2 Decibel levels with examples

Decibels ratio	Power	Typical examples
30	10^3	Speech in studio
40	10^4	Suburbs at night
50	10^5	Average house
60	10^6	Quiet office
70	10^7	Near main road; train at 30m; vacuum cleaner at 3m
80	10^8	Inside box van at cruising speed; pneumatic drill at 20m
90	10^9	Ship's engine room; train at 6m; some discotheques
100	10^{10}	Near noisy industrial plant; operating pneumatic hammer
110	10^{11}	Very noisy plant; operating heavy riveting equipment
120	10^{12}	Deck of aircraft carrier at take-off

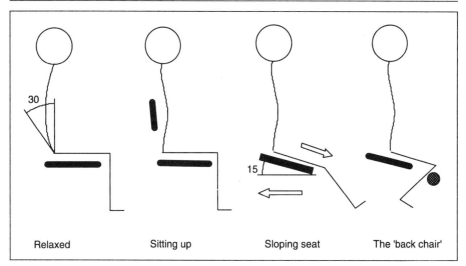

Figure 6.3 Sitting positions to maintain lordosis

4. Health and safety at work

Many items discussed so far in this chapter have an impact on the health of staff and the safety of work place operations. On both ethical and legal grounds, the safety of all people affected by an organisation's operations must be of major concern to the manager. In the countries of the European Union, national legislation has been supplemented by a series of EU directives aimed at harmonising standards and practices. Some of these directives are general while others, such as goods vehicle drivers' hours or standards for the shoring of trenches, are specific to certain industries and practices. Safety, in the way that it has an impact on costs, has economic implications. European governments are anxious to avoid the possibility of some countries becoming havens for cheap and unsafe industrial processes.

In the United Kingdom, the Health and Safety at Work Act 1974 provides the basic framework. In setting basic principles, it imposes the following duties on those involved:

- Every employer should ensure the health and safety at work for all employees.
- Every employer and self-employed person must conduct business in such a way as not to expose third parties to risks for their health and safety.
- Every employee must, at work, take reasonable care for his or her own safety and that of others and must cooperate with the employer on matters related to safety.

Standards are not fixed since the Act frequently uses the phrase 'as is reasonably practicable' to qualify its provisions. With innovation in safe procedures and new awareness of hazards, what may be acceptable and practicable in one era may be seen as hazardous and unacceptable in another. For example, since the Act was passed, more attention has been paid to the dangers of asbestos, radioactivity, noise, effluent and passive smoking.

In giving expression to the above general principles, the following duties are specified for employers:

- To produce a statement of general safety policy and how it is to be implemented and to distribute it to all employees.

- Ensure that work places and their plant and processes are safe and do not have health risks.
- Ensure that all materials are transported, stored, handled and used in a safe manner.
- Provide safe means of entry, exit and escape from all premises and work areas.
- Instruct, supervise and train all employees in good health and safety practices in the work place.
- Consult with, according to published codes of practice, employees' representatives on all matters related to health and safety; set up safety committees if asked by the representatives.
- Ensure that persons who are not employed are given information on safety and hazards both in relation to their working within the premises and their use of equipment and materials.

To give force to its intentions, the Act defined for the first time several criminal offences that would arise from failure to discharge duties, breach of specific sections or non-compliance with the requirements of an inspector working under the Act. Personal responsibility for safety was thus imposed on the directors and senior managers of companies and other organisations.

5. Accidents

Both employers and employees do not want accidents to occur for they know that they can result in personal suffering as well as impose costs. Accidents do occur, not only because there is no such thing as a perfectly safe design but also because people tend to place themselves in positions where some risk is being taken. They intuitively trade off the risk of the accident against the cost of reducing that risk. As the risk becomes smaller, further reductions become prohibitively expensive or inconvenient. The risk assessment made by individuals can be very poor. For example, although the UK has among the safest roads in the world, measured by accidents per distance travelled, this is in spite of some common bad driving practices - jumping red lights, tailgating and driving too fast in fog. In the work place, specific regulations and policies are required to prevent practices such as using grindstones without wearing goggles, entering certain areas without protective clothing and smoking near hazardous chemicals. If these did not exist, some staff would take the chance, thinking, 'It could never happen to me.'

Safety policies require an understanding of both events and their consequences. Take the example given in Box 6.3. One can see that the event of the brick falling arises from more than one cause. The brick is loose and the man trips. The outcomes of the event depend on yet further conditions. In the first case, the hazardous event occurs yet it is not noticed and it has no unfavourable effects. In the second case, the person knows of the hazardous practice but relies on personal vigilance to avoid any consequences. The third and fourth cases illustrate the use of safety equipment to eliminate negative effects of accidents.

An accident is *an unplanned, unwanted and uncontrolled event in a process involving people, objects or substances.* Accidents may result in injury to people, damage to objects and equipment and loss of materials and production output. While attention tends to be directed towards those major accidents with macabre results, there are many more incidents that are hazardous yet, for one reason or another, have no negative consequences. In the industrial setting these are equally worthy

---

Causes and consequences

A labourer is carrying a small stack of half a dozen bricks. The top brick is loose and, as the man trips slightly on a plank, it falls. There could be several outcomes of this event.

1 The man may be unaware that the brick is loose and not notice that it falls to the ground.
2 He may be aware that the brick is loose and is able to move his feet out of the way when it falls.
3 Whether aware of the looseness or not, the brick hits him on the toes with painful consequences.
4 The man is wearing safety boots which protect the toes when the brick falls.

Box 6.3 Accidents have causes and consequences

of investigation yet, generally, they go unreported. Riggs[4] quotes insurance company data to show that, for every 300 work accidents that result in no injury, there are 29 causing minor injuries and one resulting in major injury, see Box 6.4. This means that, for each major injury, there are 330 events whose recognition and investigation could lead to improved safety.

Non-injury accident Non-injury accident Non-injury accident Non-injury accident Non-injury accident Non-injury accident
Non-injury accident Non-injury accident Non-injury accident Non-injury accident Non-injury accident Non-injury accident
Non-injury accident Non-injury accident Non-injury accident Non-injury accident Non-injury accident Non-injury accident
Non-injury accident Non-injury accident Non-injury accident Non-injury accident Non-injury accident Non-injury accident
Non-injury accident Non-injury accident Non-injury accident Non-injury accident Non-injury accident Non-injury accident
Non-injury accident Non-injury accident Non-injury accident Non-injury accident Non-injury accident Non-injury accident
Non-injury accident Non-injury accident Non-injury accident Non-injury accident Non-injury accident Non-injury accident
Non-injury accident Non-injury accident Non-injury accident Non-injury accident Non-injury accident Non-injury accident
Non-injury accident Non-injury accident Non-injury accident Non-injury accident Non-injury accident Non-injury accident
Non-injury accident Non-injury accident Non-injury accident Non-injury accident Non-injury accident Non-injury accident
Non-injury accident Non-injury accident Non-injury accident Non-injury accident Non-injury accident Non-injury accident
Non-injury accident Non-injury accident Non-injury accident Non-injury accident Non-injury accident Non-injury accident
Non-injury accident Non-injury accident Non-injury accident Non-injury accident Non-injury accident Non-injury accident
Non-injury accident Non-injury accident Non-injury accident Non-injury accident Non-injury accident Non-injury accident
Non-injury accident Non-injury accident Non-injury accident Non-injury accident Non-injury accident Non-injury accident
Non-injury accident Non-injury accident Non-injury accident Non-injury accident Non-injury accident Non-injury accident
Non-injury accident Non-injury accident Non-injury accident Non-injury accident Non-injury accident Non-injury accident
Non-injury accident Non-injury accident Non-injury accident Non-injury accident Non-injury accident Non-injury accident
Non-injury accident Non-injury accident Non-injury accident Non-injury accident Non-injury accident Non-injury accident
Non-injury accident Non-injury accident Non-injury accident Non-injury accident Non-injury accident Non-injury accident
Non-injury accident Non-injury accident Non-injury accident Non-injury accident Non-injury accident Non-injury accident

Minor injury Minor injury Minor injury Minor injury Minor injury Minor injury Minor injury
Minor injury Minor injury Minor injury Minor injury Minor injury Minor injury
Minor injury Minor injury Minor injury Minor injury Minor injury
Minor injury Minor injury Minor injury Minor injury
Minor injury Minor injury Minor injury
Minor injury Minor injury
Minor injury
Minor injury

Major injury

Box 6.4 The background to major injury accidents

Multicausality is typical of accidents. There will be unsafe acts taking place in unsafe conditions. A complex combination of acts and conditions can lead to an accident. Unsafe acts stem from recklessness, anxiety, obduracy, distraction, ignorance and poor training, poor health and inability to learn. They take many forms including:

- Operating without authorisation or training
- Taking short cuts
- Overriding safety devices or rules
- Not using the correct equipment
- Not wearing appropriate clothing
- Horseplay.

Unsafe conditions originate in the design, layout and condition of the workplace and its equipment. The following are some examples:

- Floors, paths and walkways, stairs and ladders that are uneven, slippery, cluttered or lack guard rails; inadequate side and overhead clearances; blind corners.
- Unsuitable or unreliable equipment for processing, handling and storage of materials.
- Unclear controls on plant and machinery and ambiguous warnings and alarms.
- Poor ventilation, high noise levels and light flashes that can cause distraction and loss of vigilance.
- Fire risks; processes that create unguarded flames and sparks; poor insulation; unnecessary presence of inflammable materials; inadequate means of fire fighting and escape.
- Poor equipment maintenance and housekeeping.

6. Safety policies and programmes

The Health and Safety at Work Act requires that a safety policy be published and that there should be programmes of instruction and training to ensure its accomplishment. Typical company safety policies reiterate the general principles of the Act, expressing them in the company context. They should identify where the senior management responsibility lies and how managers and staff should work together through identified committees to identify and resolve problems.

A safety programme follows from the policy by applying it to each department or group of staff. It should set out how health and safety will be promoted, planned and controlled within the section. For example, Box 6.5 outlines a programme for fork-lift truck drivers in a despatch warehouse. Note that the safety problem is addressed through a process of continuous improvement. There is a legal requirement to record all accidents resulting in loss of work time but this department encourages the reporting of other hazards and incidents. These are the 'non-injury accidents' of Box 6.4. Improvements come from analysis of these events and a search for new ways of working which will reduce their incidence or their impact.

7. Work study

In addition to its application in the field of health and safety, the study of humans and their employment has great economic impact in the design and development of work systems. The purpose of work study is both to establish the best means of

Safety programme for fork-lift operations

Policy statement
1 All staff are responsible for their own, each others' and outsiders' safety.
2 The departmental safety committee, with representatives from all sections, is charged with monitoring and improving safety standards.

Operations
1 The company will, in the purchase of equipment, select only that which is known to have a good safety record. New equipment will not be used until staff are trained in its safe operation.
2 Equipment will be inspected, maintained and modified to keep it in safe running order and will never be used if it is unsafe.
3 New applicants will be tested for their ability to work safely. All staff will be fully trained in the use of equipment before they are expected to use it.

Reporting
1 All accidents resulting in personal injury must be recorded in the accident book.
2 All staff are requested to inform the safety representatives of potential hazards or incidents which do not cause injury. The representatives are to bring this information to the safety committee.

Investigation
1 The safety committee will consider all accident and hazard reports at its meetings and will arrange for investigation and analysis as required.
2 The safety committee may require that any procedure or method of working is immediately suspended. It may make recommendations to management on any matter related to health and safety in the work place.

Improvement
1 The safety committee may nominate individuals for rewards under the company safety scheme where they have demonstrated improved working in their own jobs or have made suggestions that have been successfully applied in other departments.

Box 6.5 Safety programme in a despatch department

carrying out tasks and then to set standards for, and measure, the times which jobs take. While the two aspects of work study, method study and work measurement, are here discussed sequentially, it should be understood that they are closely connected. Practitioners, often called *work study engineers* or *industrial engineers*, use time data when analysing methods or, when collecting time data, always have an eye on the question of whether the optimal methods are being used.

Wage systems frequently include some form of output bonus, based on achievement of standards set by work study. Sound costing systems use data based on staff or machine timings. These are but two examples of the ways operational systems benefit from having a reliable and respected analysis of their methods and times. Such data can have significant impact both within operations and between it and other elements of the organisation's value chain. The following list identifies some of these links:

Impact within operations
Better methods improve output, quality, wastage rates, reliability and safety. Standard times help the planning and control of plant and labour.

Inbound and outbound logistics
Batch sizes, time and place of deliveries and packaging systems all interact with operational processes.

Sales and marketing
Improved methods and reduced times lead to cost reductions and quality improvements. These in turn improve product competitiveness.

Service
Improvements through better working methods, whether service is part of the sale or is after-sales.

Procurement
Process improvements imply new or changed equipment but may lead to less use of raw materials.

Technology development
Designs of products and processes both determine, and are influenced by, the methods in use.

Human resource management
Equity in pay systems can be based on respected time standards. Planning for personnel requirements can be related to output plans through standards.

Firm infrastructure
Organisation structures and information systems have implications for work methods and can themselves be changed because of studies of working practices.

Since work study involves an external investigation of what employees do with their time, the industrial engineer is commonly seen as posing something of a threat. If the study is successful its result will be some change in the status quo, a change that some employees may not want. In the worst case, for example, a study ostensibly directed at method improvement may discover widespread inefficiency and the carrying out of unnecessary tasks. The threat is a carry over from the early emphasis on time studies where the 'time and motion man' was seen as an instrument for employers to increase the speed of output by driving the workers harder.

The industrial engineer has to be sensitive to these issues and carry out the function diplomatically. In particular, the following should be done:

- Communication with staff and managers as to the purpose and methods of the investigation.
- Ensuring that the contribution of every person is recognised.
- Avoidance of criticism of any person, or of their skills and practices.
- Sharing the results of the study with those affected.
- Maintenance of a professional approach including quality of work and presentation, discretion with personal information and fairness in assessment.

8. Method study

Method study, sometimes called methods analysis or process analysis, is concerned with the way a task is carried out, whether this be delivering a parcel or forging a piece of metal. The industrial engineer is not simply trying to drive down the cost of operations but may be asked to carry out an investigation because there are problems with product quality, service reliability, personnel safety and so on. The techniques used are applied to all types of organisational activity from shop floor manufacturing to information handling in the office.

Studies have three phases – data collection, analysis and synthesis, and presentation of results. Data collection is aided by specially developed charts used to record events and can later be used to consider and compare alternatives. Analysis involves questioning every part of the current process as a basis for synthesising new patterns. The aim is to eliminate, consolidate or resequence operations. To help with this critical process, industrial engineers use the investigatory, 5W+H, questions, see Box 6.6:

Who does the task? Why?
(Could another person be better or less costly?)
What is achieved? Why?
(Does it need to be done in whole or in part?)
Where is the task performed? Why?
(Could the task be done better or more cheaply elsewhere?)
When is the task done? Why?
(Could the task be done earlier or later or in a different part of the sequence?)
How is the task carried out? Why?
(Is there a better way?)

The charts enable the 5W+H questions to be investigated and alternatives, for example to sequences, readily compared. We shall look at these charts to illustrate the approach to, and applications of, method study.

Charts are especially useful in method study because of the complex and multifaceted nature of the information. Not only do they help in investigation but they also help in communication of results. In presenting 'before and after' designs in diagrammatic form, the practitioner can make a convincing case for the necessity and practicability of change.

9. Flow diagrams

Flow diagrams are often used to investigate the movement of objects or people around a workshop, office or other work space. They provide a means of examining processes that have a relatively long cycle and where the movements themselves form a large proportion of the time. A line is superimposed on the work place layout for each movement, the accumulation of lines showing the paths most commonly taken. The questioning process then concentrates on whether equipment could be moved to reduce the distance travelled, especially along the frequent paths. Other questions concern the elimination or combining or processes, as suggested by passing through the 5W+H sequence.

I keep six honest servingmen (They taught me all I knew);
Their names are What and Why and When and How and Where and Who

Rudyard Kipling, *The Elephant's Child*

Box 6.6 The 5W+H questions

161

Figure 6.4 shows the way a flow diagram can be set out during a study in a railway repair shop. In this section, laid out in a crowded corner of a large workshop, wheel sets were being turned in a lathe. Turning is used to restore worn pairs of wheels to true circularity and tyre profile. In the original plan, the wheel sets ready for turning were left on a track by an overhead travelling crane. The machinist pushed the wheels along the track to a small turntable set in the floor. This enabled them to be directed towards the lathe jaws. The wheels rolled into the lathe and, after adjustments by the operator, the lathe did the turning. After unloading, the operator pushed them to the turntable and thence to the output track. Because of irregular flow patterns, extra wheels had to be stored on the shop floor beside the lathe.

The operator's movements during the cycle of one wheel set are shown in Figure 6.5. Besides handling one set into and out of the lathe, the operator had to help the crane driver to place a reserve set in the input queue and move an extra set to the output. Furthermore, he had to push the output line along to make space for the set being turned. The major movements, however, can be seen as those between the loaded wheel set and the lathe controls and the turntable and its control box. The former resulted from the need of the operator to rotate loaded wheel sets to inspect their condition before the cutting took place. This was improved when better lighting and windows in the machine guards enabled most inspection to be carried out from the control position. The latter problem arose from the installation of the control box away from the turntable for safety reasons. It was necessary to keep the floor uncluttered. Again, however, some improvement followed the moving of the box round to the front of the lathe.

Many variants of flow diagram are used in projects from kitchen design to planning new roads. In one form, a pin is placed at each node; in the case of a kitchen these would be the sink, refrigerator, cooker, larder, table, door and so on. A thread is then run from pin to pin to represent the travel of the person carrying out whatever task is being studied. This accounts for the diagrams being often called *string diagrams*. The string and pin technology has largely been replaced by computer drawings. Possibilities of working in three dimensions, such as when studying traffic within a department store, or with more than one type of movement, such as people and goods, should also be noted.

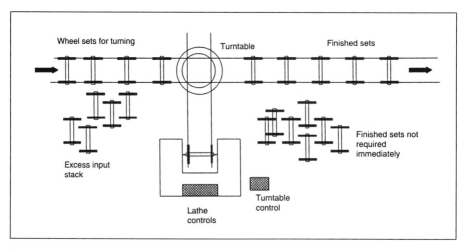

Figure 6.4 Layout of wheel turning section

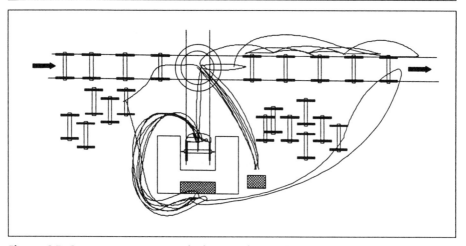

Figure 6.5 Operator movement during turning cycle

10. Process charts

While flow charts focus on transport, process charts look at all the activities that go to make up a process. They separate activities into five categories, each with its own symbol as shown in Figure 6.6. This separation encourages the analyst to ask the 5W+H questions about the different types of activity. Broadly speaking, operations involve working on the product while the others, especially transport, delay and storage, can be combined or eliminated without loss. Charts are often printed with the symbols for convenience of use. It is also possible to record distances travelled and times taken for the various activities.

Figure 6.7 gives an example from a study of office work. It depicts the process for staff to order printing through the busy administrative office. The chart, which has had its headers removed for reasons of space, enables the analyst to quickly set out the steps of the process and record distance moved and time taken.

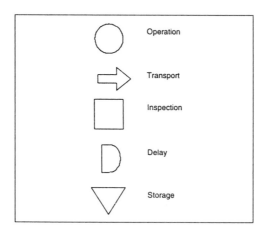

Figure 6.6 Symbols used in process charts

Print requests: current method

mtrs	secs	symbol	Operation description	Comments
	90		Fill out printing request	Combine?
50+			Take to clerk's in basket	
			Await clerk's attention	
	30		Copy details to 3-part requisition	Eliminate?
	20		Note details in progress book	Necessary?
30			Take to supervisor's desk for authorisation	
			Await supervisor's attention	
	10		Supervisor checks and signs	Why?
30			Pass to clerk's desk	
	20		Add date and time to forms	Sequence?
	10		Detach bottom two copies	
	10		Place requisition in internal mail	
	10		Send second copy to finance	
	40		Third copy to file	File and book?
	15		Note date and time in book	Sequence?

Figure 6.7 Process chart for print ordering

In this chart, there is space for comments that arise from the 5W+H questions. The case illustrates the way processes often develop for no apparent reason.

At one time, staff had been issued with three part forms but, later, there was a shortage of supply. The office conserved its stocks by issuing single sheets to staff which then had to be copied. During another budgetary crisis, the office supervisor was required to check whether requests were necessary and if some could be delayed or cut in quantity. This problem had long since passed and the supervisor never did anything but initial a pile of forms every day.

11. Multiple activity charts

When the area of interest is the combination of two or more persons and machines, multiple activity charts are used to record how their work interacts. For example, one of the entities may be idle for considerable periods while the other carries out its tasks. A person may be employed to load, adjust and unload a machine, standing idle while the machine is operating. If these periods are sufficiently long, one person could manage more than one machine. In cotton spinning it has long been the practice to operate in this way, improvements to fibre quality, machine control and the working environment enabling one person to cover more and more spinning heads. The optimal number of heads is decided by comparing the costs of extra staff against the loss of output when threads break and heads are idle waiting for attention.

To illustrate the multiple activity chart, we can return to the wheel profiling example of Figures 6.4 and 6.5. To increase throughput, it was proposed that the machine operator be provided with an assistant. As the string diagram of Figure

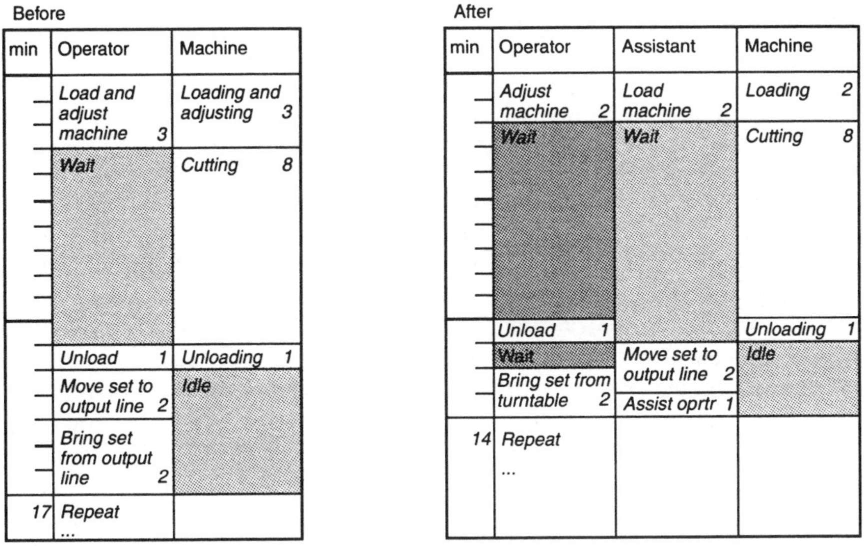

Before

min	Operator	Machine
	Load and adjust machine 3	Loading and adjusting 3
	Wait	Cutting 8
	Unload 1	Unloading 1
	Move set to output line 2	Idle
	Bring set from output line 2	
17	Repeat ...	

After

min	Operator	Assistant	Machine
	Adjust machine 2	Load machine 2	Loading 2
	Wait	Wait	Cutting 8
	Unload 1		Unloading 1
	Wait	Move set to output line 2	Idle
	Bring set from turntable 2	Assist oprtr 1	
14	Repeat ...		

Figure 6.8 Multiple activity charts for wheel profiling task

6.5 showed, the operator's walking movements during loading and unloading seemed to waste valuable time. Figure 6.8 summarises, on the left, the activities of the operator and the machine during a typical 17-minute cycle. (For simplicity, extra movements made by the operator such as housekeeping or working with the crane are left out.) The chart is arranged in a standard form with a time scale running down the page and a column for each element in the investigation.

The right-hand side of Figure 6.8 shows the effect of introducing an assistant. There are two reasons for the reduced cycle time of 14 minutes. First, by working together, the crew can cut the loading and adjusting time. Secondly, each person can perform some tasks in parallel; one takes away a finished item while the other brings a new one forward. These effects are common, some tasks are speeded up while others are done in parallel.

The awkward layout of the loading and unloading paths in this case meant that movements could not be made during the machine cutting time. Therefore the crew were idle for more than half the cycle. (Newer models of the lathe loaded and unloaded from different sides of the machine.) Despite this difficulty, management recognised that, when there was pressure to increase throughput, it was worth reducing the cycle time to 14 minutes and therefore increase output from some 26 to 32 sets per shift.

12. Motion study

Motion study refers to analysis in greater magnification than the ones presented in previous sections. Often using high-speed cameras to record action, the studies examine operations that are frequently repeated and have cycle times of, say, two minutes or less. The detailed analysis is justified because shaving a few seconds here and there can produce significant cost savings. Motion charts are adaptations of multiple activity charts using either the same symbols or a set developed specially for this purpose:

Symbol	Name	Movement
G	Get	Reaching for and taking hold of an object
P	Place	Moving an object to a target position
U	Use	Using an instrument or tool to achieve a purpose
A	Assemble	Joining two objects under control
H	Hold	Supporting with one hand while the other performs a task

These *get and place* motions are used to record arm and hand movements, for example for staff working at a desk assembling equipment or doing office work. Study of motion in even smaller cycles, *microscopic analysis*, uses a further symbol set detailing hand and finger activity.

Box 6.7 shows an example of a get and place analysis of an administrative task. In opening and checking an application form, the person has to ensure that details have been completed correctly. In the light of the checks, the form is routed to other sections. The 5W+H questions can be asked of this process. For example, the pen is held in the right hand all the time while movement tasks are carried out by the left. Is it really necessary to initial the form at every stage? Could the form be redesigned so that pages do not have to be turned over and back? Are the in-stack and out-boxes positioned optimally? Apart from these questions of detail, it could also be asked whether the task is necessary at all. In other words, it is often worth investigating the wider system before becoming involved in analysing the components that it comprises.

Review credit application before data entry: present method using form C29.

Operator seated at desk with stack of forms in front and four boxes for output to either side.

Left hand				Right hand
Take form from stack	G	H	Hold pen
Move to centre of desk	P	H	
Open at page 2	G	H	
Check completion of personal details	H	H	
	H	U	Tick any deficiencies and initial
Open at page 3	G	H	
Check if Coverplan required	H	H	
	H	U	Initial if OK for Coverplan
Open at page 4	G	H	
Check if additional card required	H	H	
	H	U	Initial if details given correctly
Turn to page 1	G	H	
	H	U	Fill in routing details
Place in appropriate box	P	H	

Box 6.7 Two-handed activity chart

13. Work measurement

Work measurement or time study is often thought of as carried out by the time-and-motion man armed with stop watch and clip board. It is widely practised in companies although much more among western companies than among Japanese. One survey found formal work measurement in some three-quarters of western firms and only one quarter of Japanese[5].

Work measurement is indeed one method that can be used for setting standards but it is only applicable to those jobs that can be observed: they must be current and regular so that the staff are familiar with what the task entails. In total, we can identify four ways to set time standards:

- *Historical data*

For many employees and supervisors, experience will tell how long tasks are likely to take or how much they are likely to cost. The data may be available from time sheets or it could be embedded in custom and practice. The small jobbing builder, for instance, will often calculate a job cost by rule of thumb, working out the cost of materials and then adding the same again for labour. The disadvantages of historical data are threefold: there is no allowance for process change or method improvement; there is usually no record of whether the previous work was carried out at a slow or fast pace; in any case, these and any unusual factors become the subject of bargaining between the manager and staff. We should note, on the other hand, that historical data is cheap to obtain and is valuable when rough estimates of times are all that are needed.

- *Time studies*

The most commonly used method, time studies use a stop watch to measure activities. The observer will focus on tasks that make up the essence of the job and will ignore irregular elements and unnecessary movements that may result from abnormal conditions, inexperience of the worker or a deliberate ploy to extend the standard time. As will be seen in section 13, time data relies on the experience of the industrial engineer to give a rating for the tempo at which work is being performed.

- *Synthetic times*

Many processes are made up of common elements that occur repeatedly in the work place. If a task can be analysed into these elements, and their normal times are already known, then they can be put together to estimate the normal time for the whole process. This approach has three advantages over the use of the stop watch. First, the assessment can be made ahead of the task being done. Alternative approaches can be studied and the benefits of investment in more plant and equipment appraised. Secondly, the cost of setting the new time standards is much lower than making the necessary number of stop watch observations. Thirdly, the elemental times have been established and checked over many hundreds of observations thus avoiding disputes over their accuracy. Section 14 illustrates how the approach is used.

- *Work sampling*

Rather than measure the duration of separate task cycles, work sampling is based on random observations of workers' activities during the whole period when they are engaged on the assigned tasks. Not only does the method enable the setting of time standards, but it measures delays between cycles, whether these result from workers resting or are caused by interruptions in the flow of production. The method is outlined in section 15.

14. Time studies

Although the stop watch may be used to measure the time taken to complete an operation, this is just the first stage of establishing the standard time for the operation. The practitioner must make allowances for two factors, namely variations in the pace of different workers and the need to allow for rest.

Stop watch times

The observer decides what tasks are going to be measured, whether it be an overall assessment of an operation taking several minutes or its individual elements that may only occupy seconds. Having taken sufficient observations, the *average cycle time* is calculated as the mean value. The number of observations required depends on their variability and can only be strictly established after the observations have taken place. The statistical analysis of this variation need not concern us here, it is sufficient to note that between ten and twenty measures are adequate for operations lasting about five minutes.

Normal times

The normal time for an operation is the time that would be taken by an operator working at a normal pace with normal skill. (It is said to be equivalent to someone walking at three miles per hour – a task that could be sustained throughout the day given reasonable rest breaks.) The observer must, while making the timings, make an assessment of the worker's pace as a proportion of the norm. The rating is difficult. Although there are benchmarks and trainees have access to special films showing work carried out at different ratings, the assessment is subjective. In spite of these difficulties, the step is necessary to discover the normal time. This is found as follows:

$$\text{Normal time} = \text{Average cycle time} \times \text{Rating factor}$$

Standard times

The final stage is to make an allowance for the fact that an employee cannot sustain the same tempo throughout the working day. There may be frequent interruptions in the work flow or many problems in the task requiring reference to instructions or the supervisor. There are also personal needs, including to wash and rest. The standard time is calculated as follows:

$$\text{Standard time} = \text{Normal time} \times (1 + \text{Allowance factor})$$

In a workshop with good conditions, the basic allowance for personal needs and rest will be a minimum of 5%, equivalent to some 24 minutes per 8-hour shift. Extra fatigue caused by working in awkward positions, the need to use physical force, bad light, high noise or poor environmental conditions is recognised by factors in the range 5 to 10%. Other elements that may be recognised are close mental attention, mental effort and monotony. These each have factors up to 5%. In heavy processing industries such as smelting, allowances for production workers will be around 35% while in machine shops, a total of 15 to 20% is typical.

In one time study, the industrial engineer took 15 observations and found the average cycle time to be 3.5 minutes. The worker's pace was rated at 85% of normal. The job required some close attention and took place in a workshop where there was intermittent high noise. Each of these merited an allowance of 2% beyond the basic.

Average cycle time = 3.5 minutes

Normal time = 3.5 × 0.85 or 2.98 minutes

Standard time = 2.98 × (1 + 0.09 + 0.02 + 0.02) or 3.4 minutes

Time measurement seems, on the face of it, to be a sensible and rational approach to the question of establishing standards. Yet the sequence of steps needed to set the standards contains several pitfalls that we can summarise:

- Measurement cannot be done before the job starts and may be done while staff are still learning the job.
- Rating is a difficult task requiring trained specialists. Even so, Das et al[6] have shown how operator bias and situational factors can combine to cause wide variations in assessments. Brisley and Fielder[7] demonstrated how, in a test, less than half of the ratings were within ten per cent of their true value.
- The cycle time is based on observations that may vary widely and be subject to statistical error.
- Allowances may be controversial. Three issues arise: the same task may have a different standard time in different departments; an employee's work may be subject to frequent delays in the supply of components; fatigue is very difficult to assess.

No measurement system can eliminate all these pitfalls, especially the last that takes a subjective view of environment, delays and fatigue. Equitable standards are especially important where firms use them as a basis for incentive payments, see **19**. Many organisations have arbitration procedures to resolve disputes in this area.

15. Synthetic times

Similar movements and tasks are repeated many times in any operational department. Therefore, the data from time studies can provide a base for estimating times for new operations that are commonly reorganised or developed from those carried out in the past. While the use of these synthetic times is both quicker and cheaper than relying on the stop watch, there is a price to pay in terms of establishing the data bank in the first place. Indeed, the cost for any firm to create a comprehensive data base would be prohibitive.

Firms can, then, take two approaches. First, they can build up a data base incrementally. This is valuable if the operations carried out do not vary much from year to year and the firm is satisfied with rough estimates. Painting and decorating businesses, for example, build up tables that give times per square or linear metre for applying different surface finishes to walls and ceilings. Other tables list correction factors to allow for: the quality of the surface being covered; the standard of finish required; the size and complexity of the surfaces; the height at which work is to be carried out; the working environment; and so on. Such data is vital to estimators and planners. In a situation where operations are much more regular and repetitive, greater attention to the quality of the data is needed and the industrial engineer will be concerned with measures of the micro-elements of work, as illustrated in Box 6.7. Fortunately, such data is commercially available.

Predetermined motion time standards (PMTS) have been established for the work elements, there being about 20 different basic motions. A scheme was originally developed by Frank and Lilian Gilbreth who coined the term *therblig* from their surname to label elements such as grasp, position, reach and assemble. The most commonly used system today is Methods-Time Measurement[8] (MTM) which has developed from work carried out and published in the 1940s[9]. The scope of the basic system of MTM is widespread and there are variants that have been developed for particular classes of operation such as small assembly or clerical work.

MTM-1, the basic system, is highly detailed and needs more than two hours to analyse one minute's worth of work. MTM-2 is higher level data in which the smaller elements are grouped into commonly used composite actions. For example:

Reach + Grasp + Move + Position + Release → Get

This simplification is at the expense of accuracy but has proved to be useful in analysing tasks with cycles greater than one minute or so. Even higher-level data, MTM-X, has been developed to further speed up analysis. Such data can be set out on a small card and is handy for quick analyses by a trained person. Table 6.3 sets out the MTM-X basic actions with their corresponding times. Each unit is 0.00001 hr, which is 0.036 sec. Hence bending down is 1.04 seconds while rising is 1.15. The approximation in the data is evident in the way times for Get and Put are given just for near, far and variable distances whereas MTM-1 tables give data for the Reach movement for each 25 mm of distance.

16. Work sampling

Work sampling is a technique for analysing activities by observation but without the need for a stop watch. It is useful for the investigation of certain types of ques-

Table 6.3 Outline of MTM-X normal times

Distance → Work element ↓	Near: less than 150 mm	Far: more than 150 mm	Variable distance
Get (easy)	8	16	13
Get (difficult)	17	25	20
Put (easy)	5	14	9
Put (difficult)	19	28	22

Regrasp	6
Handle weight	5
Apply pressure	14
Eye action	5
Step	18
Bend down	29
Arise from bend	32

tion. For example, if several random observations are made of a machine during an 8-hour shift and on half these occasions the machine is not running, then it can be concluded that the machine utilisation was approximately 50%. Because the conclusion is based on sampling, it is subject to statistical variation and so will only be accurate within certain confidence limits. We will not look into the statistics here. We can note, however, that in the case given, 100 observations would be required to obtain an estimate that was accurate within 10% on more than 95% of occasions. The number of required observations increases when the observer is trying to classify activity into more categories, say working, changing tools, waiting for material and idle.

If work sampling is to be used to set time standards it should be recognised that it is an indirect method of obtaining cycle times. Observers do not have to use the stop watch but they still have to assess the performance rating. When it comes to such detailed analysis, work sampling has little advantage over direct measurement.

Work sampling can be used to evaluate other controls and allowances:

Allocation of wage costs at the research centre of British Gas is based on weekly time sheets. Employees may be engaged on several projects during a week so they are required to keep records of the hours they spend on each. This enables charges to be made to various client departments and is typical of cost analysis of such non-routine activities. Employees will typically fill the sheets in several days late and, naturally, will ensure that the total hours shown will match those given in their employment contracts! Work sampling is a way of checking the general accuracy of the time sheets.

In the Midas exhaust fitting centre, work sampling was used to evaluate the effect of operating a 'quick-fit' service on both labour and machine utilisation. The no-reservation operation gave advantages in the market place at the expense of having staff and lifts idle for some of the day. Idle time was difficult to evaluate because, as with the previous example, staff were reluctant to record that they were doing nothing! The study required a thousand observations over twenty-five working days. Each, however, was simple to make and record.

17. Productivity

Productivity is of great interest to the operations manager and, of course, to all those who have a stake in the success of a country's organisations. Increases in productivity underpin increases in the standard of living. They represent improvements in the conversion of economic inputs, or resources, into outputs. Productivity is the measure of units produced compared with units used in their supply:

$$\text{Productivity} = \frac{\text{Units produced}}{\text{Units of input used}}$$

Note that productivity measures are not to be confined to assessment of labour efficiency. We also speak of the productivity of capital and other resources, although terms such as efficiency and yield are often used for these. The following examples are often seen:

- *Labour*
  Coal mining: tonnes per man-shift
  Car manufacture: vehicles per man-shift

Transport: passenger-km per employee
Retailing: sales per employee
Education: pupil - teacher ratio

- *Capital*
Agriculture: yield per hectare
Paper mill: output per machine hour
Transport: passengers per vehicle km
Hotels: room occupancy
Theatres: seat occupancy

- *Other resources*
Electricity generation: kWh per tonne of fuel
Stocks: inventory turnover

While many measures appear precise, they are fraught with problems and can only be used as rules of thumb for rough comparisons. Comparisons are often made between productivity rates in key industries in different countries, for example car manufacture. Yet to compare the numbers produced per shift is only valid if the cars are similar in work content and the manufacturers have the same degree of vertical integration. Even then one should not draw the conclusion that higher outputs per shift are superior. Each manufacturer has to balance the mix of inputs according to circumstances. Where wages are high, it may be better to spend more on automation; when they are low, they may employ more labour.

This discussion illustrates both the advantages and disadvantages of using *single factor productivity measures*. On the one hand, single measures of the use of key resources are valuable as rules of thumb for operations managers. For instance, when I ran a finishing department, I knew the major constraint on output, or *bottleneck* (see **12.6**). This was the spray painting line. Consequently we kept a log of line throughput (measured in square metres per running hour) and a group met regularly to review problems. The argument against single indices is that they encourage *measurementship*, the practice of managers to focus on one or a few factors at the expense of others. This can make their performance look good, at least in the short term. There may be too much emphasis on a few factors while managers lose sight of the overall reason for being in business. For example, in retailing, data on sales per metre of shelf or stock turnover can be improved if prices are drastically cut. Senior managers are particularly sensitive about the latter ratio as it is available to outside observers through the published accounts.

Multiple factor productivity measures address these problems by incorporating more outputs and inputs into the productivity equation. In the ultimate, this assembles all outputs and inputs into a single equation:

$$\text{Total productivity} = \frac{\text{Output}}{\text{Cost of capital, labour, and purchased goods and services}}$$

This ratio gains because it provides a more rational basis for analysing change. It has two disadvantages: the breadth of its coverage means that it is unsuitable for use as a regular guide to the individual operations manager and it has now become a cost function, the inverse of cost per unit of output, commonly called *unit cost*.

Japanese managers are committed to productivity that they tend to define in broad terms to include among the outputs quantity, quality and service. For each operation, broad assessments of productivity indices are made. The purpose of measurement is to find areas for improvement and ways to make the change. Detailed measurements are less common than in the West. Japan has about one twentieth of the number of qualified accountants in the United Kingdom[10].

The terms productivity and efficiency are often used interchangeably. Yet there is a difference in that efficiency is often measured as a percentage while productivity is often assessed with different variables as in the above list. We shall see in the next section how wage systems often pay bonuses based on productivity. In this case, outputs (standard hours) and inputs (actual hours) use the same units and therefore labour efficiency and labour productivity are used to mean the same thing.

18. Payment systems

Work measurement almost inevitably leads on to the question of payments. Indeed, one main reason for the introduction of formal work measurement systems is that employers seek to rationalise incentive payment systems that have grown up from bargains between supervisors and staff, see Box 6.8.

We discussed in Chapter 5 the question of whether wage incentives increase motivation. Whether they have a direct effect depends on the individual and on circumstances but it is important that, whatever system of payment is in operation, it must be clearly understood and be seen to be fair. It is common, therefore, to base wage incentive plans on measured work on the grounds that the standard hours form a rational basis for the payments. Measurement is, however, only the first step in the setting up of an effective payment scheme. The following need to be put into place:

In my first job as a foreman I had to authorise bonus payments for all the staff in the workshop. These payments, amounting to some 20% of earnings, were based on amounts to be paid for each job, such as overhauling a valve or brake cylinder, or making and fitting a run of pipe work. Each job had an agreed price. When a new job came into the shop, a new price was set by bargaining between one of the foremen and the respective charge hand. The job price incorporated the expected wage levels to be achieved at the time. Consequently, prices represented a mix of bargains made over a period of twenty years or more. The bonus for a job depended more on when its price was set than any other factor.

The foremen and charge hands used to connive at ameliorating the worst effects of this system. Documentation was slow and manual. In a good week, charge hands did not put in all the job tickets for bonus payments. Such action might have caused an investigation as the management became aware of high bonus levels. They kept a float of tickets 'in the back of the book' for the weeks when the job mix was not so favourable. Bonus levels were a little higher just before Christmas.

Box 6.8 The back of the book

- *A payment plan*

The plan should relate to management's objectives in terms of output. There should be consistency of treatment between individuals, groups and departments. The work should be assessed by a rational process.

- *Scheme operations*

The scheme should be installed and maintained by trained personnel whose competence at assessing work should be underpinned by effective training. The measurement of actual work carried out should be through a good administrative system that calculates bonuses accurately. Special payments for non-standard work should be strictly limited.

- *Quality*

Checks should be made on the quality of work output to ensure that any increased output is not at the expense of slipshod work.

- *Agreement*

All aspects need to be agreed by those involved. In particular, there should be a process of resolving disputes and difficulties, possibly through arbitration.

19. Payment plans

There are many payment plans, each being adapted to suit local circumstances. They frequently compare productivity with a standard performance. Productivity is calculated as follows:

$$\text{Productivity} = \frac{\text{Standard hours produced}}{\text{Actual hours taken}}$$

The standard performance is 100% and this is often used to trigger bonus payments. We shall review some of the main payment plans.

Piece rate

The most straightforward incentive plan is the piece rate system under which the only payment is for each unit of output. If based on measured work, each job has a standard time, usually measured in hours. A rate per hour is established for the period in question and an employee's earnings are simply:

Earnings = Payment rate per standard hour × Output in standard hours

Many types of contract labour, out-workers and casual workers are paid by this method. It enables the employer, for example a farmer employing fruit pickers, to know costs in advance and it can be highly motivating. On the other hand, piece rates are not popular among many permanent employees whose earnings would be very sensitive to circumstances beyond their control. See Figure 6.9, graph 1.

Piece rate with guarantee

To overcome this risk of loss of earnings, the guarantee is often brought in to set a minimum rate of pay for work below an agreed level, say standard performance, graph 2. The effect of this is as follows. Below 100% performance, there is no bonus. Performance above 100% is paid as if it were piecework. Modifications of this approach relate to the level at which incentive payments come into play, see graph 3. The point of this is to include in the scheme those who perform at rates a little below standard. Those who work above standard are not affected.

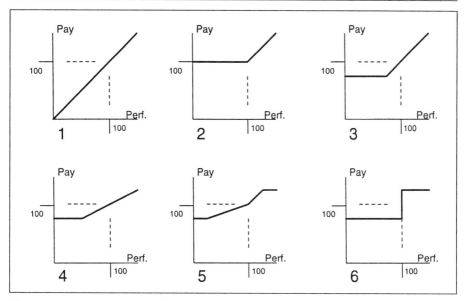

Figure 6.9 Some patterns of productivity payment

Gain sharing incentive

Gain sharing, or profit sharing, plans reward output over standard performance but at a bonus rate that is lower than the average rate per standard hour, see graph 4. The benefits of output above standard are thus shared with management. This reduced proportionality is one example of a *regressive* scheme that is designed to give some reward for extra output but not allow bonus levels to soar out of control. Outputs apparently very much higher than standard would be more likely to result from defective work measurements than workers' extra efforts. Sometimes, there is a *limit on bonus earnings* that sets a ceiling on the effect of loose times. In other cases, *staged incentive rates* may apply, with the rate of payment varying depending on performance. Graph 5 shows a scheme that combines two *progressive* steps with a ceiling.

Step incentive

A single bonus is paid for performance that reaches the standard as in graph 6. There are no other bonuses.

The design of the payment system should be matched to circumstances. In some cases, where there is plenty of work, where standards are established and where the pace is decided by the employees, simple systems with guarantees may be the most effective. Elsewhere, work may involve the interaction of many different staff and skills and it may be paramount to operate at an even, standard pace rather than encourage some to race ahead. In such cases, a single payment for standard performance will be more appropriate.

Organisations must also decide whether to tailor payment plans to individual performance or to assess output by work group or department. Again, the answer to this question depends on circumstances. Group incentives recognise that many staff are expected to work in teams and they are generally less divisive than individual incentives. On the other hand, the larger the group the less direct relationship there will be between the efforts of any person and his or her bonus, especially if the pace of activity is determined by machines. It may be, therefore, that where machine-paced work is carried out by groups, the notion of a productivity bonus should be dropped.

20. Job evaluation

The rate of pay for jobs in many organisations may be determined systematically by the personnel function. Otherwise, it may be the result of a long history of bargains and adjustments in response to changing individuals, roles and environment. It is widely accepted that some jobs have higher pay than others, tradition being that skilled workers are paid more than so-called semi-skilled and so on. Box 6.9 gives an example of a traditional system in place at Crewe in the 1960s.

Job evaluation schemes attempt to rationalise the widely held notion that payments should be higher for more difficult and responsible jobs held by people who are more skilful and scarce. It is used to set both the base rates in incentive payments schemes and the fixed rates where there are no output bonuses. Job evaluation tries to ensure that the relationships between the rates paid for different jobs is seen to be fair. It is, therefore, often the case that the basic lists are made by a small job evaluation committee consisting of both managers and staff representatives. The committee both creates the lists and arbitrates in any review.

Grade	Rate
Patternmaker	83/6
Toolmaker	
Blacksmith	78/6
Brass Fitter	
Boiler Maker	
Coach Body Maker	
Coach Finisher	
Electrician	
Fitter	
French Polisher	
Painter Class I	
Plater	
Plumber	
Sheet Metal Worker	
Turner	
Foundry Man	75/6
Machinist	

Box 6.9 Grades at Crewe Locomotive Works, 1960

The simplest method of evaluation is *job ranking*. It is based on the notions of ranking, key jobs and interpolation. Taking first the general criterion of benefit to the company, the approach lists all jobs in rank order. Then, the rates for certain key jobs, spread out through the list, are decided by negotiation. This process may consider the rates paid elsewhere and is not part of the evaluation committee's function. Finally, the rates for the rest of the jobs are filled in between the key jobs.

Job ranking is difficult in large organisations or where the committee is unfamiliar with the requirements for all the jobs. The *job classification* method improves upon ranking by setting out a list of bands or classes into which all jobs are to be fitted. For guidance, each band is given a general description and examples are often included. The salary range for each band is then set by the pay review, an individual's earnings within the range being related to service or merit. This method is common in many branches of government and large commercial organisations. However, since the job fitting often means comparing chalk with cheese, fitting into bands becomes the subject of much dispute as employees seek to be regraded.

To improve upon the problem of comparing different jobs, a *point plan* assigns points to agreed job-related attributes. In an industrial setting, the four factors of skill, responsibility, effort and working conditions may be assessed. In turn these may be broken down into sub-factors. Each job is then scored and the resultant sum is the points value related to that job. Key jobs are selected as before for negotiation and the points values for the other jobs enable interpolation to be made on an agreed basis.

Job evaluation gains by bringing out into the open the basis for different payments for different jobs. Managers may rue the lack of flexibility that an *ad hoc* system permits. For example, the procedure is inflexible and may not enable the organisation to retain a very good employee who is offered a position at a higher salary elsewhere.

Case study: Change at Barr and Stroud [11]

Until 1987, when it was taken over by Pilkington, 96% of the work of Barr and Stroud was for defence. This long-established Glasgow engineering company was a world leader in thermal imaging equipment for tanks and submarine periscopes. With the collapse of defence contracts, profits fell in two years from a sound £8.6 million, on £85.3 million turnover, to a loss of £10 million.

Pilkington's new team found a bureaucratic and heavily overmanned business. There were nine management levels, seven graded canteens and four car parks with ranked distances from the factory. The new business strategy looked for a wider spread of international markets and productivity gains through computer integrated manufacture (CIM). With the aid of consultants, a ten-year, four-stage programme of development was devised.

Initial results indicated dramatic change:

- Profitability restored within 2 years
- Inventories down by £15 million
- Stock turnover up from 2.4 to 8.7
- Sales/employee trebled to £79,000
- Scheduled delivery up to 97%
- Lead times halved to 7 months
- Design changes halved
- Backlog of orders down from 9000 to 900.

The organisational change included the creation of teams around key processes. 200 job titles were cut to 30, banded into four broad grades each with a spread of jobs and salaries. Job titles abolished included departmental managers, turners, fitters, assemblers, senior and junior clerks and expediters. Many functions carried out in the personnel office became the responsibility of team leaders. The 9 management layers became 4.

The setting up of new multidisciplinary teams unearthed some supervisors and young engineers with high leadership potential while other managers found the change too great and left. Salaries were related as much to skills as to management responsibility so that some managers complained that subordinates were earning more than them.

Phase 1 of the change included coordinating all manufacturing processes using a Manufacturing Resources Planning (MRPII) system (see Chapters 12 and 14). The system improved communication and enabled layers of management to be removed. The inventory cut of £15 million financed a move to a new site. This change enabled many bad habits to be left behind. The three project phases to follow were:

2 'Right first time'
3 Computerisation
4 Full CIM.

Phases were used in this way because, according to the Chief Executive, the people acted as a constraint to change and could not take on the whole project at once.

Employee numbers fell from 2500 in 1990 to 740 by 1993. There were 50 compulsory redundancies, the rest leaving by natural wastage. The four trade unions were involved from the start in both the jobs reductions and the design of the new pay structures. Skill-related pay is based on acquiring competences that must be relevant to business needs. A bonus scheme offered £50 to all if the budgeted profit was achieved. Better performance than that would increase the share in increments up to a maximum of £500. In the first year, the payment was £280. It rose to £500, leading managers to consider raising the maximum. Payment is made just before the summer holidays.

Teamwork is important. Groups are expected to set monthly improvement targets focusing on quality. The company is now looking for a pay scheme that rewards cooperative effort by linking teams, instead of individuals, to business performance.

Questions

1. *What would you expect to be the benefits of, and problems with, paying the annual bonus?*
2. *Specialist workers at Barr and Stroud can, after the change, earn more than their line managers. What consequences might there be with this policy?*
3. *What comments and suggestions would you have for the company in its search for a pay scheme designed to reward quality and continuous improvement?*

References

1. Pheasant, S. (1986) *Bodyspace: Anthropometry, Ergonomics and Design* London, Taylor and Francis, p. 160
2. Pheasant, op. cit. p. 162

3. Mandal, Åga C. (1976) 'Work-chair with tilting seat' *Ergonomics* **19.2** pp. 157–64

4. Riggs, J.L (1987) *Production systems: planning, analysis and control* 4th edition New York, John Wiley & Sons, p. 279

5. Stainer, A. (1993) 'Competing on productivity – the Japanese way' *Management Services* April, pp. 12–17

6. Das, B., Smith, D,R. and Yeager, R.J. 'Situational factors affecting performance-rating ability' *International Journal of Operations and Production Management* **13.3** pp. 49–56

7. Brisley, C.L. and Fielder, W.F. (1982) 'Balancing cost and accuracy in setting up standards for work measurement' *Industrial Engineering* **14.5** pp. 82–9

8. Data is published by MTM Association for Standards and Research, 16–01 Broadway, Fair Lawn, NJ 07410, USA

9. Maynard, H.B., Stegmerten, G.J. and Schwad, J.L., (1944) *Methods-Time Measurement* New York, McGraw-Hill

10. Stainer, A., op. cit.

11. Based on Kennedy, C. (1994) 'Re-engineering: the human costs and benefits' *Long Range Planning* **27.5** pp. 64–72

7

FACILITY LOCATION

Chapter objectives

When you have finished studying this chapter, you should be able to:

- Explain different location strategies followed by organisations.
- Describe the main factors to be considered in picking locations.
- Outline and show the key elements that are required for a rational approach to selecting an operational location.
- Describe in general terms the principles and processes involved in four techniques applied to the choice of location: factor rating, break-even analysis, the centre of gravity method and the transportation method.
- Identify the special issues in the siting of retail outlets.
- Give examples of location decisions in practice.

INTRODUCTION

One of the most critical strategic decisions made by an organisation is where to locate its facilities. Relocation decisions are most frequently made by small and medium enterprises faced with pressure to increase space, improve the scale and quality of their processes, reduce costs and so on. Many of these moves occur over short distances, maintaining continuity of managers and staff as well as proximity to local markets for purchases and sales. Larger facilities are moved less frequently. Manufacturing plants employing more than 100 people relocate at the rate of 1 per cent per annum compared with 3 per cent for all establishments[1]. Put another way, the former move on average every 100 years!

More common than relocation, especially for large organisations, is the establishment of one or more new facilities. Firms, from energy companies to retail chains, reach out to new supplies and markets by locating near to resources or to customers. In some cases, the new facility will be unique, in that its inputs come from clearly defined sources and its outputs are supplied to an equally clear customer or group of customers. The location decision can then follow a search for the most economic place. In other cases, the firm seeks to serve its customers from a network of points, each of which can, in principle, supply any of them. Now the pattern of supply is more complex and the choice of new locations more difficult as any new capacity will disturb the existing pattern.

This decision area is one for which many optimisation models have been proposed, the model specification being influenced by factors including the number of sources and outlets. We shall be examining the application of some of the most important models in this chapter. While doing so, however, we should bear in mind that there are many qualitative factors in the choice that the more formal models do not capture. While the main points are outlined here, the models should be seen as pointers to the best choice rather than determinants of the outcome.

1. Location strategy

Whatever the type of establishment being set up, the best location involves the selection from among alternatives. The criterion for this selection comes itself from the total strategy of the organisation. For manufacturing plants, the best location may simply be the one where the total costs are minimised. Where the firm is service orientated, see **1.15**, the customer is more closely engaged in the supply process and factors such as ease of access and speed of delivery come to the fore. We discussed, in Chapter 1, how many organisations in reality see themselves as producing a bundle of goods and services. In those cases, they have to combine ideas of cost, accessibility and speed of delivery into the assessment of location.

External and internal factors combine to influence facility location. Three basic strategies can be identified, see Box 7.1 for examples. *Product-based location strategy* is probably the most popular in large organisations. It reflects the product organisation structure, see **5.3**, in which different operating divisions are each responsible for limited product ranges. A company, therefore, can have several semi-independent facilities in the same market area or even on adjacent sites. Their separation, however, enables each to adopt and utilise the appropriate process technology, work force and staff expertise, service level, style and image and so on. Factories or service facilities that are too large and attempt to supply a mixed range are often beset with problems of focus and control.

A *market-based location strategy* places facilities to serve market areas and again reflects an organisation structure, this time one based on geographic divisions. Markets are the basic reasons for the location of retail outlets and distribution centres. Additionally, spatial considerations can justify plant locations where transport costs are high and other cost elements such as tariff barriers are important. Market-based location allows quick response to customer requirements.

A *vertically differentiated location strategy* means that different stages of the supply process are in different places. Some industries have vertically integrated firms who combine several stages of the manufacturing cycle. Rather than locate the whole operation on one site, location decisions are made for each stage. They have different economic characteristics and these influence the number and location of facilities. For instance, scale considerations may lead to a choice of just one plant at some stage, whereas, for the next stage, several plants located close to customers may be preferred.

It is useful to distinguish between *push* and *pull* factors in the decision. Push factors stem from dissatisfaction with existing arrangements and cause the organisation to consider alternatives. A recognition of a problem forms the first step in the decision process. The push factors include:

Location strategy	Examples
Product-based	General Motors makes different model ranges at its plants, for example the Astra at Ellesmere Port, Cheshire. Kingfisher serves different markets through its retailing subsidiaries B&Q, Superdrug and Woolworth. The patterns of retail outlets and support warehouses are created independently to suit each product range.
Market-based	Cement manufacturer Castle serves the UK market from four plants whose location combines access to raw materials with proximity to four regions where demand is highest. New printing and facsimile data transmission technologies have enabled national newspapers to print closer to their markets, permitting later news to be included and reducing distribution costs. Subcontractors are often used, boosting the fortunes of regional printing companies. The *Independent on Sunday* is printed in Derby, Northampton, Preston and Burgess Hill, near Brighton.
Vertically differentiated	Coca Cola produces its concentrate in one plant in order to protect quality and the secrecy of its formulation. The concentrate is delivered to some 4000 bottling plants throughout the world where water, sugar and carbon dioxide are added. Isolated service operations, see **3.6**, are examples of vertical differentiation of location. Max Spielmann processes film at one Liverpool plant. Customers are dealt with at several dozen retail outlets throughout the region.

Box 7.1 Location strategy examples

- A recognition that serving customers from the present site is awkward, slow and expensive. This could include a recognition of customers costs if they have to visit.
- Labour shortages or industrial relations problems.
- Competitors' location strategies.
- Rising costs of site-related factors such as rents and property taxes.
- Changes in space needs related to shifts in total demand, changes in the product mix, new operating methods or pressure from staff for better facilities. These changes may create a shortage of, or surplus, space.
- Constraints set by regulatory authorities related to safety, effluent, noise or planning issues.
- The need to realise capital tied up in land and buildings.
- Unusual events or risks such as flood and fire.

The pull factors come later in the decision process. They represent a set of forces that draw the organisation to one area and site or another. As explained in Chapters 2 and 4, the strategy of the organisation is expressed at lower levels as a set of objectives. In location decisions, there may be conflicting objectives, such as cost versus service, which have to be balanced. The factors to be taken into account, and the method of achieving the balance, vary from firm to firm and from time to time. Sometimes, the decision will be dominated by one factor, such as the search for skilled labour or the need to be close to a known market. On other occasions, a firm will be short of time and only carry out a limited evaluation of one or two alternatives. Some organisations will carry out detailed location and site evaluations, whereas others will rely on judgement with very little quantitative assessment.

We can think of the choice among pull factors as made in two steps. First, depending on its size, an organisation selects a trading bloc, nation or region in which to create a new facility. Then it will pass on to detailed issues of site selection. In practice, these steps are run together because the number of sites that are available, *or the number that the organisation is able and prepared to evaluate*, is small. The managers often search for a satisfactory, rather than an optimal, solution.

> When constructing facilities to form part of an existing supply network, such as the telephone or electricity grids, sites very close to existing nodes are strongly favoured. Existing cabling means that new telephone exchange capacity is best constructed within, or next to, present plant. The miniaturisation resulting from System-X exchanges has enabled this to happen in city centres without much need for new buildings.
>
> A replacement electric power station was needed at Peel, Isle of Man. To be commissioned by 1995, the favoured site was next to the existing facility. Since this was near to houses, permission for its construction was only given under stringent design conditions. This included the remarkably low noise level of 39 dB at 100 metres (see Table 6.2).

2. Factors in location selection

The general criterion for location is to optimise economic benefit to the firm. This simply stated aim hides the complex nature of both benefits and costs. For example, it is not easy to assess the impact on profits of faster delivery times or easier access for customers. This is a common problem with decisions that combine many factors both quantitative and qualitative. It is useful to break the criterion down into its constituent elements, some of which can be measured financially, others of which are the subject of judgement. The factors to be considered are:

- *Economic policies of governments at the supranational, national, regional and local levels.*
  Governments and organisations each have their own agendas when it comes to location policy. In contrast to the firm seeking to maximise its own economic benefit, governments look for benefits to their economies as a whole. Within the EU, governments support firms setting up in the weaker regions through a series of grants and tax incentives. Competition policy within the EU prevents governments from subsidising businesses unfairly but allows them give this limited support to help alleviate the effects of decline. Local governments and other agencies provide land, services and premises at low cost.
- *International risks.*
  There are many risks associated with development. These are compounded by the financial risks of moving abroad, especially exchange rates and interest

rates. Furthermore, for global companies, there are the political risks linked to operating in countries with unstable regimes or whose tax policies and currency controls shift frequently.

- *Raw materials and energy sources.*
  Access to raw materials, components or supplies of energy is important, yielding cost advantages when these elements are expensive to transport or are perishable. This explains the siting of canning factories near to pea fields, iron works close to ore fields or ports, and aluminium smelters near to electric power stations.

- *Location of markets.*
  The reasons quoted for raw materials sources also apply to markets for goods. Transport costs of heavy, awkward or very bulky materials limit the range that can be supplied from one source. With self-service and personal service, clearly they must be offered close to the customer. How close depends on the service. Regular trips to the supermarket will be less than three miles for most customers. On the other hand, some people are prepared to travel the length of the country to attend an occasional concert or study at an attractive university.

- *Transport links.*
  Quick and safe transport is needed at reasonable cost. While large organisations can afford to develop their own transport infrastructure at, say, ports, most have to rely on the communications networks provided by national governments.

- *Climate and quality of life.*
  Climatic considerations used to influence the siting of certain processes, such as cotton spinning. Modern air-conditioning means that climate now has less direct impact. It is now one of the factors that can be bundled into the general notion of quality of life. Firms are aware that, to attract and retain good staff, the local quality of life can be important. This is especially true of more mobile employees, for example managers and engineers. Population drift to the sunbelts in the United States and southern France are an indication of many individuals' preferences for sunnier climes.

- *Labour supply and training opportunities.*
  While some staff are recruited on a national or international level, cost considerations usually mean that most are drawn from local labour markets. The lack of availability of a potential work force, educated to appropriate levels, will be a factor in rejecting some possibilities. Training schools and colleges will also aid the new company in building up its expertise. Cheap labour is not always the best as the productivity of healthy and educated workers tends to be higher than for those without such advantages.

- *Competitors and allies.*
  We have already noted that location is a strategic decision that will have an impact on the interaction with other organisations. A business may open a new facility on competitive grounds, to forestall the expansion of a major rival. An organisation whose work is interdependent with another will find it beneficial to operate close by.

- *Availability of sites.*
  Sites with planning permissions and connections to utilities are in restricted supply in some areas. National and local governments use such controls and

developments to influence industrial location. Prepared factory, distribution and office premises enable the new location to be developed quickly without the cost, delay and risk of individual development.

Government policies and changes in technology have changed the patterns of office location away from traditional sites in business districts close to urban centres. The city still has its attractions but congestion and high rents have led to the setting up of alternatives. These include peripheral office and business parks, sites close to airports or, nearer to the city centre, urban rehabilitation schemes. *Docklands* in London, *La Défense* in Paris, *EUR* in Rome and *City-Nord* in Hamburg are all examples of planned office centres designed in response to the demand for commercial premises.

It is worth noting that there is, in the above list, no generally dominant location factor that applies to business overall. When examining particular industries, however, different factors come to the fore. For example, there has been concern among car assemblers, component suppliers and electronics companies over trading bloc import tariffs and quotas. This has led to many deciding to establish manufacturing facilities in the European Union and the United States. Given a decision to move to Europe, the UK government's regional selective assistance has played a large part in persuading large foreign firms to set up in the country. Local factors then come into play. The willingness of Clwyd County Council to support Welsh Office grants with non-financial benefits such as the provision of special language classes is typical of the reasons for some 20 companies setting up in that county. Box 7.2 shows some examples of Japanese manufacturers' investments in the UK since the late 1980s. These benefitted from government assistance.

It should be noted that global corporations have great freedom in deciding where to locate, access to resources or markets being very important. These issues are brought out in Box 7.3, which is based on a survey of foreign firms' views of London compared with other European centres[2]. Studies of firms more closely tied to regional or national sources of supply or markets show that government tax reductions and other inducements tend to have only marginal effects[3]. The availability of suitable labour is frequently quoted by all types of firm.

Nissan	Sunderland car plant. £900 million; more than 4,000 jobs
Fujitsu	Semiconductor plants in Durham. £700 million; 1,800 jobs
Toyota	Car plant near Derby; engine plant in Clwyd. £700 million; 3,000 jobs
Honda	Car plant at Swindon. £370 million; 1,300 jobs. Further investment of £330 million to come
NEC	Semiconductor plant at Livingston. £530 million to expand in 1990s; extra 430 jobs.

Box 7.2 Some major UK investments by Japanese manufacturers

Locating in London

- Size and depth of financial markets make it vital for financial sector firms to be represented in London. Professional firms (consultancy, advertising, insurance, law) are represented in proportion to the financial sector. A London location is not vital for manufacturing firms.
- Access to markets such as insurance, shipping, and energy and the concentration of customers are further attractions.
- The availability of staff with appropriate skills is highly rated.
- Communications, law, language and jurisdiction contribute to the selection decision but to a lesser extent.
- London's social and entertainment values are important.

- Access to governments and international financial institutions is not significant in the decision.
- Second only to Tokyo, costs are high but not a deterrent to financial institutions.
- Lease contracts with upward-only rent reviews are not popular.
- Local transport is poor.

Box 7.3 Why financial sector and related firms set up in London

EVALUATING ALTERNATIVE LOCATIONS

We shall, in the next sections, be examining some main methods that have been proposed for comparing locations. The computations become more complex with each method. This should not suggest that the methods become in any way more valid. It is just that the way the location questions are presented leads to the use of a different approach. Therefore, before we examine the methods, we should examine the general way in which questions are posed and responses obtained.

3. Optimising decisions

Location decisions are among many found in operations management in which one is asked to find a best answer to a question. Here, the question may be framed in several ways. For example: 'Where should we build this distribution centre?' or 'How many plants would we need to best serve this market and where should they be?' or 'Which of our existing outlets should serve which customers?'

To discover the optimal answer to these questions, the following are required:

- A clear statement of the objective that is being sought. This must be unambiguous so there is no room for having several objectives (for example speed, quality and cost) which are in conflict and have to be traded off, one against the other.
- A recognition of constraints. These may be drawn from the list given in section 2 or be other business constraints. An example of the former would be, 'The facility must be within 2 km of a deep water port,' while the latter would be represented by, 'The total spent on the project must not exceed £5 million.'

- A recognition that the output, or objective, is dependent upon a combination of known inputs. This is the so-called *objective function* that can be expressed in general terms as:

Objective = Function of (Input$_1$, Input$_2$, Input$_3$, ...)

or, simply:

O = f (I_1, I_2, I_3 ...)

Saying 'function of' means that we acknowledge that there is a relationship between the stated factors but may not have figured out what it is. For example, expressing all the factors in cost terms, we could say that the cost of operating at a site is a function of land and building costs, transport costs, labour costs and so on.

- There needs to be an efficient technique for discovering the optimal solution for the objective function within the stated constraints. As we shall see, this is straightforward when only a few possibilities are to be investigated. Then it is a question of calculating the value of the objective function for each site and making a choice. On the other hand, when the number of options is greater, some kind of formal search or optimisation method makes the problem solution much more efficient.

Optimisation techniques have been developed for many common problems in operations management. Some, such as the critical path method and linear programming, are widely used and we shall be reviewing their application in later chapters. Others are elegant processes of mathematical interest that may never have had much practical application or have been superseded by computer-based search methods. In a third category worthy of note are problems for which only partial solutions have been found. The 'travelling representative problem' is not a locational problem as such but it is a famous example of this category.

The travelling representative problem can be stated very succinctly (see Figure 7.1). Given that the 'rep' wants to visit several places, what is the shortest, or quickest, route? With three places there are just six routes, with ten there are 3,628,800 and with 100 the number would be 10^{156}! Search methods which reach near optimal solutions have been proposed[4] but there is as yet no known method of homing in on the optimum other than by using computer power to try most combinations. While appearing to become unreal with large numbers, the travelling representative problem does come up frequently in business. In transport departments, for instance, dispatchers may plan lorry tours with 30 or 40 drops so that goods are stowed in reverse order of their unloading.

With respect to location choices, the four methods we shall look into are: factor rating, break-even analysis, the centre of gravity method and the transportation model.

4. Factor rating

The factor rating method is a general means by which some objectivity can be introduced to the process of comparing many factors in a decision. We are examining it here in the context of location choice but it can be used for many other cases. These may be where costs are hard to evaluate and there are several intangible factors such as quality of life, workforce education and so on.

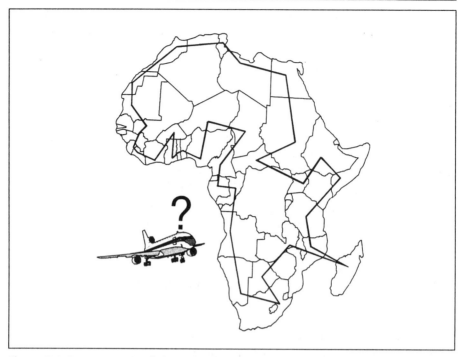

Figure 7.1 Rep's tour. But is it optimal?

The simplest form of factor rating starts with a list of factors to be included in the decision. Managers are then asked to rate each alternative, either using a simple opinion scale (poor, satisfactory, good, very good, excellent) or by assigning a numerical value. Before debating the site to be selected, the decision makers then review each others' ratings.

Table 7.1 gives an example of a telephone-based service company faced with choices about its enquiries service. It needs to update its present facility in London (alternative A) or could move the service to one of three other locations, these being available because of spare capacity in the leased trunk network. Capital and running costs are expressed in millions of pounds, the latter being represented as savings in space and labour costs compared with the current operation. Other factors considered important are scored on a scale from 1 (disadvantageous) to 5 (advantageous). One important consideration is the ready availability of staff with accents close to standard English.

Study of the approach shown in Table 7.1 will show that it is little more than the setting out of an agenda. The factors chosen are merely listed and the decision makers are not faced with having to state, in advance, which factors are more important than others. In the case shown, the company may be very short of capital. In such a case, immediate expenditure will be the key factor and the option with the lowest installation cost will be favoured. On the other hand, the organisation may be stressing the need to improve service levels and staff education and accent may come more to the fore.

To achieve greater objectivity and satisfy the requirement to develop an objective function as described in section 3, it is necessary to apply weighting to the decision factors. The steps in the weighted factor rating process are as follows:

Table 7.1 Factor scoring for location decision

			Alternative locations	
Factor	A	B	C	D
Installation costs (£M)	7	10	12	16
Change in annual running costs (£M)	0	−1	−1	−2
Room for expansion	1	3	3	3
Technical simplicity	4	2	2	1
Availability of workforce	1	3	2	4
Acceptability of accent	3	2	4	2

a Agree a list of relevant factors. These could be drawn from a broader list such as the one given in section **2**.

b Assign a weight to each selected factor that expresses the relative importance of that factor to the organisation.

c Ask each person involved in the decision to assign a rating to each location for each factor. The rating is to a number on an agreed scale, say 0 to 5, 0 to 10, or 0 to 100.

d Multiply each rating by the factor weight and add the results to produce a score for each location.

e Make a recommendation based on the scores.

The recommended location will then be the one whose score is highest. In Table 7.2, the company is using a rating scale of 0 to 5. The weights add up to 20 so the maximum score for a location would be 100. It can be seen that location D has the highest weighted total, closely followed by C. A sensible recommendation may be that both D and C are acceptable, adding that the differences between the two hinge on the availability and acceptability of staff. This question could be further investigated before a final decision is made.

5. Break-even analysis

We have already come across break-even analysis in **2.30** in our study of fixed and variable costs. It can be readily applied to location choices if good cost estimates are available and the decision is going to be made mainly on cost grounds. The steps in location break-even analysis are as follows:

a Identify the costs for each location and figure out whether they are fixed or variable.

b Produce a graph showing how costs vary with volume for each proposed site.

c Make a recommendation based on the results.

Table 7.2 Weighted factor scoring

	Raw scores					Weighted scores			
Factor	A	B	C	D	Weights	A	B	C	D
Installation costs	2	3	4	5	3	6	9	12	15
Change in annual running costs	2	3	3	4	3	6	9	9	12
Room for expansion	1	3	3	3	2	2	6	6	6
Technical simplicity	4	2	2	1	2	9	4	4	2
Availability of workforce	1	3	2	4	5	5	15	10	20
Acceptability of accent	3	2	4	2	5	15	10	20	10
Totals					20	43	53	61	65

Plant location

The approach can be illustrated by reference to the location of a single plant.

In the Pilbara region of north-western Australia lie many large mineral deposits, especially iron. The largest iron deposits lie some 800 km inland. The climate of the region is very harsh, the land is desert and very few people lived there before the mining started. Several contractors mine and export the iron ore to markets mainly in Japan.

The basic processes involved in iron production from the Pilbara ore are mining, sintering and smelting. Material is brought down from the mines to the port in 10,000 tonne trains and then loaded into bulk carriers for shipment. Mining clearly has a fixed location and smelting takes place in a large, sophisticated plant in Japan. The question is, where to locate the sintering process? This is partial refining, enriching the iron content of the ore and dumping the waste. Sintering requires energy. The choice is made on the grounds of costs, almost unhindered by space considerations because there is so much available. Three locations are possible: the mine, the port and Japan.

Sintering at an early stage would reduce transport costs because only enriched ore would be moved. However, to sinter at the mine would involve the transport of energy, plant and employees to that remote site, making the sintering process itself more expensive. Operating at the port would be cheaper and several mines could be served simultaneously, thus creating scale economies. To sinter in Japan would be cheaper than in the Pilbara because of lower input costs and possible further economies of scale. Yet the bulk carriers would be carrying reduced nett payloads of iron and large amounts of waste.

Figure 7.2 presents the break-even chart for the Pilbara example. A recommendation would be based on the conclusion that to sinter at the port is the cheapest

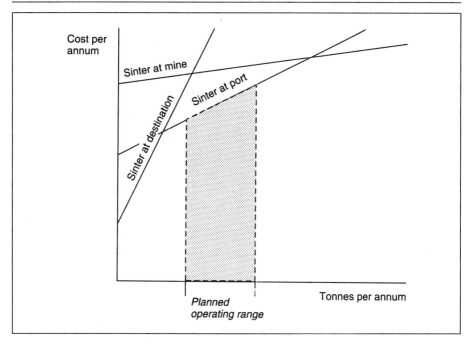

Figure 7.2 Location break-even chart

option for the planned mine output. To do this first stage of refining at the mine would only gain if volumes were much higher and to sinter in Japan is only preferred for small outputs.

6. Centre of gravity method

The centre of gravity method is the first of two techniques that use formal methods to search for the optimal value of the objective function. This contrasts with the previous two methods which merely examined each of several possibilities in turn. The centre of gravity method is also applied to a special type of problem: What is the optimal location for a warehouse that is to serve several stores?

The framing of this question allows the problem to seen as one where the search is for the minimum transport cost. Assuming that the costs per unit of distance moved are uniform (for example, all despatches are by road) then the cost of supplying each store can be represented by loads and distance. The objective function, to be minimised, is:

Transport cost = f (loads, distance)

We can use tonne-kilometres to represent costs. The total cost is represented as the sum of the individual tonne-km. That is:

Transport cost = (loads$_1$ × distance$_1$ + loads$_2$ × distance$_2$ + loads$_3$ × distance$_3$ ...)

Loads$_1$ and distance$_1$ represent, respectively, the number of loads carried and the distance from the warehouse to store number 1. The lowest value for transport cost occurs when the warehouse is located at the so-called *centre of gravity* of the stores. Its location can be found from the following equations:

191

$$x_c = \frac{\Sigma q_i \times x_i}{\Sigma q_i} \qquad y_c = \frac{\Sigma q_i \times y_i}{\Sigma q_i}$$

x_c and y_c are the co-ordinates of the centre of gravity.

x_i and y_i are the co-ordinates of location i.

q_i represents the number of loads to be delivered to location i.

The co-ordinates can be taken from any scale or grid, using any units of measurement. (This is not, of course, a real centre of gravity in the physical sense. The term is used, nevertheless, because the formulae are the same as those used in basic physics.)

The method, then, consists of the following steps:

a Determine the depôts to be supplied and the quantities they require according to a measure that is directly related to costs, for example tonnes, number of containers or volumes of liquid.

b Using consistent scales, tabulate the geographical co-ordinates of each site. The coordinates could be units on a map or actual distances.

c Calculate and total the quantity–distance products, that is $q_i x_i$ and $q_i y_i$.

d Calculate the coordinates of the centre of gravity by dividing the above by the total quantities.

e Make a recommendation in the vicinity of these coordinates.

Baglin et al[5] show how the method could be used to decide the site for a single main distribution centre for products to be supplied to existing depôts throughout France. Table 7.3 shows the basic data and calculations. The x and y coordinates represent east and north coordinates on a map.

The calculation locates the optimal distribution centre somewhat to the east of Orléans. Based on this analysis the recommendation would be to search for a suitable site in that area.

Table 7.3 Distribution centre location

Town	tonnes (q_i) × 100	x_i	y_i	$q_i x_i$	$q_i y_i$
Angoulême	34	13.3	12.4	452.20	421.60
Besançon	46	28.2	18.6	1,297.20	855.60
Caen	60	12.2	25.5	732.00	1,530.00
Lille	391	20.5	30.9	8,015.50	12,081.90
Limoges	35	16.2	13.1	567.00	458.50
Lyon	515	25.5	13.0	13,132.50	6,695.00
Meaux	1025	20.0	24.3	20,500.00	24,907.50
Moulins	36	21.5	15.8	774.00	568.80
Nancy	233	28.3	24.0	6,593.90	5,592.00
Rennes	77	8.9	21.7	685.30	1,670.90
Toulouse	85	16.7	4.8	1,419.50	408.00
Tours	52	14.7	18.8	764.40	977.60
Totals	2589			54,933.50	56,167.40
Centre of gravity at:		21.22	21.69		

Weaknesses of the model

The centre of gravity model as set out here has several weaknesses: it assumes that costs are linearly related to load and distance; 'crow-flies' distances are used, making no allowance for mountainous terrain or road tolls; there is no allowance made for regulatory constraints such as drivers' hours; finally, it assumes that the supplies originate at the distribution centre. In this last case, if the centre is to be supplied from a plant or plants at other locations, then its optimal coordinates will be found by including those sources in the centre of gravity calculation. More advanced versions of the gravity model are designed to overcome some of the other weaknesses.

7. The transportation method

In common with the centre of gravity method, the transportation method uses a formal algorithm to search efficiently for an optimal value of the objective function. Now, the question to be addressed is the best pattern of shipments from several sources of supply to several destinations of demand. We will start with the basic model. Here we are looking for the best way to *interconnect* an existing arrangement of facilities rather than find the optimal location for a new one. Let us represent the flow from source i to destination j by the term $flow_{ij}$, and the cost per unit transported along the same link to be $cost_{ij}$. Furthermore, let us assume that the cost per unit transported along a link does not vary with the flow. The objective function is:

Transport cost = Sum of $(flow_{ij} \times cost_{ij})$ for all values of i and j

There are several methods of finding the optimal value for this equation. We shall use the *stepping-stone method*. This is typical of a family of linear programming techniques that moves from an initial estimate to the optimal solution in a series of stages. The sequence is as follows:

a Determine quantities that each source supplies and each destination demands.
b Identify the costs associated with the carriage of one unit between each source and each destination.
c By working systematically through the data in a table, work out an *initial feasible solution*. At this stage, this is not a search for an optimal solution but for one where every source supplies and every destination is supplied to its capacity requirement.
d Use the stepping-stone routine to progressively move towards the optimal solution.
e Make a recommendation based on the resultant flows.

The procedure

To illustrate, let us assume that a supplier of special stone to the building industry has three quarries in Derbyshire, Cleveland and Cumbria. There are four depôts, at Kilmarnock, Manchester, Bristol and Leeds. The capacities in tonnes per week, and the link costs, have been established and set out in Table 7.4.

The values in the clear cells are the costs of each link in pence per tonne and those in the shaded cells are the capacities. In this example, we have chosen the case where the total production capacity, at 3500 tonnes, equals the demand.

193

Table 7.4 Capacities and costs, stone transport

to from	Kilmarnock	Manchester	Leeds	Bristol	Demand
Derbyshire	528	260	258	320	900
Cleveland	558	488	292	614	170
Cumbria	400	332	132	556	900
Production	1000	1400	700	400	Total: 3500

An initial feasible solution can be found by the *north-west corner* method. This involves starting at the top-left cell, and filling each in turn up to the production capacity of the row or the demand of the column. The Derbyshire–Kilmarnock cell thus has 900 tonnes per week, leaving zero for the other links in the first row. There will be 100 tonnes from Cleveland to Kilmarnock, and so on. Going down and across in steps, we produce Table 7.5.

The total weekly transport cost of this allocation is £15,610. To find a reduced cost solution, consider each empty cell in turn. For the unoccupied cell, calculate the effect on total costs if one tonne were carried along its route. The extra tonne will mean a change in flows on other links. Taking the Derbyshire–Bristol link as an example, the routine is as follows:

i) Trace a closed loop from the empty cell back to the original cell. Right-angled turns are only allowed at occupied cells. The only possible closed loop turning at occupied cells is shown in Table 7.6.
ii) Since we are exploring the possibility of moving a tonne along the Derbyshire–Bristol link, place a +1 in that cell. Then pass round the route inserting –1 and +1 at alternate angles of the loop. A review of the rows and

Table 7.5 Initial allocation

to from	Kilmarnock	Manchester	Leeds	Bristol	Demand
Derbyshire	528 900	260	258	320	900
Cleveland	558 100	488 1400	292 200	614	170
Cumbria	400	332	132 500	556 400	900
Production	1000	1400	700	400	Total: 3500

Table 7.6 First step in optimisation

to from	Kilmarnock	Manchester	Leeds	Bristol	Demand
Derbyshire	◄◄◄◄ ▼	◄◄◄◄◄◄◄◄	◄◄◄◄◄◄◄◄	◄◄◄◄ ▲	900
Cleveland	▼ ►►►►	►►►►►►►►	►►►►	▲ ▲	170
Cumbria			▼ ►►►►	▲ ►►►►	900
Production	1000	1400	700	400	Total: 3500

columns will show that these changes are needed to keep their totals constant. Table 7.7 shows the effect.

The change in weekly costs for the 1 tonne would then be: +320 – 528 + 558 – 292 + 132 – 556, which is a reduction of 366 pence. This is the *improvement index* for the cell.

iii) Go on to calculate an improvement index for each empty cell. The improvement indices are shown as italicised figures in Table 7.8.
iv) Select the link with the largest negative value of the index. The greatest cost improvement comes from switching as much tonnage as possible on to the link. This is done by adding and subtracting tonnes round the relevant closed loop, making sure that no tonnage value becomes negative. Here, 200 tonnes are switched to Derbyshire–Bristol as this then empties the Cleveland–Leeds cell. The effect of this move is shown in Table 7.9.
v) Repeat stages i to iv. After several iterations, the result in Table 7.10 appears.

Table 7.7 Results of first step

to from	Kilmarnock	Manchester	Leeds	Bristol	Demand
Derbyshire	528 **900-1**	260	258	320 **+1**	900
Cleveland	558 **100+1**	488 **1400**	292 **200-1**	614	170
Cumbria	400	332	132 **500+1**	556 **400-1**	900
Production	1000	1400	700	400	Total: 3500

Table 7.8 Table with improvement indices

to \ from	Kilmarnock	Manchester	Leeds	Bristol	Demand
Derbyshire	528	260 \ −198	258 \ −4	320 \ −366	900
Cleveland	558	488	292	614 \ −102	170
Cumbria	400 \ −2	332 \ +4	132	556	900
Production	1000	1400	700	400	Total: 3500

Table 7.9 Improved solution

to \ from	Kilmarnock	Manchester	Leeds	Bristol	Demand
Derbyshire	528 \ **700**	260	258	320 \ **200**	900
Cleveland	558 \ **300**	488 \ **1400**	292	614	170
Cumbria	400	332	132 \ **700**	556 \ **200**	900
Production	1000	1400	700	400	Total: 3500

Table 7.10 Optimal solution

to \ from	Kilmarnock	Manchester	Leeds	Bristol	Demand
Derbyshire	528 \ +198	260 \ **500**	258 \ +196	320 \ **400**	900
Cleveland	558 \ **800**	488 \ **900**	292 \ +2	614 \ +66	170
Cumbria	400 \ **200**	332 \ +2	132 \ **700**	556 \ +166	900
Production	1000	1400	700	400	Total: 3500

At this stage no empty cell shows a negative improvement index. In other words, further shifts of tonnage cannot improve the objective function and the optimal solution has been found. The flows now represent the minimum total cost of £13,160 per week.

There are many variants and improvements in the above procedure which result in a quicker optimisation of the objective function. However, since most linear programming problems such as this are solved by routine processes, they lend themselves to solution by computer. See Box 7.4 for some early applications[6]. The purpose of the above demonstration is, therefore, less to do with teaching the method than in developing an understanding of the basic principles.

The transportation method can be extended to situations where the total capacities of sources and destinations are different. This is advantageous because, in practice, it would be rare for the whole system to be in balance. For example, a supermarket chain expanding into a new part of the country may first service its new outlets from existing distribution centres. Then, when the time is right, a new centre may be constructed in the new region. This itself would be built to cope with the planned growth in the number of shops. The company will draw up a short list of potential sites for the new centre and, for each, use a transportation algorithm to look for optimal supply patterns. The transportation method is thus changed from being a means of optimising flows in an existing system to being part of a facility location decision.

8. How many sources and destinations?

So far we have examined optimisation questions that have been narrowly defined and are capable of solution by standard methods. A much broader question is the definition of the number of depôts with their siting. This is a complex question even if it is limited to a consideration of costs. Five cost relationships can now be brought into the objective function.

- *Links from factory to depôts*
  With a few depôts, the supply costs will remain low since the company can take full advantage of full lorry or container loads. However, as the number of depôts increases, each outlet will have to be supplied with part-loads and the costs per unit will rise.

Transportation studies were carried out by the National Coal Board from the mid-1950s. The calculations required desk-top calculators and much effort; a 60 colliery to 60 customer problem took 3 days to solve! The Central Electricity Generating Board conducted similar studies at around the same period. Efficient movement from pit to power station was the focus. A regional model with 135 mines and 32 stations needed 71 iterations even though the most efficient procedures were used.

Such problems were ready made for the expanding computing facilities. By the late 1960s, BP was one of the largest computer users in the country. Most of its usage was devoted to optimisation problems, concerned with forecasting, marketing, supply and so on.

Box 7.4 Early applications of the transportation method

- *Links from depôts to customers*
  With more outlets, the average length of these links will fall, thus gradually reducing the cost of this transport.
- *Depôt stocks*
  The total stocks held in many outlets will be greater than that held in a central facility. This is because each has to carry a safety stock as a buffer against random variations in demand. Theoretically, for the same level of service, the stock required increases in proportion to the square root of the number of depôts; a doubling of outlets means a stock increase of 41%.
- *Storage and handling costs*
  These costs increase because of the rise in stock levels described above. Furthermore, as the number of depôts increases, each handles fewer orders and becomes less efficient.
- *Administration costs*
  With decentralised order processing and an increase in the number of information links required, the administration cost per unit of throughput increases with the number of outlets.

The effect on the total distribution costs of these contradictory factors is summarised in Figure 7.3. The first five graphs in the figure correspond to the costs identified in the list above. The sixth graph suggests the likely form of the total cost curve. (Note that the graphs are merely conceptual and are not drawn to a common vertical scale.) There will be a range of depôt numbers that will result in operating costs close to the minimum. Companies considering how many centres they require and where they should be located will use such an approach to search for the ideal number.

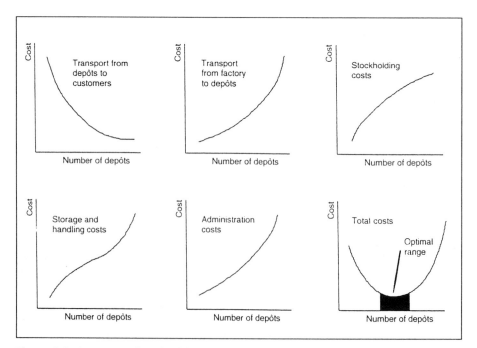

Figure 7.3 Costs associated with multiple facilities

Similar considerations inform decisions on the number and location of health centres and hospitals. Depending on the degree of specialisation, a hospital serves a district of variable size. Current thinking sees General Hospitals as serving populations of around 400,000. With larger catchment areas travel distances for patients and visitors become too far; smaller populations mean that the range of medical and support services expected in a general hospital can only be provided inefficiently.

9. Retail location

The selection of sites for retail outlets, whether they be shops, garages, pubs or restaurants, presents us with a set of considerations that are not normally of concern when locating factories or distribution centres. Retailers require visits from customers. This simple statement points to many *micro* issues in site selection that are not of interest to the factory or warehouse operator. The sales performance of sites even a few metres apart can differ substantially.

Bowlby and others[7] describe the ideal decision sequence for retail location as gradually narrowing the search from area to identified premises:

- *Geographical area*
  Choice of area may be based on identified area demand or may be part of a broader strategy such as aiming for full national coverage. For instance, Brewers Fayre is a growing chain of over 200 pubs with informal dining areas serving both individuals and families. Its location policy is to achieve national coverage using sites in the countryside or on the edges of towns. Each location has standard features such as parking and other facilities while preserving the character of the inn.
- *Site identification*
  The search for sites that fit broad selection criteria, such as nearness to markets, will generate a short list. In most areas the number of viable sites is limited. Land values, existing developments and planning controls often cut the choices to a handful. For example, the growth of superstores in Great Britain was most rapid in the old industrial areas where there were many decaying sites within and between key towns. Local authorities welcomed the developments as they helped with land reclamation and tidying up. Sites have been much more difficult to find in the south east.
- *Micro issues*
  Detailed examination of a site will cover many issues that contribute to potential performance. For location comparison, there are league tables published by estate agents such as DTZ Debenham Thorpe. These identify the sites which traders report to be the most successful. Some 300 locations are compared, retailers being asked to identify and rank those which they find to be most successful. Measures include turnover and profitability.

A drawback of the league table approach is that it measures past performance and neither directly assesses the potential of a new site nor evaluates different retailing strategies. Starting from such a data base, therefore, the major chains use sophisticated mapping models to compare different locations. The approach includes the use of *analogues* and *trade area mapping* underpinned by long experience.

Using the analogue procedure, the firm will assess features of the location that it expects to have influence upon store performance. It will compare these assessments with data from existing stores, using their grouped experience as a model for the new site. With many outlets, correlational studies become possible. Trade area mapping is a more extensive analysis based on the notion of catchment areas. It addresses the question of demand in relation to distance from the store and the location of competitors. Maps, based on electoral wards, give the population distribution according to distance. Furthermore, they give an analysis of income groups and family types. This information can then be used to suggest likely demand, possibly through the analogue procedure. Geographical distance is not necessarily the determining factor. The perception of accessibility is as much a factor of travel time and general feelings of convenience. Large shopping centres, such as the Metrocentre at Gateshead and Sheffield's Meadowhall, are known to have overlapping catchment areas. While they are some 200 km apart, they lie on the same motorway, the M1.

Firms without formal data bases may use checklists and, possibly, factor rating as in section 4 above. Four major decision factors in site evaluation are population, competition, accessibility and cost.

Population

The size and structure of the population in the assumed catchment area are recognised as having a strong influence on demand. Laura Ashley has a policy of opening stores in country towns such as Bath, Chester, Salisbury and Tunbridge Wells; Netto, the discount food retailer, entered the UK market by taking up sites within, or very close to, low-income residential areas in northern England; a newsagent will study the local estates.

Competition

Competition is a mixed blessing in retailing. Where outlets compete directly with similar product ranges, prices are likely to fall and the operator with the higher costs will suffer. On the other hand, customers are drawn to places where there are sufficient shops to render meaningful the idea of 'going shopping'. The significant role of anchor or magnet stores is noted in **9.13**. In a shopping centre, however, not only are there shops but supporting services from banks and building societies to bars and bistros. A store that depends for trade on *comparative shopping* is best located among others. There is indirect competition between related ranges of goods but within a much greater market. A remarkable example is the town of Hay on Wye which is the world's largest centre for the sale of second-hand books.

Accessibility

Accessibility should be considered from the point of view of customers, staff and suppliers. While customers are the prime consideration, inward and outward transport of goods has become an increasing problem in restricted town centres. Analysis of pedestrian flows (through *pavement counts*) and how they relate to nodes such as car parks and public transport termini is important, especially to those outlets that depend on passing trade. Confectioners do well near bus stops and it is said that there is always a flower shop at a Dutch railway station. Passing trade also applies to vehicular traffic; sites on different sides of roads or junctions can affect demand for petrol or places for rest and refreshment.

Robinson's case study of the Brown's lodging business[8] illustrates the importance of site position. The Congress Motel incorporated a camp site and trailer park next to the main Interstate highway in south Georgia, see Figure 7.4. It had

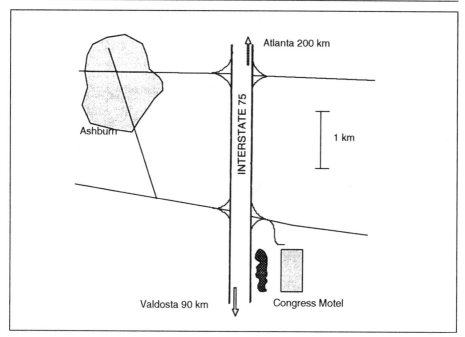

Figure 7.4 The Congress Motel site

an attractive setting alongside its own lake in full view of the I-75 close to an exit ramp. The I-75 is used by people driving between the northern states and Florida during the holiday season.

A serious drawback of the site was that, while it lay in full view of the highway, it would be seen by southbound travellers *only after they had passed the intersection*. This group would be the more likely to be looking for somewhere to stay in the Ashburn district. As Calvin Brown put it, 'This location is just too short a distance from Florida. A northbound traveller can leave from anywhere across the middle of the state of Florida and pass this area in one day.' Picking up the southbound trade may also have generated repeat business at the end of the holiday. The Browns were further frustrated by the proposed new planning controls restricting roadside advertising. This would have meant the removal of the signs they had placed by the southbound carriageway ahead of the junction.

Cost

Site operating costs in urban centres are dominated by rent and business rates. For superstore sites, the development cost may have to include land values of around £5 million per hectare, the store needing between 2 and 3 ha depending on the size of its car park. Typically, costs of demolition and removal of contamination may double the above figure. Large car parks may be necessary at peak periods but careful design is required if they are not to give an impression of a failed business at off-peak times.

10. Planning controls

Retail development takes place within a complex system of planning controls. Local authorities are the first assessors of planning applications. They work within the Town and Country Planning Acts and a set of Planning Policy Guidance instructions. Some, usually large, developments are *called in* by the Secretary of State for the Environment. This usually occurs when it is judged that the development has implications beyond the remit of the individual local authority. The current argument over the harm inflicted on high streets by edge-of-town developments is a case in point, see Box 7.5[9]. The likelihood of permission being granted for a site is a key consideration for developers. Authorities cannot use competition with existing businesses as a ground for refusal except in as far as a new centre may be shown to damage the general viability of existing ones.

Common grounds for refusal of permission may, in fact, hide underlying fears over competition. The reasons most commonly cited are changes of land use, effects on traffic and the wider impact. *Land use* restrictions on developments include building on open land, especially in the Green Belt found around many urban areas. The need to consider *traffic flows* springs from the experience of many early out-of-town developments where it was found that the road network was unable to cope. In many modern cases, developers offer, or are expected, to pay for road improvements if permission for land development is to be given. In 1994,

---

At the end of 1994, there were four large out-of-town regional shopping centres. These were Metrocentre at Gateshead, Meadowhall at Sheffield, Merry Hill at Dudley and Lakeside at Thurrock. Not only had these sites come to dominate in terms of numbers of shoppers but they were also highly profitable. On the Saturday before Christmas 1994, some 437,000 people visited these centres and 335,000 went on the Sunday. Eastgate Street in Chester is the only traditional high street in the top five.

The growth of out-of-town retail parks has been rapid, Throughout the latter half of the 1980s, space was being added at the rate of $\frac{1}{2}$ million square metres per year. This meant that, by 1994, they accounted for one quarter of all shopping space and some 27 per cent of turnover. Profit was higher than for equivalent high-street stores because of lower costs of premises and operations. The effect of the growth on town centres began to be noticed, no more so than in Dudley but also in Newcastle and Sheffield. Pressure mounted on the government to exercise some restraint.

The Secretary of State issued updated versions of various Planning Policy Guidance notes. PPG 6, reissued in mid-1993, focused on protection of existing towns. It indicated that developments would not be allowed if they could be shown to harm nearby centres. PPG 13, of March 1994, drew on the commitment to reduce carbon dioxide emissions by casting doubt on schemes which would increase the use of the car.

The immediate effect of the new policies will not be seen on the ground since many projects already have planning consent. England is likely to get two new regional shopping centres, at Cribbs Causeway near Bristol and Bluewater Park near Dartford. Another is being built at Brayhead in Glasgow. Furthermore, there are plans to relocate some 1,600 stores to retail warehouse parks selling a mixture of furniture and carpets, electrical and do-it-yourself goods.

Box 7.5 The politics of retail planning

202

GMI offered £400,000 for this purpose to back its application to Chester City Council to build an indoor tennis, squash and swimming centre on industrial land[10]. The *impact* on individual existing businesses cannot be used in judging an application. However, proposals for developments or change of use of premises can be refused on the grounds of impact on the local neighbourhood. Nuisance from noise, for instance, may be a reason in cases as different as night clubs, pleasure parks and kennels.

The general impact of planning controls is mixed. Local authorities often face strong objections from groups in areas where development is proposed and, therefore, seek grounds for refusal. Given that these grounds are limited, especially in shopping development, councils recognise both the dangers of refusal, and the costs to their budgets, if the applicants go on to appeal, and win. Consequently, they reach an accommodation, hedging permission with conditions such as the provision of open space, and restrictions on hours of operation, deliveries and types of goods sold.

Case study: Car assembly plants

In common with many other industries, the growth of vehicle manufacturing in any country concentrated in a few areas. It followed metal working which had built up around sources of materials by the time the car industry was born. Building on this, there were advantages in the close communications between the vehicle assemblers and the vast network of suppliers that sustained them. Hence were established FIAT in Turin, General Motors in Detroit, Toyota in the Aichi prefecture near Tokyo, and Rover and Jaguar in the West Midlands of England.

Perhaps the earliest large-scale plant planned in a wholly new location was that of Volkswagen at Wolfsburg where construction began in 1938. The site was by the Mittelland canal, close to *autobahnen* and railways. Wolfsburg was, however, deliberately chosen to avoid disturbing existing industrial complexes and busy traffic flows. Workers were to be housed in a new town of about 100,000 people for which room had to be allowed. As it happened, the new town was not built immediately. After production restarted and expanded after the war there was considerable commuting. For instance, in 1953, 3,000 employees (14%) were travelling daily the 80 km from Hannover. Further expansion plans could not be accommodated at Wolfsburg so, from the mid-1950s, the company expanded elsewhere, first at Hannover and then in other places in north-west Germany.

During the 1950s and 1960s, many governments became concerned about the location of their own motor industries. Through persuasion and financial incentives, they encouraged manufacturers to locate new facilities in regions of high unemployment. Thus, the car industry became an instrument of economic policy. In Britain, Ford and General Motors set up successfully on Merseyside, yet Rootes had a disastrous experience when it moved to Linwood in Scotland. In Italy, FIAT was persuaded to build a new plant south of Naples for the Alfa-Sud. Labour problems at Alfa-Sud included high absenteeism during the harvest season!

The 1970s saw a rise in international competition for government incentives. Ford, for example, discussed the location for a new plant for the Fiesta with several governments, including Austria, Britain and France, before deciding to move to Valencia in Spain.

Gradually, the motor industry has become globalized. For the producer, it is no longer a question of where in a country a plant should be located but in where in

203

each trading bloc. The barriers to trade in goods among EU countries had virtually disappeared by 1991. The United States–Canada Free Trade Agreement also had the effect of creating a bloc. Plant location, especially of Japanese companies concerned about being excluded from these blocs by tariffs and quotas, has become a matter of politics and persuasion on an international scale. In the UK there have been several developments by the well-known assemblers. Nissan is at Sunderland, Toyota at Derby and Deeside, and Honda at Swindon. In their train have followed many component manufacturers setting up offices and plant.

Volkswagen has a complex network of links among its production facilities. Figure 7.4 shows the flows among its major sites outside Europe.

Questions

1 *Compare VW's location strategy of 1938 with that which it follows today. What elements have changed?*
2 *How has government policy towards vehicle plant location shifted over the years? How do manufacturers respond in their location decisions?*
3 *Competition is pushing manufacturers towards offering customised products whilst simultaneously improving the speed of delivery. What implications do these trends have for the location of plants and the design of distribution systems?*

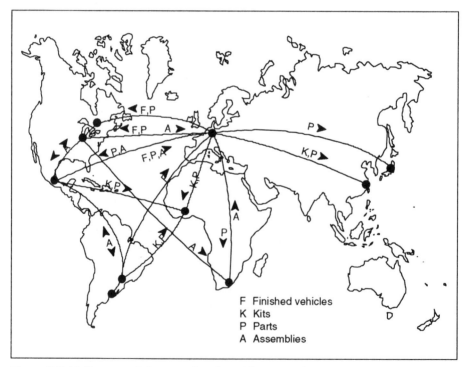

Figure 7.5 Volkswagen's international supply network

References

1. Data for the United States from Schmenner, Roger W. (1993) *Production/Operations Management* New York, Macmillan p. 440

2. Society of Property Researchers (1992) *London as a Business Location* SPR, c/o RICS Research Officer, 12 Great George Street, London SW1P 3AD pp. 1–2

3. For example, see Artikis, G.P. (1992) 'Financial factors in plant location decisions' *International Journal of Operations and Production Management* **13.8** pp. 58–71

4. Amin, S. Fernandez-Villacanas, J–L. and Cochrane, P. (1994) 'A natural solution to the travelling salesman problem' *British Telecommunications Engineering* **13.2** pp. 117–122

5. Baglin, G., Bruel, O., Garreau, A. and Greif, M. (1990) *Management Industriel et Logistique* Paris, Economica p. 369

6. Ranyard, J.C. (1988) 'A history of OR and computing" *Journal of the Operational Research Society* **39.12** pp. 1073–1086

7. Bowlby, S., Breheny, M. and Foot, D. (1984) 'Store location: problems and methods 1' *Retail and Distribution Management* **12.5** pp. 31–33

8. Robinson, R.B. (1982) 'Congress Motel and Brown's Overnite Trailer Park' Case Study in Pearce, J.A. and Robinson, R.B. (1985) *Strategic Management* 2nd edn. Homewood, Ill. Irwin pp. 939–968

9. Cowe, R. (1994) 'The high street fights back' *The Guardian* 24 December p.32. Location rankings are drawn from a DTZ Debenham Thorpe survey mentioned in Section **9**.

10. Body, C. (1994) 'Tennis centre is back on' *The Chester Chronicle* 2nd December, p. 7

8

FACILITY LAYOUT: MANUFACTURE AND ISOLATED SERVICE

Chapter objectives

When you have finished studying this chapter, you should be able to:

- Describe and explain different production system layouts, both ideal types and hybrids.

- Compare process and product layout design.

- Suggest the main advantages and disadvantages of fixed-position production.

- Illustrate the use of diagrams and models in the improvement of jobbing shop layouts.

- Discuss the advantages of group technology and show how its application could be investigated.

- Explain why line balancing is needed on production lines and summarise how this is done.

- Show how component reliability and line balancing are considered in continuous plant design.

- Suggest ways in which human factors should be considered when planning layouts.

INTRODUCTION

The appropriate layout for each operational process is unique. In its design, many factors have to be considered. These include the scale of operations, the technology involved and the links with processes at other stages of the supply chain. Layouts could be classified according to these factors. The most important difference, however, lies between, on the one hand, manufacture and isolated service and, on the other, personal service and self-service, see **3.2** to **3.5**. The dominant question in the former is the flow of goods through processes. In the latter, it is the avoidance or management of queues. Since each of these questions is a substantial one, we have devoted separate chapters to them.

In Chapter 3 we saw that manufacture and isolated service provision could be classified into five basic systems: project, jobbing, batch, line and continuous. We shall study layouts for these systems in the sections that follow. In studying layouts in this way, we should recognise that modern plants are often hybrid arrangements, combining different principles at different stages of manufacture. Furthermore, there are approaches, such as group technology, which lie at the boundary of two of the basic systems and can be applied in either.

1. Project production systems

The project, or fixed-position, layout is required when the item being made remains stationary. The staff, materials and equipment are brought to the work area when they are needed. We see that industries from civil and marine engineering to film making and research centres use such layouts. This is because of the uniqueness, complexity or sheer weight and volume of the items they produce. Civil engineering contractors are engaged in the supply both of unique products, such as roads and bridges, and of those that they produce in batches, such as houses.

Difficulties that arise in fixed-position layouts include:

- Severe limitations of space for safe working and material storage.
- The flow of materials to their installed position is difficult to plan and implement.
- The number of staff required and the rate of use of materials varies so services from accommodation to transport are difficult to plan.
- Hazardous processes are troublesome to isolate.
- Many projects involve working out of doors or at remote sites, thus imposing extra costs and risks of delay.
- Supervision and inspection are difficult.

These difficulties can be alleviated by carrying out as much work as possible away from the assembly position or site. In heavy engineering such as the manufacture of oil rigs, the policy is to make subassemblies indoors and bring them to the site only when needed. This approach is limited only by constraints in the transport system. House building in the UK has moved towards off-site assembly, notable developments being the use of preassembled roof trusses and ready glazed windows. Gradual developments such as these have been successful both in reducing costs and time and in improving quality. The building industry is, however, used to a slow rate of innovation and to making minor adjustments to components as they are fixed. The system building movement of the 1960s illustrates the difficulties of a switch to off-site assembly without proper control of manufacture and supervision of installation, see Box 8.1.

2. Jobbing production

In the jobbing factory, work is carried out either on single items or small batches, each of which is under a different contract. In principle, the type and sequence of tasks are unlimited but the sensible jobbing company will specialise in some way. It will either restrict the acceptance of orders to work within its capacity or put out work to subcontractors when the work is beyond its capability. The nature of the specialisation may be as follows:

System-built flats were erected in many towns and cities during the 1960s. The low cost and rapid construction were attractive to local authorities pressed by housing shortages and budget constraints. After some ten years, however, investigations began to show that many of the structures were seriously defective.

The flats were built from room-sized concrete panels reinforced and insulated during factory manufacture. Built-in rubber seals were intended to make them watertight. Problems of dimensional accuracy in manufacture and careless assembly on site meant that gaps between panels were not watertight. Rain penetration led to dampness in the flats, the growth of black mould and rusting of steel reinforcing bars. These problems were often made worse by ill-fitting windows or poor ventilation and insulation.

In the poor working conditions, often many metres in the air, it was difficult for inspectors to spot errors before they had been covered with wet cement or concrete, action which only made the resultant problems worse.

Most of the system-built flats have been demolished.

Box 8.1 Failure of system building

- By facilities. The jobber may have facilities such as printing machinery, lathes or saws which means that certain classes of work can be taken on. The specialisation allows the jobber to offer competitive rates for the work.
- By knowledge of customers or markets. The jobber may be willing to carry out work connected with a particular prod·uct area or customer. The business is targeted at a set of consumers rather than a set of needs.

In motor car repairs there are examples of each type of specialisation. Tyres are changed at depots that stock a range of sizes and have invested in efficient changing and balancing equipment. Many repair shops, on the other hand, offer comprehensive service focused on a named range of models. There are specialists for Rolls-Royce, VW, old MGs and so on.

For layout decisions, jobbing shops usually have little obvious work sequence. Since the orders received are very unpredictable and the sequence of operations required to fulfil them equally so, there is usually no linkage of machinery into a production line. There is likely to be a range of general-purpose machines and equipment with a demand for space for the storage of partly finished work around them. Some processes will be carried out in separate rooms or buildings because they require special conditions such as a clean atmosphere or quiet. Examples of these are painting, electronic assembly and testing.

This grouping of related machines and tasks into departments is called a *process-based* or *functional* layout. It gives high flexibility but at the cost of close control of flow by supervisors or production controllers. They arrange for orders to pass between the groups, or departments, as required. Because of uncertain loads in any department, jobbing shops tend to fill with part-finished orders. This makes them appear cluttered and increases the capital tied up in work-in-progress.

3. Functional layout design

Optimisation of the functional layout in a jobbing shop is a decision made under uncertainty about the pattern of future orders. Given this uncertainty, most organisations will be content with an approach that creates a sensible layout. This will consider cost estimates and an assessment of departments that need to be adjacent for technical reasons.

The cost approach examines the material flows among departments. This is broadly similar to the transportation models of the previous chapter. Yet here we are concerned with flows of materials at different stages of their manufacture, each involving different unit handling costs. We can use n_{ij} to represent the number of loads that pass between the pair of departments i and j and c_{ij} for the cost of moving one of these loads. The latter takes into account the distance as well as the handling difficulty of the material. There are d departments. The objective function here is then:

$$\text{Total cost} = \sum_{i=1}^{d} \sum_{j=1}^{d} n_{ij} \times c_{ij}$$

A practical approach to this problem is to compare layouts by trial and error. The method is as follows:

a Produce a matrix that shows all the flows between the departments.
b Take a proposed layout and, for each flow, calculate the cost of moving one load.
c Calculate the total movement cost.
d Repeat with adjusted layouts until an optimum is found.
e Make a recommendation based on the outcome.

We will show the first steps of this process here. There is no general optimising algorithm so, in principle, all possibilities have to be tried. But many companies will only be considering a few possible layouts or a minor modification to an existing arrangement. The number of possibilities to be searched will, therefore, be small. Otherwise, computer software is available. The Computer Relationship Layout Planning (CORELAP) package is an example.

Figure 8.1 shows the departmental layout at a jobbing machinist's. Apart from installation costs, there are no constraints on the position of any department, their positions having been laid out in the two buildings by historical accident. The string diagram suggests that the milling department is badly placed and this can be investigated by further analysis.

Table 8.1 presents, in the upper left corners of the cells, the number of pallets moved among the departments in a typical week. In the lower right corners are figures giving estimated costs for each type of pallet movement. The total cost for this arrangement is £1,313, the cost of maintaining a fork lift truck for this purpose. Were the company able to consider a rearrangement, the movement costs could be reduced. The costs would only be saved *if the idle time for the fork truck could be put to a useful alternative purpose.* In practice, it is difficult both to have such a facility on standby and to require it to perform other functions.

The cost approach is only useful if the focus is on the costs of one type of linkage, say material flows. Furthermore, it depends on the quality of the data for both the number of movements and the amount spent per movement. Where such

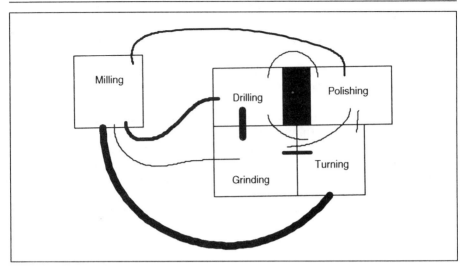

Figure 8.1 String diagram: jobbing machinist

Table 8.1 Movements and costs in jobbing shop

Two-way flows ...	Turning		Grinding		Drilling		Polishing	
Milling	128	4	24	3	70	3	44	4
Turning			55	1	30	2	12	1
Grinding					92	1	32	2
Drilling							30	2
Total costs £	512		127		362		312	

information is not available, it may be better to rely on a more qualitative approach. A *relationship chart* can be used to set out opinions of how close one department needs to be to another. Figure 8.2 shows, in outline, the relationship chart for a telephone-based credit control office. Each cell in the grid expresses how far the planners think the relevant staff or activity areas should be separated. For instance, a few pairings, centred on the receptionist, are seen as absolutely necessary. These are links with the office entrance and the fax and coffee machines. This would be because the receptionist receives the occasional visitor and would offer the person coffee while taking incoming calls and distributing fax messages. Also, it is thought desirable for the senior managers not to be close to

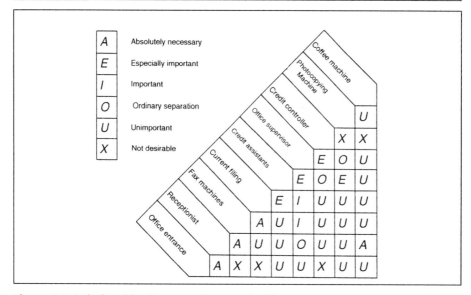

Figure 8.2 Relationship chart: credit control office

the entrance. Note that a full version of the grid would have many more cells. One should also recognise that office layouts can be as much about the representation of status as the desire to pursue efficiency.

4. Batch production

As we saw in chapter 3, batch processing is a step up from jobbing in terms of scale. Batch firms concentrate their attention on a more limited range of products produced in larger quantities than in the jobbing shop. The process-based layout is still used in such operations. With increasing volumes of orders it becomes economical to dedicate a family of machines and a team of specialists to use the *product-based* layout. This is often called the production line. Batch firms are often torn between the flexibility offered by the process system and the efficiency that comes from specialised lines. The balance between the two can shift as changes occur in the business environment. IBM found this to its cost, see Box 8.2[1]. An intermediate position can be achieved with group technology which is discussed in section 5. Section 7 addresses production lines themselves.

5. Group technology

Section 3.17 referred to how batch firms can achieve some of the benefits of line production through *group technology*, also called *cellular manufacturing*. The typical process layout is transformed into a product layout not for the whole production system but for subsystems or cells. These are devoted to the manufacture of families of similar products. In other words, rather than examine the scale of individual orders, none of which would be large enough to justify the setting up of a line, these orders are clustered according to predetermined criteria. These may be:

In 1986, IBM at Greenock spent £6 million to set up a robotic assembly line for PC monitors. Yet, by 1993, the company had decided to dispense with the robots and increase the line manning. Before 1993, some 25 assembly staff, with their robots, produced 550 monitors per shift. Afterwards, 50 assembly workers made 700.

IBM gives the reasons for the change as the rapid pace of technological development and the different safety standards which had been imposed in different countries. Both factors caused the product variety to increase and the line was not flexible enough to cope. To alter the product on the line, it had to be shut down and all the tools and holding mechanisms had to be changed. Now, the only remaining robots pack the finished items into cartons for shipment.

Box 8.2 Removal of robots at IBM, Greenock

- items of a similar size requiring similar processes, although not necessarily in the same sequence
- items with special features that require the use of a particular process.

Group technology cells are then established depending on which criterion has been used. In the former case, the cell may consist of machines that are the same as those used throughout the factory, the mix depending on the product family. In the latter case, the cell may consist of the key machine or process, supported by others as necessary. The arrangement can be seen as involving the establishment of several mini-factories each of which specialises in a subset of the whole product range. Skinner[2] introduced the term *focused factory* to stress the advantages of focus and simplicity in gaining efficiency.

Group technology recognises the value of involving skilled craftsmen in decisions concerning work flow, sequencing and so on rather than restrict them to controlling the machines themselves. Machine operation often requires skilled attention at the setup stage, then the machine can run with occasional checking until another job needs to be set up. Moreover, it is very difficult to avoid some machine idle time in a jobbing shop so to have one person per machine can waste labour costs.

Kumar and Hadjinicola[3] show how cellular manufacturing (CM) was introduced to Champion Irrigation Products. The firm specialises in the manufacture of bronze irrigation products, in particular sprinkler nozzles. End uses include golf courses as well as the domestic market, reached through do-it-yourself stores. CIP was facing problems of highly seasonal demand and the lack of capacity to satisfy the peak. It sought to simplify and improve the production process. 16 products, representing some 70 per cent of sales, were selected for study. For these products, string diagrams were produced to show the routes that they took to pass through the factory. The left-hand half of Figure 8.3 is a sketch of the original layout, The machines are shown as shaded boxes, and the connecting lines, by their thickness, indicate the main flows. The overall impression gained was of long and tortuous sequences through the machines.

For reasons of space, the following explanation has been simplified from the original study. The machining required by each product was identified and recorded. This data is summarised in Table 8.2. The rows in the table represent

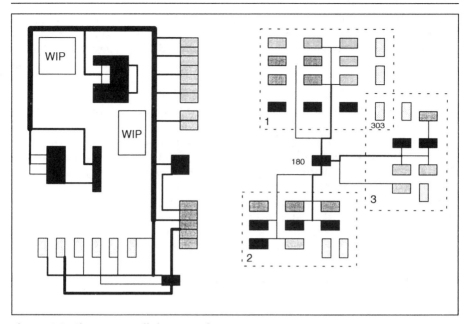

Figure 8.3 Change to cellular manufacture

Table 8.2 Products and their machining, CIP

↓Product codes   Machine codes→

	180	202	208	216	217	219	300	303	311	322	323	325	404	409	410	416
12	X			X	X		X			X		X		X	X	
13	X				X		X			X						
14	X				X		X			X						X
15	X		X	X	X		X			X		X			X	
17	X	X	X				X		X				X			
18	X	X	X				X	X							X	
19	X				X		X			X		X				
20	X	X	X					X					X			
21	X		X					X					X			
21a	X						X							X		X
22	X						X			X				X		X
23	X	X	X				X						X			
24	X			X	X							X			X	
25	X	X	X				X	X					X			
26	X	X	X					X					X			
26a	X					X		X						X		X

each product, the columns the machines. An 'X' entry in a cell indicates that the product required the corresponding machine for its manufacture. At first sight there does not seem to be much of a pattern but product families were identified using a grouping algorithm. This algorithm changed the order of rows and columns to put similar ones together.

Table 8.3 shows the arrangement after the application of the algorithm. It can be seen that the products and machines fall into three distinct families along the matrix diagonal. These families are outlined for emphasis.

The table also shows one of the problems of implementation. Products do not always fall neatly into families and some, such as 12, 17, 18, 23 and 25, overlap into other groups. Furthermore, all products needed to pass through machine 180, shown in the first column.

Installation of cells was subject to several constraints. Some machines could not be moved because of their size or the need to remove large amounts of waste. Reorganisation had to be planned carefully to minimise disruption. The right-hand part of Figure 8.3 sketches how the machines were divided into the proposed cells. Machine 180 was moved to a more central position in the plant and 303 could be shared between Cells 1 and 3. Installation went on in small stages.

Benefits reported by Kumar and Hadjinicola were:

- Work in progress reduced by 70 per cent.
- Simplification of production planning and control.

Table 8.3 Product–machining list after sorting

↓Product codes   Machine codes→

	180	219	303	323	409	416	216	217	300	322	325	410	202	208	311	404
13	X	X	X	X												
14	X	X	X	X		X										
21a	X		X		X	X										
22	X		X	X	X	X										
26a	X	X	X		X	X										
12	X					X	X	X	X	X	X	X				
15	X						X	X	X	X	X	X		X		
19	X							X	X	X	X					
24	X						X	X			X	X				
17	X								X				X	X	X	X
18	X		X									X	X	X	X	
20	X												X	X	X	X
21	X												X	X	X	
23	X		X										X	X		X
25	X		X										X	X	X	X
26	X												X	X	X	X

- Elimination of the need to number intermediate components.
- Quality improvements: the defect rate fell to about a quarter of the previous.
- Increased productivity.
- Greater flexibility and quicker response to demand.

Group technology will work best when there is a clear separation of products into families. Furthermore, given the costs involved, the reorganisation necessary to achieve a cell structure will only be justified if the company can rely on having a regular product mix.

Cells for machining work, or combinations of machines and hand assembly, will work best if they are set out so that staff can work in close proximity. In this way, informal communication can do much to smooth the flow of work as well as increase job satisfaction. It may be possible, in theory, to simulate group technology without moving the equipment. Staff would have to move frequently and the implied complexity of the communication and control systems will rule out this option.

6. Flexible manufacturing systems

Cell-based manufacture does not rule out the possibility of automation. Indeed, at higher throughput volumes, there remains the option of investing in robots and transfer lines to help or replace the human element. An automated cell dealing with a variety of manufacturing tasks is called a *flexible manufacturing system*.

Flexible manufacturing systems, FMS, are generally found in high-volume batch production. In effect, they apply microelectronic control and computer technology to automate group technology. Transfer lines connect a family of machines. In contrast to the traditional mass production line where all items pass through the same processes along a conveyor, the FMS takes up the cell idea in being able to pass any component through the set of machines in any number of ways. FMS has been made possible by the following developments:

- software to optimise production sequences and control the machine family
- robots to load equipment from the conveyors on to the machines
- multi-functional machines with modular tools and jigs fitted using a cartridge system.

The falling price of electronic components has gradually brought down the cost of FMS equipment. This in turn has reduced the break-even volume of output for which it is worth while making the investment. Furthermore, the design of machine tools themselves has developed so that single machines perform an increased variety of functions. The trend in flexible manufacturing is to set up cells with one or two robots handling products and tools for a single machine.

7. Line production

In line, or mass, production the manufacturer produces standardised designs in large volumes. These volumes are sufficiently high and stable to justify the equipment investment. The ideal type of line production system produces just one item. In practice, however, many lines can cope with a narrow range of similar products. They have highly specialised machine tools and other equipment connected by conveyors. In principle, each machine in the system operates at the same rate so that buffer stocks are not required between stages.

Mass production owes its efficiency to a combination of mechanisation and specialisation. The assembly line is both the symbol and the outstanding achievement of industrial engineering.

Ford's first moving car assembly lines, for the Model T, had work carried out while the product was fixed to the line and moving with it, see Box 8.3. Compared with previous methods, it was successful for the following reasons:

- The amount of skill required was reduced. Jobs were divided into elements each requiring a small cycle time, sometimes as low as 30 seconds. This then reduced the training time for workers.
- It stimulated careful attention to the optimisation of work methods that became integrated with the line design and the associated equipment specifications. Work stations could be designed to be highly efficient, for example the four or five nuts on a car wheel could be tightened to the correct torque simultaneously using an electric or pneumatic spanner.
- It reduced the stock of work in progress. Feeder lines, acting as tributaries to the main line, could be tuned to deliver items at the rate required and therefore avoid excessive stocks.

Another line arrangement is where production takes place at static work positions and the line conveys items from one station to another. Small variations in output between stations can be accommodated by fluctuations in buffer stocks that can build up either on the conveyors or at storage points. The packaging of kit toys is an example of this type of work.

Most line production plant is of hybrid form in that it can produce a limited number of products with common characteristics. The plant is then involved in *large batch* production, switching from time to time from one product type to another as in the examples of Box 8.4.

At the planning stage, line production can be seen as either machine-paced or labour-paced. In the former, used for the fabrication of standardised components, the string of machines is designed so that they all work at the same rate. In the latter, characterised by assembly operations, the operating speed must be related to the tasks given to the staff running the line. When this is done, the times needed by each individual to complete the cycle are made as equal as possible. This is based on assigning groups of tasks among individuals to achieve both efficient use of their labour and equity among them. These processes are called *line balancing* which is a critical problem in product-focused production systems.

8. Line balancing

In theory, each stage of the production line is designed to operate at the same rate. In practice, things may not be that simple, especially where the line is used for several products and the processes themselves are subject to gradual develop-

---

Henry Ford is usually acknowledged as having been the first to introduce the modern line. In 1913, Ford's magneto assembly line reduced the labour content per item from 20 minutes to 5. By 1914 a vehicle line had reduced assembly time from 12.5 to 1.5 man-hours.

Box 8.3 The inventor of the line

The most popular canned vegetable is baked beans. Demand is so high that manufacturers such as Heinz are able to run canning lines solely dedicated to this product. Other vegetables and soups are canned in large batches and their lines are stopped for cleaning in between runs.

Carbonated drinks plants operate with large batch production. Bottlers, who may be owned by the drinks companies or simply bottling under licence, mix syrup, water and gas in their process. Most flavours can be handled on each line. Cans and bottles are of standard designs so as to be interchangeable. It is only with very large plants located close to major markets that there are lines dedicated to one product, often one of the colas.

Box 8.4 Examples of line production

ment. It is usually not possible to operate at 100% efficiency. The following worked example of a single line illustrates the difficulties.

A model kit packing line has three separate stages. It starts with operators assembling the boxes from cardboard outers and polystyrene filling pieces. The normal time for this operation is 0.2 minutes. The packers place each box on a conveyor that runs along behind a series of benches occupied by the packers. A packer picks a box from the conveyor and fills it with the appropriate mix of parts from trays located within reach on the bench. Normal time for filling is 0.45 minutes after which the box is returned to another conveyor. This feeds the last process, an automated wrapping machine that covers each box with cellophane with a cycle time of 0.04 minutes. Figure 8.4 shows the layout.

Questions for the production manager are:

- What is the maximum output of the line?
- What manning is needed?
- What is the labour efficiency at this output?

The wrapping machine, which can wrap a box every 0.04 minutes, determines the maximum output of the line. This is 1/0.04 items per minute. That is 25 per minute or 1500 per hour.

An assembler can make up a unit every 0.20 minutes. For the assembly section to achieve the 0.04 minute cycle time, the number of staff would be 0.2/0.04, which is 5. Similarly the number of packers required would be 0.45/0.04, which is 11.25, or 12. Hence the line requires 17 operators in all.

The labour efficiency of this arrangement can be calculated from the ratio of output to input, each measured in minutes of work. Since the line output is 25 per minute, the labour content of such output is 25 × (0.2 + 0.45) minutes. With 17 staff, the input per minute of operation is 17 minutes. Line efficiency is then:

$$\frac{25 \times (0.2 + 0.45)}{17} = 96\%$$

Such a performance would be high for any production line, 85% being a good figure where complexity is great. Note that the normal times given here only measure short-term performance and the industrial engineer would have to build in

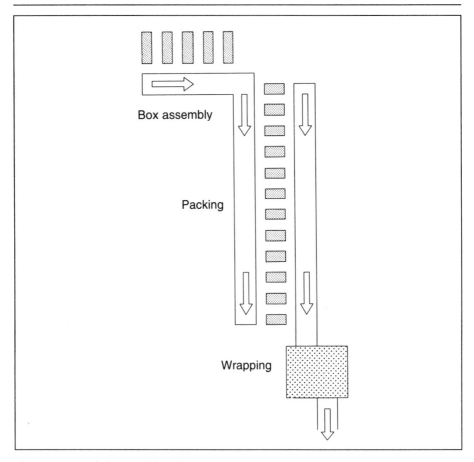

Figure 8.4 Model kit packing line

allowances for rest and breaks. A further difficulty lies in the errors made in the original measurements and the variations in performance between individuals. Fine tuning of lines is often done by experimentation and the intervention of supervisors where bottlenecks occur.

The packing example is simple because the three steps take place in a defined sequence. On many assembly lines, some of the tasks can take place simultaneously and the balancing problem includes the allocation of these among the various staff. The following example shows how this is done.

Let us say that the assembly of an item consists of 9 tasks. An initial study shows how these tasks can be set out in a *precedence diagram*, Figure 8.5. Each rectangle in the figure contains a number giving the time in minutes taken for the task; the arrows indicate the sequence in which the assembly must take place. This is a network using *activity-on-node* notation, a topic dealt with more fully in Chapter 13. The diagram means, for example, activity A must precede both B and C; C precedes F; and so on. Further, C can occur at the same time as B, D, E and so on.

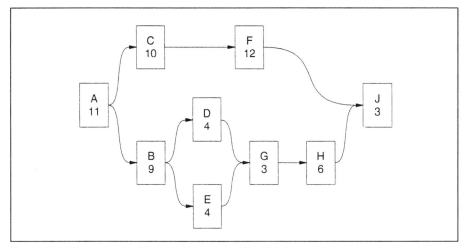

Figure 8.5 Precedence diagram for assembly tasks

Note that the precedence diagram does not relate directly to shop-floor layout, conveyors, machines or whatever.

If only one of these assemblies is required, it can be carried out by one person and the time would be simply a sum of the task times, which is 62 minutes. If more products are required at a faster rate than one every 62 minutes, then more staff are required. Layout constraints mean that it is not possible to double up on any of the tasks. The number of work stations depends on the specified cycle time.

Suppose demand means that an output of 5 units per hour is needed. How can the tasks be most effectively grouped? The method has three steps:

a Calculate the cycle time implied by the demanded production rate. This is found from the relationship:

$$\text{Cycle time} = 1/\text{Production rate}$$

Here the cycle time is 1/5 hr, or 12 min.

b Calculate the minimum number of staff or work stations needed. This is:

$$\text{Number of work stations} = \frac{\text{Total task time}}{\text{Cycle time}}$$

Here, the minimum number of work stations is 62/12, that is 6.

c Allocate the tasks among work stations, ensuring that each station has minimal idle time. This is the core of line-balancing. In our example, the solution can easily be found by inspection and the tasks fall readily into the groupings shown in Figure 8.6.

In the proposal for a 12 minute cycle time, stations B and H/J are idle for 3 minutes, C is idle for 2 minutes per cycle while A and D/E/G would lose 1 minute. The efficiency of the operation is given by:

$$\text{Efficiency} = \frac{\text{Total task time}}{\text{Number of work stations} \times \text{Cycle time}}$$

In this case the figure is 62/(6 × 12) or 86%.

219

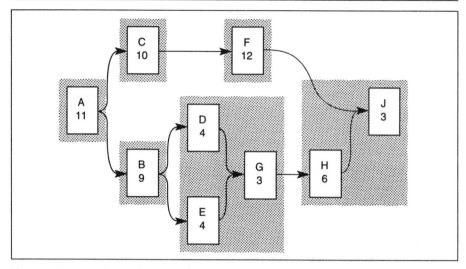

Figure 8.6 Precedence diagram showing one solution to balancing problem

The optimal arrangement of the work stations varies according to the output demanded. Further, although optimal arrangements are made, the efficiency of the line varies with the demand. Table 8.4 shows the different numbers of stations required, together with their corresponding efficiencies, for various production rates.

In Figure 8.6 it will be seen that station F is fully loaded whereas others are idle for up to 15 minutes per hour. This has two implications. First, a good supervisor will be careful to share out the work, possibly, through job rotation. see **5.16**. Not only will this aid motivation but it will provide opportunities for rest breaks. These are needed since the data being used are normal times, not standard times, see **6.14**. The second implication is that station F is the *bottleneck* that decides the maximum speed of the whole assembly operation. As we shall see in Chapter 12, bottlenecks require careful attention and control if output is not to suffer.

The graphical approach, as shown in Figures 8.5 and 8.6, is adequate for small line balancing tasks. There are algorithms that enable solutions to be found by hand. For long lines with many stages programs have been developed to enable grouping of tasks to be optimised. This means that managers can continually adapt the grouping to consider staffing available, output required and any technical problems that may arise.

9. Continuous production

The ideal process plant runs continuously producing an even flow of product to match market demands. While there are, nevertheless, many plants that approach

Table 8.4 Stations and efficiencies for different planned cycle times

Production rate per hour	2	3	4	5
Number of work stations	3	4	5	6
Efficiency	69%	78%	83%	86%

this level of continuity, most have to be closed down at regular intervals to main-tain or replace worn components. Whether the plant can be kept going during such changes is a matter of design and, frequently, safety. Too many accidents to chemi-cal plants take place during periods when repairs are being carried out.

Continuous process manufacturing is carried out for heavy chemicals, oils, polymers, paper, glass, beer, cement and some foods. The plant used is charac-terised by large scale and high capital costs. Changes to capacity are often only available in large increments so that close attention needs to be paid to market demand before investments are made. For instance, in brewing for the mass market, increments of about 90 million litres per year are required if the plant is to maintain economies of scale.

Plant layout is usually decided by the nature of the product being produced. Machines are designed to have, theoretically, the same capacity and to allow the product to flow straight through the plant without stopping. Such would be the case in an oil refinery where there is little room to store intermediate products.

As with the case of mass production lines, the theoretical balancing of all the components of a process production plant is often not achieved. We shall examine two important issues related to this, reliability and line balancing.

10. Reliability

The operation of a straight line process plant requires that all its components are operating at once. Figure 8.7 sets out the components of a process plant in the form of what is known as a *series reliability structure*. Failure of any piece of equip-ment in the line means that the whole has to stop.

For most pieces of equipment, it is possible to estimate the reliability, usually expressed as the probability of surviving for a given period. This could be the time between annual shutdowns. Let us express the reliability of the components as R_1, R_2 etc. We can then find the reliability of the whole plant surviving from one shutdown to the next from combining these probabilities as follows:

R_{plant} = (Item 1 survives) and (Item 2 survives) and etc

That is,

$R_{plant} = R_1 \times R_2 \times R_3 \times \ldots \times R_n$

In the case of 5 stages, 4 of which have a reliability of 98% (one breakdown in 50 years) and the fifth having a reliability of 90% (one breakdown in 10 years), the reliability is

$R_{plant} = 0.98 \times 0.98 \times 0.98 \times 0.98 \times 0.90$

That is 0.83, or 83%. The greater the number of components, the more the plant reliability will reduce. What could managers do about this problem? The most obvious step would be to improve the component with lowest reliability. For

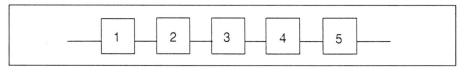

Figure 8.7 Series reliability structure

example, if the lowest was increased to 95%, the reliability of the system would rise to 88%. Let us say, however, that it is not possible to achieve improvements in the individual components. What then? It may be possible to duplicate the weakest ones to incorporate a parallel reliability structure. In such an arrangement, the failure of one component does not mean that others will fail too. Such arrangements are not prone to sudden failure but deteriorate gradually. These structures are very common. For example it would be extremely foolish to wire all the bulbs in Blackpool illuminations in a series structure!

Figure 8.8 sets out the same process plant as in Figure 8.7. Now the weakest (say, no. 3) component is backed up by several others in a parallel reliability structure at that stage.

For the parallel stage only, let us express the reliability of the components as R_a, R_b etc. We find the reliability of the stage surviving from one shutdown to the next by combining these probabilities as follows:

$$R_{stage} = \text{(Item } a \text{ survives) or (Item } b \text{ survives) or etc}$$

Expressed another way, if F represents probability of failure,

$$F_{stage} = \text{(Item } a \text{ fails) and (Item } b \text{ fails) and etc}$$

That is,

$$F_{stage} = F_a \times F_b \times F_c \times \ldots \times F_n$$

Since R and F are connected by the equation, $R = (1 - F)$,

$$R_{stage} = (1 - ((1 - R_a) \times (1 - R_b) \times \ldots \times (1 - R_n)))$$

Now, the more components in a parallel stage, the more its reliability. For example, in the case of duplicating a weak component, whose reliability is 90%, with another of the same capacity and reliability, the stage reliability is given by

$$R_{stage} = (1 - ((1 - 0.90) \times (1 - 0.90)) = 0.99 \text{ or } 99\%$$

Adding another parallel component increases this to 99.9%.

The reliability of plant can be increased by the provision of parallel structures at points where the equipment is unacceptably unreliable or when the provision

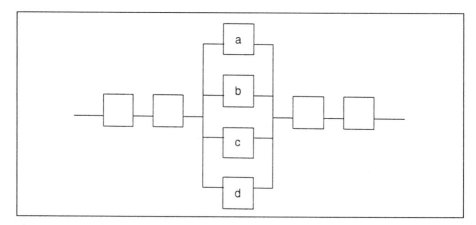

Figure 8.8 Parallel reliability structure

of standby capacity has a low enough cost. Such decisions depend on achieving the right investment balance between the value of increased plant reliability and the cost of providing the spare capacity. Parallel reliability is built into the designs of many process plants; the cost of a standby motor or pump being far less than the consequences for the whole system of an avoidable shutdown. Safety is also a critical criterion in many cases.

The transmission networks of the gas, water, electricity and telephone companies can be thought of as very large, and widely distributed, process plants. Their purpose is to maintain interconnection, either from sources to consumers or, in telephones, between any pair of users. They incorporate many duplicated routes and items of equipment. This is partly the result of historical development but also, in creating these distribution grids, there has been a deliberate policy of building parallel reliability structures. In 1994, Thames Water completed its ring main for supplies in London. The ring allows for any section to be closed without interrupting supplies. The National Electricity Grid and the National Gas Transmission System are further, more complex examples. A schematic map of the gas grid is shown in Figure 8.9[4]. It clearly shows parallel links on many primary routes. Grids have their own problems of line balancing to ensure the most efficient distribution of energy.

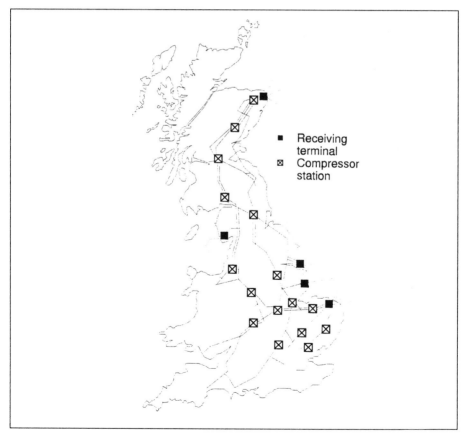

Figure 8.9 Sketch of National Gas Transmission System

11. Line balancing in process plants

Although a process plant may be designed with balanced stages, in reality the capacity of each is not fixed in the longer term. Continuous development of components and experience of operation may lead to the discovery of ways of increasing potential output of the stage. The plant will, of course, only operate at the speed of the lowest capacity stage. Managers will need to focus their attention on this bottleneck if they want to increase output. Yet, in the decision to increase stage capacity the question arises of how much to increase the capacity by.

Consider a plant made up of five stages whose capacities, in units per hour, are as labelled in Figure 8.10. Here, component D, with the lowest capacity, would be the target for attention. To what level should its capacity be increased? Any size above that of C would clearly be wasted in the immediate future but such a policy would not consider possible developments in C itself. Prudent management may, therefore, consider adding a higher capacity to D to take this into account. Improvements that are made must be part of a plan that considers the development possibilities of each stage of the process and assesses likely market demand.

12. Hybrid layouts

We should note that many manufacturing plants do not follow the typology set out at the start of this chapter. There are many that combine two or more of the five basic systems - project, jobbing, batch, line and continuous - into hybrid layouts. It is important that these differences are recognised as the processes of planning and control will have to adapt to each system. Some examples of hybrids are shown in Box 8.5.

Schmenner points out that common hybrids, namely *batch flow–line flow* and *batch flow–continuous* systems have the typical characteristic of imbalance between the two sections[5]. Significant blocks of time are needed in the batch system to set up machines to work on different components. This means that it is impossible to match continuously the intermittent output of the batch process with the need for continuous input to the next stage. Pressure can be brought to bear to increase batch sizes but, as we shall see, this only increases total stocks and makes the difficulty worse. It is not possible to achieve a balance hour by hour in these hybrid systems. It is normal to separate them by a *decoupling* stock or *buffer*. The continuous system feeds off the buffer which is replenished intermittently by the upstream batch processes. Many food processing companies prepare ingredients in batches and then mix and pack continuously. Therefore, managers must not only manage each part of these systems but they must also pay attention to their interface.

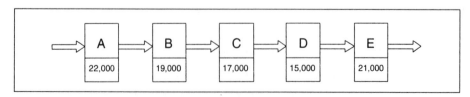

Figure 8.10 Five-stage plant with unbalanced component capacities

A pharmaceutical manufacturer produces aspirin in a process plant. Batches are then packaged in bottles and packets of various sizes.

A maker of sinks and other bathroom fittings uses vitreous china. Raw materials are blended in a process plant; items are moulded in both small and large batches; glazing and firing are mass production; lastly, the assembly of special lines is done on a jobbing basis.

A film processor develops film in a process plant and prints it in batches.

In the iron industry, casting used to be done as batch production. Recent years have, however, seen the growth of integrated steel works. This followed the invention of continuous casting. Downstream activities such as coating or galvanising are also continuous production but the cutting is done in batches to suit demand.

Box 8.5 Examples of hybrid production systems

13. Human factors in layout design

In **5.16** and **5.17** we noted the importance of job rotation and job teams in motivation. A good work layout will consider these motivational aspects as well as other factors such as flexibility and control. Taking the traditional example of the assembly line, a straight line design is often the one that is chosen. It suits the ideal case of balanced work stations and well-controlled staff sticking to their separate tasks along the way. Yet we know that the balanced line is unusual. Then the linear arrangement may separate workers by such distances that any flexibility that may be gained from sharing tasks is not available.

The traditional linear arrangement, as in example A of Figure 8.11, makes it difficult for the workers to form a coherent working group. A U-shaped layout, as in B and C, may help in the development of communication. This can help in smoothing of the flow on the line and problems being anticipated before they occur. Plan B allows easy observation and eye-contact at the expense of increasing the distances between staff, if they cannot cross the conveyor. Plan C, on the other hand, has workers facing away from each other when at their work stations. But their proximity will make line balancing easier when the cycle speed demands only a reduced number.

The advantages of U-shaped layouts should also be recognised in noisy working environments. These should, of course, never be regarded as good conditions, and staff should be provided with good ear protection. Where noise reduction is infeasible, non-verbal communication becomes more important in running the line. Further, the ability of workers to see each other easily contributes to safe working.

Case study: Warehousing operations [6]

Warehousing is an isolated service whose planning focus is on operating efficiency. Group Technology principles can be used to take advantage of similarities among key elements. There are four ways of doing this:

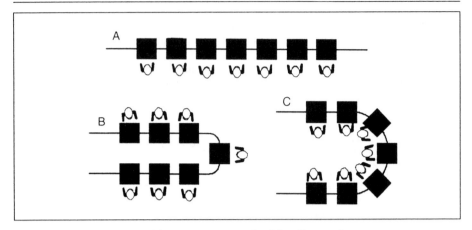

Figure 8.11 Two U-shaped layouts compared with a linear plan

1 Products with a high chance of being 'picked' simultaneously. These could be stacked in the same area.
2 Products with a high chance of being loaded to the same group of vehicles. These could be picked simultaneously.
3 Matching individuals or teams of staff to product groups. This would cut the number of staff trips into the warehouse.
4 Dedicating bays on board vehicles to products.

A 4,000 square metre beer distribution warehouse held 55 product lines. The following day's deliveries were loaded each night onto 60 delivery lorries. Of these, 34 had 12 bays, 10 had 16, and 16 had 18 bays. Loading was carried out by eight forklift drivers, working in four pairs. High volume products, loaded on pallets, were brought as needed from the warehouse and loaded straight into the lorry bays. Some stocks of low volume items were kept in the loading area where the staff could select the required number of cases for their vehicles.

The potential GT improvements listed above were investigated.

1 The forklift trucks could not handle more than one pallet at a time, although heavier ones could do so. Consequently, the idea of simultaneous picking did not apply. Further, grouping similar products in the same area cuts across the need to change the stock balance in response to promotions and rotate it to keep it fresh.
2 Simultaneous picking for several vehicles was ruled out for the reasons given in 1. The bottleneck in operations was forklift trucking.
3 It was possible to dedicate staff to groups of product lines. This policy was already in operation informally. One loader concentrated on high volume lines while the other looked after the low volume stock kept in the loading bay itself.
4 Dedicating vehicle bays to products was the most promising approach for efficiency improvement. Loading instructions showed goods by bay and these varied each day. Some customers had to have their loads placed in identified positions because of access difficulties in, say, narrow alleys. Apart from this, bays could have the same products each day, as opposed to the current haphazard allocation. The low volume stocks could then be stacked close to their dedicated bays and loading teams would spend less time sorting pallets that had been put in the wrong ones.

Questions

1 *How would a cluster analysis be used to study any of the four proposed operating policies?*

2 *Simultaneous picking was not favoured here. What conditions would make this policy advantageous?*

3 *Suggest other operational activities that might be improved by using GT principles.*

References

1. Hallahan, S. (1994) 'All hands to the production lines' *The Times* 29 July p. 15
2. Skinner, W. (1974) 'The focused factory' *Harvard Business Review* **52.3** May–June pp. 113–121
3. Kumar, K.R., and Hadjinicola, G.C. (1993) 'Cellular Manufacturing at Champion Irrigation Products' *International Journal of Operations and Production Management* **13.8** pp. 53–61
4. Based on maps in the annual reports of British Gas.
5. Schmenner, R.W., (1993) *Production/Operations Management* 5th edition New York, Macmillan pp. 6–7
6. Shafer, Scott M. and Ernst, Ricardo (1993) 'Applying group technology principles to warehouse operations' *International Journal of Purchasing and Materials Management* **29.2** pp. 38–42

9

FACILITY LAYOUT:
PERSONAL AND SELF SERVICE

Chapter objectives

When you have finished studying this chapter, you should be able to:

- Explain the causes and consequences, for the service organisation, of the imbalance of supply and demand; suggest responses to this problem.

- Describe the basic elements of a queuing system; show how statistical distributions can be used to model these elements.

- Discuss the characteristics of some common queue structures, identifying where each may be appropriate.

- Clarify the purpose of simulation and outline its advantages and disadvantages.

- Show how the Monte Carlo method works and how it can be applied to simulate queues.

- Explain why the acceptability of queue length varies from case to case.

- Outline the role of operations planning in the avoidance of waiting.

- Demonstrate how an awareness of customer perceptions can lead to improvements in the waiting process.

- Summarise the important issues in store and shopping centre layouts.

INTRODUCTION

Many features of layouts described for manufacturing systems apply also to services. This is especially true for those service facilities that have been isolated from direct contact with customers through a 'front office' or sales function. These are the *service shop* and *service factory* described in Chapter 3. Direct service activities, in contrast, have a particular problem in that they cannot easily cope with fluctuations in demand. On the one hand, personal service cannot be stocked. On the other hand, organisations can only cope with maximum demand at the expense of unused capacity at other times. Queues are an inherent part of the personal and self service functions.

Queues are not wholly outside the control of the organisation. Having understood the ways in which queues form and are sustained, the manager can take action to limit their extension beyond acceptable lengths and also influence the

228

perceptions of those who are in the line. The way in which a service provider manages queues offers it an opportunity to display to customers positive aspects of its attitudes towards them. A clear, active and fair approach to queue management is a key element of good service.

The involvement of the customer in service has other implications for layout design. Especially in self service, a layout must be attractive and convenient for customers. Good layout is an important element of sales promotion.

1. Balancing demand and capacity

It is rare that a service system achieves the ideal, an equilibrium between demand and capacity. At times when the system is out of balance, there is either a queue or over capacity at the service points. Before investigating how to cope with these, we should note that, typically, there is scope for influencing either the demand or the capacity. The following are possible actions:

Demand

- Segment the demand and restrict access to the facility at busy times to certain categories of customer.
- Charge different prices at busy and slack periods.
- Use other promotional incentives to encourage off-peak demand.
- Have a reservation system, either continuously or at peak periods.

Capacity

- Provide flexible capacity: employ extra staff at peak periods; ensure that staff are multi-skilled.
- Adapt the service that is offered, switching, as demand varies, between *standardised* and *customised* service as shown in Figure 3.1.
- Switch between self service and personal service, the processes of *attachment* and *detachment* of Figure 3.1.
- Share capacity with other organisations.
- Automate some operations to reduce service times.

Many service organisations follow one or more of the above policies. For instance, many restaurants use differential pricing between lunch and evening and weekday and weekend; promotional offers may run from Mondays to Thursdays; they may offer a fixed-price quick service lunch menu and a fuller one at dinner; reservations may be advised on weekend evenings; staff are employed according to anticipated demand.

In carrying out the balancing policies, managers must recognise constraints that exist both in the market and in their operating system. These include:

- The complexities of introducing and managing differential pricing structures. These have to be communicated to customers before they can influence behaviour and may not, therefore, have much effect on infrequent users.
- The danger of cheapening the service in the eyes of full-price customers.
- Significant deterioration in service quality.
- Limits to the flexibility that can be built in to the service design.
- Perceptions of unfairness if some customers are treated differently to others.

The extent to which the policies work is influenced by the traditions of each industry. Customers expect restaurants to vary their policy at different times, although perhaps not at *The Ritz*. The convention of higher fares on commuter trains is well established. Yet higher prices for some long-distance tickets on 'Fridays, certain Saturdays in July and August, and 23rd December' are not well understood and cause frustration for some travellers. Complex charging structures for telephone calls are also not well understood and do not affect those business users who do not pay for the bills themselves.

2. The queuing problem

While some smoothing of demand and capacity can occur, an imbalance is inevitable in personal and self service systems. Variability results in queues. Given this difficulty, the basic question is to reconcile the following objectives:

- To provide a service capacity that keeps waiting lines down to a tolerable length while not inducing excessive costs, and
- To limit the risk of creating dissatisfaction among customers, or even a loss of their business if excessive service times lead to their 'voting with their feet'.

Performance against these objectives can be assessed as follows. First, operations managers accept that there needs to be some spare capacity at the service points. In other words, the ratio

$$\text{Service capacity utilisation} = \frac{\text{Service time demanded}}{\text{Service time made available}}$$

is less than 100%. Secondly, the effectiveness of managing queues can be assessed by counting their average length or measuring waiting time. Either figure gives an estimate of the likely customer responses. This means of appraising responses will be imprecise because, as we shall see in section **12**, there are many ways for managers to influence customers' perceptions of the queuing experience and therefore their attitudes towards it.

In summary, the following detailed measures of a queuing system's performance are readily obtained and used for assessment:

Assessing the queue

- Average time spent, either in the queue or in the system (including being served)
- Average number of customers in the queue or in the system
- The probability that the number in the queue (or the system) will exceed a defined level or threshold.

Assessing efficiency

- Service capacity utilisation, as defined above
- The probability that a service station will be idle.

The relationship between queuing time and service capacity utilisation is not linear. Figure 9.1 shows how the gradient steepens as utilisation approaches 100%. Increasing capacity reduces utilisation. To take the case of supermarket checkouts, when many are in operation, it is possible to close some with little

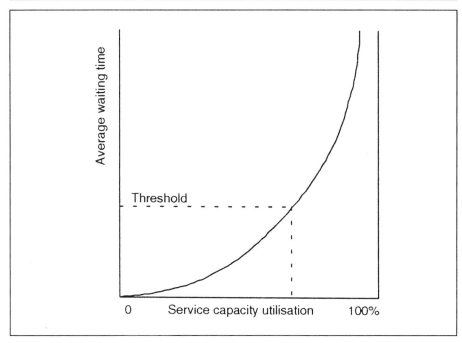

Figure 9.1 Queuing time and capacity utilisation

effect on the average waiting time for customers. As the utilisation of the operators rises, however, attempts to further increase their efficiency will lead to proportionately greater increases in queuing time. It would be foolish to attempt to achieve zero waiting times, so one way of managing the lines is to aim for a performance threshold, as in Figure 9.1. The supervisors then adjust their capacity, and therefore utilisation, in order to keep waiting times below the threshold.

MODELLING QUEUES

Before investigating how managers can cope with queues in a positive way, we need to develop a deeper understanding of why and how they form and operate. After all, Figure 9.1 merely sketches the link between queuing and capacity. We will investigate some models of common situations in later sections. First we must grasp the three basic elements of a queue system – the pattern of arrivals, the queue discipline and the service process.

3. Pattern of arrivals

There are two main factors to be considered when studying the pattern of arrivals at a service point: the size of the population from which the arrivals come and the time distribution of the arrivals themselves.

Source population

Most queuing models consider that the arrivals are *drawn from an infinite population*. The implication of this assumption is that the arrival of one customer for

231

service does not affect the chances of the arrival of another. Demand, therefore, follows a consistent pattern. Although this pattern may be random, it is assumed to be governed by constant parameters. The arrival of customers at booking offices, calls to the fire service, approaches of vehicles to bottlenecks on the road and returns of faulty consumer goods for service are all assumed to have these characteristics.

Where service demands are *drawn from a finite population*, things get a little more complicated. Here, one demand for service will have an impact on the likelihood of another arising because the number of items not being serviced is reduced. The example of a vehicle service workshop will clarify the difference. A car arriving at a Kwikfit service centre will have negligible impact on the pattern of future demand at that or any other centre. It is, in effect, drawn from an infinite population. On the other hand, if the maintenance shop is set up to service a limited number of special vehicles, such as aircraft or railway locomotives, the arrival of one machine for urgent repair in itself reduces the likelihood of another arriving. The existence of the finite population is, therefore, important in the establishment of service policies. This question frequently arises in plant maintenance. Consequently, detailed discussion will be left until Chapter 10.

It has been found that the random pattern of arrivals at service facilities matches closely the *Poisson distribution*. This probability distribution describes the probability, P_x, of x events occurring within a period of length t. The relationship is

$$P_x = \frac{e^{-\lambda t} (\lambda t)^x}{x!}$$

The symbol λ (*lambda*) is the average arrival rate. Therefore the average number of arrivals that occur in time t is λt. [$x!$ stands for factorial x, being the multiple of x. $(x-1).(x-2).(x-3). \ldots .1$.]

Figure 9.2 shows Poisson distributions for three values of λt. It shows that, if the average arrival rate is 2 customers per period (in this case one minute), the probability of exactly 2 customers arriving in any minute is 0.27, which is 27%. Further, the number of arrivals is spread across values from zero to 9 or more, although the probability of high numbers arriving is very small. For instance, in some 13% of the intervals no-one will arrive, whereas less than 1% of the minutes will see 7 come. Even smaller chances apply to values higher than 7. The Poisson distribution, then, models the variability of the pattern of incoming demand. Note that, in the examples of Figure 9.2, the numbers of customers can only take integer values, hence the bar chart. The bars are connected by lines merely to enable the groups to be seen easily.

Arrivals at a service point are not always distributed according to approximations of the Poisson formula. It is necessary to compare observations before this assumption is confirmed. Many cases do conform, however, and the simplicity of the formula's outcomes (if not its construction) helps its use in modelling common forms of queue. Simple statistical points are that the mean value of the distribution is λ and the standard deviation, the measure of spread, is $\sqrt{\lambda}$.

4. Queue discipline

Queue discipline refers to behaviour on arrival. Most models assume that customers are patient. They wait in queues until they are served; they do not switch

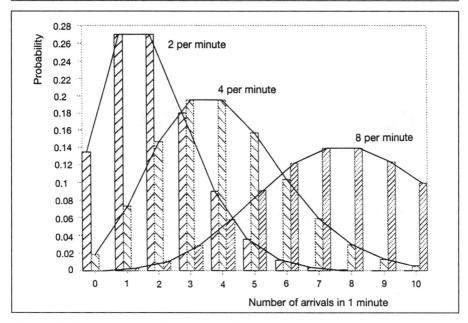

Figure 9.2 Examples of the Poisson distribution

from line to line; they do not decline to join if the file is too long; they do not back out after joining. We know that in real life such behaviour does occur. Indeed, it is possible to observe and model deviations from patient behaviour but this will only add complexity to our discussions. For instance, the likelihood of backing out will be affected by how easy it is, by how important the service is to the customer, by the individual's estimate of the wait and by his or her perception of the waiting experience itself. It is almost impossible to renege from a line of vehicles in a one-way street but much easier to pull out of a queue for a ride at a funfair.

Another possible response is for some people to cheat. We are used to FIFO, which is *first-in-first-out*, as the basic rule. Queue jumping is more common in some cultures than others and, even within one country, more common at some times and places than at others. Compare, for example, your local newsagent's or bank with the frenzied atmosphere of the theatre bar during the interval. In the former, short queues and the fact that you are known support conventions of politeness; the latter, in contrast, is more like warfare among strangers. Such circumstances are difficult to model usefully. Hence our discussion of queue models assumes, for simplicity, a discipline where all customers line up according to the same rules.

Figure 9.3 illustrates some common situations.

- The first is the simple system. There is one line to one station at which all service is given in a single phase. Typical examples are book returns at the library, stored telephone calls to a single-manned enquiry desk and vehicles at a toll booth.
- The second line is less common. Specialist service stations perform functions in sequence. Waiting twice makes such arrangements unpopular. Figure 9.3 could illustrate a queue of vehicles at a frontier where passports are checked by security

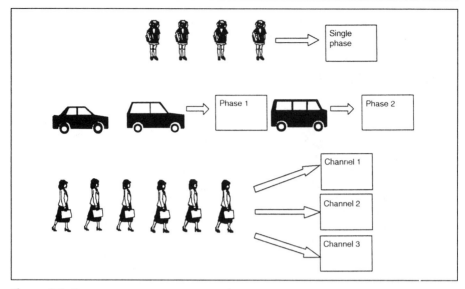

Figure 9.3 Common queue arrangements

officials and goods by customs. Banks in Italy often have separate cashier desks at which customers have to queue a second time. Sometimes they are found in hospitals where diagnosis is carried out in stages. A variant is at a blood donor centre where the first station screens out unsuitable candidates.

• The third arrangement shown in Figure 9.3 is the single line to multiple channels. This is commonly found in post offices but is also used in telephone queuing, ballot counting and entries to large car parks.

Other arrangements can be studied as variations on these themes. For example, the multiple lines in supermarkets can be understood as a set of simple systems, that is single-line single-channel systems. This is provided that customers follow the queue disciplines set out above.

5. Models of the service process

It can be seen that there are many possible queue arrangements and as many models to go with them. Rather than go into excessive detail, we will examine in this section three that are commonly met with. They are listed, with their main characteristics, in Box 9.1.

Referring to Box 9.1, we will take the simple case first and then consider two changes to that case – increasing the number of channels and fixing the service time. The first two models allow for the cases where the service given to each customer is not constant. It is decided more by the customer's requirements than by the process or equipment used to supply the service. The statistical distribution that approximates closely to this type of service pattern is the *negative exponential* distribution. This allows for the observation that much service only takes a very short time and the probability of very long times is low. As with the Poisson distribution, the negative exponential is fully defined by its mean value, here the average number served, μ (pronounced *mew*), per unit of time.

234

Name of system	Number of channels	Service time	Example pattern
Single channel	1	Exponential	Simple purchase or enquiry
Multiple channel	> 1	Exponential	Bank; AA or RAC telephone support
Single channel with fixed service time	1	Fixed	Photograph booth; fairground ride

Box 9.1 Simple queuing systems with variations

The curves in Figure 9.4 are distributions with different μ values. They show the probability that service will take longer than the number of minutes shown on the horizontal axis. Clearly, the family of curves all start where the probability = 1 as all service lasts longer than zero time. The graphs can be interpreted as follows. In the case with a mean service time of 4 minutes, the probability of the time exceeding 4 minutes is 0.36 or 36%. Further, some 28% of the customers require more than 5 minutes. Thus the number requiring service of between 4 and 5 minutes is 8%.

As with patterns of arrival times, one must take care with fitting curves to observed data. We have noted that some services, being machine-paced or

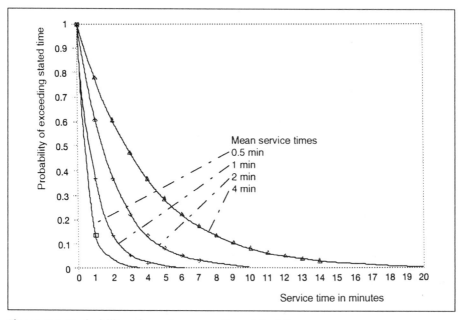

Figure 9.4 Probability of service exceeding stated time

timetabled, have fixed durations. Even in personal service, however, patterns do not always approximate to the exponential distribution. Hair cutting is one example; such times may be better represented by a normal distribution about a mean value.

Considering all the assumptions we have made, we can now present results for the three systems being studied. These are as follows:

Single channel

Probability (P_0) of zero customers in the system $= 1 - \dfrac{\lambda}{\mu}$

Average number of customers in the system $= \dfrac{\lambda}{\mu - \lambda}$

in the queue $= \dfrac{\lambda^2}{\mu\,(\mu - \lambda)}$

Average time spent in the system $= \dfrac{1}{\mu - \lambda}$

in the queue $= \dfrac{\lambda}{\mu\,(\mu - \lambda)}$

System utilisation $= \dfrac{\lambda}{\mu}$ proportion of idle time $= 1 - \dfrac{\lambda}{\mu}$

Multiple channel

Probability (P_0) of zero customers in the system

$$= \cfrac{1}{\left[\displaystyle\sum_{x=0}^{N-1} \dfrac{1}{x!} \left(\dfrac{\lambda}{\mu} \right)^x \right] + \dfrac{1}{N!} \left(\dfrac{\lambda}{\mu} \right)^N \dfrac{N\mu}{N\mu - \lambda}}$$

Average number of customers in the system

$$= \cfrac{\lambda\mu \left(\dfrac{\lambda}{\mu} \right)^N}{(N-1)!\,(N\mu - \lambda)^2} P_0 + \dfrac{\lambda}{\mu}$$

Average time spent in the system

$$= \cfrac{\mu \left(\dfrac{\lambda}{\mu} \right)^N}{(N-1)!\,(N\mu - \lambda)^2} P_0 + \dfrac{1}{\mu}$$

System utilisation $= \dfrac{\lambda}{N\mu}$ proportion of idle time $= 1 - \dfrac{\lambda}{N\mu}$

Single channel with fixed service time

Probability (P_0) of zero customers in the system $= 1 - \dfrac{\lambda}{\mu}$

Average number of customers in the system $= \dfrac{\lambda^2}{2\mu(\mu - \lambda)} + \dfrac{\lambda}{\mu}$

in the queue $= \dfrac{\lambda^2}{2\mu(\mu - \lambda)}$

Average time spent in the system $= \dfrac{\lambda}{2\mu(\mu - \lambda)} + \dfrac{1}{\mu}$

in the queue $= \dfrac{\lambda}{2\mu(\mu - \lambda)}$

System utilisation $= \dfrac{\lambda}{\mu}$ proportion of idle time $= 1 - \dfrac{\lambda}{\mu}$

These results illustrate three important points about the study of queues:

- Congestion at a service point begins to become a problem even when the system utilisation, λ/μ, is much less than 100%. The single line to two service channels, shown in Figure 9.5, illustrates the problem. Here, the service capacity of the two channels is 80 customers per hour. It can be seen that, when the arrival rate is 60, implying a utilisation of 75%, the *average* queue length is two persons. For an arrival rate of 70, the queue stretches to 5.
- Modelling can show potential improvements that flow from changing queue structures. Figure 9.5 enables us to compare a single line with two independent ones. The two arrangements have the same nominal capacity, $2 \times 40 = 80$ customers per hour. To model the separate lines, it is assumed that customers arrive at each at random and do not switch from one to another. This would often be a rather artificial assumption but applies where there is no communication between the queues. Sometimes customers enter buildings such as theatres or stadia through different doors; telephone queues may have this structure.

  Figure 9.5 shows the potential improvements to be gained from combining the two into a single line. For the same service level, represented by average queue length, the system could offer less capacity or, with the same capacity, the queue length is roughly halved. Combining lines while keeping the number of service points constant always increases capacity.
- Fixed-time service systems perform better than variable ones. The equations allow a simple comparison to be made. They show that, for a given standard of system utilisation, the numbers of customers in the queue, and therefore the time spent in it, are halved in the fixed-time case. This takes us back to the original problem of service provision – *it is the intrinsic variability of service that creates efficiency problems*.

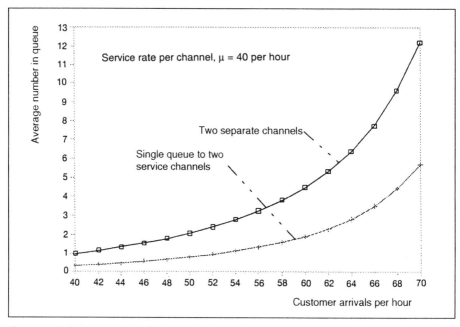

Figure 9.5 Separate and single queues compared

Many queuing situations have characteristics similar to the cases we have illustrated here. Theoretical models have been developed to cover many of them. In practice, however, managers are less concerned with the details of theoretical differences and more with taking practical steps to improve their operations. Therefore, they need some understanding of queue behaviour and some means of testing alternative approaches. These aims can be achieved through simulation.

6. Simulation models

As an alternative to mathematical modelling, simulation avoids some theoretical pitfalls. For example, the assumptions of Poisson distributions for arrival times and negative exponential distributions for service times need to be checked before the above results can be used with confidence. Simulation can approach each situation more directly.

A simulation model duplicates the relevant features of a real system. Since the important features are dynamic, the model is constructed to represent the way they change through time. Simulation refers to the process of operating the model and, by observing its behaviour, drawing conclusions about the performance of the real system.

Models for simulation range across the full spread of model types: iconic, analogue and symbolic.

Iconic

Iconic models represent the key properties by duplicating them directly within the model itself. There is often a change in scale so that, in a (say) one-tenth scale model of an aircraft, each dimension is replicated in this proportion. This shows

238

one immediate difficulty for such modelling in that not all properties scale down in the same proportion. The flying characteristics of the model aircraft are affected by the fact that the mass depends on the cube of the linear scale and the lift from the wings is proportionate to their surface area, which is their linear dimension squared. Thus even the most accurate scale model of an aircraft could not fly in the same way as the original.

In addition to widespread use in engineering design and architecture, iconic models show their value in full size mock-ups of plant and equipment. These are used to test designs and to train operators before 'letting them loose' on the real thing. Examples include flight simulators, driving simulators and full-scale control rooms operating dummy nuclear power plants.

Analogue

In analogue models, system properties are represented by different, yet equivalent, properties in the model. For instance, the flow of goods through a distribution system may be compared to the flow of water through a system of channels and sluices, the latter representing bottlenecks at which delays occur. Study of such an analogue model *may* give insight into critical issues in the system itself. Analogue models are sometimes used for training, especially of people who are not used to thinking in abstract terms. Box 9.2 shows an example given by Kinnie and Staughton[1]. JIT, or Just-in-Time, is covered in **12.10**.

Role plays, case studies and related exercises are often seen as analogue models to be used in management training. Both interviewers and interviewees, for example, are coached by means of such methods. While being of some value in bringing out issues for both parties, they often turn out to be inadequate preparation for the 'real thing'. This difficulty arises because the real interview and its analogue model diverge in critical ways. Clearly, for the interviewee, the level of stress will be significantly different.

Symbolic

Symbolic models are more abstract than analogue ones. While being sometimes more difficult to understand at first, this class of model can be immensely useful to the manager in understanding and solving problems. Algebraic models, such as the ones used throughout this book, have wide application. Other symbolic models use plain numbers, geometry or further notational forms such as logical symbols and pictograms. Graphs are also important although it can be argued that the fact that distances on the graphs correspond to real-life values places them in the analogue category.

Whatever the type of model, it will have one or more uses. First, the most straightforward use is *description*. By this we mean that, through mimicking rele-

---

Simulation was used to introduce JIT to the workforce at a company producing vehicle components. Managers used cardboard boxes and spacers to demonstrate the working of a production line. They were able to show the differences between push and pull production control systems. The demonstration proved to be 'a very persuasive tool for introducing employees to the principal benefits of JIT.'

Box 9.2 JIT simulation at 'Engines'

vant elements of a system's structure or of its processes, we can describe the system itself. Thus an architect's drawing describes a structure, a map shows a route, a production plan sets out a series of tasks to be done and a profit and loss account summarises the process of a business. Secondly, the model enables us to *understand and explain* features of the system. Through investigation of the models form and dynamic behaviour, we can identify and explain key relationships. Not all models allow this to happen. My son's 1/132 scale model of a Klingon Battle Cruiser tells me little about space travel, hyperspace or how the *Enterprise* always wins. On the other hand, leave an experienced accountant with your cash flow account for an hour and you will be presented with a series of questions and comments on the health of your business.

In each of the above purposes, description and understanding, the emphasis is on communication. This takes us to the third function of models, *control.* Understanding through the model leads to the notion of predicting system behaviour by use of the model and therefore taking control of it. This is the essence of *feedforward control* as discussed in **4.21**. Finally, given that the controller has an objective, we see that the model can be used for *optimisation.* It can be available for use when the controller needs assistance with a decision or be placed in permanent control of part or all the operations. This is *real-time process control* and can be seen in may process manufacturing plants, automatic pilots and computer managed traffic signals.

Box 9.3 summarises the pros and cons of using simulation models. Because they can be set out in a more analogous way than the mathematical models described above, many people find them easier to use and understand, at least in their simple forms. Their greatest disadvantage lies in the fact that each is unique and, therefore, needs to be independently tested before it can be used for its intended purposes. Computer packages, many with associated graphical outputs, simplify the simulation of hundreds of system cycles. On the other hand, the internal modelling logic of the package becomes more mysterious to the average

Advantages	Disadvantages
Relatively straightforward to understand.	Can be expensive and time consuming.
Can be used where there is no alternative model.	Each model is unique; results from one simulation cannot be generalised.
Valuable where distributions of events, such as the pattern of customer arrivals, cannot be fitted to standard formulae.	While standard distributions can be avoided, not using them can increase the effort involved in the modelling process.
Often brings out the complex and interactive nature of system components as the simulation is taken through time.	Model does not produce answers; optimal solutions must be found by trial and error.

Box 9.3 The value of simulation models

user. In the next sections we shall 'walk through' a queue simulation to explain the elements from which large models are built. First, however, we shall examine how the Monte Carlo method is used to simulate chance events.

7. The Monte Carlo method

The strength of many simulation models lies in the fact that they can incorporate chance events into their behaviour. This is the key to the approach. Once a simulated stream of activities has been generated it is often a simple task to set out their sequence in a multiple activity chart of the type shown in **6.11**.

The Monte Carlo method is so called because much of the thinking about probabilistic events was developed through study of games of chance. It can be set out in a sequence of five steps:

- Create a probability distribution for each variable in the model.
- Build up a cumulative frequency distribution from this data.
- Set out groups of random numbers to be associated with each interval in the cumulative distribution.
- Generate random numbers.
- Generate streams of simulated values for each variable in the model.

We shall look at each of these steps in more detail.

1 Generate a probability distribution
This is often done by observing behaviour, such as collecting data on customer serving times. It can, however, also be done by theoretical analysis. The chance of drawing a named card from a fair pack can be found by counting the pack and is 1 in 52. This probability can be confirmed, roughly, by drawing many times. On the other hand, the chance of winning the National Lottery is $49!/(43! \times 6!)$, or 1 in 13,983,816. This figure cannot be confirmed by experiment.

The normal method in practice is to collect data on actual behaviour. For customer arrival times at a busy service office, we could collect data on typical periods over several weeks. The periods themselves should be chosen at random although care would have to be taken to avoid those times when (say) the counter is just about to open or close. The results of such a collection are shown in the first two columns of Table 9.1. The second column shows the frequency of minute intervals when the stated number of customers arrived. This data can be converted to a probability distribution by dividing each observation by the total, here 500. This produces the third column.

2 Build a cumulative frequency distribution
The cumulative probability distribution is readily worked out. Each value in column 4 is found by adding its corresponding probability to the cumulative value that appears in the cell above. In a spreadsheet, the formula for D8 would be +D7+C8.

3 Assign groups of random numbers
A random number is a series of digits each of which has been chosen at random. There are, for example 100 two-digit random numbers from 00 to 99, each of which has an equally likely chance of occurrence. Thus, if we wanted to simulate an event that occurred 1 per cent of the time, we could assign to the event the

Table 9.1 Assignment of random digits to occurences

Customers arriving within minute	Frequency (Number of observations)	Probability of event Freq./500	Cumulative probability	Random number interval
0	10	0.02	0.02	00 to 01
1	35	0.07	0.09	02 to 08
2	75	0.15	0.24	09 to 23
3	95	0.19	0.43	24 to 42
4	100	0.20	0.63	43 to 62
5	85	0.17	0.80	63 to 79
6	55	0.11	0.91	80 to 90
7	30	0.06	0.97	91 to 96
8	15	0.03	1.00	97 to 99
	500	1.00		

digits 00. Indeed, any other digits would do equally well. Then, running through lists of random numbers, we could simulate the occurrence every time our chosen digits came up.

Using ranges of random digits, we can cope with frequencies greater than 1 per cent. For instance, 19 per cent of the occasions are when 3 customers arrive. To simulate this possibility, all we have to do is allocate a range of 19 digits to the 3-customer event. The process of building cumulative probabilities enables us to do this conveniently. Column 5 of Table 9.1 flows on from column 4. It can be seen that the range of digits allocated to each occurrence corresponds to its probability and that all the random digits from 00 to 99 have been used.

Note In our example, the numbers in column 2 were rounded to give figures exact to two places of decimals in the next columns. If we are interested in probabilities to an accuracy finer than 1 per cent, they can be calibrated out of 1000 or more and the random numbers can be chosen with three or more digits. This is rare for a business problem.

We should also note that some authorities present the range of digits starting at 1 and finishing at 0, that is from 01 to 00 when two-digit values at used. This does not affect the outcome but the ranges should be checked to ensure that they work as intended.

4 *Generate random numbers*

Random numbers are often presented in lists as in Box 9.4. The layout in columns of two digits is designed for easy reading rather than to suggest that the digits come in pairs. Numbers, of any length, can be read in any direction. It is wise, of course, to choose the reading rule before looking at the page in order to avoid the possibility of unconscious selection. Tables can cover many pages. This enables many experiments to be carried out using independent streams of simulated data.

73	08	19	93	63	48	20
67	24	97	17	03	84	73
71	14	37	09	38	31	43
97	04	13	67	44	63	93
55	86	72	66	58	02	79
27	49	16	50	52	74	54
35	54	75	11	70	86	30
41	30	75	44	55	09	26

Box 9.4 Random number table

Leading spreadsheets incorporate a random number function. In Lotus 1-2-3®, for instance, the formula @RAND will generate a random value from 0 to 0.99999999. To create two digits from 00 to 99, the formula @INT(100*@RAND) can be used. It multiplies the original value by 100 and then removes the digits after the decimal point. Box 9.4 was generated this way.

5 Simulate values of the variable
By taking each random number in turn, values of the variable being simulated can be figured out. The numbers are fitted into column 5 of Table 9.1 and the type of event can be read in column 1. Therefore the digits 81 stand for 6 customers arriving and 15 stands for 2.

Taking each value separately is effective when only a short stream of numbers has to be produced. For longer lists, or if the test has to be repeated many times, stages 4 and 5 can be combined in the spreadsheet. Table 9.2 has been made using Lotus 1-2-3®. It works as follows. The left-hand shaded area is a *vertical look-up table* given the range name ARRIVALS. The columns in ARRIVALS correspond to the last and first columns of Table 9.1. Each cell of the right-hand column, which can be placed anywhere else in the spreadsheet, contains the formula

> @VLOOKUP*(100*@RAND, $ARRIVALS, 1)

This can be explained as follows: @VLOOKUP is a function whose purpose is to look into a vertical table whose name appears as the second argument of the function; it is not necessary to take the integer value of 100*@RAND; the $ sign before ARRIVALS ensures that reference to the table is anchored when the formula is copied from cell to cell; 1 means that the result of the look-up is to be found by moving 1 column to the right in the ARRIVALS table.

The list of values in the right-hand part of Table 9.2 contains random arrival rates. With such a short list it is difficult to draw any conclusions but, in the long run, the list would contain values whose frequency corresponded to the original observations. This is the output of the Monte Carlo method. We should note that it is not a prediction of the arrivals in any particular interval.

8. Simulating a queue

We can use Monte Carlo data for arrival rates and service times to simulate a queue. This can best be set out on a multiple activity chart, following the conventions shown in **6.11**. We shall illustrate the case of a single line to 15 service points. It could represent a large post office, or a telephone home shopping company. A

Table 9.2 Assignment table in spreadsheet

digit range	customers
0	0
2	1
9	2
24	3
43	4
63	5
80	6
91	7
97	8

0
2
6
5
2
4
6
2
5
6
5
6
4

multiple activity chart records the behaviour of each element of the queuing system as time progresses. In Table 9.3, the time scale in minutes runs down the page and is shown in the first column labelled 't'. The second column, 'a', gives the number of customers arriving in each minute; this is the same data as in Table 9.2. The third column records the queue, if any. Then, for each of the service points, there is a column that records whether it is idle (blank) or serving a customer. The asterisks at the top of the diagram are included because it is assumed that some stations are busy from unidentified customers who arrived before the trial started.

For our illustration, each customer is identified by a letter and tracked individually through the service facility. The behaviour to be simulated for the customers is the number arriving per minute and the service times. The table for generating serving times through random digits is not shown here. Table 9.3 shows that customer 'A' arrives in the second minute and is served for 3 minutes at point number 7, this being the first one available. Customer 'n', on the other hand, arrives in minute 11 and waits in the queue until being served in minute 13 at point number 3. These examples are highlighted in the diagram.

The simulation could continue for several hours. While Table 9.3 shows individual progress, it is not usual to track each customer. The software will print a graph of queue length and station idle time during the simulated period and provide summary statistics. The experiment can then be repeated with different management policies. These could, for example, be to increase the number of service points always open or to add to the basic number when the queue reaches a defined length.

Table 9.3 Simulation of single queue to 15 servers

t	a	In queue	1	2	3	4	5	6	7	8	9	10	11	12	13	14	15
1	0		*	*	*	*	*	*	*	*	*	*					
2	2		*	*	*	*	*	*	A	B							
3	6		*	*	*	*	C	D	A	B	E	F	G	H			
4	5		*	*	I	J	C	D	A	B	E	F	G	H	K	L	M
5	2		*	N	I	J	C	D	O	B	E		G	H	K	L	M
6	4	S	P	N	I	J	C	D	O	B	E	Q	G	H	R	L	M
7	6	VWXY	P	N	I	J	S	D	O	B	E	Q	T	H	R	U	M
8	2	YZa	P	N	I	J	S	D	V	W	E	Q	T	X	R	U	M
9	5	cdef	P	N	Y	J	S	D	V	W	Z	a	T	X	b	U	M
10	6	fghijkl	P	N	Y	b	c	D	V	W	Z	a	d	X	b	U	e
11	5	hijklmnopq	f	N	Y	b	c	g	V	W	Z	a	d	X	b	U	e
12	6	nopqrstuvw	f	h	Y	b	i	g	j	k	l	a	d	X	b	m	e
13	4	stuvwxyzα	f	h	n	o	i	p	j	q	l	a	r	X	b	m	e
			f	h	n	o	i	p		q	l	a	r		b	m	e
				h	n	o	i			q			r			m	e
					n		i			q							e
										q							

MANAGING QUEUES

We have seen that queues occur in many service situations. They consist not only of customers standing in line but also the following:

- Waiting for service to arrive. This could be in a restaurant, by the side of the road waiting for a breakdown van or lying in bed having called the doctor.
- Waiting for an item to be serviced. The item could be a tool or a piece of household equipment.
- Waiting in an electronic queue. These lines do not require that the customer be physically present but they can, nevertheless, be frustrating. Examples are waiting at the computer terminal and for telephones to be answered.
- Waiting one's turn over a long period. Long-term queuing may be for entering hospital, admission to a golf club or buying a Morgan car. The frustration felt by the person waiting depends largely on the desirability of the result.

We have also examined how it is possible to model the behaviour of queues, either to produce measures of mean lengths and times or to simulate their dynamic behaviour. Yet none of this is of direct interest to the operations manager unless it can be turned to positive effect and lead to an understanding of *how queues can be managed.* Given the inevitability of waiting occasionally, the successful organisation will be one that can show its customers that it is aware of, and responding to, the situation in a positive way.

9. Acceptable queue lengths

The acceptable length of a queue depends on many factors that vary from individual to individual and from case to case:

- *The significance of the wait.* Some people have more time than others; they are prepared to wait for some services more than for others, possibly because these services are more important or there are few alternatives. It is accepted that there is to be some waiting time for a free hospital bed in non-urgent cases, although there is little consensus over how long this interval ought to be!
- *Perception of queue length.* Customers perceive the length of a line in different ways. For instance there is the difficulty of comparing a short but slow-moving line with a longer one that is moving more quickly. Queue structures can, therefore, have an impact on customer response. Another issue is the sense of urgency felt by the customer. Lining up for a railway ticket well ahead of departure will be a more comfortable experience than if the train is about to leave.
- *Information.* Besides the time lost in the line, another customer anxiety is uncertainty. Some organisations relieve this problem by informing customers of the likely period of the wait. For this policy to be successful, customers need to be confident that the estimated delays are accurate and that there is a commitment by the organisation to keep to them. Theme parks offering free rides, such as Alton Towers and Disneyland, incorporate signs in the queuing areas with such information.
- *Competition.* Standards may be set by competitive forces in industries where service quality can be defined as including the time spent waiting. Many airlines are installing fast or automated check-ins available to premium-price passengers as part of their strategies to gain in this important market sector. In supermarkets, the lengths of delay at the crowded discounters was one reason behind Tesco's advertising campaign of late 1994[2], an example of which appears in Box 9.5.
- *Priorities.* Competitive forces may be one of many factors that encourage organisations to discriminate among customers and replace the common first-come-first-served rule. Alternative priority criteria include:

  Urgency. Medical services in an out-patients' clinic are given according to arrival times with emergencies being treated immediately

---

If there's ever more than one other customer in front of you at the checkout we'll aim to open another until all our tills are open.

TESCO *Every little helps*

Box 9.5 Competing over waiting lines

Consequences. Emergency services will normally be sent to answer any call but, in case of overload, they are allocated according to the potential consequences of the fire or other crisis.

Special customers. Those who place large orders or who buy premium services, such as first class tickets.

With our study of structures, these points suggest three approaches that may be taken to improve service operations: queue avoidance; queue differentiation; and changing the experience of queuing.

10. Queue avoidance

A sensible alternative to the pressure and problems resulting from queuing is to avoid them through some form of reservation system. This will aim to regulate demand for service, either to cut it altogether or to shift it to more favourable times. One policy is to use price premiums at peak times but, as we have seen, this tends to be a relatively blunt weapon. Other approaches have been adopted in various industries; in some it is commonplace while in others it is not expected. Reservations are, for example, normal for international flights.

> Passengers expect to have to book in advance for international flights yet the practice of selling 'open' tickets, under which a customer may not show and incur no penalty, works against filling all seats. To cope with this uncertainty, airlines offer a range of tickets at different prices. Open tickets are expensive. The cheaper, APEX tickets are only valid for identified flights. Holders of standby tickets have to queue!

One problem with reservation systems is that they can replace one type of waiting with another – lining up to make a reservation. This happened to cinemas as credit card booking systems replaced the need to stand in line to get to a popular film. UCI found that up to 60 per cent of sales at some southeast cinemas were made by telephone. While busy centres had four operators, many calls were abandoned due to engaged tones or the long wait. In response to this problem, UCI has invested in a centralised reservation system that, in effect, has become a single line to multiple servers covering all its cinemas. Further details are in Box 9.6[3].

A further difficulty for some customers is that a reservation system may increase the time spent waiting for service. A person with an urgent need may prefer to queue straightaway rather than enter a slower queue or make an appointment for later. The former applies to people who have forgotten to renew their passports. For the latter, doctors operate dual systems as does the admissions system to higher education in Germany.

> Admission to Fachhochschulen, Technical University Colleges, in northwest Germany is made on the following basis. Candidates apply after having passed the Abitur, the school leaving certificate giving entry to higher education. In any year, one half of the places is offered to those in a list ranked by grade gained in the Abitur. The other half of the places goes to those with lower grades who have been waiting the longest.

In some industries it is possible, through the integrated management of flows and timetables, to avoid delays. This approach is used in large-scale transport facilities such as airports and the Channel Tunnel.

United Cinemas International operates 28 cinemas throughout the country. It has installed, in Manchester, a computer answering system which is designed to answer 95% of calls in less than 20 seconds. Customers make up to 23,000 calls per day using a range of Freephone numbers, each of which enables the computer to recognise from which cinema catchment the call originates.

When answering, the operator's screen shows the programme of the caller's local UCI together with prices and availability. After booking, all details are transmitted to the customer's cinema where tickets and receipts are prepared for collection. The facility is staffed for almost 100 hours per week. At other times, a touch-tone telephone can be used to make reservations

Sales rose by about 6 per cent in the year after the system was installed. Since the cinemas were connected to the network in stages, it was possible to separate the effects of the better service from the impact of the films being shown.

Box 9.6 UCI's growing reservation system

Airport landings are restricted by 4 km separation distances on the downward glide path towards the runway. Aircraft are kept apart to avoid the risk from one flying in the turbulent wake of another. Conventionally, those airports that operated near to full capacity required aircraft to queue, at 'stacks', until a path was available. Nowadays, the flow control system in use throughout much of Europe has done much to avoid this irritating and wasteful practice. Using short-term forecasting models, controllers make detailed landing plans several hours in advance. Flights do not leave their points of origin until they are, in effect, cleared to land. In flight, the plans can be continuously updated and the aircraft speed adjusted accordingly.

The Channel Tunnel has a capacity of 12 trains per hour in each direction. The headway of 5 minutes is the minimum allowed for safety reasons. Like a runway, if a slot is lost, it represents capacity lost for ever. The late arrival of an express train would mean loss of business unless it could be replaced by another train from a queue, for example a freight train or *Le Shuttle* car transporter service. Therefore, it is in the interests of the tunnel company to expect some of its traffic to queue in case one planned train is late.

Both facilities operate most efficiently if the separation distances are fixed and planes or trains move through at a constant rhythm. Planes are instructed to approach runways, and trains pass through the tunnel, at the same speed as all the others.

The policies for queue avoidance laid out in this section remain constrained by the need to maintain capacity that exceeds demand. While many businesses view excess capacity as wasteful, others will compete through promising that it will always be available. McDonald's and other quick-service restaurants, for instance, have high capacity, simple technology and flexible staffing that enable them to offer their service effectively under a wide range of demand conditions. The success of the investment in this approach to service is represented by the corresponding business growth.

11. Queue differentiation

As we have seen, the most common form of queue is the one that operates on a first-come first-served basis. This system is generally operated and accepted in single server facilities in shops, banks and so on. When the operator provides several servers, complications arise, particularly where the layout and atmosphere of the serving area conflicts with the need for orderly lines to form. The theatre bar has already been mentioned as a case in point. Several arrangements are possible for multiple servers:

- *Multiple lines to full range servers*
  This is the typical standard supermarket checkout or the arrangement found in many banks. Servers are not specialised so that customers choose queues they think are going to move quickly. Where the variability of service time among customers is high, customer frustration can become acute as queues move at different speeds. The problem is exacerbated for those with few purchases. Customers may switch lines.
- *Multiple lines to specialised servers*
  One common way of separating lines is to have some servers dedicated to particular transactions such as selling stamps in the post office or dealing with those with a few purchases, or paying cash, in the supermarket. This reduces the anxiety caused by multiple queues where service variability is high. A disadvantage is that some customers may see other lines empty while they are still waiting. Furthermore, excessive specialisation of the servers would mean that some customers have to wait in more than one queue to have their needs attended to. This is the experience of out-patients in some hospitals who, requiring several tests and examinations, have to move from queue to queue for several hours.
- *Single lines to multiple servers*
  Perceived by many to be the fairest method, customers are served in order of arrival. This arrangement has been introduced into many banks and applies in telephone systems. Where volume of demand is high, the queue can appear to be very long, although it can move quickly. The arrangement requires that the waiting area can be set out in a convenient manner to maintain the queue organisation and that the servers are all able to provide the full service. As a variant, banks and others combine this scheme for most business with specialist counters for transactions such as share dealing and currency exchange.

12. Changing the experience of queuing

As with all service business, excellence will only be achieved if the perspective of the customer is fully considered in planning what is on offer. This clearly includes the customers' perceptions of having to wait for service.

Both Maister[4] and Davies and Heineke[5] propose sets of hypotheses concerning personal queuing which draw together the above discussion. They are combined in Box 9.7. Note that some aspects are more under the provider's control than others. Customers' attitudes and value systems cannot be immediately changed by the firm and it will succeed by learning as much as it can about them before tailoring its service to suit. This is an important theme in quality that we shall return to in **15.13**. Using the ideas in Box 9.7 as a basis, managers should consider the following actions:

1 Queuing before the process feels longer than waiting during it.	↑↑↑↑↑
2 Uncertainty makes queuing seem longer.	Under
3 Unexplained queuing seems longer than explained queuing.	firm's
4 Unfair queuing seems longer than when lines are seen to be fair.	control
5 Uncomfortable waits seem longer than comfortable ones.	
6 Idle time feels longer than occupied time.	Shared
7 Anxiety makes queuing seem longer.	control
8 The more valuable the service, the longer the customer will be prepared to queue.	
9 Queuing alone seems longer than queuing in a group.	
10 A customer's current attitude leads to a particular perception of the wait.	Under customers'
11 Customers' value systems lead to different perceptions of waiting.	control ↓↓↓↓↓

Box 9.7 Hypotheses concerning the perception of waiting

- *Reducing the anxiety* that comes from uncertainty. Informing customers of the likely length of wait both enables them to plan what to do meanwhile and gives the impression that the managers care about their circumstances.
- *Influence the perception* of queuing time by distracting customers. Distractions include drinks in a restaurant, Mickey at Disneyland, videos in the post office, coffee at the garage and ensuring that parallel parts of the service are not too fast, see Box 9.8[6]. There is also the well-known story of the up-market New York hotel where customers complained of having to wait for the lifts. Grouses became fewer when full-length mirrors were installed on each landing.
- *Identify stressful elements of the environment* and take steps to relieve these. Problems include room temperature and noise. The latter may, of course, be caused by the queue itself!
- *Make the queuing time part of the service* by taking orders, handing out registration forms or briefing customers about what to expect.
- Use numbered tickets to *maintain the principle of first-come-first-served* while allowing people to leave the queue. For instance, this is done at the delicatessen counter within supermarkets.

Whatever the queue structure and management policies chosen by an enterprise, it is essential to show to clients that the operation is under control, for there is nothing more disheartening for the anxious customer than to feel that events are following their own course.

The baggage reclaim hall at Dallas – Fort Worth airport is close to the gate area. Passengers have a short walk to collect their luggage but usually arrive first. At Los Angeles they have to walk much further and arrive after the luggage. Dallas passengers grumble more about luggage delays.

Box 9.8 Walking as a distraction

SERVICE FACILITY LAYOUTS

In this chapter we have, so far, concentrated our attention on the waiting line. While this is a critical issue in the design of service layouts, we must not forget that the customer is present in other areas of the service operation. Retail stores and shopping centres use design to create shopping environments that are both efficient and stimulate demand through their presentation.

13. Store and shopping centre layout

Retail managers have, through years of experience, developed many tricks of the trade to promote sales. For example, it is expected that goods presented at eye-level are more likely to sell, as are goods displayed towards the ends of rows of shelves. These rules of thumb are reinforced by research studies using direct observation of customer behaviour and analysis of sales mixes drawn from scanning checkouts. Leading supermarket chains now plan their layouts centrally. They allocate some 50% of shelve space to own-label goods, perhaps 40% to the leading proprietary brand and 10% to other brands that may well have some local following.

Store design is a critical component of company image and influences shoppers' perceptions of value. Compare the small cramped aisles of the discounter with the spacious layouts of the leading, quality-orientated superstores. Each attracts customers through messages concerning its price-quality image. Dividing a large store into sections, each with its own ambience created by scale, colour and, perhaps, smell, is an extension of the overall design philosophy. Box 9.9[7] shows how a Safeway bakery department is created with its own identity to support the company's image of high quality goods sold at reasonable prices.

Designers of shopping centres have not only to consider safe and comfortable conditions but also seek to persuade leading companies to take space within the

---

'We aim to foster a clear customer awareness of quality. ...

'In-store bakeries, seen as one of the fresh food specialist areas in a store, must personify this expectation by the selection of range and the way we display our products. Expectations are just as high regarding the surroundings and fittings in which products are displayed. Atmosphere and interest are highly valued and a well designed attractive department layout will provide a favourable background to product and service. ...

'The department [is] defined with a distinct character by bringing all of the elements together, pre-pack sections, service counter, bread back rack and self-selection chilled cake cabinet, all linked by a strong livery and unique fittings. ... Strategically placed promotional units are an integral part of the department, creating extra volume sales. ...

'Customer expectation in terms of service hygiene quality and choice is rising all the time, so we must never become complacent. A quality bakery department serves as a point of difference.'

Box 9.9 Some issues in in-store bakery design: Safeway

development. Indeed, developments are often not started until such agreements are in place. Another aim is to achieve a mix of stores so that customers can be confident of having their needs satisfied 'under one roof'. This may appear to limit competition among the outlets but most are subject to indirect competition from other retailers as each pursues some diversification of its range. For the smaller operator, the negative effects of competition can be outweighed by the benefits from the 'pull' of the so-called anchor stores[8]. There is even positive interaction among sales of the major retailers. Sainsbury does well in areas where Marks and Spencer has high sales. The Metrocentre at Gateshead was developed with Carrefour, House of Fraser and Marks and Spencer among the main anchors.

Not only do store designers have to consider the presentation of goods to customers to achieve sales, they should also pay attention to the needs for deliveries, storage, space for staff and security of staff, stock, cash and fittings.

Case study: Francis Thomas [9]

Francis Thomas is a family business selling fruit, vegetables and a few cut flowers from small premises in Town Hall Square, Chester. It was set up close by its present address in 1947 and has moved twice since. During the 1950s the family had, for a time, two shops in the street and, in 1959, opened a branch in a suburb. The focus in town was on fruit (70%) while the suburban shop, in a poor area, sold mostly vegetables. The latter business was sold in 1962. The shop is now one of two the family owns, another suburban branch having been taken over in the early 1990s. There is also a substantial delivery business, accounting for some 25% of turnover, serving hotels and restaurants throughout the city. This shares the city shop premises. Competition comes from about six greengrocery stalls in the market hall, about 100 metres away, and several other shops within 200 metres. Thomas' prices are lower than those of competitors, and up to 30% below those of the Tesco supermarket (about 200 metres away).

In 1994 Thomas' was unusual in that it is one of the few food shops in which customers were still served with most of the items they wanted. Apart from the market stalls, all of the other greengrocers in the city centre were self-service.

Figure 9.6 shows the layout of the shop. There was always bustle. Because of the delivery business, staff were continually carrying goods through the shop, to and from a van parked outside. Until about 1990, customers used to stand around waiting until they estimated it was their turn. Then Mr Thomas introduced a makeshift barrier of steel posts and string to regulate the flow. The barrier was made permanent so that customers queued between it and a stack of empty boxes that usually stood against the adjacent wall. Then Mr Thomas fitted shelves on the same wall. These displayed some prepacked fruit and vegetables that the customers could select while waiting. The shelves reduced the space in the shop so that about five customers could queue inside, two in the doorway and the rest in the street.

The shop assistants used weighing equipment that automatically produced an itemised bill for each customer. They then paid at the till on the way out. Flowers were displayed by the till and sold separately because they attracted VAT. Customers wanting to buy flowers only could bypass the main queue. At busy times up to six assistants served customers along the counter and the movement was considerable. When it was quieter, the assistants made up orders for delivery, refilled the shelves and did other shop work.

1994 saw another change. The Thomases had found that the self-service experiment made it easier to display and sell a greater variety of fruit, including exotic varieties which customers were reluctant to ask for. The itemised sales records enabled them to track this change. At the same time, they were aware of the labour intensity of their current operation, accepted that there was a trend towards self-service, and felt a switch would give a faster service to most customers.

The shop closed for a week in November and was rearranged as shown in Figure 9.7. The place was redecorated and fitted out with new lighting, simple racks and shelves designed to carry fruit boxes. Over the next few months, the decision proved itself in higher turnover and margins. The mix of customers changed towards more of both younger and older people. The former had been brought up to expect self-service while older folk liked the opportunity to shop regularly for small quantities. The proportion of those whom Mark Thomas described as 'middle-aged fuddy duddies' fell.

Questions

1 *What methods did the Thomases use to manage the queue?*
2 *What happens to queue management when a shop changes to self-service? Does the relative importance of each approach change?*
3 *What criteria do greengrocers use to arrange the goods in their shops? How important is each of these?*
4 *Can you account for the different appeal of self service to different types of customer?*

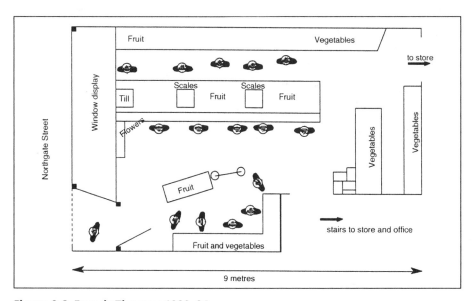

Figure 9.6 Francis Thomas: 1990–94

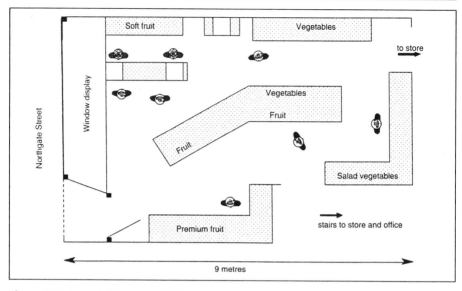

Figure 9.7 Francis Thomas: 1995 on

References

1. Kinnie, Nicholas and Staughton, Ray (1994) 'The problem of implementing manufacturing strategy' in Storey, John (ed.) *New Wave Manufacturing Strategies* London, Paul Chapman p. 54.
2. Tesco plc (1994) Media and handbill compaign, November
3. Morton, Nuala (1994) 'Cinemas dial box-office hit' *The Independent on Sunday Business News* 17 July p. 8
4. Maister, D.H. (1985) 'The psychology of waiting lines' in Czeipel, J.H., Solomon, M.R. and Suprenant, C.F. (eds) *The Service Encounter* Lexington, D.C. Heath
5. Davis, Mark M. and Heineke, J. (1994) 'Understanding the roles of the customer and the operation for better queue management' *International Journal of Operations and Production Management* **14.5** pp. 24–31
6. Render, Barry and Heizer, Jay (1994) *Principles of Operations Management* Boston, Allyn and Bacon p. 356
7. Jenkins, Ray (1993) 'The evolution process of the in-store bakery' Paper no. 379, *Proceedings of British Society of Baking*, 76th Conference, October
8   Anderson, P.M. (1985) 'Association of shopping centre anchors with performance of a non-anchor speciality chain's stores.' *Journal of Retailing* **61.2** pp. 61–74
9. I am grateful for the help given by the Thomas family in producing this case study.

10

MAINTENANCE

Chapter objectives

When you have finished studying this chapter, you should be able to:

- Outline the extent of terotechnology.
- Describe the patterns of failure which occur and explain the roles of FMEA and fault tree analysis in their investigation; show how reliability is defined and how it changes through time; use the bath tub curve to illustrate.
- Identify different maintenance policies and suggest situations in which they may be applicable; explain preventive and predictive maintenance; use examples to show how these can be applied.
- Describe the main advantages of TPM in raising the availability of equipment.
- List and briefly compare repair and replacement policies.
- Explain key issues in how the maintenance department may be managed.
- Demonstrate the contribution of the concept of maintainability to the analysis of costs-in-use.
- Discuss briefly how maintenance itself can be seen as a business and the disadvantages this may entail.

INTRODUCTION

Often regarded as the poor brother by other functions of the business, maintenance is seen as imposing a cost that really ought to be avoided. Equipment failures or shutdowns are readily put forward as reasons why an order could not be completed or a delivery made. On the other hand, the perfectly reliable item of equipment has yet to be devised and, in any case, most items wear out in use.

Maintenance is an essential part of the operations function and the question is not how it can be avoided but to work out and carry out effective maintenance policies that contribute to added value.

Maintenance is usually seen as related to the physical assets of the business. Such is the growing recognition of its importance that a special branch of technology, *terotechnology*, has emerged. It is defined, following BS 3811, in Box 1[1]. This definition tries to be broad by incorporating several lists. We should focus on how the core of the discipline is on a coordinated approach to optimisation of costs throughout the life of an asset. Indeed, the interest goes beyond this life for, with information feedback, there is the intention to incorporate experience into the next generation of equipment. We could go beyond simply looking at costs, for good maintenance can also be a route to higher outputs, productivity and quality that are key elements of offering greater *value* to customers of the competitive environment.

We can examine the maintenance question from three interrelated points of view. First, the aspect that will take up most of the chapter is terotechnology itself, the control of costs-in-use throughout the life of a physical asset. Secondly, since these physical assets are supplied before they are used, there is the issue of maintainability, the incorporation of best practice into design and construction so that the user is satisfied. Thirdly, there is the way that maintenance itself becomes a business. This ranges from the small neighbourhood car repairer to specialist contractors with turnovers worth many hundreds of millions of pounds. For them, maintenance is not a tiresome burden but a major opportunity in the service sector.

The maintenance activity is concerned with preventing or responding to failure. Therefore, before we go on to compare maintenance policies we need to consider why and how assets fail. These events have consequences that can vary from a complete plant shutdown to a gradual loss of efficiency or quality of output.

1. Patterns of failure

It is understood that equipment should be reliable. To achieve this end, it should incorporate proven designs and be assembled from high quality components using methods that have been tried and tested. Further, in cases where critical components have an uncertain, limited life, these should be duplicated, see **8.10.** Finally, equipment should be designed to fail safely and, preferably, slowly.

Yet, as mentioned above, no item can be 100% reliable even if the amount spent on its manufacture is unlimited. In practice, capital budget restraints mean that equipment is likely to fail at some point. For a start, it is useful to distinguish

---

A combination of

> management, financial, engineering, building and other practices

applied to physical assets in pursuit of economic life cycle costs. Its practice is concerned with the

> specification and design for reliability and maintainability

of

> plant, machinery, equipment, buildings and structures,

with their

> installation, commissioning, operation, maintenance, modification and replacement

and with

> feedback of information on design, performance and costs.

Box 10.1 Terotechnology defined

differences in the scope and the rate of onset of failure. These are described below and illustrated in Table 10.1.

Scope

- *Total failure*
  The asset is no longer able to perform its function. This is common in many simple machines from hair dryers to vacuum cleaners; the absence of redundancy in the design and a failure of a key component means that they will not work. On the other hand, it is to be hoped that redundancy in insulation (*double insulation*) means that the safety function of the design does not fail.
- *Partial failure*
  The asset continues to perform its function but less effectively than expected. A vacuum cleaner will function with worn beater brushes but not so well as when they are new. They can be replaced. The redundancy built into large plant, systems and networks ensures that partial failure is the common pattern. Under partial failure it may be possible to maintain a service to customers, yet sometimes at higher cost or lower quality. Transport companies reduce the frequency or speed of service, for example.

Rates of onset

- *Gradual failure*
  The deterioration in use of many items takes place in small increments. They can be monitored, often very readily. The worn bearings will make the motor noisy; the brushes can be checked periodically. Monitoring of component condition is often a key element in the maintenance of large plant and systems.
- *Sudden failure*
  While in principle such failures may be predictable, it is not practicable to anticipate them in practice. Rather than regularly dismantle a vacuum cleaner for inspection, one would prefer to take the risk of being without it for a few days if it suddenly fails. The same is not true for facilities that are more important, where the consequences of failure are more serious. Therefore, we have regular inspection. Examples include vehicle braking systems as well as major components in many industrial plants and structures.

As we have seen in the above examples, failures may result from wear in components or from damage. The latter may be the result of unrecognised weakness in the original design or assembly or from misuse. In the business setting, the sensitivity of much equipment to failure from misuse means that it is important to

Table 10.1 Modes of failure and their rates if onset: domestic vacuum cleaner

		Rate of onset	
		Gradual	*Sudden*
Failure scope	*Total*	Wear out of motor bearings	Control switch malfunction
	Partial	Fraying of beater brush bristles	Cracked handle

involve everyone in the checking, reporting and maintenance of the equipment that they use. This is a feature of Total Productive Maintenance (TPM) to which we shall return in section **8**.

Many physical assets are indeed complex systems with many components. They can fail in many ways and these events can have different consequences. A component failure may result in one of the following conditions:

- *Fail-safe*
  The equipment or system is shut down or run to a safe state, preferably in an orderly manner. This is the case when electrical systems fail and trip fuses or circuit-breakers operate. Railway signals are designed to switch to red if there is a communication failure and train brakes are applied if key system components are damaged.
- *Fail-soft*
  The equipment functions partially. Automatic controls may have failed so that continued operation is dependent on human intervention. Passenger aircraft have multiple engines so they should be able to remain airborne if one is shut down.
- *Fail-run*
  Under fail-run conditions, equipment continues to operate in the normal way. While sounding dangerous at first sight, fail-run is the desirable mode in systems where the consequences of a shutdown can themselves be dangerous or inconvenient.

These three results can exist in the same plant. Because of their complexity, and the critical nature of many assets, a formal study of failure is a first step in the creation of a maintenance plan. Such studies are known as Failure Mode and Effect Analysis (FMEA).

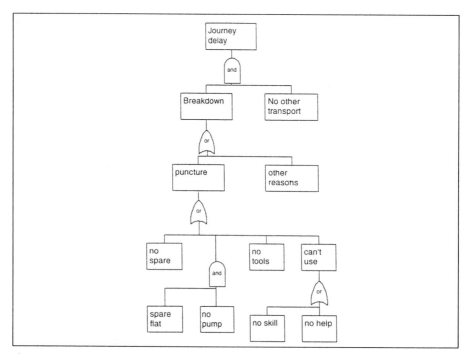

Figure 10.1 Simple fault tree

2. Failure Mode and Effect Analysis (FMEA)

In complex systems where failures may result in safety risks or financial losses, FMEA is used at all stages of the life of equipment from design through operations and improvements. It addresses the question: What could the consequences be for the system because of a failure of a component? This is a detailed approach that starts from a definition of a system, its components and how they work. Each is then studied to see the ways in which it can fail. A gas valve, for example, can fail in both the fully closed and fully open positions as well as many in between. Electrical wiring can suffer breakage and loss of current flow or insulation failure and leakage to earth. These are all failures but the modes differ.

Looking more closely, for each *failure mode* there may be more than one *failure mechanism*. For example, the gas valve stuck in the closed position may be the result of damage to any part of the control mechanism as well as seizure of the valve components themselves. Such studies will lead to a better understanding of the risk of each failure mode occurring.

Having studied the ways in which components fail and assessed the expected frequencies of these events, FMEA goes on to examine *failure effects*. In some designs with little redundancy, one malfunction will lead to system failure. In others, however, the outcome will require deeper investigation since the effect of one component going down will depend upon the state of others. The fault tree (see section 3) helps with this analysis.

The last step in the analysis forms the lead-in to maintenance planning. It identifies means by which failures can be detected, either in advance or in sufficient time after occurrence to relieve the failure effects noted previously. Further, the terotechnology approach is completed by noting corrective action, either that which is taken at the time or what may be done to reduce the frequency of breakdowns in the future. In conducting FMEA, engineers use standard forms along the lines of Table 10.2.

Quantification of the FMEA approach is widely adopted. Safety engineers work on risk assessment of complex systems such as oil platforms and compare different designs and operating procedures using quantitative measures. This data is needed not only by operators but by regulators and insurance assessors. Muhlemann et al. [2] propose an extension to FMEA which they call Failure Mode, Effect and Criticality Analysis. Their *criticality index* is a product of rating indices given for probability of occurrence, severity of failure and difficulty of detection. They would add columns to Table 10.2 to include assessments and index calculations. Harris and Ramsey [3] show how London Underground Ltd estimates the impact of failures of different parts of its system using a generalised cost equation common in public transport modelling. The social cost, from the passengers' point of view, is made up of a combination of price and time spent. Each element of time is weighted with a different constant. The equation has the form:

Generalised cost = Fare + (b_1 × Access time) + (b_2 × Waiting time) + (b_3 × Running time)

To this value can be added changes in operating revenue and cost because of diversions and so on.

While quantification has the advantage of setting out an agenda of issues and giving estimates of the impact of different events, there is a danger of placing too much reliance on the total scores. These depend to a large extent on the choice of weighting factors applied to the equation components. For example, in the social

259

Table 10.2 FMEA: Illustration of space heating boiler controls

Item	Failure mode	Failure mechanism	Failure effect	Failure detection	Corrective/ preventive action
Space Thermostat – T101	Fail closed	Breaker points welded Springs failed Insulation damage in capacitor	Space overheats – waste of energy	Discomfort of occupants	Manual override until replacement
	Fail open	Connections open circuit Thermometer worn out	Space not heated	Discomfort of occupants	Immediate repair
Boiler Thermostat – T102	Fail closed	Breaker points jammed Capacitor insulation	Boiler fails to cut out	Alarm – A41	Duplicate thermostat with indicator Immediate manual shutdown
	Fail open	Connections open circuit Thermometer worn out	Boiler does not cut in	Discomfort of occupants	Immediate repair
Alarm – A41	Fails to operate	Faulty installation Disturbed during maintenance Wiring failure	Failure of T102 and gas valve not detected	Unlikely during service	Regular testing and shutdown if fault detected

cost example it is assumed that passengers regard increased travel time in a negative light and would assign notional costs to this time. Further, it is supposed that different values are placed on each minute depending on whether it is spent actually on the move, reaching a stop or waiting for the service. Since, for example, I read on the train but not when standing in the underground, time spent in transit is less of a loss to me than time spent waiting. Similar difficulties apply to all factor-weighted models, the location decision of **8.4** being but one.

3. Fault trees

Studies of component failures would be incomplete without consideration of the interaction among them in the development of a failure. For instance, while it is difficult to forecast and hence prevent the occasional puncture in a car tyre, its impact can be lessened by carrying a spare. Strictly, one should also say that the following are required: a spare *and* ((tools *and* the strength *and* the skill to use them) *or* (the availability of assistance)). Such statements can become complicated!

Failure effects, then, are conditional on combinations of circumstances. Representing these can be done using a *fault tree*. Figure 10.1 gives an example of how a tree can be set out, using a series of events, drawn as rectangles, connected through *and* and *or* gates shown as special symbols. The tree is then a logical description of the combinations of events that can result in the failure shown at the top of the tree. Thus the statement: (Spare flat *and* no pump) *or* (no spare) *or* (no tools) *or* (no skill *and* no help) will lead to serious delay if there is (a puncture) *and* (no alternative transport) can be traced through the diagram.

4. Reliability through time

Reliability has already been defined, in **8.10**, as a measure of the probability that an item survives a given time. This can be formally expressed as:

$$R_t = \frac{\text{Number surviving until time } t}{\text{Number existing at time } t = 0}$$

Failure is the complement of this measure, expressed as:

$$F_t = \frac{\text{Number failing before time } t}{\text{Number existing at time } t = 0}$$

$$F_t = 1 - R_t$$

In studying failures of existing equipment, we are less interested in the overall expected failure rate from the start of the equipment's life and more in what is likely to happen in the future. This parallels the recognition that, on average, a person aged 50 is expected to live to a greater age than one aged 10. This is because the adult has already survived the risks and hazards associated with the intervening 40 years. As a practical measure of current failure risk, then, the *failure rate* is calculated as:

$$f_t = \frac{\text{Number failing during unit time at time } t}{\text{Number existing at time } t}$$

Here, reliability and failure rates have been expressed as ratios; for single items of equipment they can be represented as probabilities. For instance, the failure rate is simply the probability of failure in unit time.

Lastly, risks of breakdown are sometimes expressed in terms of the *mean time between failures* (MTBF) which helps the maintenance manager in planning how much attention needs to be given to each item. This is the reciprocal of the failure rate:

$$\text{MTBF}_t = \frac{1}{f_t}$$

If the failure rate is measured in hazards per day, then the MTBF is the number of days between hazards.

The plot of a typical breakdown rate through time is known as the *bath-tub curve* (Figure 10.2). It has three marked phases:

- *Burn-in or Infant phase*
  Manufacturing, assembly, transport or installation defects become apparent early in the life of a product. Commissioning work on new installations concentrates on eliminating defects quickly. Vehicles have a running-in period and

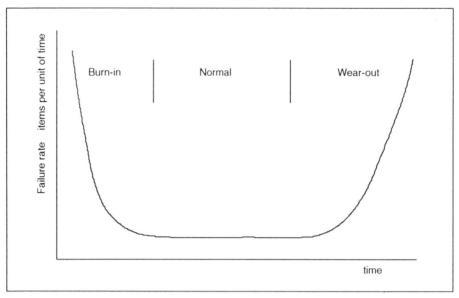

Figure 10.2 Bath-tub curve

short service intervals during their infancy. Some items, such as electronic equipment, can be run on test benches for a few hours before despatch to ensure that the burn-in phase has passed. Replacement of defective systems is not recommended if burn-in is a significant problem as all that would happen is a return to the high failure rates of early life.

- *Normal or Adult phase*
  After the initial burn-in, the failure probability remains low as the equipment works through its designed life. Provided that it is properly maintained at regular intervals, and not misused, the MTBF can be a high, and constant, figure.
- *Wear-out or Aged phase*
  The equipment moves towards the end of its designed life. While it is possible to rejuvenate it by replacement of key items, the expense of this is often high and so the failure risk increases as one or another component reaches the end of its life.

While the three bath-tub phases are seen in the lives of many items from simple machines to buildings, some have small or nonexistent burn-in and wear-out periods.

Car manufacturers used to stipulate speed maxima during the early life of their products to allow engines to run in. Such demands were not always heeded, especially as the consequences would not show up until much later in the engine's life. Mass-produced engines are now made to much finer limits, rendering running in unnecessary and cutting early-life service costs.

Electronic components tend to have a high initial failure rate followed by a very long normal life with very few malfunctions. When servicing such systems it would be foolish to replace these components and move back into the burn-in phase. Hi-fi equipment usually breaks down through the loss of electromechanical ancillary items such as switches, tape transport mechanisms and sliding resistors. The solid-state components become obsolete before failure.

Having examined relevant properties of components and systems, we can use this knowledge to investigate maintenance policies.

5. Maintenance policies

In the business organisation, maintenance supports the operating function in that it responds to demands from that function to keep its facilities in working order. The increasing trend towards lean production, operating just-in-time with very low buffer stocks at all stages, means that the unplanned shutdown of an asset can have significant effects. The asset may be a vehicle, ship, plant, small machine or personal computer. Maintenance makes a contribution towards operational efficiency.

Maintenance policy should, therefore, be integrated with operational policy. Gits[4] expresses the closeness of this relationship by means of the diagram shown in Figure 10.3. There is an immediate feedback loop between the two activities. Deciding upon capacity within the maintenance function is part of the strategic decision involving the supply of operating capacity. The maintenance function is thus part of the whole operations team. For instance, when the RAF supplies the United Nations with a fleet of helicopters to aid in a peace-keeping rôle, each aircraft requires 13 people to keep it operating; the maintenance staff cannot be considered as an afterthought to the supply of the helicopters and flying crew.

Maintenance supplies the operations system with its planned capacity. This statement suggests two main areas to be considered when establishing a policy to support operations:

- *Reducing the frequency of failures*
  This can be achieved through ensuring correct installation of suitable equipment, preventive maintenance and replacement of items as they move into their wear-out phase.
- *Reducing the impact of failures*
  To relieve the effect of operations of a component being out of service, approaches will include the provision of standby capacity at key points, see **8.10**, and organising the maintenance activity in such a way that repair times for critical items are minimised.

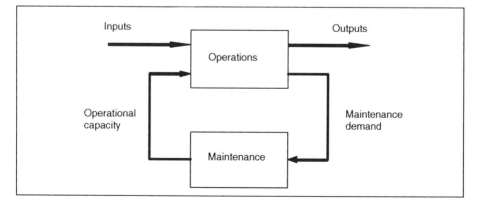

Figure 10.3 Operations and maintenance

The criterion for choice should be the effect on the value offered by the operations function. We will return to this question of optimisation in the next section but first we should look at the different types of maintenance that are practised.

While a small business may approach its maintenance in an unplanned way, it is unlikely to avoid problems once it begins to use buildings, vehicles and equipment of any substance. Maintenance policies can be grouped into two broad categories[5]:

- *Run to breakdown*
  This may be the rational course in cases where failure is unpredictable, consequences are limited and the equipment can be readily substituted. Within such an unplanned policy, maintenance should respond to problems in one of two ways. *Emergency* action is called for if there is a breakdown with potentially serious effects. Work must be done immediately. *Corrective* action, on the other hand, may be delayed. It involves routine work that must be done within the near future, perhaps because there is not the immediate operational demand.
- *Preventive*
  This work must be carried out on a planned basis. The service intervals are established by experience, by manufacturers or, in the case of equipment such as aircraft or power stations, by external authorities. Its aim is to forestall failure and to reverse the gradual degradation caused by wear in equipment components. The continuous painting of the Forth Bridge is a famous example of structural preventive maintenance intended to stave off high repair costs in the future. *Diagnostic* or *predictive* maintenance is another approach to prevention based not on predetermined service intervals but on the condition of the equipment. Hence an important part of the maintenance function is inspection. This is especially true for items that are expensive to replace. Experience shows that it is prudent to shut down plant for inspection at regular intervals; vehicles have to be tested at least once a year; many organisations carry out safety tests at regular intervals. The inspection is regular and the maintenance is conditional on the inspection.

It is also useful to distinguish when maintenance is carried out in the operations cycle. In many cases, *running maintenance* can be done while assets are performing their functions. In others, *shutdown maintenance* is necessary for safety or other practical reasons. Finally, three levels of action can be distinguished. The first is *servicing*, the replacement of components that are consumed while the equipment is in use. Examples are printer cartridges, engine oil, air and fuel filters, and lamps of all kinds. *Repair* action is the restoration of assets to an acceptable standard by repairing or renewing worn or damaged components. Changing worn or stiff bearings or seals in gear boxes are instances of repair. *Overhaul* refers to the comprehensive inspection and repair of assets to bring them up to the acceptable standard. It includes a detailed search for signs of wear that would not be noticed when the item is in service.

The relationships among the different categories introduced here are summarised in Figure 10.4 which is based on a Department of Industry model given by Hill [6]. The model distinguishes between planned and unplanned policies yet recognises that breakdowns occur even though planned maintenance is in place. Preventive maintenance in the diagram includes the diagnostic approach mentioned above. The two are similar in intention but the latter is based on active monitoring of equipment and using the results as the basis of the planned actions.

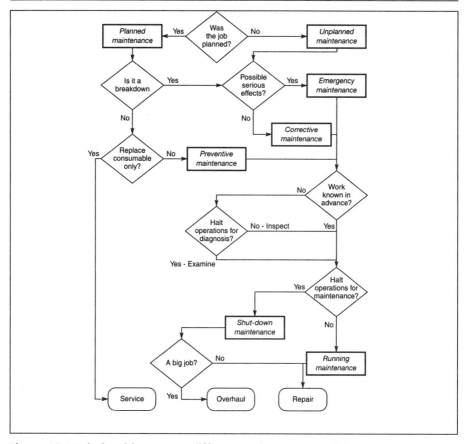

Figure 10.4 Relationships among different maintenance policies

An operations facility may combine the policies set out above. Items which are in use intermittently are not critical and are readily repaired and can be attended to in an unplanned way. On the other hand, when items are critical and repairs are expensive, planned maintenance is called for. This assumes, of course, that there is sufficient knowledge of failure modes and their corresponding rates, as in the bath tub curve, to make preventive maintenance a practicable proposition. Thus, if the variation about the mean expected life of an asset is low then a simple policy of disposal just before the life has expired would be effective.

6. Preventive maintenance

Since the policy has the aim of reducing the frequency of events that are the traditional bread and butter of repair shops, there is the danger that, with few breakdowns, the repair function begins to be seen as an expensive luxury. Much work, especially inspection, can appear to have no output. It is also difficult to get users to accept that inspection and service intervals cannot be extended. From the operations point of view, there is the argument, 'If it ain't broke, don't fix it.'

A valuable test of the usefulness of preventive maintenance is to examine how it influences the total costs associated with the operations-maintenance subsystem of the business. These costs have three components:

265

- Costs associated with the preventive or predictive maintenance itself. These clearly increase as the effort devoted to prevention expands.
- Costs of emergency and corrective maintenance. These will be reduced under a planned maintenance programme but in a nonlinear way. A little preventive maintenance will bring the greatest benefits when planned maintenance itself is low. It will be applied to the critical and easiest items first.
- Costs associated with lost output. Again, these will fall as more planned maintenance is introduced. Not only will the repair down-time be cut but much of it will take place at off-peak periods so as to minimise the disruption of operations.

Figure 10.5 sketches the pattern of these costs to show that there may be an optimal mix of breakdown and planned maintenance where total costs are minimised. Some assets are best treated in one way while others are treated the opposite. In principle, each asset's maintenance requirements ought to be assessed. Various algorithms have been suggested for the decision. Osborne and Taj[7] propose a procedure, shown in Figure 10.6, which can be used for machines in high volume operations. It can be seen that the algorithm establishes key points of interaction, namely periodic need, shutdown, time savings and range of components. The authors are particularly concerned with the integration of maintenance into manufacturing schedules and with the coupling of components that need repair or replacement. Thus, if a machine is taken out of service for the repair of one component, it can be worth giving attention to others although they have not reached the end of their useful lives. Osborne and Taj report examples of poor practice[8]:

'... while machinery was down for scheduled PM, the workers did not replace many of the inexpensive components that may reach failure in just a short time. When a component had yet to reach its prescribed useful life, it was left in the machine even when a component adjacent to it was replaced. Components costing just a few cents were preserved in the machine, sometimes costing hundreds of dollars in lost production in replacing them later.'

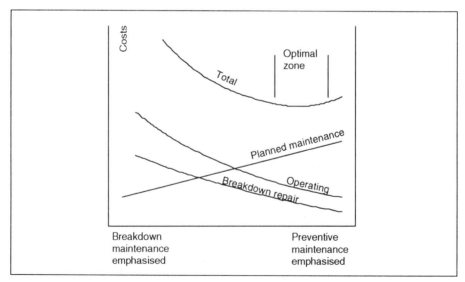

Figure 10.5 Cost variations depending on maintenance policy

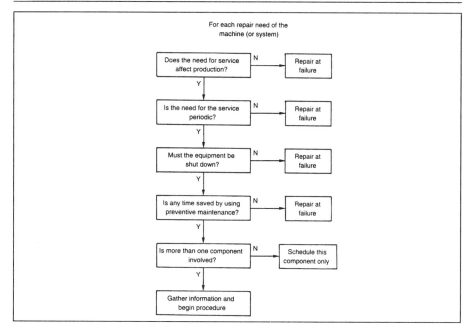

Figure 10.6 Algorithm for breakdown – preventive choice

The comparison to be made is between the value remaining within the partly used component and the cost of having to stop the machine again to repair it in the future. A practical example is in car servicing. When a worn clutch plate is replaced, it is normal to replace the clutch release bearing irrespective of its condition. The item is cheap compared with the cost of having to strip down the car for further work in the future. Such ideas point the way towards practical benefits from planned maintenance. Similar ideas can be applied in many other operational settings.

7. Preventive maintenance in practice

Preventive maintenance, in its basic form, is founded on statistical analysis of an asset and its component parts. This data is obtainable from several sources. Initially it is available from equipment suppliers who propose, in the light of their own experience, values of MTBF for major components of the equipment. Preventive maintenance is suited to parts that follow the bath-tub curve into the wear-out phase. In other words, they are subjected to mechanical wear or fatigue which is correlated with use. As an operator develops experience in the use of assets in the local circumstances, maintenance plans can increasingly be based on internal records. In this way, operators of fleets of vehicles, such as buses, refine manufacturers' recommendations in the light of experience. Furthermore, in some industries, manufacturers are expected to be involved with customers throughout the life of a product. Since safety is such an important requirement, aircraft manufacturers and users are required by regulatory authorities to share maintenance records so that patterns of common faults can be recognised.

Maintenance intervals can be based on use or time. For many machines, deterioration is dependent on use, often measured in number of times used, running hours or kilometres travelled. It is common to fit critical items of equipment with meters or recorders to collect this data. In other cases, deterioration follows the elapse of time. For instance, building and grounds maintenance is normally carried out at regular calendar intervals. Frequently the two policies are combined: installations such as railway tracks, cable ways, pipelines and roads deteriorate both through weight of use and weathering.

Preventive maintenance using estimates of MTBF is valuable to the smaller business that is unable to build up the record base of the large user. Replacement on a conservative basis may be preferable to the high costs associated with breakdown. For the heavy user, on the other hand, unnecessarily early replacement will result in excessive costs. Predictive maintenance comes to the fore in these cases.

Predictive maintenance

Predictive, or diagnostic, maintenance is important where there is uncertainty over time between failures. This can be where there is no known expected life or where there is significant uncertainty over this life. Then it is better to use a diagnostic policy. The keys to predictive maintenance are:

- The possibility of regular collection of information on defined properties of the system.
- Effective linking of this information to potential failures.

Data for diagnostic maintenance needs to be available at a cost that is low compared with the value of the components being examined and the cost of breakdown. It is available from several sources:

- *Inspection*
  Regular checks carried out by operators or maintenance staff. Preferably, these checks should be made without interruption to operations, either while in service or at normal breaks such as tool changing, end of trip turnarounds and so on. The length and detail of tests vary from the single hammer blow of the wheel-tapper walking along the train to the ultrasonic weld tests (scanning of joints) of the nuclear inspectorate. Good equipment design includes ease of access for inspection.
- *Performance monitoring*
  As we will see in Chapter 15, statistical control systems monitor process outputs and highlight variations in quality. Trends in product properties can be traced to needs for equipment servicing or overhaul.
- *Built-in diagnostic systems*
  Many items of equipment have built-in diagnostic devices. Depending on their level of sophistication, these indicate either simple warnings or full details of the state of internal components. The ignition or oil pressure warning lights in popular cars are examples of the former while we can see the latter in the more complex engine systems of Formula 1 cars. They have on-board computers to pass data on many parameters to the pits. This data is valuable during development testing but is also useful during a race in planning pit stops.
- *Indirect diagnosis*
  There have been many developments in the field of indirect diagnosis in recent years. They are analogous to diagnostic practice in medicine where doctors use equipment from stethoscopes to scanners to assess patients' state of health. Two examples, which are both non-intrusive and provide good predictions at low cost, are given in Box 10.2[9].

Motor Current Signature Analysis
Detailed analysis of the current taken by electric motors shows small changes in the wave form through time. It is as though each motor develops its personal 'signature' which it imposes on the basic alternating current. These changes can be associated with bearing wear and other variations in operating conditions. MCSA has been applied in nuclear plant where motors for items such as cooling fans can be difficult to reach.

Lubricating Oil Diagnosis
Lubricating oil contains a history of wear in engines and other heavy plant. Not only is the user interested in when to change the oil - basing this on condition rather than on a predetermined period - but details of the content can provide information on plant condition.

Oil companies such as Shell and Century Oil offer diagnostic services. Customers send regular samples to the laboratory. Automated lines carry out a series of tests which include:

- Metal content. Minute particles of worn metal from bearings accumulate in the oil. Their formulations can be matched with known bearing materials to establish their source.
- Carbon content. The build-up of soot in the oil originates as it is burnt on the sides of valves, pistons and cylinders and leaks past sealing rings.
- Water content. Water should not be present in lubricating oil. Small quantities may leak from cooling systems.
- Fuel. Again, fuel should not be present. It may indicate leakage or incomplete combustion in one section of the engine.
- Viscosity. The 'thickness' of the oil is a measure of its effectiveness and monitoring this property will indicate when the lubricant is reaching the end of its useful life.

Each set of test results is compared with trends and reported to clients. Any unanticipated change, indicating the imminent onset of failure, generates an urgent communication.

Box 10.2 Examples of non-intrusive diagnosis

Many examples of maintenance involve combinations of preventive and predictive approaches, the latter using a variety of data sources. Table 10.3 shows an extract from the schedule for a family car. Since the average user cannot diagnose engine oil quality, planned maintenance recommends a change of oil and filter every 10,000 km. This interval is shortened for harsher, dusty conditions. Other items require an inspection at regular intervals and replacement if necessary. Note also the first service after 1,000 km. This is to diagnose faults during running in, that is during the burn-in phase.

The philosophy of integrating maintenance more closely with the productive process also applies to prevention. For instance, many parts of steam locomotives used to be given running attention by the driver. He took charge of tasks from replenishing supplies of oil to feeling the state of bearings. Only very few locomotives were fitted with any electrical device at all so there was a tradition of a close monitoring relationship between the operator and the machine. The coming of electric machinery running at high speed broke such links in many industries and the operators lost their commitment to maintenance. This became a specialised,

Table 10.3 Extract from maintenance schedule for typical passenger car

Number of kilometres in thousands		1	10	20	30	40	50
Check torque of cylinder head bolts, exhaust and carburettor nuts, manifolds		x					
Adjust valve clearances		x		x		x	
Check drive belts for wear, fraying etc		x		x		x	
Change engine oil (a)			x	x	x	x	x
Change engine oil filter (a)			x	x	x	x	x
Replace fuel filter						x	
Distributor points	Check	x		x		x	
	Replace		x		x		x
Check brake linings, drums and other components for wear (b)				x		x	

(a) Change oil and filter every 5,000 km if: driving mainly short distances; city driving; driving in dusty conditions.

(b) When driving in salty or other corrosive conditions, check every 10,000 km or 6 months, whichever comes earlier.

technical activity somewhat remote from the operators. Osborne and Taj argue that there has been an overemphasis on seeing planned maintenance as an exercise in data gathering and implementation:

> The dynamic nature of all maintenance, and the large number of machines that must have maintenance programmed, necessitates that the majority of scheduling for PM be done by those close to the actual work. Supervisors, foremen and skilled trades leaders will do much of the day-to-day scheduling of preventive maintenance. Only a decision making process that can be used and interpreted by these people can have any real chance of being applied in the typical workplace[10].

While these concerns are expressed here in terms of the hierarchy of those who should be involved, they do represent a return to recognising the operator-machine link. This link has been rediscovered with the arrival of Total Productive Maintenance.

8. Total Productive Maintenance (TPM)

TPM is an approach involving all employees from the shop floor to top managers. It is based on the notion of teamwork where those who carry out the operation are also encouraged to control quality, change tools and do some equipment maintenance. In many cases, operator awareness is an excellent form of diagnosis and can lead to successful early intervention. Operators are aware of minor faults, unsuitable operating conditions, defective procedures and lapses in the regular attention required by preventive maintenance schedules.

TPM, then, is preventive maintenance in which all employees participate. Operators are responsible for routine adjustments and repairs. This approach would not work, however, unless it were based on changes in attitudes towards the responsibility for performance of equipment. TPM tries to break down traditional rivalry between maintenance crews and operators in which each group attempts to protect its narrow interests. Working practices and cultures have to be changed and culture is the biggest factor in implementation.

According to Nakajima, TPM surfaced in Japan during the 1970s[11]. The notion of preventive maintenance had been borrowed from the west in the 1950s, followed by productive maintenance in the 1960s. TPM took these ideas and adapted them to the Japanese industrial situation. This unique working environment included a strong emphasis on cooperation with employees unconcerned with job categories. Consequently, when the idea of all employees participating in the development of maintenance policies and practice was put forward, it was readily accepted. Toyota Motor Corporation was one company in which TPM was developed, alongside the new production (JIT, see **12.10**) and quality (TQM, see **15.8 – 15.13**) systems. The company saw that none of these would be effective without the others.

A TPM programme is built up incrementally. Successful installations have been in those companies who are already carrying out basic preventive maintenance and trying to integrate it more closely with the production system. The programme starts with common sense switches of responsibility, for example for routine maintenance tasks that do not require much skill or training. These encompass cleaning, lubrication, inspection and minor adjustments. Unfortunately, even some limited applications have led to regressive steps, including:

- Converting skilled maintenance staff into routine machine operators
- Shifting line authority for maintenance crews to production managers
- Pushing TPM as a means to reduce the apparent overhead of the maintenance department
- Applying TPM principally to reduce maintenance costs. [12]

Taking the short-term perspective embodied in the above points, the effect of TPM is to transfer a few tasks, that seem costly when carried out by skilled workers, into the hands of cheaper workers. Without training and further development, the advantages of having an experienced eye regularly look over equipment are lost. Maggard and Rhyne[13], however, give a more positive view, explaining how TPM was successfully put in place at Tennessee Eastman, see Box 10.3. They chart the rise in TPM and point out how the Japanese firms learnt that it is a necessary concomitant to JIT and TQM.

9. Repair and replacement

Whatever maintenance policy is adopted, the question of repair or replacement of components eventually arises. Low-cost items should be replaced whenever it is convenient to do so. For more expensive items, the question is more difficult. This is because of difficulties of estimating the remaining life of an asset after it has been repaired together with further costs in use. These should be compared with

The need
The process plant produces a wide range of polymers on a scattered, 1,800 ha site. Maintenance, carried out by 1,200 personnel, was seen to be operating satisfactorily overall with formal procedures in place. Yet, as the plant implemented its Total Quality Management programme, it was clear at shop-floor level that maintenance support was not as good as it should have been. For instance, formal requests for work to be done often had to pass through many hands and organisational levels to gain approval. At a minimum, they involved an operator, supervisors for both production and maintenance and the skilled mechanic who actually performed the task. In addition, machine operators felt little sense of ownership of the equipment and the repair staff little sense of urgency to cut repair times.

Studies
It was found that 40% of conventional maintenance work could be done, with minimal training, by another employee. A further 40% required extra training, yet still not up to the competence level of the skilled mechanics. Therefore, there was a large element of task responsibility that could be transferred from mechanics to operators. The company saw that TPM should be more than this. Each group should be trained in the other's activities. The operators can do much more maintenance, sufficient for them to assume 'ownership' of the equipment. The mechanics can be trained in operations to help with prevention and make repairs easier.

Planning
The change to TPM was treated as a project with a leader, steering group, organisation, office and so on. Managers and team leaders were all trained in the principles. Work areas were selected on the basis of 'opportunity audits' which assessed current operations and maintenance according to: improvement potential; readiness for change; interest among the staff in a new approach; and whether visible success would have effects elsewhere. Goals and rewards were established. The former covered scope, costs, extension of TPM and detailed measures such as machine availability. Recognition events for successful work groups ranged from lunches and celebrations to managers giving written and oral praise and even washing employees' cars.

Results
The programme was launched in 1987. By 1991, there were 120 functioning TPM teams with over 85% of the 5,000 staff participating. Productivity has risen, the annual benefits being estimated at $8 million. Failures of critical equipment have fallen, sometimes dramatically. In one year, a rise in availability of 1%-2% was attributed to TPM. There were several examples of serious failure incidents being avoided by timely operator intervention. Management estimated a payback period of 6 months for the project investment.

Box 10.3 TPM at Tennessee Eastman Kodak

the cost of replacement by new equipment combined with associated operating costs and changes in productivity and quality.

Some items have to be replaced regularly. When a business has to maintain a group of such items in working order it is faced with several choices:

- Replace items when they fail.
- Replace failed items at predetermined intervals.
- Replace all items at predetermined intervals.
- Replace failed items when they fail and all items at predetermined intervals.

While at first sight some of these alternatives may be rejected, their selection does depend on the operating situation. Factors to be considered include:

- *The bath-tub curve for the items.* Many electronic components have an indefinite normal life after relatively high failure during burn-in. Replacement of items before they develop faults would only increase the average failure rate. Fixed interval replacement is preferable when the variation in expected life is small.
- *Costs of the replacement activity.* Difficulties of access mean that special equipment has to be used and processes interrupted. Thus, the cost of replacing a group of items hardly differs from the cost of replacing one. Light bulbs on a tall mast or along the centre of a motorway are cases in point.
- *Tolerance of failure.* Often a component is critical to an operational process and needs to be attended to without delay. In other cases, action could be delayed until a convenient break or until a defined proportion of items are out of service. Blackpool Illuminations is a fail-soft system in which odd failed lamps are not attended to.
- *Item costs.* As already indicated, items whose value is low compared with maintenance and associated lost output costs should be replaced more frequently.

10. The maintenance function

Since the function can itself be seen as a cost-effective supplier of capital productivity, maintenance is a service operation in its own right. It is a Type 5 operation (see **1.15**) or, more specifically, a service operation, as in **3.3**. The model presented in Figure 3.1 is also helpful if one starts from the conventional perspective that maintenance delivers *professional service,* that is an individualised service delivered in the presence of the customer, the operations department. The Type 5 operation is one of instant service without queues which could isolate it from variations in demand. Managers have to face the problem of internal inefficiencies caused by the need to give instant emergency service. At the same time, non-essential maintenance work can tolerate some level of queuing.

Figure 3.1 and the above discussion point the way towards improving the efficiency of the department. Among possibilities to be considered are:

- *Isolation*
  Moving the maintenance service activity away from operations. This can be done through *unitisation* in which large components or subsystems of equipment can be quickly exchanged with service replacements. The faulty units are then taken away for overhaul. This policy is applied to many electronic components such as telephone exchange equipment, aircraft engines and, of course, motor vehicle tyres. Gains are achieved when the cost of obtaining and carrying spare components is lower than the lost output when repairs take place on the job.

  As we have seen, isolation is also achievable through planning. Planned maintenance enables attention to be provided at off-peak times or when equipment is not in use.

- *Standardisation*

  Standardisation, both of equipment and repair procedures, enables scale advantages to be obtained. Among other benefits are ease of training and development of staff together with limitation of the range of spares and special equipment which needs to be carried. Replacing a whole group of items after a specified interval is an example of standardised activity.

- *Detachment*

  The discussion of TPM has picked out the possibility of much routine maintenance being carried out by the operators on a self-service basis.

Such policies can be incorporated into maintenance planning. While retaining the capability of responding to any sort of urgent repair request, good planning should ensure a significant proportion of non-urgent work. In this way, the department maintains a satisfactory level of internal efficiency.

Subcontracting

Subcontracting is an option that is increasingly being taken up by business. Subcontractors will be favoured when some of the following factors apply:

- There is a need for specialist equipment
- There is a need for special technical knowledge
- Regulations or policies require external supervision or certification
- Internal costs are too high
- The need is irregular.

It is not surprising that many firms use subcontractors for at least some of their maintenance work. Examples range from telephones to toilets and lifts to landscape gardening.

On the other hand many prefer to keep regular service operations in-house. This helps with coordination, especially within a TPM context. When new equipment is obtained, a customer will commonly rely on the suppliers' service engineers, especially during the warranty period. Then the business will develop its own skills through courses, documentation and on-the-job teaching.

11. Modelling the maintenance function

As suggested in the previous section, general models of service activities are also applicable to maintenance. Techniques include Monte Carlo simulation to compare, for example, different patterns of resource deployment, the use of subcontractors, the number of spare items of equipment required and so on. The service element also suggests that queues are important.

The queuing models of 9.3 were based on the assumption that arrivals for service were drawn from an infinite population. Maintenance situations commonly do not match this assumption. The number of machines, ships, cranes or computers is limited. The arrival rate is now *dependent* on the length of the queue. To take an extreme case, if all of Britain's four nuclear submarines were at their Faslane base at once, then the arrival rate would fall to zero!

The calculations of queue lengths and waiting times in such situations are beyond our scope and data are published in tables[14]. Figure 10.7 gives an example of an operator with 5 machines. The choice is whether to have 1 or 2 repair teams available to service them. The graph relates the average number of

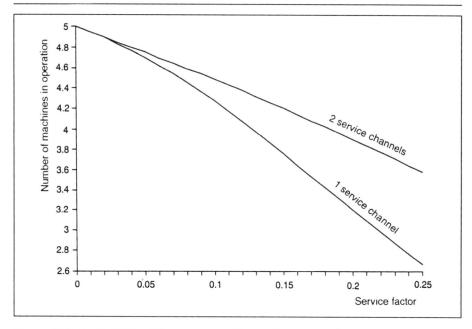

Figure 10.7 Availability of 5 machines with varying service factors

machines available for operations to the *service factor*. This is a measure of the amount of service each machine needs, that is:

$$\text{Service factor} = \frac{\text{Mean service time}}{\text{Mean service time} + \text{Mean running time between service}}$$

It can be seen that, where machines have a high interval between maintenance (a low service factor), little improvement in availability comes from the extra service team. However, the data for higher service factors show a widening performance gap. Let us look at the case of a 20% service factor. If one were to ignore queuing, one may expect an average of 1 of the 5 machines to be out of operation at any time. Yet, with just 1 service channel, there are only 3.2 machines available on average - one is being serviced and 0.8, on average, is waiting. Introducing a second repair team brings the availability close to the maximum of 4 (3.9 on average) and waiting for service is almost eliminated.

The combination of computer simulation and queuing theory has been applied to the planning and development of maintenance systems. Moffat[15] reports a study of the maintenance of aircraft in war conditions, see Box 10.4.

12. Monitoring maintenance performance

For many organisations, the cost of maintenance is a significant fraction of total costs. Control needs to be exercised to ensure that the department adds value to the business through delivering productive and reliable assets. Performance ratios are convenient ways of assessing performance and comparing it with benchmarks. These can be industry standards or other divisions within a group of companies. An operator of a fleet of buses may look at accounting ratios, operating ratios and then performance within the maintenance garage itself.

Modern wars have provided the lesson that the ability to repair returned aircraft after a mission will make an important contribution to winning. Having no recent practical experience, the RAF used detailed computer models to represent engagements and simulate the sort of damage which might be sustained. This in turn produced data on those repairs that could be made in the field. Since this was highly unpredictable, Battle Damage Repair (BDR) teams were set up to deal with the wide variety of problems.

In peace time, aircraft are repaired to very high standards before being returned to operations. In war, however, the standards could not be the same: the aircraft should be repaired only to achieve the next mission.

Having defined the tasks and standards, the simulation then took aircraft and teams through the processes related to each sortie. These were pre-flight inspection, take-off, transit to and from the target, post-flight inspection, repair of battle damage and other faults which may have arisen. It can be seen that the relationship between aircraft and BDRs is one of a single queue to multiple servers, the inspection sorting out queuing priorities on the basis of shortest service first.

The results helped to establish the optimal number of BDRs per base. Having more teams increased the number of sorties which could be generated but each extra team brought a declining benefit. Further work was done on dispersed landing grounds, such as used for the Harrier GR3. With several bases, the problem became one of multiple queues to multiple servers.

Box 10.4 Aircraft battle damage repairs

Accounting ratios are based on accounting records. One simple assessment is to compare the amount spent on maintenance to sales revenue. To explore this total further, it can be divided into four cost components:

$$\frac{\text{Labour costs}}{\text{Revenue}}; \quad \frac{\text{Materials costs}}{\text{Revenue}}; \quad \frac{\text{Overhead costs}}{\text{Revenue}}; \quad \frac{\text{Subcontract costs}}{\text{Revenue}}$$

Operating ratios evaluate the efficiency and effectiveness of the department in terms of its main objectives. From the point of view of minimising breakdowns, the MTBF (mean time between failures) gives a good indication of how well the work is being carried out. Failures in service are serious hindrances to maintaining good relations with customers. The speed of dealing with such incidents could also be assessed.

The total efficiency of delivering capital productivity can be measured by:

$$\text{Availability} = \frac{\text{Time vehicle available for use}}{\text{Time vehicle available for use} + \text{Time awaiting and undergoing maintenance}}$$

This ratio has to be used with care as demand variations mean that not all buses available for use will be running at all times.

276

With fuel costs running at some 10 per cent of the total, managers should take note of consumption of fuel and other factors. Industry habits compare these and other measures to vehicle movement:

$$\frac{\text{Fuel consumption}}{\text{Vehicle-km}} \; ; \; \frac{\text{Consumables}}{\text{Vehicle-km}} \; ; \; \frac{\text{Maintenance costs}}{\text{Vehicle-km}}$$

This data can give a picture of departmental performance and also, when looked at in detail, of each vehicle in the fleet.

Dep   artmental ratios look inside the garage to assess the quality of planning and organisation. Speed of service is important and any backlog of vehicle repairs can be assessed by measuring the length of the queue in days or weeks. Planned maintenance backlog can be measured by:

$$\frac{\text{Number of PM tasks outstanding}}{\text{PM tasks carried out per week}} \quad \text{or} \quad \frac{\text{Hours of PM work outstanding}}{\text{Hours of PM planned per week}}$$

For efficiency measures, if records allow work to be measured in standard hours, see **6.14**, then:

$$\text{Labour productivity} = \frac{\text{Standard hours of maintenance work carried out}}{\text{Actual hours worked}}$$

An allowance has to be included in such a formula to allow for unscheduled and emergency work. It is common, however, to have standard times for planned maintenance which suggests another advantage for developing PM systems.

13. Maintainability

There may be a tendency, both here and in many published articles, to regard maintenance as an operational activity that has to react to, and look after, whatever assets in terms of buildings, plant and equipment have been obtained. We have, however, shown how the maintenance function should be optimised by integration with mainstream operations.

There is a further, longer-term perspective in that it should be integrated into the process of selecting and obtaining assets in the first place. Maintainability, which is the *capability of being maintained*, should be considered within the procurement process. This is rather like the discerning shopper looking at garment care labels with the intention of rejecting those that state, 'Dry clean only.'

When faced with the choice of obtaining an extra asset, or replacing a current one, the organisation compares choices according to total costs throughout the asset's life. The maintenance cost inputs to this total include all of those set out in Figure 10.4 (p.265). Briefly, these are:

- *Servicing*: costs of replacing consumable items including the price of the items themselves; whether they can be fitted without interrupting operations; if interruptions are needed, the time taken to carry out the servicing; whether they require specialist skill or equipment.
- *Preventive maintenance*: ease of inspection and whether it can be carried out while the equipment is in service; arrangements for monitoring of performance and direct or indirect diagnosis.

- *Emergency or corrective maintenance*: whether the asset is fault tolerant; access; time and skill required to repair or correct; recommended frequency of over-hauls; MTBF.

Good estimates of this data are very difficult to obtain. Even when equipment is in use, accounting information tends to be unreliable. As Walker [16] points out, there are problems in respect of:

- Allocating fixed and semi-variable costs to a single asset and establishing which change through time
- Disaggregating grouped data
- Filling in gaps in records
- Allocating operational losses from down-time
- Converting costs spread over several years to present values.

A further difficulty is that older machines are often 'relegated' to less arduous duties with the younger ones having to take more of the strain. Therefore, some of the operating costs of these younger machines should be counted as unreliability costs of the older group.

These difficulties mean that decisions should not be based purely on the poor cost data. On the other hand, an overall comparison of costs-in-use should be made as part of the asset acquisition procedure.

Flint and Donoghue[17] report on emerging questions of maintainability in the aircraft industry. Advances in commercial aircraft materials and systems are rapid. Operators cite the examples in Box 10.5 as cases of technology for technology's sake. Other authors point to maintenance being a significant portion of running costs in information technology[18] and road haulage[19] and these should be considered in procurement and operations.

14. The maintenance business

We noted in section **10** how subcontracting of maintenance is an option that is increasingly being taken up by organisations. Needs for specialist facilities and knowledge, and the ability to carry a range of spare parts, are clearly examples of benefits of scale that could flow to a service provider doing business with many customers. We have noted how many service businesses focus on a limited range of activity from tyre depots to telephone answering services. Many domestic services gain because of their specialist focus. They are frequently protected from direct competition by franchise agreements. Examples are Hotpoint's service centres, Dynorod's drain cleaning and wood preservation offered by Rentokil.

Composite structures These lead to weight savings, increased malleability and lower corrosion. They are, however, more expensive and there is concern over a lack of standardization in composite materials as well as price increases in replacement parts.	*Advanced electronics and avionics* These allow for better control and safer operations. Yet designers are led by the technology. Higher prices and greater sophistication are not matched with corresponding gains in reliability.

Box 10.5 Technology for technology's sake?

Users of subcontract maintenance services also benefit from the speed and flexibility that may be difficult for an organisation to provide internally. For instance, oil production platforms require many different types of attention during the annual shutdown, such work not being needed at other times. In effect, the production workers take a break and are replaced by teams of subcontractors during this period.

Ultimately, subcontractors gain because they offer their services at low cost. This may be because their customers have high internal labour rates or high overheads. Both are reasons why many local authorities have passed functions from highways and grounds maintenance to computer servicing to private sector contractors.

British Airways is both a user of subcontract maintenance services and has been developing its own business as a supplier in this field[20], see Box 10.6. The advantage to BA is that, with increased scale, there are possibilities of greater efficiencies in the use of all resources. These include the specialist equipment and supply of spares dedicated to each model of aircraft. The danger is that the outside maintenance work may become an end in itself. The engineering department, recognising that it wins orders based on price, speed and flexibility, may be tempted to lower the priority given to internal work. Having been set financial performance targets, it would develop its own business strategy to ensure that a continuous supply of work was available. This shows how there is a conflict between a function being a contributory part of one value chain compared with it being a complete value chain itself. The author worked in a heavy engineering company where this happened. External business was taken on to smooth out demand between internal rebuilding projects. Eventually, the works was so busy with a major refurbishment programme for a third party customer that a large internal job had to be sent to a subcontractor abroad.

Maintenance is a critically important function for any airline. Standards are normally closely regulated by governments. British Airways was the first European airline to receive Joint Airworthiness Requirement approval. The 19 nations in the JAR agreement agree to accept joint standards without resort to their own legislation.

The JAR approval gave BA competitive advantage in being able to offer its services to other airlines. From 1991 to 1993, it quadrupled its revenue from these sources to some £140 million. This was out of a total budget for the engineering department of £550 million. Most of the maintenance activity of BA is carried out at Heathrow and Gatwick airports. The company is, however, developing new facilities at Cardiff and Llantrisant where costs are lower.

Subcontractors are widely used in BA's operations. For example, FLS Aerospace Engineering at Stansted has a five year contract to refurbish most of BA's 747 fleet. FLS has facilities for overhaul, anti-corrosion treatment and coating of this aircraft. It also does modification and overhaul work for major US airlines at Stansted and Manchester.

Box 10.6 BA as a subcontractor

Case study: Maintenance of fire-fighting vehicles [21]

The Greater Manchester Fire Brigade has more than 300 items of mobile equipment. To improve maintenance activity, a study of some ten years' records was carried out on a sample group of equipment. Each type was divided into levels, namely system, subsystem and component. Typically, there were about 7 subsystems per vehicle, each having 8 components, making 56 components in all. The maintenance data covered dates, times and costs for each component group with information on the type of failure that had occurred.

Failure analysis identified components which were most subject to fault and the impact of these faults on system performance. Measures included: frequency of failure, mean time between failures (MTBF) and down-time. Failure rates were also related to equipment age to figure out the lengths of useful lives. By eliminating the wear-out phase of the bath-tub curve, it should have been possible to improve reliability and availability while reducing costs. These studies showed the highest failure rate in the first year of operation.

Cost analysis examined planned and unplanned repairs. There were three aims: to find subsystems and components with the highest costs; to compare planned and unplanned maintenance; and to compare costs of internal, as opposed to sub-contract, work.

Figure 10.8 shows a plot of faults occurring among 12 Dennis RS131 fire engines during their first 6 years of service. It shows a typical Pareto frequency distribution, at both subsystem and component levels. The results, combined with cost analysis, led to further investigation of causes.

The failures in the electrical subsystem, ancillary equipment and cab body can be ascribed to corrosion of construction materials or terminals, connections and switches, resulting from the high volume of water being carried and used. Water leaks were a problem and the electrical systems lacked a sufficiently high standard of waterproofing.

The semi-automatic gearbox, also used on other fire engines in the fleet, appeared not to cope with:

- the weight of the vehicles and their loads, including special equipment and 2 tonnes of water;
- driving practices which included many rapid accelerations and decelerations.

Data on the maintenance of Vauxhall Chevette vans showed high repair costs for the cab and body, electrical equipment and the suspension system. These were attributed to the use of these general-purpose vehicles by large numbers of different personnel.

There were two trailers used as mobile headquarters. These presented high costs among ancillary equipment, electrical subsystem, body work and brakes. The equipment repair costs were due to technical complexity, possibly enhanced by the two vehicles being over 11 years old.

Questions

1 *Use a fault-tree approach to explore the faults, including malfunctioning of a vehicle gear box en route, that may combine to prevent the fire service achieving its normal standard.*

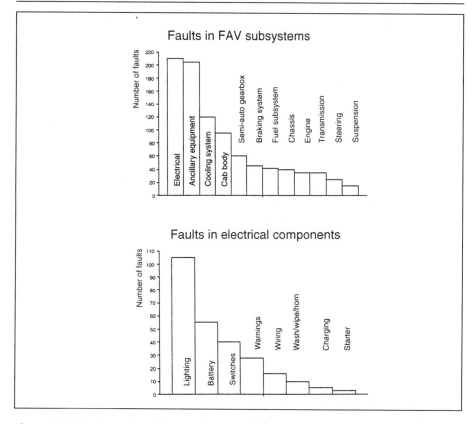

Figure 10.8 Fault analysis: Fire appliance vehicle

2 *What is the significance of the Pareto analysis?*

3 *From what you know of the way the fire service is organised and the special problems it faces, what issues would be raised by a proposed move towards a TPM approach?*

4 *What implications in terotechnology does this study have for the fire appliance vehicle manufacturers?*

References

1.   British Standards Institute (1984) *BS 3811 Glossary of Maintenance Terms in Terotechnology* London, BSI

2.   Muhlemann, A. P., Oakland, J.S. and Lockyer, K.G. (1992) *Production and Operations Management* London, Pitman p. 116–7

3.   Harris, N.G. and Ramsey, J.B.H. (1994) 'Assessing the effects of railway infrastructure failure' *Journal of Operations and Production Management* **14.6** June, pp. 635–640

4.   Gits, C.W. (1994) 'Structuring maintenance control systems' *International Journal of Operations and Production Management* **14.7** pp. 5–17

5.   There is no generally accepted categorisation. Some authors use more than two. See, for example: Paz, N.M. (1993) 'Maintenance scheduling issues, results and research needs' *International Journal of Production and Operations Management* **14.8** pp. 47–69; slightly different groupings are used by Gits, C.W. (1994) 'Structuring maintenance control systems' *International Journal of Operations and Production Management* **14.7** pp. 5–17; yet another set is

given by Hill, T.J. (1991) *Production and Operations Management: Text and Cases* Hemel Hempstead, Prentice-Hall p. 418

6. Hill, Terry (1991) *Production and Operations Management: Text and Cases* Hemel Hempstead, Prentice-Hall p. 422

7. Osborne, D. and Taj, S. (1992) 'Preventive maintenance in a multiple shift and high volume manufacturing operation' *International Journal of Operations and Production Management* **13.10** pp. 76–83

8. op. cit. p. 77

9. Gradin, L.P., Cartwright, W.B. and Nissen, M. (1994) 'Test method improves bearing wear assessment at Calvert Cliffs' *Power Engineering* **98.6** June, pp. 32–3; information on Oil Diagnosis from company sources

10. Osborne and Taj, op. cit. p. 77

11. Nakajima, Seiichi, quoted in Teresko, J. (1992) 'Time bomb or profit centre?'*Industry Week* **241.5** 2 March, pp. 52–57

12. Windle, W.W. (1993) 'TPM: more alphabet soup or a useful plant improvement concept?' *Plant Engineering* **47.2** 4 February, pp. 62–63

13. Maggard, W.N. and Ryne, D.R. (1992) 'Total Productive Maintenance: A timely integration of production and maintenance' *Production and Inventory Mangement Journal* **33.4** pp. 6–10

14. Peck, L.G. and Hazelwood R.G. (1958) *Finite Queuing Tables* New York, John Wiley

15. Moffat, J. (1992) 'Three case studies of operational research for the Royal Air Force' *Journal of the Operational Research Society* **43.10,** October, pp. 955–960

16. Walker, J. (1994) 'Graphical analysis for machine replacement' *International Journal of Production and Operations Management* **14.10,** pp. 54–63

17. Flint, P. and Donoghue, J.A. (1992) 'The hidden cost of high tech' *Air Transport World* **29.7** July, pp. 22–34

18. Corbitt, T. (1993) 'The computing iceberg' *Accountancy* **111.1198** June, pp. 67–68

19. McKinnon, A.C., Stirling, I. and Kirkhope, J. (1993) 'Improving the fuel efficiency of road freight operations' *International Journal of Physical Distributions & Logistics Management* **23.9** pp. 3–11

20. Shifrin, C.A. (1993) 'BA sees explosive growth in third-party maintenance' *Aviation Week & Space Technology* **138.20** 17 May, pp. 44–45; Reed A. (1994) "Fishing an 'overtrawled puddle' " *Air Transport World* **31.3** March, pp. 91–92

21. Based on: Keller, A.Z., J-Fendi Al-Saadi, S. and Leckie, L. (1992) 'Reliability assessment of fire-fighting vehicles and equipment' *International Journal of Quality and Reliabilty Management* **9.2.** pp. 42–51

11

CAPACITY MANAGEMENT

Chapter objectives

When you have finished studying this chapter, you should be able to:

- Distinguish between designed, effective and achieved capacity and illustrate how they can be measured.
- Show how different flow layouts affect capacity.
- Relate the problem of capacity planning to organisation strategy.
- Explain the role of forecasting in responding to uncertainty; outline different forecasting procedures and how they relate to time horizons.
- Outline the application of time series and causal forecasting models in anticipating demand and exemplify their use with examples.
- Differentiate between financial and strategic views on capacity investment choices.
- Suggest how operational managers need to be aware of learning effects in their planning.
- Clarify the role of aggregate planning. Compare policies of chasing demand and output levelling in the medium term.

INTRODUCTION

Capacity management is concerned with matching the size of an operational facility to the demands that are placed upon it. This is a two-way process in which both the scale of the facility and the size of demand should be managed or, at least, influenced. The issues can be examined from short, medium and long term points of view. In the short term, balancing is tactical. Routine adjustments are made to sway individual orders and adjust output within the framework of a facility having been set up and other resource commitments made. In the medium term, the firm plans to cope with the bulk of orders it expects to receive without becoming involved in the detail of any one. It looks for means of adjusting resources such as personnel and subcontract activity, again within the fixed facilities. In the long term, all is variable. The scale of the facility can be altered and the organisation needs to make choices with respect to market and product policy.

Choosing long-term capacity is one of the riskiest decisions an organisation has to face. Not only is the business relying on its ability to modify itself over a period of years but it is making the decision without knowing what its competitors are likely to be doing over the same period. In addition, forecasts of future demand are notoriously prone to error. We shall look at the long, medium and short term aspects of capacity decisions. Before we do so, however, we must consider important questions of definition, measurement and general process structure.

1. What is capacity?

In everyday use, the term *capacity* is used in several ways. Perhaps the most common is the way it refers to the stocks that can be held in a container, building or other space. Examples include: the 50-litre capacity of a family car's fuel tank; the 37,000 seating capacity at Arsenal's Highbury stadium; the 340 megabytes of my hard disk. In another use, the word describes *capability*, as in: 'She has a tremendous capacity for hard work'; the boxer who has a 'tremendous capacity for soaking up punishment'; or my nephew who has an 'enormous capacity' for strawberry ice cream. Finally, capacity is used to describe *flow rates* along chains or through operating processes. For instance: the road has a capacity of 3,000 vehicles per hour; the canning line can pack 10,000 litres per shift; the pipeline can carry 800 cubic metres per hour.

In operations management, capacity is used to describe both stocks and flows. To avoid the confusion that this may cause, it is important to attach units of measure to any values under discussion. Stocks are measurable and can either be counted as numerical quantities or be expressed in units of measurement such as litres, tonnes, square metres and so on. Flows relate to the production or supply of items over time and should always be expressed in terms of the movement of stocks per interval. Thus, we have the tap delivering 8 litres per minute; the Renault line producing 17 R25s per hour; the polyethylene plant running at 200,000 tonnes per year.

Operations managers are primarily interested in flows as they represent the transformation of inputs into outputs that can be sold in the market place. Indeed, as we have seen, stocks are increasingly scrutinised for the way they add dead weight to the business. They occupy space and their cost acts as a drag on profitability. Just-in-time management focuses on optimising flow rates through manufacturing facilities.

Flows can, however, quickly transform themselves into stocks. In service settings they become the queues that we have discussed in Chapter 9. Queues have to be accommodated. An airport may have a peak outward flow capacity of 10,000 passengers per hour. A problem, such as an accident or fault in the traffic control system, may cause an average flight delay of one hour. This will place an immediate demand on the facilities of the terminal building. The queue may not seem very long in terms of time but the lounges must cope with a backlog of 10,000 passengers who would otherwise be on their way.

The capacity of an operating system is, therefore, normally expressed in terms of throughput per period. Good management will recognise, however, how the system must be capable of holding stocks or queues at intermediate points. Warehouses, storage yards, lounges and waiting rooms must have the stocking capacity to cope with flow variations.

2. Measurement

Where a process is producing a standard product, it is usually easy to express its capacity in terms of output per period. When products develop some variety, difficulties arise. These can, in the first instance, be handled by expressing the work content in standard units. Typically, in a jobbing or small batch business, the capacity of any work station can be expressed in terms of standard hours (or estimated hours) per week. If all the jobs have corresponding estimates then, on the face of it, output can be planned using weekly available hours as the basis.

Variety becomes more apparent in service organisations, particularly those offering personal service. What, for instance, is the capacity of a waiter-service restaurant? It is often expressed as the number of seats, a measure of stock. Yet it could be seen that the work-cell is the table. Let us say that, in this restaurant, the table is taken to be occupied whether there is any number, from one to four, of diners. A working average may be 3 and, on this basis, a waiter may be expected to handle 8 tables. Each meal may take an hour. The capacity of the section of 8 tables is, therefore, 24 meals per hour. If, by chance, all tables are filled with 4 customers, can the system cope? It all depends on whether the waiter can serve the meals. Furthermore, can the kitchen produce the dishes at this rate? Thus, the capacity of the section may not rise to 32 meals per hour. There are many other possible variations in this situation; some customers want a light meal while others will order five courses; tables may be split or shared, and so on. The capacity of the system depends on the assumptions made in measuring it and is usually equal to that of the limiting resource – the seat, the table, the waiter or the kitchen.

A further problem in assessing capacity arises from the fact that facilities do not run full out all the time. We can distinguish between:

- *Designed capacity*
  Otherwise known as *theoretical capacity*, this is the maximum achievable under ideal conditions. To keep the conditions in this state usually requires such an effort that, in almost all cases, facilities operate at a lower rate. Allowances have to be made for breaks, planned maintenance, tool changing and so on. Change-over problems become more important when the product variety is higher.
- *Effective capacity*
  This is the proportion of designed capacity that the organisation achieves given its plans for product mix, maintenance, shift patterns and so on. Otherwise known as *utilisation*, this proportion is a key factor in operational success. While never being able to operate at 100%, organisations that manage to increase utilisation to a few per cent higher than their rivals will tend to have lower costs and, therefore, be more profitable. The 1994 liberalisation of shopping hours in England and Wales meant that many shops could increase their utilisation. This was particularly true of large self-service stores for whom fixed costs account for a greater proportion of the total operating cost. Sunday shopping and later opening hours thus brought them relative advantage.

Throughout the construction period of the Channel Tunnel there was argument over its effective capacity. Eurotunnel claimed that it would eventually be able to handle 20 trains per hour in each direction. This view was challenged partly on the grounds of tunnel and terminal design but also because of the service mix. The freight trains, travelling more slowly, would hold back the high-speed passenger trains. Critics quoted figures as low as 10 for the effective capacity[1] .

In many industries, especially during recessions, demand is less than the total effective capacity and it is that, rather than internal factors, which acts as the constraint. Falling demand in the European chlorine industry meant that plants were

The 5 years up to 1993 saw a 15% decline in European demand for chlorine. This resulted from the elimination of its application in paper bleaching and the steady reduction in the use of chlorofluorocarbons and chlorinated solvents. PVC takes 39% of the European output but this product has, in turn, become an issue with environmental groups. PVC usage in packaging will suffer as governments introduce recycling targets.

Box 11.1 Declining demand for chlorine

operating well below their effective capacities, see Box 11.1. With chemical plants having high fixed costs and already operating near to break-even point (see **2.31**), many were reporting losses.

- *Achieved capacity*
  Effective capacity is reduced by inefficiency. This can arise from many sources from the lack of skill of operators or weak organisation through to the use of poor materials, tools and equipment. External factors range from weather to congestion and poor organisation of suppliers and subcontractors. These items either are under management control or management can take steps to limit their influence. A 100% efficiency target is realistic. Commonly, the output is less than effective capacity; operating speed may be lower than planned or the *process yield* may be reduced by the production of poor quality product.

Achieved capacity is otherwise known as *net output*. This focuses on the *yield* created by the process. Managers will have targets to maintain or increase the yield and therefore increase achieved capacity. It is wise, nevertheless, for schedulers to base their plans on whatever net output the facility is currently achieving. The measures stated here are linked by the following equation:

Achieved capacity = Designed capacity × Utilisation × Yield

3. The effect of work flow layout

In finding out how different processes contribute to deciding total system capacity, we must consider how they are connected, if at all. There are three possible arrangements:

- *Processes in parallel*
  The capacities of independent, parallel processes can be added to assess total system capacity. This is most clearly seen when two facilities are separated geographically. Very simply, two gas production platforms, each producing 100,000 cubic metres per day, supply a total of 200,000 cu.m. per day. Even in such simple additions, care must be taken to ensure that the facilities do not use the same resource or share a common distribution system, either of which could set a lower limit.
- *Processes in series*
  The capacity of a system that is made up of a set of processes arranged in series is equal to the rate of the slowest. This is the *bottleneck* whose output decides the output of the whole system. We shall look at the significance of bottlenecks in the philosophy of Optimised Production Technology in Chapter 12.

Highways have bottlenecks. Whatever the length and state of a motorway, its capacity between two consecutive junctions is limited to the worst lane restriction. This is the world of the *contraflow* and the *tailback*. In contrast, the capacity of an urban road system is most affected by the design and operation of the junctions themselves. Links between junctions have little effect on network capacity provided they can take more vehicles than the intersections that they connect, which is usually the case. It is worth improving these roads but only to make them easier or safer, not to increase network capacity. This realisation, together with developments in control technology, has led to a resurgence of interest in the use of city-wide traffic light systems and other methods of regulating traffic behaviour at junctions.

- *Joint processes*
  Often, the production of an output requires the supply of many inputs that, while not being delivered from the same source in series, are nevertheless interrelated. The system capacity is again equal to the lowest among the elements. One example is in the restaurant where different resources are brought together in the supply of the meal service. There is a series of processes from kitchen preparation, through waiter delivery to eating at the table. Yet these take place in parallel with the supply and maintenance of the seating capacity, clearing up and so on. In manufacturing, two lines may produce components that only come together at the last, final assembly, stage. The system cannot produce at a rate that exceeds the lower of the two supply lines and that decides its total capacity.

The question of system capacity was raised in the context of line and process production in Chapter 8. In **8.11** it was shown that a production system with a bottleneck and much spare capacity was out of balance. While irregularities of demand and operations make its achievement difficult, it is one aim of capacity management to ensure that processes run close to a balanced position. This irregularity is especially apparent in jobbing shops.

4. Forecasting long-term capacity needs

The relationship between capacity and demand in the long term is summarised in Figure 11.1. It shows that product and market policies are intertwined. Demand for the products of an organisation are assessed by means of a forecast, first of the industry sales and then of the expected market share. In the light of this long-range view, the firm develops its product and marketing policies designed to satisfy the forecast demand. These strategic decisions will, in turn, influence the demand through feedback loops. This will often be seen through changes in market share as the organisation offers enhanced products and promotes them more effectively. At the same time, the business has to decide whether to satisfy some or all demand itself or whether to use subcontractors.

This last option is frequently seen as a tactical measure where companies need extra capacity in the short term. This is common and many firms offer very flexible capacity in order to act as subcontractors in this way. Longer-term relationships are needed in cases where the contractor has to invest in space, plant, tooling, vehicles, training and soon. Such long-term links are often seen as a form of *strategic alliance*.

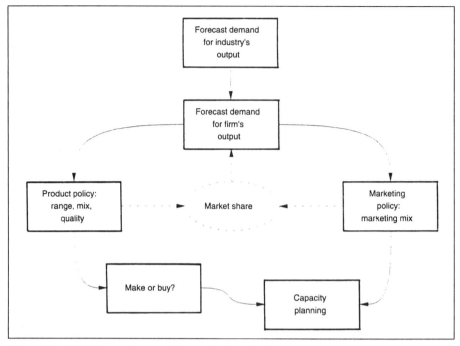

Figure 11.1 Markets, share and capacity in the long term

5. The forecast

As Figure 11.1 shows, a key element in the long-term capacity management process is the forecast. This is but one of the steps that are susceptible to the types of uncertainty set out in **4.2**. We can illustrate this by reference to the planning of airports.

Box 11.2 gives a snapshot of the debate over runway planning in south-east England[2]. In the report, we can identify references to state, timing, effect and response uncertainty.

- *State uncertainty*
  The key driver of the decision making process is the demand forecast. If one ignores short-term fluctuations caused by fuel shortages or war, one can note that the underlying growth in air travel throughout the world has followed an exponential pattern. Passenger numbers have doubled every ten years. This corresponds to a cumulative 7 per cent year-on-year increase. Whether demand in the south-east region of the United Kingdom will continue to grow at this same rate is the problem. The equations below show that, if the actual rate fell to 6 per cent each year until 2015, the forecast 170 million passengers would be in error by some 18 million. Since the planning range is so long, the forecast is sensitive to small changes in the growth rate assumption.

  $$75 \times 1.07^{12} = 169 \qquad 75 \times 1.06^{12} = 151$$

- *Timing uncertainty*
  In investments that are designed to provide capacity that is confidently expected to be required, the question is not how much is required but when. In other

'The Government will announce this week ... that it is to wait until 2019, when a ban on a second runway at Gatwick expires, before expanding runway capacity in the south-east. ... [This change] will revive worries that inadequate capacity could end the dominance of London as the European hub for intercontinental flights.

'A 1993 report of a Ministry of Transport working group ... forecast a continuation of the 7 per cent growth rate ... the number of passengers using airports in the south-east would rise from the present 75 million to 170 million by 2015. [The report proposed] a further runway at Heathrow or Gatwick by 2010 or, if this were not provided, at Stansted by 2015.

'The Government will announce instead that better use should be made of existing runways. There is under-used capacity at Luton and particularly at Stansted which ... could handle four times as many passengers ...

'Redhill could be used for the large number of smaller aircraft that now use its big neighbour, Gatwick. At the moment, half the flights at Gatwick generate only a fifth of the passengers. Transferring them to Redhill would increase its capacity by 10.5 million passengers a year.'

Box 11.2 Uncertainties in runway capacity planning

words, when will demand reach a certain level. Again, if there were to be a 6 per cent annual growth, the forecast demand of 170 million in 2015 would not be reached until 2 years later. Here, the event timing is sensitive to the growth rate.

- *Effect uncertainty*
  The variable being forecast is passenger demand in south-east England. Yet the capacity being planned is runways. The relationship between the two is not constant. Box 11.2 mentions some means by which existing runway capacity can be increased. These are changing the mix of aircraft and the operating procedures. Beyond this are developments in technology including aircraft design. For example, larger aircraft use runways more efficiently and quieter aircraft may be able to make more night movements. Therefore, we have uncertainty in the effect of changes in passenger demand on runway capacity needs.

- *Response uncertainty*
  The fourth difficulty concerns responses to whatever decisions are made for capacity provision. For example, if the government directs British Airports to develop Stansted, what will be the reactions of airlines? Will they accept the extra costs of transferring connecting passengers and baggage among three airports or the competitive disadvantages of operating from a base further from the metropolis? Some may decide to move their 'hubs' for either passenger or freight business to other United Kingdom or European centres. Paris and Luxembourg, for instance, are both investing heavily in freight handling facilities [3].

The example used here is unusual in the length of the period the forecast is covering. Yet it should be borne in mind that to build a new runway at an existing airport can take at least ten years, including the time taken for public enquiries and related approval procedures. There are two management actions that can alleviate some of the uncertainty. First, while in the end there may be a need for a significant investment in a single new facility, much can be done to incrementally improve existing assets to make them work harder and be more flexible. Adding terminals at airports increases capacity in large increments so that, for some time after opening, they tend to be under-utilised. The 1986 opening of Terminal 4 at Heathrow raised capacity to about 38 million passengers per annum. A further increase of 4 million was achieved by refurbishment of Terminal 3 and more efficient use of all the terminals. Secondly, when an investment decision is eventually made, operations and marketing managers need to team up and run it to make it work. In other words, they commit their organisations to making the forecasts come true.

6. Forecasting demand

The passenger demand forecast illustrated in 4 is but one of several approaches to prediction that are used. We should remember that the purpose of forecasting is to reduce uncertainty. To this end, attempts are made to anticipate the future in many fields. These range from the broad areas of economics, international relations and technology to the more specific ones of demand for the products of an individual firm. The former are not usually the province of the operations manager although an awareness of trends should be part of the development of operations strategy. As we noted in Chapters 2 and 4, organisations that are involved in planning require some sort of forecasting method. Otherwise they must take their chances as events unfold. That is, they must behave entrepreneurially.

Forecasts are usually made with *time horizons* in mind. This term relates to the future period they are trying to cover, the horizon being the moment beyond which one is not able to see. The passenger demand forecast had a horizon in the 2010s which contrasts with the supervisor planning the despatch of an order today. Forecasts are often classified by three time horizons as shown in Box 11.3. There is no strict rule separating the three bands in terms of time, issues or responsibilities. Indeed, Box 11.3 shows the periods as overlapping and it should be noted, for example, that capital projects falling into the long-term band will contain many elements that are planned and executed within shorter cycles. The point of the description is to show that longer-term forecasts involve broader issues. Because of their scale and relationships with great uncertainty in the environment, more senior managers tend to be involved.

Medium and short term forecasts focus on narrower issues, often down to estimating the behaviour of one variable. This could be sales, the price of fuel or the congestion on a particular route. The accent is on producing firm, numerical values. Long-term forecasts incorporate many more factors and tend to include much qualitative data.

Qualitative forecasting techniques attempt to gather experience, intuition and value systems of experts and leaders to reach a description of the long-term future. We can list some here:

- *Delphi methods*
  The Delphi method (named after the oracle) is made up of a series of surveys of expert opinion. The experts, about ten in number not necessarily gathered in one place, are asked to speculate on questions about their field in (say) ten or

Time horizon	Years	Issues	Responsibility
Long-term	2 to 10 or more	New products, markets, large capital projects, location	Led by senior managers
Medium-term	$\frac{1}{2}$ to 3	Planning of operations, sales, budgeting, smaller capital investments	Middle managers
Short-term	0.0001 to 1	Task schedules, job allocation, loading, dispatching, routing	Junior managers and supervisors

Box 11.3 Time horizons, examples and responsibilities

more years time. Assuming that there is a lack of a consensus after this first stage, the organisers circulate all responses to all members of the panel. There is then a second round of opinion gathering in which it is expected that there will be some move towards a consensus. Rounds continue as necessary. Questions asked may be, for example, 'What do you think the average size of intercontinental passenger aircraft will be in 2015?' or 'What changes will there be in steel production methods before the middle of the next decade?'

Delphi methods are usually seen as gathering together expert opinion. A similar approach can use a group of senior managers who are asked to forecast the business environment. This activity often takes place in a workshop setting away from the normal work place. There is support from background data, statistical trends and so on. These techniques are called jury methods.

- *Sales force surveys*
  In the short-term, sales data can be extrapolated to forecast demand. Using the opinion and contacts of the sales people themselves can considerably enrich this approach. They spend much time with customers, hear about developments and gain a feel for the actions of competitors. This qualitative information can be systematically gathered in sales force surveys.

- *Customer surveys*
  Many customer surveys attempt to gather accurate, quantitative data by customer research. They ask about or, better, observe actual behaviour. Hence the question, 'How often do you eat pub meals each month?' More future orientated information may be gathered by asking about future spending plans; this is gained either by surveys or through consumer panels who meet to discuss ideas and assess product proposals. Since customers themselves are being asked to speculate, the results from these studies should be used with care in making firm forecasts.

Quantitative forecasting techniques use numerical techniques and historical data sometimes combined with models of relationships among the variables being studied. We shall look at two types here:

- *Time series models*

  A time series model is based on the simple assumption that the future depends on the past. For instance, the sales of newspapers in the next three months can be discovered by combining data about past sales in some way. These methods are often effective if there is no major upheaval in the industry sector being covered. In the case of newspapers, if things remain more-or-less as they are, the best forecast of future sales in probably one based on recent trends. On the other hand, the outbreak of a price war (*The Times* was reduced to 20 pence in 1994) disturbs patterns so much that trends are no longer followed.

- *Causal models*

  These models try to discover and use the patterns of relationships that determine the behaviour of the variables under investigation. Sales of do-it-yourself goods are known to be related to people moving house. Therefore, the modeller attempts to represent the relationship between store sales, house purchases and any other variables that have an impact. Rather than use a time series to forecast the DIY sales, the causal model would be used instead. We should recognise, however, that the input data to this model, such as house sales, may itself have to be generated through a time series. Since, however, this data is readily available and the house moves precede the higher spend on DIY, doing the forecasting this way enables the user to get 'ahead of the game'.

7. Time series forecasting

A time series is simply a list of values each of which is labelled with the time of its occurrence. We shall outline how time series forecasts are made from this stream of historical data. First, the time series must be decomposed. Actual data streams are affected by factors such as seasonal variations that tend to hide the underlying trends. Decomposition splits the data into information about these components. Secondly, we shall review techniques for forecasting itself.

Decomposition consists of splitting the past data into its components each of which can be forecast. There are, typically, four components:

- *Trend*

  The trend, often called the *underlying trend*, is the basic change in the data as time advances. It is captured in statements such as, 'Demand is doubling every five years,' and is represented by the 7 per cent annual growth in the airline passenger example.

- *Seasonality*

  This not only refers to quarterly or annual changes such as represented by 'The Christmas Rush', 'The Spring Collection' or even new potatoes but also to patterns that repeat hourly, daily, weekly and so on. Some of these are readily observed by the public, the rush hour and the weekend being obvious examples. Others are internal to the organisation such as the weekly, four-weekly or monthly cash flows of wages and salaries, and quarterly or annual variations in work load of the accounting office as it prepares financial statements.

- *Cycles*

  Occurring over periods of several years, cycles are important in those industries that experience peaks and troughs. They are, in principle, similar to seasonal factors but, since they are notoriously difficult to forecast both in size and in time period, they are often treated separately. They are, however, important in sales and capacity planning.

- *Random variations*

  Changes that cannot be explained and captured in the above three categories are treated as being the result of random events. Since these are treated as random, they cannot be included in a forecast. A causal model may help in understanding these variations yet even then may not help in their forecasting. For example, demand for taxis is clearly affected by the weather. This is known as a causal relationship. Yet it does not help in assessing the likely demand over the next few years and therefore deciding the number of licence plates to issue.

We can see how these components combine in Figure 11.2. Sales of a consumer product are shown over a period of several years. Clearly there is an annual cycle whose size seems to be quite consistent. The actual sales line has the 'jagged' random component and, within this, there is clearly a combination of a regularly falling trend with seasonal variation. Any long-term cycle, such as may be based on industry cycles or the product life cycle, would not show up over the three-year time scale.

The decomposed demand formula is the assembly of the components described above. There are two forms, the multiplicative and the additive. In the more common multiplicative equation, the components are multiplied:

$$\text{Sales} = \text{Trend} \times \text{Seasonal factor} \times \text{Cyclical factor}$$

The additive equation looks like:

$$\text{Sales} = \text{Trend} + \text{Seasonal value} + \text{Cyclical value}$$

Since seasonal and cyclical values are assumed to be regular and random variations cannot be controlled, the forecasting stage of the time series approach is essentially one of moving the trend line forwards. There are various methods that can be used for this. These are:

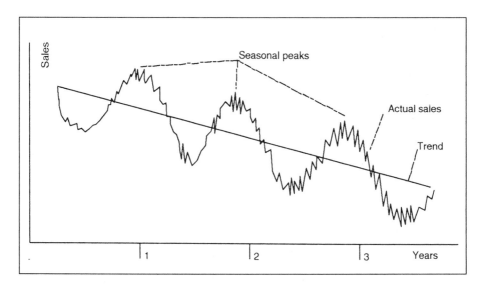

Figure 11.2 Sales graph showing seasonal and random variations

- *Simple approach*

  A quick approximation can be made by extending the trend line, often by sketching on the graph. For short-term trends, it is quick and efficient.

- *Moving averages*

  Moving averages base immediate forecasts on the averages of previous periods. For example, where little trend is expected, an average of the past six months' sales will give a guide to future monthly sales as it will cut out the random variations. If a trend is expected, recent sales can be given more emphasis by given them greater weight in the formula. This is the technique of *weighted moving averages*. Moving averages are easy to use and work well in stable conditions. They are good at smoothing out the random fluctuations. Yet if the time over which averaging is made too large, they become less sensitive to underlying change. Indeed, they are poor at picking out trends. Since they are averages, they will, of course, always make a forecast within the range of the past data.

- *Exponential smoothing*

  Exponential smoothing places little reliance on averaging a stream of past data. Instead it corrects the previous period's forecast according to the error in that forecast. A basic formula is:

  Forecast = Previous forecast + $\alpha \times$ (Previous actual sales – Previous forecast)

  The term α is the *smoothing constant* that takes a value from 0 to 1. Our new forecast is equal to the one we made for the previous period adjusted by the error that occurred in that previous forecast. The amount of adjustment depends on the value chosen for the smoothing constant. If set near to zero, the forecast never changes. If set near to 1, the forecast is always equal to previous sales.

  For $\alpha = 0$ Forecast = Previous forecast

  For $\alpha = 1$ Forecast = Previous sales

  Since forecast depend on previous forecasts which in turn depend on the ones before them, exponential smoothing does take into account previous data in its projections. Choice of α affects how these previous periods are weighted. If the constant is set at 0.5, only the last three periods have much effect on the forecast, whereas if it is 0.1, recent demand is downgraded and about 20 data values are smoothed out.

- *Trend analysis*

  In contrast to the extrapolation methods mentioned above, trend analysis works on the trend line by trying to fit a mathematical equation to it. Then future values can be forecast using the equation. The trick is to choose a line that is most likely to represent the behaviour being forecast. Figure 11.3 shows two examples, the linear trend and exponential growth. The former is simple and is used where no other model is thought better; the latter is applicable to cases of explosive growth where, say, sales double every several years.

  Having chosen the general form of the line, the regression analysis technique will establish the closest fit to the past data.

8. A practical example: electricity generation

We saw in **1.14** how electricity was a special kind of Type 4 product in that it cannot be stored. Generating companies, therefore, place great emphasis on

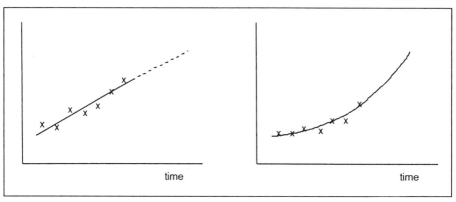

Figure 11.3 Two examples of trend projection

forecasting. They use a mixture of quantitative and qualitative techniques to predict demand.

Electricity generation is carried out in power stations the most efficient of which are operated almost continuously. These produce the so-called base load. Stations do not usually run at full power, the turbines and generators are most efficient when operating at about 70 per cent of maximum. This spare capacity is known as the *spinning reserve*, being machines that are running at the correct speed and whose power output can be increased in fractions of a second.

As demand increases in, say, cold weather, older, less efficient stations are started up. The maximum demand is about 50,000 MW at 6 o'clock on a cold winter's evening. Peaks can usually be related to the breaks between programmes at peak viewing times, and are catered for by the spinning reserve, gas-turbine systems, which can be run up to full power in about 30 seconds, and pumped storage hydroelectricity. There can be demand surges of 10% or more. To anticipate these changes, operators use data from sources as varied as the meteorological office and *Radio Times*.

Figure 11.4 shows the time series of demand through the evening of 4th July 1990. It shows the moderate summertime base load of about 26,000 MW with some remarkable peaks. This evening was the occasion of the famous (or infamous) semifinal match between England and Germany in the football World Cup. The three increasingly unpredictable surges occurred at half-time, full-time and the end of the penalty shoot-out[4]. The largest leap in demand was 2,800 MW, equivalent to a large power station.

Medium and long term forecasting are also critically important to the success of the electricity generators and distributors. They seek to produce clear operating budgets as well as take a longer view for the planning of new networks and power stations. MANWEB[5] found that during the 20 years to 1990, sales changed as follows: an average annual increase of 1.5 per cent to industrial customers; sales to commercial units increased by 4.1 per cent per annum; domestic consumption remained stable. A simple time series extrapolation of each sector would be a first stab at future forecasting. However, the company experienced a 15 per cent fall of sales to industrial customers in 1980-81 when there was a significant recession. It also recognises the effect of the

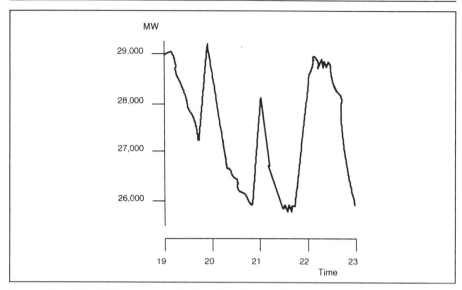

Figure 11.4 Electricity demand in Britain, 4 July 1990

weather and the relative prices of other energy sources in those markets where there is competition. The identification of these links in its market sectors means that causal forecasting, using time series extrapolations of underlying variables, can give clearer pictures of the future.

9. Causal forecasting

Beyond trend analysis, regression analysis is also used in causal forecasting. Here, instead of using time as the independent variable, other factors are considered. In the simplest case, there is assumed to be one independent variable and the relationship is assumed to be linear. This relationship is similar to the first graph of Figure 11.3. The form of the regression equation is

$$\hat{y} = a + (b \times x)$$

$\hat{y}$ is the variable being forecast, x is the independent variable and a and b are constants. Regression methods allow a line to be fitted to a data set and an estimate made of how well the line matches this known information. An extension of this basic approach enables a model to be built with several independent variables x_1, x_2, x_3 and so on. This has the form:

$$\hat{y} = a + (b_1 \times x_1) + (b_2 \times x_2) + (b_3 \times x_3) + \ldots$$

Known as *multiple regression*, this is a powerful technique. It enables the analyst to explore interconnections between large numbers of variables within a system. We should note, however, that it needs to be used with care and still requires the independent variables to be predicted if it is to be used as a forecasting technique. Box 11.4 gives an example of how the method can produce usable results[6]. It was shown how Dettol sales could be related to four variables, two of which they could control and the other two they could forecast. Managers were then able to insert their own pricing and advertising plans, as well as time series forecasts for the other variables, in order to estimate future sales.

296

The study sought to identify the main factors affecting the sales of Dettol, the leading domestic disinfectant and antiseptic. Sales were found to have statistically significant relationships with:

- real personal disposable income (purchases tended to fall when consumers had relatively less money)
- the seasons (sales of all disinfectants and antiseptics are higher in the warmer months)
- price (adjusted for inflation)
- the weight of advertising.

With the first two factors being outside the company's scope, the effects of price and advertising are of greatest interest. The study not only identified these factors but also measured their effect. Price elasticity was estimated at -0.44 and advertising elasticity at 0.19. This data, coupled with cost figures, enabled the company to show that rises in price and advertising expenditure were profitable.

Box 11.4 Factors affecting sales of Dettol

10. Committing resources to long-term capacity changes

In Chapter 2 we saw how an organisation uses modelling techniques such as break-even analysis to weigh up the relative advantages of different mixes of fixed and variable costs. Further, the various methods of evaluating investments were reviewed. Typically, investments that take some years to complete and bring benefits should be analysed using discounting methods, see **2.39**.

While these methods are widely used and are to be recommended for an initial appraisal, they fall down on two counts. First, there are technical weaknesses in the accounting processes themselves. They include: difficulties in establishing values for risk, discount rates, inflation estimates and so on; over-optimistic appraisal of the benefits of new projects compared with maintaining the status quo; problems of coping with benefits that may flow a long time in the future; underestimation of the costs of change, including organisational disruption. Secondly, there is the increasing recognition by managers that long-term benefits to the organisation flow not from a narrow concentration on financial return but on developing competitive advantage. Thus changes, such as increased flexibility, broadening the range of products on offer and improving quality and service, may be difficult to evaluate in financial terms yet be crucial to long-range success.

Render and Heizer[7] list five strategic considerations that they recommend should be called upon to enhance analysis of investments in operations. These are:

- Investments should be part of a coordinated strategic plan. Rather than be considered in isolation, they should be seen as working together to win customers.
- Investments should yield competitive advantage through, for example, flexibility, speed of delivery or service, quality, reliability and so on.
- Investments should consider product life cycles.
- The analysis should consider a variety of operating factors. Changes may affect scrap, rework, space requirements, inventory, maintenance and training needs.
- The analysis should be subjected to sensitivity tests on the key strategic variables.

The football industry illustrates many of these questions. Following the Hillsborough tragedy and the subsequent Taylor report, there have been huge investments to create all-seater stadia. The eventual cost of several hundred millions is being borne by an industry that loses about £10 million per year. In their conversion, most grounds now have reduced capacity. This has, more often than not, occurred by default rather than because of a concerted plan. How should an individual club decide the size of its stadium?

The changes have increased the difficulty of forecasting both short-term and long-term demand. Dobson and Goddard[8] showed that different influences affect demand for standing and seating places. Standing fans depend on form, significance of the game and geographical distance whereas seated customers are most influenced by historical record. In the switch to seating, the question is whether those who used to stand will behave as in the past or more like their seated counterparts.

A narrow financial appraisal may base ground capacity investment on current attendances. At a construction cost of approximately £1000 per seat and known ticket prices, it may be possible to assess the rate of return for each extra block or row of accommodation. Yet, for small clubs, this policy would create a poor image, display a lack of ambition and give no flexibility in holding the occasional big game, see Box 11.5. Again, large clubs always hope to increase attendances, stage internationals and other events, and need an impressive stadium to attract the crowd. A further argument against relying on investment appraisal is that only a few clubs are explicitly led by the profit motive. Manchester United and Tottenham Hotspur are public limited companies. For many of the rest, to fathom the decisions that have actually been made, one must go into the boardrooms to understand the motivation of club owners and directors.

Chester City F.C. opened its new 6,000 seater stadium during the 1993-4 season. The club was leading the Third Division and heading for Division Two. Yet within weeks of the opening there were problems of unanticipated demand.

The *Chester Chronicle* (8 April 1994) reported, 'Chester City have been savaged by their own fans and supporters from Preston following last Saturday's Third Division promotion clash at Deva Stadium.

'An estimated 300 Preston fans were locked out of the ground and, despite several appeals for them to leave, dozens forced their way in 25 minutes after the kick-off.'

A letter in the *Lancashire Evening Post* (2 April 1994) said, 'What a pathetic capacity for a League football club. Chester should be stripped of their League status.'

One year later, the team's form had slumped. They were bottom of the Second Division and average gates were 1,500.

Box 11.5 How big to build a stadium?

11. Learning

Many facilities, such as the football stadia we have just looked at, have a capacity which is obviously fixed. In other cases, where the capacity we are discussing refers to flow rate through a complex set of processes, it has been observed that productivity tends to improve as the tasks are repeated. Throughput or output may not be affected because there may be a limiting factor such as the speed of a single machine, the size of a lorry or the number of beds in the hotel.

One simple explanation of the productivity improvement is that people do better with practice. As individuals, they gradually find ways to avoid interruptions, skip unnecessary movement, set up the machine more quickly and so on. Well trained staff can switch from one job to another and apply their experience to the new task. This learning occurs quite quickly and is known as the short-term learning curve. A further development lies in the way organisations learn. Not only does carrying out the tasks improve with practice but all departments and functions find ways of improving their performance, linking themselves together and creating a more efficient value chain. Therefore all costs may fall and, unless there is a limiting factor, output will improve. This is the long-term effect.

Learning curves are of negative exponential form as shown in the first sketch in Figure 11.5. The exponential relationship can be demonstrated by the existence of a linear relationship when observed times are plotted against output set out on a logarithmic scale. See the second sketch graph of Figure 11.5.

Many cases of rising productivity have been established, at least over short periods. The slope of the learning curve is often expressed in terms of the fall in costs which occurs with each doubling of output. Gradients, known as *learning rates*, in practice lie in the range from 70 to 85 per cent. This means that the standard hours required for the twentieth task are about 0.7 or 0.85 of those for the tenth. The fortieth requires a similar proportion of the ones used in the twentieth and so on. More formally, if the hours are measured for a base item b, then they can be estimated for item n by the formula:

$$\frac{\text{Standard hours for unit } n}{\text{Standard hours for unit } b} = \text{Learning rate} \times \ln \frac{n}{b}$$

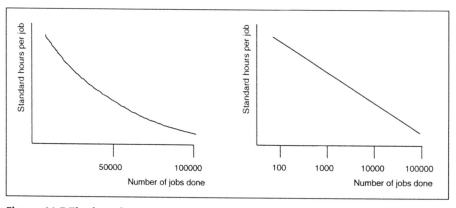

Figure 11.5 The learning curve

The function ln is the logarithm to the base 2. This takes the value of 1 when $n/b = 2$. Using the learning rate as the cost ratio for output doubling thus simplifies understanding and application.

The exponential nature of the decline should be noted. It is always prudent to ignore times for the first few items since there may be many irregularities in the way that the tasks are carried out. Afterwards, the tenth, twentieth, fortieth and so on may show reductions. As the output doubling occasions spread out, the curve represents the slowing down in learning which is inevitable. It is, however, assumed that the benefits are based on *total cumulative volume*. They are, therefore, different to *economies of scale* which result from current capacity.

We have noted that short-term learning is readily observed and easily measured. In discussing the long-term curve Henderson argued that it hardly matters why the experience curve happens. It is a rule of thumb whose characteristic pattern is observable. 'That is all the experience curve says. Everything beyond this is an inference, a hypothesis, a corollary, or a theory. ... The cost characteristics of experience curves can be observed in all elements of cost.'[9] We should note that this is a controversial view. Data supporting the existence of the long-term effect is hard to come by. Cost changes may originate elsewhere in the system. It has been argued that costs only seem to fall because of the way capital is depreciated and other difficulties of accounting comparisons over several years.

Much of the data that does exist is based on prices which only give a rough guide to costs. Render and Heizer[10] quote the example of the Model T Ford whose long production run lasted from 1910 to 1926. The learning curve seems to have a slope of 0.86 but the data observed is the showroom price. Henry Ford may have reduced his prices because of cheaper raw materials, larger scale of production and, probably more importantly, the emerging competition from General Motors. In another example, labour-hours per tonne of steel are quoted. From 1920 to 1955, this line sloped at 0.79 per doubling of output. Yet, over this period there were such changes in steel making and associated technology that the gains cannot be ascribed solely to learning. Technical innovation often originates in small companies or equipment suppliers and its application does not require huge cumulative volumes already having been produced.

While care must be taken to not assume too much in relation to learning curves, there are several implications for the operations manager:

- Cost budgets, especially for labour costs, may take into account expected productivity rises. Some firms involved in long production assembly runs, such as Texas Instruments, allow for these changes in their initial pricing. Alternatively, in assessing the amount to pay in a cost-plus contract for 250 special vehicles, the Ministry of Defence assesses productivity after (say) 20 have been made, perhaps repeats the exercise after another 20 and then negotiates improvements for the next batches.
- Changes in scheduling assumptions as some tasks are speeded up.
- The possibility that learning may result in increased shop capacity.
- The strategic opportunities flowing from improving performance.
- Increase the gradient of the learning curve. Take steps to maximise the rate of learning for the organisation as a whole. Use suggestion schemes and quality circles to encourage sharing of minor innovations.

12. Adjusting capacity in the medium term

We have seen in our discussion that there is no sharp divide between the different time horizons for planning. As Box 11.3 shows, medium term suggests a period of six months to three years. Here we are referring to the possibility of making some changes to flexible parameters within a defined plant capacity. It is often known as *aggregate planning*. This is distinguished by making provision for operations over the medium term without changing the fixed capacity or getting down to the scheduling details of each order. It may, for example, be possible to change the number of weekly operating hours of a facility by increasing the number of staff. This may be possible at short notice but usually requires a build up and training of staff over several months.

Aggregate planning approaches diverge in different operating systems. They depend on whether stocks or queues (or both) can be used to smooth out variations in the match between demand and capacity.

Service systems

We noted the possibilities in **9.1**. In summary, these are:

- Flexibility of staffing through both multi-skilled and extra people
- Switching between standardised and customised service
- Switch between self service and personal service
- Sharing capacity with other organisations including subcontractors
- Automation.

A coach operator will use aggregate planning to cope with changing demand at, say, public holiday weekends. The firm will expect a significant rise in sales and, consequently, will strive to have a full complement of vehicles and drivers ready for service. Detailed routings for each coach will not be worked out in advance; these can be left until enough seats have been sold for the destination pattern to become clear. This short-term planning may even run up to the last minute. The aggregate plan determines how the demand, as a whole, is responded to.

Process and mass production

Many process plants operate at their technical limits, constrained by the performance of the slowest link in the chain. It is not usually possible to increase output of such plants through using additional personnel. In the longer term, managers may consider improvements to the slowest link through line balancing explained in **8.8**. In the medium term there may be opportunities based on replacing or bypassing the link. This would become urgent if there is a steady rise in sales.

The fibre board mill at Queensferry, Clwyd, had its output limited by its capacity to grind timber chips into the main board ingredient, wood fibres. The grinding machines were expensive and had a long lead time. A short-term improvement, arranged at one month notice, was gained by buying wood pulp from a firm that did not compete in the same market. This was fed into the process after the grinder. Although the bought pulp was more expensive than the in-house variety, the effect of increasing total throughput improved profits.

The net output of product is the key variable of concern to process plant managers. We noted in **2** that the net output of a process plant is given by:

Achieved capacity = Designed capacity × Utilisation × Yield

The medium-term management of process plant will concern itself with maintaining plant utilisation and reducing the amount of trim and waste. Yield is also an issue in other manufacturing systems; an item rejected for a defect that shows up close to the finishing stage represents a use of production capacity that can never be recovered. This is one of the benefits of aiming for zero defects in manufacture.

Mass production is similar to process production when it comes to considering the above factors. Beyond these, however, many mass production lines have variable speed depending on the amount of personnel allocated to them. They can readily reduce their throughput provided the surplus staff can be redeployed elsewhere.

Jobbing and batch production

Jobbing and batch production have complex capacity matching problems. As will be shown in Chapter 12, there is so much interference between products waiting for processing that scheduling a jobbing shop to anything approaching 100% is impossible. The idea of an achievable, fixed capacity does not apply. The capacity of the shop for a given pattern of work is found from experience. This does not mean that nothing can be done. Capacity utilisation is a key feature of MRP systems. Further, Optimised Production Technology defines capacity not according to all the processes in the jobbing shop but just of those that act as bottlenecks.

Managers have, therefore, many opportunities to vary the capacity of these manufacturing facilities. If they are to do so efficiently, however, they need the back-up of good data and good modelling techniques, from rules of thumb to computer-based MRP systems. Staff flexibility is an important feature of the successful implementation of approaches such as Just-in-Time systems. They depend on the ability to allocate resources to wherever processing delays are likely to occur. These questions are again addressed in Chapters 12 and 13.

13. Limits to chasing aggregate demand

Attempts to continually adjust capacity to match current and anticipated sales, known as *chasing demand*, are constrained by the problems of quickly adjusting capacity. In some industries, the use of casual labour and other temporary resources is well established and a necessary part of operations. In other cases, however, employees are more highly trained and well organised and attempts to have total flexibility in their employment would fail. Many organisations prefer to uncouple demand and throughput rates not because they are unduly constrained by pressure groups but because they believe that this is the way to run operations more effectively.

From the narrow point of view of optimising operating costs, the policy of *levelling output* looks attractive. The capacity is not changed in the short term and the facility can focus its efforts on being as efficient as possible. Japanese firms such as Nissan believe that stable employment and consistent shop floor work lead to more experienced staff, easier supervision and better quality. Furthermore, the costs of change are eliminated and overtime working does not become habitual. As we have noted, level output requires either demand management or stocks and queues to isolate the market and operating systems.

Level output policies are common in service industries. Passenger transport organisations have to plan their timetables months in advance and can only respond to random variations in customer flow by accepting queues and congestion. Shops and personal service outlets have fixed opening hours. Mail order companies accept variations in order backlogs according to random demand changes.

Many organisations plan a mixed system with no shifts in capacity in response to short-term demand changes but occasional adjustments in the medium term. In this way, the operating core of the organisation is only changed to match established trends in the time series data rather than respond to its every 'blip' or seasonal fluctuation.

Figure 11.6 illustrates the policies of chasing demand and levelling output. A manufacturer attempts to satisfy demand that is on an upward trend but has seasonal variations. The chase demand approach adjusts capacity based on short-term forecasts using, in this case, exponential smoothing. The level demand policy makes annual adjustments according to the trend. Differences between demand and production are absorbed by stock. Stock changes are roughly represented in the figure by the area lying between the actual sales line and the relevant production line. If the demand line is higher, stock is falling, and *vice versa*. It can be seen that even the chase demand policy does not avoid the need for buffer stocks. Such variations and imperfections in whatever matching method is chosen mean that manufacturers follow a mixed policy. They combine capacity adjustments with both order backlogs (queues) and finished goods inventory.

The aggregate planning process creates a broad schedule for operations managers. As we can see in Figure 11.7, it bridges the gap between the strategy and the short-term scheduling, such as MRP, that we will study in Chapter 13. For instance, at a cable manufacturer such as BICC, the aggregate plan would cover a period of about a year. It would be expressed in terms of tonnes of cable to be produced by each plant. Without being able to identify any order or size in detail, the plan would help to integrate the business. The personnel department will ensure that any needed staff are recruited, purchasing will place orders for those raw materials with long lead times and accounting will prepare the budgets. In a similar way, the seaside quick-service restaurant estimates demand a few weeks ahead, the mail order company plans the resources it needs to back up a new advertising campaign.

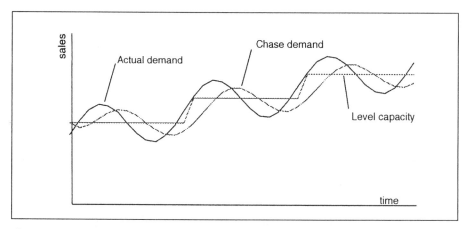

Figure 11.6 Approaches to smoothing capacity through aggregate planning

303

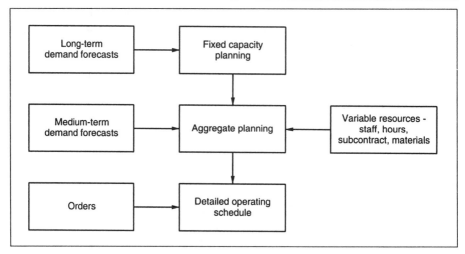

Figure 11.7 Aggregate planning as the link between capacity planning and detailed scheduling

Case study: Manchester Airport's second runway

Manchester Airport[11] is the third busiest in the UK after Heathrow and Gatwick. In 1992 it handled 11.7 million passengers (mppa). There are some 100 airlines offering 170 charter and scheduled services. The airport has one 3,048 metre runway served by two passenger terminals and a separate World Freight Terminal. Other airfield activities include maintenance and support such as fuelling.

Demand is forecast to rise to 22 mppa by 2000 and 30 mppa by 2005. These figures imply compound growth rates of 8% until 2000 and 7% thereafter. Based on 100 passengers per air transport movement (ATM), corresponding ATMs are forecast to be 220,000 in 2000 and 300,000 in 2005.

Manchester Airport plc is a company established in 1986. Its shareholders are the ten local authorities of Greater Manchester with Manchester City Council holding the majority stake. The company has a licence to operate its airport from the Civil Aviation Authority. The CAA ensures fair access to all aircraft, allows for distribution of landing slots among airlines and sets hourly runway capacities consistent with safe working.

The primary purpose of an airport is to act as a node connecting air routes with those on the ground. Passengers and freight are processed through stages whose capacity must match demand and be balanced if the airport resources are to be used efficiently. The system can be seen as having three key subsystems: the runways, the terminals, where the interchange occurs, and the local ground network.

Terminals
Manchester opened the first phase of Terminal 2 in 1993. Extensions and improvements to both terminals will take the capacity to around 30 mppa. Domestic flights are handled by a special section of Terminal 1.

Runways
The airport is dependent on a single runway which achieves a 'best in class' performance of 42 ATMs per hour. This output is not achieved at all times of the day

nor all year. Peak daily demand occurs from 0700 to 1000 and 1600 to 1930. Summer demand, especially for charter movements, is higher than in the winter. Furthermore, the runway is closed from time to time. Planned closure for maintenance occurs usually at night. Unplanned closure can happen at any time and results in a complete shut-down of the airport.

Airlines' response to congestion and the unavailability of slots can be to increase the size of aircraft or to move their business elsewhere. Management estimates, however, that the 300,000 ATMs in 2005 will require a capacity of at least 60 per hour. If this were the case, the annual capacity utilisation would be 57%.

Ground transport

Road vehicle movements generated by the Airport were estimated to number 52,000 during the effective 16-hour day. The projected growth would increase this to 124,000 by 2005. About 80% of the road traffic uses the M56 motorway and the airport expansion would increase the total on this road by 13%. The M56 and the connecting M63 are being widened and a new link to the M6 is planned.

The airport has a new railway station with some 70 trains per day. This figure is to increase when the link line to the south is completed. Other proposals include a light rapid transit line and promotion of the use of buses.

The second runway

The airport company sees the construction of a second runway as crucial to its expansion plans. The proposal has attracted widespread support and protest. Objections are based on unnecessary environmental damage and the better use of capacity elsewhere, especially at Liverpool. The proposed extension would cover part of the small, picturesque Bollin Valley and require the demolition or removal of several historic farm buildings. To the south-east of the site lies the village of Styal with its important heritage of the early industrial era, see Figure 11.8.

In its planning application, the airport company tried to anticipate and respond to many of the objections. It considered impact on the physical environment in terms of noise, air and water quality, landscape, wild life and so on. The proposed runway would be parallel to the existing one. While the impact on some sensitive sites would have been relieved by a different orientation, safety requirements meant that the two runways would have to be parallel. In response to the special nature of the Styal area, the new runway would be built to the west of the existing one and would be used in such a way that aircraft would not fly any closer to Styal than at present. In the prevailing westerly winds, it would be used for take-off. On the 20% of days when easterlies blow, it would be used for landing.

Questions

1 Show, in a diagram, the processes passed through by a passenger after arriving for a flight. From the capacity management point of view, where can problems arise?
2 What would be the role of aggregate planning in the airport context?
3 Identify the types of forecasting mentioned in the case. What are the implications of errors?
4 Are there any other systems or subsystems, not mentioned here, that restrict or influence the operating capacity of Manchester Airport?

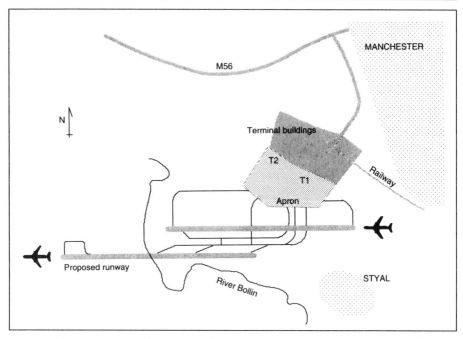

Figure 11.8 Manchester Airport showing runway use in the prevailing wind

References

1. Hellier, David (1994) 'Eurotunnel capacity challenged' *The Independent on Sunday: Business* 1 May, p. 1
2. Faith, N. (1995) 'Third Heathrow runaway to be ruled out in bid for terminal' *The Independent on Sunday: Business* 29 January, p. 1
3. DuClous, P. (1993) 'Cream of the continent' *World Trade* **6.8** September, pp. 136–140
4. National Grid Company plc (1994) *Highways of Power*
5. Kleinwort Benson Limited (1990) *Mini Prospectus: The Regional Electricity Companies Share Offers* 21 November, pp. 23-4
6. Cannon, Tom (1992) *Basic Marketing* Third edition London, Cassell pp. 156–171
7. Render, R and Heizer, J. (1994) *Principles of Operations Management* Boston, Allyn and Bacon p. 216
8. Dobson, S.M. and Goddard J.A. (1992) 'The demand for standing and seated viewing accommodation in the English Football league' *Applied Economics* **24.10** October, pp. 1155–1163
9. Henderson, B. (1984) *The Logic of Business Strategy* Cambridge, Mass., Ballinger p. 49–50
10. op. cit. p. 307
11. The case study is based on: Manchester Airport plc (1993) *Runway 2: Planning Application Supporting Statement* July, mimeo.; Cobham Resource Consultants and Consultants in Environmental Sciences Ltd (1993) *Runway 2: Environmental Statement – Non-technical Summary* Manchester, Manchester Airport plc, July, mimeo.

12

SCHEDULING

Chapter objectives

When you have finished studying this chapter, you should be able to:

- Distinguish between scheduling issues in intermittent and repetitive manufacture and service operations.

- Use Gantt charts to explain the complexity of task sequencing in a simple job shop; suggest how it may be managed.

- Explain the context and use of the MRP family of systems in batch scheduling; describe some difficulties that arise in implementation.

- Outline the Theory of Constraints and its contribution to resolving scheduling dilemmas; demonstrate the operation of a simple OPT system.

- Show how Just-in-Time philosophy has been applied to relevant manufacturing situations; illustrate how a basic kanban link works and show how it can be used to gradually achieve a reduction in waste.

- Compare the use of techniques in intermittent and repetitive manufacture and discuss how they interact with the people who use them.

- Set service scheduling needs in a comparative framework; show where keeping to time is a key element in service competition.

INTRODUCTION

Scheduling deals with the timing of operations. To produce schedules, an organisation may start from capacity and aggregate plans, if it has them, and produce detailed instructions on the sequence and times for each operation it intends to carry out. This suggests that planning has to be carried out in advance and in detail. Although this is true in principle, we shall see in practice that the problem can be eased by repetition, focus on key elements and the skills and experience of the people on the ground.

Schedulers not only plan jobs as they pass through the operations system. They must also assign personnel, equipment, materials and other resources to each stage. The purpose is to optimise operational performance according to a combination of the following objectives:

- Time the order spends within the system
- Waiting time for the customer

- Efficiency of use of resources
- Inventory levels.

Having to optimise, or at least cope with, many factors simultaneously makes scheduling a complex job. Box 12.1 outlines four situations where resources have to be brought together for the activities to take place. Sometimes, the allocation of resources is automatic, having been established by practice over many repeats. In others, however, details of each element need to be worked out in advance.

To discuss the scheduling of manufacturing processes, we can return to our classification of process technologies. Operations scheduling in jobbing and batch production, that is *intermittent* systems, is different from that in mass and process production, called *repetitive* production. The former systems are characterised by separate processes that can produce a variety of items either individually or in batches. Managers have to focus their attention on these processes, possibly in groups, and the orders that have to be moved through them. The job shop has the highest variety and the more *ad hoc* procedures. The batch operation frequently runs batches of the same product and therefore finds it worthwhile to make and keep more detailed plans. In repetitive manufacturing, attention is not so much given to the detail of individual orders but to the steady flow through the whole production system.

The manufacturing process not included here is the project. Project planning and scheduling usually focuses on the delivery of one contract. The scheduling techniques differ from those used elsewhere. Consequently, we shall discuss project management in a separate chapter.

Direct service operations are often designed to respond to demand as it arises. Therefore, they cannot be scheduled in detail. Self service systems need no scheduling. On the other hand, isolated services, where order processing takes place away from the customers, have, as we noted in **3.4**, many characteristics in common with both intermittent and repetitive manufacturing systems. The examples we shall use to illustrate production scheduling questions will be drawn from both manufacture and isolated service.

Business	Some items for scheduling
Jobbing printer	Order sequencing; machine allocation; employee assignment; paper and ink supply; print setting
Parcel service	Collection and delivery routing; consolidation; vehicle allocation; crew assignment; sorting times
Film studio	Set construction and access; crew assignment; actor and extra recruitment; wardrobe, props etc; support on location
Brewery	Product sequencing; fermentation times; raw material flows; bottling, barrelling or despatch; employee assignment

Box 12.1 Some scheduling tasks

INTERMITTENT MANUFACTURE

1. Job shop scheduling difficulties

Job shops are noted for their high variety of work and their low volume. Production is usually carried out to customers' orders, each differing in their requirements. Consequently, each order has to be planned and tracked all the way through to its conclusion and despatch. Depending on the firm's previous experience and the variety of tasks to be undertaken, there can be considerable uncertainty about how much time each will take and planners have to allow enough flexibility within the system to enable it to cope. We can understand this more clearly when we recognise that new orders with yet further patterns of requirements are continually being received and inserted into the production process.

There are many scheduling techniques available. They are often designed to suit particular patterns of orders and the nature and complexity of tasks. They will focus on defined objectives, such as the minimisation of machine idle time or the maximisation of throughput volume. Reliable and appropriate techniques are vital in the jobbing shop. Ranging from the simple rule of 'first come first served' to full-scale manufacturing requirements planning, they move scheduling from a hit-and-miss affair to a consistent and dependable management activity. What a job shop cannot achieve, however, is a pattern of constantly working machines, busy staff and no delays in orders being passed. Slack is needed somewhere.

To illustrate the difficulties let us look at scheduling in a car repair shop. Take the following example of basic servicing:

When I was last in Crane Bank Garage, I overheard a customer complaining that a two-hour job took all day. It looked as if the manager must have a scheduling problem. To simplify things, we shall consider all cars as requiring the same sort of service. In reality, the variety of tasks that customers ask for makes matters much worse! So let us say that there are four stages as follows:

C Cleaning. The garage does not carry out full service work without cleaning. This process takes place in a bay equipped with steam lances and ramps.
U Under body inspection and lubrication. Brake check and adjustment. This is done on a hoist fitted with oil changing equipment.
E Engine check and adjustment using the Krypton tuner to bring emissions into line with the regulations.
A Ancillary equipment check and repair.

Normal times for these jobs are well established for different makes of car. For our customer's model, the manager estimates them to be: C = 0.25; U = 0.5; E = 0.75; A = 0.5. Consequently, we might agree with the customer's assertion that they should take 2 hours all together.

To begin to investigate why the job takes longer, we could start by plotting the schedule for each task as shown in the left half of Figure 12.1. This is a Gantt chart, a widely used form of presentation for sequenced events. In its standard form, the times for each task are plotted as horizontal bars, on a time scale ranging from minutes to months as appropriate.

The first Gantt chart suggests that the job should be finished by 10:00. This would be the case if this were, as many clients believe, the only car in the shop.

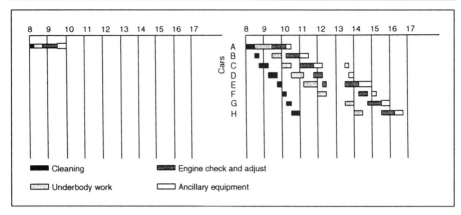

Figure 12.1 Servicing schedules for a single car and many cars

The difficulty is that our customers' is not the only one in. It has no particular priority over the others and the supervisor has used the usual scheduling rule - process cars in the order in which they are booked in. Cars waiting for each stage are, therefore, taken in the same sequence. The second Gantt chart of Figure 12.1 shows the effect of the scheduling rule. Each row of the chart represents the progress of one vehicle. The four tasks are indicated. It is normal to code different tasks using a shading or colour scheme.

We could just as well use each row to plot the activity of each process and identify the cars by a shading code. This would be rather like a horizontal version of the multiple activity chart of section **6.11**. Which way the chart is drawn depends on the number of processes and jobs and on the reason we are producing it. Here our interest is on the progress, against the clock, of cars through the shop. Note that the irate customer's car is G and the garage closes from 12:30 to 13:30.

Because of the irregular pattern of task times, cars have to wait between stages. A two-hour job can indeed take all day. Of course, car G could be serviced more quickly if it were started earlier. Since not all customers can be given this priority, the manager has to decide whether to concede in this case and then explain the decision to this and other customers. Such diplomacy is part of the role of the front office in isolating service operations.

The repair shop example, although simplified, is typical of scheduling problems in jobbing and batch production. On the one hand, orders are being pushed through task sequences in as short a time as possible. On the other hand, these tasks have to be carried out efficiently. Harrison[1] quotes Shingo's description of the complexity of the system, see Figure 12.2. The production system is a multidimensional network of operations and processes. Workers and machines work on various processes. Provided there is always work waiting at each stage, these can appear to be very efficient. Yet jobs have to pass through these stages in many sequences. As Figures 12.1 and 12.2 both show, they may have to wait ahead of every process they come to, whether these are direct operations or inspection, transport and the like. A balance has to be achieved between the efficiency of the production system and the throughput of the jobs.

A moment's further inspection of the situation at Crane Bank Garage shows that, with a little planning, the time taken for most cars and the waiting time of

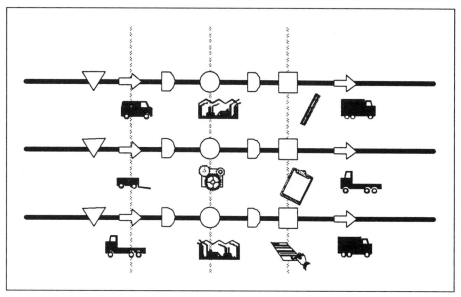

Figure 12.2 Conflict between production flow and operational efficiency

each process could be reduced. For example, the day could start with car B because it requires the shortest period in the cleaning bay. The next process could start earlier and so on. It looks as though the business could improve its performance by better scheduling. Is it possible to formalise the scheduling decision so as to make this possible?

Our repair shop example, although simplified, is typical of job shop scheduling problems. There are four principal elements:

- Several *work stations*: in our case these are the stages through which cars are processed.
- Several *jobs*: these are the cars themselves, the work on each being a complete job.
- A *sequence for each job*: for the purposes of our illustration there was one standard sequence but it is easy to see that even these operations could be done in a different order provided the first was cleaning.
- A *time for each operation*: in a simple case this is assumed to be known in advance and the uncertainty connected with it is ignored.

Sequencing rules, of which many exist, take the elements of the scheduling problem and, using a procedure, work out a plan. The rules include the following:

FCFS – First come first served
LPT – The longest processing time goes first
SPT – The shortest processing time goes first
EDD – Earliest due date goes first

It is, indeed, possible to think of many rules, each of which has application in different circumstances. For instance, the ones suggested above do not consider cash flow or profit. In cases where jobs takes weeks or months, it may be best to start on those that generate the quickest cash return.

311

2. Job shop loading: sequencing through one process

The simplest sequencing problem occurs when several jobs have to be passed through one process only. Take the following example of a job shop providing isolated service:

> Bithell's Boats has a small dry dock that can take one canal cruiser at once for cleaning and repainting. At the time of our investigation, the dock has just become free and there are five boats waiting. They have been examined and Mr Bithell is confident about the work time required in each case. The trouble is that he has given estimated completion times to each customer. Table 12.1 shows the relevant data. The question is, in which order should the boats be repaired?

Table 12.2 sets out the progress of the yard if it follows each of our decision rules. Which pattern is optimal will depend on what Mr Bithell is trying to achieve. To help in the assessment we can calculate three measures of performance: the mean time to complete, the mean number of boats in the system and the mean number of days late.

$$\text{Mean time to complete} = \frac{\text{Sum of total times}}{\text{Number of boats}}$$

$$\text{Mean number in system} = \frac{\text{Sum of total times}}{\text{Sum of servicing times}}$$

$$\text{Mean number of days late} = \frac{\text{Sum of days late}}{\text{Number of boats}}$$

Table 12.3 compares the four decision rules against these measures of performance. It can be seen that no rule beats the others on every count. LPT is clearly worse than the others but Mr Bithell could benefit from changing his work order from FCFS to either SPT or EDD. The snag would be that if the customers were aware of this new policy, they may object because they regard FCFS as the most equitable form of queuing. SPT may seem slightly better than EDD and it often helps employees' morale to see the quick jobs 'got out of the way.' SPT does have one disadvantage. We must remember that the real business is dynamic and would be receiving a stream of new orders and enquiries. Any new work whose estimated processing time was less than for boat E would push it further back down the queue, so much so that E may never be attended to! Therefore, if SPT is to be used, a regular review of the longest jobs must be carried out.

Table 12.1 Boat maintenance times

Boat	Servicing time (days)	Promised time ahead
Alexandra	12	16
Barbara	4	12
Caroline	16	36
Daphne	6	30
Ester	18	46

Table 12.2 Bithell's Boats with different decision rules

FCFS: First come first served			
Boat	Serve time	Total time	Prom. time	Days late
A	12	12	16	-
B	4	16	12	4
C	16	32	36	-
D	6	38	30	8
E	18	56	46	10
	56	154		22

LPT: Longest processing time first			
Boat	Serve time	Total time	Prom. time	Days late
E	18	18	46	-
C	16	34	36	-
A	12	46	16	30
D	6	52	30	22
B	4	56	12	44
	56	206		96

SPT: Shortest processing time first			
Boat	Serve time	Total time	Prom. time	Days late
B	4	4	12	-
D	6	10	30	-
A	12	22	16	6
C	16	38	36	2
E	18	56	46	10
	56	130		18

EDD: Earliest delivery date first			
Boat	Serve time	Total time	Prom. time	Days late
B	4	4	12	-
A	12	16	16	-
D	6	22	30	-
C	16	38	36	2
E	18	56	46	10
	56	136		12

Table 12.3 Comparison of sequencing policies at Bithell's Boats

	Mean days to complete	Mean number in system	Mean days late
FCFS	30.8	2.8	4.4
LPT	41.2	3.7	19.2
SPT	26.0	2.3	3.6
EDD	27.2	2.4	2.4

3. Job shop loading: sequencing through more than one process

Things become more complicated when there is more than one stage to be gone through. There are very few theoretical solutions to the problem of scheduling several jobs on two or more work stations. We shall, however, illustrate Johnson's rule for two stations. It is designed to minimise both processing and idle time. Johnson's rule has four steps:

1 List each job with the time it needs at each station, including set-up time.
2 Choose the job with the shortest processing time at either station. If this is at the first, put this job first. If it is the second, put the job last.
3 Take the selected job out of the list.
4 Repeat steps 2 and 3, filling in the intermediate positions in the sequence.

The data in Table 12.4 is processed as follows: #104 has the shortest time. It is on machine X so #104 is placed first in line. #101 then has the shortest time, also on X, so it is put second in line. Then #102 is selected, but this time the shorter time is on Y so it goes at the end. We continue with #103. It goes next to the end and finally #105 is placed in the middle. The sequence is 104, 101, 105, 103, 102.

The outcome of Johnson's rule is depicted in the Gantt chart of Figure 12.3. The upper part of the diagram shows the preferred order while the lower depicts what would happen if the processing took place in the arbitrary sequence of issue of job numbers. The advantage of using Johnson's rule can be clearly seen.

Table 12.4 Five jobs, two machines

Job No.	Machine X hrs	Machine Y hrs
101	5	8
102	11	6
103	13	7
104	4	11
105	9	10

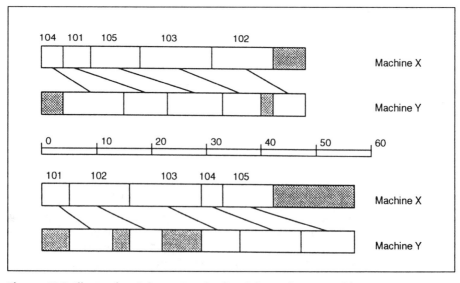

Figure 12.3 Illustrating Johnson's rule: five jobs and two machines

Note the weakness of the analysis in that no allowance is made for tasks that either precede or follow the five in question. It could be that the idle times for X at the end and Y at the start could be absorbed by further jobs in the sequence. Consequently, the difference in performance under the two rules may be exaggerated by our presentation.

Modelling longer sequences is beyond our scope and, anyhow, rare are the occasions when Johnson's rule can be applied in practice. For the job shop supervisor, however, there is a suggestion of an applicable rule of thumb. This could be stated as: *Ensure that the machines early in the sequence do sufficient jobs of short duration to keep the later machines busy.* With this approach, most of the machines would be filled with work and the efficiency figures would look satisfactory. Yet we must not fall into the trap of stressing machine efficiency as the single goal. The result would be a pile-up of work in progress with its associated slow-down in flow through the business. Giving the downstream machines too much work is as bad as giving them too little.

Job shops with many work centres have to cope with complexity. They do so with a mixture of policies that can include:

- Rough planning and sequencing in the office, together with some indication of priorities
- Surplus capacity
- Decentralisation of detailed sequencing decisions to manufacturing cells or individual employees
- Flexible staff
- Employment of progress chasers or expeditors to track orders and arrange for local sequences to be changed
- Intervention by supervisors and managers through progress meetings.

The job shop is characterised by limited planning resources in comparison to the number of orders it receives. Usually, the size and complexity of each job mean that anything more sophisticated and expensive than these policies does not bring a return. Many businesses, however, can group jobs into batches of items that are the same or very similar. This reduces the variety of work going through the factory and makes more thorough initial planning more worthwhile.

4. Batch scheduling: MRPII

Batch production shops could work in similar ways to job shops by treating each order as a job and following more fully the policies set out in the above paragraphs. By so doing, however, they would not be taking advantage of the relative scale of each order and associated reduction in variety. With the development of information systems that gather and combine data very efficiently, opportunities have opened to integrate the planning, scheduling and control of batch production more effectively than in the past. Among the best known applications is MRPII, Manufacturing Resources Planning Mark Two.

There is not one MRPII method, rather a family of approaches with the same general principles. They are supported with proprietary hardware and software from specialists in the field. Its origins lie in the earlier MRP, Materials Requirements Planning, which was using IT in leading companies in the 1960s. This was *dependent* materials control (see **14.9**) where material ordering was scheduled to satisfy actual orders received rather than the earlier methods of

315

obtaining quantities of raw materials and numbers of components based on historical statistics.

MRPII goes beyond material ordering. In its various forms, it is a method for planning all manufacturing resources. It cascades down from the aggregate business plans, through the Master Production Schedule (MPS) to provide detailed instructions to the purchasing department, suppliers, stores and the shop floor. Extensions can allow for tool supply, maintenance planning, personnel allocation and financial analysis. Figure 12.4 outlines the links between the core functions that should be integrated to comprise MRPII. This diagram shows what is known as an open-loop system because the feedback links that are needed for control are not shown. These are covered in Chapter 14. The core functions are:

- *Aggregate Sales and Operations Plan*
  Aggregate plans, see Chapter 11, cover the medium term. Without detailing individual orders, they identify the range of products expected to be ordered, with batch sizes, expected delivery schedules and so on. In making commitments at this stage, including estimated throughput times, advanced purchases of raw materials and short-range adjustments to capacity, the aggregate plan creates a framework for the MPS to be produced.

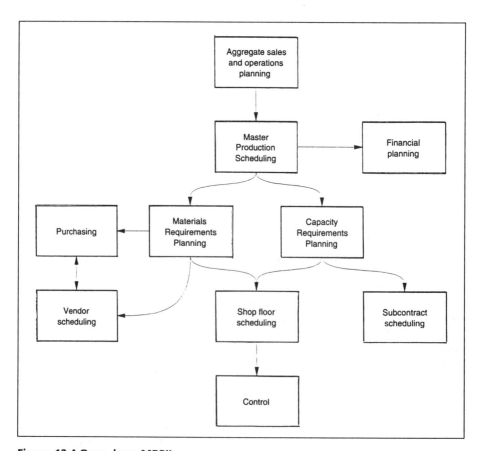

Figure 12.4 Open-loop MRPII

- *Master Production Schedule*

  The MPS is the linchpin of the MRPII system. It is a specification of what is to be made and when. Continually updated, the MPS fits in with the aggregate plan, financial plans and constraints, and known capacity. It has to consider not only shop floor capacity but lead-times of vendors and subcontractors where these are used.

- *Material Requirements Plan*

  The master schedule can be itemised into the MRP through bringing together several modules. The Bill of Materials is an item by item list of the materials needs for each order. Stock records identify what material is already available *and uncommitted to any other order*. The MRP then sets out the further materials that need to be obtained before the order can be completed.

- *Capacity Requirements Plan*

  The CRP produces, in the first pass, daily or weekly estimates of the work load in each department of the plant, even analysing it down to key machines or processes. Its purpose is to anticipate difficulties in good time so that short-term adjustments can be made to capacity, if that is possible, or the MPS can be revised to bring forward or delay orders as appropriate.

Figure 12.5 suggests the way variations in capacity requirements may be handled. The MPS has 6 weeks of *released orders*, that is orders for which details have been prepared for the shop floor, suppliers and subcontractors. Resources have been committed to these orders at this stage. Variations in weekly load at a particular work station are shown in the diagram. They are relatively small and are coped with by idle time in week 2 and overtime later in the period. After week 6, there are a further six weeks for which orders have been planned but not yet released. Schedules have to be confirmed as the picture becomes clear. For example, customers may wish to alter their own schedules. At the moment, the load at the work station is not balanced and some of it must be

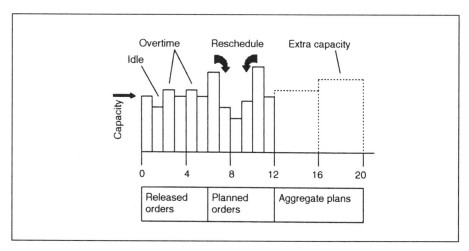

Figure 12.5 CRP at the level of one work station

rescheduled. Work from week 7 may be delayed and from week 11 brought forward. Beyond the twelfth week we return to the field of aggregate planning in which rough capacity needs are identified monthly. Here, the MPS will show that the current aggregate plans will lead to considerable overload at our work station and arrangements must be made to provide extra capacity.

- *Detailed schedules for shop floor, vendors and subcontractors.*
  The power of MRPII systems shows through when detailed schedules are produced. The information system brings together component-by-component vendor lead times, shop floor manufacturing sequences and times and assembly sequences. For the first time any item is produced, the creation of this information requires substantial investment but, once in place, the files can be adapted and updated as changes in design and production processes are introduced.

MRPII is not an automatic scheduling system. While its software can contain algorithms for sequencing jobs at various stages as well as constraints and alarm functions to give warnings when lead times or capacity limits are likely to be violated, the basic decisions have to be made by managers. Factories will have a scheduling office manned by a few key persons whose role requires a blend of knowledge of the production processes with diplomatic skills to absorb the stress caused by changes in the plan.

MRPII can bring considerable benefits in terms of reduced costs and improved response to customer needs. Standards reported include more than 95% of deliveries on time and manufacturing efficiency also higher than 95%. While we have presented it here in the context of batch production MRPII has been used in other types of production technology, sometimes under other names. Spreadbury[2] describes its successful use at Dista, a pharmaceutical plant in Liverpool. There, continuous process technology is used.

5. Problems with MRPII

There is a danger in the technical power of MRPII in that it can encourage too frequent rescheduling. It is normal to review the whole MRPII weekly, moving the planning horizons forward and updating all changes that have occurred in the intervening period. Changes could vary from the receipt of a rush order from a valued customer to a difficulty at a vendor's leading to supply delays, see Box 12.2. This *regenerative* approach is wasteful if it creates many small changes to the released order sequences with the consequent need to issue revised instructions. This problem is worsened if the updating is done more frequently. Unfortunately, this action is encouraged by efficient computing facilities. Using *net-change* MRPII, however, only those areas that have changed significantly will be modified. It requires more sophisticated software but will reduce the dithering or *system nervousness* that can lead to stress among users. The operations system should respond to major changes but should absorb minor ones through its own flexibility.

Plant in the vicinity of Kobe, Japan produce a substantial proportion of the world supplies of integrated circuits. Two days after the earthquake of January 1995, prices of processors for PCs had risen by 70 per cent.

Box 12.2 Supply and demand for PC chips

The change of beliefs and behaviour throughout the operations functions of the business are significant parts of successful implementation. Luscombe describes two MRPII failure modes in this connection[3]. Both relate to the compromises needed in developing a workable MPS. First, the sales department finds that it is being asked to provide regular sales forecasts and that these forecasts are being used to decide the aggregate plan, the quantities and types of products that are to be available for sale. Often this requires sales to change their behaviour from taking what orders they can get, including 'slipping in' the odd urgent one where possible. The MPS now enables the scheduler to point out the knock-on effects of accepting an urgent order. Other orders, possibly already released with promised delivery dates, will have to be put back. In the past, such changes would not have been noticed amid the general chaos. The second problem follows on from the first. Even if the new relationship between sales and production can be established, it may not be supported by senior managers and by key customers. A valued customer may find that, suddenly, sales is unwilling to push a rush order through the system. The frustrated customer telephones a senior manager who decides that 'for once' the wishes of the customer must be satisfied. The order is accepted. The MPS credibility is weakened. Other orders become late. Fire-fighting and progressing return and 'normal service' is resumed.

Is MRPII too dominated by production? Is it a return to a production orientation for the business in circumstances where greater efforts should be made in giving high levels of customer service? Luscombe answers these questions in this way:

'To give all customers the best possible service all the time, much better planning and control is required than has previously been possible. There was never any difficulty in rushing one urgent job through production to satisfy a particularly demanding customer. The price was in the poor delivery performance, inability to forecast despatch dates, high production inventory costs, and long lead time that were accepted as the norm for the bulk of customer orders.'[4]

Several surveys[5] point to frequent failure with MRPII implementation. It is not clear whether these amount to reductions in performance of the whole production system or a lack of achievement of high expectations which had been set out at the start of projects. In any case criticism has been levelled at MRPII schemes because of their attempt to manage the whole production system in detail. The more complex the system, the more difficult this task becomes.

Box 12.3 is drawn from notes made in interviews by a colleague at Liverpool John Moores University[6]. The first module of an MRP system at this factory had been installed in 1977 and had been added to over the following 17 years as MRPII became available. It appears that the factory managers had never been happy with the system except in as far as it gave them something, other than themselves, to blame! Our report invited the managers to return to the recognition that MRPII is merely a planning tool with known rules and logic. It will not optimise schedules itself and cannot cope with frequent changes imposed from above. The three product ranges were offered in different industrial markets and, although they shared some common components and processes, mixing them in the same plant did create problems of conflicting pressure. The factory had not given sufficient status to the role of the scheduling office so that decisions made by the small team that maintained the MRPII were not supported. The person responsible for the MPS had the same rank as first line supervisor.

There is widespread recognition amongst the members of the manufacturing management team that the factory is not performing effectively. High inventory levels, poor due date performance and manufacturing times all appear to be excessive. The general opinion is that major problems were encountered in achieving the manufacturing plan, and the levels of expediting by management in trying to achieve the plan are excessive. The group gave the impression that individual responsibilities for scheduling the factory, inventory management and product delivery performance are not clearly established.

For example, the product-led expediting practice appears to set expediter against expediter in a battle to establish order priority within the manufacturing areas. One comment from the management team was that 'the right hand does not know what the left hand is doing here' and so one has to question the effectiveness of communicating shop floor data. As a result, a disproportionate number of manufacturing shop orders are on the highest priority, due dates are changed to effect queue jumping, and real priorities, i.e. customer delivery dates, are masked.

The whole factory appears to be shortage and priority driven and, as a result, management appears to be reactive, jumping from one crisis to another ...

... the real culprit is the [name] MRPII system as there are clear and obvious planning and control difficulties ...

One possible explanation for this lies in the nature of the three product lines manufactured by [company name]. One application of [name] MRPII is used to control all of them yet factors in one may be different from the other two.

Box 12.3 MRPII failure. Or was the problem deeper?

The key to successful implementation lies in recognising that an approach such as MRPII is not a technical 'fix'. If treated in this way it becomes a rigid, bureaucratic extra burden which managers find they have to override to regain the flexibility which successful batch systems require. Sillince and Sykes[7] point to the major *management* changes that are required if benefits other than inventory reduction are to be obtained. We shall return to these themes in Chapter 14.

6. Batch scheduling: OPT

If batch production is so complex, and it is so difficult to create a management system whose complexity is a match for it, where should management focus its attention to cut lead times and inventories as well as improve production performance? An alternative to MRP lies in the recognition that it is not necessary to plan much of the plant at all. A plant does not consist of a set of machines that can and should be fully loaded. According to Goldratt and Cox [8], several basic ideas of the way plants are planned and organised are wrong. They challenge three assumptions about the way production systems ought to be managed:

- Capacity to be balanced with demand, followed by attempts to maximise the use of the capacity.

- Incentives to be based on the utilisation of workers in the tasks they have been set.
- Activation and utilisation of resources amount to the same thing.

These assumptions mean that the drive at the shop floor level is to keep as much as possible running for as much as possible of the time. Yet much of this effort does not lead to progress. In a real manufacturing system there are few *bottlenecks* and otherwise a great deal of slack. There are only a few key points on which managers should concentrate. Maximising the use of resources, including paying incentive bonuses to workers who are not working at bottlenecks, is not benefi-cial. All that happens is a build up of partly finished items waiting for their turn at the bottlenecks.

It was around this simple realisation that Goldratt created the *Theory of Constraints* and developed the software system known as *Optimised Production Technology. The Goal*, in which Goldratt and Cox present the theory, is written as a novel [9], a 'thriller' according to the dust jacket. In telling the story of the turn-round of a factory, the Theory of Constraints is both advanced and explained by the authors. Early in the novel , they use a parable of a scouts' route march to point to the essence of the problem. Scouts walking in line need a small gap between each pair to allow for statistical fluctuations in their speeds. These gaps tend to increase, for while it is possible for each to slow momentarily, it is not so easy for them to catch up. In any case, each is limited by the speed of the one in front. The statistical fluctuations do not quite average out. They simply accumu-late as the line gradually lengthens. Taking the broader picture, the whole group has to be constrained to move at the speed of the slowest member. These are fun-damental notions in the Theory of Constraints.

The theory is then worked out in a batch manufacturing setting. The extract in Box 12.4[10] shows how the notion of bottlenecks is applied in a factory. The hero persuades an old friend of how he should improve things. Attention should be focused on constraints. In any operating system, there are relatively few bottle-necks (constraints caused by internal resources) and constraints that exist outside the organisation. Apart from the obvious constraint of market demand, we can identify both in the examples of Box 12.5. Goldratt's contribution lies in simplifi-cation and focus.

7. Bottlenecks, batches and inventories

Besides providing managers with a means of focusing their attention on those parts of the production system that really matter, Goldratt shows how his ideas can be extended to cut stocks of partly finished work. There are two aspects to inventory reduction, the first coming from recognition of bottlenecks and the second from batch size reduction.

First, it is clear that work done upstream of a bottleneck, if it is done ahead of when it is needed, does not contribute to delivery on time. While an hour lost at the bottleneck is an hour lost from the whole system, an hour saved at a non-bottleneck is worthless. All that happens is that stocks of partly finished goods are increased in value and the workshop looks more crowded. Commitment to the Theory of Constraints would encourage managers to allow resources at the non-bottleneck to remain idle rather than work unnecessarily. There are echoes here of the Kanban system that we discuss in **13**.

'...we know that a very small number of constraints in a manufacturing system govern its overall level of performance.'

'Right. So you've got to identify what they are,' said Eric.

'Exactly,' said Alex.

Then he explained that, thanks to Jonah's experience, he knew that most companies are affected by a set of several constraints.

'For instance, you may find that the capacity of every resource in the organization exceeds the demand from the market,' he said. 'The resource with the lowest capacity in the system can handle 200 units, but the market can only handle 100.'

'So the market is the bottleneck,' said Eric.

'Well, no, a market is not a resource,' said Alex, 'So, by definition, it can't be a bottleneck. It can be, and often is, a constraint, but never a bottleneck.'

'Okay, gotcha,' said Eric.

'In other cases, you'll find that demand exceeds the capacity of at least one resource. And so this bottleneck resource is the constraint,' said Alex.

'Gotcha again,' said Eric.

'Most companies will be subject to several constraints. But, whatever they are, let's say you've found them,' said Alex. 'In a process of ongoing improvement, what do you think you would do next?'

Eric said, 'Run the entire system according to the constraints.'

'That's right,' said Alex. 'But how does everybody in the system know what to do?'

'Okay, you need awareness,' said Eric. 'You need to make sure everybody knows what the constraints are.'

Alex nodded. 'And every move they make is done with due consideration of the effect that their actions will have with respect to the constraints. It becomes the focus of attention for the entire organisation.'

Box 12.4 Bottlenecks and constraints

Operation	Constraint (in environment)	Bottleneck (in operations system)
Brassware manufacturer	Supply of castings from foundry	Any process, eg turning, milling, plating
Retail shop	Access; parking; deliveries	Number of tills
Open-air pop festival	Roads near site	Number of sets; food and water supplies; toilets
Chocolate factory	Raw materials supplies	Any processing plant; distribution system
Hospital specialising in transplants	Donors	Theatre access; trained teams

Box 12.5 Operations systems, bottlenecks and constraints

Secondly, batch size reduction can reduce inventories and improve delivery performance. To illustrate, imagine 1,000 items scheduled to pass through two system bottlenecks A and B. If A can handle the job in 4 hours then it seems that B can be scheduled to start 4 hours after A starts. But what if the batch size is reduced to 250? B can start one hour after A starts provided that 4 deliveries of items are made from A to B. This simple change may involve some slightly higher administration costs. Yet it will take 3 hours out of the total time taken to supply the order. Furthermore, it will reduce the stocks within the system as the product goes through more quickly.

8. Drums, buffers and ropes

Drum-buffer-rope, DBR, is a scheduling technique based on the Theory of Constraints. Its name comes from the story of the scouts' march. The drum is the schedule at the constraint; through following its beat the rest of the system will proceed at the rate of the slowest. The rope represents the line behind the constraint; it prevents the line from lengthening. In the factory the rope 'pulls' work into the system at the right time so as to avoid the build up of unnecessary stocks of work in progress. There is a small buffer just ahead of the constraint to allow for minor fluctuations and ensure that the constraint keeps going.

Figure 12.6 shows three simple work sequences that may arise in batch production[11]. The first shows a production line with market constraint. Material release into the system, either from stores or direct from a supplier, is scheduled some time ahead of delivery. This period is the *shipping buffer* that acts as a rope to pull the material through.

The second layout is paced by an internal constraint. This stage is the drum. A rope, now the *constraint buffer*, pulls the material through to the constraint. Afterwards, the shipping buffer links the constraint schedule and the schedule for delivery. The third example shows flows into final assembly operations. One part has a constraint. The non-constrained parts are started according to a combination of the shipping buffer and the assembly buffer.

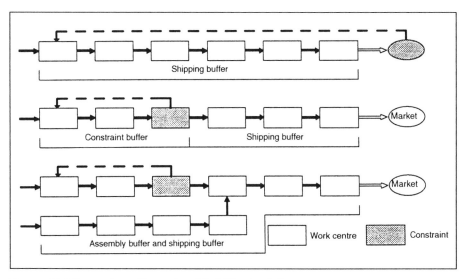

Figure 12.6 Examples of layouts with DBR scheduling

Control of this system is only required at key points. These are material release, where material enters the system, constraints and assembly and divergence points. These last two are where lines join. At the assembly point for example, the schedule ensures that the constraint part is the last to arrive, thus ensuring that there is no excessive stock and the system does not wait for non-constraint items.

Other resources do not need detailed schedules but can operate according to local conditions and simple rules. One could be, 'Work if you have materials, do not if there are none.' There is no attempt to schedule each operation, thus setting DBR in sharp contrast with MRPII.

Figure 12.7 gives a practical example of one of the systems in the previous diagram. The batch order being produced has a known sequence and times to be spent at each work centre have been established. It must pass through MC100, which is a bottleneck. The MC100 schedule for this part is worked out according to the required delivery schedule and the shipping buffer, taken to be the sum of the times after the constraint. Similarly, material release into the first stage occurs at a time before the constraint schedule equal to the sum of upstream times. The Gantt chart shows what might happen. MC100 must work according to schedule but the other centres have flexibility. Rules ensure that these centres keep the constraint going and the expeditors will check to ensure that there are no undue hold-ups. As discussed in **12.7,** away from the buffer the batch can pass through overlapped stages very rapidly.

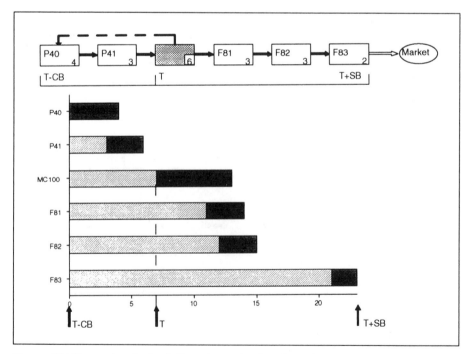

Figure 12.7 Example of scheduling through a bottleneck

9. Impact of DBR

Gardiner and others[12] summarise the impact of the DBR approach as follows:

- The complexities become understandable
- The number of resources that must be scheduled is cut dramatically
- Early warnings of potential disruption are given
- Lead time is reduced
- Guidance on continuous improvement is given
- Significant improvements over other systems are gained
- Measures of performance at different organisational levels are aligned.

We shall return to some of these points in later chapters. The main one, however, is that DBR mounts a challenge to conventional planning philosophy in that it deliberately sets out to eliminate unnecessary controls. Therefore, there is a reduction in scheduling complexity down to the five simple steps of Goldratt and Cox[13]:

Step 1   Identify the system's bottlenecks ...

Step 2   Decide how to exploit the bottlenecks [how to make them work as hard as possible] ...

Step 3   Subordinate everything else to the above decision ...

Step 4   Elevate the system's bottlenecks. [Find ways of bypassing or duplicating them]

Step 5   If, in a previous step, a bottleneck has been broken go back to step 1.

What then? OPT does not eliminate scheduling. Companies have used Goldratt's OPT or modified MRPII systems to match bottlenecks with external constraints. At the John Deere Engine Works an MRP system was simplified using the ideas expounded in *The Goal*[14]. Bottlenecks and upstream material release were scheduled in detail.

REPETITIVE MANUFACTURE

On the face of it, the scheduling of repetitive manufacturing processes, line or continuous technology, should be easier than for intermittent manufacture. This is, in some senses, true since variety is more limited. On the other hand, many firms are large and the nature of costs and competition in their industries means that there is a continuous pressure to reduce waste, improve throughput times and make the most of the resources that have been invested. Scheduling has significant impact on stock levels and many improvements have generated much of their pay back through elimination of the costs related to inventories.

We will concentrate our attention on the just-in-time production system because it is widely used in industries such as automotive assembly and is spreading into many others. Seen by many as ideal for high volume repetitive manufacture, it is also being developed in large batch production situations and some of its techniques are applicable in jobbing and small batch companies[15].

10. Just-in-time production

The basic purpose behind JIT is to minimise stocks of work in progress and to keep all materials in motion through the production system. This means that firms must be able to:

- supply goods just in time for them to be used
- create subassemblies just as they are needed in the final assembly shop
- make components just in time for fitting to subassemblies
- receive bought-in items at the time they are needed.

In its origins in Japan, JIT grew by linking many series of small factories each with hundreds, rather than thousands, of employees. Each plant made daily deliveries to its successor, the quantity being the exact amounts required for the following day's production. For this to be stable and efficient, all the suppliers knew the monthly production schedule that was set by the final assembler. This company became the driver that pulled the supplies through the system. *Kanban* is a widely quoted description of the way the information was recorded and process rates regulated. The name refers to the card attached to each component bin in the original system. Development of the kanban system was helped by the proximity of the factories. For example, until Toyota began to develop overseas plants in the 1980s, all of its plants were located in Aichi prefecture close to Tokyo. This has the area of a small British county.

Toyota, led by Taiichi Ohno as Manufacturing Director, was a pioneer of kanban. Its performance after the sudden oil price rises of 1973-74 excited the interest of rivals both in Japan and elsewhere. Toyo-Kogyo, whose brand is Mazda, was almost bankrupted by the same oil shock. Its recovery had much to do with its introduction of the Toyota production system that was already regarded as good practice throughout the country. Ford's close connection with Toyo-Kogyo began when it bought a 25% stake in 1976. Then followed an intensive programme of training of Ford managers in Japanese techniques.

JIT is different to conventional production planning with its *push* philosophy. JIT *pulls* work through the system. Having deliveries at least once a day implies small batches and little stock. Yet, in many people's minds, it goes beyond stock minimisation to continuous improvement and incorporation into other business functions. To operate flow systems with such little stock implies, for instance, that: each item must be of the correct quality, hence Total Quality Management; that machines are highly reliable, hence Total Productive Maintenance; and that all staff are well trained and motivated. In other words, JIT is as much a philosophy of the way the whole business should operate as a technical approach to the problem of scheduling.

11. Waste elimination

The advantages of JIT come from the elimination of waste at all stages. Waste arises in many ways in the production system:

- *In the process itself*
  Some processes add no value. Fitting and other adjustments, or removing scale or burrs, are only required because of defects in upstream processes. If a machine cannot produce to defined tolerances, it should be replaced or the tolerances themselves reviewed and the design changed.

- *Running the process too fast or too early*
  Overproduction leads to the build up of inventory which not only wastes investment but wastes space and transport resources as the stock often has to be moved several times to keep it out of the way.
- *Waiting*
  Waiting time between processes is wasteful because the inability to deliver quickly loses the firm market opportunities.
- *Stock*
  Just-in-Time replaces the idea of 'Just-in-Case'. This meant that inventory was held only because there were problems in the production system. These made it impossible to supply within a period when customers wanted orders.
- *Material movement*
  The effect of excessive distances between processes is often disguised in a production system. Such movements, and the associated stock that has to be in transit, add no value.
- *People movement*
  Excessive movement of people may arise from poor job layouts but also from their having to go and look for materials for the next task. Shops crowded with inventory lengthen this search.
- *Defects*
  An example of the interaction between the scheduling and quality systems, defects cost more than the value of the lost item. Habitual defects rates mean that: schedulers set batch sizes to allow for loss; correction delays waste time; customers become annoyed.

12. JIT techniques

Beyond the general statements of principle and the declaration of war on waste, JIT consists of a family of techniques that can be assembled and integrated. These fall into two groups: *JIT1* is preparatory, making the facility ready for high flow, short lead time production; *JIT2* techniques are the tactics used to cut waste. A summary list appears in Box 12.6. It is based on details given by Harrison[16]. Some selected points are amplified in the following paragraphs.

Small machines
Installing several small machines, each dedicated to one process, may appear less economical than having fewer, more powerful general-purpose machines. Yet the gain in flexibility may enable inventory to be reduced and this in itself may fund the extra equipment and space. Fewer changeovers will themselves save cost and batch sizes can be cut.

Set-up reduction
Many firms have bad habits when it comes to set-ups. They may not, as a habit, have the next set of tools ready for installation; they may not allocate the optimal size of team; they may not train and practise enough. If set-ups cannot be avoided, there are many ways of reducing the time needed for changeovers. Introduction of such changes requires the cooperation of many members of staff.

Scheduling
The JIT factory has a Master Production Schedule that is used to create detailed instructions for the final assembly stage. From there, upstream processes are

---

JIT1: Preparation

Design	*Design for manufacture* to reduce number and range of components. Defining quality to match capability.
Focus	Limit scope of manufacturing task by setting up groups, cells or focused 'plants within plants' each of which concentrates on a limited range.
Small machines	Several single-purpose machine may be superior than a few large multi-purpose ones.
Work flow	Careful attention to layout to control the stock of goods in transit cuts waste.
Maintenance	Planned maintenance to avoid wasteful breakdowns and their associated buffer stocks will benefit flow rates.
Set-up times	Reduced set-up times mean that smaller batches can be run more economically.

JIT2: Waste reduction

Scheduling	The kanban system of pulling inventory through the system avoids the futile build-up of stocks of partly finished items.
Inventory	Inventory levels are to be cut by running smaller, regular batch sizes and ensuring that goods move on when they are ready.
Visible controls	Simple, readily seen controls enable staff and supervisors to see the state of any batch of work at any time.
Continuous improvement	In the JIT philosophy, problems are 'jewels to be treasured' rather than embarrassments. From learning about problems comes improvement, the furtherance of the attack on waste.
Scheduling techniques	JIT can be integrated with MRPII, OPT and so on.
Vertical integration	JIT works best if the whole productive system works to the rhythm of the Master Production Schedule. Waste can be cut from all stages.

Box 12.6 The family of JIT techniques

scheduled in detail by signals that come from the next ones down the chain. Originally, *kanban* was a simple visible method of allowing routine material flow decisions to be made at shop floor level. This is still widely used but has also been developed through the application of information systems. Detailed operations of a link in the chain are explained in **13**.

Integration with other scheduling techniques
While in some ways being presented as rival approaches to the question of shop-floor scheduling, MRP, OPT and JIT can be combined. As Harrison points out[17], possibilities for synergy include:

- Preparation along JIT1 lines can be of use to all manufacturers.
- JIT simplification can be carried out before the installation of an MRPII system, reducing the number of transactions and therefore the scale required.
- All systems should avoid predefined batch sizes and lead times and they should not accept that scrap rates are fixed and to be planned for.
- JIT is good at control but is only good at planning for regular repetitive manufacture. On the other hand, MRPII plans in detail but is weaker at control because of the amount of detail required by the central MRP office.
- JIT techniques can improve the capacity of OPT bottlenecks, for example design improvements can be made to avoid time in the bottleneck processes and set-up reduction can increase available machine capacity.

Vertical cooperation

A JIT factory cannot work alone. JIT works best if the whole productive system operates at the speed of the Master Production Schedule. This means that, throughout the supply chain, there can be only one MPS. It is most likely to be decided by the final assembler who is in contact with details of customer demand. Assemblers beat the rhythm for the rest to follow.

The links between organisations require the development of a great deal of trust and cooperation. They must, for example, share plans and understand each other's capabilities and constraints. These relationships mean that JIT philosophy has entered the purchasing and supply arena with the ability to deliver to daily or even hourly schedules being an important element in vendor selection. One instance illustrates the impact of JIT ideas on supply channel planning.

In late 1992, Sunderland Football Club announced a plan to build a new 40,000 seat stadium and leisure complex away from its cramped Roker Park base. Among the objectors to the application for planning permission was Nissan. The motor company's £900 million plant stood next to the 60 hectare green belt site. The company feared that congestion on roads leading to the 11,000-space car park would upset its JIT delivery schedules from seven local manufacturers. These flows, according to the engineering director, had a tolerance of minutes[18].

13. How a kanban link works

In contrast to job tickets in other planning and scheduling systems, the kanban (ticket) does not follow pieces of work all the way through the production chain. A set of kanbans circulates at the link between every pair of stages in the production system. Each kanban travels down the stream with the material and returns from the next stage each time its bin in used. Thus, the number of tickets, and the information they carry, regulate production at the upstream stage. The kanban records:

- Details of the operation to be carried out on the piece
- The origin and destination
- The number of pieces per standard container
- The number of pieces to be made in one lot
- The number of kanbans in circulation within the link.

In order for the system to operate consistently, there is a set of rules that must be followed:

1 Each bin (or trolley, rack, container etc.) must have a kanban card with details of the parts, their routing and quantity.
2 Parts are pulled by the next process.
3 Work is not started without a card.
4 Bins contain exactly their stated number of parts.
5 Defective parts must not be sent to succeeding processes.
6 When parts are taken by the next process, only enough to replace them can be made.

We can now look at how kanbans regulate the flow. The link between two production stages is akin to that between supplier and client. The kanban represents an open manufacturing order placed by the client on the supplier. When the consignment is made by the upstream, or supplier, stage, a kanban is placed on each standard container, see step **A** in Figure 12.8. There the ticket remains while the container passes to the downstream, or client, stage and waits until it is used, **B**. At the moment that consumption starts, the kanban is removed from the container and passed back upstream, **C**. It becomes again an open order for manufacture. There is usually a rack at the upstream stage where several kanbans are assembled until processing starts, **D**. While each container carries a standard quantity of parts, and has one kanban, economic lot sizes for the supplier stage may be greater than one container-full and are set at levels of multiples of kanbans.

Kanbans, therefore, take up different roles during their circulation. Flowing downstream, they are stock tickets indicating quantities and destinations. Moving upstream, they are job orders, communicating the requirements of the client stage. It will be clear that the number of kanbans circulating in the link limits the amount of work in progress. Note that the two stages need not be close, as suggested in Figure 12.8, but could be separated by workshop walls or even the distances between factories.

From the outstanding kanbans in the rack, the supplier can see the stock ahead of the next stage and can, therefore, decide work priorities. This will be important where the supplier is engaged in supplying more than one client with different components. It could, for example, be a multi-purpose miller in a brass machining shop or a press to make covers in a bindery. Simple rules are used. Figure 12.9 shows the planning rack for a stage with four customers.

Kanbans in the rack show fewer than maximum full containers in circulation. For each link, a different number of kanbans will trigger the production of new

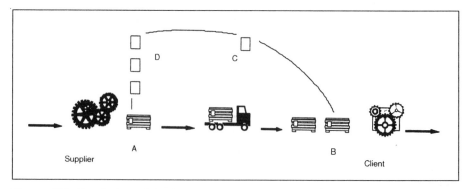

Figure 12.8 Circulation of kanbans

supplies. In the simple system, this will be shown by (say) a green line on the rack. Work may not start straightaway so the kanbans continue to accumulate. A red line on the rack shows danger level, signalling that unless work is started immediately, the customer runs the risk of being out of supplies. The stress in such presentation is simplicity and clarity. The status of the system can be easily seen by all staff: the supplier knows the state of the client's work; the supervisor can tell if things are going wrong; the group can investigate areas for improvement. We examine how the green and red levels may be estimated and changed in **14**.

14. The number of kanbans

The number of tickets in circulation corresponds to the economic lot size[19], ELS, for the supply stage plus the stock ahead of the client that is consumed during the reaction time that the link requires. In other words, when the planning rack reaches the green trigger, the stock of items waiting ahead of the next stage continues to fall until the next consignment is produced and delivered.

The reaction time, RT, is made up of several elements: time to produce a container full; transport of stock; machine setting; movement of the tickets up the chain etc. If the client's use rate is CUR, then the client uses RT × CUR items during the delay period. To allow for unforeseen variations and the possibility of delay if the supplier has more than one customer, a safety margin, SM, is added. SM may be 10 to 20 per cent.

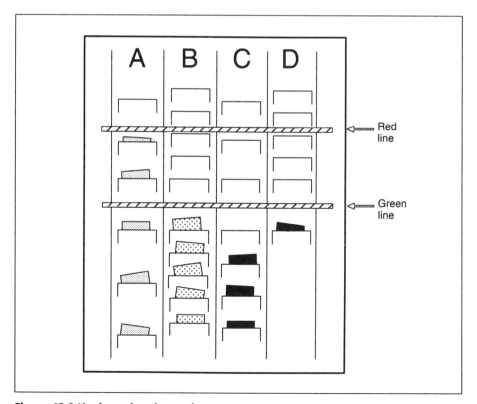

Figure 12.9 Kanban planning rack

It can be seen that the stock in circulation reaches a maximum given by:

Maximum stock = ELS + [RT × CUR × (1 + SM)]

This corresponds to the number of kanbans, K, required by the system. When each container holds n items,

$$K = \frac{ELS + [RT \times CUR \times (1 + SM)]}{n}$$

To illustrate, suppose that the client stage consumes 1,200 pieces per day, that is 150 per hour. The supplier, which serves more than one client, can produce at the rate of 600 items per hour with a set-up time of 15 minutes. The economic lot size has been set at 400, or 5 containers of 80 items. The reaction time is 90 minutes and the safety margin is 10%.

The consumption during the reaction time is $90 \times 1.1 \times 150/60 = 248$ pieces. Adding the ELS of 400 gives 648, corresponding to 8 kanbans of 80 items in circulation.

Including the set-up, the time taken by the supplier to produce the ELS is 15 + 400/10, or 55 minutes. During this period, the client consumes $55 \times 1.1 \times 150/60 = 151$ pieces. This corresponds to 2 containers that should be the minimum number ahead of the client when the supplier starts the next lot. The red line on the planning rack should, therefore, be set at 2 fewer than the number of tickets in the system, that is 6. With these 6 tickets on the rack, the supplier will know that the client has reached danger level.

The simplicity of the system is a strong part of its appeal. The formulae given here enable all to establish clear procedures and to make adjustments and improvements. For instance, the effect of cutting set-up times is plain. Not only will the ELS itself be reduced but the required safety margin will also fall. Alternatively, having a dedicated small machine in the above example could reduce the ELS to 1 kanban, cutting the total in circulation to 4.

The empty containers themselves can sometimes be used instead of tickets. If each small loop has its own clearly identified containers, then their number determines the maximum stock in circulation. Where two work stations are within sight of each other, the height or length of stacks on the floor can act as signals for production to recommence.

15. Applications of kanban and the JIT philosophy

While the last worked example makes kanban operations look in some ways like the events in a job shop, there are two features that confine its application to repetitive manufacture. First, the volume of any individual item passing through the system must be large enough to make it worthwhile setting up loops that are continuously active. The variety of items produced at any stage must be limited, otherwise simple rules will not enable operators to decide priorities and keep all clients satisfied. These points emphasise that JIT is applicable in high volume industries such as automotive and domestic equipment manufacture. Secondly, the daily production rate must be level. It can easily be shown, through simulation, that the kanban system would amplify variations in the demand placed upon the chain by the final assembler. The MPS of the final assembler must show level demand. Variations are handled through the build-up of some stock of finished goods. If the MPS is to change, then due notice needs to be sent to the whole chain so that the planning boards and numbers of tickets in circulation can be adjusted.

JIT methods have been extended and adapted within high-volume repetitive production. For example, the need to focus and increase flows through chains has led automobile assemblers such as Peugeot Talbot to develop *partnership sourcing* with one supplier per component.

At Ryton, Coventry, the 8,300 components come from 380 suppliers, instead of the 600 before the programme was started. Hills Precision Components is a partly owned subsidiary company situated close to Ryton. Here, Peugeot orders for fascia assemblies arrive twelve times a day. Each specifies models, colours, left- or right-hand drive and so on. The fascias are assembled from a range of standard components and delivered within two hours. This speed of response means that fascia orders for any car do not have to be placed until after the build has started. HPS also makes components with fewer variations, such as seats, door casings and steering wheels. These are on continuous flow orders. Tickets are not used for any of these links because electronic data interchange is the favoured system. Kanbans are replaced by bar codes.[20]

The pressure in volume manufacturing is to improve speed of response through squeezing inventory out of the system. The philosophy of continuous improvement has led car assemblers to reexamine bottlenecks in their lines, especially the problems of switching from one type to another. Increasing the variety available from any plant satisfies the growing demand for individual cars, the process of customisation.

A typical car assembly line copes with a family of cars with related characteristics.Thus, the General Motors Astra lines at Ellesmere Port cope with: cars and light vans; diesel and petrol engines from 1.2 to 1.8i; hatchbacks, saloons, estates and convertibles; two doors and four doors; trim from 'Base' through L, LX, LA to GTE. The wide range means that it is normal to supply cars to customers' orders. This only works if it is possible to offer short lead times. Customers do not want to wait!

Colour is not easy to change frequently. This is because the paint booths and spray lines have to be cleaned out and primed at every switch. This costs time in terms of lost output and loses paint. A good time for change is during pauses between shifts as the plant does not run continuously.

Some colours are more popular than others. White is at least five times more popular than blue, for example. The limit to the range of colours is the lead time that can be offered. Currently, the least popular colour at the plant accounts for 5% of the demand. This means that if the colour change occurred daily, the least frequently requested one would be applied once a fortnight. Waiting time for these customers would be, on average, one week longer than for those wanting white. In the highly competitive situation of the car industry, this is hardly satisfactory.

In the 1990s, GM developed its paint equipment to cut changeover time and costs. This allowed the lines to switch colours more frequently and reduce lead times. Ironically, one of the effects was to encourage arguments from marketing to take advantage of the improved lead times to offer a wider range of less common colours. If this proposal were implemented, the paint shop investment would have saved little in cost but allowed greater customisation.

16. People and scheduling systems

A comparison of scheduling systems from MRPII to JIT would not be complete without a note on the interaction between these systems and the people who work with them. Apart from different technical features, a major difference between MRPII and JIT is the degree of centralisation. OPT lies between the two. MRPII systems are centralised, the scheduling decisions becoming a set of instructions issued by the office for the shop floor to follow. In many respects in the western factory, this amounts to more of the same thing. The tradition of management control by taking over all aspects of decision making has grown out of the tenets of Taylor's scientific management. MRPII is an extension of Taylorism, being a better way for the scheduling office to operate.

JIT, in its basic principles, encourages the involvement of shop floor staff in detailed scheduling and control. This is a move towards decentralisation, although constrained by the strict rules without which JIT would not work. There are moves towards autonomy and pressures for more discipline. Storey, in one listing, mentions the following as essential features of 'people preparation'[21].

- Discipline – 'the critical essence of a manufacturing company'
- Flexibility – growth in the long term through training
- Equality – removal of divisions
- Autonomy – having authority to stop the line, solve problems, control materials
- Quality of Working Life – developing security and a sense of involvement and enjoyment
- Creativity – harnessing the 'natural curiosity of company members to make improvements which affect the work they do.'

Whether these factors can live happily together both defines, and depends upon, the culture of the organisation. Whether this can in turn stand apart from the culture of a nation, either permanently differentiated from it, or as an instrument of change, is a further difficulty.

There is no doubt that the best production management systems bring improved competitiveness to organisations. At the same time, there have been arguments that many have pushed 'Japanese style' management practices into place by taking advantage of the weak labour market. Forcing people to work as hard as possible merely builds up resentment that might explode the next time workers feel they have more power. Further, those companies that have cut out stocks and switched to single suppliers have compounded their strategic risk by increasing their vulnerability to any discontinuity that may arise[22].

17. Intermittent and repetitive systems

The job shop and the dedicated production line represent the two extremes of the scale of repetition - every unit different to every unit the same. Scheduling in the job shop consists of many *ad hoc* decisions over material, capacity, sequencing and delivery. In the dedicated production line, scheduling involves establishing a uniform daily rate for all operations and maintaining the flow continuously.

De Toni and Panizzolo[23] give a useful summary of the characteristics of the two types of process, see Table 12.5. It can be seen that intermittent manufacturing is highly uncertain and requires concentration on detail in order to make it operate. Therefore, it is necessary to delegate much of the decision making to the shop

Table 12.5 Nature of scheduling decisions in two manufacturing processes

	Level of detail	Decision making latitude	Time horizon of decisions	Amount of uncertainty
Intermittent manufacturing	High	High	Short	High
	↑	↑	↓	↑
	↑	↑	↓	↑
	↑	↑	↓	↑
Repetitive manufacturing	Low	Low	Long	Low

floor. This policy is supported by the fact that each decision is relatively small, having an impact within a short time horizon. At the other extreme, the dedicated, repetitive line needs planning well in advance to match market demands. The low level of detail and high certainty make central planning possible. Given the desire to integrate the whole system, there is little decision-making latitude at shop floor level.

The family of techniques we have discussed in this chapter fit between these extremes, each being adapted to local circumstances to aid shifts towards more uniformity or flexibility. Kanban, for example, is a means of allowing some flexibility into a high-volume manufacturing and assembly system. If there were to be a single product with no variation, kanban would be unnecessary because all stages could be specified to operate at the constant rate. As we mentioned in **16**, however, the latitude for decision making within the kanban system is constrained by strict rules. For example, shop floor staff may decide priorities when tickets on the planning board rise above the green line but they cannot decide for themselves the number of tickets within each loop.

SERVICE SCHEDULING

18. Service patterns

For a framework in which to discuss service scheduling, we can return to the model set out in Figure 3.1. Three patterns of service delivery were identified: isolated service, self service and personal service. We can focus our discussion by recognising that the first is similar to manufacturing and the second needs no scheduling. This leaves personal service as the problem area. In addition, it was shown that in each case the impact of scale was important. Increasing scale corresponds with standardisation while reducing it implies customisation.

Isolated service

Isolated service takes place away from the customer, either on a small scale in the 'back of the shop' or on a large scale in service factories. An important part of the process design is the interface between the isolated service activity and the customer. This is, in effect, either personal or self service so the isolated service function is always combined with another pattern that acts as a 'front end'. Questions of scheduling have already been discussed. The off-line clock repairer, design service or bookkeeper offer intermittent jobbing whereas the hospital laundry, film processor or credit card company are engaged in repetitive processing.

Self service

Unless the service capacity is limited, self service needs no scheduling. The provider offers capacity that the customer will use when required. In the ideal case, there is no personal interaction, the user consumes any amount of the facility at any time. Payment systems, unless fees can be collected automatically, often need personal service as at the supermarket checkout. The supermarket is not, therefore, self service in its pure form. Examples of the ideal type range from free facilities such as municipal parks, through those where access requires a fixed payment, such as cable television or toll bridges, to cases such as telephones where billing is automatic.

Some telephone services with limited capacity have to be booked, as do keyboards in a busy university learning centre. In these cases, the self service requires some personal service to regulate the flow.

Personal service

Personal or *direct* service is a recurrent problem. Why is it so difficult?

- Demand for direct services is variable and cannot be levelled as with a master production schedule. Unless the operator can rapidly adjust service capacity, queues will form.
- Customisation is normal in many service activities. This ensures that variety is high.
- The presence of the customer impedes adherence to any schedule that may have been planned. What if the customer asks for a change of service half way through?

We shall examine some approaches to these problems in the next section.

19. Scheduling direct service

As noted above, the processes of *isolation* or *detachment*, see Figure 3.1, are important first steps in protecting most of the service facility from the effects of variability. But, having laid out the facilities and designed the service process, there is little that the service operator can do but fine-tune capacity and service levels in response to demand. Reservations or appointments systems work in some circumstances, from doctors' surgeries to theatres. Yet these are designed to manage demand to fit the chosen medium-term schedule rather than adjust the short-term schedule to fit demand.

In circumstances where demand is variable and unregulated, how can a business adjust to maintain a high standard of customer service? It uses a combination of anticipation and changes in staff and service levels. Telephone home shopping is an example of mass personal service. In such bureaux, the capacity is established to cope with anticipated demand but local, short-term adjustments are always necessary.

> Home shopping grew out of mail order. The leading companies, such as Great Universal and Littlewoods, now take about three quarters of all orders by telephone. Networks enable customers to call at local rates.

For the customer, order placement is easier, deliveries are faster, and, when stock-outs occur, alternatives are offered. Service quality is improved. Operators check customers' credit records on-line so that satisfactory orders are immediately placed in the despatch schedule and picking instructions sent to automated warehouses.

Better service raises expectations. Mail allows short-term queuing. Telephone users, however, find waiting frustrating and require quick responses. Typical targets are to answer within 20 seconds. Littlewoods needs a telephone bureau whose size balances the response target against the cost of having staff idle for much of the time. At peak times over 100 operators are working.

Callers join a single queue and are answered in sequence. The equipment connects desks in rotation. The call queue length is displayed prominently in the operating room to warn of excess demand.

Demand varies hourly and daily. Experience enables a forecast to be made for each half-hour interval. Enough staff are recruited and trained to cover the forecast pattern Yet changes occur by the minute. To cope with short-term surges the supervisors can:

- Reduce the time staff spend with each caller. When time permits, staff remind customers of special offers and pass on other information about the company. This activity is cut.
- Ask staff to delay breaks or getting a cup of coffee from the machine.
- Call to the manager to bring in more staff from other activities, although this usually takes several minutes to arrange.

20. Scheduling isolated service

Many mass service operators have refined their process design to give it many of the characteristics of repetitive manufacture. Nowhere is this more apparent than in express parcels delivery which concentrate on establishing flows and schedules to meet customer needs. The hub and spoke system of Federal Express, which carries one half of all overnight packages in the United States, is a leading example of the way transport can be thought of in flow-process terms. It is, in effect, a distributed service factory that communicates with the customer either through personal or, as we shall see, self service.

Each evening, freight aircraft fly parcels along inward spokes to FedEx's sorting hub at Memphis, Tennessee. Here they are sorted and loaded for the outward trip to arrive by early morning. A late afternoon consignment from the main European capitals has a guaranteed delivery by 10.30 anywhere in North America. The system works by having clear fixed flight and sorting schedules and parcel tracking software. Plane loads out of Memphis are thus defined well before the parcels arrive for sorting.

Computer developments mean that more than 25,000 United States businesses have direct access to the information system to track their own parcels and time consignments accurately. For example, Laura Ashley clothes shops are restocked within two days, thus cutting out the risk and expense of local warehousing. Federal Express has more than 460 aircraft and delivers over two million packages a day. Excess demand is coped with by delaying consignments on lower grade services.

Scheduling transport operations is an art in itself, especially for public services such as air and rail travel where use of terminals and track has to be explicitly shared with other services. Railway timetablers have used graphical methods since the 1840s. They were developed by the French engineer Charles Ibry[24] who hoped that both operators and the public would use them. Systems of great complexity, with hundreds of stations, can be shown. Figure 12.10 is an example, showing a few hours of the weekday service between Manchester and Chester.

The time scale is read across the top of the diagram and stations, positioned according to their distance along the track, appear down the side. Diagonals running from upper left to lower right show trains heading towards Chester. The other diagonals depict trains for Manchester. Some trains start from, or continue to, places beyond Manchester, hence the 'spikes' at the top of the chart. Chester is a terminus for all.

The advantage of the Ibry timetable is that it captures relevant dimensions of the service and enables problems to be visualised, anticipated and, therefore, managed. Steeper diagonals represent faster trains (although there are few here), Xs mark where trains meet and minutes spent waiting result in horizontal lines (although the scale prevents them from being shown). Like the kanban planning board, the visualisation enables experienced operators to cope with the adjustments that are continually required.

Even our simple example repays study. Two short stretches of the route are single track. These are marked by grey bands across the chart. Strict safety procedures prevent two trains entering these sections. However, it can be seen that

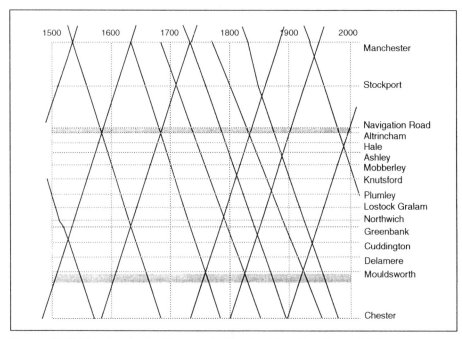

Figure 12.10 Manchester to Chester via Northwich – Monday to Friday

careful management will be required if the late running of, say, the 1720 out of Chester is not to delay the next incoming service by making it wait at Mouldsworth.

Beyond looking at features of the service, we can use the chart to follow the path of rolling stock and crews through their working days. For example, it is easy to visualise the trains turning round at the Chester terminus. During the middle day off-peak period, trains run faster because six of the small stations close. This saves trains. For instance, the 1541 arrival at Chester is in time to form the 1550 departure.

Compared with Gantt charts, Ibry diagrams emphasise different aspects of the system being studied. Gantt was concerned with representing time spent at fixed points, either queuing or in process. Ibry focused on plotting locations in a space-time continuum. Gantt represents tasks and time in the factory although variations of Ibry can be used to picture, for example, the movement of products through a long process such as a series of glazing and firing stages in a kiln.

Case study: Engineering and Manufacturing – Oiso [25]

E&M-Oiso is a manufacturing plant of the NCR Corporation located some 65 km from Tokyo. It has 550 employees developing and assembling cash registers, point-of-sale terminals and financial terminals. The first two product groups are sold throughout the world.

In principle, the plant works by building to order. There is an aggregate production plan drawn up as 'a hedged version of marketing's sales forecast.' It considers factors such as capacity and lead times for subassemblies and suppliers' availability and delivery times. Risk is involved and has to be managed since sales never turn out to match the forecast. The monthly plan is based on firm orders. Variability in the flow of orders has to be matched with flexibility. Kanban systems are used to regulate the assembly of products to customers' orders. Certain processes, however, have long lead times that would not allow quick enough supplies.

Such lead times exist in the printed circuit board manufacture where the capacity of the surface mount technology is limited. The solution is to build controlled lots of basic boards for stock. When firm orders set the kanban system in motion, these boards can be withdrawn for further components to be built on. Therefore there is a mixture of 'push' and 'pull' production scheduling. This achieves delivery requirements without the need to add SMT capacity.

E&M-Oiso uses Computer Integrated Manufacturing to manage the JIT programme. Its aim is to minimise lead times. Having set schedules that aim to have components arriving at assembly just when they are needed, the CIM system captures data on the status of all orders to ensure that they are progressing satisfactorily. All items carry bar codes.

The company works closely with its 192 suppliers to gain and share benefits from the JIT system. It sees relationships with these companies as sharing responsibilities for minimising the cost of ownership of bought-in components. Suppliers are involved in the process of design for manufacture.

Daily delivery is not required in the JIT system. Attention centres on those items that make up most of the value. Figure 12.11 shows how parts have been split into four categories from A-prime to C. The A-prime items are just 3.4% of the number but represent some 70% of the value. They are all in the JIT programme which is to be extended to the whole A category. JIT will then cover 85% of parts by value. (See Chapter 14 for ABC analysis.)

Of the 192 suppliers, only three are off-shore. The company wants to increase this number. The tight schedules make such sourcing difficult. Not only are shipping times longer but risk is higher. Off-shore supplies will have to be based more on the aggregate forecast than on actual orders and this will create inflexibility.

Visualisation is seen as important in the presentation of performance results. Data on weekly results, such as delivery performance, are prominently displayed in consistent graphical formats throughout the plant. Even the untrained eye can recognise the degree of goal attainment. While details are given of who is responsible for each element of the output, the intention is not to allocate blame but to contribute to team building and continual improvement. The company believes that cooperative performance depends on common knowledge.

Questions

1 *What is E&M-Oiso doing when it says it uses a hedged version of the sales forecast? Why?*
2 *Identify the type of production systems likely to be found at E&M-Oiso. Suggest applications of MRPII and OPT in this situation.*
3 *What are the production and supply risks involved with off-shore sourcing into Japan?*
4 *Why does the company set such store by presenting performance data?*

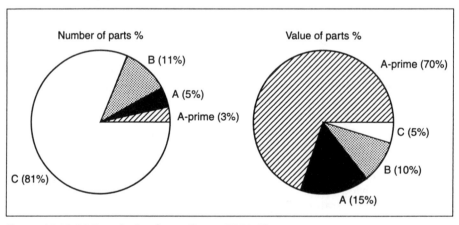

Figure 12.11 ABC analysis of supplies to E&M-Oiso

References

1. Harrison, A. (1994) 'Just-in-time manufacturing' in Storey, J. (ed.) *New Wave Manufacturing Strategies* London, Paul Chapman Publishing, p. 188
2. Spreadbury, A. (1994) 'Manufacturing Resources Planning' in Storey, J. (ed.) *New Wave Manufacturing Strategies* London, Paul Chapman Publishing, p. 154
3. Luscombe, M. (1994) 'Of course I'm commited to MRPII but . . .' *Management Services* March, pp. 12–13
4. ibid.
5. For example: Waterlow, G. and Monniot, J. (1986) *A Study of the State of the Art in CAPM in UK Industry* London, SERC/ACME, 1986; Whiteside, D. and Ambrose, J. (1984) 'Unsnarling industrial production: why top management is starting to care' *Industrial Management* March, pp. 20-26
6. Turnover of this branch plant of a large combine was some £50 million. The interviews were conducted in 1994.
7. Sillince, J.A.A. and Sykes, G.M.H. (1993) 'Integrating MRPII and JIT: a management rather than a technical challenge' *International Journal of Production and Operations Management* **13.4**, pp. 18–31
8. Goldratt, E.M. and Cox, J. (1989) *The Goal* Aldershot, Gower
9. ibid. p. 95
10. ibid. p. 270
11. Gardiner, S.G., Blackstone, J.H.Jr and Gardiner, L.R. (1992) 'Drum-buffer-rope and buffer management' *International Journal of Production and Operations Management* **13.6** pp. 68–78
12. op.cit.
13. op.cit. p. 297
14. Spencer, M.S. (1991) 'Using 'the Goal' is an MRP system' *Production and Inventory Management Journal* **32.4** pp. 22–28
15. Harrison, A., op.cit. p. 181
16. Harrison, A. (1992) *Just-in-Time Manufacturing in Perspective* Hemel Hempstead, Prentice-Hall
17. Harrison (1994) op.cit. p. 190
18. 'Company News' *The Financial Times*, 23 January 1993, p.4; Tighe, C. (1993) 'Nissan and Sunderland FC cry foul in a local derby', *ibid.*, 15 October, p. 1; 'Sunderland gives stadium approval', *ibid.*, 11 March 1994, p. 7
19. Economic lot size is found by balancing the savings in work in progress through smaller lots against the savings in set-up time through larger lots. It is akin to economic order quantity, see Chapter 14.
20. Gooding, C. (1993) 'Technology: On the road to a slicker operation' *The Financial Times* 22 July, p. 16
21. op. cit. pp. 183–4
22. Industrial Relations Services (1993) *The impact of Japanese firms on working and employment practices in British manufacturing industry* London, IRS
23. de Toni, A. and Panizzolo, R. (1993) 'Operations management techniques in intermittent and repetitive manufacturing: a conceptual framework' *International Journal of Operations and Production Management* **13.5**, pp. 12–32
24. Tufte, E.R. (1990) *Envisioning Information* Cheshire, Connecticut, Graphics Press p. 108. The book includes several beautiful examples of this form of presentation.
25. Based on: Tanabe, Masaru (1992) 'Making JIT work at NCR Japan' *Long Range Planning* **25.5** pp. 37–42

13

PROJECT MANAGEMENT

Chapter objectives

When you have finished studying this chapter, you should be able to:

- Explain the basic principles of project planning and how it is carried out in various types of organisation; note the role of specialist project companies and why they exist.

- Compare the key features of project management with other management settings.

- Show how modern project scheduling methods have grown from Gantt schedules and the early networking techniques.

- Detail the procedure for setting out a project as a network and, from it, producing a schedule of work packages.

- Show the use of the techniques to manage resource allocation within constraints, time-cost trade-offs and approaches to project restructuring.

- Outline how risks of duration overrun are estimated and how these estimates can be incorporated into total project management.

- Summarise the main items covered by project control and relate these to the control model.

INTRODUCTION

Sooner or later an organisation will take on a substantial and complicated project. As we have seen earlier, there are those firms that specialise in such work as a business. They supply one-off products whose creation requires the bringing together and coordination of many activities. Some of this work falls in the manufacturing category, such as the construction of new plant or buildings, laying down of new roads, developing a mine or making special items of equipment. For other firms, the emphasis is on service such as refurbishment of a building, installation of new software systems, major business consultancy or moving a service centre to a new site.

While there are firms that specialise in project management, most organisations become directly involved in it from time to time. They may, of course, hand over such tasks to the specialists as a matter of course. The supermarket chain, electric company or shipping line are not specialists in the building of stores, stations or tankers and will normally issue turnkey contracts to specialists requiring them to deliver a fully functioning facility that they can use at the agreed date.

In contrast, many changes and developments should be, and are, handled internally. Since they are often outside the mainstream of the organisation's operations, they present managers with difficult problems. An organisation set up to manage, say, a JIT production process will not readily cope with a one-off reorganisation or installation of a new process. Project organisation is, therefore, usually handled by a special team that is then disbanded when the work is complete.

This chapter is called *Project management* because it considers the full cycle through which well-run projects pass. First there is *planning*. After the initial feasibility study and approval to go ahead, this comprises the setting of goals and the selection and organisation of the team. Second there is *scheduling*. Here, there is the specific sequencing of tasks to be done and the allocation to them of resources of people, plant, materials, cash and so on. Project scheduling uses specially developed tools that differentiate it from other types. Third, there is *implementation*, the carrying out of the plans right through to the end of the job. Inherent in all this activity is the need for *control*, which involves monitoring progress against time and budgeted cost and taking steps to steer the project along the planned route. Again, the project management tools are valuable for control.

1. Planning and organising the project

The initial feasibility study for a project may result, for a specialist company, in a tender to carry out the work. Alternatively, an internal project will require a proposal to be approved. Whether a contract is awarded or internal approval given, a project will start from a definition of the following:

- The scope of the project. This covers the output to be achieved and an outline of how it is to be done, including the responsibilities of the various groups or firms associated with it. The outputs are often called *deliverables*.
- The time within which the project is to be achieved.
- The budget within which the work is to be carried out.

Given the total plan, the approved tender document or feasibility study will have included a breakdown of the work to be done into broad categories and identification of the resources needed for each. This *work breakdown structure* gives a framework for the detailed planning and scheduling which is to follow. It will summarise the deliverables expected from each stage.

An early decision concerns how project work is to be organised. The outcome depends on factors such as the firm's prior experience, how many projects are to be carried out at once, the significance of any project and the expertise and preference of decision makers. A comparison of vertically divided hierarchies and matrix organisations was made in **5.3** and **5.4**. This applies in the context of projects where approaches can vary from making no special provision through to setting up either temporary or permanent units:

- *No special provision*
  A project that may involve the functional departments within the typical small firm may be managed from the top with work tasks assigned through normal processes. The policy is advantageous where the organisation is small and the project cuts across the whole hierarchy, making it worthwhile involving all departments with it.

- *Minimal provision: project coordinator*
  While the project is still carried out through the normal managerial hierarchy, an individual is appointed to act as coordinator. Where the duties are not seen as onerous, the work could become the responsibility of a senior manager as an extension of normal duties. On the other hand, the task could require the appointment, or secondment, of a full-time person. While this appointee has the advantage of being able to focus effort on progressing the work, setting up the role outside the normal hierarchy may not provide them with sufficient authority to make progress. The backing of senior managers is essential.
- *Project matrix*
  In the matrix arrangement, staff besides the coordinator are assigned to the project. Since the attachment is temporary or intermittent, there may be difficulties in balancing the demands of the special work with the employees' normal duties.
- *Project team*
  When the project has major significance or is likely to last a long time, it is worthwhile to build a team of staff whose work is solely related to it. The project group then has its own internal budget and controls and can coordinate its work as though it were a separate department. This arrangement is common in organisations whose business is project work. Examples range from defence contractors supplying external clients such as national governments to research departments that work through a series of development 'contracts' on behalf of their client functions. The permanent project team is difficult to arrange for a single task in a conventional organisation. The necessary flexibility may be lacking and there may be problems of re-entry to the mainstream for staff who have been seconded.
- *Joint ventures*
  In some industries it is common to form consortia, now usually called joint ventures, to bid for and deliver project work. This arrangement stems from the clients' desire to negotiate the turnkey contracts mentioned in the introduction to this chapter. The arrangement replaces previous systems where the client itself either managed and coordinated several separate contracts or appointed a main contractor whose responsibilities included coordination of the work of many others. Increased complexity has meant that only the largest firms have the capacity to, say, build new power stations or telecommunications networks, or reorganise large administrative structures or transport systems.

The external coordination among two or more firms engaged in a joint venture can present operating problems. The extra dimension of difficulty involves the coordination of project teams who are jointly and equally responsible for making progress within budgets.

In most of the arrangements listed above there is a project manager. This person is responsible for achieving the defined aims but this sometimes has to be done in spite of a lack of the normal line authority. In such a case, a combination of technical expertise and diplomatic skills is needed for success. Technical expertise goes beyond knowledge of disciplines involved in the various parts of the work breakdown schedule. It involves the ability to use project management techniques to help in the scheduling and controlling of tasks. Moreover, it includes the management of a mixed team of professionals, each of whom is in the team because of his or her expertise.

Very large projects will be broken down into a hierarchy of levels. The lower-level work packets will themselves be seen as projects, each under the control of its own project manager.

2. Features of managing projects

Project management differs in significant ways from both the intermittent and repetitive operations we have discussed in previous chapters. In discussing the question of control, Anthony[1] identifies a range of special features that have to be considered:

- *Single objective*
  In contrast to the multiple objectives faced by managers of most operating units, the project manager has the aim to achieve a stated outcome within a stated time. Some performance measures are, therefore, more clear cut.
- *Superimposition*
  This point was examined in the previous section. For many organisations, superimposing a project on an existing structure means that it is regarded as ambiguous. Relationships must be built with preexisting departments and the conventional budgetary control system may be inappropriate.
- *Control*
  Conventional control, whether of accounting budgets or other performance measures, is usually built around fixed periods, say weeks, months or quarters. Since time is so important, projects are best reviewed at key moments, or *milestones*, when reviews are meaningful. Milestones are illustrated in an example later. They do not necessarily occur at regular intervals. The implication of non-conventional control is that a dedicated information system will have to be created.
- *Trade-offs*
  Within the single objective mentioned above, managers can make trade-offs between costs and time and even adjust the scope of the project if circumstances change.
- *Unique performance standards*
  Since project work involves assembling tasks in a unique combination, the performance standards that can be applied have to be less finely honed than for repeated operations. In the latter, long experience allows for standards to be developed for all aspects of the work from quality and quantity to cost and productivity.
- *Frequent change*
  Again, the absence of practice and learning means that project work is inherently less predictable than conventional operations. Clearly, leading firms in industries such as heavy mechanical or civil engineering are well practised and able to transfer learning from one project into another. A similar case can be made for professional service organisations such as management consultants and software houses. In this sense it pays the client to use their expertise to reduce uncertainty. In contrast, more unusual developments are more prone to changes as the outcomes of one stage influence progress on the next.
- *Project rhythm*
  The tempo of activity in project work differs from that in conventional tasks. It builds from a slow beginning to a peak and then tapers towards the end. The

types of work being done, and the corresponding skills needed, change continuously. During plant construction, for example, the work of civil engineers reaches a peak earlier than for other disciplines. After the two-thirds stage they have usually disappeared.

- *Environmental influence*
  While all organisational activity is affected by the environment, the influence is more marked in project work. Manufacturing and isolated service functions are deliberately separated from changes in the environment by boundary spanning functions such as marketing. Their purpose is to allow operations to work as efficiently as possible. The influence of the natural environment is obvious in large construction projects. Furthermore, the very size of all projects excites interest and response from individuals and groups who could be competitors, customers, lobbyists, protestors and so on.

- *Resources are brought to site*
  In most project work where the output is a physical good, materials and components are brought to site. This is the stay-put layout. Not only does the movement often need special equipment but the sequencing of materials, components, plant and staff requires special skills that differ from those needed in conventional factories.

In noting the distinctions set out in the above list, we should recognise that they are not clear cut. Project work, for example, can involve the creation of readily movable goods or the delivery of a service. Further, what may be treated as a special item by one organisation may be seen as part of the routine of another.

3. Project scheduling

The scheduling task involves taking the elements of the work breakdown structure, WBS, and arranging them in the optimal sequence. To this end, these *work packages* should be of fairly uniform duration, have clearly recognisable starting and finishing points, and be under the control of one manager[2]. Therefore each manager runs a 'mini-project' with defined scope, time scale and budget. This, in turn, may have its own WBS and be divided into smaller elements. Given the possibility of many hundreds of work packages within a large contract, firms need special tools to help them decide sequences and control progress. They create a *network schedule* that shows all the work packages and their sequential relationships.

When the number of tasks is small, the Gantt chart allows sequences to be set out conveniently. Following Gantt's development in 1917, the next great advances in project scheduling came in 1956 when two network planning techniques, CPM and PERT, were developed independently, see Box 13.1. The techniques had much in common although there were some differences whose importance has gradually declined as planning has moved from the drawing board to the keyboard.

Some forty more years on, the growth of software[3], which even on a personal computer outperforms manual methods, has led to an integration of the techniques and the elimination of most minor differences of notation and layout. While some still recognise PERT as laying more emphasis on the probabilistic distribution of work package durations, both traditions now include the possibility of time-cost trade-offs and the generation of the full range of control reports. Furthermore, the limitations of the computer screen and printer have favoured the production of tabulated plans rather than large schematic diagrams whose

<table>
<tr><td>

Critical path method (CPM)

CPM grew out of the desire of the du Pont company to improve the planning and scheduling of work done during maintenance shutdowns. It was developed in 1957 by du Pont's M. R. Walker and J. E. Kelly of Remington Rand Corporation.

Since the method was intended to schedule work packages whose separate durations were already well known, CPM treated the duration of each element as if it were deterministic, that is it had a fixed value. The context is of limited total time available and CPM included routines for making a trade-off between time savings and extra costs.

</td><td>

Programme evaluation and review technique (PERT)

PERT was a 1950s development among the United States Navy's Projects Office as customer, the contractor Lockheed and the consultants Booz, Allen and Hamilton. It was created to improve the management of special projects, including the Polaris undersea missile programme. There were more than 3,000 organisations involved in that project.

Since many of the Polaris work packages had not been carried out before, it was decided to include the uncertainty surrounding their duration as part of the scheduling technique. PERT, therefore, treats times as probabilistic distributions.

</td></tr>
</table>

Box 13.1 Background of CPM and PERT

setting out was part of the training of many planners and designers. The Gantt chart has made a comeback. We shall use it in this chapter as the basic means of presenting our discussion.

4. Procedure

There are three phases in the network scheduling procedure:

- **Network planning**
  1 Define the project with its work breakdown structure of all significant elements.
  2 Identify all the direct links between pairs of elements. Decide the logical sequence which links each with its immediate predecessors and successors.
  3 Draw the network to represent this set of planned sequences. A network is drawn according to conventions established within CPM and PERT and now modified by authors of computer software.

- **Network scheduling**
  4 Estimate the duration of each work package. This may result in a single time value or a distribution, depending on policy.
    [If time-cost trade-offs are to be investigated, assign costs to each work package. This information, as we shall see, may also cover the costs associated with shortening or extending their durations.]

5 Work out the longest time path through the network from start to finish. This is the *critical path* that decides the total time for the project. Ascertain the schedules for the rest of the activities within the network.

[Again, if time-cost trade-offs are to be investigated, use the network to test alternatives to create more economical or faster project delivery.]

- **Monitoring and controlling**
  6 Use the results to work out detailed work schedules against which progress can be monitored.
  7 In the light of regular review, update the plan and reallocate resources to keep the project on track.

The first step is to create the work breakdown structure of events and activities. An *event* is a moment marking the start or finish of a work package. An *activity* is the work package itself, having a finite duration between its starting and finishing events. The network is a graphical representation of the linking of activities and events in logical sequences. Although usually read from left to right, a network represents links; it is not scaled to depict the elapse of time.

Unfortunately, there are two conventions used to represent activities and events in networks. One, *activity on arrow* (AOA), depicts the activities as arrows joining the nodes as events. Arrows are labelled with durations and their directions represent the passage of time between nodes. The other notation, *activity on node* (AON), is almost the reverse. Activities become the nodes in the network while the arrows represent not the events but the logical sequence of the activities. The arrows are not scaled.

Selecting one or other notation depends on personal preference. To avoid confusion, only one is used here. There are two reasons for selecting AON. First, while AOA has been more common, it seems that most software generates reports in AON format. Second, AON avoids some technical difficulties in setting out sequences. Although the use by AOA of *logical dummies* hardly matters in computer models, they can complicate manual presentations.

5. Network planning

We can best show how a network is created through a simple example. Let us imagine we have been asked how long it would take to plan and carry out a survey of the condition of prewar houses in the inner city. Our client, the local authority, wants us to interview a large sample of householders and note the state of key features of the dwellings.

In approaching this problem, experience tells us that preparation for the survey task itself requires work on two parallel, yet interconnected, tracks. These are creating the survey instrument and staff recruitment and training. The size of the project requires a substantial number of temporary staff who, because of the skills they need, will be recruited from among construction faculty students. They will need training in interview and survey techniques.

Step 1
Table 13.1 lists the main activities that make up the WBS.

Table 13.1 Activities and precedences: survey project

Activity	Predecessors	Successors
Agree detailed plan		Develop questionnaire Recruit survey staff
Develop questionnaire	Agree detailed plan	Select sample and locations Train and allocate staff
Select sample and locations	Develop questionnaire	Carry out survey
Recruit survey staff	Agree detailed plan	Train and allocate staff
Train and allocate staff	Develop questionnaire Recruit survey staff	Carry out survey
Carry out survey	Select sample and locations Train and allocate staff	Analyse data
Analyse data	Carry out survey	Write report
Write report	Analyse data	

Step 2
For each activity, the table shows those tasks that must directly precede or succeed them. Stating both forward and backward links in this way is redundant but we shall give a full layout for this first example.

Step 3
Figure 13.1 depicts the network that corresponds to the activities and precedences set out in Table 13.1. The AON notation has the activities in boxes and arrows showing logical sequences.

6. Network scheduling

We can now return to the activity table to work out estimates for the times that each task will take. Then we can schedule all the activities in the network.

Step 4
For this example, let us imagine that we have carried out similar tasks before and, therefore,we can estimate their durations with confidence. This information is given in Table 13.2.

Step 5
These values are incorporated in the network diagram in the following way:

a) Label the lower left-hand cell of each node with the activity duration, D. (The scheduled network appears as Figure 13.2.)

b) Work out the *earliest starting time*, EST, for each activity by passing through the network from start to finish. The EST for the first activity is set at 0. Then we can compute the *earliest finishing time* as:

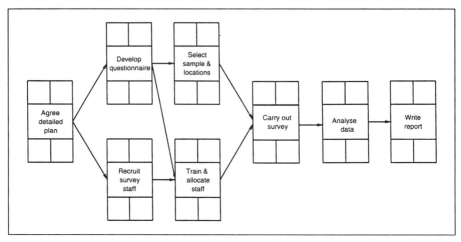

Figure 13.1 Basic network: survey project

Table 13.2 Activity durations: survey project

Activity	Duration (days)
Agree detailed plan	3
Develop questionnaire	8
Select sample and locations	2
Recruit survey staff	6
Train and allocate staff	5
Carry out survey	10
Analyse data	5
Write report	5

$$EFT = EST + D$$

For other activities, the EST depends on when predecessors finish. Since the start of any activity depends on all of the previous ones having been completed, its EST is the greatest value of their EFTs. That is:

$$EST = Max\ (EFT_{previous})\ or\ EST = Max\ ((EST + D)_{previous})$$

Thus, in our case, the EST for the activity *Train and allocate staff* is the greater of (3 + 8) or (3 + 6), that is 11. The remainder of the ESTs are computed in the same way.

The EST for the last activity is 31 which means its EFT is 36, the total time for the whole project. The ESTs appear in the top left-hand corners of each node in Figure 13.2.

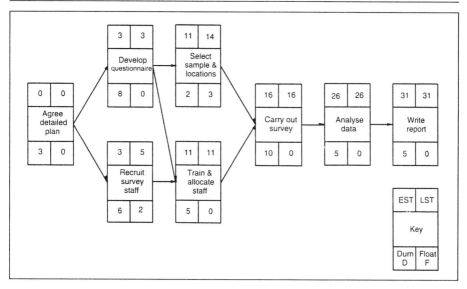

Figure 13.2 Scheduled network: survey project

c) Work out the *latest starting* times for each activity. This is done by reversing the procedure for ESTs. Starting at the last activity, its *latest finishing time*, LFT, is set as the same as its EFT. (In the case of projects where a known finishing day has been stated, then this can be used as the LFT.) The process works backwards by computing *latest starting times*, LSTs, and LFTs in turn. For any activity, LST = LFT – D. Clearly, the latest starting time for the last activity is 31 if the project is to be completed on time.

At junctions in the logical sequence, reasoning similar to the ESTs is applied. Yet it is reversed. For any activity,

$$\text{LFT} = \text{Min (LST}_{following}) \text{ and so LST} = \text{Min (LST}_{following}) - \text{D}$$

Therefore, in the case of *Develop questionnaire*, its LFT is the smaller of 11 and 14 and its LST is (11 – 8).

It is conventional to enter the LSTs in the top right-hand corner of each node. It would, of course, be possible to enter EFTs and LFTs in the diagram. While this has often been advocated, it does tend to clutter all but the simplest diagrams and, in any case, does not appear in many computer printouts. The key used here is taken from BS 4335: 1987.

d) The longest path through the network is the critical path that decides the minimum total time within which the project can be done. Activities on the critical path can be identified by their having equal ESTs and LSTs.[†] In those cases, there is no room for manoeuvre. In the other activities (just two in our simple example) there is a difference between the EST and the LST. In the case of *Recruit and survey staff*, the task could begin any time from day 3 to day 5 without having an impact

---

† But the project may be working to a stated target date which is later than the EFT for the last activity. In this case, the critical path will be made up of those activities where the LST–EST difference is the same as for the last activity.

351

on the total project duration. This 2-day reserve is known as *float* or *slack*. It is easily found from:

Float = LST – EST

Sometimes, as in our case, the activity can be delayed by the time of the float without having an effect on the start or finish of any other activity. This is sometimes called *free float*. In other situations, the float is shared with other activities along a chain. Whatever the type of float, its value is placed in the lower right-hand cell of each node. This confirms the activities on the critical path which is usually a single path through the network that connects all those activities that have zero float.

The point of identifying float is that it highlights the manager's freedom for scheduling within the LST–EST window.

7. Monitoring and controlling

Monitoring refers to collecting relevant information about project progress. The process of controlling involves comparing this information with standards to detect deviations and then decide whether to act and what can be done. Comparison of progress is made against detailed work schedules.

Step 6
Rather than use the network diagram for detailed work schedules, it is usual to present the results as tables or a Gantt chart. The latter forms an excellent visualisation of the network with the added advantage of the time scale. Indeed, using appropriate codes, the Gantt chart contains much information and repays careful study.

The chart, in Figure 13.3, shows the schedule for each activity in the network. Those which lie on the critical path have dark shading. The non-critical activities not only have float but they are coded in a lighter grey. They are shown as starting at their ESTs but they could, of course, be scheduled later. The vertical dotted

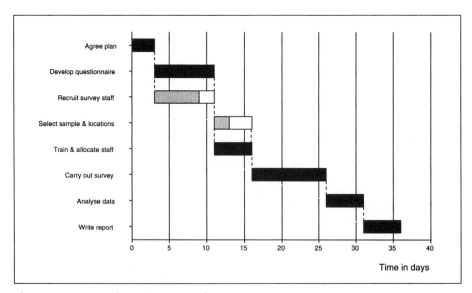

Figure 13.3 Gantt chart: survey project

lines are drawn here to emphasise the links with the network diagram. They suggest the ways that activities come together at key moments. In joining up time paths through the Gantt chart they have echoes of the Ibry chart of Chapter 13. Although vertical in this case, suggesting instantaneous transfer from one activity to another, they could slope. In this way the lines could suggest delays between finishes and starts connected with, for example, the time needed to move staff or equipment. In more complex project networks, Ibry lines would clutter and confuse and they are not shown.

Step 7
The information generated during planning and scheduling forms the basis of control. Reports, such as in Table 13.3, allow actual progress compared with the plan. It identifies areas for action to be taken.

In Table 13.3, the AST and AFT columns refer to actual starting and finishing times that are entered as the project progresses. In this Day 13 report, a critical activity is noted as running one day late. Managers will have to consider if some changes must be made to catch up.

If the project management tools went no further than to provide fixed schedules for monitoring and control they would remain valuable items in any manager's kit. But they go beyond this basic analysis to enable exploration of means of improving project performance through resource allocation and exchange, and task restructuring. They also permit estimates to be made of the risk of overrun and means of reducing this risk where it is unacceptable. To illustrate these points we need a more complex worked example.

8. Resource allocation

For this example we take the role of manager in a small firm that develops traction equipment for special underground railways. These are used in applications as diverse as silver and tin mines in South America and sewers in Southampton. In preparation for the industry's biennial trade fair, the firm wants to create a new

Table 13.3 Progress report: survey project

Activity	D	EST	LST	F	AST	AFT	
Agree detailed plan	3	0	0	0	0	3	OK
Develop questionnaire	8	3	3	0	3	10	✓
Select sample and locations	2	11	14	3	12		✓
Recruit survey staff	6	3	5	2	3	9	OK
Train and allocate staff	5	11	11	0	12		LATE!
Carry out survey	10	16	16	0			
Analyse data	5	26	26	0			
Write report	5	31	31	0			

high efficiency locomotive. The prototype, to be called ProtoLoco, will be shown at the fair to gain contracts for the supply of units or small batches to a wide range of potential customers.

The project manager has drawn up a work breakdown schedule and has estimated durations that the various work packages will take. These, with precedence relationships, are shown in Table 13.4. This listing then enables the network to be drawn up, Figure 13.4. Compared with the conventions used in our introductory example, several have been added or changed. Additions are the *milestones* at the start, finish and a key point during the project, and the outlining of critical activities to stress their pathway. The milestones are events (treated as activities with zero duration) which mark out significant points in project development. They can be placed anywhere in the sequence to mark occasions, say, of major review or moments when connections with events outside the detailed project schedule are possible. Examples of the latter are planting seasons, weather windows for oil rig installation, seasonal market opportunities or the juxtaposition of planets.

The next diagram to be created is the Gantt chart, Figure 13.5, which shows all the activities and milestones. The time scale is marked in intervals of 20 days, that

Table 13.4 Work breakdown schedule: ProtoLoco

Label	Activity	Duration	Successor (days)
A	Receive approval	-	B
B	Agree project outline	5	C, D
C	Equip working area	8	F
D	Schematic design	10	E, F
E	Power system specification	10	G, H
F	Model construction	15	G
G	Mechanical design	40	I, M
H	Electronic design	50	I, N
I	Design stage complete	-	J
J	Obtain materials and components	40	K
K	Component manufacture	20	L
L	Subassembly manufacture	20	M
M	Final assembly	30	P
N	Produce promotional materials	15	R
O	Programming	20	P
P	Test	10	Q
Q	Deliver and instal	5	R
R	Open exhibition	-	-

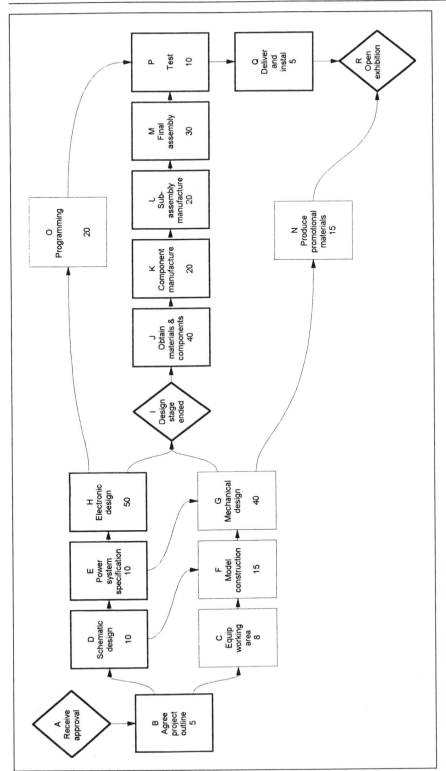

Figure 13.4 Network diagram: ProtoLoco

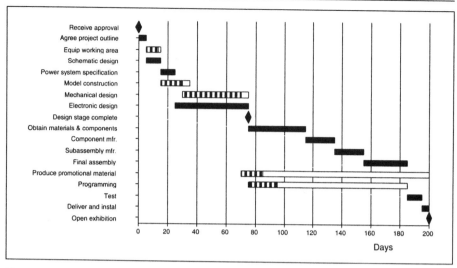

Figure 13.5 Basic Gantt chart: ProtoLoco

is periods of four working weeks. Darker shading indicates the critical path. It can be seen that activities not on the critical path mainly have free float. Exceptions are Model construction and Mechanical design which, in effect, share the 5 days float. This means that a delay in the first affects the second although it will not necessarily change the total project time.

Starting from this base, we can explore some further ways in which a project manager uses network analysis.

9. Resource constraints

So far we have assumed that, except for the logical sequences, the work packages can be carried out at any time, including simultaneously. Yet, in reality, the tasks may use common resources of people and equipment. This limitation may prevent them from being done at the same time. It is important, then, to check that sufficient resources are available to cover the tasks. If not, further constraints must be introduced.

For example, in our small firm we employ one mechanical and one electronic engineer. Their work includes trying out ideas in the laboratory as well as theoretical design. Let us see what happens when these engineers, along with the project manager, are allocated to the tasks in the network.

Table 13.5 sets out the work packages again. This time, however, it shows, in the last column, the staff who are primarily involved with each. With this information we can pass across the Gantt chart to check whether the proposed sequence breaks any of our people constraints. Thus we find that, between Days 25 and 30, the electronic engineer is required for two activities - MODEL CONSTRUCTION and ELECTRONIC DESIGN. We are now faced with a problem. If there were no alternative personnel, we would have to schedule the tasks at non-overlapping times, for instance making the second job follow the first immediately. Since neither activity has float, any extra time required will push out the total project length.

Moving further to the right in Figure 13.5, we will find that the project manager is down for two tasks between days 75 and 85. These are OBTAIN MATERIALS... and

356

Table 13.5 WBS with staff allocation: ProtoLoco

Label	Activity	Duration	Staff (days)
A	Receive approval	-	
B	Agree project outline	5	PM,EE,ME
C	Equip working area	8	PM
D	Schematic design	10	EE,ME
E	Power system specification	10	PM
F	Model construction	15	ME,EE
G	Mechanical design	40	ME
H	Electronic design	50	EE
I	Design stage complete	-	
J	Obtain materials and components	40	PM
K	Component manufacture	20	Wkshp
L	Subassembly manufacture	20	Wkshp
M	Final assembly	30	Wkshp
N	Produce promotional materials	15	PM
O	Programming	20	EE
P	Test	10	ME,EE
Q	Deliver and instal	5	ME,EE
R	Open exhibition	-	

PRODUCE PROMOTIONAL MATERIAL. Here, however, the latter activity has ample float. One simple solution is to split it so that it does not put back OBTAIN MATERIALS... which lies on the critical path.

The effect of these two changes is shown in Figure 13.6. It can be seen that the need to allocate the one electronic engineer has caused MODEL CONSTRUCTION to replace POWER SYSTEM SPECIFICATION on the critical path and the total project time is increased by five days.

When project work involves the use of teams of people, it is normal to plot the numbers required during each period. It may be possible to even out peaks and troughs by adjusting the schedules of non-critical activities. Otherwise, where the peaks are the result of critical or near-critical work packages, extensions to the total time may be considered. This process, known as *resource smoothing*, is an important part of project management.

10. Trade-offs between time and cost

As an alternative to letting the finish date be put back by five days, the problem of the overload on the electronic engineer may be resolved by drafting in a col-

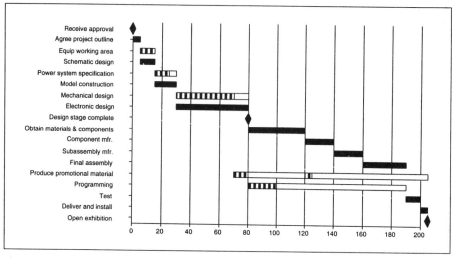

Figure 13.6 Gantt chart after personnel constraints: ProtoLoco

league for the critical period. The ability to do so will, of course, depend on the size of the firm, other work going on and the availability of a suitable candidate. Using the extra help from, say, the fifth to eighth weeks will bring two benefits. First it will allow the two tasks already shown to be clashing to go on simultaneously. Secondly, it may allow the time for the work package ELECTRONIC DESIGN to be cut from 50 to, say, 35 days. Again, we can examine the effect by rescheduling. The Gantt chart lets us compare the effect of these changes with the original plan by relating Figure 13.7 back to 13.5.

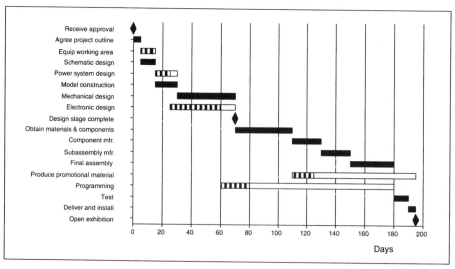

Figure 13.7 Gantt chart with time-cost trade-off: ProtoLoco

The comparison shows a 5-day saving on project finish and the route for the critical path again changing, this time to include the MECHANICAL DESIGN activity. Cutting the time for ELECTRONIC DESIGN by 15 days does not show through into a corresponding effect on total time. Indeed, the 10 days float created in that activity may be a waste of resources.

The results shown here are commonly experienced by project managers. Delivery times can be brought forward by spending extra funds. This raises two questions: whether it is worth spending these funds and, if so, which activities will yield the best returns.

- *Whether to spend extra*
  Sometimes, such as with our ProtoLoco, it may not be advantageous to deliver early as the project is aimed at a fixed target date. In other cases, for example where the early introduction of new process technology would permit extra cost savings, early completion pays. If a new process were to save, say, £40,000 per month, then it would be worth spending an amount less than that for any month saved.

- *Where to spend the extra*
  Selection of which activities to reduce is not so straightforward. A basic study would start with those on the critical path. Of these, some items will be of fixed duration (such as waiting for suppliers or for concrete to dry) whereas others can be cut using known extra resources. The snag among the latter is the non-linear link between time saved and cost.

These points can be illustrated in the ProtoLoco project. Suppose that another opportunity arises to show the prototype earlier than the proposed trade fair. How can weeks best be saved? Table 13.6 shows four activities where duration reduction is feasible.

It is often cheaper, per day, to save a few days rather than many. For a few days, staff can be encouraged to work overtime or delay holidays. For more than that, it may be necessary to reorganise, bring in new members to the team or use different methods and equipment. This is shown in the data of Table 13.6 which gives daily costs of duration reduction up to 3 days and 10 days. Days 4 to 10 have a higher marginal cost for activities G and L.

We can use Table 13.6 as follows. On a first pass it seems that, for any time saving up to 3 days, the extra resources should be put into FINAL ASSEMBLY. Then

Table 13.6 Selected activities with daily costs of duration reduction: ProtoLoco

Label	Activity	Duration (days)	Reduction up to 3 days	Reduction 4 to 10 days
G	Mechanical design	40	£140	£170
H	Electronic design	50	£150	£150
I	Obtain materials and components	40	£180	na
L	Final assembly	30	£130	£170

follows MECHANICAL DESIGN. But MECHANICAL DESIGN is not on the critical path so spending on that activity would be wasted. Therefore, for the next five days of crashing, funds should be spent on ELECTRONIC DESIGN. At this point, we know that MECHANICAL DESIGN itself becomes critical but forms a duplicate path. Further spending on the design area would have to crash both activities to gain total time savings. This would cost £290 per day. Attention, therefore, switches back to FINAL ASSEMBLY for up to 10 days in total. Lastly, it passes to OBTAIN MATERIALS. The daily costs of crashing rise as we seek more and more time saving.

Resource exchange

We have seen how extra spending can be targeted on network items to reduce project time. We also noted those projects where time savings are not looked for. Even in these cases, time-cost trade-offs should be examined. Here, instead of shortening total time, resources are exchanged among work packages to save total cost. This approach involves both a shift of resources from non-critical to critical lines and a shift among the critical ones. In the latter case, the time savings in one activity may counterbalance the extra duration of another. The switches are made without moving the target completion date.

11. Restructuring the project

After the work packages have been laid out, with their links and precedences, it is useful to reexamine them to see whether the links have been stated too conservatively. An area for investigation is suggested by the string of purchasing and manufacturing processes lasting for 110 days from day 75 of the ProtoLoco project. We could ask whether the detailed elements of these packages could be organised to allow overlap between the end of one and the start of another. This idea has echoes in the policy of batch size reduction in the OPT system, see **12.6.**

In Figure 13.8, the four activities from OBTAIN MATERIALS to FINAL ASSEMBLY have been reorganised to allow each to start before the previous one is complete. This is

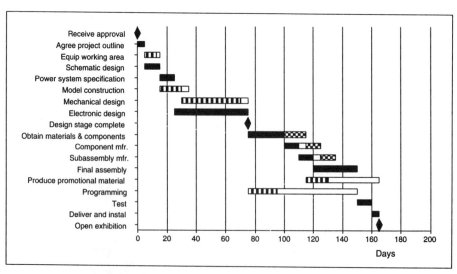

Figure 13.8 Gantt chart with critical activities restructured: ProtoLoco

common practice and worth the extra planning and coordination required. For instance, when obtaining raw materials, the project manager must ensure that those required early in the manufacturing process are obtained first. It may be worth issuing special orders or arranging for special deliveries if such actions would save time. For illustration, each activity has been divided into two roughly equal parts, identified by shading. The reorganisation saves 35 days.

12. Managing time variations

We noted in Box 13.1 that, during early development, PERT was distinguished from CPM by the attention paid to the effects of errors in time estimates. This difference has disappeared with the emergence of flexible software on which quick analyses of sensitivity can be performed. We shall, however, note the way in which time estimate variations were originally handled.

PERT used the Beta distribution to combine estimates and provide the manager with insights into the way errors may affect the project duration. The distribution allows for the possibility of very late work packages while recognising that their being very early is most unlikely. The method is to ask managers to make three estimates for task duration: the optimistic, OE; the pessimistic, PE; and the most likely estimate, MLE. From this information, the expected time, T, for the activity is given by the formula:

$$T = \frac{OE + 4\,MLE + PE}{6}$$

Its variance is found from the formula:

$$V_T = \left(\frac{PE - OE}{6}\right)^2$$

For example, the three estimates may be 30, 40 and 80 days. This gives an expected time of 35 days with a variance of 70 (corresponding to a standard deviation of 8.3 days).

The variance of the project completion time is the sum of the variances of all the activities on the critical path. Further, the fact that it is normally distributed allows for the probability of any completion time being achieved to be computed. This brings out the advantage of the approach. A manager can estimate the risk of a project exceeding a stated duration. This is essential, for instance, if a stadium is to be built or remodelled in time for a major public event, such as the Olympic Games. The contractor will not only estimate the construction time but be anxious to avoid the risk of missing the deadline!

Now that projects can be readily scheduled and rescheduled on computers, the PERT approach to time estimations is less important. Managers conduct sensitivity analysis by asking direct *what if?* questions of work packages and simulating various possibilities.

13. Controlling time, cost and cash flow

CPM and PERT were developed in circumstances where organisations found difficulty in delivering projects on time. The early focus was, therefore, on scheduling and continually allocating resources to meet deadlines. While this task remains important, cost control and resource management now receive equal attention. This change reflects the changed grounds on which many project contracts are let. There are two basic forms:

- *Cost reimbursement*
  Under this contract, frequently called *cost-plus*, the client agrees to pay all the supplier's costs plus a reasonable margin for profit. It is suited to circumstances where many changes are expected during the work and many risks have to be coped with. There are problems. For the contractor, there is little incentive to control costs, except in as far as the firm will seek to protect its reputation of giving value for money. The client will need to control costs in detail and assign substantial resources to this task.

- *Fixed price*
  The fixed-price contract states total price and delivery date. There are usually penalties for late completion. On the face of it, the client is better off in that all problems of risk and control are taken on by the contractor. Given that the latter is an 'expert', the job may be in better hands. Yet difficulties arise when unexpected circumstances are met or the client has a change of mind on some part of the specification. These lead to the issue of a *change order* to alter the contract terms. The scope, duration and price of the contract are, in effect, renegotiated with each change. In major projects, there are many hundreds of these orders. For instance, during the construction of the Channel Tunnel, the British and French governments changed regulations and the terms of the operating licence in response to new concerns over fire risks. It is often said that the key expertise in the management of fixed-price contracts lies in the negotiation of profitable change orders.

Given the difficulties with both forms of contract, it is not surprising that many hybrids exist. For instance, under a fixed-price contract, a supplier may be protected from inflation or exchange rate risks through variable pricing. In another case, a cost-plus contract may include estimates for cost and time with incentives to beat certain targets. In exchange, the supplier must provide information on detailed internal costs and agree to auditing and arbitration in disputes.

It can be seen that monitoring and control are essential aspects of project management. Whatever the form of agreement, progress review is indispensable. At each review, the remaining work packages should be examined, replanned and rescheduled as if they formed a new project.

Figure 13.9 suggests the way both costs and time must be reviewed. The original budget planned the way costs were to be spent. Variances from this budget appear in two ways:

- *Cost variances*
  At the current date, a review shows that the actual costs exceed the budget. This may warrant investigation of causes or it may represent the fact that the work is ahead of schedule. Managers tend, then, to do variance comparisons according to milestones, or *deliverables*, rather than calendar dates.

- *Value variances*
  To give a general measure of how close the performance is to schedule, the value variance comes from a comparison of the budgeted cost of work scheduled with the budgeted cost of work carried out. In Figure 13.9, the 'Value achieved' line plots the latter. The 'Current delay' arrow shows how much the value achieved lags behind the planned delivery.

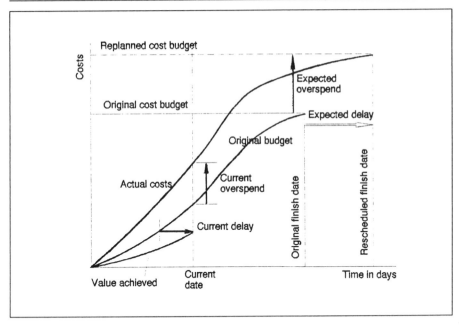

Figure 13.9 Project replanning at review stage

Now, the management team makes a new cost and time budget, shown as an extension, beyond the current date, to the line for actual costs. Both overspend and delay are anticipated in this new budget. The managers then have to investigate whether the changes are acceptable or they should allocate more resources to catch up.

To support the decision making process, managers will produce special reports. Project management software will readily generate forms such as time sheets, progress tracking charts and statements of the remaining work to be done. Among the more important are:

- *Delay statements*
  Comparisons of the planned schedule for each work package with outcomes will identify whether and where action should be taken.
- *Costs and costs to complete*
  At any review, many tasks will be partially complete. This analysis prepares an estimate of progress for each task to work out its expected total cost. From this statement, a revised budget can be presented as in Figure 13.9.
- *Cash flow analysis*
  It can often be a mistake to complete operations too soon. This can create problems from the physical to the financial. For the former, it may be that assemblies ready for final installation arrive on site too early and stand around wasting space and deteriorating. Perhaps what is more important, completing a large work package too early means that cash will have been spent when it should have been conserved. Therefore, for jobs not on the critical path, managers should consider their sequence not only in terms of resource smoothing but also in their impact on cash flow. Strictly, this means identifying a schedule that maximises the net present value of all cash transactions. It may be practicable to

delay those work packages in which expensive purchased components are brought together. Working to latest starting and finishing times does, of course, bring with it an increased risk of delay. Managers must, therefore, be cautious in planning tasks down to the last possible moment.

A variation is in the case when cash receipts can occur before project completion. This can occur when a facility is partly opened, as in a new tramway or sports stadium, or if a client pays in instalments according to reaching agreed milestones.

- *Exceptional reports*

While routine reporting may form the basis of good control, managers should also be aware of unusual problems. These may have occurred or may be anticipated. Such difficulties include: unexpected geological conditions; changes in legislation; entry of new competitors in a market; delays in supplies and so on. Events like these need to be reported so that responses can be made. It may be that a change in the business environment means that the client agrees to a delay. In this case, the schedule needs to be restated with new plans for resource allocation and cash flow.

In the above examples of the ways that managers run projects, we can see examples of the classes of control introduced in **4.21**. While the work is being carried out, there is a constant stream of reports that cause adjustments to schedules, new allocations of resources and so on. This is *concurrent control*, where the control action follows very closely upon the performance itself. To the extent that managers are also regularly updating their plans, they exercise *feedforward control*, anticipating the changes to outcomes that will result from their control actions. Finally, at various stages throughout the project, and most certainly after completion, teams should review progress and reflect on ways they may change the way the work was managed. In this way, learning can be incorporated into arrangements for next time. This is *feedback control*.

Concurrent control within the work packages dominates the scene during the process of the project. While modern computer systems allow new optimisation to be carried out in the light of each event, a surfeit of minor changes creates *system dithering*, a problem mentioned in connection with MRP systems. Changes made too frequently are stressful and demoralising.

Project management is an art carried out in a dynamic setting. In spite of the decision aids embodied in modern software, finding the optimal balance remains a matter of judgement. Theoretical work in the years since the CPM and PERT developments of the 1950s has sought solutions to various aspects of project scheduling. While these exist for some management questions, however, there is no general rule that will enable a manager to optimise time, cost and cash flow simultaneously[4]. The best outcomes must be judged by scheduling, rescheduling and careful attention to cost and cash budgets.

Case study: Britannia Airways' new fleet [5]

Britannia is the world's largest charter airline and the second largest carrier in the UK. In April 1990 it announced plans to introduce the modern Boeing 757 aircraft for the start of 1991.

To achieve the target, tasks as varied as obtaining Civil Aviation Authority approval, crew training and carrying out engineering modifications had to be performed. The short deadline was the result of market pressure. To meet it Britannia had to lease aircraft until the ones it intended to buy from Boeing were available. Three new aircraft were due in the spring of 1992 and three a year later.

1st November was the target date for the first leased planes to be in the air. They were identified in June 1991. Within two months they were in service, using crews from the lessor. But Britannia needed a CAA certificate permitting it to use its own people aboard. Its own pilots began flying before the end of the year. To support the transfer there were new training manuals, crew training, development of operating procedures and inspection and planned maintenance schedules.

Since the company already flew the similar Boeing 767s, it decided to make small changes to the cockpit layout of the 757s to make the two fleets closely compatible. This took time but the firm decided it was necessary. The main reason was safety, although the change also eased personnel flexibility and made training quicker.

To fit in with Britannia's own standards, the leased aircraft were fitted with new in-flight entertainment systems. This was in line with company policy to have the best standards of video in all its planes. Again, the process involved more than obtaining and fitting the equipment. The design had to be carefully carried out and installation approved.

Throughout the changeover, the project team consisted of staff drawn from pilot training, engineering, cabin and airport services, and the scheduling, commercial and finance functions. Team meetings were held weekly to review progress and reschedule future tasks when required. Planning and control reports were produced using PC software.

The leased planes, with full Britannia crews, were airborne by January 1991.

Questions

1 *Identify the characteristics of the situation that supported the use of formal project management techniques.*
2 *With which other company planning and scheduling systems would the conversion project have to have interacted?*
3 *How would you manage this project?*
4 *How would you evaluate success?*

References

1. Anthony, R.N. (1988) *The Management Control Function* Boston, Mass, The Harvard Business School Press, pp. 102–4
2. ibid. p. 107
3. Well known project management packages include Hoskyns' *Project Management Workbench*, Microsoft's *Project* and Mantix Systems' *Cascade*. The analysis in this chapter used the first of these, although the drawings were made separately.
4. Icmeli, O., Erenguc, S.S. and Zappe, C.J. (1993) 'Project scheduling problems: a survey' *International Journal of Production and Operations Management* **13.11** pp. 80–91
5. Based on: Meall, L. (1994) 'Britannia Airways: The sky's the limit' *Accountancy* **113.1206** February p. 57

14

CONTROL OF PROCESSES AND INVENTORIES

Chapter objectives

When you have finished studying this chapter, you should be able to:

- Differentiate between planning and control as management functions.
- Apply key control ideas to operations and inventory management. Show where feedback, concurrent and feedforward control are used.
- Explain how control works in different manufacturing and service systems and how effective monitoring is carried out.
- Evaluate the relative advantages of different classes of inventory; distinguish between dependent and independent inventory and explain the implications for management.
- Demonstrate basic replenishment procedures.
- Illustrate the use of ABC analysis in inventory management.
- Explain the application of EOQ inventory models under different assumptions; show how the reorder point is calculated when conditions are uncertain; explain the use of safety stock to maintain service levels.

INTRODUCTION

In this chapter we return to the control models introduced in **4.21**. Here we use the models to investigate the processes that follow the setting out of detailed operating plans. We are concerned with the closing of the feedback loop through monitoring and control action. The range of applications of these ideas is very wide. The broader management control issues, such as budgeting, were dealt with in Chapter 4. Here we investigate the application of control ideas to two shop floor areas, namely operations and inventory. The operations discussion concentrates on the control of MRPII systems and process plant but also recognises the issue of control in service operations. Inventory management is itself a service operation. Its success in maintaining availability levels within realistic expenditure limits makes an important contribution to business performance. Quality is another area where control ideas have application. Indeed, the establishment and maintenance of quality standards are so important as to merit separate chapters.

THE CONTROL CONCEPT

1. Planning and control

In this book we make a distinction between *planning*, choosing and organising what to do, and *control*, checking and ensuring that the desired results are achieved. Some see this as an arbitrary distinction. For instance, Anthony argues, 'Although planning and control are definable abstractions and are easily understood as calling for different types of *mental* activity, they do not relate to major categories of activities actually carried on by an organisation, either at different times, or by different people, or for different situations.'[1] He continues by pointing out that most people in organisations engage in both planning and control. Furthermore, the definitions of the terms in the literature are inconsistent; the function referred to by some authors and in some companies as 'operations planning' is called 'operations control' by others. Few texts have separate sections on operations control, either treating the issue as an adjunct to scheduling or hardly mentioning it at all.

The view taken here is that it is worth making the distinction. We have argued that managers fill many roles including leader, decision maker, motivator, negotiator and communicator. Planning and controlling are another two ways of looking at what managers do. Despite the fact that they are carried out by the same person in different proportions at different times, they are no less worthy of analysis. At the strategic level, managers spend a greater proportion of their time planning whereas shop floor staff have functions that are much more specific and include a greater proportion of control. Therefore, in spite of his grand title, it

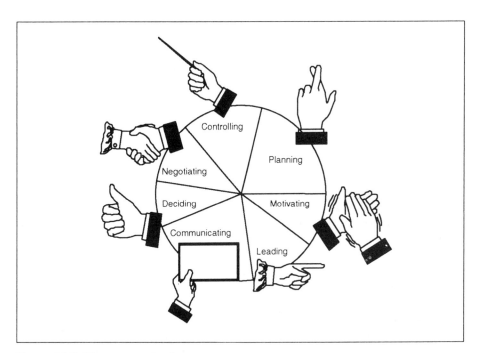

Figure 14.1 Management roles

would be surprising if the Fat Controller spent more time on control activity than did Thomas's driver[2].

On the shop floor, control is focused on what Anthony calls *task control*[3], which means ensuring that defined tasks are carried out according to objectives. The framework in which the task control is carried out will have already been established as part of the management process. In many cases, the tasks are clearly prescribed and, barring unforeseen events, control can be exercised automatically without human intervention. Since much of this work is routine, from the stock clerk making out a purchase order to a coating machine operator adjusting application thickness, questions of employee motivation and attention are relevant. These were discussed in Chapter 6.

2. Control models

In **4.21**, we identified three types of control. Their key points can be summarised as:

- *Feedback control*
  Feedback control depends on monitoring outputs, comparing them with goals and learning from discrepancies. Changes are made to avoid the errors in the future, see Figure 4.11. One criticism is that corrections occur after the event when the errors have been made and waste created. The focus is on information about the past.

  Feedback control has an advantage in that it provides a check on the objectives and standards in use. If standards are not being achieved consistently, then there may be a case for changing them to make their attainment easier. This should not be seen as an argument for lowering standards arbitrarily; there are many opportunities in product and process design to make such adjustments without affecting the satisfaction of customers.
- *Concurrent control*
  Otherwise known as real-time control, this works as closely as possible with the current system performance. The steps of data collection, comparison and adjustment are closely integrated as the controller is, in effect, part of the system, see Figure 4.12. A supervisor may receive daily time sheets that record the activities on which the department has been engaged. This is feedback control. Most supervisors, however, prefer to operate concurrently, maintaining regular, but not excessive, checks on progress in the section.
- *Feedforward control*
  In feedforward control, the accent is on anticipation. As Figure 4.13 shows, not only is there a feedback loop but the feedback data runs through a forecasting stage that provides information on the future consequences of current performance. This enables managers to actively anticipate problems and, therefore, prevent them. We have seen examples of feedforward control in preventive maintenance and project rescheduling after review.

We noted in **4.21** how concurrent control can be seen merely as a variant of feedback control. To see the difference, we need to recognise the importance of perspective. If we study a job shop employee using a lathe to turn a few components, we will see a series of machining, measurement and adjustment steps until the workpiece diameter is just right. At this level of detail we can identify stages of feedback control as shown in the lefthand part of Figure 14.2.

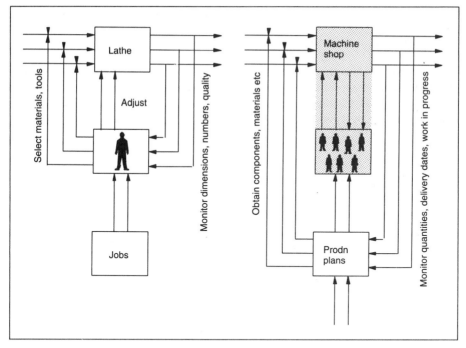

Figure 14.2 Perspectives on feedback and concurrent control

If, on the other hand, we see the person-lathe system within the context of the whole production process, the perspective will be better represented by the right hand part of the diagram. The staff and equipment within the machine shop operate as if using concurrent control. The people in the control office, however, gather information not about individual dimensions or pieces of work but about the progress of orders through stages of production. The machine shop's detailed operations exist, as it were, in a *black box*. This is shown shaded in the diagram. From the point of view of the office, shop floor control is concurrent.

We can summarise the two reasons for the different perspective:

- *Time*
  Shop floor operators work on tasks measured in minutes, while work schedules may be planned in days or weeks. The feedback intervals perceived by the machine operator are simply not seen by the production controller.
- *Detail*
  Job planning and scheduling, especially in job shops, do not go down to the detail of the separate elements of each operation. It is neither feasible nor obligatory to issue such instructions. Within the broad production plan, staff use their skills to carry out tasks and control them concurrently.

There are similar problems of blurred distinctions when feedforward and feedback control are compared. To see the latter solely in terms of correction of past mistakes would underestimate the staff involved. After all, decisions should be taken with an eye on the future. Yet there are two common cases showing an over reliance on feedback control. First there is the sort of expediting that merely attends to overdue orders and then attempts to push then along. Second, there are stock holding systems where inventories are determined by past performance with no attempt to forecast future patterns of demand. The point of modern control systems is that the anticipatory element should be incorporated. In so doing, we see a merger between planning, or looking forward, and controlling, which focuses on the past as the basis for decisions. To suggest that feedforward control is simply feedback with forecasting is to underplay the different management attitudes required to back such a system.

In spite of the issues mentioned here, the distinctions between control methods are worth drawing. They will be used throughout this chapter.

CONTROL OF OPERATIONS

3. Manufacturing

In a manufacturing environment, control fits into the sequence of activities from order receipt to despatch as follows:

- *Rough cut planning*
  Broad resource allocation from sales forecasts, analysis, process planning, advance material ordering and capacity analysis.
- *Detailed planning and scheduling*
  Order receipt, documentation, allocation of resources of labour, materials, machine time etc. to each order. Establishment of priorities at each stage. Issue of manufacturing instructions.
- *Monitoring*
  Obtaining up-to-date and relevant data on order progress, resources used and available, completions, delays, stock levels and shortages, and so on.
- *Feedback and corrective action*
  Evaluating the data in the light of plans and schedules. Short-term changes to the plan at shop floor level can be made. If these will not correct the variations, feedback into the planning system is required.
- *Completion and despatch*
  When the order is complete, instructions are removed from the operations system. Yet this is not the end of the story for control. Records should be assembled of manufacturing cost, scrap levels and, later, defects that occur in service.

As de Toni and Panizzolo[4] point out, these five activities are carried out in very different ways in intermittent and repetitive production contexts. We noted the differences in planning and scheduling decisions in **12.17**, so we will concentrate on control here. The issues are summarised in Table 14.1.

In the intermittent, that is to say, job shop, environment, the basic unit of control is the order. The materials and components for this order are moved around the plant, grouped together in batches if necessary. The items are connected by being under a single order number that the system uses for transmitting instructions and monitoring progress through all the production stages. After each key stage, data on the order is assembled to provide information about its status. In the light of this information, corrective actions range from local expediting, see Box 14.1, to rescheduling. The latter relates to either the order or others that are interfering with its progress. As the job is completed, data on costs or profits and

Table 14.1 Control in intermittent and repetitive manufacture

Control activity → Manufacturing system ↓	Monitoring	Corrective action	Post despatch analysis
Intermittent manufacturing	Order by order; stage by stage	Local expediting; rescheduling	Cost/profit, delivery dates per order
Repetitive manufacturing	Emphasis on sufficient checkpoints and rapid feedback to maintain the flow.		Cost/profit per unit of output

delivery performance are collected. This can be fed back into the sales system to ensure that future prices and terms of delivery are realistic.

In repetitive manufacture, materials and components pass through stages in a continuous stream and not in predetermined batches. Each stage has limited scope, being capable of working on a narrow family of parts or assembling a known range of finished items. The purpose of the five activities is to instigate and maintain the flow of work without interruption. Since the plant is dedicated to the narrow product range, the first two stages, order review and release and detailed planning, are merged, the aim being to establish the speed at which the whole system must operate and ensure that corresponding resources are available. Much of the order-oriented activity of intermittent production, such as identifying different quantities of raw materials, is unnecessary, these tasks having been routinised within the plant design. Detailed plans are not needed. The same sequence of orders is used throughout the line. Data collection for progress control may be confined to the end, unless the line is so long that intermediate steps are worthwhile. These checkpoints should be sufficiently frequent to allow rapid data feedback to support concurrent control.

When I was a supervisor in the wagon works, one of my staff, Watmough, spent his days pushing a small handcart around the works. The works was extensive, covering some 48 hectares. My section assembled bogie frames at about forty per week. Although Watmough could not read, he knew every inch of the production process and every component that we needed. Work was frequently late from the machine shops. When this happened, he would pick the first few items from the finished stack and bring them over in his cart. He would also let me know when things were running behind so I could slow the job down and put the welders on other work. When the people from the 'top office' came across Watmough in the yard, they used to ask him where the problems were. They could then go to their Monday scheduling meetings with grass roots information.

Watmough's rewards were recognition and an occasional cigarette from the Works Manager, something never offered to supervisors. He was a great expediter, using a mix of concurrent and feedforward control to run his personal MRP system.

Box 14.1 Watmough the expediter

In repetitive manufacture, concurrent control is oriented to maintaining the flow as opposed to tracking each order. Since orders are carried out in sequence, as on a car assembly line where basic models are customised to personal requirements, the issue of an order instruction into the line will inevitably lead to a product. With short lead times and interdependent sequences of machines, emphasis is placed on rapid feedback of data about the flow so that hold-ups can be detected and correction taken. At the level of each section of the line, supervisors use concurrent control to ensure that sufficient crews are available, machine defects are corrected and any difficulty with supplies overcome. Data on profit or performance is not collected after each item is despatched. The interest is on the performance through time, measured in terms of revenues per week or per unit of output such as tonnes.

4. Monitoring

The bridge from planning to control is monitoring. To be effective the collection system must provide data that is:

- *Relevant*
  It is a simple point but the data must be about the process and values being controlled. Sometimes it can be too easy to collect the data that can readily be observed and expect the user to interpret it to form the basis for action.
- *Comprehensive*
  Measuring performance using just a few parameters runs the risk of encouraging staff to ensure good performance in these areas at the expense of others.
- *Sufficient*
  Sufficiency implies that there is adequate information to form the basis of control decisions. At the same time, the receiver can suffer for a surfeit of data that only served to hide the key values.
- *Timely*
  The frequency of monitoring and reporting is an important issue in the design of effective control systems. For concurrent control, a continuous stream of data must be available to the staff. This is usually direct observation. Feedback, and feedforward, control systems will collect data at regular intervals. The choice of their duration has an impact on the effectiveness of the control system.
- *Reliable*
  The temptation of fraud in some areas of business means that checks and audits are required, especially where funds are being handled. Yet some manoeuvring, sometimes called measurementship, is driven by individuals' desires to appear good, although manipulating the data brings them no direct personal gain. All business control systems should, therefore, be transparent in their operation and subject to external checks and audits.

Questions under these headings have been regularly raised in the operational control of financial markets and trading in them, see Box 14.2[5]. This is compounded by the shortage of staff able to understand and evaluate newly devised financial instruments such as derivatives. Control is difficult in the culture of the city dealing room where cunning and risk-taking seem to be encouraged and traditional values of honesty and caution are seen to demonstrate gullibility[6].

The choice of frequency of process monitoring must balance the cost of this monitoring, with its concomitant data interpretation and control action, with the

'When things go wrong at securities firms, they often go wrong in the back office.' The successes and failures of those who buy and sell securities, such as derivatives, are the material for newspaper headlines yet some of the greatest losses have come from a failure of the control system to identify a potential risk and take action. This problem may have caused the collapse of the 230 years old Barings Bank in March 1995. Those responsible for control were unable to prevent a dealer taking a huge gamble on the Nikkei index of the Tokyo stock exchange.

Deals are recorded as they are made and traders make daily reports on the positions they take. In the Barings case, the roles of making the contracts and settling them were not separated and it was possible for these reports to be confused. Headquarters' monitoring was too slow. If the controls had been effective, the scale of trading could not have occurred.

The bank is not the only one to have failed in this way. Saloman Brothers lost well over £220 million from inaccurate recording of swap contracts. Another New York trader, Kidder Peabody, failed when one executive created false profits to boost his 1993 salary bonus to $9 million. The accounting system recorded each contract profit on the day it was formed, not on the day it was due to be settled. Deals could be rolled over to extend their life and thus delay settlement. It was only then that the false paper profits would be exposed. In 1982, Chase Manhattan Bank failed to detect that a $285 million loan was being made to a firm that was much too small to carry this size of debt.

Supervision cannot be left to the annual auditors. The difficulties can grow very quickly. Barings' 1994 audit had not been completed by the time of its 1995 collapse.

Box 14.2 Feedback in financial dealing

benefits gained from the closer control. The sketch in Figure 14.3 shows the effect of changing the frequency of monitoring. Suppose we are trying to control the value of a single variable to keep it as close as possible to a target value. The solid line shows what happens if the monitoring occurs every hour. Corrections are made to push the value back towards the target. The chained line shows the effect of less frequent monitoring. The variable can change at the same rate as before but, given the greater time between adjustments, it can deviate further from the target. Clearly, if the intervals are made too great, the variable being controlled can surpass sound or safe limits. A tightrope walker must continuously monitor balance and practice leads to automaticity in this respect. In other cases, intervals are set according to statute, informed analysis or merely habit. Intervals are extended if the data stream shows stability and can be shortened if the risk of variability appears to rise. This question is returned to in the context of quality control in Chapter 16.

5. Closing the MRPII loop

Figure 12.4 presented MRPII as a series of stages within an open-loop model. Without feedback, this would be unsatisfactory. As Burcher argues[7], there are at

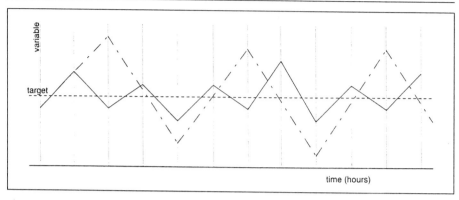

Figure 14.3 Varying the monitoring intervals

least three levels of planning at which resource checks could take place. These are shown as dashed lines in Figure 14.4. The first level checks whether the Master Production Schedule meets the needs of the aggregate plan; the second compares materials availability and production capacity with the MPS to see if the 'rough-cut' capacity estimates are adequate for the proposed master schedule; the third is concerned with whether detailed shop floor and subcontract scheduling are likely to meet the CRP. Each of these levels should be part of the planning system, amendments being created as part of planning and scheduling control that is dynamic and monitors changes as new orders and requirements come in. Since the plan is continually being modified ahead of production actually taking place, this is feedforward control and is one of the strengths of full MRP systems.

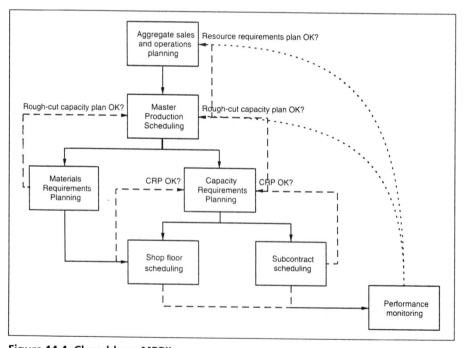

Figure 14.4 Closed-loop MRPII

Control can also be exercised after the event. Figure 14.4 shows how performance monitoring should gather data about the whole system performance. This is sent back to all decision making stages although the diagram shows only two feedback loops for clarity. It will be too late to use this loop to change current orders so the information is employed to modify the way future decisions are made. The system, therefore, learns from its successes and mistakes.

What happens in practice? While the model in Figure 14.4 suggests an ideal situation, many companies find difficulty in its implementation and, consequently, are disappointed with the results. Burcher was interested in the extent to which MRPII was used in UK manufacturing in 1990. He found that more than half the 349 companies responding to a questionnaire used capacity planning, with rough-cut capacity planning (58%) occurring most frequently. Yet perhaps one third of these did not regard the approaches as working successfully. The most commonly cited reasons for planning difficulties were:

- Absence of either job time standards or detailed routing paths through processes.
- Lack of efficiency or utilisation information that would allow machine or process effective capacity to be calculated realistically.
- Poor sales forecasts with resulting large volumes of unplanned orders.

In many companies, feedback from the capacity requirements plan to the master production schedule was not used. Reasons given included a preference to change capacity using overtime or subcontracting, the lack of a master production schedule and a view that rough-cut planning was sufficient.

Closed-loop MRPII is, therefore, only partially implemented in many companies. The nature of the business and its environment strongly affect the ease with which it can be put in place. Measured times are critical. The survey showed that companies engaged in more repetitive manufacturing, or with products that were relatively unchanging, tended to have most output under standard times. Examples with a high proportion (95%) were brick, pottery, glass and cement industries. On the other hand, textiles, leather, clothing and footwear average 68%, hardly a base for the establishment of detailed capacity plans.

The rewards to be gained from full MRPII implementation are great. Spreadbury refers to the payback available from achieving excellent standards[8]. These include delivery more than 95% on time, more than 95% manufacturing schedule performance, improved inventory turnover, reduced waste, and so on. Many European companies have reached these standards, including Kodak, ICI, Reckitt and Colman, Formica and Courtaulds Films. Implementation of full MRPII involves major reorganisation and can seem to take a long time. Spreadbury argues that such changes ought to be treated like full-blown projects, divided into work packages with individual managers identified as responsible for each. The key to success lies not merely in the first stage of application but in the continuous improvement that must follow. It is there that the learning loops, mentioned above, come into their own.

The paradox of MRPII implementation is that its greatest successes have been reported from those plants whose production organisation is closest to repetitive manufacture. This is hardly surprising since these plants handle a narrow range of products and orders. So the plants that need MRPII systems the most – those with greatest complexity – find the most difficulty with its installation and, so far, have benefitted the least from it.

6. Control of process plant

In contrast to the complexity in many intermittent environments, dedicated process plants have control loops designed in. They often lend themselves to computer control because:

- There can be a large volume of data.
- Many variables in the process can be continuously monitored using instruments. Examples are temperatures, flow rates and so on.
- Processes are well understood. This means that the computer can hold an internal decision model enabling it to operate automatically.
- Accurate control is required over long periods. Humans are notoriously poor at maintaining long-term vigilance when tasks are simple.
- Computers are cheap.

The simplest form of feedback control in a plant would be to monitor the quality of the finished product and, were it not to standard, make adjustments until it was so. This approach is unsatisfactory because of the waste that would be created. The lags between adjustments to the process and monitoring would result in large deviations from standards. In control of process plant, therefore, there is a need for monitoring of each stage of the system to ensure that the corresponding intermediate product is satisfactory. This shortens the feedback loop to the extent that the plant works under concurrent control.

This monitoring provides information on discrepancies earlier than before. In a fermentation process of a brewery, for instance, the reactions may not proceed at the normal rate and the whole plant is slowed down. Adjustments to the system are made almost as soon as the discrepancies occur. Is this the best that can be done?

In many cases it is possible to use feedforward control, provided the system is well enough understood. To use a motoring analogy, a good driver anticipates danger and is in a position to take avoiding action. On the other hand, a bad driver anticipates others' actions incorrectly.

Much of the monitoring of process plant is concerned with the variables that underlie the rates of production and its quality. Returning to the example of fermentation, monitoring of the temperature of the wort would enable one to anticipate a slow-down in alcohol production. Corrective action, through adding more hot water, could be carried out almost before the problem, low conversion rate, had arisen.

Concurrent process control requires, therefore,

- Monitoring of many variables at many points
- Rapid feedback of data
- Computer systems to handle the high volume of data.
- Models permitting feedforward control.

Do computers run such plants? The answer depends on how well understood and predictable the processes are. It is normal to have automatic control of the system, provided it is operating between expected limits, and to require human intervention under unusual conditions. Yet to design a system that can work safely under human control is extremely difficult. The case of the Three Mile Island power plant was mentioned in **6.1**. A further example comes from an incident on the Docklands Light Railway.

The Docklands Light Railway, in east London, uses computer-controlled trains without drivers. The first collision, in 1991, occurred at a junction. One train was running to schedule under computer control. The other, which should not have been there, was under human control because of an earlier computer failure.

7. Control of service delivery

Much of the activity in personal service involves concurrent control as the server continually decides what to do in the light of the customer's needs. The range of customers also means that it is difficult to set service standards that can be monitored other than through the eyes of each individual. We shall return to this theme when discussing quality in service provision in Chapter 16.

Many personal service organisations set internal standards that act as yardsticks against which performance is measured. They serve as indirect indicators of customer satisfaction. Marriott Hotels, for instance, supplements the comment cards handed to every customer with monitoring against formal performance targets. In 1985, the company set a 15-minute standard for in-room breakfast service, otherwise it would be free. This increased demand by 25% and meant that employees had to develop new ways of handling the orders, transmitting them to the kitchen and delivering the trays to the rooms[9].

Box 14.3 outlines the control process used in the management of another personal service, Manchester's emergency ambulances[10]. Collecting performance data in this way enables operations managers to spot discrepancies from standards and anticipate when and where problems may arise. Besides supporting day-to-day control, the data can be summarised and used in periodic reviews of targets and operating procedures.

We discussed in **13.18** how, except where capacity is limited, self-service needs no scheduling. Capacity is made available and the customer takes it up when

---

The service deals with about 3,800 emergency cases a month. Targets are set as follows:

- *Activation* The time from receiving the call until there is a vehicle moving towards the incident should be no more than 3 minutes.
- *Response time* The time from receiving the call until arrival at the emergency should be no more than 7 to 14 minutes (depending on the area).

While the emergency call is being received and the response arranged, a log is kept of the sequence of events on a special form. In addition to recording the nature and location of the incident, and the names of people involved, the operators note the following times:

Call receipt
Information passed to vehicle
Arrival at incident
Departure to hospital
Arrival at hospital

These records are checked every 24 hours to ensure that the targets for activation and response are being achieved.

Box 14.3 Manchester ambulance service targets

wanted. In the same sense, control action is not required in relation to each customer. A provider must, however, ensure that the service remains available at the appropriate level. To this end monitoring of stocks, facilities, cash and so on is needed at appropriate intervals.

The other form of service, isolated service, takes place away from the customer and, like scheduling, has control characteristics related to its manufacturing counterparts.

A summary of control issues matched with different processes is set out in Box 14.4. The lists show that the features of control of the different processes vary considerably from one to another.

Process	Key control task	Focus	Information
Repetitive manufacture and isolated service	Rate of flow of all stages linked together. In mass production not all products need all components; in process plant each process modelled and managed.	Maintaining full use of plant capacity to optimise the flow.	Centralised control to monitor each stage and balance all continuously.
Intermittent manufacture and isolated service	Progressing individual orders and batches through multiple stages; meet planned assembly schedules and/or promised delivery dates.	Each order tracked through processes.	Instructions to shop floor to establish sequences and priorities. Monitoring of order progress and expediting.
Project (manufacture or service)	Progress against planned milestones; obtaining and using constrained resources at the right time.	Optimisation of single contract; close watch on critical activities.	Creating network; comparing time and cost progress against master schedule; regular rescheduling.
Personal service	Matching service to customer's changing needs.	Satisfying each customer within constraints.	Stream of information from customers; queue lengths; reservation systems.
Self-service	Maintenance of self-service 'offer', eg stocks of goods, money, equipment.	Following customer flow.	Inventory levels; customer demands.

Box 14.4 Summary of control in different manufacture and service processes

INVENTORY CONTROL

8. Inventory

Our studies of the different operational processes have brought out many stages where inventories are found. One conventional way of classifying them is into categories of raw materials, work-in-progress and finished goods. While all of those appear as assets in financial accounts, it is the case that most companies would prefer to operate with very low stocks, or even none if this were possible.

Inventory is often viewed as imposing dead weight on the business. Indeed, followers of the JIT philosophy see inventory in a negative light as it hides problems that should be brought to the surface. These are valid points. The cash tied up in stock could be used more profitably in other activities and so there is an *opportunity cost* associated with carrying any stock at all. Heaps of stock typify the inefficient job shop. We must recognise, however, that inventory does perform various functions that ought to be seen as contributing to the firm's need to add value through its processes. Functions of the three classes of inventory are as follows:

- *Raw materials*
  - To protect the operating processes from shortages caused by uncertain supplies.
  - To reduce materials costs by enabling purchases to take place in the optimal quantities at the most appropriate times.
  - To hedge against inflation and unstable prices.
- *Work-in-progress*
  - To enable each stage in the process to operate to optimal batch sizes.
  - To decouple different stages so they operate at different rates according to their technologies.
  - To provide buffers at points along the whole process that allow for the unreliability or technical uncertainty of one or more stages.
- *Finished goods*
  - To enable instant service to be offered.
  - To smooth out production when demand is known to be seasonal.
  - To protect the operating processes from unexpected shifts in customer demand.

Some reasons are defensive in nature and are only required to cover weaknesses in the production system or uncertainties in the business environment. Others are the result of choices within the scheduling system, where work-in-progress levels are the result of decisions on questions such as batch sizes. Finally, some reasons can be more directly related to gaining competitive advantage. Raw material policies can be adjusted to optimise input costs and keeping a good stock of finished goods will affect sales rates in many cases. Box 14.5 shows how FAI makes a virtue of carrying large stocks[11].

9. Dependent and independent demand

Different firms arrange their production systems partly with the intention of restricting stock levels. The job shop that supplies to order is not concerned with inventory of finished items and may carry little raw material because of space restrictions and uncertainty of the requirements in future orders. Such stocks are

The Montreal-based FAI company distributes electronic components to customers throughout America. Starting from scratch in 1968, it reached an annual turnover of over $800 million in 1994. In the volatile semiconductor market, FAI emphasises service as its strong selling point. It aims to supply from stock a much wider range than its rivals and has, in consequence, a turnover ratio lower than the 2.5 industry norm. The volatility means that many distributors buy on 'price protection' contracts from the major manufacturers such as Motorola and Intel. If the distributors can show that goods have had to be sold on at lower than anticipated prices, the manufacturers will give rebates. Therefore, the latter take on the price risk in the market.

FAI is the only major distributor that does not participate in these contracts, seeing them as letting the manufacturers control the distributors' margins. FAI buys at fixed prices and uses its good service levels to 'gets its price'. That is, it sells at margins comfortably above those of its rivals.

Box 14.5 High stocks, high margins, high performance

only carried if substantial quantity discounts are available or local suppliers cannot deliver within short lead times. The job shop's problem is work-in-progress!

At the other extreme, the process or dedicated mass production plant operates with the smallest possible level of work-in-progress, there being just enough of it to fill the relevant pipes and vessels or load the cradles on the assembly track. The steady, planned input flow means that these plants can limit raw materials stock by arranging long-term JIT supply contracts. At the other end of the production line, in contrast, problems arise. The driver, usually the assembler, in the JIT system, sets the rhythm of the steady daily production rate. As a result, it needs to hold stock to decouple the manufacturing process from the variable market demand.

Process technologies between the job and the highly repetitive seek different equilibria among the three types of stock.

The most significant difference between operating processes and the way they affect stock management lies in whether the inventory is held to satisfy dependent or independent demand. Items in the former category are those that can be directly linked to demand for another item. It is derived from demand for the assembly of which it will form a part. These stocks are materials, components and subassemblies that can be connected to each manufacturing order by a definitive bill of materials. An order placed by a customer automatically generates *pro rata* demand for the constituent parts. The materials requirements plan, MRP, will be the aggregation of the bills. It will form the basis for purchase orders and shop production whether the firm is using MRPII or other planning procedures. The quantity and timing of supplies can be figured out precisely. There will be some non-dedicated stock held when a MRP system is in place. It will cover advanced orders for components and materials whose lead time is too great to fit in with customers' normal requirements and casual items used around the plant for maintenance and related activities.

The independently demanded category of items includes, besides the non-dedicated stock just mentioned, finished goods and materials that are bought to underpin production as a whole rather than the aggregation of individual orders. The most important of these is the stock of finished goods. The quantities needed, and the times when they are wanted, cannot be worked out from definite orders. This, therefore, is the philosophy of *just-in-case*, as opposed to just-in-time. Stock levels have to be estimated from production and demand patterns using special techniques. Their management and control are thus very different to the time-dependent items.

Order-oriented production systems depend on a firm's willingness to adopt a MRP system. The length of time required, up to three years, and the high cost of computer systems, training and so on mean that they may only be adopted by the larger companies. Therefore, rather than go to the trouble of setting up MRP, a company that makes to order may choose to manage its own inventories as independent systems. Service organisations that distribute goods, namely distributors and retailers, face independent demand and therefore have inventory control problems similar to the finished goods stage of the manufacturer.

MRP systems were covered in **5** so independent inventory systems will now be discussed.

10. Independent inventory control structure

The inventory system consists of three main subsystems, shown at the centre of Figure 14.5. The *inventory holding system*, with receiving, holding and despatching components, consists of one or more stores, warehouses, stockyards or similar depots. This is controlled by the *inventory control system* that monitors the behaviour of the holding system to maintain stock levels according to policy and to monitor security. At a level higher than the control system is the *inventory management system* that monitors total performance and sets the goals and rules to be used.

The typical method of operation is for the control system to monitor levels of stock from the records of inputs and outputs, the so-called *perpetual inventory* method. Stock checking validates these calculations and identifies shortages caused by damage, deterioration or theft. Checks take place either at fixed intervals, say monthly, or continuously. The former is convenient where the store can be closed for the count to take place but may require personnel to be drafted in at

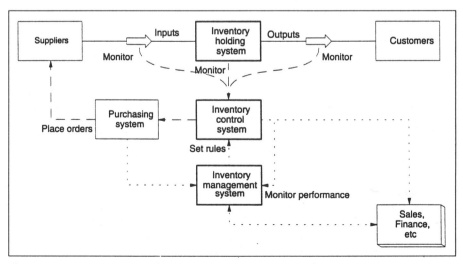

Figure 14.5 Inventory holding, control and management systems

an inconvenient time. The latter is better when the store operates without interruption and can take place during normal working hours.

The inventory control system uses the stock information and the control rules to generate orders, via the purchasing system, for suppliers to provide replenishment. General direction is provided by the inventory management system that gathers performance data, such as the frequency of stock shortages, and changes the control rules if necessary. We see, therefore, two levels of control. First, there is concurrent, operated continuously to replenish stocks as they are depleted. Second, there is feedback, carried out after intermittent reviews to change the way the control task is carried on. Feedforward control will also be seen if the inventory management system uses, say, information from the sales department on anticipated demand changes or from the purchasing department if input prices or suppliers' lead times are expected to shift adversely.

Firms that fail to keep up with industry standards of inventory control suffer competitive disadvantage. Pentos is an example of a company not keeping up with its competitors in this critical area, see Box 14.6[12].

11. Replenishment procedures

Even small firms may stock thousands of different items. Consequently the inventory control system needs a set of rules to show when levels of each item are to be reviewed and refilled. We can look at four methods: fixed quantity, fixed interval, min-max and constrained budget. Of these, the first two are most common, the third is a variant of the first two combined and the fourth recognises the constraints imposed by cash budgets.

Fixed quantity procedure

The pattern of inventory level under this procedure is set out in Figure 14.6. We can note the following features:

• The inventory is replenished from time to time with a predetermined quantity of stock. This amount is chosen to be the most economic and depends on a combination of costs and prices that are further investigated in section **14**. Here, the new supplies are assumed to arrive in a single batch, producing a vertical step in the inventory line. In other cases, these supplies are delivered as they are made and the line has a rising slope instead, see section **15**.

The Pentos group, owners of Dillons bookshops and Ryman office supplies, went into receivership on 1 March 1995. The Dillons/Hatchards chain had been built up from one shop in 1977 to 140. It had 11 per cent of the UK book trade and was strong in the specialist sector, with some 40 per cent. Profit, however, had been hit by the 'high cost of leases and antiquated information technology'. Pentos still monitored stock levels manually.

By 3 March, the receivers announced acceptance of a purchase offer from Thorn EMI, owner of HMV. In addition to recognising overlap in the customer base of specialist bookshops and music stores, Thorn planned to transfer its management talent into development of Dillons.

Box 14.6 The fall of Pentos

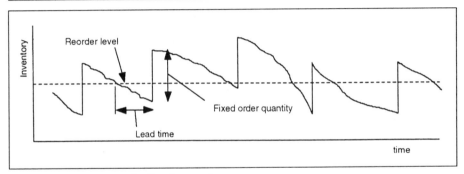

Figure 14.6 Inventory in fixed quantity system

- Replenishment occurs at irregular intervals depending on consumption.
- Orders for new supplies are triggered by the inventory falling to the *reorder level*. Delivery of these consignments follows the order by a delay called the *lead time*. The reorder level is set high enough to limit the risk of there being a stock-out before the next batch arrives. Risk arises from uncertainties in consumption during the lead time that is itself variable.

The fixed order procedure is best suited to items whose demand is relatively constant, although with some variation, as shown by the irregular slope of the inventory line in Figure 14.6. Calculations of economic order quantities are based on usage estimates. Further, since it is the inventory level that triggers fresh orders, the procedure requires a continuous record of this level. Perpetual inventory, aggregating each transaction as it occurs, is clearly the most effective. Alternatively, the stock count needs to be checked at intervals that are short compared with the expected intervals between reordering. Keeping permanent track of stocks of many items can be expensive but its cost falls if it is incorporated into other processing such as the checkouts of self-service stores. The bar-code system enables the organisation to keep detailed stock records at very low cost.

In cases where item value does not justify detailed control, simple physical methods have been devised to check stock levels. A bin of screws in a workshop may have the lower half of its inside surfaces painted red. This will warn that an order for new supplies should be sent out. This is a cheap variant of the *two-bin* system that, conventionally, has a separate container for the stock to be consumed during the lead time. Other interpretations include areas painted on the floor or lines around walls of storage bays. Small motorcycles have reserve tanks giving, say, a 60 kilometre range. In this way they avoid being fitted with fuel gauges.

Fixed interval procedure

The main features of this procedure are shown in Figure 14.7. They are:

- Orders for stock replacement are triggered by the passage of time and are independent of current stock levels. These are indicated along the time axis of the figure.
- The intervals between deliveries are intended to be constant, although there may be variations due to lead time uncertainties.
- Order quantities vary. They are aimed towards replenishment of the stock to a target level, making an allowance for the consumption that occurs during the lead time. In effect, the order replenishes the most recent demand.

383

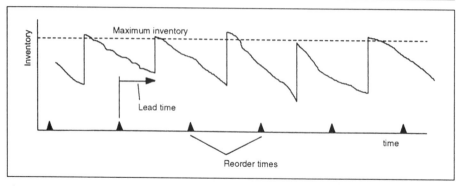

Figure 14.7 Inventory in fixed interval system

The fixed interval procedure is most appropriate when:

- Several items are ordered from one supplier simultaneously. These *joint-replenishment* items can, therefore, be bundled up to achieve economies. The supplier may offer discounts based on order value and there may be transport savings. The firm's own ordering costs may also be cut if orders are consolidated.
- Supplies are sent out at regular intervals. Many distributors have regular rounds whose intervals balance service quality with efficiency. Carpet wholesalers try to visit most areas in a region each week and many exporting companies make fortnightly or monthly runs to each target country throughout Europe.
- The firm does not operate a perpetual inventory monitoring. Order-placing work can be spaced out to smooth the load on the buying office. Clerks check each stock area on regular dates.

Difficulties with the procedure occur when the above arguments clash. For example, different suppliers may have different delivery patterns and joint replenishment items may have different optimal order intervals. Furthermore, seasonal demand variations may mean that the target maximum stock level is too high much of the time. Clearly, a shopkeeper knows to vary targets for Easter eggs or Christmas puddings.

Minimum–maximum procedure

One disadvantage of the fixed interval procedure is that it can result in small orders being placed. The min-max procedure avoids this by setting a minimum inventory above which orders are not placed. It works as follows (see Figure 14.8):

- Stock levels are reviewed at regular intervals.
- Replacement orders are made only if the stock has fallen below a defined minimum level. The figure shows orders placed at the first, third, fourth and sixth reviews. Consumption before the other two has been lower than average and a new order is not placed.
- When orders are placed, their size is judged to return the inventory to the target maximum.

Min-max combines features of both previous systems. Stock review is regular but the decision whether to place an order is contingent on the stock level prevailing at

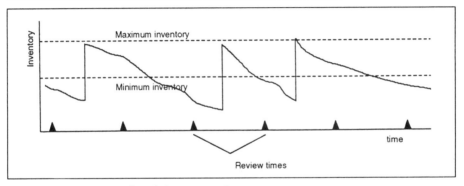

Figure 14.8 Inventory in minimum–maximum system

the time. If the most recent demand is the best indication of the future pattern, then the curtailing of orders in response to slackness is advantageous. Yet in other case the opposite will be true. Low drawings of an item from stock may simply mean that its main users are not engaged on the irregular work. Demand during the next period may return to normal and there may even be an element of catching up.

A related disadvantage is that the average stock levels may be too high. If the minimum holding is sufficient for one period, then why not apply this to all periods and operate the inventory according to the fixed interval procedure? As always, attention must be paid to achieving a balance between the cost of holding larger stocks and the administrative costs of placing more orders. This argument suggests that the min–max procedure is best suited to low value items where the cost of administering small orders outweighs any savings that should flow from holding lower average stocks.

Constrained budget

The constrained budget policy is less of a procedure applicable to each item and more a general policy that limits the overall level of stock holding. It is especially applicable in retailing where sales are discretionary. To say that an off-the-peg fashion store sells what it stocks may be a truism yet it emphasises the basis of inventory policy in such establishments. Analysis may suggest the optimal range of sizes to be stocked but, when it comes to achieving a balance among, say, coats, suits, shirts, woollens and accessories, buyers have discretion. To ensure a balanced offer in the shop, the budget allocates totals to each category.

Normally, the budget is financial, the sum being set by the owner or head office or, commonly, agreed with the insurers. Space also acts as a constraint. We can observe the varying allocation of shelf space in, for instance, supermarkets throughout the year. Many leading retailers limit their stocks to the amounts they can display plus a small back-up behind the scenes. Firms such as Marks and Spencer know that discretionary sales depend upon display and, therefore, space allocation. Items that are not selling well mean a loss of profit opportunity and their allocation is reduced, subject to the need to offer a balanced product range.

In industrial companies, the impact of budget constraints is not felt directly except in two circumstances. First, the firm may have liquidity problems such that there is a pressure to reduce order quantities whatever procedure is being used. Second, there is often a desire to delay supplies at the end of the financial year to massage the stock figures in the balance sheet.

12. ABC analysis

We have mentioned several times how inventory control policies need to be matched to the cost of the items being stocked. Their worth varies from many thousands to that of a paper clip. This is an example of the Pareto principle that contrasts the critical few and the trivial many. The ABC classification recognises this contrast and divides items into classes, usually three, to which different procedures are applied. It could be that there will be different review and order intervals or that some items will be managed under the fixed interval regime and others with fixed order.

The ABC classification, see Figure 14.9, creates an initial sort of stock items into groups according to the annual expenditure on each. The intention is to give greatest attention to those with the highest expenditure. These Category A items may only number some 10% or 15% of the total yet may account for more than 60% of the annual spend. Among the trivial items in Category C, numbering more than half the total, the expenditure may be less than 10%. Between these two extremes lies Category B, making up perhaps one third of the quantity and amounting to about the same proportion of the cash flow.

The procedure is as follows:

1 Estimate the annual amount to be spent on purchasing each item of inventory.
2 Rank all items in descending order of expenditure.
3 Divide the list into A, B and C categories at, say, the 15% and 45% points. This requires the exercise of judgement. It may be that there are 'break points' in the list to serve as a guide. Alternatively, certain products may be selected to serve as markers.
4 Adapt the list using other criteria if necessary. For instance, problems with delivery, the critical nature of a component, the need for special storage and limited shelf life, quality difficulties or scarcity may result in an upgrading.

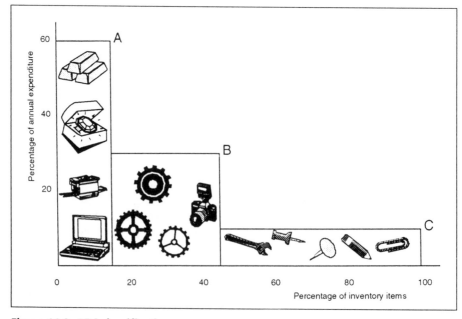

Figure 14.9 ABC classification

The analysis is then used to choose inventory control policies:

- The resources put into controlling the A items should be much greater than for C. Even a few months' extra inventory for A will be very expensive whereas for C it will not make much difference.
- Forecasts for A category demand require more care, especially if there is a risk of obsolescence.
- Security for the A category should be more rigorous. C items are ideal for min-max, including the kind of open two-bin system mentioned above.
- Control records for the A category should be kept in more detail. In a repair shop, for instance, the costs of A items should be allocated to orders but the C parts, kept in open bins, can be regarded as general expenses.

Items in the B category fall between A and C when it comes to policy, combining medium security and control rigour. On the other hand, it may be that the firm does not wish to differentiate this as a group and, therefore, is content with a two class system.

13. Independent inventory models

The basic EOQ model is perhaps the oldest and is certainly the best known inventory control policy. It is widely used as a basis for decisions. Yet its renown could be because it has been so widely taught in business courses. Its value may be overrated because it is very difficult to estimate the data that the formula requires. We shall consider the method here, with some variants, before going on to summarise these limitations.

The policy decisions that have to be arrived at in independent inventory control processes seek a balance among a number of costs. Besides the cost of the inventory itself, the significant items are those associated with placing, receiving and paying for orders with others associated with holding the stock itself. In the first instance, let us assume a constant price for the incoming material. Since a given annual amount has to be obtained and paid for anyway, we see that the main variable we have to consider is the amount ordered each time. Larger batches mean higher average inventory and higher holding costs, see Figure 14.10. On the other hand, larger batches mean fewer orders are placed each year so the ordering cost goes down. The costs that are sensitive to order quantity are shown in Box 14.7.

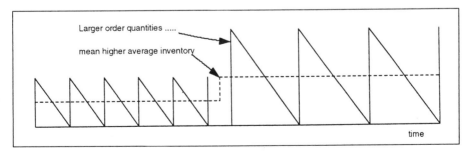

Larger order quantities .....

mean higher average inventory

time

Figure 14.10 The impact of order size on inventory

Costs which increase when order quantities increase and orders are placed less frequently	Costs which fall when order quantities increase and orders are placed less frequently
Capital invested in inventory	Ordering
Storage, monitoring and handling stock	Changeover costs between batches (if these can be avoided)
Storage space	
Insurance	Order tracking, receiving and, possibly, transport
Obsolescence due to design changes	Risk of supply interruption as low points are reached less often
Damage and deterioration	

Box 14.7 Costs affected by changes in order quantity

One difficulty becomes immediately apparent. Many of the costs in the list have to be imputed and averaged across a large number of items. Furthermore, order administration and set-up costs are frequently, in effect, fixed. Removing one order from a buyer's workload will have an imperceptible effect on administrative overhead. These are important practical problems. What is widely accepted, however, is the principle that there is an optimal cost position between ordering large quantities infrequently and small quantities very often, see Figure 14.11. Here, the holding cost is shown to rise approximately in proportion to the amount of inventory held while the ordering cost falls. The total cost reaches a minimum at a point known as the EOQ, the *economic order quantity*.

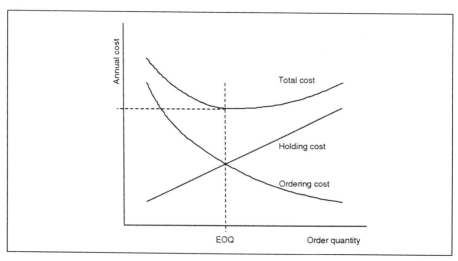

Figure 14.11 Costs as functions of order quantity

14. The basic EOQ model

In calculating the EOQ in a simple case, the following conditions and assumptions must apply:

- The demand rate is known and constant. This allows us to estimate the average inventory to be half the order quantity, see Figure 14.10.
- There are no quantity discounts.
- Orders arrive in one batch, so the upward steps in the inventory line are vertical.
- The lead time is known so that orders arrive just as stock is exhausted.
- Order placement and receiving costs are known and are independent of order quantity.
- Inventory holding costs are a fixed proportion of inventory value. There are no economies or diseconomies of scale in this function.

These assumptions underpin the lines in Figure 14.11. It happens that, with smooth curves of the form shown in the figure, the minimum value of the total cost occurs at the point that the constituent cost lines intersect. This then suggests the following method of determining the EOQ:

1 Create an expression for the holding cost as a function of order quantity.
2 Create an expression for the ordering cost as a function of order quantity.
3 Set the two costs to equal each other.
4 Solve to establish the EOQ.

We shall use the following variables:

S = Cost per order
C = Cost of each item of inventory
i = Carrying cost per period (usually one year) as a fraction of inventory value
D = Demand during the period (again, say, one year) in numbers of items
Q = Order quantity

1 Ordering cost
The annual ordering cost is found from the number of orders placed and the cost per order. Since the number placed is equal to D/Q, then:

$$\text{Ordering cost} = \left(\frac{D}{Q}\right) \times S$$

2 Holding cost
The annual holding cost is found from the average inventory value and the annual holding cost per pound of inventory. The former is equal to $C \times Q/2$, see Figure 14.10, and the latter is i. Hence:

$$\text{Holding cost} = i \times C\left(\frac{Q}{2}\right)$$

3 EOQ equation
The EOQ is found when the two costs are equal. That is:

$$\left(\frac{D}{Q}\right) \times S = i \times C \left(\frac{Q}{2}\right)$$

whence the EOQ is given by:

$$Q = \sqrt{\left(\frac{2DS}{iC}\right)}$$

For example, in a company where: ordering cost is estimated at £5; holding cost is 20% of stock value; annual demand is 1,000 units at a supplier's price of £20; the EOQ is found from:

$$EOQ = \sqrt{\left(\frac{2 \times 1000 \times 5}{0.2 \times 20}\right)} = 50 \text{ units}$$

Fifty units should last about $2\frac{1}{2}$ weeks and reordering should take place with this interval.

Reorder point (ROP)

Having decided how much stock to order, the second question for inventory control is when to place the order. The time between placing the order and receiving delivery is the lead time. This is based on suppliers' promises and the accumulation of experience. Given our assumption about steady, predictable demand, we can estimate the reorder point from the demand and lead time:

$$ROP = \text{Demand} \times \text{Lead time}$$

Weeks or days, or even hours, could serve as time units in this equation. Hence, if rolled steel sections are available on a 14-week lead time, and we use a particular size at the rate of 200 linear metres per week, the ROP should be set at a stock level of 14×200, or 2800 metres.

Depending on the importance of the item to the firm, and experience, it may be felt necessary to raise the ROP by an amount called the safety stock. When the delivery arrives, the *safety stock* will not normally have been used. On the other hand, it is there to allow for both demand and lead time variations. More details on the ROP appear in **16**.

15. Variations on the EOQ model

In **14** we set out several assumptions to simplify the EOQ presentation. It is possible to modify these to make the model more representative of different circumstances. We shall look at two practical cases – simultaneous production and quantity discounts.

Simultaneous production

We can examine the case where the replacement inventory is not received in one batch but 'trickles in'. This models a common situation where goods are supplied from another department in the same plant or organisation. Now, instead of resembling the sharp sawtooth graphs of Figure 14.10, the inventory line looks like that shown in 14.12.

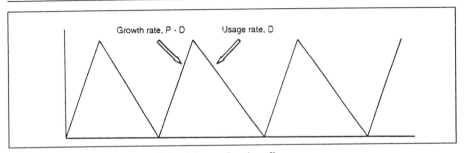

Figure 14.12 Inventory model with production flow

For a given order quantity Q, the average inventory under the revised assumption will be lower. This is because of the time it takes for the product to be supplied. If the production rate is P, the time for that production will be Q/P. Further, we know that the usage rate is D and so, during the production period, D × Q/P will be consumed. Hence the stock will rise by the order quantity *less* this consumption, which is $(Q - D \times Q/P)$.

Calculations of the EOQ under the new conditions follow the previous procedure. We shall only give the result here:

$$Q = \sqrt{\left[\frac{2DS}{iC} \times \frac{P}{P-D}\right]}$$

We can extend our previous numerical example. If we note that our supplier produces the items at the rate of 100 per week, which is 5,200 per year, then:

$$\text{EOQ} = \sqrt{\left[\frac{2 \times 1000 \times 5}{0.2 \times 20} \times \left(\frac{5200}{5200-1000}\right)\right]} = 56 \text{ units}$$

Price discounts

There is an endless assortment of price discount arrangements offered by suppliers. They range from reductions for large quantities of a single item to discounts for total order value, accumulated annual sales or even for repeat orders for the same items. Clearly, each case must be assessed on its merits. We shall confine ourselves to one example here, the price discount for larger quantities of a single item.

Let us say that the vendor lists three prices. Since the inventory holding cost is related to the value of orders placed, we can relate it to order quantity by the stepped line shown in Figure 14.13. Note that, besides the steps, the gradient of this line reduces at each price break to reflect the lower price per unit. The ordering cost is not affected by the discount structure.

The graphical representation of Figure 14.13 suggests that the EOQ lies at the second price break. This can be confirmed by sketching the complete cost-quantity curve. This, however, is unnecessary since the points for comparison are confined to the price breaks and any minima in the total cost curve. A full approach is as follows:

1 For each price, calculate an 'EOQ' as though the price were fixed for the full range of quantities. Having done so, check that this EOQ lies within the quantity range that qualifies for the given price. If it does not, reject it. Otherwise, accept it and calculate the corresponding annual total cost.

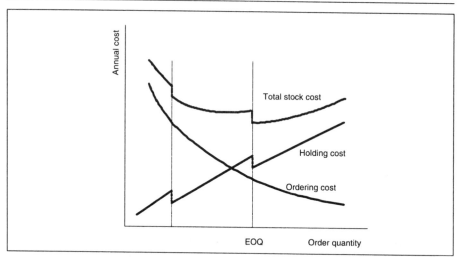

Figure 14.13 Costs related to order quantity: price breaks

2 Work out total costs for quantities just above each price break. This time, the purchase costs have to be included, since they vary among the price breaks.
3 Choose the quantity corresponding to the lowest value of the total cost function. This is the EOQ for this item.

Example

Mineral fibre ceiling panels have a basic price of £6. As is common in the distribution trade for building materials, quantity discounts apply. Here, there is a 10% discount for orders over 1,000, those over 2,000 are at list less 15% and over 10,000 it is list less 20%. A distributor estimates the ordering cost to be £25 per order and the cost of holding this type of stock to be 25% per annum. The current demand is 1,000 panels per month, which is 12,000 per year.

The first step is to compute 'EOQs' for each price range. These are:

$$Q_{list} = \sqrt{\left[\frac{2 \times 12000 \times 25}{0.25 \times 6}\right]} = 632 \text{ units}$$

$$Q_{>1000} = \sqrt{\left[\frac{2 \times 12000 \times 25}{0.25 \times 5.4}\right]} = 666 \text{ units}$$

$$Q_{>2000} = \sqrt{\left[\frac{2 \times 12000 \times 25}{0.2 \times 5.1}\right]} = 685 \text{ units}$$

$$Q_{>10000} = \sqrt{\left[\frac{2 \times 12000 \times 25}{0.25 \times 4.8}\right]} = 707 \text{ units}$$

Clearly, only the first of these applies here. The next step is to compute the total annual purchase, ordering and holding costs for Q_{list} and at the three price breaks. These are set out in the following table:

Quantity	Price £	Annual purchase cost £	Annual ordering cost £	Annual holding cost £	Total annual cost £
707	6.00	72,000	474	474	72,948
1000	5.40	64,800	300	675	65,775
2000	5.10	61,200	150	1275	62,625
10000	4.80	57,600	24	6000	63,624

It can be seen that the 15% discount for order quantities of 2,000 panels looks attractive. This means that orders will be placed every two months.

16. The reorder point

A brief note on the reorder point was given in **14**. There, as in the rest of our discussion, it was assumed that the system behaviour was regular and the inventory could be forecast. After all, in figuring out the reorder point, the inventory manager is, in effect, making a forecast of likely demand during the lead time. To allow for errors, a safety stock is added to the reorder level so that the inventory line looks like Figure 14.14.

How is the safety stock decided? If experience and judgement of buyers and inventory managers are used as the basis, its size will inevitably tend to increase. This is because the purpose of the inventory system is to give service, either to customers or to other departments within the firm. A stock-out, lack of service, is to be avoided as far as possible. On the other hand, it can be seen that the safety stock directly increases the average stock on hand. In a fixed order system it will rise from $Q/2$ to $Q/2 + SS$. The safety stock is, therefore, not cost free. As with the

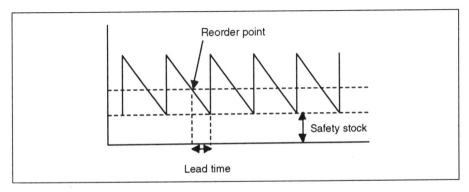

Figure 14.14 Inventory line with safety stock

393

rest of the inventory, it has to be paid for, stored, checked and eventually discarded when obsolete.

Let us look a little more closely at the pattern of demand during the lead time. Clearly, it is reasonable to expect the mean demand rate to remain the same as in the recent past. Furthermore, we could forecast a maximum demand during the period. If this can be done, the reorder point should be set to cover this maximum. The possible stock movements during the lead time are then as shown in Figure 14.15. In practice we will rarely be able to establish a maximum demand with certainty, we can only estimate probabilities. We must accept that there will be occasions when demand exceeds the maximum and a stock-out occurs.

Recognising this problem, inventory managers establish service level targets. If a retail store is to maintain a reputation for keeping a wide range of goods, it will set a service level of, say, 98%. This means that 98% of the product lines are on the shelves at any time. In setting the service level, a balance has to be struck between the cost of achieving a high service level and the cost of not having the item available. Box 14.8 summarises the issues.

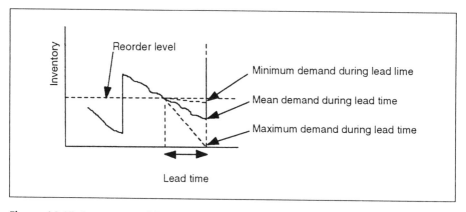

Figure 14.15 Inventory with uncertain demand during lead time

Higher levels of safety stock are preferred when ...	Lower levels of safety stock are preferred when ...
The cost, including opportunity cost, of stock-out is high.	The cost of a stock-out is low; alternatives are available or back-up can be obtained.
Ordering frequency is high so the risk is met repeatedly.	Orders are placed infrequently so the stock rarely dips into the safety zone.
The cost of carrying safety stock is low.	Stockholding costs are high.
Demand is variable and uncertain.	Demand varies little and is expected to remain steady.
Lead times are long.	Lead times are short.

Box 14.8 Factors affecting safety stock policy

Table 14.4 Demand and probability

Demand per month	Probability
120	0.05
140	0.20
160	0.50
180	0.20
200	0.05

It is possible to go beyond simple judgement to set safety stock levels if there are enough data to attach probabilities to lead time demand. Table 14.4 shows the pattern of demand for an item established over recent months. Since the goods are boxed in 20s, the numbers are rounded to the nearest box size. The question is as follows. If the lead time for delivery is one month, what should be the reorder level?

Evidently the most likely demand during the lead time is 160 and this could be a sensible point to trigger a new order. Yet, using this policy, a stock-out would be encountered once in every four replenishments. To cut this to 5%, the reorder point must be set at 180. This means that the firm would be carrying a safety stock of 20 items and the demand for 200, leading to a stock-out, would occur on only 5% of the reordering occasions.

Rather than make detailed appraisals of the demand–probability relationship, the statistical distribution of demand can be estimated from recent data. It follows the normal distribution. Computer stock control systems can maintain up-to-date information on this distribution for each stock item and therefore continually adjust the reorder point in the light of given service level targets.

Leading companies adopt ABC analysis to discriminate among inventories that should have different service levels. For example, ICI's engineering division purchases each year more than £1,000 million of materials, equipment components and other supplies. Items are categorised according to the effect of stock-out and hence are managed to different service level targets.

- Category A items are those whose absence would cause a plant shut-down. Examples in the limestone quarries include spare drive motors and their components, conveyor belting and so on. In the salt mines, there are many items of equipment critical to safety. These include lifting cables and other hoist components, many of which are on long lead times. A fault in any of these demands an immediate replacement.
- Category B items are close to those in A except that it is recognised that the consequences of a stock-out are less severe and problems can be avoided at some cost. Service targets of 99% are set for these items.
- Category C items are covered by 95% service targets. The consequences of a stock-out are not so serious. Sometimes, alternatives can be used. Otherwise, the result can be extra administrative and transport costs as an order is speeded up. As one buyer reported, 'In the end, we can always send out to B&Q!'

Many retailers and service companies rely on the back-up of regional stockists to cover the vast range of components and spares that may be demanded and for which they cannot carry any level of stock. Halford's service centres carry spares for popular cars and endeavour to obtain any other within an hour. Within the same industry, car assemblers support their distributors with rapid delivery systems. VW has its own aircraft and Rolls Royce claims to be able to supply a spare for any car it has ever made to anywhere in the world. These policies need to be supported by highly effective information systems.

Before we leave this discussion of the impact of demand variations, we should recognise that the lead time itself is variable and uncertain. While this adds complexity to the records and calculations, its impact is similar to the above discussion. Safety stock needs to be held to cover the risk of lead time extensions. Firms can respond to some of the problem by gathering up-to-date information on lead times in different supply sectors. It is to be expected that these vary throughout economic cycles and summary data is published regularly in trade magazines. Good buyers will maintain regular contact with their normal suppliers and issue warnings of changes into the inventory control system.

17. Comment on inventory models

The models presented in this chapter are basic and many extensions and adaptations are possible to suit different circumstances. One difficulty with all of them is that their application depends on the use of data of dubious quality. This is particularly true of values used for estimating ordering and stockholding costs. Weaknesses include the marginal effects of small changes and the assumption that holding cost relationships are linear. Clearly, the formulae can be modified to respond to the problems, but the advantages of doing so are doubtful. The general principles, however, hold. These are:

- There is likely to be an economic order quantity and it is worthwhile trying to estimate it. Since the total cost curve tends to be flat around its minimum point, errors in estimates of the EOQ will have only minor effect. Depending on their circumstances, firms are likely to use some variant of the EOQ formula and then modify it by judgement and trial and error. In the light of the modern pressure to reduce average inventory holdings, pushing levels down to slightly below the ideal EOQ will have only minor cost effects and the released capital could yield greater benefits elsewhere. In another approach, reducing the cost of placing orders, such as by setting up long-term contracts with call-offs, feeds directly through to the EOQ formula and therefore reduces inventory.
- The fixed quantity reorder procedure, which uses the EOQ formula, is attractive in that it directly addresses the question of the cost of holding stocks. It is not, however, applicable in all situations. The expense of operating the perpetual inventory system that underpins the process, the lack of past data and the uncertain effects of seasonal demand changes are just three reasons why some firms operate other procedures for at least some of their inventory.
- Safety stocks are required because companies do not know in advance what demand during the lead time is likely to be. Again, procedures based on historical data will suggest safety stock levels corresponding to service targets. Companies will take these as a starting point and modify them in the light of

experience. The models suggest that policies to reduce stock will increase the frequency of stock-out. Whether this is tolerable will depend on the items and how they are used. ABC analysis will help in this decision.

- Reorder points are, in the first instance, determined independently of the EOQ. Yet small EOQs result in frequent orders and more regular exposure to the risk of stock-out. Therefore safety stock levels may be increased, countering some of the benefit of the reduced EOQ.

- The optimisation of independent demand inventory is a difficult task. Many firms have to face it, especially at the end that deals directly with retail customers. Upstream from this point, however, there is a trend to share information between different stages of the supply chain. Thus each supplier in the chain is presented with derived or dependent demand from its immediate customer business. The effect of this conversion is that JIT, MRP and related systems are brought into play. Safety stocks are supplanted by information; control replaces buffers.

Fast response distribution systems yield competitive advantage. The stock–service relationship can be balanced more effectively. One trick learnt by leading companies is to delay customisation to as late as possible in the chain. This means that both the upstream dependent systems and the independent demand inventory operate with less variety and hence lower cost. Carpet supplies are an example of operating with very little stock.

The large rolls of broadloom carpet on display in carpet shops give the impression of high variety and quick service. Yet most are dummies, consisting of a single loop of carpet stapled to a cardboard former. Most customers have their purchases delivered and fitted so the stores' main function is to take orders. Deliveries from regional warehouses are made on a weekly schedule.

For the lower-cost tufted carpets, changes in the production system have separated carpet making and printing. To reduce lead times, firms keep intermediate stocks of base colours such as grey and beige. The low batch sizes needed for printing mean that stocks of patterned carpets are topped up regularly. This manufacturing and distribution strategy allows a wide pattern range to be offered without the high risk of holding safety stocks.

Case study: The Home Shopping Bureau

We saw in **12.19** how supervisors in the telephone service bureau coped with sudden peaks in demand by reducing the time spent with each caller, delaying rest breaks and calling for reserve staff. Of particular value to the supervisors is the prominent display showing the length of the queue at any moment.

Outcomes are reviewed at three levels. First, each week, the supervisors receive information on operators' performance levels including the times that each individual takes to handle calls. They are expected to check on operators whose performance appears to be out of line. Difficulties are usually resolved by discussion. It is important not to over-stress the times as the quality of customer service is vital. The trick, at peak times, is to give good quality while maintaining an efficient tempo.

At the second level, the departmental manager is responsible for achieving service standards within cost constraints. Enough staff must be allocated to the operation to enable more than 99% of calls to be answered within 30 seconds but this has to be done within operating cost budgets.

The manager plans the allocation of staff according to latest demand forecasts. Beyond taking into account hourly, daily and seasonal fluctuations, they are adjusted for growth trends in the business. These forecasts are updated weekly. In addition, the manager has available summarised information on costs, staff performance against standards, average time to answer calls, average length of call and the number of enquirers who hung up before their calls were answered. Using this information, the manager discusses the weekly programme with the supervisors.

The third level of control is with the divisional manager who receives summarised performance information each week on all departments including both telephone and mail order. Problems and possible changes are discussed with the departmental managers. Additionally, the divisional manager works with other departments on methods of improving the ordering activity in the longer term. These include: changes to the information system; new order processing methods; improved query handling; and clarifying instructions and information given to customers. The divisional manager must also consider increasing use of the telephone, the possibilities of using Fax or E-mail, and new marketing policies. Some new products, such as insurance and other financial services, may require specialist advice at the point of contact.

Questions

1 *Describe the different patterns of control that are used in the management of the order bureau.*
2 *To what extent does the control guarantee first class service every time? List any other objectives that are aimed at.*
3 *What further areas of activity could be monitored? Explain how and why you would collect and use data in these areas.*

References

1. Anthony, R.N. (1988) *The Management Control Function* Boston Mass., The Harvard Business School Press p. 27
2. Awdry, W. (1961) *Thomas the Tank Engine* London, Edmund Ward
3. Anthony, op.cit. p. 37
4. De Toni, A. and Panizzolo, R. (1993) 'Operations management techniques in intermittent and repetitive manufacturing: a conceptual framework' *International Journal of Operations and Production Management* **13.5** pp. 12–32
5. Cohen, N., Kelly, J. and Urry, M. (1995) 'The Back Office: when things go wrong, the first place to look' *Financial Times* 28 February, p. 2
6. Donkin, R. (1995) 'When preservation takes precedence over profit' *Financial Times* 1 March, p. 13
7. Burcher, P.G. (1992) 'Effective capacity planning' *Management Services* October, pp. 22–25
8. Spreadbury, A. (1994) 'Manufacturing Resource Planning' in Storey, J. (ed.) *New Wave Manufacturing Strategies* London, Paul Chapman
9. Phillips, S. and Dunkin, A. (1990) 'King Customer' *Business Week* 12 March, p. 91
10. Based on a case study, Armistead, C. (1985) 'Operations control for emergency services in Greater Manchester' in C. Voss et al. (eds) *Operations Management in Service Industries and the Public Sector* Chichester, Wiley
11. Source: A private communication.
12. Buckingham, L. (1995) 'David-like attack distracted Maher from main task' *The Guardian* 2 March, p. 22, and 'Thorn plans new chapter for Dillons chain' *The Guardian* 3 March, p. 17

15

QUALITY MANAGEMENT

Chapter objectives

When you have finished studying this chapter, you should be able to:

- Define quality and recognise the difficulties encountered with the many definitions in use; show how meanings may differ between goods and services.

- Explain the importance of quality both in terms of costs and in creating competitive advantage.

- Identify the costs of quality and show how an organisation can benefit by changing the balance among them.

- Apply control models to quality issues; compare these issues as they arise in various production technologies.

- Outline the contributions made over the past 50 years by leading advocates of the quality message; identify the important elements of the work of Deming and others.

- Evaluate the contribution of product and process standards and suggest why the latter have gained ground at the expense of the former.

- Define and explain the key features of Total Quality Management; outline its limitations in practical application.

- Show how quality concepts can be applied in the management of service functions and in relating design to operations.

INTRODUCTION

Over the past twenty years or so, the critically significant importance of quality has been recognised as industry after industry has been challenged by innovation and international competition. While manufacturing and service organisations who could not keep up have suffered in the new climate, those who have absorbed the quality message have prospered. Success has bred success as customers respond to rising standards and have their demands satisfied like never before.

Companies whose products fall below the new specifications and do not carry industry standard warranties have only themselves to blame. Quality, as we shall see, requires good management to mobilise the whole organisation in its achievement.

The discussion of quality is divided between two chapters. This one deals with policy issues, that is definitions, standards, organisation and mobilisation in manufacturing and service settings. The next chapter deals with tools and techniques of problem analysis, change and control. The two areas form a whole such that to discuss one without the other is somewhat artificial. There is, therefore, some overlap where necessary.

1. Quality definitions

People use different definitions of quality in different contexts. Consider the following examples:

> A European company ordered some semiconductor components from a Japanese supplier. The order stated something like, '10,000 items required, with a defect rate of 0.02%'. The consignment duly arrived in two containers. The larger carried 9,998 good components and the smaller held the two defects, clearly labelled. The supplier could not understand why the customer wanted the defects but they were sent all the same[1].
>
> In the recession of 1991, a traditional, family-run clothes shop near my home closed down. Its place was taken by a 'Factory Seconds' chain store selling rejected textiles, mainly clothing. Prices are much lower and the new shop has a brasher and cheaper image compared with its predecessor. There were complaints. The local newspaper carried letters grumbling about the way such shops have lowered the tone of the town and the quality of the shops in the centre[2].

What do the above examples say about quality? Are there such things as high quality and low quality? Is the bespoke tailor better than the factory seconds store?

In general use, we tend to speak of high quality as being superior to low quality. In so doing, we imply that some attribute, such as designed life, has a higher value to us. A pair of shoes is, in these terms, of high quality if it gives five years wear instead of two. Yet, what of the people who do not want shoes to last five years? To these customers, fitting the fashion may rank more highly than fitting the foot! In short, they prefer a different combination of attributes. Clearly, in any product, there are many. Customers search for those that most closely fit what they want.

We can summarise the overlapping ideas about quality as follows:

- *Quality personally defined*
  This perspective, preferred by marketing managers, looks for quality definition through the eyes of the customer. It is particularly critical in the delivery of personal services, where it is expected that each customer comes along with individual needs and criteria. Yet the variety of interpretations that the definition implies poses a problem for mass producers. They must interpret varied needs into more formal standards when they design their products and delivery systems.
- *Quality in use*
  Many individually specified attributes relate to the use to which a product is to be put. These include *performance* (will it do the job?), *reliability* (under individually defined conditions), *serviceability* (again, after particular use) and *fit* (especially the aesthetic relation to other products to which it will be related). *Safety* is another feature that many would include, although it is not easy for individuals to make detailed appraisals. Government, industry and independent organisations provide some data for some products, see Box 15.1[3].

> 'Some cars are better than others in protecting their occupants in a crash. You can substantially reduce your risk of injury by a sensible choice of car.
>
> 'To help you with your choice, we have drawn up tables that show ... how well particular models have protected their occupants ...
>
> 'No doubt the size of car you choose depends on a number of interrelated features, but having decided on a size of car, you should compare the safety ratings ... and choose accordingly.'

Box 15.1 Quality as safety

- *Quality as grade or features*
  In referring to quality, many customers are using the term to mean *grade*. For instance, Rhodes' *Carron Lodge* Cheshire Cheese (First Prize, Nantwich Show, 1994) is a higher grade (said to be better quality) and more expensive than a basic product. The range of *features*, such as the number of cycle options on a washing machine, is another aspect of this confusion.
- *Quality to guide processes*
  Operations managers need standards, preferably defined by or agreed with the customer, to provide clear yardsticks. They can then decide whether they have achieved their targets of 'getting it right first time.' In this view, if different bottling plants all produce their cola drinks to the specifications laid down by each syrup maker, then their quality is satisfactory. Customer brand preferences are not factors in this assessment.
- *Quality as product attribute*
  For some, the notion of quality is an attribute of the product itself, independent of the use for which it is intended. Legal standards for marmalade, sausages, petrol and electric cable are defined within such frameworks.

While there are similarities between manufactured goods and services, other ideas come into play in the assessment of the quality of the latter or, indeed, the service aspects of manufactured goods. Zeithamal and others[4] give five factors which are important in service quality assessment:

- *Reliability* – giving the promised service precisely and dependably.
- *Responsiveness* – helping customers promptly with their varying needs.
- *Tangible factors* – the condition of facilities and the appearance of staff.
- *Assurance* – the demeanour and knowledge of staff and the way they convey trust and confidence.
- *Empathy* – caring and offering individual attention.

A working definition

Not only are the above definitions in common use but they are often mixed within the same usage. We need, therefore, a more usable definition of quality that combines attributes and standards with the purpose to which the product is to be put. As Crosby argues, 'Quality has to be defined as conformance to requirements, not as goodness... The setting of requirements may simply involve only answers to questions. Requirements, like measurements, are communications.'[5]

In stressing *conformance to requirements,* Crosby is emphasising two features. First, quality is about matching, that is conforming to, some standards. Secondly, these standards, or requirements, have to be established and communicated in some way from their origin, be it customers or some other external source. If we are talking about individual service, it may be possible to adjust operations for each client. On the other hand, mass production and free markets work because standards have been created and imposed across whole industries.

Quality is, therefore, about setting standards and conforming to them. We shall examine these aspects throughout the chapter. A formal definition, adopted by both the British Standards Institute and the American Society for Quality Control[6], captures the range of issues:

The totality of features and characteristics of a product or service that bear on its ability to satisfy stated or implied needs.

2. The importance of quality

The story of a supplier sorting defects from good items emphasises how Japanese companies gained competitive advantage from supplying quality goods. The remarkable progress of the Japanese consumer goods manufacturers is further, more solid evidence. Quality is a strategic factor that works through virtuous cycles to build market share and reduce costs. Figure 15.1 illustrates some key relationships. The *quality improvement* area of the diagram has two zones related to product improvement, making it more suited to customers' needs, and process improvements, ensuring better conformance to standards. Improved quality increases demand and enables the firm to charge higher prices for the value differentiation that it offers. An important second-order effect is the way customers learn about quality and continue to feed back their demands into product design. Achieving customer satisfaction is not, therefore, a one-off process; rising standards create demand for even higher standards in the competitive market place. Within the organisation, process improvements have direct impact on costs and also show feedback as the habit of continual development is self-reinforcing. Lastly, the increased profits both provide the funds for, and justify policies devoted to, quality improvement.

Managers in Japanese firms have recognised these interactions since the 1950s[7]. It may be difficult, initially, to accept that improving quality will lead to improved productivity but the fewer delays, mistakes and rework more than pay for themselves in terms of rises in net output.

Deming used a simple example to make the point[8]. He referred to a production line running with 11% defective output, a level that the management was unaware of. The line was well controlled, showing consistent performance over time. The main cause of the defects was that both operators and inspectors did not understand sufficiently the kind of work that was acceptable or unacceptable. To them, 11% was normal. The manager and two supervisors made a special study and, in seven weeks, came up with a practical definition of work standards. This was posted for everyone to see. Defects fell to 5%. The corresponding benefits, shown in Table 15.1, were achieved at very little cost. Productivity rose 6% and, as Deming noted, 'Customer happier. Everybody happier.'

Defects are not free. Someone is paid to make them, resources are used and, as Deming's example shows, opportunities of making saleable products are lost.

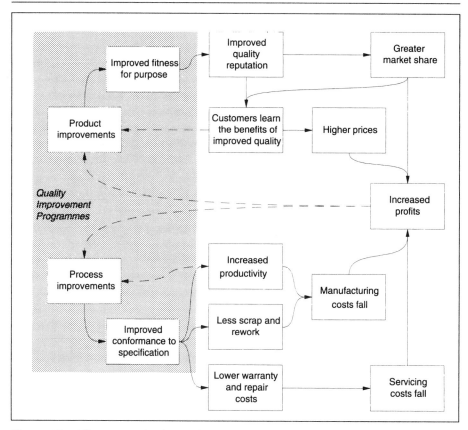

Figure 15.1 Virtuous cycles in quality improvement

Table 15.1 Quality up, costs down

Item	Defects before change: 11%	Defects after change: 5%
Total cost	100	100
Number of good items	89	95
Cost per item	1.12	1.05

There is a danger if this argument is over-stressed. We must not interpret the example as suggesting, in Crosby's words, that *Quality is Free*[9]. The reasoning should be that there are many operational situations where some improvement in quality will bring reduced operating costs, so much so that there will be nett gains to the organisation.

Service operations often echo the manufacturing line of Deming's case. Quality standards are ill defined and consequently difficult to implement. At the same time, their effect can be critical in winning and holding on to customers. As cost pressure reduces the firm's service-offering capacity, so competitive forces and the experience of good quality intensify demands, as in Figure 15.1. The solution is not to spend more and do more but to be more effective. Quality must be seen through the eyes of the customer who only recognises what he or she *gets out* of the service process, not what the firm *puts in*.

Why provide quality service? There are good reasons. The satisfied customer will not only do more business in the future but will recommend the firm to others. On the other hand, the dissatisfied customer will not only directly reduce profitability but will deter new customers. In addition to these interactions with customers, poor service is demoralising for staff as they spend time handling complaints and are demotivated when nothing seems to be done to relieve them. Lister refers to data on the effects of poor service[10]. Depending on the industry:

- For each complaint there may be 26 unresolved problems.
- Of those who do complain, between 50 and 70% will do business again if their complaints are handled effectively.
- Dissatisfied customers will tell between 10 and 20 people whereas satisfied customers tell between 3 and 5.
- Customers stop doing business for the reasons shown in Figure 15.2.

The importance of quality is to recognise that, although '... everyone is doing his best,' the 'best efforts are not sufficient.'[11] As in other fields, without guidance, focused on consistently improving quality, best efforts cause a random walk. (In a random walk, each step has a uniform size but its direction is independent of all the others, see Figure 15.3.)

3. Costs of quality

The costs that are incurred as a result of poor quality and those which are spent to prevent these costs are together referred to as the *costs of quality*. They are often

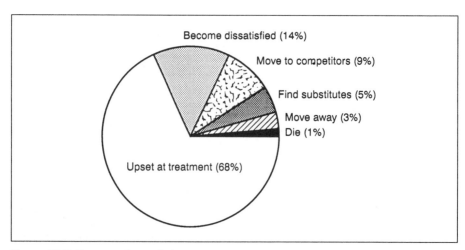

Figure 15.2 Reasons for quitting

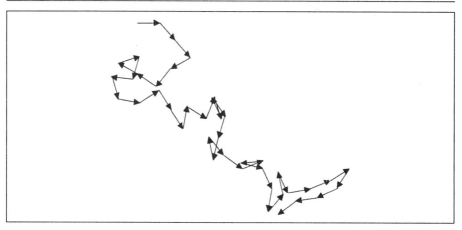

Figure 15.3 A random walk

divided into three categories, failure, appraisal and prevention. We can summarise them in the following list:

- *Failure*
  This category can be split into failures that occur within the process and those that occur, or become apparent, after the product is supplied to the customer. In both cases, failure means that the product has not reached intended standards.
  Internal failure costs include:
  - Costs of producing items that are scrapped or downgraded to be sold as second quality;
  - Costs of rectification of defects to raise the items to the specified standard;
  - Waste of time and materials incurred at all stages including design and planning as well as manufacture and supply;
  - Re-inspection and investigation of causes.
  External failure costs include:
  - Repair, extra servicing, replacement under warranty;
  - Extra handling of returned items;
  - Loss of goodwill through any of the above and customers' complaints in general;
  - Consequential losses that may result in litigation and damages;
  - Financial compensation paid to customers but not as a result of litigation;
  - Further inspection, investigation and administration.

- *Appraisal*
  This group of costs is related to the assessment of all incoming materials, components and services and all processes within the organisation's value chain to ensure that standards are achieved. Specifically, there are:
  - Inspection of all materials whether bought in or produced by intermediate processes;
  - Final inspection of products and services;
  - Quality audits to assess whether the quality control system is operating satisfactorily;

405

- Vendor rating, part of which involves a quality audit of suppliers' standards and procedures;
- Equipment and processes explicitly devoted to inspection;
- The costs of quality appraisal, control systems and organisation.

- *Prevention*
Prevention costs refer to the investments made in quality before production begins. They relate to the setting up and maintenance of processes that are aimed at preventing failures while also limiting appraisal costs. Frequently called *quality assurance*, the prevention costs cover:
  - Identification of customer requirements for quality and identifying or producing relevant specifications to cover all components, assemblies and services;
  - Creating the system to optimise the balance between prevention, appraisal and failure costs;
  - Time and effort required to build-in quality to all products. The cost of quality research, good design and prototyping is included;
  - Training of all staff to appreciate their own contribution to quality, especially failure prevention;
  - Administration of quality programmes.

As explained in **2**, the failure to control quality results in extra costs. Put another way, the failure to plan and manage quality means that too much is spent on the total of the quality costs listed above. Almost certainly the excess will lie in the *failure* category. Gador quotes the experience of Tennant, the world's largest manufacturer of floor sweepers and scrubbers[12].

A steering committee of six senior managers was set up to redirect corporate culture towards quality and productivity. As shown in Figure 15.4, the change resulted in a substantial reduction in quality costs and a shift in the balance of these costs towards prevention and away from correction.

This is an example of a more general relationship between the ability to match quality to customers' expectations and the direct quality costs. This is shown in Figure 15.5. Where the quality capability is low, failure costs are high and dominate the total. With improving capability, both failure and appraisal costs can be cut, resulting in better performance overall. The change takes time and the response is itself dynamic. Consequently, the organisation should not seek a stable optimum position. The costs of quality should continue to fall as it learns new approaches within an ever more exacting environment.

The two main thrusts of a quality plan are, therefore, prevention (quality assurance) and appraisal (inspection and control). We have seen that failures are to be avoided. This is the so-called ZD or zero-defects policy although it should be recognised that the cost of avoiding *all failures* may be prohibitive and the technology to do so may not be available. In such cases of failure, the organisation must make an effective response, especially if the problem occurs as, or after, the product is supplied.

4. Quality and the control model

Quality runs through the whole production process. The need for integration becomes more apparent as organisations learn to prevent failures and incorporate this learning into standard procedures. Shifting to prevention is a shift towards

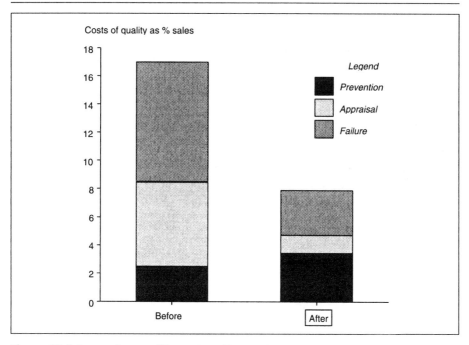

Figure 15.4 Improving quality costs at Tennant

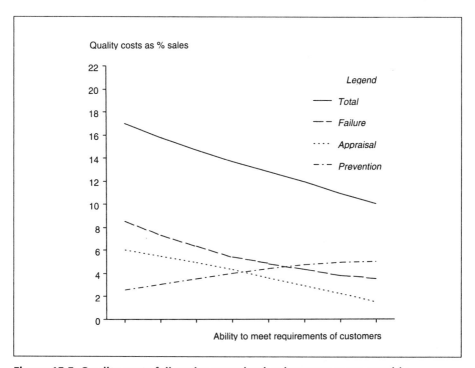

Figure 15.5 Quality costs fall as the organisation becomes more capable

407

feedforward control as it implies that getting the inputs to each stage right will have a significant effect on their outcomes. Choosing the appropriate form of control is not only relevant to the timing of interventions but also has an effect on employee motivation. Finished product inspection has an important function, yet if it is separated from operators and staffed by a separate group of employees, the former group will come to regard it as merely a burden that restricts their ability to earn bonuses.

In the quality system we see all three forms of control at work:

- *Feedforward quality control*
  This covers all the inputs to the production process, from materials and components, whose standards are measured by agreed means, to design, specification and planning processes whose effectiveness has such a great impact on outcomes.

- *Concurrent quality control*
  Covering the monitoring and continual adjustment of work as it takes place, concurrent control is needed to ensure that defective parts are never passed on to the next stage. Tools of quality management, see Chapter 16, and recognised standards come into use here.

  While being concerned with monitoring work 'as it happens', prudent managers will focus their efforts at points where defects and rework make a substantial difference. Adopting ideas from Optimised Production Technology, **12.6**, inspection is best carried out:
  - *Before*: costly operations; operations on expensive or sensitive machines; operations that temporarily disguise defects; irreversible assembly or installation; storage.
  - *After*: operations with high defect risk; sequences where inspection can easily be built in as the last step.

- *Feedback quality control*
  Inspecting the quality of finished products is carried out by all prudent organisations. Feedback data should be drawn from more sources, however. These include orders for spares, investigation of all complaints and product returns, debriefing of the sales force, studies of products in use, and evidence of brand loyalty (or the lack of it).

5. The impact of production technology

It is unfortunate that effects of some production technologies run counter to the desire to mobilise all employees in quality improvement. Deskilling tasks, a process that ran alongside the development of both mass production lines and mass service operations, changed the approach to quality. Concentrating on establishing inspection as the most important means of ensuring quality output from such facilities had two deleterious outcomes. First, the presence of the inspectors themselves meant that the production workers became less interested in building quality into their own work and discussing the issue with their colleagues. The fact that the role of inspector was often a promoted grade only reinforced the alienation. Secondly, the inspection task began to be surrounded with its own mystique. Staff in the 'Inspection Department' wore white coats to emphasise the scientific nature of their roles. They used special equipment to assess quality and their analysis and reports were couched in the technical language of statistical process control. The precision measuring equipment had, of course, to be housed in a separate room. In service operations, inspectors would require separate access to customers or other means of observing the service delivery activity.

The coercive nature of inspection often represented the lack of trust between managers and workers. Beynon quotes a senior shop steward at Ford's Merseyside plant shortly after production had started in the 1960s. Referring to supervisors who had been transferred from the main plant at Dagenham, the steward said, 'They thought they could treat us like dirt, them. We were just dirty scousers who'd crawled in off the docks out of the cold. We'd never even seen a car plant before and these sods had been inside one since they were knee high.'[13]

Similarly, in France of the 1950s and 1960s, immigrants obtained the dirtiest jobs in industries such as car assembly. Etcherelli has a supervisor, indicating Algerian track workers, emphasise to an inspector, 'Listen, you are here to control *their* work.'[14]

Specialised, efficient and even necessary as these inspection methods may be, organisations have come to recognise the illogicality of separating the responsibilities of doing a task and taking care of its quality. Contrast the above examples with the long period of training and team building which have typified the start up of the new United Kingdom car plants of Honda, Nissan and Toyota.

The separation of quality responsibility from operating tasks has been less of a problem in job shops, process plants and professional service. Job shops and professional service maintain the intimate relationship between the individual provider and the output and it is natural that quality is built in to the process. Continuous process plants have quality embedded in the work in a different way. It comes from the design of the plant itself and it could be said that all staff are, in effect, quality controllers. These points are drawn together in Box 15.2 which brings out the difficulties of delivering quality in key sections of business and industry, namely mass production and mass service.

6. Leaders in attitude change

Perhaps more than in other fields of management, the move of quality to the top of the operations agenda has been associated with the names of experts who have moulded the attitudes of a generation of managers. Interest in quality as a competitive weapon took root in the West with the tide of imports of Japanese consumer products. The ideas then spread from the factory into all organisations from service businesses and non-profit organisations to government operations and administration. We shall pick out a few names of advocates of this slow process.

W. Edwards Deming

In the late 1930s, Deming was responsible for mathematics and sampling at the United States Bureau of Census. His methods of statistical control achieved great improvements in the productivity and quality of the 1940 census. This work led to invitations to train industrialists and military personnel and he worked with many thousands of US military engineers and technicians to improve quality. In 1947, he was in Japan with the government of occupation to prepare a census there. At that time, the Japanese business community became so impressed by the standards of American military equipment that it invited Deming, in 1950, to advise on industrial recovery. While Deming based his work on advanced statistical methods, his contribution lay in presenting the ideas in a simple way. The results were both impressive and influential, so much so that eventually the Deming prize was created. It remains Japan's leading quality prize.

Technology	Relationship between task and person	Who is responsible for quality?
Intermittent manufacture		
Unit and small batch (project and job shop)	Integrated in the craft skills and experience of the worker.	Mainly the person who carries out each step of the process.
Repetitive manufacture		
Large batch and mass	Deskilling and lack of training means the individual takes little responsibility for any aspect of the job.	While the employee remains responsible in theory, lack of involvement and the inability to trace many problems back to the individual mean that quality is taken over by inspectors and quality control systems.
Continuous	Integrated into the process and plant design.	The same person or group is responsible for all aspects of output which cannot be separated.
Personal Service		
Professional service	Provider, customer and task closely interlinked.	Professional ethos emphasises personal responsibility.
Mass service	Frequently suffers from deskilling, lack of training and low expectations of customers.	Taken over by inspectors and supervisors who are faced with external failures and customers 'voting with their feet'.

Box 15.2 Technology and responsibility for quality

Deming's main argument against traditional quality control was that it focused on the product rather than the process. Keeping down the number of delivered defective products typically meant high expenditure on inspection and rework and, in any case, many defects slipped through. Deming advocated the use of statistics to measure process variability which was the chief culprit of poor quality. He then argued for continual investigation and fine-tuning to incrementally improve the production system. He proposed a framework for this continuous improvement, the PDCA cycle, which we shall return to in **14**. Participation of everyone in the process was, at the time, a revolutionary notion.

It was not until the early 1980s that Deming's work was recognised in his own country. He spent the last part of his life spreading his message to large audiences throughout the United States, dying in 1993 at the age of 93.

Kaoru Ishikawa

Ishikawa was a professor at the University of Tokyo who advocated quality ideas before the second world war. He founded the Union of Japanese Scientists and Engineers which became the focus of Japan's quality developments as its economy recovered. The UJSE was responsible for Deming's 1950 invitation. Ishikawa advocated the notion of customers being both internal and external to the organisation and popularised the fish bone diagram as a problem investigation tool as well as other techniques.

Ishikawa saw that western management practices could not be grafted on to Japanese habits. He was a pioneer of quality circles, see **9**, which emphasised the role of the group in working and learning. His first circles were at Nippon Telegraph and Cable in 1962; by 1978 there were more than one million quality circles in Japanese manufacturing industry.

Joseph M. Juran

Like Deming, Juran's background was in statistics. He also had strong influence on Japanese managers, being linked to Ishikawa's UJSE. Many Japanese workers were illiterate, this problem being a serious hindrance to the introduction of quality processes. Juran took advantage of this situation. Large businesses had already started 'reading circles' led by supervisors and others with the necessary skills. Juran had his ideas published in forms suitable for learning materials for these groups. The pamphlets were even sold through newspaper kiosks. For the reading circle using Juran's material, it was a short step to the quality circle.

Later, Juran founded a training consultancy, the Juran Institute, and through this, spread his ideas about partnerships and teamwork, internal customers, problem solving techniques and application of Pareto analysis to quality issues. He was concerned about fitting quality improvement programmes into a company's current strategies and plans to minimise the risk of their being rejected. For him, quality was *fitness for purpose*, a wider definition than conformance to specification which he regarded as very limiting. In this approach he differed from Deming's more conservative adherence to the idea of matching specifications. Like Deming, however, Juran spoke in public into his nineties.

Genichi Taguchi

In 1989, Taguchi was honoured with the award of MITI's Purple Ribbon from the Emperor of Japan for his contribution to the development of industrial standards in that country. His strength has been in the application of statistical methods, not to quality control where they had already found wide application, but to improving products and processes. He applied methods in novel ways to: making products less sensitive to variations in their components and in the environment in which they are made; improving reliability; and improving testing procedures. A family of techniques called 'Taguchi methods' has grown up. Yet Taguchi himself did not like the use of the term, especially when it was used to describe standard statistical methods. Moreover, while many acknowledge his contribution to the engineering design of experiments, they criticise his use of statistics as being inefficient and cumbersome[15]. We shall refer to Taguchi methods in **16.7** and **8**.

Philip B. Crosby

Author of *Quality is Free*, Crosby's career as a quality advocate grew from his experience as a manger in ITT where he developed the Total Quality Management programme. With credibility founded on his experience and well-documented examples of uncovering the costs of waste, scrap and rework, Crosby has become well-known in the field. He argues that *getting it right first time* is an achievable goal. This zero-defects strategy is important because the costs of poor quality are seriously underestimated.

ZD is part of the 'four essentials' of quality management:

1 Quality is conformance to requirements. To Crosby, a product either conforms or it does not. There is no such concept as 'good' quality and quality has nothing to do with notions such as elegance.
2 Prevention is the route to achieve conformance, not appraisal.
3 Zero defects is the only acceptable performance standard.
4 Quality is assessed by the cost of non-conformance.

Compared with the work of the other authorities described above, Crosby's change programme is more behavioural. It stresses management and organisational processes rather then the application of statistical methods. While this enables a fit with current cultures and hierarchies it gives little detail of the practical tools of analysis that are essential in quality improvement.

7. The development of standards

International trade has implications for quality standards. Standards, as Crosby argued, are communications. They pass between customers and suppliers to convey information about the clients' needs summarised in conventional form. The European Union made harmonisation of standards one of the main planks of its construction of the single market.

Product standards have existed ever since the creation of assay offices to ensure that gold was not being diluted with other metals by unscrupulous traders. Gradually, the British Standards Institute, along with parallel organisations such as Deutsche Industrie-normen (DIN) and the American National Standards Institute, have developed product standards covering items from reinforced concrete and rolled steel sections to cables and thread. Table 15.2 gives a small extract from one of the early British Standard specifications, for steel I-beams. In its many

Table 15.2 Extract from I-beams, BS 4: 1932

Depth × Breadth in.	Wt/ft. lb.	Area in^2	Modulus in^4
3 × 3	8.5	2.52	3.81
4 × 1¾	5	1.47	3.66
4 × 3	10	2.94	7.79
5 × 3	11	3.26	13.68

tables and multiple editions, BS 4 set out the dimensions of standard steel sections that could be used by engineers to select and specify beams to use in their designs. Standardisation in specification and manufacture reduced design time for engineers, stimulated a competitive market and enabled more efficient producers to gain economies of scale.

Industry standards and norms have also been established, either by agreement, such as the emerging specifications for digital television, or by the success of a leading design or brand, the PC being notable in this respect, or almost by chance, as evidenced by the dimensions of wallpaper, cloth, railway track and vinyl records. Product standards are, in many cases, backed by statute, often at the international level. There are many EU regulations covering product specifications from the strength of vehicle seat belts to the noise emitted by domestic lawn mowers.

Several drawbacks with product standards can be noted:

- *Limited scope*
  The time taken to agree standards, and the difficulty of reaching agreement, means that they relate to only a limited range of products that are in general circulation.
- *Limited applicability to assemblies*
  Product standards often only apply to those parts of assemblies of complex equipment that are in common circulation. It is, for example, hardly of interest to know that the bolts inside a washing machine are made to BS dimensions.
- *Applied only to some properties of a product*
  BS 476, for example, specifies testing methods for fire resistance of building materials. The attachment of this label to a batch of, say, decorative panels will say nothing about their acoustic or other properties.
- *Complexity*
  The multiplicity of standards almost takes away the point of having them. Lacking common standards, many companies and purchasing authorities have felt obliged to issue their own specifications. Government purchasing, especially of military equipment, became subject to standards and conventions such as the 05 standards of the Ministry of Defence and NATO's Allied Quality Assurance Publication.

Since many items of military hardware were very complex and had to have quality built into every component, defence procurement authorities required suppliers to have their manufacturing processes open to inspection. Indeed, when small companies manufactured supplies for the MoD, they were not allowed to progress the job unless an external inspector was present. From the frustration, confusion and costs of this system, and the burgeoning number of standards in the civil sector, grew a new approach, concentrating on the processes themselves.

BS 5750 was, therefore, created in response to the needs of industry seeking to gain recognition in those many situations where product certification was not practicable. It is a practical, national standard that can be used by organisations of all sizes. It is built around the basic quality disciplines, specifying the procedures that are necessary for outputs to satisfy customers' requirements. Quality is built in to every process and must be evidenced with relevant documentation. Compliance with the provisions of the standard, validated by an inspection organised by the British Standards Institute, leads to certification and an inclusion in the *Register of Quality-assessed UK Companies*. Unannounced checks are made about four times a year. Box 15.3 outlines the general and specific provisions of the various sections of BS 5750.

While the weight of the demands made under BS 5750 may seem onerous at first, they do not go beyond what is recognised as good operating practice in leading companies. The spread of the certification throughout the UK is stimulated by the need for any company seeking registration to have procedures to validate the supplies it uses. Either it must be able to demonstrate input quality through inspection of all its incoming goods and services or it can rely on the supplier itself being certified. Therefore, many leading companies are introducing registration as a condition of joining their list of approved suppliers. For instance, one further education college in north-west England gained recognition for its engineering department because it wanted to maintain, and increase, its involvement in training for British Aerospace. Given the haphazard organisation

---

General provisions

- Good quality organisation with responsibilities clearly allocated.
- Regular reviews, carried out systematically, to identify defects and problems. The impact of proposed changes to be audited to check that the problems have been resolved.
- Clear integration of the quality system with other key functions, including design, research and development, subcontracting management, manufacturing and supply and installation.
- Planning of new approaches to testing and assessment.
- Monitoring of all measuring and testing equipment with results clearly recorded.

Specific provisions

- Design activity to be clearly planned and controlled to include: development programme; code of practice; studies of new methods; control of communications and interfaces with other departments; preparation and control of drawings, specifications, procedures and other instructions; incorporation of appropriate statutory provisions; studies of new materials; validation of the reliability of engineering and value studies; design review; incorporation of feedback from previous designs. (Where an organisation supplies to another's designs then this section becomes the responsibility of the customer.)
- System of managing relations with subcontractors and suppliers of goods and services; appraisal of capability and performance; agreements on inspection procedures; all arrangements to be documented.
- Manufacturing to be clearly controlled. The standard sets out the required contents of work instructions and operational procedures.
- Quality appraisal activities during the process to be specified; sampling and acceptance rules to be laid down and the options to be chosen for failed work to be set out in advance.
- Final test procedures, personnel, conditions and control are to be specified.

Box 15.3 BS 5750

and documentation that prevail in the 'education industry' the decision to make the application demanded a significant change in both practice and attitudes!

Sponsored by the European Union, the ISO 9000 series comprises five sections (90000 to 90004) based largely on BS 5750. Again, it is a process standard, this time developed with the express intention of achieving uniform and fair practice throughout the EU. It has gained acceptance outside the continent, first through foreign companies seeking to do business in the EU and then through their own suppliers and partners. Some 60 countries have recognised it formally but the push behind its acceptance comes from companies for whom it cuts out the confusing and conflicting standards met with in international trade. There are more than 30,000 certified organisations[16].

The question raised by the switch to process standards is whether the average quality of products is affected by them[17]. ISO 9000 leaves three problems outstanding:

- *Universality means average*
  Through establishing norms that are achievable across a wide range of organisations, the excellent standards of leading companies are not affected. ISO 9000 is valuable neither to them nor their customers. They simply register and continue unchanged. Following a meeting of the European Foundation for Quality Management, Dickson reported on 'The fuss over European-wide certification – notably complaints by small and medium-sized suppliers about the time and money spent on acquiring the quality standard ISO 9000 to appease their demanding customers ...'[18].
- *Narrow definition*
  By fastening its attention on the consistency of the supply process in achieving its own product standards, ISO 9000 ignores other dimensions of customer satisfaction that many authorities would include in a broader definition of quality. Possibilities are speed of response, customisation and continuous improvement. As we shall see later, service element of manufacture, or the extra dimension that can be given along with basic service, are critical elements of customer satisfaction.
- *Products*
  Moving products from the centre of the stage allows for wide coverage for registration and does not restrict innovation. In taking this approach, however, ISO 9000 does not guarantee any particular product. Makers of lead balloons can be certified so long as they make them consistently according to the procedures declared during the registration process.

While the last point suggests that absurd positions may arise, it is worth making the point that ISO 9000 is not intended to replace product standards. They remain relevant in many industries. Furthermore, an organisation seeking product approval is likely to require process registration as a prerequisite of an appraisal.

TOTAL QUALITY MANAGEMENT

8. TQM defined

In section **1** we saw the many and varied definitions of quality that are in use. Given the intense debate that is taking place over what it means, it is not surprising that Total Quality Management also has a number of interpretations. This divergence is underpinned by the fact that many advocates are consultants anxious to advocate their own line or nuance. In essence TQM brings together the ideas we have covered so far in this chapter and links them to detailed methods and techniques which we shall cover later. In that sense TQM is a philosophy of quality that links policy and operational practice. The need for quality products in the competitive market place is clear. What is sometimes lacking, however, is the setting of appropriate organisational goals and the mobilisation of all members to commit themselves to achieving them.

Of the three elements of TQM:

- *Total* suggests wholehearted commitment of everyone in the organisation.
- *Quality* means, following Juran or Crosby, continuously meeting customers' requirements.
- *Management* implies an active process led from the top.

For our discussion, therefore, we shall use the following definition:

Total Quality Management is a process of involving everyone in an organisation in continuously improving products and processes to achieve, on every occasion, quality that satisfies customers' needs.

Key implications of this definition are:

- Involving everyone in the company through teamwork, trust and empowerment
- Continuous improvement
- Identification of customers and their needs, and then focusing on them
- Using tools and techniques to jointly resolve quality problems.

In the next sections, we shall discuss these items in more detail.

9. Teamwork, trust and empowerment

The holistic approach of TQM distinguishes it from conventional approaches where the responsibility is assigned to a 'quality department'. For some, it even goes beyond the Quality Circle (Box 15.4) which can be seen as a means of management delegating some quality responsibilities while retaining most of the control. Indeed, QCs are sometimes seen as coercive by Japanese workers. The holistic goal is commitment and sharing of the quality issue among all employees so that the contribution of each is both recognised and influential.

Empowerment can only occur when people are well trained, given access to relevant information, know and use the best techniques, are involved in the decisions and receive appropriate rewards. Most quality problems relate to materials, designs, specifications and processes and have little to do with poor employee performance. Yet these same employees are usually well aware of the shortcomings of the production system and can be valuable in finding solutions.

10. Continuous improvement

Many programmes for operational change are based on the notion of restructuring the system and moving it from one state to another. This requires three stages: preparation for change, the change itself and the confirmation of the new arrangement. In contrast, advocates of improvement, or *kaizen*, see striving for quality as

Quality Circles have made major contributions to the success of Japanese companies. Conventionally, staff are organised into groups of, say, 6 to 12. Training and guidance in the concepts of quality and problem solving techniques are given by middle managers. The group meets regularly to select problems to work on, and then analyse and solve them. It sets its own targets, not only for quality improvement but also for related issues such as production flow, planned maintenance, working conditions and safety.

Among many variants, QCs may:
- have people from one or several work groups;
- have people from one or several levels in the organisation;
- have a nominated leader or decide to rotate the leadership role;
- be stimulated by a scheme which rewards suggestions through financial incentives.

From the first QC in Japan in 1962, the number has expanded to, perhaps, 100,000 registered with the Union of Japanese Scientists and Engineers. (There are an estimated 1,000,000 further circles not formally recorded.) In 1990, Yamaha had 700 circles, Toyota 6,700 and the medium-sized Toppan Printing 150 among a mere 2,000 workers. More than 13 million Japanese people participate, always voluntarily and usually outside working time. Each QC generates about 50 suggestions a year. The movement is seen as a driving force behind the continuous improvement of products and processes.

The QC fits well into the Japanese organisational culture with its emphasis on the group, as opposed to the individual, its lifetime loyalty (at least in major firms) and lack of serious demarcation of job roles. Although tried in the West with some success, the different context makes the idea difficult to transfer without removing or diluting some of the key principles that make QCs work.

Box 15.4 Quality circles

an endless journey rather than a trip to a known and fixed destination. Normal behaviour, in this view, is experimentation, adjustment and minor improvement to every detail. If *kaizen* is accepted, employees expect small developments and do not see them as challenges to existing working practices and relationships. No-one is ever quite happy with the *status quo*.

According to Imai, every person's work comprises two parts, continuation and improvement[19]. The former, which Imai calls maintenance, refers to the current work. People must know what they are supposed to be doing and follow these standards and agreements. The second half of everybody's job is improvement. This means finding a better way of doing the job and raising the standard. It happens that people find new ways of doing jobs without raising the standard. Imai argues that this behaviour should be seen as deviation rather than improvement because the key factors of quality, cost and delivery have not been affected. For improvement to take place, the standard must be raised. *Kaizen*, then, implies continuous challenges to the standards we have in our daily jobs.

As shown in Figure 15.6, the majority of work at shop floor level is directed towards continuation. The role of managers is to take on more responsibility for

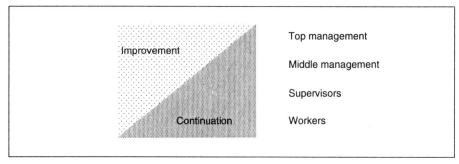

Figure 15.6 Proportions of improvement and continuation

improvement. Imai suggests a set of questions to act as guide when problems occur. Did it happen as a result of:

- there being no standard?
- the present standard being inadequate?
- staff not following the standard?
- staff not trained to follow the standard?

When problems arise, the manager's job is to find out what has happened, using the above questions. A better standard or method can be worked out. This, in Imai's view, is most important for standards guide both continuation and improvement. There can be no quality without it. With it, recurrence of problems can be prevented and the variability within all processes can be controlled. The history of quality improvement in Japan is the history of standardisation.

Closely associated with this commitment to involvement in the detail of standards and improvement is *Gemba*. *Gemba* means the place where the activity takes place. It can refer to: the shop floor; the customer's offices where a salesperson is calling; the customer's site where an installation is being made; the screen or drawing board where an engineer is working out a design; or the hotel reception area, bedroom, restaurant or sauna. Imai sets out the improvement process based on five *Gemba* principles, Box 15.5[20].

Many solutions can be made in the first two steps. Yet the real solutions are achieved only after the last ones are taken. Otherwise, managers not using the discipline remain fire-fighters. The principles have implications for the roles of senior

---

1 When an abnormality occurs, go to *Gemba* first and right away!

2 Check with *Gembutsu. Gembutsu*, in Japanese, means something you can touch, such as machine, material, failures, rejects, unsafe conditions, etc.

3 Take temporary countermeasures on the spot.

4 Find and remove the root cause.

5 Standardize for recurrence prevention.

Box 15.5 The five principles of *Gemba*

managers. They should be there to remove restraints on *Gemba*, that is to help people lower down the hierarchy to investigate and solve problems without excessive constraints. Since managers are ultimately responsible for everything that happens in *Gemba*, they need to stay in touch and become involved when problems arise. Hence the opening maxim, 'Go to *Gemba* first and right away!' For Imai, the problem with most managers is that they believe their workplace is their desk.

11. Being customer-centred

We have seen that both Ishikawa and Juran advocated the notion that, in the TQM organisation, everyone has customers. They may be internal or external. Internal customers are other members of the organisation who rely on the individual next along the quality chain for the inputs to get their work done. Usually, it is another internal customer who receives the 'output' from whatever the individual is responsible for. Sometimes, people's work can be so interconnected that they are *mutually dependent*, that is each is the other's customer. Whatever the relationship, they are all part of quality chains. When it comes to quality, it follows that the internal customer is very much like an external one. The difficulty of the customer's work, and the quality of the output, are strongly affected by the quality of the input.

As for external customers, it is obvious that the TQM company will require *all employees* who deal with them to be committed to satisfying their needs. Being customer-focused entails:

- Appreciating situations through customers' eyes so that needs are anticipated.
- Listening to customers, especially the detail of what they want.
- Understanding possible ways of satisfying customers' wishes.
- Providing the appropriate response.

Box 15.6 illustrates how leadership can be so negative. The point of the tale is that it represents BR's customer service failure[21]. It starts by putting on one side any discussion of who is responsible for the problems. Then it does not recognise that it is not possible in a mass service organisation for a small elite of managers to deal with customers in the way suggested. The TQM business acknowledges this and, rather than criticise the inadequacy of recruits, develops its people to achieve high standards. This means leadership, training, standards and rewards.

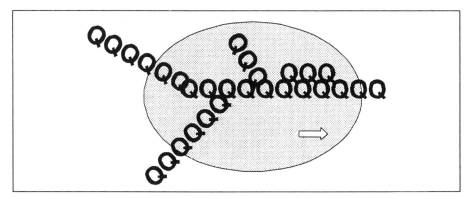

Figure 15.7 Quality chains

A senior railway manager once told me, 'The trouble for British Rail is that the people in the organisation who deal with the public are the people at the bottom.' Without too much reflection, I accepted the statement and went on to discuss something else. Later, I saw the serious implications of the assertion. The critical points of contact between travellers and railway staff are not at ticket sales or general enquiries but when a passenger has a problem or a complaint. Then, the manager is implying, 'the sort of people we employ' on the shop floor (porters, train crew and so on) are ill-equipped to handle the problems. If only the complaints were immediately handled by intelligent and articulate staff (like the manager himself) passengers would be better satisfied.

Box 15.6 The blaming trap

Retailing can teach a great deal about customer orientation for the whole organisation. Writing on excellence, Peters likens retail, in the classroom or the showroom, to a performance art. True, to locate, build and stock a store, or to organise a management seminar, require skills from purchasing to project management. Yet, when everything is in place, and the shop opens or the class begins, success is down to personal delivery. Just as there are good and bad actors and actresses, so there are good and bad shopkeepers, receptionists, ticket collectors and teachers. Being good means giving the customer the best of what they want every day. 'You are the absolute master, ruler, tsar. You alone bring that space, or those five restaurant tables, to life. Ninnies or saints, fearful or fearless, management can't hold you back.'[22]

12. Tools and techniques

We shall investigate in Chapter 16 the more important tools for solving quality problems. Imai warns, however, that too much stress can be laid on the need to learn the techniques[23]. He believes that most quality problems can be resolved by simple steps using common sense. Imai's procedures for putting common sense into practice are:

- *Go to Gemba*
  This is the most important rule.
- *Standardisation*
  Standards are the basis of both continuing activity and improvement. If there are no standards they should be introduced. If the standards are failing, they should be modified.
- *Don't get it, don't make it, don't send it*
  Based on the premise that quality is everyone's job, one should be determined not to receive rejects, create them or pass them on.
- *Speak with data*
  Collecting data is the starting point of analysis. People should be prepared to measure before changing anything.
- *Ask why*
  Problem solving means asking why as often as necessary to find the root cause. Only then can the problems be eradicated.

Others argue that quality cannot be sustained without quality measurement techniques. This is undoubtedly true, but the emphasis in the TQM organisation is less on the measurement and more on the use of appropriate measures to support continuous improvement. Rather than use detailed recording and trend analysis at the end of the production process, it may be much more effective to enable a process worker to take some simple measurements earlier on and make adjustments immediately if such action were necessary. Matching the complexity of quality tools with the training and experience of the users is a vital part of involving people at all levels. The tools are clearly a necessary but not sufficient basis for a TQM programme.

13. Limitations of TQM

At its core, Total Quality Management is a simple idea. The search for competitive advantage through quality is best sustained by applying basic ideas right across the organisation. Yet to the simplicity have been added a great deal of jargon and extra techniques that take the focus off quality. The controversy over registration under ISO 9000 was mentioned in section 7. The large firms may register because to do so is easy; the small may feel forced to do so and grumble about the costs of consultants and the appraisal process itself. European firms may not have committed themselves to TQM as much as Japanese and, it appears, North American ones. We can examine this further by looking at costs and people.

Costs

When examining the costs of quality and changing the balance among them, in sections 2 and 3, we came across the idea that quality programmes would eventually pay for themselves. 'Quality is free' because the total costs of prevention are less than the costs of failure. This begs two questions. First, what happens in the firm once it has cut its costs of failure to a more moderate level? Usually, this will be the easy part of the improvement and, from then on, gains will become more difficult to come by. Further quality developments may be difficult to justify on financial terms, especially when there may be other problems on the managerial agenda. Secondly, quality programmes are an investment. As with other development programmes, there is an additional short-term cost before the benefits start to flow. Figure 15.8, which draws on Figure 15.5, shows how the quality spending may be changed during a 5 year development programme.

The graph tracks cash flow to cover all spending, whether treated as expenses or as investment. Note how, over the first two years, there will be a bulge in prevention spending before it settles to a new level higher than before. This is mainly related to reorganisation and training. The benefits come after the prevention investment peak. Failure cost problems reduce as the programme begins to take effect and, as confidence in the new system rises, the resources put into appraisal systems can be cut.

Human resources

Dawson sounds several warnings when discussing changes in technical and social processes during the introduction of a TQM programme[24]. He first of all points out that TQM is not a panacea. Many plants have problems which need to be resolved either as a prerequisite of a quality programme or separately from it.

421

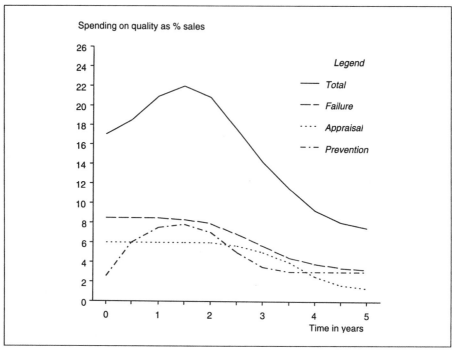

Figure 15.8 Cash flow associated with quality investment

Further points concern social issues:

- There may be problems within the work groups during the transition. To participate in TQM, through quality circles for example, is voluntary. Yet to work under the restructured operating system is mandatory. Those employees who, because of pre-existing problems, find it impossible to join in will not support the change. The TQM development may, therefore, make current social tensions worse.
- Employee involvement may be difficult to mobilise at first and may have to be considered as an eventual objective. Cultural, language and structural constraints create barriers.

    Culture and language

    Dawson quotes a Pirelli plant in Adelaide, Australia, where there were language differences among shop floor workers, many of whom were recent immigrants. These hindered the deep levels of communication which cooperation requires, a problem that would not arise in the remarkable homogeneity of Japanese society.

    Structure

    The relevant structures at shop floor level include plant layout and the shift system. Both may hinder participation in TQM, either through physical or temporal separation of individuals and groups. In such circumstances, workers will have grown used to relying on supervisors for coordination and they are likely to see TQM in the same light. Night shift workers, often fewer than day staff, often perceive themselves as being independent of management and are reluctant to commit themselves to personal involvement.

- Employee ability may be limited, not only by cultural and language diversity but by general levels of education. Dawson comments that the value of TQM techniques, especially statistics, had been exaggerated. Groups used brainstorming methods at first but relied on one or two members or coordinators to produce simple graphical material. A further problem for those left out of the discussions by such barriers was that they were expected to go along with the decisions that were made.

In a wider context, it may appear that the emphasis on personal and group development, backed up by training, would provide great opportunities for the development of personnel policies and practices generally. Yet personnel functions are not heavily involved. TQM accomplishment is very much an operations activity, often established under a project leader who is a line manager. Therefore, the stress will be on business results rather than long-term development of employees.

14. Deming's contribution to the management of quality

Paramount among the developers of quality principles was Deming, of whom a brief biography appears in 6. Although he did not invent the term TQM, Deming's teachings covered the full range of issues from quality practice to commitment and top management support. In the context of the 1950s, where narrow scientific management was strongly adhered to in the best companies, the ideas were revolutionary. Some of them were so challenging to existing management attitudes that it is not surprising that Deming was ignored for so long. Nowadays, however, many have become incorporated in conventional management training and practice. They seem, perhaps, less surprising and, sometimes, rather quaint. In proposing his *14 points*, Deming emphasised that they are the permanent obligations of top management none of which is ever completely fulfilled. The points are set out, with comments, in Box 15.7[25].

Deming may have made more progress with a more subtle attack on the backward ways of western management. Yet, in spite of a rather curmudgeonly approach, Deming was eventually listened to because of his experience of Japan and the simple rigour of his problem-solving approach. He pressed for the adoption of informed decision making based on good quality data. He advocated the plan-do-check-act (PDCA) cycle, Figure 15.9[26]. He called this the *Shewhart cycle* in recognition of the founder of statistical quality control but the Japanese, and others, call it the *Deming cycle*.

In using the PDCA cycle, managers are encouraged to start with small changes about things that are really important. The approach is set in the tradition of research and trial-and-error experimentation. Actions and reflections are grounded in observed data. In this belief in experimentation, Deming is close to Taguchi, see 6 and 16.8. The four stages of the continuous PDCA loop are:

- *Plan* Work out changes based on observed data. Decide whether a pilot experiment is needed and how one is to be conducted.
- *Do* Make the change or carry out the planned pilot experiment.
- *Check* Observe the effects of the change or collect the results of the small experiment.
- *Act* Study the outcomes of the work and establish the lessons to be learned. Confirm the change, or otherwise. Interpret the results of the experiment. Start to plan again.

1 *Create constancy of purpose*
Constancy refers to the long term view; innovate with materials, methods, services and in all aspects of the business. Put resources into research and education. Put resources into equipment of all kinds.

2 *Learn the new philosophy*
Managers must adopt new attitudes which are not satisfied with current levels of defects, unsuited materials, poor training and management. It is possible to learn to be smart.

3 *Ask for evidence of process control along with incoming parts*
Purchasing managers must learn about control methods to be able to include them in their requests to suppliers. Relying on inspection is futile.

4 *Be prepared to reduce the number of suppliers*
Companies must consider the costs of having more than one vendor. If they decide to cut the number, they must work out how to trade off quality and price and not just buy on the basis of the cheapest.

5 *Use statistical methods to find out, in any trouble spot, what are the sources of trouble*
Judgement, according to Deming, always gives the wrong answer when it comes to finding out where a fault lies. (Here his background in statistics is revealed in the confidence he places in those methods. Note how this contrasts with Imai's reliance on common sense explained in **11**.)

6 *Institute modern aids to training on the job*
Deming argued for major changes in training, using statistics to discover whether training would be beneficial. A person fully trained and in control of the task can do no better. If unsatisfactory, the person should be moved.

7 *Improve supervision*
Deming said that many supervisors were deplorable. The common practice of calling attention to every defect or mistake may be wrong and counterproductive. Supervisors should provide leadership and use statistics as aids to improving the production system.

8 *Drive out fear*
When employees do jobs the wrong way it may be because they are afraid to ask how and why. Security means an absence of fear. When insecure, people will not ask questions, report difficulties or discuss with colleagues how to do things better.

9 *Break down barriers between departments*
Bureaucratic barriers make it difficult to achieve the common goal: customer satisfaction. Deming quotes the case of two suppliers each meeting the specifications for certain components. Yet the differences between the two sets of supplies imposed heavy costs on the production department. It was the specification that was too loose, a problem not picked up by the bureaucracy because it was not included in the reporting system.

10 *Eliminate numerical goals, slogans, pictures, posters, urging people to increase productivity, sign their work as an autograph, etc., so often plastered everywhere in the plant.*
Posters such as 'ZERO DEFECTS' do not lead to people doing better jobs. Numerical targets lead to frustration, they just indicate management's lazy attempts to convert their budget promises into shop floor action.

11 *Look carefully at work standards*
Consider whether quotas and numerical targets bring the benefits so often claimed. They encourage people to forget quality. Deming rejected the practice of Management by Objectives.

12 *Institute a massive training programme for employees in simple but powerful statistical methods*
Deming's belief in statistics as a medium for investigation and communication made him see that it should be part of everyone's training. Further, there should be many experts who can guide the rest.

13 *Institute a vigorous programme for retraining people in new skills*
The programme should match developments in models, processes, materials, machinery, rules and so on.

14 *Create a structure in top management that will push every day on the above thirteen points*
Since development is everyone's job, leaders should recognise this and take full responsibility for the changes that are needed.

Box 15.7 Deming's *14 points*

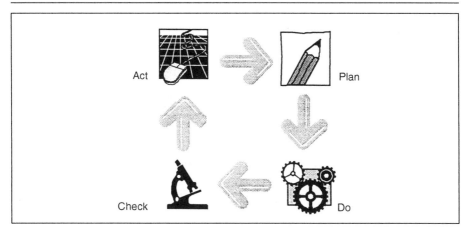

Figure 15.9   The Deming-Shewhart PDCA cycle

The cycle is not original. As with many of his ideas, Deming's contribution was to draw them together and apply them both rigorously and vigorously to the quality question.

APPLYING QUALITY IDEAS

The basic process improvement tools of TQM are just some of the techniques applicable in the quality context, either for continuation and control or for improvement. We shall study these in the next chapter. There remain, however, some wider issues concerning the application of 'quality thinking' in different settings. These are the special problems associated with service delivery and the integration of the operations function with other business disciplines.

15.   Quality in the service dimension

We have emphasised that almost all supplier–customer transactions include significant service. The quality of the whole transaction is, therefore, strongly affected by the way the service is provided. Although one could not support the railway manager's attitudes expressed in Box 15.6, one should, nevertheless, recognise that service is vulnerable at its weakest points, the moments of direct interaction with customers. These are the *moments of truth*. In the restaurant, good food can be spoiled by indifferent service, while in the supermarket passing through the checkout can be a positive or negative experience. The TQM service organisation pays attention to all the interconnected factors that contribute to quality. They are shown in Figure 15.10 and we shall deal with each in turn.

Organisation and staffing for service quality

The nature of the service will, to a great extent, determine the way it is provided. Personal service is delivered in the presence of the customer and with the customer's participation. Otherwise the isolated service is organised out of contact with the customer who is contacted through the 'front office'. Separation of back room personnel from customer contact can be a retrograde step if the organisation,

425

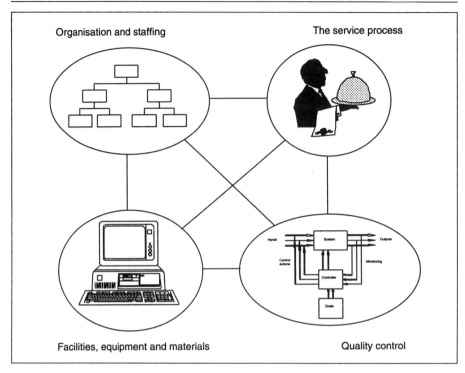

Figure 15.10 Factors in the service-quality mix

for the most part, loses its orientation towards service quality. Maintenance of this orientation can be helped by use of quality circles, training, job rotation and appropriate controls. Matching the needs of service organisations with selection and training of appropriate staff is the first step towards providing good service. It may even be possible to automate the customer contact aspects of the delivery, as in the case of simple banking transactions.

Much service delivery is prone to uncertainty. We tend to forget that even making a small purchase in a shop is an acquired skill. Usually, however, both parties to the transaction are familiar with its usual course and duration. In other service situations, uncertainty can be the result of genuine unpredictability of outcomes or unawareness on behalf of the customer as to what to do. Customers may not know many of the things that service personnel regard as normal. Does one help oneself or wait to be served? Can one sit anywhere? May one make a noise? Who, in Box 15.8, was wrong?

> I visited the snack bar of a ferry on a Holyhead to Dublin sailing. Having bought tea, I settled at a table in a quiet corner. After a moment a staff member came over to tell me I should not be sitting there because the area had just been cleaned. I replied that seemed to be an excellent reason for sitting there and refused to move. I suppose I went down in the log as an 'awkward customer'.

Box 15.8 Awkward customer

Difficulties caused by uninformed customers may result in perception of lower quality not just for them but for other customers who are disturbed or displaced in some way. Customer 'training', through advertising, announcements, personal guidance and notices, can go a long way to overcoming these difficulties. In other words, not only should it be clear what is on offer, but also when and how it is offered and the best way for the customer to become involved. There is little worse than having a customer expect one quality of service and the firm deliver another. In the spring of 1995, Eurotunnel had launched its *Turn-up-and-go* car transit service. Difficulties with train capacity and underestimation of demand, however, meant that, at weekends, long queues formed at the terminal and angry passengers blocked the roads. Eurotunnel was forced to require bookings for Saturdays.

The TQM organisation, then, recognises that customer satisfaction depends on matching perception and expectation as closely as possible. We saw in **9.12** how important this was in the design of processes where queuing may occur. Yet narrowing the perception–expectation gap is critical in all service situations and requires the commitment of all to achieving it.

The service process

Imai's arguments about standardisation apply equally to manufacture and service. Good management of the service process must include specification of standards to be achieved at all operational stages. Standardisation is crucial in mass service but it is difficult to be so specific when it comes to personal service. In either case, the production thinking of manufacturing may get carried over with unfortunate consequences. Focus on standards and uniformity in the service organisations run the risk of too much attention being paid to delivering the 'hard' aspects of service at the expense of the 'soft'. 'Getting it right first time' is important in service quality but the slogan hardly helps if the business wrongly defines the *it*.

The specification of quality standards in service functions is difficult and tends to concentrate on quantifiable elements, especially the time taken for various stages of delivery or the frequency at which certain tasks are carried out. The non-quantifiable aspects, such as the overall impression of the helpfulness and politeness of the staff, are more difficult to assess although they can be observed by supervisors and monitored using sample surveys. Unfortunately, the latter do not give the detailed immediate feedback needed for concurrent control. Vandermerwe distinguishes between 'hard' and 'soft' capabilities, arguing that customers evaluate the service they receive on what they *get out*, while firms, using conventional quality measurement and control, concentrate on what they *put in*[27]. The contrast between the capabilities is shown in Box 15.9.

Facilities, equipment and materials

Facilities, equipment and materials have differing degrees of importance depending on customer expectations and the nature of the service. In food retailing for example, they are all very important whereas professional advisers make little use of materials and equipment.

Development of information systems has enabled more services to be provided through self service. In these cases ergonomics and the study of human-machine interaction should play a significant role in the design of equipment. The quality of

Hard thinking		Soft thinking	
Minimise variation	Deviation avoided	Maximise adaptation	Be able to respond
Get it right first time ...	... without fail!	Ensure relevance over time	Make it work for the customer
Measure attributes	Assess the facts of the service	Measure customer experience	How the service functions
Zero defects	No faults at any time	No breaks	Do not interrupt the flow of service
Fitness for purpose	Build value in	Ease of application	Getting value out
Standards...	... and adhere to rules	Resilience	Adaptation, renewal
Uniformity	Everything the same	Consistency	Can provide the customer's needs each time
Durability	Product lasts	Reliability	Things work
Cause and effect	Clear links	Interactions	Solutions in complex situations

Box 15.9 Hard and soft thinking about service attributes

such equipment will itself have an impact on the customer's perception of the service package as a whole. Its reliability is critical, as witnessed by any customer who has been let down by a cash machine when trying to obtain £10 for a late night taxi.

Quality monitoring in services

Effective quality control requires the establishment of clear standards and the ability to measure conformance to these standards. Only then can action be taken to ensure compliance and also decide where standards themselves can be improved. The example of Marriott hotels, given in Box 15.10, is typical of the best companies. It shows how monitoring of both objective and subjective measures can be carried out. But note that the effectiveness of the audit will depend on its covering the factors that are important and relevant to the customer. Furthermore, the way the information from the survey is used will have a strong influence on whether quality levels are maintained and improved. Used as a basis of cooperative problem solving it can do much to advance the cause, but if it is used punitively, or mainly for financial incentives, then the benefits will not be realised.

The question for service quality monitoring is how to combine hard data with the much more difficult soft data. The latter may say a great deal more about the customers' responses to the service. Vandermerwe[28] argues that it is the language of monitoring that has to change. Box 15.11 lists *hard* and *soft* factors to illustrate this point. The aim, for instance, is to evaluate the rapport achieved with each customer rather than measure average satisfactions.

428

The Marriott Corporation is one of the world's leading hotel chains. It stresses service quality as a basic tenet of its strategy. Whether they have stayed overnight or attended a conference, every guest is invited to complete a questionnaire to evaluate the hospitality. In an accompanying letter, the Chairman, Bill Marriott, promises to share the comments with the hotel manager and follow up all comments and recommendations.

The four page computer-marked form has 36 questions and a space for open-ended comments. The following questions are typical:

12 Please think about the bathroom and bedroom areas of your hotel room and rate the following items:

Overall cleanliness of bathroom	10 9 8 7 6 5 4 3 2 1
Cleanliness of tub and tile	10 9 8 7 6 5 4 3 2 1
Cleanliness of vanity area	10 9 8 7 6 5 4 3 2 1
Supply of bath towels and wash cloths	10 9 8 7 6 5 4 3 2 1
Overall cleanliness of bathroom	10 9 8 7 6 5 4 3 2 1
Condition of carpet in bedroom	10 9 8 7 6 5 4 3 2 1
Condition of bedspread	10 9 8 7 6 5 4 3 2 1
Condition of furniture in bedroom	10 9 8 7 6 5 4 3 2 1

14E   Please rate the following items if you ordered from the *breakfast menu*:

Server's knowledge of menu	10 9 8 7 6 5 4 3 2 1
Server's familiarity with items on menu	10 9 8 7 6 5 4 3 2 1
Friendliness of server	10 9 8 7 6 5 4 3 2 1
Timeliness with which you received your beverages	10 9 8 7 6 5 4 3 2 1
Food prepared the way you wanted it	10 9 8 7 6 5 4 3 2 1
Timeliness of beverage refills during meal	10 9 8 7 6 5 4 3 2 1
Timeliness with which you received check	10 9 8 7 6 5 4 3 2 1
Value for price paid	10 9 8 7 6 5 4 3 2 1

Box 15.10 Marriott's customer survey

16. Design and quality

Successful designers have always recognised customers' needs and devised means of satisfying them through the design and supply process. Many organisations today, however, are unwilling to rely on intuition as the dominant basis for decision making and prefer to apply one or more formal methods. We shall look briefly ·t formal ways of identifying customer needs and controlling the design process so that these are effectively incorporated into product specifications.

Customer needs

Customers' needs in relation to quality are difficult to establish. This stems partly from the many definitions in use but also from the inexperience of customers in separating quality from other factors involved in the purchase. In response to these problems, Quality Function Deployment has been developed. It recognises the strategic role of design and integrates design activities which, hitherto, had been independent. These are:

Hard		Soft
Calculate	▶▶▶▶▶▶▶▶▶	Assess
Quantify		Observe
Average	▶▶▶▶▶▶▶▶▶	Case specific
Figures		Language
Single-level	▶▶▶▶▶▶▶▶▶	Multi-level
Static		Directional
Inspect	▶▶▶▶▶▶▶▶▶	Reflect
Change		Improve
Schedule	▶▶▶▶▶▶▶▶▶	Prioritise
Replicate		Originate
Set routine	▶▶▶▶▶▶▶▶▶	Improvise

Box 15.11 Assessing hard and soft factors: language contrasts

- *Conceptual design*
  Finding solutions which will satisfy the market demand.
- *Preliminary design*
  Giving priorities to design features in isolation from customers.
- *Detailed design*
  Detailing the key characteristics that will enable manufacturing to create the product.
- *Process design*
  Specifying how the product is to be made.

At the later stages of the sequence, design changes may be required to enable the product to be made and these will necessitate a review of the previous work. It has been estimated that the lack of integration of the stages means that 45% of design time is spent on adjusting to such changes. Further, when it comes to manufacture, 75% of all problems, and 40% of quality problems, are those which have been created during the detailed design phase[29]. When designs are changed early on, the costs can be small; if modifications happen after manufacturing starts, the costs can run into millions.

QFD has been adopted, in various forms, by companies who believe that the extra cost incurred at the 'finding out' stage, and integrating the design process around the results, is more than balanced by the savings from avoiding expensive mistakes later on. The challenge is to transform the attributes of a product that are recognised as important by the customer into characteristics that can be expressed in engineering terms and therefore can be made. The particular QFD factor association procedure uses a special matrix called *The House of Quality*. For the details of the procedure, see **16.6**.

Controlling the design process

In many circumstances and industries the design process is seen as quite separate to production. Nowhere is this more acutely seen than in building and construction where design is frequently let as a separate contract. Since the cost of design is usually a small proportion of the total project cost, its significance is often ignored. Yet, an increase in design expenditure can often reduce the total life costs, that is the combination of investment, operating and maintenance costs of the building. McGeorge quotes an example where design of a hospital cost 5% of the total. If more resources had been put in to that stage, increasing by half the expenditure to $7\frac{1}{2}$% of the total, it is not infeasible that the rest would have fallen sufficient to cut the total by 7%, even allowing for the extra $2\frac{1}{2}$% spent on design[30]. The normal practice of awarding design contracts on criteria heavily weighted towards price militates against quality.

Designers have to be flexible as the process they are engaged in is one of learning and interaction with other designers, suppliers, manufacturers and so on. Poor process quality in the design office is one reason for poor eventual product quality. Unless the production of designs and specifications is well controlled, with adjustments recorded and checked, it is unlikely that those who follow can do a good job.

Table 15.3 shows what might happen throughout the engineering design process in three design departments[31]. In the first there is no control, in the second things are improving while the third has a good quality set of procedures. It is fair to say that only the last would receive accreditation under BS 5750 or ISO 9000. The importance of design in the whole quality process makes it inevitable that large sections of both of these standards should be devoted to the control of procedures in this area.

17. Design, process capability and manufacturability

Another area in which habit and tradition play leading parts is the common ground shared by design and production. In many engineering companies, the designers have considerable shop floor experience and are very familiar with manufacturing capabilities. Yet, when faced with an engineering challenge, the unwise are likely to say, 'The works? They're good, they can make anything.' This enthusiasm needs to be tempered with an awareness of direct costs and the indirect effects of adding complex tasks into a production system that may already be overloaded. This caution is embedded in the notion of *manufacturability*.

Manufacturability is a measure of a design's ability to consistently satisfy product goals while being profitable.[32]

The product goals referred to in the definition of manufacturability include performance, reliability, availability and quality. Taken together, they are a specification of the conformance to customers' specifications. To understand how designs can satisfy this definition, we need to examine the nature of defects and how they arise.

A defect is the variation of any specified parameter outside the customer specification. Defects occur because the manufacturing process cannot consistently make the product exactly to the design specification. To investigate this we will consider one parameter, a single dimension.

Component with one parameter

Here we refer to a parameter as some measured property of a product which needs to conform to a customer requirement. While we will consider length here, the parameter may have any value, for example, a weight, a colour, a strength,

431

Table 15.3 Changing the way the design process is controlled

Procedure	Department's control of design process		
	1 No quality	2 Improving ...	3 Good quality
Requirements specification	Intuition based on experience	Occasional meetings Sales department	Regular interaction between Sales and Design
Drawing control	Engineer makes sketches and notes for craftsmen to interpret	Supervisor reviews sampled drawings	Regular reviews using multi-disciplinary teams
Changes	Verbal instructions	Written notices	Changes to be assessed for impact before approval
Calculations	Handbooks and experience combined	Calculations reviewed by supervisor	CAD systems operated by specialists
Non-conformance control	None	Consultation by Production over problems	Reviewed by specialists
Engineering records	Not prepared	Drawings and notes sent to filing	Integral part of organisation's record management procedures
Evaluation by management	Little evaluation from outside department	Management only involved when problems occur	Internal audits to look for improvements in all processes

electrical resistance etc. Whatever the material, it is not possible to produce products to an exactly consistent dimension. Furthermore, many substances, such as wood and paper, change continuously after they have been made.

We can note that it is usually the case that items can be measured more accurately than they can be manufactured. Therefore, random variations that occur in all processes can be detected by inspection equipment. To allow for these variations, specifications are usually written in the form, for example, of 600 ± 2 mm. Here the ± 2 mm is called the *specification width* about the central value of 600 mm. How is this value to be determined?

The random variations in parameters usually approximate closely to a normal distribution. The distribution can be described by its mean, μ, and standard deviation, σ. One of the properties of the normal distribution is that 16.6% of the values lie more than 1σ above the mean value and a further 16.6% are more than 1σ below the mean value. Therefore, if we produce our product, whose specification width is ± 2 mm, in a process which happens to create a standard deviation also

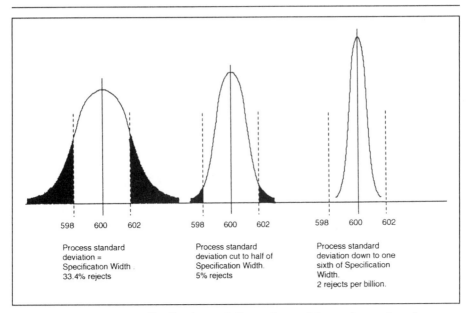

Figure 15.11 Frequency distributions of dimensions with varying ratios of process capability and specification width

of 2 mm, more than 33% of the output will be defective. These defects are shown as the shaded areas under the first graph of Figure 15.11. This shows the frequencies with which different dimensions occur.

Clearly, two courses of action are available if the defect rate is to be reduced. The specification width can be increased or the process can be improved in some way to reduce its variation. A third choice, to check all items and reject the one in three that lie outside the limit, would be a last resort.

The normal distribution tails off quickly. For example, while 33.4% of measurements lie outside ±1σ, 5% lie outside ±2σ and only 0.3% lie beyond ±3σ. This effect is shown in Table 15.4 which compares defect rates with the ratio of specification width to process standard deviation. Two cases from the table form the second and third graphs of Figure 15.11. (The heights are not to scale.) The second shows the 5% rejects if SW/σ is set at 2 and the third shows the much tighter process capability of SW/σ = 6. This last case has often been mentioned as a quality target – the Six Sigma specification – where, at 2 items per billion, the Zero Defects standard has virtually been achieved.

It is worth noting that the data in the three right-hand columns of the table is repetitive and is only included to emphasise the effect. For instance, in the sixth data row, 99.99%, 100 defects per million and 10,000 parts per defect are merely different ways of saying the same thing.

Table 15.4 assumes that a defect is defined as any item lying outside the specified range on either side of the central value. That is why each range is expressed as ± (SW/σ). In some processes however, defects will only lie to one side of the value. Then the defect rates will be half of those in the table. This is illustrated by drink dispensing. Serving too much is not illegal and customers will not complain. But see the consequences for the landlord illustrated in Box 15.12.

433

Table 15.4 The effect on defect rates of changes in specification width

SW/σ ±	Yield %	Defects per million parts	Number of parts per one defect
2	95.0	50,000	20
2.5	99.0	10,000	100
3	99.7	3,000	333
3.3	99.9	1,000	1,000
3.9	99.99	100	10,000
4.0	99.994	60	16,666
4.4	99.999	10	100,000
4.9	99.9999	1	1,000,000
6	99.999998	0.000002	500,000,000

An automated beer pump dispenses pints (545 ml) with a standard deviation of 3 ml. What volume should the machine be set to so that only 1 in 2,000 customers do not get their full pint?

Defects in this case are defined only as deviations on one side of the target value. Therefore, a 1 in 2,000 defect rate is equivalent to an SW/σ corresponding to 1 in 1,000 in Table 15.4, that is 3.3. This means that, given the known standard deviation, 3 ml, for the pump, the SW must be chosen as 9.9 ml and the pump set to 554.9. The result is that, to avoid more than the stated failure rate, the publican dispenses almost 10 ml extra per pint. Solution: Get a better pump.

Box 15.12 Landlord's burden

It is clear that, to achieve very low defect rates, careful attention should be paid to product design and the specification of key dimensions and other parameters. Why is it necessary to aim for such low defect rates? The answer to this question lies in the fact that most products have a number of parameters specified simultaneously. Components with many parameters can quickly show defects as explained below.

Components with many parameters

Suppose our design policy is to make all product specifications such that SW/σ is equal to 3. Table 15.4 shows that, for one parameter only, the number of good parts will be 99.7%. What about if we consider two parameters together?[33] This is a case of joint probability. The overall proportion of good parts will be given by:

$$0.997 \times 0.997 = 0.994 \quad \text{that is } 99.4\%$$

Table 15.5 Defect rate per thousand assemblies of all parameters have SW/σ equal to 3

Parts	Parameters			
	1	10	20	40
1	3	30	59	114
10	30	260	452	699
20	59	452	699	910
40	114	699	910	992

In practice, products are made up of many components, each of which can itself have many parameters. Table 15.5 expands the joint probability calculation to show how the combination of components and parameters increases the defect rate of an assembly. For example, with 20 components each with 20 parameters, we are considering 400 measurements and the overall success rate will be given by:

$$0.997^{400} = 0.301 \quad \text{that is 301 parts per thousand}$$

In a practical design, things are more complicated because parameters are not all independent and it is possible to easily arrange for some ratios of SW/σ to be much higher than others. This is where the parameter is much less critical from the user's point of view. The results demonstrate, however, that in order to achieve quality standards it is necessary to incorporate two factors into the design:

- *Specification width high*
  The specifications should be wide compared with process capabilities.
- *Number of parameters low*
  There should be as few critical parameters as possible.

The purpose of this discussion is to bring out the way the design and manufacturing departments must cooperate closely in designing and specifying items to be made. The debate is by no means complete. For example:

- The definition of quality is based on conformance to specification – a manufacturing concept. Taguchi would point out a flaw in this approach. With a specification of 600 ± 2 mm, a panel of 601.9 mm would be good quality and 602.1 would be rejected. Yet the difference between the two, 0.2 mm, is much less than the 1.9 mm deviation of the former from the target size of 600!
- Uncontrolled irregularities about a target mean value are only one of the problems of process variability which the quality organisation must cope with. Other factors have to be monitored.

We shall discuss these and other issues of quality appraisal in Chapter 16.

Case study: Kobe Steel Company, Kakogawa Works [34]

The Kakogawa Works, built in 1968, can produce 6 million tonnes of steel per year. The site employs 9,000 people, including subcontractors. The plant has been designed for high productivity, energy recycling, clean processes and low pollution levels.

The basic quality policy is to meet quality, delivery and cost requirements. Standardisation is an important element in achieving these aims. Quality improvement is included in the 10-year long-term plan whose objectives include:

- Make an increased proportion of higher grade steel and steels with higher added value
- For products whose quality is seen to be lower than competitors' products, take steps to equal and then overtake these quality levels as soon as possible
- For products whose quality is seen to be satisfactory, reduce manufacturing cost without reducing quality
- Enhance the effectiveness of the quality assurance system.

At Kobe these long-term objectives have been converted into short-term plans that include specific targets which are to be met. Overall responsibility for quality assurance rests with the works manager. The quality system manager provides instruction, advice and coordination on issues such as quality problems, standardisation and quality control.

In 1989, Kobe was facing problems because customer requirements were advancing faster than the production technology could cope. For example, electrical appliance manufacturers had become particularly severe on surface imperfections on rolled sheet steel. This was the main cause of non-conformance at Kobe. As one countermeasure, operators clean and paint the plant and the floor in bright colours between production runs. This is to minimise the dust in the atmosphere.

Manufacturing control is carried out by computers. These measure product dimensions, surface finish and chemical content, and check for internal flaws. Data is assembled each day and analysed using statistical techniques. Results are available to all employees.

Questions

1 *Select from the case study one example of each of the three costs of quality.*
2 *How does Kobe Steel seek competitive advantage through quality? What factors are relevant to customers?*
3 *What features of a TQM organisation are mentioned in the case study?*

References

1. Besides illustrating a point about quality, I find this story interesting because it shows something about the development of organisational myth. I have heard it in presentations and conversations from buyers who were sure that the events, albeit with different numbers, happened to someone in their own organisation. I took to asking speakers to give more details and have learnt that they never know but could refer me to someone who might. My conclusion is that such incidents are common or that they do not happen at all. In either case we have a simple story told to audiences who are ready to believe. Truth and myth are indistinguishable.
2. There is even another shop, in a cheaper part of town, that sells 'thirds'.
3. Department of Transport (1993) *Buying a Car? Choose Safety*, Leaflet No. T/INF/271.
4. Zeithamal, V.A., Parasuraman, A. and Berry, L. (1990) *Delivering Service Quality: Balancing Consumer Perceptions and Expectations* New York, Free Press p. 26.
5. Crosby, P.B. (1984) *Quality without Tears* New York, McGraw-Hill p. 60
6. British Standards Institute (1987) *BS 4778 Part 1* Section 3; Johnson, R. and Winchell, W.O. (1989) *Production and Quality* Milwaukee, American Society for Quality Control p. 2.

7. Ho, S. (1993) 'Transplanting Japanese management techniques' *Long Range Planning* **26.4** pp. 81–89

8. Deming, W.E. (1981) 'Improvement of quality and productivity through action by management' *National Productivity Review* **1.1**, reprinted as Reading 7 in Latona, J.C. and Nathan, J. (eds) (1994) *Cases and Readings in Production and Operations Management* Needham Heights, Mass., Allyn and Bacon pp. 223–236.

9. A best-seller that did much to bring quality ideas to a wide audience: Crosby, P.B. (1980) *Quality is Free: The Art of Making Quality Certain* New York, Mentor.

10. Lister, Richard (1994) 'Beyond TQM ...' *Management Services* May pp. 8–13.

11. Deming, op.cit. p. 223.

12. Gador, Brad (1989) 'Quest for Quality – Tennant Company, Minneapolis, MN' *Target* Fall, pp. 27–29.

13. Beynon, H. (1973) *Working for Ford* Harmondsworth, Penguin p. 77.

14. Etcherelli, C. (1985) *Elise ou la vraie vie* London, Methuen p. 137.

15. In a special issue of *Quality and Reliability Engineering International* 4.2 (1988) on Taguchi Methods, a number of articles show how the statistical methods can be improved. A general evaluative paper is: Box, G., Bisgaard, S. and Fung, C. (1988) 'An explanation and critique of Taguchi's contributions to quality engineering' ibid., pp. 123–131.

16. Henkoff, R. (1993) 'The hot new seal of quality' *Fortune* 28 June, pp. 116–117.

17. Ho, op.cit. p.87.

18. Dickson, Tim (1993) 'Management quality street cred – TQM is struggling to make an impact in Europe' *The Financial Times* 20 October, p. 16.

19. Imai, Masaaki (1992) 'Solving quality problems using common sense' *International Journal of Quality and Reliability Management* **9.5** pp. 71–75.

20. ibid. pp. 72–73.

21. It should be noted that BR, and its successors, have worked hard to improve in this area in recent years. The change from 'passengers' to 'customers' is a minor symbol of the development of a retailing philosophy.

22. Peters, Tom (1994) 'Theatre on the retail stage' *The Independent on Sunday: Business* 6 March, p. 26.

23. op.cit. p. 74.

24. Dawson, Patrick (1994) 'Total quality management' in Storey, John (ed.) *New Wave Manufacturing Strategies* London, Paul Chapman pp. 103–121.

25. Deming, op.cit. pp.229–235. Various versions and interpretations of the points can be found. For example: by Deming himself, (1985) 'Transformation of Western style of management' *Interfaces* **15.3** pp. 6–11, (1986) *Out of the Crisis* Cambridge, Mass, MIT Press, pp. 23–96 and (1991) 'Philosophy continues to Flourish' *APICS – The Performance Advantage* **1.4** p. 20; Aguayo, R. (1991) *Dr Deming: The man who taught the Japanese about quality* London, Mercury pp. 121–122. Curiously, Aguayo has 16 points in his list of 14.

26. Deming (1986) op.cit. p. 88.

27. Vandermerwe, Sandra (1994) 'Quality in services: the 'softer' side is 'harder' (and smarter)' *Long Range Planning* **27.2** pp. 45–56.

28. ibid. p. 53.

29. Ansari, A. and Modarress, Batoul (1994) 'Quality function deployment: the role of suppliers' *International Journal of Purchasing and Materials Management* October pp. 28–35.

30. McGeorge, John F. (1988) 'Design productivity: a quality problem' *Journal of Management in Engineering* **4.4** pp. 350–362.

31. Based on: Burgess, John A. (1988) 'Assuring quality in design engineering' *Journal of Management in Engineering* **4.1** pp. 16–22.

32. Heidenreich, Paul (1988) 'Design for manufacturability' *Quality Progress* May, pp. 41–44.

33. Strictly, we must assume that the different measurements are independent for the following analysis to be sound.

34. Based on Dale, Barrie and Asher, Mike (1989) 'Total Quality Control: lessons European executives can learn from Japanese companies' *European Management Journal* **7.4** pp. 493–503.

16

INVESTIGATING AND CONTROLLING QUALITY

Chapter objectives

When you have finished studying this chapter, you should be able to:

- Demonstrate the use of charts and other forms of data presentation in the investigation and communication of quality issues.

- Show how control charts are set out, used and interpreted for both quality variables and attributes.

- Summarise the key features of benchmarking for establishing standards and evaluate the associated benefits and problems.

- Outline the quality function deployment process and use a simple illustration to illustrate the House of Quality.

- Discuss Taguchi's work in developing the quality loss function and proposing the idea of robust quality.

- Identify sources of dominance and their implications for quality control.

- Evaluate the advantages and disadvantages of sampling in quality systems.

- Explain the nature and role of acceptance inspection and how sampling plans balance producer's and consumer's risk against the cost of inspection.

INTRODUCTION

The important contributions of Shewhart, Deming, Juran and others to the development of the management of quality originated in the application of statistical theory to the questions of sampling and control. In this lay the danger of inspection and quality control becoming the domain of the expert rather than quality becoming the general responsibility of everyone on the organisation. Fortunately, the stress on statistics, in practice as well as in training, has been toned down and new techniques and approaches have been brought to the fore to enable more people to be involved.

In this chapter we shall examine some tools and techniques that help the investigation of quality problems and enable realistic standards to be set. These have to match the needs of the market place with the capabilities of the enterprise.

438

Statistics retains a key role in the TQM context. Within the scope of the book we shall examine the two most common applications, in statistical process control and acceptance inspection.

INVESTIGATION

Among the skills that are part of the repertoire of both analysts and quality circle members is the ability to use charts. They help in problem awareness and break-down and act as valuable records of group discussion. As an aid to the communication of complex ideas, a well-designed chart is difficult to beat. In the next paragraphs, we explain several graphical means of analysing quality issues and communicating ideas about them.

1. Cause and effect

The cause and effect diagram is a valuable way of starting an investigation into, and opening up discussion about, quality questions. It is also known as an *Ishikawa diagram*, after one of its advocates, or a *fish-bone diagram*, after its form. While often drawn to suggest a fish, there is no conventional method of presentation. Stars or sprays will do equally well. The essence of the diagram is to record discussion and ideas and connect them by lines. In the version of Figure 16.1, the starting point, at the fish's head, was the problem of egg damage in a supermarket. The other boxes represent main limbs where causes may lie and the small

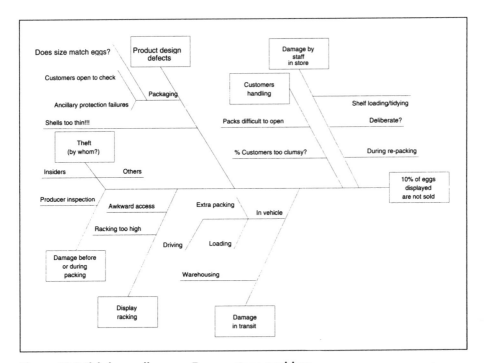

Figure 16.1 Fish-bone diagram: Egg wastage problem

439

bones suggest some detailed reasons for these areas. Therefore, the diagram can summarise ideas of cause and effect in an informal, hierarchical way.

Having established a visual agenda, a team, or quality circle, can use the fishbone diagram to plan further investigation. This can follow Imai's instructions for kaizen as explained in **15.12**. We should: *use common sense, go to Gemba* and *speak with data*.

2. Speaking with data

Before a study becomes too involved in the complexities of statistical analysis and control, it is remarkable how much understanding can be gained from collecting some simple data and presenting it in basic, visual ways. To illustrate, let us look again at the case study of Kobe Steel, given at the end of Chapter 15. Suppose we were to discuss the question of product faults with staff throughout the plant. We would be given responses such as, 'We get a lot of surface markings because ...,' or 'It's quite common to find ...,' or 'Sometimes it's as though ....' Staff will be very aware of at least some issues but are unlikely to agree on what the main causes are. Furthermore, their awareness would not be dependable as a source of frequency data for the various faults.

The next step is to collect data. Instead of gathering scrap material and sending it back for recycling without examination, we would assess the imperfections of each piece. In fact, one would expect this to be normal procedure in a steel rolling mill. The point of the exercise is to examine the data on reasons for failure in order to make some sense of it. Juran was one who pointed out that Pareto charts are useful for making the point. This form of presentation shows the frequency of events in ranked order. Figure 16.2 gives an example for one rolling mill during two study periods in consecutive years.

The data suggests that, between the two studies, great strides were made in the reduction of failures, especially those caused by roll marks in the steel. Yet pockmarks in the surface remained the most serious problem, dominating the others in terms of material spoiled. The Pareto presentation helps to focus the efforts at problem solving.

The data compared in Figure 16.2 is a mixture of attribute quality (Was the surface quality acceptable or not?) and dimensions. The latter can be further analysed because, as mentioned in Chapter 15, dimensions can usually be measured more accurately than they can be made. Carefully measuring thicknesses, rather than simply using a *Go-NoGo* gauge (see Figure 16.3) to test whether a dimension meets a specification, enables us to dig more deeply into the causes of variations. This is a prerequisite to reducing them. In the TQM firm, it would be normal to keep records of critical parameters, not merely to appraise whether a product is acceptable, but also to aid understanding of the process. We shall return to this question of detailed process control in **10 to 14** but first let us see what can be done with data and some simple charts.

3. Using simple charts

Imagine we are watching a rifle shooting competition. In the first series, competitors shoot ten rounds each. Figure 16.4 shows two of the targets. The left-hand competitor, LH, has scored 4 inners with the rest of the shots spread around the next ring. The right-hand competitor, RH, has all shots very closely clustered but

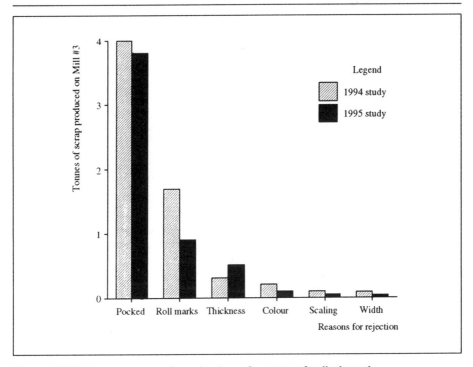

Figure 16.2 Data on reasons for rejection of output of rolled steel.

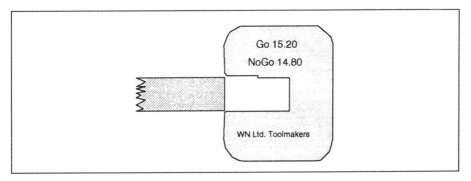

Figure 16.3 Go-NoGo gauge testing panel thickness

none are in the centre. If hitting the inner is the sole criterion for success, then LH scores 4/10, RH scores zero and LH wins. We can say that LH is the better quality shot. Yet whom would you back for the next round?

In the next round, RH can clearly improve by adjusting aim. This can be done either by pointing 'a little to the right and down a bit' or by adjusting the gun sight. On the other hand, there is little that LH can do. It looks as if the aim is good but slight shakiness means that not all shots are true. The competitor suffers from random variations (nerves?) which cannot be overcome by simple adjustment. LH is already shooting at maximum performance.

441

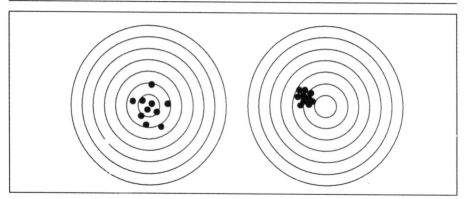

Figure 16.4 Whose is the quality shooting?

This illustrates an approach to manufacturing quality investigation. We have a sanding machine that finishes timber furniture components. If the sander produces a good surface finish, the key dimension is thickness. One way of tracking the process is to take samples every 15 minutes. 5 panels each time will be sufficient. What story can we glean from the data? The answer to this question will clearly depend on the data itself.

Before going on to look at general cases, we can study one example, shown in Figure 16.5. The top half of the diagram shows the measurements taken for each of the five panels in each sampled set. Note that we have set out the raw data first. Working with means and measures of dispersion at this stage unnecessarily loses some of the data variety. The plots are rather like the rifle range results. Looking at the raw 'x' data, we can see that, each quarter hour, the machine setting changes but it remains capable of performing close to that setting. To confirm our impression, we can calculate summary data. The line in the upper graph shows the mean values of the samples, emphasising how the product thickness falls by about 0.05 mm during the whole hour covered by the observations; the lower graph measures the dispersion of each sample by simply measuring its *spread* or *range*, the difference between the maximum and minimum.

Naturally, we do not know whether the machine is being adjusted to move it towards a target thickness or whether it is simply drifting out of control. Yet we can conclude that the sanding process is capable of consistent quality output provided that the setting is under control. To this end we would recommend regular monitoring of sample thicknesses and machine adjustments if necessary. Quality would be improved if the cause, or causes, of setting changes were discovered and then eliminated.

The observations do not reveal whether the sanding machine is actually producing quality products during the trial. Investigation of this aspect requires targets and limits to have been set in advance. These boundaries form the framework for control charts, proposed first by Shewhart in 1924. Shewhart's statistical approach was aimed at separating common causes from special causes in process variation. Deming acknowledged that this formed the basis of much of his later work.

4. Control charts

Control charts are used to set out process variables in a standard form. The horizontal axis shows time and the vertical axis represents a variable. This could be a

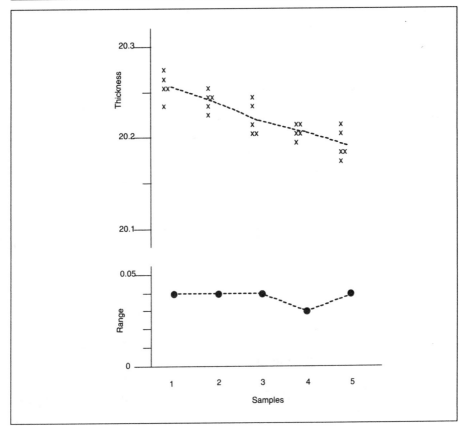

Figure 16.5 Sanding machine performance

product property, such as length, weight, electrical resistance and so on, or it could be a process variable, for example the temperature of a fluid or its density or viscosity. The vertical axis shows the target value and two *control limits*, upper and lower. They may be the specification width but not necessarily so, usually being set more narrowly than this.

Typical patterns are shown in Figure 16.6. As with other charts, visual inspection can reveal a great deal:

A Normal behaviour.
The results are scattered around, and close to, the target.
B C One measurement outside the control limits.
The matter should be investigated and further samples taken to see if the results are freakish or part of an emerging pattern.
D E Two measurements close to the control limits
These are danger signs. The result could be by chance or the process may need adjusting. Again, further samples should be taken before any action is taken.
F G Six to one side of target
While being well within the control limits, the results are suggesting that the process needs adjustment. Again, the reason for the drift should be established.

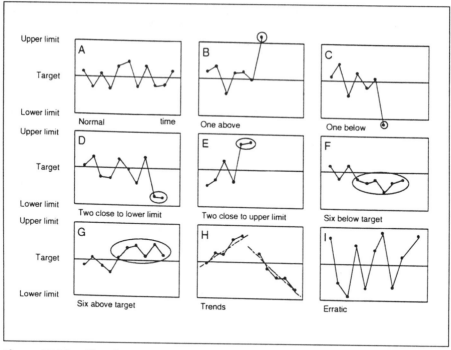

Figure 16.6 Looking for patterns in control charts

The number on one side that will trigger investigation will depend on experience with the process.

H Trends

Clear trends, which can be confirmed by collecting more data immediately, show that the output is likely to move out of range shortly. Immediate adjustment may be required. Again, the cause of the pattern should be looked for.

I Erratic behaviour

This may be the expected pattern for the process and all is well. Yet it does suggest that the machine is not good enough to operate within the chosen limits. It would be very difficult to control, for one could ask how to set this machine to the target and how one could pick out any of the behaviour patterns shown in D to H.

SETTING STANDARDS

We noted at the end of section **3** the need for setting targets and control limits. To look into this process, we must go back several stages from the operations scene to examine where the standards come from. Processes to be covered are *benchmarking, quality function deployment* and study of the *quality loss function*.

5. Benchmarking

As a source of ideas and standards of quality, service and other operational attributes, benchmarking has obvious attraction. After all, why not look to the best for the standards that should be used? We can define the term as follows:

444

Benchmarking is the practice of recognising and examining the best industrial and commercial practices in an industry or in the world and using this knowledge as the basis for improvement in all aspects of the business.

This is not imitation. It is about taking the best features from all other organisations and finding ways to combine them so that they are equalled or bettered. There are, in the definition, two modes of benchmarking. The more straightforward is done within the industry. The firm monitors competitors' products and processes and uses this knowledge to improve its own. Outside the industry, imaginative comparisons can be made between common or related functions. For instance: ICL has measured its training methods against those of the Royal Mail; a US regional airline compared its aircraft turnarounds with motor racing pit stops; other companies have looked worldwide to set best practice standards for research and development[1].

Done effectively, benchmarking produces data on which new policies can be created. It will examine:

- Internal and external *products*
- *Operational processes* used in the production and distribution of these products
- *Infrastructure* including people, capital assets and other resources and how well they are used
- *Management processes* especially strategy and the management of change.

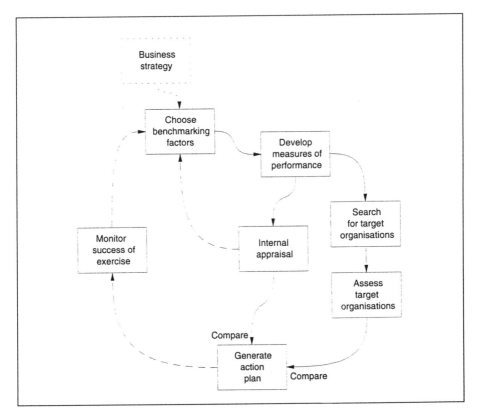

Figure 16.7 Benchmarking cycle

The benchmarking cycle has several steps (ranging from about 4 to 9 depending on which authority or organisation is being quoted). As shown in Figure 16.7, we shall present 6, as follows:

1 *Choose the factors to be benchmarked.* These can be selected according to the headings of products, processes and infrastructure listed above. Strategic value chain analysis will help to ensure that the items chosen are of critical importance.
2 *Develop measures of performance.* This is relatively straightforward if they relate to financial risk but much less clear cut if one is investigating customer satisfaction. Methods of collecting the same data about other organisations will also have to be considered and may limit the variables that are to be studied.
3 *Make an internal appraisal* of performance measured against the benchmarks. This will be limited to current assessment and historical comparison. Furthermore, it may uncover some further factors for study.
4 *Search for organisations* that are leaders according to the benchmark parameters. The start of this search is likely to be the organisation's direct competitors but world-class standards can be found anywhere. Box 16.1 summarises some selection criteria[2].
5 *Assess the target organisations* on the relevant performance measures. Use this information for comparison and as the basis of questions such as, 'What are they better at?' or 'Why are they better?' or 'What can we learn?'
6 *Generate a plan of action* based on analysis and comparison.

As Figure 16.7 shows, these steps are linked in sequence and form a loop with a monitoring activity. This stage, having reviewed how the exercise has turned out, suggests modifications to the benchmarking criteria as well as to other elements.

Presented in this way, the process sounds straightforward but can, of course, run into problems with other companies, particularly fierce rivals. Yet much information is already formally published, products contain a wealth of data and can be readily bought or observed, and responses to different companies can be discussed with customers. Main gives some advice for use when approaching other companies[3]:

Target organisations	Advantages	Disadvantages
Other in-house organisations	Ready access to information	Insufficiently convincing; biased
Domestic and foreign competitors	Much information accessible; very convincing	New information not easy; supply resistance; concern over leaks
'National class' of excellent organisations	Innovative; cooperation most likely	Different operating environments
'World class' of excellent organisations	Highly informative and innovative	Cultural differences hinder transfer; costly and time consuming

Box 16.1 Picking the target

- *Don't go fishing* This means that study should have a clear purpose and its scope should be limited to support areas that need improvement
- *Send out the people who will have to make the changes* This means letting people see for themselves. Raising awareness in this way is a great step along the path of change.
- *Exchange information* The target company may well be involved in its own benchmarking exercise. Information exchange is a possibility and a firm should not be asking any question that it is not prepared to answer itself. Commonly, a study will be welcomed by the target organisation.
- *Steer away from legal problems* Sharing information on price, market share and related issues may suggest price and market fixing which are illegal. Some companies forbid their managers even talking to people from rivals for this reason. The need to protect sensitive information about new products is also a factor.
- *Keep obtained information secure* An organisation that shares information with a benchmarking partner may be alarmed if this is passed on to a competitor.

Benchmarking can be both eye-opening and a stimulus to action. When studying engine repair processes, British Airways found that technicians on Japanese Airlines took 40 minutes to turn round a 747 while BA's people took 3 hours. The process also has its limits, however. It works well for high performance companies whose internal appraisal compares well with the best. Yet for moderate performers, the exercise may only generate confusion and low morale. It is rather like my swimming which I do to keep fit. I sometimes check my lengths against the clock to see whether I am improving at all. To compare my times with the Olympic champion is pointless. Low performing companies should think in the same way. There are plenty of basic actions they can take, from team building to improving links with customers, before they start to worry about becoming world class.

Benchmarking is best used for evaluating existing products, processes and infrastructure among firms that are aiming for excellence. As mentioned, it does not help in the innovation area where firms jealously guard their proposals from competitors' eyes. Anyhow, innovation is neither about imitation nor catching up. To develop standards for the future, one must go to the customers.

6. Quality function deployment (QFD)

Good companies incorporate customers' needs and expectations into their product planning processes. Market research takes the lead in finding out about these expectations. The design process converts them into specific products with specified performance. These should both satisfy the expectations and be capable of being supplied at reasonable cost. A major difficulty with this rational procedure is that customers' needs are expressed in different terms to those used by the suppliers.

Take, for example, the design of a popular camera. Customers may not know very much about camera design, especially as the average replacement rate spans several generations of technology. For the most part, they are likely to express their needs in terms such as convenient, flexible and simple to use. Of course there are those with more knowledge who will talk in terms of centre field autofocus, zoom ratio and red-eye reduction. But we are talking about a popular camera here and the firm is trying to reach the mass market. How does the company convert the customers' wishes into a viable product?

Quality function deployment is a methodology which enables firms to evaluate their current products and assess new proposals and the processes needed to supply them. It is both a philosophy, in that it implies a set of beliefs about the way products should be designed and supplied, and a communication tool, for it is used to underpin the links among marketers, designers and operations people. The goals are improved interpretation of what elements create customer satisfaction and dissatisfaction, quicker and more successful design, and more effective teamwork among all parties.

QFD is defined as:

A system for translating consumer requirements into appropriate company requirements at every stage, from research, through product design and development, to manufacture, distribution, installation and marketing, sales and service.

The procedure was introduced at Mitsubishi Heavy Industries in 1972. By 1976, it had been taken up and further developed at Toyota and among its suppliers, reaching the West in 1983, through the motor industry. Toyota, which in the 1970s had had a bad reputation for 'body durability' (that is to say, rust) made rapid strides, both on that dimension and in shortening and improving the design process. Through QFD, the start-up costs (those attributed to implementing the design in the production process by adjusting virtually every element) were drastically reduced. By the mid-1980s, the effect was such that 90% of design changes at Toyota were complete *before the manufacturing start-up*. The typical western company was still revamping its designs months later.

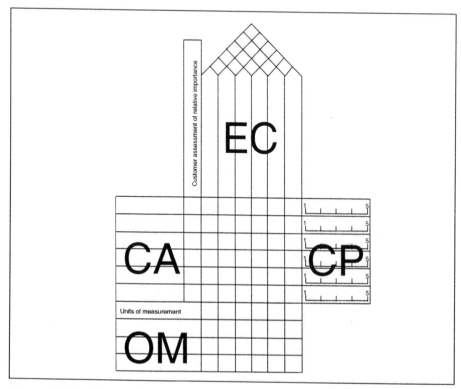

Figure 16.8 The House of Quality

QFD has been applied using seven steps whose results are laid out in a set of special matrices and tables linked as in Figure 16.8. The form of the figure gives the technique its name - *House of Quality*. The steps are as follows:

1 *Identify customer attributes, CAs*
   At this stage it is important to record these attributes in the customers' words. Using the *voice of the customer* avoids having their needs interpreted (that is, misinterpreted) by designers and engineers. Note that the customers need not be for consumer goods. The approach works equally well for services or for intermediate products sold to other organisations. Customers' requirements will, in some industries, be backed up by those of regulators. For instance, many standards covering motor car design are set by the government.

2 *Identify engineering characteristics, ECs*
   Now the process uses the language of the engineer. Product features specify components, layouts, sequences, performance and so on. The features should be measurable so that they can be evaluated in comparison. The units of measurement can be recorded in the diagram.

3 *Compare CAs and ECs*
   This step uses the central matrix with the CAs listed to the left and the ECs across the top. Any cell where there is a relationship has an entry. The symbol indicates the strength of the relationship. An EC can affect several CAs. For example, incorporating a high-quality wide-range exposure meter in a camera addresses the CAs of ease of use and flexibility. On the other hand, it may be found that an engineering characteristic does not bear on any CA. In that case, the question is whether the EC makes a contribution to product value or is unnecessary.

4 *Establish links between pairs of ECs*
   Another matrix, forming the 'roof' of the house, is used to set out interrelationships between the EC pairs. Again, symbols represent strong or weak links. Recording them in a matrix enables the team to understand how changes in one element affect others. For instance, thickening the material in a vehicle frame will increase strength and safety but will add weight and therefore reduce acceleration.

5 *Evaluate competitors' products, CPs*
   The method here is to rank or score rival products against the CAs. An extension is to establish weightings for the CAs so that trade-offs among them can be manipulated clearly. This evaluation process is readily done with existing products through standard market research procedures using interviews or contact groups of various forms. The weightings or rankings appear as the 'chimney' of the house.

6 *Assess the ECs of the rival products as the basis for development targets*
   This step is achieved by testing, inspecting and dismantling the rival products, if they are goods. Assessment of services can be made through field observations. They appear as a set of objective measures, OMs, to form the house foundations. From a comparison of rival OMs of ECs, development priorities will be set out.

7 *Select ECs for development into detailed design, process design and operations*
   This step not only confirms the main design specification but underscores the detailed attributes that need to be incorporated into the product to satisfy the CAs. The House of Quality is, therefore, feeding the *voice of the customer* right through into the manufacturing or supply processes.

To show how this works out in practice, let us return to the example of camera design. We will consider the sector for compact automatic cameras without zoom lens. This is a crowded sector with about a dozen leading suppliers and much 'feature' competition. Figure 16.9 shows how information would be set out. The CAs include notions such as 'easy to use', which ranks first, to 'easy to carry' which ranks fifth in the abbreviated list shown here. ECs list the main devices to be included in the EC specification. The roof matrix shows that the firm knows how to, say, design an automatic focus and exposure system with integrated flash and low power consumption. Yet the flash itself consumes more battery power, particularly if it incorporates the red-eye reduction system. Further, electric film winding consumes power and adds weight. Hence the negative symbols The central matrix relates the ECs to the CAs. ECs of auto-focus and exposure strongly support 'easy to use', as does, to a lesser extent, electric film winding.

Units for the ECs are shown below the central matrix. They are metres, grammes, milliwatts and f-numbers. OMs for the firm's current product and two

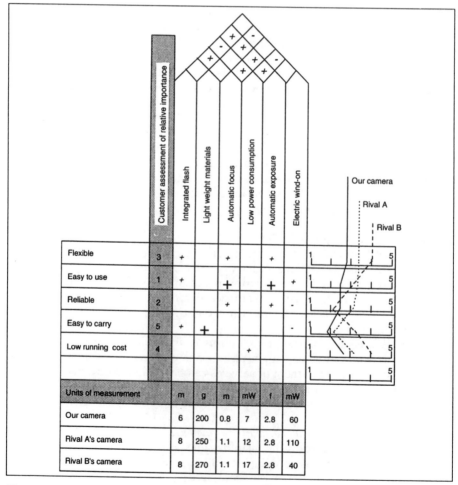

Figure 16.9 House of Quality: Camera development

450

leading rivals are given below. The three are compared against CAs in the CP area on the right. The array presents designers with a view of the problem they face and suggests where they may concentrate their efforts. At present, the firm's camera compares poorly with rivals on CAs, especially the most important, ease of use. Improvements to the controls for the focusing, exposure and, possibly, flash units seem to be a development priority. Naturally, studies would have to be conducted in much more detail and a practical House of Quality would contain many more rows and columns than the cut-down version shown here.

Hauser and Clausing [4] point out that the house is not a rigid procedure. It helps teams to set targets and summarise data in usable form. Like any good methodology, it acts as a guide, framework and agenda setter. The decisions still have to be made by the participants. The procedure is not rigid in another sense. Although one form of the process has been set out here, development teams would be expected to customise the House of Quality to suit their own needs. Details of how rivals' products are selected and evaluated, for example, depend on the industrial setting. It is also clear that the process will differ if the firm intends to develop a new product, in which case the comparison procedure would be more open ended.Yet again, in the supply of services the terminology would change. The essence of the House of Quality, however, remains the same. It sustains the effort to convert the voice of the customer into real product dimensions.

The house, or a 'row of houses', can be used through the whole development sequence. 'If our team is truly interfunctional, we can eventually take the 'hows' [ECs] from our house of quality and make them the 'whats' of another house, one mainly concerned with detailed product design.' [5] The ECs can become the equivalent of CAs in a 'parts deployment' house and so on. The four houses, shown in Figure 16.10, take the voice of the customer through to manufacturing. Ansari and Modaress show how QFD can be used as a vehicle to bring suppliers in to the development activity[6].

7. Quality loss function (QLF)

Taguchi argued that what has become the conventional way of looking at specifications is too naive. The conformance perspective, with its *specification width,*

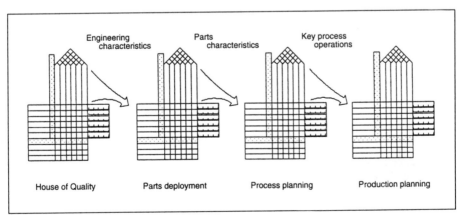

Figure 16.10 Row of Houses of Quality

creates too sharp a distinction between acceptable items just inside the boundary and unacceptable ones just outside. The existence of the tolerance band, moreover, creates an attitude of mind that believes that all items falling inside the band are of equal value. Therefore, compared with real concentration on the target, this conformance-oriented quality leads to a greater proportion of products being further from it.

The difference is illustrated in Figure 16.11. The left-hand graph shows the outputs of three conformance-oriented manufacturing processes. It does not matter whether the frequency distribution is centred on the target, nor indeed whether there is any evidence of the process producing a peaked value, all of the output is acceptable. In the right-hand graph, on the other hand, it is clear that the process has been set to achieve the target.

Taguchi proposed a *quality loss function*, QLF, to underline the need to aim close to the target. It estimates the total cost in the long run of poor quality resulting from a product moving away from exactly matching the target value. The cost covers all losses from the time the product is delivered, including those incurred during use and the consequential effects of failure. It comprises service and warranty work, customer dissatisfaction, extra inspection and scrap as well as what Taguchi refers to as the general cost to society. There is practical support for this view in the manufacture of many goods. For instance, a high-speed drive shaft may be made within tolerance but very slightly out of true. The consequences of the error may never reveal themselves but, if the assembly is used often enough, the defect will lead to extra bearing wear and premature failure compared with one that is 'spot on'.

The QLF has a simple squared formula, that is the loss increases by the square of the distance from the target:

$$L_x = C \times D_x^2 \qquad TL = C \sum_1^n D_x^2$$

Here L_x is the loss for item x that deviates D_x from the target, and C is a constant. TL is the total loss from all n items of output.

Taguchi and Clausing [7] use the formula to estimate that, if a car manufacturer fails to spend $20 on getting a gear exactly on the target, then it would eventually spend $80 for two standard deviations, $180 for three, $320 for four and so on. On this rather shaky estimate they comment, 'Actual field data cannot be expected to

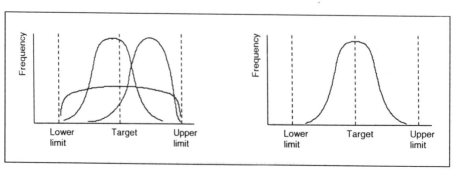

Figure 16.11 Conformance versus target-oriented quality

vindicate QLF precisely, and if your corporation has a more exacting way of tracking the costs of product failure, use it.' [8] More convincing is their use of the experience of Sony to contrast the two attitudes to quality specifications, see Box 16.2. Quigley and McNamara [9] look at the question from the buyer's point of view. Purchasing can, in principle, be improved by recognising the quality differences between acceptable suppliers. If this is to be done, the buyer must be able to *decide the value of quality differentials* that exist within the specification. They propose the QLF for this purpose.

8. Robust quality

Taguchi uses the QLF in developing the idea of *Robust Quality*. Robustness refers to *quality in use*, that is the performance of a product when it has been used, misused, overloaded (a little), knocked about in service, not overhauled on schedule and so on. Customers assess products as much by how they perform outside the specification as how they conform to it in the first place. Naturally, designers attempt to overcome the effects of degradation by building in extra strength at key points. But, as Taguchi and Clausing emphasise[10], many problems come not from weaknesses in individual items but from the interactions between slight variations in one item with others with which it forms systems.

In one case, it was asserted that very slight design deficiencies in the foundations of a power station hall allowed the alignment of an electric generator set to move a few thousandths of a millimetre out of true. The vibrations increased significantly the rate of bearing wear and damaged the generator windings[11].

In the late 1970s, Sony had found that customers preferred a particular colour density in their television pictures. We can call this value 10. Dissatisfaction rose with deviation from 10, so Sony set limits at 7 and 13.

Sets were manufactured in San Diego and Tokyo. The ones produced in the American plant had colour values uniformly spread throughout the range 7 to 13. All output was inspected and no sets outside the limits were despatched. A customer was just as likely to be given a set with a 7.8 screen as one with 10.2. Meanwhile, the Tokyo products clustered near the target of 10, although about 3 per 1000 fell outside the range. The output was not inspected.

Colour differences were not easy to perceive but they could be noticed. If a customer compared a new television, made to 13.1, with a neighbour's which was at 12.9, there would be no detectable difference and no dissatisfaction. Yet if it were compared with a demonstration model built to 10, the customer would see the difference and demand repair visits until the set had been put right. Sony San Diego produced 100% to company specification but received more complaints that Sony Tokyo, which could achieve *only 99.7%*.

If American workers were asked to produce to a specification of 10 ± 3, they would readily do so. The Japanese, in addition, would automatically strive to get as close to 10 as possible.

Box 16.2 Identical specification, identical televisions?

Taguchi's argument may follow the following lines in this case. The generator building should be built properly. Yet unexpected conditions make it possible for building foundations to move. Therefore, good design of the electrical equipment should recognise this and be robust, that is operate successfully in spite of some slight variations.

Through the work of Taguchi and others, Japanese engineers became familiar with the design of experiments to test the robustness of their products. Taguchi's own contribution focused on: making products robust compared with environmental conditions; making products insensitive to variations in their own components; and minimising variation in manufacture[12]. We shall look at each in turn.

Robustness under environmental variations

To design for robustness, engineers have to understand the environments under which products are to be used. In the case of mechanical equipment, for instance, users will understand something of a product's limitations and look for good service within these limits. At the same time, they want to cope beyond this and will often look for the extra reliability, or at least ease of repair. The *Land Rover*, for example, built its reputation on both counts. Taguchi's contribution to the study of robustness was to propose a formal method for its investigation. Box 16.3 gives an example set in the field of home economics.

Making products insensitive to variations in their own components

Since many products are assembled from many components, it is clear that the performance of the product will vary if the component performances vary. Given

---

Let us say we are considering the launch of a new muffin mix. We can, in the laboratory, develop mixes and test them under ideal conditions. Yet the success of such a product depends to a great extent on its quality in use, that is whether it will produce good outcomes in domestic environments. In the home, for example, oven temperatures are unreliable and, as anyone who cooks will know, baking time often over runs.

It may be that the mix that gives the best muffin under experimental conditions is not the one that should be sold. Alterations in the formulation may result in a product that is slightly less good. Yet the design may be more robust in that it produces an acceptable output over a wider range of baking temperatures and times.

A Taguchi experiment would then vary the *design factors* - the amounts of plain flour, baking powder, salt, egg and milk powders and sugar - and assess the sensitivity of the outcome to the *environmental factors* already mentioned. The difficulty is that it is possible to conduct an endless number of trials. Taguchi proposed a means of designing the experiment in terms of which variables to change and by how much. These are set out in special arrays intended to allow the trials to home in on good results quickly. The search is not for the best muffin mix but for one that gives good results across a wide range of conditions.

Box 16.3 Robust muffins

454

the inevitability of some component variation, engineers seek ways of minimising these effects on the assembly. To illustrate the point, let us look at the choice of length of a clock pendulum.

The relationship between the period T and the length l of a pendulum is not linear, see Figure 16.12. If a clock manufacturer can make pendulums with a known variation, these will be transmitted into variations in period. As Figure 16.12 shows, however, these period variations depend on the length of the pendulum and are smaller when the pendulum is longer.

The effect can be seen for the formula for period and its differential:

$$T = 2\pi\sqrt{\frac{l}{g}} \qquad \frac{dT}{dl} = \frac{\pi}{\sqrt{(l \times g)}}$$

Therefore, if the manufacturing variation is independent of the length of the pendulum, the designer should incorporate the maximum length of pendulum into the clock.

This simple example demonstration is not valid if it is assumed that the manufacturing variation itself increases with the pendulum length. The basic notion is important, however. It is possible to design components such as electronic circuits, whose performance is insensitive to components, especially those components that can neither be made nor adjusted precisely.

Minimising variations in manufacture

Variability is the enemy of mass production. If variability can be reduced, so will waste and scrap. As with the above examples, Taguchi argues that well-designed experiments will find ways of reducing variability caused by combinations of process factors. The approach can be illustrated by reference to a machine for filling detergent cartons.

It is commercially important for the weight of detergent entering each carton, and hence the fill rate, to be carefully controlled. Three factors affect the fill rate (kilogrammes per second) of the cartons: the chute diameter, the particle size of the detergent and the shape of the chute. Table 16.1 shows the experimental results using two values for particle size and chute diameter and with two

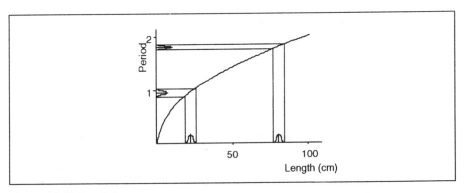

Figure 16.12 Pendulum errors

Chute A		Particle size	
		Low	High
Diameter	Small	1.2 (0.011)	1.4 (0.031)
	Large	3.5 (0.008)	3.3 (0.045)

Chute B		Particle size	
		Low	High
Diameter	Small	1.0 (0.015)	1.3 (0.027)
	Large	2.8 (0.009)	3.2 (0.030)

Table 16.1 Flow of detergent in experiment

chute shapes. The figures give average flow rates and standard deviations, both in kg/sec. It can be seen that only the chute diameter greatly affected average fill rate. On the other hand, the variation in the fill rate was affected strongly by particle size, it being reduced if the particles were smaller.

If, then, the aim was to achieve a stated average fill rate with the smallest variation, this could be done by choosing small-diameter particles and adjusting the chute diameter to hit the target rate.

9. Dominance

Related to the idea of robustness is the one of dominance. Depending on which process is being considered, the production of quality frequently hinges on one specific element rather than others. Therefore, to attain optimal quality, that part of the process must be the one that is most effectively controlled. Dominance, according to Juran, falls into four classes: set-up, machine, operator and component. We can compare them as in the table on page 457.

It can be seen from the fourth column of the array that different methods of appraisal are to be applied under different assumptions about dominance. Clearly, if more than one factor arises, then more inspection is needed. But this would then be a poor quality process. As the column suggests, much inspection relies on some form of control chart. These use the basic ideas set out in Figure 16.6 but are more formal in that chart boundaries and decision rules are worked out so that operators know what to look for in sample results. Their design depends on the application of statistical models to the field of quality. It is to this area that we now turn.

Dominance	Explanation	Examples of processes	Control system required
Set-up	Setting-up is the most important activity since the process is stable, equipment reliable and so on.	Many operations in the machine or printing shop if equipment is in good condition; checkouts in supermarket.	Inspect first piece to check setting; inspect last piece to confirm nothing went wrong.
Machine	Tool wear, machines getting hotter, changes in environment, or similar changes cause drift from target.	Many processes require adjustment because of minor changes in conditions.	Continuous control using charts to spot drift.
Operator	Variations in operator skill and experience cause output differences.	Judgement of bakers, painters and similar craft workers; cooks and waiters in restaurants.	Comparative use of control charts; feedback control to evaluate operator performance.
Component	Stable process has variations in material or component inputs that affect product quality.	Many assembly plants; processes using natural products from grapes to grain.	Inspection of incoming materials to accept or reject; measure key parameters.

STATISTICAL QUALITY CONTROL

We have looked at many examples of the application of statistical techniques, such as graphs and charts, experimental analysis and studies of variation. Going beyond these, there are two applications of great importance. These are statistical process control, SPC, which underpins concurrent control of products as they are made, and acceptance sampling, which concentrates on screening out batches of items containing an unacceptable proportion of defects. Acceptance sampling is corrective control in that it covers items that have already been made and is concerned with picking out defects. SPC, if used at the very end of a process, will also have a corrective emphasis. Yet, if properly integrated at key stages of the production cycle, SPC can take on characteristics of concurrent and even feedforward control. Therefore, it is valuable in preventive control too.

10. Sampling

Before going on to examine the statistical techniques themselves, we need to consider the role of sampling. It is convenient but brings with it problems and risks.

457

Why do organisations use it? The following reasons explain why samples are frequently taken instead of having full inspection:

- *Sampling is quicker*
  A manufacturer may not need to know the exact value of a parameter, just whether it lies within the acceptable range. Sampling enables this to be done speedily and with enough accuracy to enable process adjustments to be made.
- *Sampling is cheaper*
  Some tests are expensive in comparison with the value of the item being produced. Anyhow, the work done in inspecting a sample will be less than that required for all items. The manufacturer has to consider the cost advantage of sampling compared with the costs associated with making wrong decisions as a result.

  Customer satisfaction surveys are often based on samples for cost reasons and because continuous surveying of regular customers would eventually annoy them.
- *Some tests damage or destroy the product*
  There are many good reasons for *destructive testing* of product samples, especially where the sample size can be small and the results valuable. Examples range from bolts to biscuits and fuses to flame-proof fabrics.
- *Sampling may be more accurate*
  This curious notion can be explained by tests that show that inspection accuracy decreases as the number of tests made increases. The trade-off between well-conducted sample trials and 100% inspection done badly may favour the former on this ground alone.
- *Sampling smooths out random variations*
  We need to be able to discriminate between random effects that arise in the process and events to which it is sensible to assign causes and, if necessary, make corrections. We do not want operators to adjust machines in response to every variation. (In fact, the Central Limit Theorem tells us that, whatever the distribution of the parameters we are studying, the means of samples taken from it will be normally distributed. Therefore, since the normal distribution is well known, we can say much about risks and trends from sample data.)

The risk involved in sampling is that the wrong decision about the whole batch may be made from the data about the sample. There are two types of error:

- *Type I errors*
  Type I errors are decisions that something is wrong when, in fact, the process is operating according to plan. The consequences of finding something wrong may be small, for example the rule may be to take further samples immediately. On the other hand, the rule could be that all products made since the previous inspection have to be individually inspected. In either case, extra costs are involved and these are incurred unnecessarily since there was nothing wrong in the first place.

  How does a Type I error arise? In process control, the limits on the control chart are usually set more narrowly than the specification width. This is to ensure a safe, early warning of, say, process drift. Yet it does mean that samples will come up which lie outside the control limit yet which still lie within specifications. The decision is to weigh the cost of a Type I error against the risk of its occurring.

  Familiar Type I examples from life are: convictions of innocent defendants; unneeded tonsillectomies and dismantling your car's engine only to find nothing wrong.

- *Type II errors*

The Type II error can be more serious than the Type I. It occurs when the process is not working as planned, yet the sampling procedure suggests that it is running satisfactorily. The consequences may be confined to the organisation, involving a great deal of rework at a later stage, or they may not be detected and result in problems in the market from complaints to legal action.

How does a Type II error arise? It may occur in what seems to be a highly reliable process where sampling frequency is low. Somehow a fault arises and it does not show up in any of the samples. Alternatively, one fault is detected but is explained as a random event whereas it is actually a symptom of a process problem. Again, the costs of the errors must be balanced against the gain to be had from sampling.

Examples from life include: not convicting the guilty; failing to detect geological problems in a sample site survey; and a sample audit not picking up stock losses.

Referring to Table 16.2, the sampling strategy should seek to maximise the hits in the 'right decision' cells

11. Classes of control chart

Deming reported an example of an employee at the Nashua Corporation, a producer of carbon paper.

The carbon was sprayed onto the paper through an adjustable nozzle. The employee running the process would measure the amount on the paper and, in the light of whether there was too much or too little, would open or close the nozzle. Was there anything wrong with this? Even with a perfect process, random variations mean that half the product turns out below the mean and half above. And this is true whether or not the mean is fixed on the target value. Taking single sheets and adjusting the spray process in response to them meant that the operator was trying to adjust *randomness* out of the system. In fact it was found that this behaviour merely added variation. It was better for the employee to collect and measure samples, take a mean value and, using a control chart, decide whether any adjustment was necessary. [13]

The apparent contrast of this response with that which Taguchi may have made should be noted. He might have argued that the carbon variation is intolerable

Table 16.2 Errors of Types I and II

		Decision	
		Look for problem and take corrective action	Do nothing
Process condition	Process is satisfactory	Type I error	The right decision
	Process is faulty	The right decision	Type II error

459

and the process should be improved. Yet what we are focusing on here is how to control a process whose random variations have been reduced as far as current knowledge permits. After all, while Taguchi methods place *reduction of variation* on the quality agenda, they do not claim to be able to eliminate it.

There are two classes of control chart, plotting either variables or attributes. The former records information about samples of specific measures, such as length, volume, diameter, temperature and pressure. Normally, plots are made of the average of the sample, $\bar{X}$, and its standard deviation or range. Sometimes, individual items are measured and plotted on an X-chart. Attribute charts do not deal in measurements but in the number of defects within the sample. All of these charts can be used in combination as they can support each other in diagnosing whether and why a process has a problem. They are summarised in Box 16.4.

12. Control charts for variables

To demonstrate how control charts for variables are set out, let us return to the example presented in Figure 16.4. Consider first the chart for $\bar{X}$. It requires a mean line, corresponding to the process target, and upper and lower control limits to warn when the process is straying too far from the mean. The mean line is decided by:

- The standard specified at the design stage; or
- A process capability study as in **15.17**; or
- A study of at least 50 recent samples.

Type	Measure recorded	Explanation
Variable charts		
$\bar{X}$	Averages of small samples of measurements	Very commonly used to pick out changes in process settings.
R	Standard deviation (or range) of small samples of measurements	Used in combination with $\bar{X}$ to detect any sudden increases (or decreases) in process variation.
X	Measurements of single items	More difficult to interpret than $\bar{X}$ but used where only one observation in practicable.
Attribute charts		
P	Proportion of defective items	Used when decisions are whether to accept or reject.
C	Number of defects	Used when samples are of same size; identifies different types of defect when decision is whether to accept or reject.

Box 16.4 Common types of control chart

The choice is merely a starting point and such is the dynamic nature of control that the mean would be kept under continuous review until the process was well settled.

The control limits are usually set at ±3 standard deviations (of sample means) from the mean line. Referring to Table 15.4, we can see that this corresponds to 99.7% of the normal distribution lying within the limits. Put another way, 0.3% of the sample means would fall outside the control limits due to random causes.

To establish the standard deviation of the process, two related approaches are possible:

- Take a series of, say 25, samples and measure their mean values. The number in each sample should equal the number intended in the future. Calculate the standard deviation directly. (The sample size should be consistent as the standard deviation of sample means depends on the chosen number, see the equation below.)
- Take a set of, say 100, individual measurements and calculate the standard deviation, σ. The standard deviation of the means of samples, sized n, is always smaller than this, the two being related by the equation:

$$\sigma_{\bar{x}} = \frac{\sigma}{\sqrt{n}}$$

Rather than use σ as a measure of dispersion, the *range* of the sample measurements could be used, as in Figure 16.5. This is why the chart is called an R chart. The idea is easier to pick up when no calculator is available but the preferred method is the one shown here. Again, as with $\bar{X}$, data accumulates as the process is run and the boundaries can be checked in the light of more recent information.

Finally, the chart layouts should be checked against the product specifications. We are looking here at keeping processes under control by getting close to the target and staying there. The specification width should be much wider than the between-limits band we have established.

A completed chart is shown in Figure 16.13. The top half is the $\bar{X}$ chart for sample means. Six such samples have been plotted. It can be seen that, while the means lie well within the control limits, it does look as if the process is drifting towards a lower dimension. This could be accounted for by machine or tool wear but other upstream factors may be relevant. The R chart suggests that the process is basically healthy. Investigation of the drift and adjustment are called for.

13. Control charts for attributes

The problem with attribute data is that values for means and standard deviations do not exist. The data often concerns just two attributes for example: does the light bulb work or not; did the bus run on time or not; is the loaf ready or not. Sometimes there may be more than two classes as in: is the steak rare, medium or well done; is the dress tight, the correct fit or loose; is the porridge too hot, too salty or just right. The data collected tells us how many elements of the sample fell into one or other category. This is usually summarised by the value p, which is the proportion of defective items in the sample. Hence the P chart records the data and monitors the process to see if it is getting out of control.

As with control of variables, the P chart requires control limits. The target value can be set up initially and modified by experience. With a continuing process, it may be based on a long data run. The P chart assumes that the data for percentage defective follows a *binomial distribution* whose properties are used to set control limits.

461

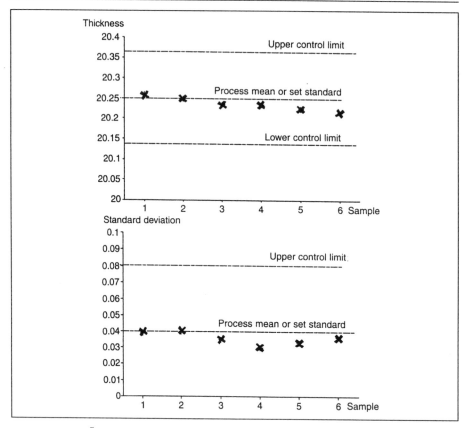

Figure 16.13 $\bar{X}$ and R control charts

For a mean value, $\bar{p}$, of the defect rate and a sample size of n, the standard deviation of the distribution of sample means is:

$$\sigma_{\bar{p}} = \sqrt{\left[\frac{\bar{p}\,(1-\bar{p})}{n}\right]}$$

From this, the control limits of $\pm 3\sigma$ are laid out in the usual way. It is usual to use sample sizes much larger than with $\bar{X}$ charts. The idea is to ensure that samples contain on average at least one defective item. Full 100% inspection of batches is used where defect rates are very small.

The C chart is similar to the P chart except that it is usually used to count the number of defects per unit of product. We may be looking for more than one type of defect although the incidence of each is small. A good example concerns typing or data entry tasks. There are many possible errors, for example hitting the wrong key, transposition, spelling and so on. The work can be sampled to check error frequency per (say) 5,000 words or 5,000 data items entered. Under these conditions, the Poisson distribution makes a good approximation. Its standard deviation is given by $\sigma_c = \sqrt{c}$ and the 99.7% control limits will again be set at $\pm 3\sigma_c$.

14. Using control charts

Figure 16.6 illustrated some patterns that may be encountered when process data is recorded on control charts. In a statistical process control system, managers must set up:

- Means of monitoring
- Means of recording the data so that it can be compared with standards – the control chart
- Rules covering what action to take in the light of different emerging patterns.

These items correspond to the steps set out in the control model. The rules for action are worked out in the light of experience and analysis of costs of defects and their correction. For example, there may be one measurement outside the control limits, see cases B or C of Figure 16.6. To adjust the process, or even stop it immediately, runs the risk of making a Type I error. The process may have been satisfactory and the sample mean may have that 1 in 333 that would have occurred by chance. On the other hand, to do nothing risks a Type II error because the process really is defective. A sensible sampling policy under these circumstances is to immediately take another sample rather than wait until the next scheduled one is due.

Similar policies can be worked out for other patterns. For instance, the variation may be increasing unexpectedly. This suggests failure of a machine component. If this can be spotted, then repair is required. On the other hand, the machine, when inspected, may appear to be working normally. Then the variation is acting as an early warning of possible trouble. In these circumstances, the time between sampling should be reduced and a careful watch kept on the standard deviation.

15. Acceptance inspection

While its most common uses are at the two ends of the firm's production process, namely goods inward and outward, acceptance inspection is used to prevent defective batches moving from any stage to the next. Acceptance sampling means taking random samples from batches to assess either attributes or variables. It assumes that there will be some level of defects, for 100% inspection is the only way of achieving none. The policy is to use the results of the sample to judge the condition of the whole batch and therefore whether to accept it, defects and all. The consequence of rejection of incoming goods can be either to return the batch to the supplier or inspect every item, returning the defects and charging the costs of the extra work. It should be emphasised that acceptance sampling should not be relied upon to make up for lack of good process control. The modern trend is to eliminate as much of it as possible by policies such as validating suppliers' quality procedures. JIT supply systems would be much less efficient if acceptance sampling delays had to be allowed for.

Acceptance sampling usually concerns two parties with different interests. They agree a sampling plan designed to judge quality fairly and avoid expensive mistakes. The *producer's risk* is of having a good batch rejected. The *consumer's risk* is of accepting a defective batch. The parties agree a *sampling plan* that identifies how samples are to be taken, their size and the decisions that follow the inspection. Each sampling plan has an *operating characteristic*. The OC is a curve showing, for a stated sample size and sample defect rate, the probability of accepting a batch compared with the real number of defective items in the batch[4]. The curve shown in Figure 16.14 is set up to satisfy the conditions agreed between producer and customer:

- Acceptable Quality Level = 2%
  The AQL is the desired quality level for the whole batch. The sampling plan must be devised so that, if the batch reaches this level, it stands a very high chance of being accepted.
- Producer's Risk = 5%
  The producer's risk is a Type I error. It is the chance of a good batch being rejected under the plan. This will be caused by a sample taken from a batch with fewer than AQL defects 'unluckily' containing more than the target number of defects.
- Rejectable Quality Level = 7%.
  The RQL, also called the Lot Tolerance Percentage Defective, LTPD, is the quality level for the whole batch that would stand little chance of being passed by the sampling procedure. In other words, batches worse than this must be highly likely to be recognised and rejected.
- Consumer's risk = 20%
  The consumer's risk is a Type II error. It is the chance of a bad batch being accepted under the sampling plan.

Using both an AQL and RQL is a means of achieving low values for the producer's and consumer's risks. If just a *single sampling plan* were used the AQL and RQL would be equal and the consumer's risk would be too high. Using the RQL set at a percentage higher than the AQL allows for three zones under the curve and the possibility of *double* or *multiple sampling plans*. With this approach, any

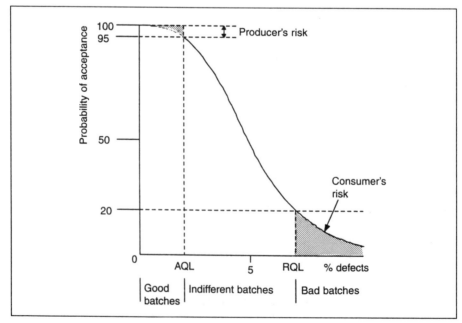

Figure 16.14 Example of operating characteristic curve

sample scoring fewer defects than AQL means its batch is accepted. Any worse than the RQL has the batch immediately rejected. For values between the two, further samples are taken and acceptance or rejection depends on the outcomes.

What happens if either party finds that its risk is too high? The quickest solution is to increase the sample size. Figure 16.15 demonstrates the effect of this. Here we are comparing two plans. In Plan A the sample size is 25 while in Plan B it is doubled. Under A only one defect (4%) is allowed in the sample, whereas under B the maximum is two, also 4%. These proportions are the same but the operating characteristics of the plans differ.

We can compare what happens if two deliveries, G and H, are tested. G truly has $2\frac{1}{2}\%$ defects. It ought to be accepted. Under Plan A it has an 80% chance of acceptance. This rises to almost 90% under Plan B. Batch H, however, is the opposite. It has some 6% defects and should be rejected. Under plan A it will be accepted 15% of the time, a figure which falls to below 10% with Plan B. This illustration shows that both the producer's risk and the consumer's risk fall when a larger sample is taken.

Increasing the sample size reduces the risks. This effect is sketched in Figure 16.16. Eventually, the sample size reaches 100% and the OC is 'squared off' as shown by the heavy line in the diagram.

To resolve the question of whether to sample, the firm should examine the cost savings resulting from sampling and compare these with the extra costs associated with the risks that they take. Essentially, 100% inspection is merited if:

- Inspection costs are low.
- Costs associated with a defect are high.
- The percentage defect rate is high.

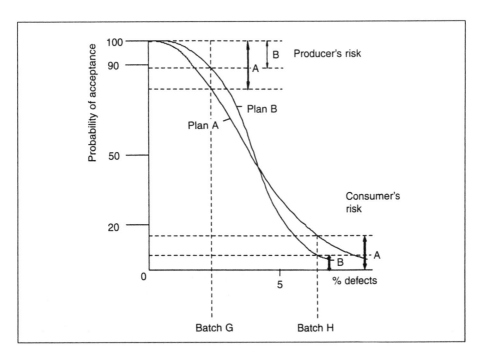

Figure 16.15 Two sampling plans compared

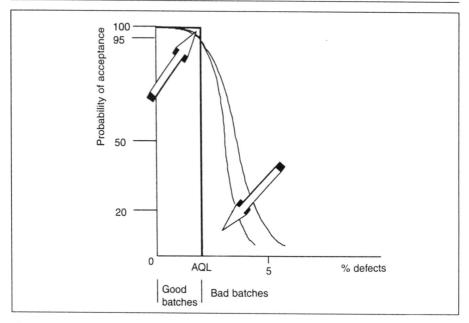

Figure 16.16 Increasing the sample size reduces risk

This question broadens into one of whether to inspect at all. No inspection is a good policy where:

- Inspection costs are high.
- Costs associated with a defect are low.
- The percentage defect rate is known to be low.

Acceptance sampling, therefore, is somewhat of an intermediate policy to be carried out in circumstances where there is some concern about inspection costs, defect costs and the defect rate. A decision about whether to set up a procedure will depend on a study of all of these costs. There is, of course, the special case where testing is destructive and so sampling will always be used.

In many cases, acceptance inspection should be seen as a last resort, in the sense that it covers deficiencies in other aspects of the quality assurance process. It is also inefficient if both producer and customer feel bound to carry out the procedure. As a first step to building confidence between partners in a supply chain, the customer could agree to accept the results of the supplier's inspection. Moving on from there, the supplier's own quality systems should be improved to ensure that faulty items never reach the despatch stage. This argument takes us back to the ideas of Total Quality Management.

Case study: Madras cheque clearing system [15]

In the Madras area there are about 800 branches of some 50 banks. Cheque clearing is the responsibility of the National Clearing Cell, a division of the Reserve Bank. Since 1987, the process has been automated around a high-speed reader-sorter system (HSRSS) for cheque data capture, linked to a mainframe computer. Cheques paid in at one bank and drawn on another are processed by the NCC.

The system sorts the cheques by bank and branch code and prints reports, including the balances for each bank.

The HSRSS reads data from the magnetic ink character recognition band along the bottom of each cheque. As with UK cheques (which use optically read characters) basic data is pre-printed. This covers serial number, account number, branch code and so on. The payment is encoded after the customer has presented the cheque. Those that have incorrect codes, or are of poor quality, are rejected by the HSRSS and are sorted and have their data entered by hand. Two batches of cheques are returned to each branch. Those accepted by the machine are fully grouped while the other has to be separated by the branch. Therefore, a faulty cheque is sorted twice.

The efficiency of the system depends on the HSRSS acceptance rate. Following complaints from banks about the amount of labour-intensive work they were expected to do, it was found that the cheque reject rate was about 10%. The manual work was leading to high error rates in data processing which in turn created reconciliation problems among the banks. The shift to computer processing had not resulted in the promised benefits.

In defence, the NCC manager pointed to the peculiarities of cheques presented in Madras and the high proportion that originated elsewhere in India.

After about a year of debate, steps were taken to improve NCC's internal processing. The tuning of the HSRSS equipment was adjusted and the whole operating area was cleaned to remove all traces of dust. This reduced the rejects by 1%. At the same time NCC sent new instructions to the banks to improve the data encoding but this had little effect.

The next step was for NCC to inspect all incoming cheques and attempt to repair the bad ones. While this succeeded in cutting another 2% from the reject rate, it was only achieved at high labour expense. The intervention was abandoned.

Finally, the NCC decided to investigate the encoding procedures at the branches. Training of staff was carried out by 5 NCC staff across a sample of 50 offices. For two months little happened, but, as more branches were trained, the reject rate fell to 4.5%. The training programme was extended, new operators had to be taught and all branches had to designate one person with the responsibility of ensuring that only quality cheques were sent to NCC. People from the branches visited the HSRSS operation to learn of the impact of proper encoding on the whole operation. These steps led to great improvements but rejects refused to come down to the international norm of 3%.

Further studies analysed the errors in more detail. The banks were answerable for only one of the five fields encoded on each cheque. The others were the responsibility of the printers. At a meeting at NCC, these were asked to submit a hundred cheques for proofing before producing an order. Print runs could run into millions. The NCC, in its turn, promised to return the test batch, with a report, in half an hour. Some printers agreed, others did not. Later, it was found that those who had co-operated produced rejects at fewer than 1%. Soon, the others fell into line and the overall reject rate fell to 2%.

The NCC manager then set about standardising the new procedures. It was found that the standards could be met by different personnel, rotated around jobs, thus proving that they were 'people proof'. A regular series of meetings with the banks was started. It shared feedback on operations and discussed suggestions for further improvement.

The project covered the work of thousands of employees. It had the backing of senior management. What had begun as a response to problems of poor service led to a transformation in the competence levels and empowerment of employees. There was a significant reduction in costs, although that was not the intention. The labour devoted to sorting was cut substantially, most cheques were sorted automatically and reconciliation errors fell to negligible levels.

Questions

1 *Use an Ishikawa diagram to express the causal links in NCC's service quality problem.*

2 *If you were investigating the causes of failure of the system, what sorts of data would you collect and how would you present it?*

3 *What would the relevance of a benchmarking study have been in this case?*

4 *For the more efficient operations after the change, explain how statistical techniques can be used to maintain control. How and where would you collect data and how would you use it?*

References

1. Trapp, Rodger (1994) 'Benchmaking moves on to bench-testing' *Independent on Sunday: Business* 9 January, p. 13

2. Ohinata, Yoshinobu (1994) 'Benchmarking: the Japanese experience' *Long Range Planning* **27.4** pp. 48–53

3. Main, Jeremy (1992) 'How to steal the best ideas around' *Fortune* **126.8** 19 October, p. 104

4. Hauser, John R. and Clausing, Don (1988) 'The House of Quality' *Havard Business Review* **66.3**, May-June, pp. 63–73; see also Whitney, D.T. (1988) 'Manufacturing by design' *Harvard Business Review* **66.4**, July-August, pp. 89–91

5. ibid., p. 71

6. Ansari, A. and Modaress, Batoul (1994) 'Quality Function Development: the role of suppliers' *International Journal of Purchasing and Materials Management* **30.4** pp. 28–35

7. Taguchi, Genichi and Clausing, Don (1990) 'Robust quality' *Harvard Business Review* **68.1** Jan-Feb, pp. 65–75

8. ibid., p. 68

9. Quigley, Charles and McNamara, Charles (1992) 'Evaluating product quality: as application of the Taguchi Quality Loss Concept' *International Journal of Purchasing and Materials Management* **28.3** pp. 19–25

10. op.cit., p. 66

11. At the time of writing, legal proceedings were expected.

12. The following examples are basd on: Box, G., Bisgaard, S. and Fung, C. (1988) 'An explanation and critique of Taguchi's contributions to quality engineering' *Quality and Reliability Engineering Journal* **4.2**, pp. 123–131

13. Quoted by Schmenner, Rodger W. (1993) *Production/Operations Management* 5th edition New York, Macmillan pp. 122–123

14. British Standards Institute *BS 6001* (1972, 1984, 1986) and *BS 6002* (1979)

15. Based on Sudhakar, Kaza (1994) 'Reject rate reduction at the Reserve Bank of India' in Dean, James W. and Evans, James R. *Total Quality: Management, Organisation and Strategy* St. Paul, West Publishing Co. pp. 167–168

17

CHANGE

Chapter objectives

When you have finished studying this chapter, you should be able to:

- Demonstrate how an organisation can use order-winning criteria to focus on areas for improvement.
- Compare and explain change directions in service and manufacturing organisations, relating these to technology and control.
- Identify changes in the balance of competitiveness, showing how manufacturing and service offers are converging.
- Show the limits of continuous improvement and indicate responses when incremental change is not enough.
- Outline key issues in achieving integration of operations in the whole organisation.

INTRODUCTION

The way organisations create value for their customers has changed dramatically in fifty years. In the production era, the stress was on operating cost which meant supply at the lowest possible price. The marketing era shifted the customer into centre stage. Finding out what the customer, or at least the average customer, wanted was seen as the beginning of the whole process of design, production and supply. Later, when this awareness had itself become established in many industries, competition shifted to quality. This took over as the key attribute used by customers to distinguish among rivals in the ever more crowded, globalised market place. So organisations became quality oriented. Now, the rules of the competitive game are shifting again. Terms such as responsiveness, flexibility, customisation and time-based competition describe the new emphasis on short cycles, rapid change and an ever more mobile and cynical crowd of end-users. It is not that the quality era is over, for most firms are still struggling to catch up. Leading companies, nevertheless, have made the great leaps forward and can no longer rely on quality as the single dimension that differentiates them from their rivals. Their customers, meanwhile, have come to expect higher standards in all aspects of business performance.

Such grand generalisations must be kept in perspective. There is no single trend. Just as some organisations are investing in expansion, others are involved in *down-sizing*. As one rationalises its product range as a prerequisite for aggres-

469

sive expansion, another decides that its skills are better focused on niche markets. Strategic shifts lead to strategic gaps.

It would, therefore, be foolhardy to risk a generalisation on the future of all operations management. Organisations, anyhow, do not work to generalisations. They must study where they are and formulate and carry out policies that are consistent with those positions. What is clear is that improvement will always be required and successful firms will gain if their operations are managed according to clear policies under which all elements are integrated.

This brief chapter considers continuous improvement from the point of view of how a firm should decide what operational areas need attention. It continues by looking at whether continuous improvement is good enough. It then returns to a theme of this book, the integration of the supply of goods and services into processes which concentrate on delivering value to the customer.

1. Improvement priorities

An important decision in operations management is the choice of areas on which to focus attention. Where such decisions are being formalised for the first time, the choice will help to set the agenda. When strategy is being updated, it will identify areas for improvement. These arise when the standard achieved in a critical area falls below that which is required. The *importance–performance matrix* is an aid to setting out managers' choices and assessments. In Slack's version, elements that comprise the product/service mix are placed in one of the 81 cells of a 9 × 9 grid[1]. The scaling is excessively complicated and Figure 17.1 is a 3 × 3 version of the matrix in which the key features are shown.

The horizontal axis of the matrix expresses the importance of each element in terms of its contribution to gaining and holding on to business. To be placed in the right-hand column, the element must provide advantage in the relationship with customers because they give it emphasis in their decision making. For the

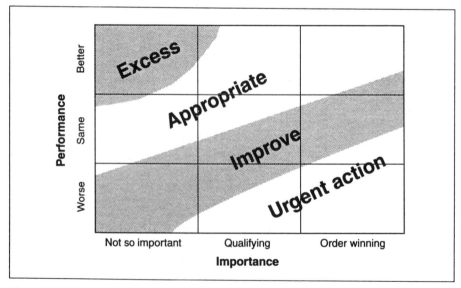

Figure 17.1 Importance–performance matrix

centre, the element must be about good enough to be acceptable to customers. Provided this is the case, customers attach little value to excellence in this aspect. The left-hand column contains elements that are rarely or never considered by customers when it comes to placing contracts.

The vertical axis of the matrix is used to record assessments of organisational performance compared with competitors. To attain the top row requires performance that is more than marginally better than benchmarks. The centre row covers performance that is almost the same. Worse achievement than rivals is recorded in the bottom row.

The significance of the model becomes apparent when the matrix area is divided into four zones, labelled *Excess, Appropriate, Improve* and *Urgent action*.

- *Appropriate*
  The lower edge of this area represents the minimum performance that should be achieved in the long term. For elements that are not seen as important by the customer, the firm must maintain a standard that is around the industry average. It must not be seen to be inferior. On the other hand, for the order-winning elements, performance must be maintained at the best industry levels. Therefore, this boundary slopes upwards towards the right.
- *Improve*
  Below the *appropriate* area come those elements where some improvement is required. Unimportant areas must be brought up to scratch as the company must not be seen to be failing while the order winning factors must not remain merely average in the long term. The boundary of this zone also slopes upwards from left to right.
- *Urgent action*
  Lying in the lower right-hand corner of the matrix come those elements of the package that are below standard even though the customers regard them as important. Clearly they must be improved urgently.
- *Excess*
  It is possible for an element to fall in the fourth zone of the area. Here, the organisation excels in its operations but on a dimension that is not regarded by customers as having much significance. It may be prudent to leave this area alone, unless it were costing excessive funds in which case it could be downgraded. There is no case for improvement.

An application of the grid is shown in Figure 17.2. The company was the sole UK producer of its type of insulating panel. It had higher costs than the importers yet could gain and hold on to business by its flexibility, personal service and weekly to-site delivery cycle. Unfortunately, the size of the niche that this marketing strategy provided was not large enough to enable the plant to run at full capacity. Therefore, the company sought to move into another end-use market where the panels had a decorative function. In this market, however, surface finish, which had not been important to its previous customers, was an order-winning criterion. (This is why this factor appears twice.) The change of policy, therefore, depended on urgent attention being given to this factor, as well as to the continuing problem of high operating costs. If improvement could be achieved, market research had suggested success as the company's other order-winning competences were either important or highly important in the new sector.

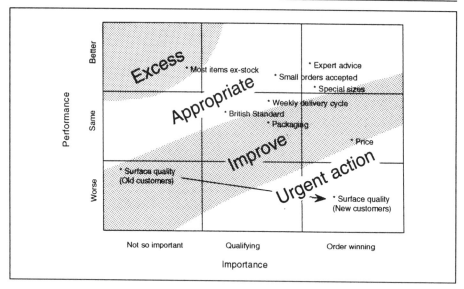

Figure 17.2 Identifying improvement priorities: Panel manufacturer

It is also worth noting that having British Standard approval for the material was regarded as a qualifying characteristic in the industry. The BS would be specified by engineers and architects in many applications. As a criterion, however, it could not be more than a qualifier as satisfying the standard was all that any manufacturer could do. This underlines a point made in Chapter 16. Common conformance quality standards do not help in differentiation once many companies achieve them.

The example given in Figure 17.2 is of a manufacturing company. Slack displays the use of the matrix in a service setting. Differences of application are, however, minor. In any case, it is clear from Figure 17.2 that many criteria used by customers in assessing manufacturers' capabilities in fact relate to service elements.

The importance–performance matrix is another way of identifying directions for improvement. They are, however, locked within current product and process definitions. We shall move on to look at directions for change in operational processes before raising the question of whether more fundamental reviews are called for.

2. Changing service directions

In which direction is business moving? The answer to this unrealistic question is that the directions are as many as the organisations themselves. For every one that expands, there is another that contracts; for each that broadens its range, another refocuses; as one enters international operations, a rival catches a cold on the foreign exchanges. The models presented in Chapter 3 to compare patterns of manufacturing and service operations can be used to picture these changes.

Figure 17.3 uses the same rows and columns as Figure 3.1 to set out the six patterns of service delivery. It has been suggested that there is a trend towards service standardisation aimed at reducing its labour intensity. Isolation and

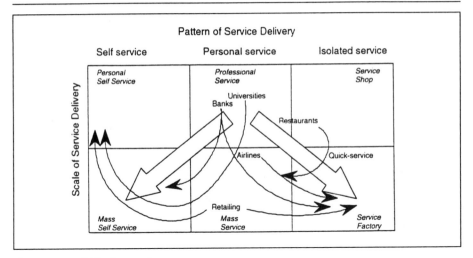

Figure 17.3 Shifts in service patterns

detachment of the service provider from the customer are also commonplace. This observation, supported by employment statistics for service industries, is represented by the broad arrows in the diagram. Service organisations that were in the *Professional Service* cell are having to change to survive. There are two general change directions. Either become *Mass Self Service* operations through the application of automation to customer service, or become *Service Factories* by moving most of the work to the back room. Banks have followed both vectors, automating personal banking to move towards the left corner and centralising the way business accounts are dealt with to move to the right. Airlines offering 'no-frills' service have followed the right-hand vector.

Yet the change process does not rest. Universities, for example, have responded to higher demand by moving first to *Mass Service* and then, in some cases, towards *Mass Self Service*. This is seen in the emergence of distance and open learning supported by information system applications. Yet the potential flexibility of the new systems in turn opens the possibility of new forms of customisation. *Personal Self Service* is seen as a goal of many institutions where students could be offered tailor-made courses supported by flexible information and control systems. These shifts are neither rational nor smooth; they are the outcomes of battles between those who argue for 'proper courses' and the advocates of 'consumer choice'.

A further point about change directions is that many operations do not currently lie close to the main diagonals, although there may be a drift towards them. Many restaurants occupy the *Service Shop* cell. McDonald's showed the way to standardise and combine *Mass Service* with a *Service Factory*. Modern retailers are, or were, offering *Mass Service* and have shifted towards both arrows, *Mass Self Service* and *Service Factory*. Yet, for each strategic shift, we see holes or 'niches' left behind. The specialised restaurant or fashion boutique come in to fill the cells left behind by the mass marketers.

What is the attraction of the two diagonals of Figure 17.3? These represent zones of less uncertainty where control can be exercised more readily. Customised service, at least of the type provided by human servers, is notoriously difficult to control. Not only is the demand varied and difficult to anticipate, but the detail of what happens in the service encounter leaves managers worrying about how customers are responding to interaction with their staff. Therefore, the move towards service standardisation, a shift down the diagram, is a move towards greater certainty and clearer managerial control. Furthermore, any trend towards the corners of the diagram is in response to the need to control labour costs that are frequently the dominant element in *Mass Service* operations. Yet, as some arrows suggest, the story does not end and, supported by new information systems, companies are inventing new ways of personalising service while retaining control of the transactions.

3. Changing manufacturing directions

We have discussed many aspects of improving manufacturing competence in this book. In the first instance these relate to, 'Doing better what you are currently doing.' We should also recognise shifts in the product–process relationship. This is illustrated by Figure 17.4 which is adapted from Figure 3.5. Again, there is a dominant diagonal in the model that firms stick to. Here the pressures to stay near the diagonal are more clear cut. On the one hand are the disadvantageous costs of putting too high a variety through dedicated production lines. On the other lies the hazard of loss of opportunity if the flexible shop decides unnecessarily to limit its range.

Manufacturing organisations do not move smoothly along the diagonal as they develop. For example, through selling efforts, a company may find that it is winning a greater variety of orders. This would move it down the diagram and it may find itself moving into the 'extra costs' zone. At this point its investment may be in converting dedicated lines to flexible manufacturing to push it back towards the diagonal. Just as easily pictured, however, is the firm whose average order size becomes larger, possibly as its main customers become more successful. The reduced variety implies a move up the diagram towards the 'opportunity costs' zone. Investment should then be aimed at improving the capability of handling

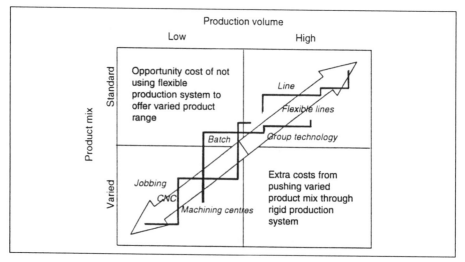

Figure 17.4 Shifts in manufacturing patterns

large volumes, a shift to the right. Whatever the details of the moves, change in a manufacturing firm throughout its life can be seen as a series of steps, moving up and down the volume/variety scale. Three notional patterns are sketched as stepped lines in Figure 17.4.

4. Competitiveness through integration

Survival of any organisation, whether it is a business or not-for-profit, depends in the end on its ability to compete. Either through direct competition in the market place, or through comparative benchmarking or other means of appraisal, the organisation is measured against the best of its rivals. The idea of 'competitiveness' applies to all organisations. There is no single dimension to the comparison for it is made across the six PQRRSS[*] factors:

- Price – not too far out of line
- Quality – very frequently an order-winning factor
- Reliability – keeping to promises every time
- Responsiveness – matching a customer's particular needs
- Service – at all stages of the interaction
- Speed – to keep down costs and offer good service.

The relative importance of the factors varies from case to case. It is clear, however, that success follows paying attention to all of them and keeping them in balance. To a manufacturing firm, for instance, service is not to be seen as an extra chore to be considered and offered after the production process has been devised. 'Service is all the rage in business. Even traditional manufacturing companies cannot prosper on the back of product quality alone. They must also achieve prompt delivery, competitive price, and after-sales back-up.'[2]

Voss points out that much operations management literature has considered the application of ideas from manufacturing in the service area[3]. He goes on to argue that the reverse ought also to be the case. Service is not incidental to the manufacturing firm: it is crucial. The so-called 'service elements' of the manufacturing process are, from the customer's point of view, as much a part of what is bought as the physical goods themselves. For Voss, service arises at three points of the manufacturer's value chain:

- *Distribution*
  The distribution system contributes to all aspects of the PQRRSS mix given above. Distribution costs have to be built into prices; quality controls should cover the whole chain; responsiveness and speed impact upon the order cycle time; service includes how and where deliveries take place and the support that goes along with them; reliability is the ability to maintain stocks and provide scheduled deliveries consistently.
- *After-sales service*
  The quality of after-sales service can be assessed by suppliers using both hard measures and impressions. Rapid and reliable service in response to customers' call-outs sustain repeat business.
- *Factory*
  While the factory's main service contribution has been in achieving delivery performance, its potential is much wider. Chase suggests four service roles,

---

[*] Remembering the initials 'P, Q, double-R, double-S' may help with the list.

shown in Box 17.1[4]. Using the manufacturing facility as part of the communication with customers can be important in shaping their perception of the value of what is produced.

This book takes the argument further. Every part of the organisation, every cell of the value chain, is engaged in providing customer service. Much of it is hidden from view but it can emerge in different places at different times. In the factory, we see just one example. Others include the purchasing department, where sources of supplies can be part of customers' specifications, and accounting, where sales invoicing and payment collection procedures often have a critical influence on the customer interaction.

As outlined in Box 17.1, we see many examples of organisations opening themselves to the inspection of the customer. At the same time, there are managers who find that this runs counter to their wish to maintain control over the interaction processes and, therefore, confine factory operations to the back room. Other

---

The factory as:

Showroom
> Supporting sales through showing off products, processes, quality assurance systems; people.
>> Disctronics showed customers difficulty of making CDs: this modified expectations.
>> ICI spent an extra £1 million on a new plant to enable customer access: this boosted perceptions of competence and enabled problems to be shared with customers.

Despatcher
> Supporting distribution, satisfying customers' delivery needs, backing up after-sales service, modifying and upgrading delivered products in service.
>> British Steel uses electronic data interchange to shorten lead times and lock out rivals.
>> EDI also at ICI Paints and Digital: in the latter case, lead time cut from 40 days to 4.

Laboratory
> Linking with R&D over experiments and improvements, working with marketing to incorporate customers' needs into products, all linked using processes such as Quality Function Deployment.
>> ICI works with suppliers to develop robotics.
>> US steel company: 'Our factory is our laboratory for testing new processes.'

Consultant
> Participating with other parts of the organisation in quality and cost improvements, design changes, new product applications.
>> Klix' shop floor staff install and service vending machines.
>> Lucas Engineering staff work on customers' quality problems.

Box 17.1 Service roles for the factory

organisations, therefore, are reducing the number and range of customer contacts to provide a higher quality service encounter. This is an example of fundamental restructuring.

5. Restructuring

In response to the changing business environment, adjustment is necessary. Critics of incremental improvement strategies, such as the shifts described in **2** or **3** or the *kaizen* of Total Quality Management, point out that small changes to improve what is currently being done may not be enough. For many organisations facing environmental pressure, rising productivity and the need for higher competitiveness on the order-winning dimensions, only a fundamental shift will do. After all, as a Polish politician is said to have remarked, 'You cannot leap a chasm in two jumps.'

There is a time for *kaizen* or continual improvement, and one for fundamental change. Too often it happens that firms try to avoid the change. Then, when the crisis eventually occurs, it is almost too late. Curiously, the firms that make big changes the most are of two types, the leaders and the crisis prone. The leaders change because they know how to. Change makes them successful. They continue because it is a means of staying ahead. The crisis-prone change because they have to.

To cope in the long term, three ways for operations to live with change emerge:

- *Flexibility*
  Responsive manufacturing and service systems enable firms to cope where they can obtain no advance warning of changes that might arise.
- *Forecasting*
  We have investigated the way that forecasts, qualitative or quantitative, place a 'buffer' of information between the operating system and the organisation's environment. This enables the firm to set limits on the change it has to cope with and therefore contains the cost of flexibility.
- *Influencing*
  Power vis-à-vis the environment can be exercised by methods from persuasion through advertising and lobbying, to adopting competitive stances aimed at limiting the scope of rivals. In this way, leading companies change the 'rules' of competition.

What if 'living with change' is not enough? In contrast to the incremental approach of the family of TQM techniques, *Business Process Re-engineering* takes a more critical stance. BPR is an innovative approach designed to improve all aspects of the customer offer. It is:

The fundamental rethinking and radical redesign of business processes to achieve dramatic improvements in critical contemporary measures of performance, such as cost, quality, service and speed. [5]

Critics would query the use of terms such as fundamental, radical and dramatic. Supporters would draw attention to the definition's use of rethinking and redesigning and the recognition that it is through their *processes* that organisations actually achieve anything. BPR is not concerned with smoothing out the bumps on the old road but with building a new one.

BPR has been given impetus by information system developments. The introduction of such systems into many organisations makes it possible to create new arrangements for work processes. For example, work that had been sequential because staff had to share the same resource, for instance an information file, can now be carried out simultaneously. Exploiting these possibilities, Hammer, a leading advocate of BPR, proposes six rules or principles as guides, see Box 17.2[6].

Hammer and Champey quote an instance of BPR. IBM Credit Corporation organises loans for customers wishing to buy from its parent company.

> Before the intervention, a credit request passed through five steps, each in a different department, and took an average of six days, although the work per request was only $1\frac{1}{2}$ hours. For the rest of the time the items were being assembled into batches and counted ready for passing on to the next step. Another problem lay in tracking each enquiry. Since no-one was in complete control of the process, queries from the field led to problems in locating at which stage the item was waiting. A direct response to this, keeping a central log of each batch, actually *increased* the average processing period.
>
> Once it was recognised that most enquiries did not require the attention of a specialist from each department, the company worked out a completely new process. One person, backed up by a database, became responsible for the whole transaction. A pool of expert advisers was made available to cover difficult cases. As a result, enquiry turnaround time fell from seven days to four hours, there was a small reduction in staff numbers and the number of deals made increased by a factor of 100.

Whether this example proves that BPR is a new approach or merely a repackaging of techniques from method study to information systems analysis is unclear. What is clear, however, is that information system developments offer new ways of coordinating the operations function. Restructuring to improve integration is concerned with making fundamental improvements to the flows of goods, services and information.

6. Integration

Four major integration thrusts are included in restructuring programmes[7]:

- *The best control is no control*
  Information systems are needed to support control systems, if they are to be introduced. Yet control systems themselves do not add customer value, merely building the 'hidden factory' of people working hard and achieving little. As we showed in Chapter 15, such control of areas like quality is best *designed out*

---

1 Organise around outcomes, not tasks.
2 Have those who use the output of the process perform the task.
3 Subsume information processing work into the real work that produces the information.
4 Treat geographically dispersed resources as though they were centralised.
5 Link parallel activities instead of integrating their tasks.
6 Put the decision point where the work is performed and build control into the process.

Box 17.2 Re-engineering principles

of the system. Similar arguments can be advanced for the management of JIT and other forms of operations planning and control.

- *Information systems should be flexible and decentralised*
  Just as control systems should be minimal, so should information systems. The attractions of the huge central database are clear but the hidden consequences not so easily foreseen. Penalties lie in inflexibility, the cost of operations and the difficulties of users to develop the skills to use more than a tiny fraction of the potential. Users demand that the providers focus on the six PQRRSS factors of section 4 and not the design of the IS itself.

The successful use of IT does not depend solely on planning or the level of sophistication of software. Of critical importance is the ability of managers to interact with the information system itself. A recent study among small and medium sized firms concluded:

' ... managers without a significant IT background showed both how to recognise the emerging opportunities for creative use of information systems and to implement changes. In other cases, the company IT specialists were well integrated with operating managers and the continuing developments grew out of their interaction.' [8]

- *Measures should match policies*
  Performance measurement is an important factor in steering the organisation along new strategic directions. For example, many cost accounting systems bedevil the introduction of JIT and OPT. We noted that, in an OPT environment, work done before a bottleneck was wasted work. Costing systems that calculate direct labour costs and machine utilisation encourage this waste.

- *New operations systems*
  The demands for new balance among the PQRRSS factors have created new operations systems. The challenge for the modern organisation is to create these systems, improve them and integrate them in an efficient and effective way. Organisational cultures, with traditional boundaries between, say, white collar and blue collar workers, are inappropriate to the ideas of sharing and empowerment implied by JIT, self control, flexibility and service demand in the modern market place.

To conclude, it is worth quoting further from the study mentioned above:

'Not only must management be flexible and creative with the firm's products and processes but it must also be able to implement and confirm successful change.'

> *Tempora mutantur nos et mutamur in illis.*
>
> Times change and we change with them.

Case study: Berghaus [9]

Founded by two walking enthusiasts in 1966, Berghaus is one of the EU's leading manufacturers of specialised outdoor clothing. The range includes outer wear, rucksacks and accessories. The company is known for its innovative design and marketing. Products are expensive, with some jackets selling at £350.

The company, with sales of £20 million, employs 450 staff in two factories in Newcastle-upon-Tyne. About half the output is exported, the main markets being Italy, Germany, Norway, Sweden, Benelux and Switzerland.

In 1989, the company installed a new computer system to book and allocate production and stock several months in advance. But the software failed to function. The second half of the year saw five months without management accounts or credit notes and two without invoicing. Then came the third mild winter in a row. Sales were down and the company and its distributors were overstocked. Berghaus pulled out of ski clothing and concentrated on its developments in all-year apparel.

Until recently, retailers have ordered stock and accepted delivery in two hectic seasons, holding stock, as a result, for up to six months. British retailers, faced with recession, high interest rates and a growing awareness of unpredictable weather led the trend away from the established pattern. Outdoor clothing shops in the UK include some chains while in Italy the fragmented market consists of some 500 small family-owned businesses.

After its 1989 experience, Berghaus began to develop a new 'stock response system', a sort of JIT for retailers as used by the main supermarket chains. Under this system, most of the risk of holding stocks is taken up by manufacturers. From 1993, UK retailers could choose to hold up to only one month's stock of an agreed range. Replenishment would occur once a month, with delivery inside a week from order placement. This contrasts with 1989 lead times of between six and twelve weeks. For export business, the minimum order quantity was cut from £1,500 to one garment with a seven-day lead time being the target.

The company could no longer rely on its eight-month order book. To cope with the uncertainty it had to increase its own stocks by 30% and work harder at forecasting and planning. The manufacturing process was redesigned to change it from mass production to short, flexible runs.

In February 1993, the founders sold the business for £7 million to Pentland, owners of Speedo and other sports brands. Pentland's intention was to develop and popularise the brand by appealing to the average outdoor enthusiast as well as the specialist. Pentland already sourced in the Far East and this would be investigated to lower costs.

Questions

1. *How have the PQRRSS factors been changing in the outdoor clothing market?*
2. *How does the operations system at Berghaus cope with change?*
3. *Propose some methods that Berghaus could use to make and use forecasts.*

References

1. Slack, Nigel (1994) 'The importance–performance matix as a determinant of improvement priority' *International Journal of Operations and Production Management* **14.5** pp. 59–75

2. Trapp, Rodger (1994) 'Products are just part of the service' *Independent on Sunday Business* 8 May, p. 15

3. Voss, Chriss (1992) 'Applying service concepts in manufacturing' *International Journal of Production and Operations Management* **12.4** pp. 94–99

4. Chase, R. and Garvin, D.A. (1988) 'The Service Factory' *Havard Business Review* **66.4** July/August pp. 61–69; the examples are taken from Voss, op. cit.

5. Hammer, Michael and Champey, James (1993) *Re-engineering the Corporation – A Manifesto for Business Transformation* London, Nicholas Brearly Publishing

6. Hammer, Michael (1990) 'Re-engineering work – don't automate, obliterate' *Harvard Business Review* **68.4** July/August

7. Collins, Robert S., Oliff, Michael D. and Vollmann, Thomas E. (1991) *Manufacturing Restructuring: Lessons for Management* Executive Report 2 August, IMD Lausanne, pp. 15–17

8. Naylor, J.B. and Williams, J. (1994) 'The successful use of IT in SMEs on Merseyside' *European Journal of Information Systems* **3.1** pp. 48–56

9. Lorenz, Christopher (1993) 'Management – Ain't no mountain high enough' *The Financial Times* 11 January, p.8; Foster, Angus (1993) 'Pentland pays £7 million for outdoor clothing company' *The Financial Times* 17 February, p. 20

INDEX